The Politics of Social Policy
in the United States

STUDIES FROM THE PROJECT ON THE FEDERAL SOCIAL ROLE

FORREST CHISMAN AND ALAN PIFER, SERIES DIRECTORS

The Politics of Social Policy in the United States
Edited by Margaret Weir, Ann Shola Orloff, and Theda Skocpol

Democracy and the Welfare State
Edited by Amy Gutmann

The Politics
of Social Policy in
the United States

EDITED BY

MARGARET WEIR,
ANN SHOLA ORLOFF,
AND THEDA SKOCPOL

PRINCETON UNIVERSITY PRESS

Published by Princeton University Press, 41 William Street,
Princeton, New Jersey 08540
In the United Kingdom: Princeton University Press, Guildford, Surrey

Library of Congress Cataloging in Publication Data will be
found on the last printed page of this book

ISBN 0-691-09436-5 (cloth)
    0-691-02841-9 (pbk.)

This book has been composed in Linotron Sabon

Clothbound editions of Princeton University Press books
are printed on acid-free paper, and binding materials are chosen
for strength and durability. Paperbacks, although satisfactory for
personal collections, are not usually suitable for library rebinding

Printed in the United States of America by Princeton University Press
Princeton, New Jersey

Designed by Laury A. Egan

To a Better Future for Social Provision
in the United States

CONTENTS

PART III. SOCIAL POLICY, RACE, AND THE "POVERTY PROBLEM"

FOREWORD

This book is one of several volumes based on activities sponsored by the Project on the Federal Social Role. The Project was a nonprofit, nonpartisan enterprise established in 1983 to stimulate innovative thinking about the future directions of federal social policy.

Americans are doubtless more preoccupied than any other people with questions about the fundamental purposes and directions of their national government. In part this concern reflects a healthy political culture. We are always searching for better ideas about government and always disagreeing about which ideas are best. In part, too, our concern reflects a longstanding ambivalence about the value of national institutions. We still honor the tradition of Thomas Jefferson, which presumes against an active federal role, in an era when programs and policies emanating from Washington permeate every aspect of our lives.

But while Americans never seem to tire of arguing about the proper role of national government, systematic thinking on this subject has been neglected in recent years. Scholars have produced a great deal of excellent research about specific policies and programs. But there has been too little careful study of what effect those measures, considered as a whole, have on the American people.

This neglect of the larger issues of public policy is deeply troubling. The federal social role is more than the sum of its parts. The various policies and programs that constitute it interact with each other in a great many ways. Collectively they have a far greater impact on our future as a nation than the study of particular issues can reveal.

More importantly, the specific measures of government are all parts of a broader commitment by the American people to employ their common resources toward achieving common goals. Only a strong sense of what those goals are and what overall directions of policy are required to achieve them can ensure that so large and diverse an enterprise as the federal government serves the general welfare.

The problems that arise when basic issues of purpose and direction are neglected have been vividly demonstrated in recent years. For half a century Americans supported an almost continual expansion of the federal social role. But the growth of federal activism slowed in the late 1970s and early 1980s, and there were dire predictions that national government had exhausted its possibilities as an instrument for social betterment. A period of reassessment followed. For over a decade, virtually every aspect of the social role was closely scrutinized by politicians, scholars, and the press.

As an exercise in public education, this reassessment was undoubtedly a success. But as an exercise in policy development it was a disappointment. No clear directions for the future emerged. The federal role was neither greatly augmented nor diminished; nor was it set on any new course. The nation remained locked in political stalemate.

Although periods of national stock-taking are often healthy, prolonged stalemate is a luxury that the United States cannot afford. While national policy has been standing still, major forces of change have been at work in our social and economic life. Transformations in the nature of our economy, evolving personal lifestyles, societal aging and worsening conditions for many of the poor are the largest and most visible developments. We are no longer the nation that we were a few decades ago, and because government pervades so many aspects of our lives, we need new measures to suit our new circumstances.

The recent reassessment of public policy failed to come to grips with the forces of social and economic change in large part because it proceeded in a piecemeal fashion. Debate was confined primarily to the merits and demerits of policies and programs already in place. As a result, the nation artificially constrained its options. We failed to examine carefully enough the need for major new initiatives by the federal government and ways to make them work.

In this static and backward-looking environment, destructive myths and misunderstandings found fertile ground—most notably the myth that there are severe limits to what activist government can achieve. This idea takes various forms, and in most of those forms it is seriously misleading. If our national history teaches us anything, it is that each generation is capable of accomplishing far more through the use of government than previous generations would have dreamed possible. History also teaches that we *must* accomplish more: that effective government is a never-ending process of responding to new needs and opportunities. This requires breaking with the ideas of patterns of the past. As often as not, the social role has evolved through large measures that defied past skepticism and cut across the categories of previous thought.

Washington, D.C.   Forrest Chisman
                                                                                 Alan Pifer

PREFACE

The Politics of Social Policy in the United States is an unusual collection because it brings together approaches usually kept apart in specialized subdivisions of academia. Long-term overviews of a country's government and politics are typically not grouped with discussions of particular public policies or contemporary social problems. The papers in this volume were assembled on the premise that social policy choices in the United States are best understood in the context of changes in the polity and society. A macroscopic and historical perspective that highlights political institutions and processes in relation to the regional, economic, and racial diversity of American society allows us to understand past policies and their effects; for example, the timing and form of the Social Security Act of 1935, the failure of efforts in the 1940s to extend social benefits or institutionalize economic planning, and the backlashes against "big government" that followed the Great Society reforms of the 1960s and the early 1970s. Such a perspective not only improves our understanding of the implications of these experiences for the present but also helps us wisely examine alternative possible futures for social provision in America.

The institutional limits and political coalitions that have shaped U.S. social policies suggest several pertinent lessons. The United States never has had, and is not likely to develop, a comprehensive national welfare state along West European lines. But certain social policies have flourished in America: those that have appealed simultaneously to middle-class and lower-income people but have not included direct bureaucratic intervention in local communities. Contemporary advocates of "a return to the free market" are not likely to succeed in dismantling broadly targeted measures such as Social Security. Yet currently fashionable "workfare" solutions to the persisting issue of how the United States should aid "the poor" may prove administratively or politically unsuccessful, and may further stigmatize welfare recipients. Instead, new family policies and full-employment programs could be devised to meet similar needs shared by lower-income and middle-class Americans. This strategy might revitalize broad political coalitions in support of social policies that effectively embody basic national values.

The editors, Margaret Weir, Ann Shola Orloff, and Theda Skocpol, have drawn inspiration for this volume from previous collaborative research projects and from books on the history of public policies in the

United States that each has in progress. Weir is writing about employment policies in the United States from the 1930s to the present. Orloff is writing about the origins of old-age pensions in the United States, Canada, and Great Britain. Skocpol is preparing a comprehensive analysis of the politics of American social provision from the late nineteeth century to the present.

This project gained not only from the prior involvement of the editors with related scholarly issues but also from the distinctive interdisciplinary context provided by the Center for the Study of Industrial Societies at the University of Chicago. The project also depended upon generous support that the center received for a series of conferences from the Project on the Federal Social Role, directed by Alan Pifer and Forrest Chisman under the auspices of the National Conference on Social Welfare. In the final stages of preparing the book, the editors also benefited from a grant to Theda Skocpol from the Ford Foundation's Project on Social Welfare Policy and the American Future.

The Center for the Study of Industrial Societies has served as a bridge between sociology and political science. When Weir and Skocpol were together at the University of Chicago from 1982 through 1985, the center allowed them to engage in dialogue with William Julius Wilson and Gary Orfield, and to become familiar with the remarkable research their collaborators have done on urban blacks and race relations in the United States. Most of the contributors to this collection belonged to the "CSIS Chicago network"; the themes of many of the papers were discussed in workshops at Wilder House, the center's headquarters. The basic policy prescription for universalistic measures that cut across racial and income divisions is a view jointly held by Skocpol, Weir, and Wilson, and one that they often debated vigorously in Wilder House sessions with Orfield.

In the spring of 1983, Alan Pifer and Forrest Chisman visited the University of Chicago. They were then planning a project that would examine the federal government's role in providing or encouraging social security. Some months later, after Pifer and Chisman had arranged funding for the Project on the Federal Social Role, several of us at Chicago proposed to them that a series of three small conferences be held in 1984–85 on "The Politics of Social Policy in the United States." The first conference would focus on social-scientific theories of the welfare state and their applicability to the American case, the second on U.S. social policies from the New Deal to the 1960s, and the third on policy debates since the 1960s concerning the situation of women and blacks. Pifer and Chisman agreed not only to fund these conferences but also to enliven them with their presence.

Throughout 1984–85, scholars from the University of Chicago and elsewhere assembled at Chicago to give papers and serve as discussants at the three conferences. Papers from the first conference were later published separately, while many primarily from the second and third meetings were revised for inclusion in the present book. The Project on the Federal Social Role also sponsored conferences and seminars at other universities. This "Chicago collection" of papers is one of several volumes offering reflections on American social policy from various disciplinary and analytical perspectives.

We gratefully acknowledge the help and stimulation we received from Alan Pifer and Forrest Chisman, and from all of the participants in the three conferences organized by Kimberly Stanton and Margaret Weir. We certainly could not have completed this volume without the collaboration and the generous support and constructive criticism we have received. Paul Moskowitz and William Skocpol deserve a special kind of thanks. We are thankful for the encouragement and comments of Michael Katz and Jennifer Hochschild, the two readers of the manuscript for Princeton University Press, as well as for the help we have received from Gail Ullman and Walter Lippincott, Jr., at the Press. Each author acknowledges the contribution of particular scholars. But no one else need take responsibility for what has been said here, or for any shortcomings of fact or argument that critics may find.

We have dedicated this volume "To a better future for social provision in the United States" because we hope the issues it raises will be discussed in the renewed debates about American social policy that are currently under way in both intellectual and governmental circles. Anyone who has worked and lived in, or visited, the South Side of Chicago recognizes the need for better measures to ensure family support and full employment in the United States.

The Politics of Social Policy in the United States

Understanding American Social Politics

MARGARET WEIR, ANN SHOLA ORLOFF, AND THEDA SKOCPOL

Along with many other advanced-industrial democracies, the United States finds itself in the midst of debates over the future of national social policies. Since the 1970s all such democracies have endured a fiscal crisis traced by some to the growth of the welfare state. International economic recession has brought the cold grip of "stagflation" to many nations at a time when Keynesian strategies of macroeconomic management no longer seem certain to ensure steady economic growth without rising unemployment. Large population cohorts covered by mature pension systems are aging and retiring, while increasing numbers of individuals cannot depend upon traditional family ties for help during periods of difficulty. Economic pressures and social trends have thus combined to spur widespread consternation about the future of public social programs in the Western nations.

As European welfare states undergo serious reevaluations of prior policies, innovative measures continue to be debated, and the existing strong responsibilities of national states to promote social welfare are not fundamentally challenged. In the United States, however, the legitimacy of the welfare role of the federal government *is* a matter for debate, and relatively paltry public social programs are being vigorously attacked. Proponents of new social policies speak in voices barely audible on the national political stage. This is a paradoxical situation, for if any one of the advanced industrial democratic countries could afford to do more to meet domestic needs through public provision—or perhaps one should say, if any country could afford to do better and, where necessary, more—that country would be the United States.

By international standards the United States has a remarkably healthy economy, one that has consistently generated new jobs at a high rate and has recovered relatively well from the recession of the 1970s.[1] At the same

---

In preparing the final version of the Introduction, the editors benefited from comments by Fred Block, Jennifer Hochschild, and Robert Kuttner.

[1] On the remarkable generation of employment by the U.S. economy, even in the face of

time, despite rising levels of social spending since 1960, the United States has never established more than a relatively inexpensive and programmatically incomplete system of public social provision. In the mid-1970s social spending for education, income maintenance, and health in the United States accounted for about 16 percent of GDP, while most European nations devoted more than 20 percent of GDP to social expenditures.[2] Although the United States is above average in educational expenditures, it lacks the national health insurance and family allowances provided by most European welfare states as well as Canada. Both public assistance and unemployment insurance in America remain ungenerous by international standards and uneven in their coverage across the states and population groups at risk.[3] Only in the area of old-age, disability, and medical insurance for retired workers who have been stably employed for most of their working lives does the United States compare well to other industrial democracies.[4] Yet benefits in these areas are not only channeled through the public sector but also (with encouragement from tax breaks) through privately negotiated fringe-benefit schemes.[5]

Why is the United States, which has one of the least generous systems of public social provision of any of the capitalist democracies, witnessing a period of unusually intense political attacks against its incomplete social programs? Contrary to the accepted wisdom among conservatives and leftists alike, the explanation does not lie in any inexorable "limit of welfare state development" or global "crisis of advanced capitalism." Although fiscal strains may be common to many countries, whether and

strong demographic pressures, see John Schwarz, *America's Hidden Success: A Reassessment of Twenty Years of Public Policy* (New York: Norton, 1983), p. 128.

[2] Organization for Economic Cooperation and Development, *Public Expenditure Trends*, Studies in Resource Allocation no. 5 (Paris: OECD, June 1978), Table 6, p. 25. For more precise comparative figures on "income security programs" in particular, see John Myles, *Old Age in the Welfare State: The Political Economy of Public Pensions* (Boston: Little, Brown, 1984), Tables 1.2 and 1.3, pp. 17–19.

[3] For comparisons of U.S. with Western European and Canadian social policies, see: Myles, *Old Age in the Welfare State*; Norman Furniss and Timothy Tilton, *The Case for the Welfare State* (Bloomington: Indiana University Press, 1977); and Robert T. Kudrle and Theodore R. Marmor, "The Development of Welfare States in North America" in Peter Flora and Arnold J. Heidenheimer, eds., *The Development of Welfare States in Europe and America* (New Brunswick, N.J.: Transaction Books, 1981), pp. 81–121.

[4] Richard F. Tomasson, "Old-Age Pensions under Social Security: Past and Future," *American Behavioral Scientist* 26 (1983): 699–723. Myles, in *Old Age in the Welfare State*, Table 3.7, cols. 1–3, p. 69, shows that of fifteen capitalist democracies, the United States is average or slightly above average in public pension levels for low-, average-, and high-income workers.

[5] See the paper by Beth Stevens in this volume (Chapter 3); also Alicia Munnell, *The Economics of Private Pensions*, Studies in Social Economics (Washington D.C.: The Brookings Institution, 1982).

exactly how a "crisis" is defined, and the nature of the policy alternatives debated for the future, depend mostly upon each nation's social structure and political arrangements. Understandings of crisis and policy alternatives also depend on the ways each nation's existing policies influence political alliances and arouse debates over further policy choices. A nation's politics creates social policies; they in turn remake its politics, transforming possibilities for the future.

Contemporary American debates over "the crisis of social security" and "the need to reduce welfare dependency" do not, therefore, simply reflect economically given limits or an inexorable international crisis. To understand the shape of these debates—and also to see where American social policy might go from here—we need to explore the historical formation and remaking of social policies in the United States from the roots of the New Deal's Social Security programs through the Great Society efforts of the 1960s and on into the present. At a time when the future of U.S. public social provision is very much at issue, there is a compelling need to grasp the fundamental patterns of American social politics in historical perspective. Such is the task to which this collection of essays is devoted.

History does not speak for itself, however. It will answer only the questions we pose, and there is always more than one way to ask questions and hear answers. So we had best be explicit from the start. What features of U.S. social policy do we seek to understand? And how does our perspective on American social politics—our way of framing questions and answers—compare to important alternative perspectives that other thoughtful people have used?

The American Version of Public Social Provision

Modern welfare states, as they have come to be called, had their start between the 1880s and the 1920s in pension and social insurance programs established for industrial workers and needy citizens.[6] Later, from the 1930s through the 1950s, such programmatic beginnings were elaborated into comprehensive systems of income support and social insurance encompassing entire national populations. In the aftermath of World War II, Great Britain rationalized a whole array of social services and social insurances around an explicit vision of "the welfare state" that would universally ensure a "national minimum" of protection for all

---

[6] Peter Flora and Jens Alber, "Modernization, Democratization, and the Development of Welfare States in Western Europe," in Flora and Heidenheimer, eds., *The Development of Welfare States*, pp. 37–80. See also Furniss and Tilton, *The Case for the Welfare State*, chaps. 5 and 6.

citizens against insufficient income caused by old age, disability, ill health, and unemployment. During the same period, other nations—especially the Scandinavian democracies—established "full-employment welfare states" by deliberately coordinating social policies, first with Keynesian strategies of macroeconomic management, and then with targeted interventions in labor markets.[7]

American "social policy" prior to the 1930s included state and local support for mass public education,[8] along with generous federal benefits for elderly Civil War veterans and their dependents. In contrast to the European tempo of welfare state development, neither old-age pensions nor social insurance made much headway in the United States before the Great Depression. Then, in what has been called a "big bang" of national legislation, the Social Security Act of 1935 established nation-spanning social insurance and public assistance programs, creating a basic framework for U.S. public social provision that has remained in place to the present.[9] Health insurance was omitted from the Social Security Act and later schemes for universal national health benefits also failed.[10] But three major kinds of social provision were included in the 1935 legislation: federally required, state-run unemployment insurance; federally subsidized public assistance; and national contributory old-age insurance.

Unemployment insurance was instituted in 1935 as a federal-state system. All states were induced to establish programs, but each state was left free to decide terms of eligibility and benefits for unemployed workers, as well as the amount of taxes to be collected from employers or workers or both. Unemployment benefits and taxation became quite uneven across the states, and it remained difficult to pool risks of economic downturns on a national basis or to coordinate unemployment benefits with Keynesian demand management.[11] Despite efforts in the 1930s and 1940s to

[7] Gösta Esping-Andersen, *Politics against Markets: The Social Democratic Road to Power* (Princeton, N.J.: Princeton University Press, 1985), chap. 7; Andrew Martin, "The Dynamics of Change in a Keynesian Political Economy: The Swedish Case and Its Implications," in Colin Crouch, ed., *State and Economy in Contemporary Capitalism* (London: Croom Helm, 1979).

[8] See Morris Janowitz, *Social Control of the Welfare State* (New York: Elsevier, 1976), p. 34; and Arnold J. Heidenheimer, "Education and Social Security Entitlements in Europe and America," in Flora and Heidenheimer, eds., *The Development of Welfare States*, pp. 269–304.

[9] The "big bang" characterization comes from Christopher Leman, "Patterns of Policy Development: Social Security in the United States and Canada," *Public Policy* 25 (1977): 261–91.

[10] Paul Starr, "Transformation in Defeat: The Changing Objectives of National Health Insurance, 1915–1980," *American Journal of Public Health* 72 (1982): 78–88.

[11] Joseph M. Becker, "Twenty-five Years of Unemployment Insurance," *Political Science Quarterly* 75 (1960): 481–99; Edward J. Harpham, "Federalism, Keynesianism, and the Transformation of the Unemployment Insurance System in the United States," in Douglas

nationalize unemployment insurance and join its operations to various measures of public economic planning, no such explicit coordination of social and economic policy was achieved in the postwar United States.

The public assistance programs subsidized under Social Security already existed in certain states by the early 1930s. Assistance for the elderly poor and for dependent children were the most important of these programs. Left free under Social Security to decide whether they would even have such programs, the states were also given discretion to decide matters of eligibility and benefits and, in practice, methods of administration. Over time, as old-age insurance expanded to cover virtually all retired employees in the United States, federal old-age assistance became less important than it had been originally. By the 1960s, the Aid to Dependent Children Program (now Aid to Families with Dependent Children—AFDC—providing benefits to caretakers as well as to the children themselves) expanded enormously with a predominately female adult clientele.[12] Labeled "welfare," AFDC has very uneven standards of eligibility, coverage, and benefits across the states, generally providing the least to the poorest people in the poorest states, and leaving many impoverished men and husband-wife families without any coverage at all.[13]

Since 1935 contributory old-age insurance, the one program originally established on a purely national basis, has usurped the favorable label "social security" that once described the whole and has become the centerpiece of U.S. public social provision. Payroll taxes are collected from workers and employers across the country. Ultimately, retired workers collect benefits roughly consistent with their employment incomes, with some redistribution to low-wage contributors to the system. After 1935, additional programs were placed under this contributory insurance rubric: programs for surviving dependents in 1939; for disabled workers in 1956; and for retirees in need of medical care in 1965. Equally important, "social security" coverage and benefits grew, as more and more employees and categories of employees were incorporated during the 1950s, and benefit levels have been repeatedly raised by Congress.[14] By the 1970s, the United States, despite the uneven and often inadequate help provided

Ashford and E. W. Kelley, eds., *Nationalizing Social Security in Europe and America* (Greenwich, Conn.: JAI Press, 1986), pp. 155–79.

[12] Winifred Bell, *Aid to Dependent Children* (New York: Columbia University Press, 1965).

[13] Furniss and Tilton, *The Case for the Welfare State*, p. 170; Harrell R. Rodgers, Jr., *The Cost of Human Neglect: America's Welfare Failure* (Armonk, N.Y.: M. E. Sharpe, 1982), pp. 56–62; David T. Ellwood and Lawrence H. Summers, "Poverty in America: Is Welfare the Answer or the Problem?" in Sheldon H. Danziger and Daniel H. Weinberg, eds., *Fighting Poverty* (Cambridge: Harvard University Press, 1986), p. 84.

[14] Martha Derthick, *Policy Making for Social Security* (Washington D.C.: The Brookings Institution, 1979).

to unemployed and dependent people, had nevertheless become reasonably generous in the benefits offered to retired people of the working and middle classes.

Properly understood, public social provision in the United States also includes many federal measures undertaken to further the well-being of broad sectors of the populace, including middle-strata employees and small property owners. Some of these measures, such as agricultural price supports to shore up the incomes of commercial farmers, were launched in the New Deal. Others—such as educational aid to military veterans and grants to localities to encourage hospital construction—were established or significantly expanded in the aftermath of World War II, when higher peacetime revenues became permanently available as a result of the extended federal income tax. Although they do not carry the explicit label of "welfare" or "social policy," these policies are often implemented by *indirect* governmental action such as "tax expenditures" (that is, incentives in the form of forgiven tax payments) rather than direct public expenditures. In other cases, federal subsidies flow to third-party providers, such as private businesses or associations or local governments, as a way to encourage the provision of goods or services to favored groups or to members of the citizenry at large. U.S. housing policies especially exemplify the use of indirect instrumentalities. Both federal mortgage insurance and the deductibility of mortgage interest payments from federal taxes have spurred widespread private home ownership; even federal programs to house the poor have relied on regulatory breaks and subsidies to private real estate developers.[15]

Welfare became an area of political controversy and policy innovation in the United States only during the 1960s, when the "War on Poverty" and the effort to create a "Great Society" were declared.[16] For the first time since 1935, major new programs of needs-tested public assistance were established in the form of in-kind aid through Food Stamps and Medicaid. In 1972, moreover, old-age and other assistance programs (originally established as federal programs under Social Security) were nationalized, ensuring more standardized benefits. Nevertheless the much larger AFDC program remained federally decentralized, and standards for

[15] On U.S. housing policies in comparative perspective, see Bruce Headey, *Housing Policy in the Developed Economy* (New York: St. Martin's Press, 1978); Arnold J. Heidenheimer, Hugh Heclo, and Carolyn Teich Adams, *Comparative Public Policy*, 2d ed. (New York: St. Martin's Press, 1983), chap. 6; and Paul Starr and Gösta Esping-Andersen, "Passive Intervention," *Working Papers Magazine* 9 (July–August 1979): 15–25.

[16] For overviews of Great Society efforts, see Sar A. Levitan and Robert Taggart, *The Promise of Greatness* (Cambridge: Harvard University Press, 1976), pts. 1 and 2; James T. Patterson, *America's Struggle against Poverty, 1900–1980* (Cambridge: Harvard University Press, 1981), pt. 3; and Eli Ginzberg and Robert M. Solow, eds., *The Great Society: Lessons for the Future* (New York: Basic Books, 1974).

other benefits such as medical care are often tied to this uneven standard bearer of the American welfare system. Welfare remains, as always, both institutionally and symbolically separate from national economic management, on the one hand, and from non-means-tested programs benefitting stably employed citizens, on the other.

In sum, a number of features of U.S. social provision require explanation. Core welfare state policies such as old-age pensions and social insurance were much slower to emerge in the United States than in Europe; some—such as national health insurance—have never been instituted at all. We need to know why America's initiation of such modern social policies was (by international standards) so belated. We also need to make sense of the two major periods of explicit social policy innovation at the national level in the twentieth century: the New Deal of the 1930s, which included the passage of the Social Security Act, and the Great Society and Nixon era reforms of the 1960s and early 1970s, which included new programs for the poor along with improvement of Social Security benefits for retirees.

The programmatic structure and modes of implementation of U.S. social provision also require explanation. The public assistance and social insurance programs established under the Social Security Act have remained disjointed and nationally uneven, and these programs operate in conjunction with a variety of indirect federal incentives and subsidies that provide scattered social benefits outside of any comprehensive vision of the goals or effects of an American welfare state. Unlike the situation in Britain following the Beveridge reforms instituted after World War II, national standards have not been established in the United States for public benefits (not even the direct ones). American "social security" has remained firmly bifurcated, both institutionally and symbolically, from welfare; and in contrast to the "full-employment welfare states" of Scandinavia, there has been little coordination of U.S. social policies with nationally rationalized public interventions in the macroeconomy or labor markets. In the United States, various social benefits remain operationally, fiscally, and symbolically separate from one another; and they are all kept quite apart from other things the national government may be doing in relation to the economy and society.

We need, in short, to understand better why the United States in the twentieth century developed *not* a Western European-style welfare state but a much more disconnected system of public social provision. Once we understand the origins and patterns of this distinctively American system, we should be better positioned to see what might come next—not what *will* come next, but what alternatives are now within the realm of political possibility.

Explaining Social Provision:
Industrialization and Liberal Values?

Among many of those seeking to understand the development of social policies in the United States, two seemingly opposite but actually complementary perspectives have long held sway. One school of thought can be dubbed the "logic of industrialism" approach because it posits that all nation-states respond to the growth of cities and industries by creating public measures to help citizens cope with attendant social and economic dislocations.[17] Once families are off the land and dependent on wages and salaries, the argument goes, they cannot easily cope with disabling accidents at work, with major episodes of illness, unemployment, or with dependent elderly relatives unable to earn their keep. As social demand for public help grows, all modern nations must create policies to address these basic issues of social security without forcing respectable citizens to accept aid under the demeaning and disenfranchising rules of traditional poor laws.

Plausible as this sounds, recent cross-national studies on the origins of modern social insurance policies have demonstrated that urbanization and industrialization (whether considered separately or in combination) cannot explain the relative timing of the passage of national social insurance legislation from the late nineteenth century to the present.[18] American social policies, in particular, are not well explained by the logic of industrialism school. Not incidentally, proponents of this perspective have tended to include data for "the U.S. case" only when doing cross-national analyses for the period after 1935. Before the 1930s the United States is an awkward outlier; this country was one of the world's industrial leaders, yet "lagged" far behind other nations (even much less urban and industrial nations) in instituting public pensions, social insurance, and other modern welfare measures.

A second school of thought—what might be called the "national values" approach—accepts many underlying principles of the logic of industrialism argument, but introduces a major modification to explain why some nations, such as Bismarck's Germany in the 1880s, initiated modern social policies at relatively early stages of urbanization and industrializa-

[17] For examples of this approach, see Phillips Cutright, "Political Structure, Economic Development, and National Social Security Programs," *American Journal of Sociology* 70 (1965): 537–50; Robert Jackman, *Politics and Social Equality: A Comparative Analysis* (New York: Wiley, 1975); Harold Wilensky and Charles Lebeaux, *Industrial Society and Social Welfare* (New York: Free Press, 1965); and Harold Wilensky, *The Welfare State and Equality* (Berkeley: University of California Press, 1975), chap. 2.

[18] Flora and Alber, "Welfare States in Western Europe"; David Collier and Richard Messick, "Prerequisites versus Diffusion: Testing Alternative Explanations of Social Security Adoption," *American Political Science Review* 69 (1975): 1299–1315.

tion, while others, most notably the United States, delayed behind the pace of policy innovation that would be expected from the tempo of urbanization and industrialization alone. The answer, say proponents of this approach, lies in the values and ideologies to which each nation's people adhered as urbanization and industrialization gathered force.[19] Cultural conditions could either facilitate or delay action by a nation-state to promote social security, and cultural factors also influenced the shape and goals of new policies when they emerged.

Gaston Rimlinger, one of the ablest proponents of the national values approach, argues that the early enactment of Bismarck's social insurance policies was facilitated by the weakness of liberalism and the strength of "the patriarchal social ideal" and "the Christian social ethic" in nineteenth-century Germany.[20] In the United States, however, laissez-faire liberal values were extremely strong, and a "commitment to individualism . . . and self-help" led to a "tenacious" "resistance to social protection."[21] The unusual strength and persistence of American liberal values explain why social insurance measures were not instituted before the 1930s. Rimlinger points out that "it was only when the Great Depression revealed in a shocking manner the utter defenselessness of the citizen in the American industrial state that the still potent individualistic tradition could be overcome." Besides, the American individualistic tradition was never really overcome, even in the 1930s, for the new contributory social insurance programs were deliberately rationalized as "quasi-contractual" measures in which individuals would "earn the right to benefits" through their own contributions. "This," writes Rimlinger, "was a shrewd formula, for it covered the inevitable element of compulsion with a veneer of individualism. . . . The emphasis on contractual rights was of strategic significance: in an individualistic society the individual was not to be left dependent on the benevolence of the ruling powers."[22]

Again we confront a highly plausible account. Americans *do* espouse liberal values, and virtually all public policies in this country *are* either supported or opposed with arguments invoking liberal ideals. All the same, proponents of this approach have yet to pinpoint the precise ways that cultural values influence processes of political conflict and policy de-

---

[19] This approach is advocated (especially for the United States) in Kirsten Gronbjerg, David Street, and Gerald D. Suttles, *Poverty and Social Change* (Chicago: University of Chicago Press, 1978); P. R. Kaim-Caudle, *Comparative Social Policy and Social Security* (London: Martin Robertson, 1973); Anthony King, "Ideas, Institutions, and the Policies of Governments: A Comparative Analysis, Parts I and II," *British Journal of Political Science* 3 (1973): 291–313, 409–23; and Gaston Rimlinger, *Welfare Policy and Industrialization in Europe, America, and Russia* (New York: Wiley, 1971).

[20] Rimlinger, *Welfare Policy and Industrialization*, p. 91.

[21] *Ibid.*, p. 62.

[22] *Ibid.*, pp. 214, 229.

bate—let alone how they help to determine actual policy outcomes. Arguments like Rimlinger's about national values offer a credible general gloss on "what happened," but they do not consider the subtlest value-related questions about the origins and the structure of U.S. social policies.

Laissez-faire liberal values were in many respects more hegemonic and popular in Britain than they were in the United States in the nineteenth-century. Yet in the years before World War I Britain enacted a full range of social protective measures, including workers' compensation (1906), old-age pensions (1908), and unemployment and health insurance (1911). These innovations came under the auspices of the British Liberal party, and they were intellectually and politically justified by appeals to "new liberal" values of the sort that were also spreading among educated Americans at the turn of the century.[23] Under modern urban-industrial conditions, the "new liberals" argued, governments must act to protect individual security; and governments may proceed without undermining individuals' dignity or making them dependent on the state. If British Liberals could use such ideas to justify both state-funded pensions and contributory social insurance in the second decade of the twentieth century, why could American progressives not have done the same? In both Britain and the United States, sufficient cultural transformation within liberalism had occurred to legitimate fledgling welfare states without resort to either conservative-paternalist or socialist justifications.

When American New Dealers of the 1930s at last successfully instituted nationwide social protections justified in "new liberal" terms, why did they end up with the specific policies embodied in the Social Security Act? Why was health insurance left aside, despite the availability of liberal rationales for it that were just as valid as those put forward for unemployment and old-age insurance? And why did the public assistance programs subsidized under Social Security actually cement the dependence of many individuals on the arbitrary discretion of state and local authorities, rather than furthering individual dignity and making predictable the delivery of citizen benefits as a matter of "right"? Finally, given the clear priority that Americans have always placed on getting ahead

[23] On Great Britain's "new liberalism," see Michael Freeden, *The New Liberalism: An Ideology of Social Reform* (Oxford: Clarendon Press, 1978). On parallel developments in Great Britain and the United States, see Kenneth O. Morgan, "The Future at Work: Anglo-American Progressivism, 1870–1917," in H. C. Allen and Roger Thompson, eds., *Contrast and Connection: Bicentennial Essays in Anglo-American History* (Columbus: Ohio University Press, 1976), pp. 245–71; and Charles L. Mowat, "Social Legislation in Britain and the United States in the Early Twentieth Century: A Problem in the History of Ideas," in J. C. Beckett, ed., *Historical Studies: Papers Read before the Irish Conference of Historians*, vol. 7 (New York: Barnes and Noble, 1969), pp. 81–96.

through hard work, why did the measures proposed in the 1930s and 1940s fail to achieve proposed measures to guarantee jobs for everyone willing to work? Arguably, the Social Security measures that were implemented were less in accord with longstanding American values than measures embodying a governmental commitment to full employment would have been.[24]

General deductions based on the national values approach simply cannot give us the answer to many crucial questions about the timing and programmatic structure of American social provision. At any given time some potential policy implications of liberal values are taken up, and others not; sometimes rhetorically well-crafted liberal arguments work, and sometimes not. To explain such subtle variations within American social politics, and to understand U.S. policy developments (and nondevelopments) in cross-national perspective, we must find more precise analytical tools than those offered by the national values approach. We should, however, retain the salutary emphasis on historical process and national distinctiveness that these scholars have introduced in response to the logic of industrialism argument.

Explaining Social Provision: Business Hegemony and Working Class Weakness?

Arguments stressing the impact of either industrialism or national values on the development of social policy tend to downplay political struggles and debates. Since the mid-1970s, however, many historians and social scientists have analyzed the political contributions of capitalists and industrial workers to the shaping of social policy in the Western democracies. Two sorts of class politics perspectives have been applied to American social politics; one highlights the initiatives of "welfare capitalists" and the other stresses "political class struggles" between workers and capitalists.

Proponents of the welfare capitalism approach take for granted that corporate capitalists have dominated the U.S. political process in the twentieth century, and they look for economically grounded splits between conservative and progressive capitalists as the way to explain social policy innovations.[25] Early in this century, the argument goes, certain

---

[24] For opinion data in support of this speculation, see Jerome S. Bruner, *Mandate from the People* (New York: Duell, Sloan, and Pearce, 1944), chaps. 8 and 9.

[25] Those who advance this argument differ in the ways they describe intracapitalist splits and relate them to policy outcomes. See, for example, Edward Berkowitz and Kim Mc-Quaid, *Creating the Welfare State* (New York: Praeger, 1980); William Domhoff, *The Higher Circles* (New York: Random House, 1970), chap. 6; Thomas Ferguson, "From Normalcy to New Deal: Industrial Structure, Party Competition, and American Public Policy in

American businesses preceded the public sector in developing principles of modern organizational management, including policies for planning and stabilizing employment and protecting the social welfare of loyal employees. Prominent "welfare capitalists" then pressed policy intellectuals and public officials to accept their ideas, so that public social insurance measures in key states and at the federal level were supposedly designed to meet the needs of progressively managed business corporations.

This perspective has served as a good lens through which to view the complementarities between public social policies—once enacted—and the labor-management practices of American corporations. For example, many American corporations accommodated nicely to Social Security's contributory old-age insurance program, meshing it with their own retirement benefits systems, especially after World War II.[26] But business groups originally opposed the passage of the Social Security Act, as well as the passage of most other federal and state-level social and regulatory measures favorable to workers, and this creates problems for the welfare capitalism thesis. Its proponents have failed to demonstrate convincingly that genuine groups or categories of U.S. capitalists—as opposed to a handful of maverick individuals not representative of any class or industrial sector—actually supported mandatory public pensions or social insurance.[27] However adaptable American capitalists have proven to be after the fact, the historical evidence is overwhelming that they have regularly fiercely opposed the initiation of public social policies. Political processes other than the initiatives of capitalists have nearly always been the cause of U.S. social policy innovations.

The "Social Democratic" or "political class struggle" perspective takes for granted that capitalists everywhere tend to oppose the emergence and expansion of the welfare state. This approach has predominated in recent cross-national research on the development of social policies in Europe and the United States.[28] To explain why American public social provision

---

the Great Depression," *International Organization* 38 (1984): 41–93; Jill S. Quadagno, "Welfare Capitalism and the Social Security Act of 1935," *American Sociological Review* 49 (1984): 632–47; Ronald Radosh, "The Myth of the New Deal," in Ronald Radosh and Murray N. Rothbard, eds., *The New Leviathan* (New York: E. P. Dutton, 1972); and James Weinstein, *The Corporate Ideal in the Liberal State, 1900–1918* (Boston: Beacon Press, 1968).

[26] William Graebner, *A History of Retirement* (New Haven, Conn.: Yale University Press, 1980), chap. 8. Also see footnote 5 to this Introduction.

[27] Many business organizations did support the state-level workers' compensation laws passed in the Progressive Era. These measures, however, did not include direct taxation or expenditures by government, and they dealt more predictably with liability issues already under the courts' jurisdiction.

[28] Those who have taken this approach include Lars Bjorn, "Labor Parties, Economic Growth, and Redistribution in Five Capitalist Democracies," *Comparative Social Research*

commenced later and has not become as generous as European public social provision, advocates of this approach underline the relative weakness of U.S. industrial unions and point to the complete absence of any labor-based political party in U.S. democracy. Given these weaknesses of working class organization, U.S. capitalists have been able to use direct and indirect pressures to prevent governments at all levels from undertaking social-welfare efforts that would reshape labor markets or interfere with the prerogatives or profits of private business. Certainly an emphasis on political class struggle between workers and capitalists helps to explain why the United States has not developed a comprehensive full-employment welfare state. As might be predicted by the political class struggle approach, American unions have frequently supported extensions of public social provision, while business groups have opposed them. Thus, policies more similar to those of Sweden probably would have been developed in the United States had American workers been as highly unionized as Swedish workers or had the modern Democratic party been a truly social-democratic party based in the organized working class.

Nevertheless, if our intention is not merely to contrast the United States to Europe but also to explain the specific patterns of modern American social policy, then the Social Democratic perspective on political class struggles is insufficient in several ways. Strict attention to conflicts of political interest between capitalists and industrial workers deflects our attention from other socioeconomic forces that have intersected with the U.S. federal state and with decentralized American political parties to shape social policies. Until recently, agricultural interests in the South and West were crucial arbiters of congressional policy making. Struggles over social welfare or labor market interventions have often involved regional, ethnic, and racial divisions. We need a mode of analysis that will help us understand why these conflicts have been equally or more influential than industrial class conflicts in the shaping of social provision in the United States.

A political class struggle approach also falls short in illuminating those

---

2 (1979): 93–128; Francis Castles, *The Social Democratic Image of Society* (London: Routledge and Kegan Paul, 1978); Francis Castles, "The Impact of Parties on Public Expenditures," in F. Castles, ed., *The Impact of Parties* (Beverly Hills, Calif.: Sage, 1982), pp. 21–96; Esping-Andersen, *Politics against Markets*; Walter Korpi, *The Democratic Class Struggle* (Boston: Routledge and Kegan Paul, 1983); Andrew Martin, *The Politics of Economic Policy in the United States: A Tentative View from a Comparative Perspective*, Professional Paper in Comparative Politics 01-040 (Beverly Hills, Calif.: Sage, 1973); Myles, *Old Age in the Welfare State*; and John Stephens, *The Transition from Capitalism to Socialism* (London: Macmillan, 1979). For an excellent overview of research using this approach, see Michael Shalev, "The Social Democratic Model and Beyond: Two Generations of Comparative Research on the Welfare State," *Comparative Social Research* 6 (1983): 315–51.

watersheds in American politics—especially the middle 1930s and the late 1960s and early 1970s—when broadly "democratic" forces were on the rise, and when many policies that business strongly opposed actually did pass and become a permanent part of the federal government's activities. At these junctures, why did not full-employment guarantees or more comprehensive national social policies become institutionalized as goals and programs? A political class struggle approach alone will not explain the failure of possibilities for national commitments to such measures as health insurance, or nationalized public assistance, or full-employment planning during the major reformist periods of the twentieth century. Nor can it account for the sudden political backlashes that quickly emerged in the wake of reform efforts at the end of the 1930s and the late 1960s. In short, while European social democracies have experienced the steady extension of established social policies in tandem with enhancement of labor's strength, the United States has experienced sudden bursts of reform and equally sudden backlashes, without such close correspondence to waxing and waning organizational capacities of industrial labor. The distinctive dynamics of American social politics have been rooted in shifting political coalitions that include, but necessarily go beyond, business and labor.

State Formation, Institutional Leverage, and Policy Feedbacks

Political class struggle theories have been argued with certain state and party structures in mind—namely centralized and bureaucratized states with parliamentary parties dedicated to pursuing policy programs in the name of entire classes or other broad, nation-spanning collectivities. For much of Western Europe, the existence of such features of political organization has given substance to the presumption that the industrial working class *may* translate its interests into social policies whenever "its" party holds the reins of national power over a sustained period. In contrast, the United States has never had a centralized bureaucratic state or programmatic parliamentary parties. Thus the American case highlights the importance of bringing much more explicitly into our explanations of social policy making the historical formation of each national state, as well as the effects of that state's institutional structure on the goals, capacities, and alliances of politically active groups.

Many of the puzzles about American social politics left unresolved by the alternative theoretical persuasions just surveyed can be addressed anew from what we shall call an "institutional-political process" perspective. This approach examines state formation and the state's institutional structure in both societal and historical context. Political struggles and policy outcomes are presumed to be jointly conditioned by the institutional arrangements of the state and by class and other social relationships, but never once and for all. For states and social structures are themselves transformed over time. And so are the goals and capacities of politically active groups, in part because of ongoing transformations of political and social structures, and in part because of the effects of earlier state policies on subsequent political struggles and debates.

Understanding of the patterns of American social provision can be improved from an institutional-political process perspective in several interrelated ways. First, the historical particularities of U.S. state formation, when understood in relationship to capitalist economic development, urbanization, and transformations of liberal values, explain the distinctive rhythms and limits of American social policy making more effectively than do socioeconomic or cultural processes abstracted from the institutional contexts of national politics. Second, as an alternative to overemphasis on zero-sum class struggles between capitalists and workers, pinpointing ways in which class and other social relations have intersected with the organization of the state and political parties greatly improves our ability to explain the complex political alliances that have sustained or opposed social policies in America. Finally, probing for the feedback effects of policies on subsequent politics reveals how changing policy agendas and alternative possible alliances emerge not only in response to new socioeconomic conditions but also on the basis of—or in reaction to—previous policy accomplishments.

The papers of this volume have been assembled to demonstrate the analytic value of an institutional-political process approach, and we do not want to preempt what the various authors have to say here in the introductory chapter.[29] Even so, we can briefly preview some of the insights about the development of U.S. social policies to be gained from an investigation of state formation, institutional leverage, and the political effects of preexisting policies.

"State formation" includes constitution-making, involvements in wars, electoral democratization, and bureaucratization—macropolitical processes, in short, whose forms and timing have varied significantly in capitalist-industrializing countries.[30] In sharp contrast to many European na-

[29] The institutional-political process perspective is not shared by all contributors to this volume, but the editors believe that the arguments of all of the papers fit within this frame of reference. Several contributors also explicitly develop analytical insights consistent with perspectives that emphasize the roles of capitalism and class relations.

[30] On variations in state formation and examples of how the U.S. case compares with others, see J. Rogers Hollingsworth, "The United States," in Raymond Grew, ed., *Crises of Political Development in Europe and the United States* (Princeton, N.J.: Princeton University Press, 1978), pp. 163–96; Samuel P. Huntington, *Political Order in Changing Societies*

tions, the United States did not have a premodern polity characterized by monarchical absolutism, a locally entrenched standing army and bureaucracy, or recurrent mobilization for land warfare against equal competitors. Instead, the American colonies forged a federalist constitutional republic in a revolution against the English monarchy, and (after some years of continued sparring with Britain) the fledgling nation found itself relatively sheltered geopolitically and facing toward a huge continent available for conquest from militarily unformidable opponents. America's greatest war—even when compared to its eventual participation in the world wars of the twentieth century—was a war about itself, the Civil War of the 1860s.[31] Both before and after that conflict, moreover, America's nineteenth-century polity was a "state of courts and parties," in which judges and lawyers made and remade private property rights, and political parties competed to mobilize the white male electorate.[32] Because such mass electoral democratization preceded state bureaucratization in the United States, public administrative arrangements were colonized by political party networks and used to nourish their organizational needs through patronage.

Not until the beginning of the twentieth century—decades after electoral democratization and well after capitalist industrialization had created private corporate giants operating on a national scale—did the U.S. federal, state, and local governments make much headway in the bureaucratization and professionalization of their administrative functions.[33] With the greatest changes coming first at municipal and state levels, bu-

(New Haven, Conn.: Yale University Press, 1968), chap. 2; Seymour Martin Lipset, *The First New Nation* (New York: Basic Books, 1963); Stephen Skowronek, *Building a New American State: The Expansion of National Administrative Capacities, 1877–1920* (New York: Cambridge University Press, 1982); Martin Shefter, "Party and Patronage," *Politics and Society* 7 (1977): 404–51; and Charles Tilly, ed., *The Formation of National States in Western Europe* (Princeton, N.J.: Princeton University Press, 1975).

[31] Northern and Southern battle deaths during the Civil War totaled about 600,000 (or 17,000 per million of the national population), compared with 126,000 U.S. battle deaths (1,313 per million) in World War I, and 408,300 U.S. battle deaths (3,141 per million) in World War II. Approximately 37 percent of Northern males then 15 to 44 years old, and approximately 58 percent of the Southern white males in that age-group, fought in the Civil War. This was also the only war that ever resulted in enormous destruction of property on the American mainland.

[32] The phrase "state of courts and parties" comes from Stephen Skowronek, *Building a New American State*, chap. 2; see also Morton Keller, *Affairs of State: Public Life in Nineteenth-Century America* (Cambridge: Harvard University Press, 1977), chaps. 7, 8, and 14, and Richard L. McCormick, "The Party Period and Public Policy: An Exploratory Hypothesis," *Journal of American History* 66 (1979): 279–98.

[33] Skowronek, *Building a New American State*, pts. 2 and 3; and Martin Schiesl, *The Politics of Efficiency: Municipal Administration and Reform in America, 1880–1920* (Berkeley: University of California Press, 1977).

reaucratic-professional transformations happened piecemeal through reform movements spearheaded by the new middle classes. As the various
levels of government were thus partially reorganized, the fragmentation
of political sovereignty built into U.S. federalism and into the divisions of
decision-making authority among executives, legislatures, and courts
continued throughout the twentieth century.[34] Meanwhile, American political parties have remained decentralized; and in many localities and
states the major parties uneasily combine patronage-oriented and interest-group oriented modes of operation.[35] Within the federal government,
Congress, with its strong roots in state and local political establishments,
has remained pivotal in national domestic policy making—even during
periods of strong executive initiative such as the New Deal and the world
wars and the Cold War.[36]

Finally, it should also be kept in mind that the United States was, par-
adoxically, both the first and the last to democratize its electorate among
the long-standing capitalist democracies. It was the first for white males,
who were irreversibly enfranchised by the 1830s; and it was virtually the
last to enfranchise *all* citizens because, except briefly during Reconstruction and its immediate aftermath, most blacks in the United States could
not vote until after the post-1930s migrations from the rural South and
the Civil Rights upheavals of the 1960s. During all of the twentieth century until the 1960s, the United States was a regionally bifurcated federal
polity: a mass two-party democracy in the East, North, and West, coexisted with a single-party racial oligarchy in the South.[37] Only since the
1960s, as a result of major transformations that are far from completed,
have American blacks been fully incorporated into the electorate, and has
two-party electoral competition made headway in the deep South.

The patterns of U.S. state formation just summarized have conditioned
the rhythms and patterns of social policy making from the nineteenth cen-

[34] Barry Karl, *The Uneasy State* (Chicago: University of Chicago Press, 1983); Skowronek, *Building a New American State*, pp. 285–92.

[35] On parties in relation to the polity, see Martin Shefter, "Party, Bureaucracy, and Political Change in the United States," in Louis Maisel and Joseph Cooper, eds., *Political Parties:
Development and Decay* (Beverly Hills, Calif.: Sage, 1978), pp. 211–65; and William Nisbet Chambers and Walter Dean Burnham, eds., *The American Party Systems*, 2d ed. (New
York: Oxford University Press, 1975).

[36] On the role of Congress in the U.S. state structure of the twentieth century, see Morris
P. Fiorina, *Congress: Keystone of the Washington Establishment* (New Haven, Conn.: Yale
University Press, 1977); Samuel P. Huntington, "Congressional Responses to the Twentieth
Century," in *The Congress and America's Future*, 2d ed., The American Assembly, Colum-
bia University (Englewood Cliffs, N.J.: Prentice-Hall, 1973), pp. 6–38; Morton Grodzins,
"American Political Parties and the American System," *Western Political Quarterly* 13
(1960): 974–98; and Richard Polenberg, *War and Society: The United States, 1941–1945*
(Philadelphia, Pa.: Lippincott, 1972).

[37] V. O. Key, *Southern Politics in State and Nation* (New York: Knopf, 1949).

tury to the present. America's nineteenth-century patronage democracy, with its proclivity for widely distributing benefits, fueled the late nineteenth-century expansion of de facto disability and old-age benefits for those who could credibly claim to have served the Union forces during the Civil War. Yet once American government began to bureaucratize and professionalize, the surviving structures of patronage democracy and elite perceptions that the Civil War pension system was corrupt discouraged U.S. progressive liberals from imitating the pension and social insurance innovations of their English counterparts. America's initial governmental "response to industrialism" was primarily local and state regulatory laws that often established agencies to take over functions from courts and political parties.

During the New Deal and in its aftermath, the United States launched a kind of modern welfare state, which included public assistance and social insurance measures. Nevertheless, the Social Security Act was rooted in state-level laws or legislative proposals still being actively debated in the 1930s; and congressional mediation of contradictory regional interests ensured that national standards could not be established in most programs. Most black people, still trapped during the 1930s at the socioeconomic bottom of the nondemocratic South, were excluded from or severely disadvantaged within America's original social programs. Blacks remained to be incorporated later, after social and political circumstances had sharply changed.

American mobilization for World War II—a mobilization less total and centrally coordinated by the state than the British mobilization for the same war—did not overcome congressional and local resistance against initiatives that might have pushed the United States toward a nationalized full-employment welfare state. Instead, this pivotal war enhanced federal fiscal capacities and created new possibilities for congressionally mediated subsidies and tax expenditures, but did not permanently enhance public instrumentalities for labor market intervention or the federal executive's capacities for coordinating social spending with macroeconomic management.

Geopolitics and war experiences, along with the sequencing of democratization and bureaucratization have thus powerfully set institutional parameters for social politics in the United States. Yet these fundamental patterns of state formation are only the starting point for our analysis. Political struggles and their policy outcomes have also been conditioned by the institutional leverage various social groups have gained, or failed to gain, within the U.S. state and political parties. By analyzing ways in which America's distinctive state structure has influenced possibilities for collective action and for political alliances, we can improve upon arguments that simply highlight struggles of capitalists versus industrial workers.

America's precociously (yet until the 1960s unevenly) democratized federal polity has always made it difficult for either capitalists or industrial workers to operate as a unified political force in pursuit of class projects on a national scale. Ira Katznelson and Martin Shefter have spelled out the situation for workers in a series of important publications.[38] Because in the United States manhood suffrage and competing patronage parties were in place at the very start of capitalist industrialization, American workers learned to separate their political participation as citizens living in ethnically defined localities from their workplace struggles for better wages and employment conditions. No "working class politics" joining community and workplace emerged; and American trade unions developed no stable ties to a labor-based political party during the period around the turn of the century when European social democratic movements were forged. Nationally, American workers were left without the organizational capacities to push for a social democratic program, including generous and comprehensive social policies. In localities where they did have considerable political clout, American workers tended to gain advantages on ethnic rather than class lines. Only during and after the New Deal was this situation modified, as alliances developed in many places between urban-liberal Democrats and industrial unions.[39] Yet the Democrats and the unions never went beyond flexible and ad hoc partnerships. Particular Democratic politicians put together unique constellations of supporters, sometimes including certain unions and sometimes not, while unions retained the option of supporting friendly Republicans as well as Democrats.

Although the U.S. polity has thus hardly served as a tool of broadly defined working class interests, American capitalists nevertheless, in the apt phrase of David Vogel, "distrust their state."[40] In part, this is an understandable response to a long-democratized polity prone periodically

---

[38] On the consciousness and collective action of workers, see Ira Katznelson, *City Trenches: Urban Politics and the Patterning of Class in the United States* (New York: Pantheon, 1981); Ira Katznelson, "Working-Class Formation and the State: Nineteenth-Century England in American Perspective," in Peter B. Evans, Dietrich Rueschemeyer, and Theda Skocpol, eds., *Bringing the State Back In* (New York: Cambridge University Press, 1985), pp. 257–84; and Martin Shefter, "Trade Unions and Political Machines: The Organization and Disorganization of the American Working Class in the Late Nineteenth Century," in Ira Katznelson and Aristide Zolberg, eds., *Working Class Formation: Nineteenth-Century Patterns in Europe and the United States* (Princeton, N.J.: Princeton University Press, 1986), pp. 197–276.

[39] J. David Greenstone, *Labor in American Politics* (New York: Knopf, 1969).

[40] David Vogel, "Why Businessmen Distrust Their State: The Political Consciousness of American Corporate Executives," *British Journal of Political Science* 8 (1978): 45–78.

to launch moralistic reform campaigns challenging the prerogatives of large-scale property holders. In addition, it reflects the frustrations that American capitalists recurrently experience in their dealings with this or that part of the decentralized and fragmented U.S. state structure. For not only does U.S. federal democracy impede unified working-class politics; it also gives full play to divisions within business along industrial and geographical lines.

Conflicts within the ranks of American business are readily politicized, and U.S. corporate interests have always found it difficult to provide unified support for national initiatives that might benefit the economy as a whole on terms favorable either to most sectors of business or to economically dominant sectors.[41] Within the ranks of business as well as beyond, the losers can always go to court—or back to the legislatures, or to a new bureaucratic agency—for another round of battle in the interminable struggles that never seem to settle American policy questions, especially when government intervention in the economy is at issue, as it usually is. To American capitalists the U.S. state has seemed neither coherent nor reliable. National episodes of democratic reform leading to strengthened state interventions have been resisted with the aid of any coalitional allies at hand, even though most businesses have proven able to accommodate, to reshape, and even to benefit from strengthened state interventions after the fact.

Within a state structure that so discourages unified, persistent class politics as does U.S. federal democracy, it is perhaps not surprising that social policy breakthroughs have clustered in widely separated "big bangs" of reform: during the Progressive Era from about 1906 to 1920; during the New Deal of the mid-1930s; and between the mid-1960s and the mid-1970s, during and right after the Great Society period. Each cluster of new policies was heterogeneous, a product of disparate plans previously pursued by networks of policy intellectuals (perhaps buttressed by voluntary associations or particular governmental bureaus) rather than by any political party or nationwide economic group. What is more, each cluster of policy innovations was put through by coalitions of groups in

---

[41] For examples in various policy areas, see Susan S. Fainstein and Norman I. Fainstein, "National Policy and Urban Development," *Social Problems* 26 (1978): 125–46; Ira Katznelson and Kenneth Prewitt, "Constitutionalism, Class, and the Limits of Choice in U.S. Foreign Policy," in Richard Fagen, ed., *Capitalism and the State in U.S.–Latin American Relations* (Stanford, Calif.: Stanford University Press, 1979), pp. 125–40; Steven Kelman, *Regulating America, Regulating Sweden* (Cambridge, Mass.: MIT Press, 1981); Theda Skocpol and Kenneth Finegold, "State Capacity and Economic Intervention in the Early New Deal," *Political Science Quarterly* 97 (1982): 255–78; and David Vogel, "The 'New' Social Regulation in Historical and Comparative Perspective," in Thomas K. McGraw, ed., *Regulation in Perspective* (Cambridge: Harvard Business School/Harvard University Press, 1981), pp. 155–86.

touch with sets of elected legislators, coalitions that emerged during nationally perceived crises widely understood to call for positive governmental solutions. But in each episode the coalitions favoring new social policies were temporary, fragile, incapable of any permanent institutionalization, and very soon undone by conservative backlashes that drew on local forces plus business and other groups resistant to enhanced state power in the United States.

In the histories of many modern welfare states, agricultural classes have proven to be important political allies of urban-industrial groups that would either promote or resist enhanced state interventions.[42] In the United States agricultural interests have been even more pivotal than elsewhere, and not only because there have always been large numbers of family farmers in American society. The American federal state, with its decentralized and nonprogrammatic political parties, has provided enhanced leverage to interests that could associate across many local political districts. Such widespread "federated" interests—including organizations of farmers such as the Grange and the American Farm Bureau Federation, along with local businessmen linked to the Chamber of Commerce, and certain professional associations including the National Education Association and the American Medical Association—have been ideal coalition partners for nationally focused forces that might want to promote, or obstruct, or rework social policies, especially when proposals have had to make their way through the House of Representatives.

Occasionally, such widespread federations have spurred the passage of national social policies; the impact of the Townsend Movement is a case in point. More often, widespread federations—especially those involving commercial farmers and small businessmen prominent in many communities—have obstructed or gutted proposed national social policies. Thus, for example, during the early New Deal of 1933 to 1935, federal agricultural policies had the not fully intended effect of strengthening interest-group association among commercial farmers across the disparate crop-areas of the South and Midwest. In turn, this meant that the American Farm Bureau Federation could ally with business organizations, including the Chamber of Commerce, to pressure congressional representatives against one liberal New Deal social welfare proposal after another, from 1936 on.

Pinpointing institutional leverage through Congress also helps us to make sense of the special role of the South in modern American social policy making—a role that certainly rivals that of either capitalists or the industrial working class. To be sure, the South's role cannot be under-

[42] Agrarian allies or opponents of welfare states are discussed in Castles, *The Social Democratic Image of Society*, and Esping-Andersen, *Politics against Markets*.

stood without underlining the class structure of southern cotton agriculture as a landlord-dominated sharecropper system from the late nineteenth century through the 1930s.[43] Nor could we ignore the explicit
racism that ensured white dominance over black majorities in all sectors
of economic and social life. Yet the South had been militarily defeated in
the Civil War, and by the 1930s this region carried little weight in the
national economy as a whole; nor were its social mores typical of the
nation's. Thus socioeconomic factors and racism alone will not explain
why Southern politicians had so much leverage during and after the New
Deal that they could take a leading role in congressional alliances opposed to the setting of national welfare standards and to any strong federal presence in economic planning.

The influence of southern agricultural interests depended on the inser-
tion of their class power as landlords and their social power as white
racial oligarchs into federal political arrangements that from the 1890s to
the 1960s allowed an undemocratized single-party South to coexist with
competitive two-party democracy in the rest of the nation. Above all,
southern leverage was registered through a congressionally centered legislative process in Washington that allowed key committee chairmen
from safe districts to arbitrate precise legislative details and outcomes.
From the New Deal onward, the national Democratic party used congressional committees to broker the divided goals of its southern and urban-
liberal northern wings.[44] This prevented the often contradictory orientations of the two wings from tearing the national party apart, but at the
price of allowing the enactment of only those social policies that did not
bring the national state into direct confrontation with the South's nondemocratic politics and racially embedded systems of repressive labor
control.

In short, taken together, the U.S. state structure as it had been formed
by the 1930s and 1940s along with the operations of the New Deal party
system, magnified the capacities of southern economic and social elites to
affect national policies—at the same time that the capacities of other interests, including those sections of organized industrial labor allied with
urban Democrats in the North, were simultaneously enhanced by the

[43] See the paper by Jill Quadagno in this volume (Chapter 6); see also Lee J. Alston and
Joseph P. Ferrie, "Labor Costs, Paternalism, and Loyalty in Southern Agriculture: A Constraint on the Growth of the Welfare State," *Journal of Economic History* 65 (1985): 95–
117, and Alston and Ferrie, "Resisting the Welfare State: Southern Opposition to the Farm
Security Administration," in Robert Higgs, ed., *The Emergence of the Modern Political
Economy*, Research in Economic History, Supplement No. 4 (Greenwich, Conn.: JAI Press,
1985), pp. 53–83.

[44] Richard Franklin Bensel, *Sectionalism and American Political Development, 1880–
1980* (Madison: University of Wisconsin Press, 1984), esp. chap. 7.

same U.S. state structure and party system. Many features of the New Deal Social Security programs—and indeed of the entire disjoint configuration of social and economic policies with which the United States emerged from the political watersheds of the New Deal and World War II—can be understood by pinpointing the social interests and the political alliances that were able to gain or retain enhanced leverage through the long-standing federal and congressional institutions of the U.S. state. As several contributors to this volume spell out for particular policy areas, the New Deal brought social policy innovators to the fore through the newly active federal executive. It also energized urban-liberal forces and created new possibilities for political alliances through the electorally strengthened and partially realigned Democratic party. Nevertheless, in the end, America's federal system and regionally uneven suffrage placed severe limits on the political alliances and policies that could prevail as the original foundations were laid for nationwide public social provision.

Especially after the New Deal (although also before that, as revealed by the effect of Civil War pensions on the social insurance debates of the Progressive Era), federal social policies themselves influenced further state formation and politics. The phrase "policy feedbacks" is used to refer to this obvious but usually insufficiently emphasized phenomenon: Once instituted, social policies in turn reshape the organization of the state itself and affect the goals and alliances of social groups involved in ongoing political struggle. Thus the Social Security Act of 1935 strongly affected subsequent possibilities for bureaucratic activism, as well as alliances and cleavages in postwar American social politics.

So many new social, economic, and military interventions by the federal government were launched in the period from the 1930s through the early 1950s that their sheer elaboration forced the growth of federal spending and employment; moreover, state and local governments expanded in response to stimuli and subsidies from the enlarged federal establishment. Because America's federal state became at all levels more bureaucratized and active, further social policy innovations were often generated from "within the state" itself. As Martha Derthick's account suggests, no better example of this phenomenon can be cited than the steady postwar extension of the one fully national program under the Social Security Act, contributory old-age insurance.[45] This program expanded to encompass virtually the entire wage and salaried population, and was also extended into related programmatic areas such as disability insurance and medicare for the elderly. According to Derthick, these developments were primarily propelled by the Social Security administrators themselves, as they adroitly deployed bureaucratic resources to man-

[45] Derthick, *Policy Making for Social Security*.

age public and expert opinion, to sooth congressional committees, and to prepare new legislative proposals for passage at opportune political conjunctures.

As they sought to expand social insurance, the Social Security administrators benefited from the increasing popularity of contributory social insurance after 1955. Within Congress and in the broader society, more and more covered groups became part of the political coalitions that protected and expanded "social security" measures. But other postwar U.S. social policies did not fare so well. In significant part this was because of the reverberations from previous policy choices, first from the internally bifurcated New Deal system and then from attempted Great Society reforms.

As has already been noted, the United States did not become a complete electoral democracy for all of its citizens until after the Civil Rights revolution of the 1960s began the process of incorporating blacks into the southern electorate, and on new terms into the national electorate and the Democratic party. The effects of these processes have been tumultuous—both on agendas for debate over social policy and on political alliances concerned with policy alternatives from the Great Society to the present.[46] Yet the incorporation of blacks into the national polity has not been happening in a social policy vacuum; it is taking place in the context of social policies inherited from the New Deal. "Social security" for the stably employed majority of citizens had become by the 1960s institutionally and symbolically separated from welfare for the barely deserving poor. And for both socioeconomic and political reasons, working-age blacks were disproportionately clients of the vulnerable welfare components of U.S. social provision.

During the social policy reforms of the 1960s and early 1970s, welfare clients temporarily benefited from the widespread recognition that the New Deal system of social policies had not adequately addressed issues of poverty or responded to the needs of blacks, who could now vote in greater numbers. As will be discussed in greater detail below, southern socioeconomic and political arrangements were finally changing in relation to the nation as a whole, and reinvigorated liberal Democrats tried to use welfare extensions and new anti-poverty programs to incorporate blacks into their—otherwise undisturbed—national and local political coalitions. But many social policy reforms of the 1960s and 1970s soon backfired to disturb rather than reinforce Democratic coalitions. National politics underwent a sea change. Since the late 1970s, conservative

[46] This is a theme emphasized by Frances Fox Piven and Richard Cloward. Although our analytic approach is different, we acknowledge their pioneering role in the study of popular impacts on social policy making.

forces hostile to expanded public social provision have found renewed strength within and beyond the Democratic party. This has left impoverished people, including many blacks, increasingly isolated in national politics, and welfare programs more than ever the unwanted orphans of social policy.

Looking Ahead

The Epilogue will further explore the historically evolved constraints and possibilities of American social politics today, and will survey current debates about the alternative lines along which future social policies may develop. Between the Introduction and the Epilogue lie twelve papers grouped into three major parts. Those in Part I illuminate overall configurations and long-term patterns of American social policy in relation to the most basic institutional features of the U.S. federal democratic state. The papers of Part II probe the programmatic innovations that have occurred within the system of social insurance and public assistance policies that originated in the New Deal. Finally, the papers of Part III explore American social politics since the 1960s, taking as their common point of reference the changing social and political situation of American blacks, who were originally left at the margins of the New Deal social policy system, but who have become central to a new round of fundamental debates about public social provision in the United States.

Readers may notice that the parts of the volume correspond to some degree with the three lines of analysis presented as aspects of our institutional-political process approach to U.S. social politics. Part I deals especially with state formation and institutional limits on social policy innovations; Part II examines the shifting leverage of social groups and political coalitions within the mid-twentieth-century U.S. state structure; and Part III especially highlights the consequences of previously established policies for present-day politics. But these correspondences are—and should be—only approximate, as each individual essay necessarily strikes its own balance among all three lines of analysis. Together, institutional limits, shifting political coalitions, and policy feedbacks constitute the political processes through which our national social policies have been made in the past—and will be remade in the future.

I

INSTITUTIONAL LIMITS AND PATTERNS OF POLICY

The authors of the papers in this part look back over decades of American political history and point out contrasts between U.S. social policies and the welfare efforts of West European nations. They highlight large-scale processes of state formation in the United States, showing how civil and international wars and phases of democratization and bureaucratization have distinctively shaped governmental institutions and political parties, and how those institutions, in turn, have affected the patterns—and limits—of social and economic policies in the United States.

We learn why the passage of the 1935 American Social Security Act was belated compared to the enactment of social insurance measures in Western Europe, and also why World War II did not result in the consolidation of the Keynesian welfare state that many New Dealers hoped they had launched in the 1930s. Further, the authors explore two important interfaces between the federal government and the nation's corporate-capitalist economy. Since the 1920s and especially since World War II, federal tax incentives and labor regulations have shaped the development of "private" social welfare benefits, which intersect in complex ways with America's limited public social benefits. Across these same decades, unemployment in the wage-economy has recurrently challenged the capacities of the federal government to stimulate macroeconomic growth and to intervene in particular industries and labor markets.

Modern "social" and "economic" policies have not been coordinated by the American national state, as they have been by many European welfare states. This part of *The Politics of Social Policy in the United States* explores why, tracing connections between the slowly changing structures of U.S. federal democracy and the overall balance sheet of policy successes and failures at key watersheds of political struggle over American social provision.

Not only what happened in the making of social policy but also what might have happened but did not, receive careful attention in this part. Ann Shola Orloff discusses the failure of U.S. social insurance proposals in the Progressive Era; Edwin Amenta and Theda Skocpol investigate the failure of National Resource Planning Board ideas in the 1940s; Beth Stevens explores organized labor's turn from public welfare shortfalls to campaigns for private-sector fringe benefits; and Margaret Weir focuses on the frustration of federal social-spending measures and labor-market interventions in both the 1930s and the 1960s. The aim is to understand the actual processes by which institutional limits have been set and reset in American public policy. Thus each author traces failed policy efforts, as well intended successes (or unintended outcomes later favorably defined).

When joined with analyses of state formation, this approach to policy making reveals the specific ways in which U.S. state structures have, at key watersheds, affected political coalitions and balances of power, and also affected the ability of federal officials to intervene in the economy. We note not only the "successful" outcomes but also the coalitions that did not come together or hold within political parties and in Congress, and the interventions, both proposed and attempted, that were beyond the reach of the executive and administrative capacities. Throughout recent American history, failed attempts to launch social welfare programs, or to more closely coordinate national social and economic policies, have periodically revealed—and also helped to reconstitute—the institutional limits of policy.

At the center of Ann Orloff's chapter is the question of why old-age pensions and social insurance were not initiated at the turn of the twentieth century in the United States, as they were in several major European nations, including liberal Great Britain. Not until the Social Security Act of 1935 did the federal government institute nationwide social insurance and public assistance. Yet the United States did not simply "lag" going down the same road as Europe, Orloff argues. A distinctive nineteenth-century U.S. "state of courts and parties" developed because enfranchisement of all white males preceded the growth of state bureaucracy. Patronage-oriented political parties were the predominant forces in this nineteenth-century polity, and they elaborated Civil War pensions into a massive social spending program benefitting many elderly northern U.S. citizens by the turn of the century.

In Britain at that juncture, civil servants in centralized ministries joined Liberal party leaders to launch pensions and social insurance, partly in response to working-class demands and partly to cement political alliances between the middle- and working-class voters. But the United States in the Progressive Era lacked strong public bureaucracies, and middle-class reformers were so preoccupied with fighting "political corruption" that they refused to ally with working-class forces to support new public spending, especially for the old-age pensions that reminded them all too vividly of the excesses of Civil War pensions. Thus Orloff shows that struggles over tardy state bureaucratization in the United States at the turn of the century helped to preclude cross-class political coalitions in support of new social benefits.

The successful reforms of the Progressive Era were mainly local and state economic regulations. Their enactment complemented the late-nineteenth-century expansion of public education and a variety of social welfare measures. Orloff does not discuss these developments, but they are well-documented in other studies from complementary perspectives.[1] In

---

[1] See especially Arnold J. Heidenheimer, "The Politics of Public Education, Health, and

the United States, the foundations of professionalized civil administration were also laid primarily in cities and states. As Orloff shows, World War I required nationalization of industrial regulation and public employment agencies, but Congress reasserted state and local prerogatives right after the war, dismantling or hobbling the "emergency" federal bureaucracies.

The Great Depression was experienced more severely in the United States than in any other Western nation except Germany. Later World War II drew the American people together in full national mobilization against foreign foes. During and in the immediate wake of these successive national crises, the federal government grew enormously and instituted many new social and economic policies. Why did these policies take the form they did? And why did they not result in the establishment of a full-employment welfare state, a counterpart to the British or Scandinavian welfare states? The chapters in this part offer relevant insights.

When the Social Security Act was passed amid the crisis of the Great Depression, Orloff shows, it built upon prior subnational administrative arrangements and was influenced by state-level policy debates. Most of the professional experts, liberal business leaders, and union leaders who took an interest in the emerging social legislation wanted national unemployment insurance and strong national standards for public assistance. But key Roosevelt administration officials and congressional committees worked to preserve state and local standards where they existed. The only national program established in 1935 was contributory old age insurance for employees, a policy for which there were no subnational precedents.

Local interests—including but not restricted to southern landlords and politicians with a stake in maintaining low wages and racial exclusion—continued to check efforts at American "welfare state building" from the late 1930s through the late 1940s. The strengthened federal executive that emerged from the New Deal spawned many new plans for national economic and social intervention. But both interagency rivalries and the leverage of congressional conservatives proved insuperable obstacles to the realization of such plans—except for such measures as veterans' benefits or construction subsidies tailored to deliver payoffs without central controls to virtually all local constituencies. Margaret Weir analyzes the frustration of Keynesian spending policies, the defeat of efforts at executive reorganization, and the evisceration of the full employment bill of 1945.

Welfare in the U.S.A. and Western Europe: How Growth and Reform Potentials Have Differed," *British Journal of Political Science* 3 (1973): 313–40; Michael Katz, *In the Shadow of the Poor House: A Social History of Welfare in America* (New York: Basic Books, 1986); and William R. Brock, *Investigation and Responsibility: Public Responsibility in the United States, 1865–1900* (Cambridge and New York: Cambridge University Press, 1984).

Continuing this story, Edwin Amenta and Theda Skocpol trace the defeat of wartime and postwar efforts to achieve the nationalization of unemployment insurance, permanent public employment programs, national health insurance, strong public housing programs, more uniform public assistance for all of the poor, and the extension of contributory social insurance to the disabled. In addition to discussing political dynamics like those analyzed by Orloff and Weir, Amenta and Skocpol attribute the defeat of most social welfare reforms in the 1940s partly to the fact that the United States mobilized for the war through business incentives rather than by imposing direct federal controls over production and labor. In Great Britain, by contrast, strong wartime administrative controls enhanced the political clout of industrial labor and eventually worked to the advantage of coalitions favoring welfare state extensions. It also helped that Britain entered the war with extensive social insurance programs already in place. In the United States, the Social Security programs had barely started by the early 1940s, and the fledgling Social Security Board barely managed to preserve the basic features of contributory insurance. Yet because it did, while more comprehensive public welfare proposals failed, old-age insurance became by the end of the war the centerpiece of U.S. social policy.

Beth Stevens reveals additional ways in which federal policy outcomes in the 1940s proved critical for channeling postwar social politics and welfare developments. Stevens highlights the federal government as collector of taxes and as regulator of industrial labor relations. The New Deal involved federal officials in regulating union organization and collective bargaining. World War II brought a massive extension of the federal income tax along with assorted special levies and tax breaks. Stevens shows that these developments, coinciding with wartime controls over wages and the failure of wartime and postwar efforts to expand public social provision, encouraged private corporations and industrial unions to bargain over fringe benefits such as retirement plans and health care coverage. As a result, postwar social provision in the United States developed on two federally encouraged tracks: expansion of direct Social Security benefits from the early 1950s onward, and the simultaneous expansion of additional retirement and health benefits provided by corporations in return for tax breaks. Stably employed unionized workers—and the unions that bargained effectively on their behalf as long as U.S. industries flourished—were the disproportionate winners, but at the expense of broader political coalitions that might have supported welfare state programs for all citizens.

Margaret Weir examines the 1960s as a period when there might have been a broad interracial coalition in support of new "full employment" policies as well as enhanced social welfare benefits. This coalition might have united unionized workers with the marginally employed or unemployed, many of whom were urban blacks who had recently migrated from the rural South. Such a coalition failed to emerge, however, and Great Society economic interventions divided into "poverty" policies aimed at changing the individual attitudes and qualifications of welfare recipients versus tax cuts to stimulate aggregate economic growth. Weir attributes the frustration of employment policies in the 1960s partly to congressional and party influence on political coalitions. In addition, she underlines the inability of the federal executive to intervene in labor markets or to coordinate macroeconomic management with social spending, a weakness that was inherited from the outcomes of earlier battles over full employment in the late 1930s and 1940s.

Like Stevens and Amenta and Skocpol, Weir connects the patterns of American social politics in the postwar era to the limits of national state capacities and interventions that had been, through political struggles, negotiated at the denouement of Depression and World War. At the watershed when major European nations were consolidating their welfare states, the United States was institutionalizing the bifurcation between social and economic interventions, between public and "private" welfare systems, and between "social security" for the employed and "welfare" or "poverty" programs for lower-income people marginal to the labor market.

Taken together, the four chapters of this part survey key aspects of American social provision from the nineteenth century to the present. They demonstrate many of the ways that political institutions have shaped social and economic policies in the United States, tracing the political conflicts through which state and party structures have affected policy outcomes. Not all aspects of social policy are covered, and many analytical questions remain to be addressed. But these papers illustrate the fruitfulness of an approach that highlights state formation and the political effects of persistent institutional arrangements. American social provision has been politically created, not only in a capitalist economy, and not only in a liberal society. It has also taken shape in a federal democracy with decentralized parties and fragmented administrative capacities. These institutions have placed severe limits on efforts to create comprehensive social and economic policies in the United States.

1

The Political Origins of
America's Belated Welfare State

ANN SHOLA ORLOFF

Against the backdrop of European welfare states, the American system of
public social provision seems incomplete and belated. Restricted coverage, lack of generosity to most beneficiaries, and a lack of systematic connections among different social programs—all mark the modern U.S. approach to public social provision as unusually underdeveloped, especially
when one considers the relative wealth of the nation's economy. In addition, the initiatives that established the programs constituting the American approximation to a welfare state were noticeably out of phase with
developments elsewhere in the industrialized West. For some time, historians and social scientists interested in the timing of policy developments
have noted only that the United States has been a "welfare laggard" relative to Europe. Policy breakthroughs leading to a nationwide system of
social provision did not occur here until the passage of the Social Security
Act of 1935, which established a national old-age insurance program, a
federal-state unemployment insurance system, and federal subsidies for
approved state programs of assistance for the elderly poor and dependent
children. In contrast, European countries launched core social programs
about a generation earlier, in the period between 1883 and World War I.
Unlike most other advanced industrial countries, moreover, the United
States has never established national health insurance.

Merely characterizing the United States as a "welfare laggard," however, overlooks some critical facts of American history, facts that doom
from the outset any attempt to fit U.S. developments into the ideal-typi-
cal, European-centered pattern of welfare state development, even with
allowances for delays and incompleteness. For it is not the case that
America has a version of a European welfare state that was simply slightly

I would like to thank John Myles, Hugh Heclo, George Steinmetz, and my co-editors,
Theda Skocpol and Margaret Weir, for their helpful comments on this paper. Thanks also
to Eric Parker for providing research assistance. Partial support for this research was provided by a grant from the University of Wisconsin Graduate School Research Committee.

tardy in arriving, or that U.S. social benefits will eventually "mature" into a European-style system. Not only is the contemporary U.S. system of public social provision cross-nationally unusual, but also the trajectory along which the United States traveled to arrive at this system has been strikingly different from what students of European social policies have led us to believe is the inevitable course of welfare state development. The aim of this chapter is to describe and to explain the development of American social policies up through the passage of the Social Security Act of 1935. Because it is customary to treat U.S. national welfare programs as beginning in the 1930s, many people know little of what preceded this period. Thus, I will begin with a fresh overview of the overall trajectory of American social policy developments.

AN OVERVIEW OF AMERICAN SOCIAL POLICY

Histories of American social provision often presume that the federal government had no role in providing welfare benefits until the 1930s, when President Franklin Roosevelt introduced social security programs as part of his New Deal. Until then, the story goes, the needs of those Americans unable to care for themselves through participation in the labor market were addressed only, if at all, by the state and—especially— local levels of government. This account is superficially accurate but potentially quite misleading. For there was one rather spectacular exception to local predominance in the welfare field in the late nineteenth and early twentieth centuries. This was the Civil War pension system, remarkable in its own right and also consequential for later social policy developments in the United States.

Originally, the federal government paid pensions only to veterans who had been disabled in the battles of the Civil War and to the dependents of soldiers killed in the war, as one might expect of a military pension system. But then, in the decades following Appomattox, the Civil War pensions were changed into de facto old-age and disability pensions that provided coverage for some one million elderly Americans, reaching about one half of all elderly, native-born men in the North around the turn of the century. While analysts today tend to overlook the social welfare function of these pensions, it was well recognized by contemporaries. In 1917, prominent social reformer Edward Devine called Civil War pensions "a main national provision for old age."[1] And University of Chicago sociologist Charles Henderson, a leading advocate of social insurance, noted in 1909 that "the military pension system has acted in great meas-

---

[1] Edward Devine, quoted in John Gillen, *Poverty and Dependency* (New York: Century, 1926), p. 284.

ure as a workingmen's pension system."[2] Isaac Rubinow, another leader in the U.S. social insurance movement, wrote of the Civil War pensions in 1913:

> After all, it is idle to speak of a popular system of old-age pensions as a radical departure from American traditions, when our pension roll numbers several hundred thousand more names than that of Great Britain. It is preposterous to claim that the cost of such a pension would be excessive, when the cost of our pensions is over $160,000,000, or more than three times as great as that of the British system. . . . We are clearly dealing here with an economic measure which aims to solve the problem of dependent old age and widowhood.[3]

Indeed, in the period between the 1880s and World War I, while reformers, labor leaders, and politicians throughout the West initially were discussing the possibilities for adopting modern social insurance and old-age pensions to protect the "respectable" working class—and especially the "worthy aged" among them—from the indignities of the traditional poor laws, many elderly working and middle-class Americans were actually already so protected.

Logically then, we might expect that U.S. reformers around the turn of the century would have been interested in building upon the Civil War pension experience to extend old-age benefits to all elderly Americans. During the Progressive Era of about 1900 to 1919, Americans were active participants in transnational debates over social insurance and pension proposals. Even so, only a few Progressive reformers advocated the extension of the Civil War pension system into a modern, universal system of old-age protection. These pensions were allowed to pass from existence with the dying of the Civil War cohorts, and there was no federal-level public replacement until the enactment of contributory old-age insurance plus assistance for the elderly poor under the 1935 Social Security Act.

During the Progressive period, most states did adopt laws establishing workers' compensation and so-called widows' or mothers' pensions—the forerunner of today's Aid to Families with Dependent Children (AFDC).[4] This period of reform also witnessed the passage of many laws regulating a wide range of industrial conditions. Yet the more expensive and admin-

---

[2] Charles Henderson, *Industrial Insurance in the United States* (Chicago: University of Chicago Press, 1909), p. 277.

[3] Isaac M. Rubinow, *Social Insurance* (New York: Henry Holt, 1913), p. 404.

[4] Elizabeth Brandeis, "Labor Legislation," in Don Lescohier and Elizabeth Brandeis, *History of Labor in the United States, 1896–1932*, vol. 3 (New York: Macmillan, 1935), pp. 399–700; Mark Leff, "Consensus for Reform: The Mother's-Pension Movement in the Progressive Era," *Social Service Review* 47 (1973): 397–417.

istratively demanding social spending programs that formed the core of nascent systems of social protection in Europe and some parts of the British Commonwealth—old-age pensions and insurance, health and unemployment insurance—were politically unsuccessful in the United States between the 1880s and World War I. And in the wake of the war, America decisively rejected new *public* social protections and embraced instead the ideal of "welfare capitalism."[5]

Only in the midst of a political crisis triggered by the Depression of the 1930s did Americans—belatedly, from the European perspective—initiate nationwide public social protections. Yet the delay was not without consequences for the character of the set of policies established by the 1935 Social Security Act, the "charter legislation" for the U.S. version of the modern welfare state. Two telling features of the 1935 legislation were the omission of national health insurance and the institutionalization of existing state-level differences in benefits and coverage for most programs. The Social Security Act did lead to the establishment of nationwide welfare programs, although they demonstrated varying levels of federal control. There was a fully national, compulsory system of contributory old-age insurance for those who worked in covered industries. Also established was a federal-state contributory insurance system for the unemployed in which the states were induced, but not mandated, to participate—and for which the states set benefit levels and eligibility requirements. In addition, there were optional programs of noncontributory, means-tested social assistance that remained under state-level administration, with costs to be shared by the states and the federal government. These public assistance programs, established at the discretion of the states, could aid dependent children in single-parent families and needy elderly people who did not qualify for insurance benefits. Significantly, the framers of the American social security system chose not to follow the European pattern of adding to the contributory insurance programs government subsidies financed from general revenues; nor did they establish *national* benefit programs financed entirely from the federal government's revenues.

How are we to make sense of the historical development of the modern system of U.S. public social provision—the trajectory of its development and the character of the Social Security Act which established almost all of the programs that compose it? Three important dimensions of analysis have emerged from previous research on the development of the welfare state; taken together, they form the elements of an *institutional-political process approach*. At the most fundamental analytic level—the develop-

---

[5] Stuart Brandes, *American Welfare Capitalism, 1880–1940* (Chicago: University of Chicago Press, 1976).

ment of institutions—we attend to the ways in which U.S. state formation shaped the American political universe, within which alliances were formed and policies were formulated. In particular, we focus on the sequence of bureaucratization and democratization, two fundamental processes that transformed the political structure of America in the late nineteenth and early twentieth centuries. This changing political structure formed the context in which modern social policies were debated and met their initial legislative fate in the United States. Then, we focus on the political process, which comprises the second and third elements of this approach: the character of the political alliances that helped to launch (and delay) the American version of a welfare state and the feedback effects of earlier social policies on subsequent politics and policy debates. Before developing an explanation for the *American* pattern of social-welfare provision, let us first see how these analytic elements central to the institutional-political process approach help to explain the emergence of modern welfare states more generally.

EXPLAINING THE EMERGENCE OF MODERN WELFARE STATES

In the last years of the nineteenth and the first years of the twentieth century, social reformers, labor leaders, and political elites across Europe and North America were actively debating social policy issues. Given the new social and political conditions created by industrialization, urbanization, the rise of capitalism, and the political incorporation of the working class, their questions centered on whether the deterrent poor law system should be replaced (at least for some groups in the population) with contributory social insurance or noncontributory pension programs. In addition, in both Europe and North America, popular movements, often based on labor organizations, pressed for new social protections, particularly for publicly funded old-age pensions that would not require tax contributions from workers. Yet neither the concern of elites about the "social question" nor the actual initiation of new welfare programs in Europe were responses simply to popular demands or to social problems newly created by industrialization, urbanization, and concomitant changes in the family.

Recent comparative research on the origins of welfare states in Europe suggests, instead, that political and bureaucratic elites instituted social insurance and pension programs, utilizing existing or readily created state administrative organizations, as part of efforts aimed at the "anticipatory political incorporation of the industrial working class."[6] The issue of

[6] Theda Skocpol and John Ikenberry, "The Political Formation of the American Welfare State," *Comparative Social Research* 6 (1983): 90.

working-class participation in the polity—on whose terms and through which organizations—was of great concern to European elites and middle classes in this period, as extensions of the suffrage to non-propertied groups were occurring across that continent. This response suggests, in turn, that some element of political incentive, flowing from a threat to political control or from an opportunity to gain organizational or electoral advantage, especially in periods of electoral competitiveness or when new voters are entering the polity, must be operating in order to stimulate elite interest and coalition-building in the social welfare field. Indeed, a review of analyses of the initiation of social insurance and pensions suggests that the political force responsible for the introduction of new public protections was that of a *cross-class coalition* for new public social spending. The support of reformist elites and new middle-class groups as well as the working classes was a necessary condition for the political success of the new programs in this early period.

European reformers within and outside the state suggested social insurance and pensions as a means for respectable members of the working classes to avoid the cruelties of the traditional poor law. These measures were also to serve as a means for governments and propertied classes to head off the threat to the social order and to their political hegemony posed by leaving no recourse to the lower classes in times of need but the poor law system. The poor law policy itself served as the starting point for debates about what should replace it. The broader analytic implications of this point are worth noting. Policy debates are regularly informed by ideas about how best to correct the perceived imperfections of past policy, rather than simply how best to respond to social conditions as such. This means that the goals and demands of politically active groups cannot be gauged simply from their current social positions or solely from ideological and value preferences. Meaningful reactions to existing policy—a part of what we have referred to in the Introduction as *policy feedback*, and what Hugh Heclo has called "political learning" about the "policy inheritance"—color the very interests and goals that groups or politicians define for themselves in public policy struggles.[7]

To implement the proposed welfare programs, policy reformers looked to state administrative organizations. In late-nineteenth-century Europe, these agencies either had been recently rid of patronage practices and been professionalized through the passage of effective civil service statutes or had longstanding traditions of bureaucratic autonomy. The European experience suggests that processes of *state formation* had important implications for the development of systems of modern, public social

---

[7] Hugh Heclo, *Modern Social Politics in Britain and Sweden* (New Haven: Yale University Press, 1974).

provision. First, for the new social insurance and pension programs to succeed, the state administration had to have the capacity to plan and administer relatively complex programs. Groups of influential public officials could then play key roles in formulating new social policies with existing administrative resources, pressing them on political executives and working out compromises with organized interest groups. This pattern of policy development was especially noticeable in the case of contributory social insurance. Because these programs, in addition to providing benefits, taxed workers and involved the state in activities previously within the domain of working-class voluntary associations, they often were less popular initially than noncontributory old-age pensions. Popular movements frequently arose to demand noncontributory pensions— which would not tax workers or threaten the autonomy of their organizations. The substantial popular support for state social spending initiatives could sometimes be utilized by leaders of political coalitions to overcome resistance to social insurances programs, especially if well-placed civil servants had laid the groundwork for those programs.

Second, elite (and, to a lesser extent, popular) support for social policy initiatives was conditioned on there being a suitable instrument for administering the new programs efficiently and honestly. After all, definitions of what is feasible or desirable in politics depend in part on the capacities and qualities that political actors attribute to state organizations and to the officials who operate them. Just as there is political learning about past policies, a kind of political learning about the government itself also occurs. Thus, the appeal of any given policy will depend to some extent on how well groups think it could be officially implemented, as well as on how it may affect the fortunes of groups struggling over the control of official organizations. When state organizations adequate to the administrative tasks at hand are believed to be available, elites are more likely to respond to political incentives arising from popular mobilization by building or joining a cross-class alliance to support new social spending for income protection.

Finally, the process of state formation affects the operating modes of the very political organizations—especially parties and state administrative organs—through which public social policies can be collectively formulated and socially supported. In particular, the sequence in which bureaucratization and electoral democratization occur is critical in this regard, as the work of political scientist Martin Shefter on patronage and political parties would suggest.[8] State bureaucratization preceded electoral democratization in most European absolute monarchies; in such instances, when political parties emerged and sought popular support, they

[8] Martin Shefter, "Party and Patronage," *Politics and Society* 7 (1977): 404–51.

could not simply offer the spoils of office as an inducement to voters and party activists, for access to jobs in civil administration was controlled by established bureaucratic elites. Thus, parties were forced to rely upon programmatic appeals, based on ideology or promises about how state power might be used for policies advocated by, or potentially appealing to, organized groups of constituents. At the same time, state administrations in these polities could (further) rationalize and professionalize their operations free from the partisan political concerns that dominated the calculations of elected officials. In contrast, in countries where mass electoral democratization preceded state bureaucratization, as it did in the United States, the civil administration was not protected from partisan use, and parties could use government jobs and resources for patronage. Under this set of conditions, parties would tend to rely on patronage rather than on programmatic or ideological appeals to mobilize their constituencies and reward activists. The electoral calculus of party politicians would dominate the operations of state organizations, rendering such organizations less able to use bureaucratic resources to plan autonomous state interventions into civil society.

By the mid–nineteenth century, all Western states were coming under pressures to become more efficient and professionalized. Industrialization, urbanization, and the need to compete internationally, both economically and militarily, generated these imperatives. In those countries where patronage still held sway over state administrations, there were struggles over how to overcome the "political corruption" of patronage in order to create an "efficient"—that is, nonpartisan, predictable, and expert—civil service. If civil service reform succeeded before full democratization—as it did in Great Britain, for example—political parties were encouraged, as more people were granted the franchise, to change their mode of operation and to reorient their electoral appeals from the patronage system toward more programmatic appeals and constituency-based organization. The civil administration could then be changed in ways that enhanced its capacity for intervention in civil society. However, if patronage was established in a fully (or almost fully) democratic polity—as it was in the United States—it was quite difficult to uproot afterwards. Mass electorates, and the party politicians appealing to them, had a continuing interest in using government as a source of patronage, and civil service reformers had to wage difficult, eventually only partially successful, struggles to overcome democratized "political corruption" in government and party politics.

Thus, to fully understand the forces that gave shape to the contemporary American social welfare system, we need to begin with the sociopolitical processes transforming the American state and party system in the nineteenth century. Critical to the entire trajectory of American social policy is the fact that the United States was the world's first mass democracy. The extension of suffrage to all white males in America had occurred by the 1830s, well before the democratization of the electorate in European countries. More importantly, this happened before the development of any political constituency interested in building an autonomous, professionalized, and nonpartisan state organization. Without such a "coalition for bureaucratic autonomy" (to use Shefter's term), positions in the state administration were used by party leaders as resources for mobilizing the mass electorate and maintaining party organizations. This was the essence of the well-known spoils system, which dominated U.S. politics throughout the nineteenth century. Reinforcing the effects of early democratization and the dominance of patronage parties over the civil administration was the relatively protected geopolitical position of the United States. Bureaucratic state-making was not stimulated by war-making, as in the early modern European cases so well analyzed by Charles Tilly.[9]

Patronage Democracy and the Civil War Pension System

In industrializing America after the Civil War, parties mobilized the electorate through popularly rooted political machines whose very life-blood was patronage. Ideological and programmatic appeals were not prominent, but politically discretionary distributional programs that provided jobs, services, or other goods, such as Civil War pensions, were quite popular with politicians and their constituencies.[10] These distributional policies were of critical importance to elected officials, for it was in the late nineteenth century that American politics were at their most competitive outside the South. In the North and Midwest, Democrats and Republicans faced each other with nearly equivalent popular electoral support, and they regularly replaced each other in office. Electoral participation was at an all-time high, and given the nearly equal division of support, a few hundred votes—however secured—in the most politically competitive states, such as Indiana, Ohio, Illinois, and New York, could mean the difference between winning and losing an election.[11]

[9] Charles Tilly, "War Making and State Making as Organized Crime," in Peter Evans, Dietrich Rueschemeyer, and Theda Skocpol, eds., Bringing the State Back In (New York: Cambridge University Press, 1985), pp. 169–91.

[10] Richard McCormick, "The Party Period and Public Policy: An Exploratory Hypothesis," Journal of American History 66 (1979): 279–98.

[11] Morton Keller, Affairs of State: Public Life in Nineteenth Century America (Cambridge, Mass.: Harvard University Press, 1977), chaps. 7, 8, 14; Heywood Sanders, "Paying for the 'Bloody Shirt': The Politics of Civil War Pensions," in Barry Rundquist, ed., Political Benefits (Lexington, Mass.: Lexington Books, 1980), pp. 137–59.

The Civil War pension system was an excellent example of the sort of policies generated by the operations of patronage democracy. It allowed politicians, especially Republicans, to channel to many individuals in numerous (non-Southern) communities pensions financed out of the surplus revenues coming from the constantly readjusted tariffs they sponsored to benefit various industries and areas.[12] Given the extensive mobilization of voters and the extremely competitive electoral conditions of late-nineteenth-century patronage democracy, it is not surprising that during the 1880s and 1890s, the pension system was changed from a provision for compensation of combat injuries and war deaths to the functional equivalent of an old-age and disability pension system for a politically important segment of the U.S. electorate. In the Northern and Midwestern states, veterans of the Civil War constituted fully 12 to 15 percent of the electorate, making the "soldier vote a prize of great worth," a "prize" that increased in value with the growth of the Grand Army of the Republic (GAR), the veterans' lobbying group.[13]

Figure 1.1 helps to show the effects of the transformation and expansion of the post–Civil War pension system by charting the trends in disbursements, number of pensioners, and private pension bills between the late 1860s and 1920. Benefits under the original 1862 law were extended only to soldiers actually injured in combat or to the dependents of those disabled or killed. As one might expect, the number of beneficiaries and total expenditures were falling off in the late 1870s. Subsequently, however, under the pressure of the intense electoral competition of the times, both Republican and Democratic Congressmen supported legislative liberalizations, the most important in 1879 and 1890, that effectively transformed the character of the pension system.[14] The 1879 Arrears Act allowed soldiers who "discovered" Civil War–related disabilities to sign up and receive in one lump sum all of the pension payments they would have been eligible for had they been receiving benefits since the 1860s! Then the 1890 Dependent Pension Act severed altogether the link between

[12] Richard Bensel, *Sectionalism and American Political Development* (Madison: University of Wisconsin Press, 1984), pp. 60–73.

[13] Leonard D. White, *The Republican Era: A Study in Administrative History, 1869–1901* (New York: The Free Press, 1958), p. 218. GAR membership increased from 60,000 in 1880 to 428,000 in 1890, when the organization included about one-third of all Union Army veterans who survived the Civil War. Yet the initial legislative liberalization of pensions—the Arrears Act of 1879—was not a product of GAR lobbying; rather, the growth of the GAR was stimulated by the Arrears Act. On the GAR, see Mary Dearing, *Veterans in Politics: The Story of the G.A.R.* (Baton Rouge: Louisiana State University Press, 1952), and Donald McMurry, "The Political Significance of the Pension Question, 1885–1897," *Mississippi Valley Historical Review* 9 (1922): 19–36.

[14] William Glasson, *Federal Military Pensions in the United States* (New York: Oxford University Press, 1918); McMurry, "Political Significance of the Pension Question."

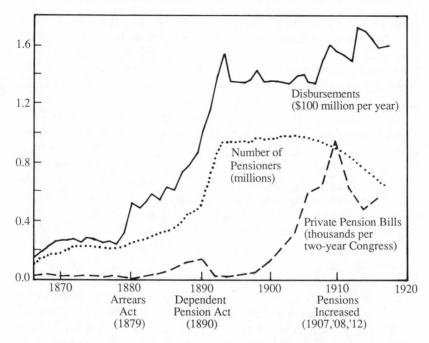

FIGURE 1.1 The expansion of Civil War pensions, 1866–1917. Source: William Glasson, *Federal Military Pensions in the United States* (New York: Oxford University Press, 1918), pp. 273, 280.

combat-related injuries and benefits under the pension system. Any veteran who had served ninety days in the Union Army, whether or not he saw combat or was injured in the Civil War, could sign up for a pension if at some point he became unable to perform manual labor. In practice, after the 1890 legislation, old age alone became a sufficient disability, and in 1906 the law was further amended to state explicitly that "the age of sixty-two years and over shall be considered a permanent specific disability within the meaning of the pension laws."[15] By this time, about 90 percent of the surviving Union veterans were pensioners. In essence, America had a de facto old-age and disability pension system for those who had served in the Civil War and a survivors' allowance for many of their dependents.[16]

Members of Congress were kept quite busy by the operations of the

[15] U.S. Bureau of Pensions, *Laws of the United States Governing the Granting of Army and Navy Pensions* (Washington, D.C.: Government Printing Office, 1925), p. 43; Carole Haber, *Beyond Sixty-Five* (New York: Cambridge University Press, 1983), p. 112.

[16] Ann Shola Orloff, "The Politics of Pensions: A Comparative Analysis of the Origins of Pensions and Old Age Insurance in Canada, Great Britain, and the United States, 1880s–1930s" (Ph.D. diss., Princeton University, 1985), p. 71.

pension system in the 1880s and 1890s. Not only were there the recurrent legal liberalizations of the terms of eligibility for pensions, but, in addition, congressmen and senators devoted a large amount of time to helping their constituents establish their eligibility for pensions through personal intervention with the U.S. Pension Bureau and by sponsoring thousands of special private pension bills tailored to allow specific individuals to collect benefits even when they did not qualify under the very liberal legislated qualifications.[17] The U.S. Pension Bureau itself was the "most uncompromisingly political branch of the late nineteenth century federal bureaucracy," where there was wide discretion in the processing of claims due to a huge backlog.[18] Under such circumstances, control of the civil administration was an important political resource. The partisan appointees in the Pension Bureau, most notably the Republicans, utilized this resource particularly at election time, when pension agents would be sent into the field to sign up pensioners—for their benefits and for the Grand Old Party![19]

Given that a considerable proportion of men then in their twenties and thirties served in the Civil War regiments, and given that these men were in their sixties by 1890 to 1910, it is not surprising that at least one-half of all elderly, native-born men in the North, as well as many old and young widows, were receiving what were in effect federal old-age and survivors' pensions during this period. Of course, the post–Civil War pension system was uneven in its coverage of the American population, with the distribution of pensions favoring native-born men and pre–Civil War immigrants living in the North and Midwest. A majority of the elderly white Southern participants in the Civil War were veterans of the Confederate Army and therefore not eligible for federal benefits, although most of the Southern states began to give (relatively meager) state pensions to disabled or impoverished Confederate veterans in the 1890s.[20] Also excluded were blacks and all post–Civil War immigrants; this meant that relatively few unskilled workers were among the system's beneficiaries.

It seems clear that benefits under the Civil War pension system flowed primarily to members of the middle class and the upper strata of the working class, rather than to the neediest Americans. Yet in Europe it was precisely the "respectable" and better-off members of the working classes

---

[17] McMurry, "Political Significance of the Pension Question," p. 28.

[18] Keller, *Affairs of State*, p. 311.

[19] Sanders, "Paying for the 'Bloody Shirt.' "

[20] William Glasson, "The South's Care for Her Confederate Veterans," *American Monthly Review of Reviews* 36 (1907): 40–47; Rubinow, *Social Insurance*, pp. 408–9; Ann Shola Orloff and Theda Skocpol, " 'Why Not Equal Protection?': Explaining the Politics of Public Social Spending in Britain, 1900–1911, and the United States, 1880s–1920," *American Sociological Review* 49 (1984): 728.

who were of most concern to those reformers proposing social insurance and pensions. The problem of the pauperization of these "worthy" (and often newly enfranchised) people through the operation of traditional poor laws, which left no alternative to destitution but degrading, insufficient, and disfranchising poor relief, was in fact a major stimulant to the consideration of social policy reform in Europe. In the United States, not every Civil War pensioner would have been a pauper without the aid of a federal pension, but as Charles Henderson wrote in his important 1909 work, *Industrial Insurance in the United States*, "Many of the old men and women who, in Europe, would be in almshouses, are found in the United States living upon pensions with their children or in homes to which paupers are not sent and they feel themselves to be the honored guests of the nation for which they gave the last full measure of devotion."[21]

Although Civil War pensions were a form of public aid expanded to meet the needs of some fortunate older Americans, not all who were elderly, disabled, or impoverished around the turn of the century received Civil War pensions. For some unemployed people, there were occasionally positions in work-relief projects funded by municipalities during business downturns, when the plight of the jobless was most visible.[22] But for the non–able-bodied poor, the only alternative to destitution was charity. Charity, whether dispensed by local public poor law authorities or private philanthropic agencies, was at best inadequate. At worst, it involved disfranchisement and residence in a semi-penal workhouse. Significantly, public poor relief was offered as an alternative to, rather than as a right of, citizenship.[23]

The financing and administration of the poor laws throughout nineteenth-century Europe and North America had several commonalities—local administration was the rule, and poor relief everywhere was meager and degrading.[24] The distinguishing feature of late-nineteenth-century U.S. poor relief administration was the predominance of patronage practices. A wide variety of governmental forms existed in American localities, but whatever the form, the patronage organizations of Democrats

[21] Henderson, *Industrial Insurance*, p. 277.

[22] Leah Hannah Feder, *Unemployment Relief in Periods of Depression* (New York: Russell Sage, 1936), pp. 168–88.

[23] Raymond Mohl, "Three Centuries of American Public Welfare," *Current History* 65 (1973): 6–10, 38–39.

[24] By the latter half of the century, some central administrative supervision of poor relief functions had emerged; in European countries, this was often at the level of the national government, while in the U.S., it was at the state level. On early U.S. poor relief administrative practices, see Josephine Brown, *Public Relief, 1929–1939* (New York: Henry Holt, 1940), chap. 1, and Michael Katz, *In the Shadow of the Poorhouse: A Social History of Welfare in America* (New York: Basic Books, 1986), pt. I.

and Republicans dominated city, town, and county governments.[25] The partisan control of American local governments meant—as did the dominance of patronage politicians in the federal government—that administration was nonprofessional and "permeated . . . to the core" by party politics.[26] Control of poor relief provided politicians with opportunities for patronage appointments and for exercising partisan preference in the awarding of contracts for building and supplying poorhouses, asylums, and other welfare institutions.[27] In addition, because local officials had discretion in granting outdoor relief and work relief, electoral considerations could enter easily into the determination of eligibility for aid.[28] Describing the use of public works as a relief measure in New York City in the 1890s, sociologist Leah Feder noted that "partisan politics entered into its expenditure; workers referred by social agencies were dropped more quickly than those sent by politicians . . . carelessness, extravagance, and misappropriation in administration were rife . . . [although] the fund undoubtedly provided an important resource in relieving unusual distress."[29] Public charity was sometimes supplemented by the gifts of party bosses, who on occasion distributed food and fuel to the poor. Typically, they paid for this largesse out of the "private" funds they garnered through graft or "macing" (the practice of levying assessments on the salaries of public employees).[30]

Late-nineteenth-century patronage democracy was effective in mobilizing broad popular support, but it also produced serious opposition. Populists and labor groups denounced the links between politicians and the "robber barons"—the capitalists dominating the economy through their control of railroads, manufacturing, and banking, newly national in scope. At the same time, university-educated professionals criticized especially the "corruption" and "inefficiency" of the personnel practices of the spoils system. They were dissatisfied as well with the kinds of policies fostered by patronage democracy, which, they charged, lacked any justification in terms of the "public interest." Instead, noted critics, the devel-

[25] Keller, *Affairs of State*, p. 377.

[26] Ari Hoogenboom, *Outlawing the Spoils: A History of the Civil Service Reform Movement* (Urbana: University of Illinois Press, 1968), p. 1.

[27] Frank Bruno, *Trends in Social Work, 1874–1956* (New York: Columbia University Press, 1957), p. 79; Sophonisba Breckinridge, *Public Welfare Administration in the United States: Select Documents* (Chicago: University of Chicago Press, 1927), sec. 4; Harry C. Evans, *The American Poorfarm and its Inmates* (Des Moines, Iowa: Loyal Order of Moose, 1926); Keller, *Affairs of State*, p. 501.

[28] Brown, *Public Relief*, p. 16.

[29] Feder, *Unemployment Relief*, p. 188; see also pp. 22, 158.

[30] John Pratt, "Boss Tweed's Welfare Program," *New York Historical Quarterly* 45 (1961): 396–411; William L. Riordan, *Plunkett of Tammany Hall* (New York: McClure, Phillips, 1905).

opment of American public policy was above all tied to the partisan political exigencies of winning elections. These exigencies did not at all preclude—in fact, probably stimulated—out and out corruption and fraud. Even the normal functioning of the patronage system was coming under fire as "political corruption." For example, the chairman of the committee on the merit system in public institutions of the National Conference of Charities and Correction (NCCC), America's leading association of charity workers and social reformers in the late 1800s, forcefully challenged the rationale and practices of the spoils system, calling that system "treasonable robbery, although not treason in the eyes of the law."[31]

The Civil War pension system was targeted as a particularly egregious example of the problems to which patronage democracy led. By the 1880s and 1890s, the pension system's partisan uses were clear to many in the broad middle-class public, despite the attempts of elected officials to legitimize the repeated expansions of the system through the use of patriotic rhetoric and waving the "bloody shirt." As one observer noted in an investigatory article appearing in an 1884 issue of the reform-oriented magazine *Century*, "It is safe to assert that most of the legislation adopted since the war closed, to pay money on account of service in the Union armies, has had for its real motive not justice nor generosity, but a desire to cultivate the 'soldier vote' for party purposes."[32] For the remainder of the nineteenth century and in the Progressive Era of the twentieth, these "abuses" of the pension system and other "perversions of democracy" associated with mass patronage politics provided a continuing stimulus for political reform, as well as a powerful symbol of all that was considered to be amiss with existing political practices.

The initial proponents of ending patronage through civil service reform in the United States were "Mugwumps," upper- and upper-middle-class reformers located in the Northeast, especially New York and Massachusetts. Like their European counterparts of the late nineteenth century, the Mugwumps wanted public administration taken out of patronage politics, so that expertise and predictability could prevail.[33] At first, however, the Mugwumps' reform proposals made only limited headway, for American party politicians had secure roots in the fully democratized, tautly

[31] Philip Garret, "The Merit System in Public Institutions," *Proceedings of the National Conference of Charities and Correction* (Boston: George Ellis, 1896), p. 369.

[32] Eugene Smalley, "The United States Pension Office," *Century Magazine* 28 (1884): 427.

[33] Martin Schiesl, *The Politics of Efficiency: Municipal Administration and Reform in America, 1880–1920* (Berkeley and Los Angeles: University of California Press, 1977), chap. 2; Martin Shefter, "Party, Bureaucracy and Political Change in the United States," in Louis Maisel and Joseph Cooper, eds., *Political Parties: Development and Decay* (Beverly Hills: Sage, 1978), pp. 211–65.

mobilized mass white-male electorate. As Stephen Skowronek has pointed out in his study of American state-building, "to build a merit system in American government, government officers would have to move against resources and procedures vital to their power and position."[34]

Through the last quarter of the nineteenth century, the conflict between politicians and the various good government reformers resulted in overall defeat for the Mugwumps. Following the extremely close presidential election of 1880 and the patronage-related assassination of President James Garfield, the Republican administration of President Chester Alan Arthur and the Republican-controlled Congress in early 1883 approved the establishment of a Civil Service Commission under the Pendleton Act, largely as a concession to the Mugwumps to avoid losing their votes.[35] Analysts agree that the impact of the law was quite limited; Skowronek notes that it dried up "selected pockets of patronage so as to improve efficiency and, at the same time, serve strategic party goals . . . ; [it] supplemented the dominant patronage relationship rather than supplanting it."[36] In fact, because of the growth in federal employment, a larger number of jobs were available for patronage by the end of the century than had been before the enactment of the Pendleton Act, even with the growth in the proportion of classified (i.e., civil service) jobs. Thus, significant civil service reform was delayed until the Progressive Era, when electoral competitiveness declined somewhat, although even then, reformers never fully succeeded in uprooting patronage. Nevertheless, the crisis of the patronage system formed the backdrop to the policy debates of the early twentieth century.

The Progressive Era: Debate and Defeat
of Proposed Social-Spending Measures

Around the turn of the twentieth century, Americans, along with people in almost all the industrializing nations of the West, took part in debates over what the state should do in the face of the increasingly well-publicized problems of income insecurity. But the political legacies of nineteenth-century patronage democracy were far from conducive to the establishment of modern social insurance and pensions in Progressive-Era America. The incomplete success of civil service reform in the late nineteenth century had left the U.S. state with relatively underdeveloped capacities for regulating an industrial-capitalist economy and administering

[34] Stephen Skowronek, *Building a New American State: The Expansion of National Administrative Capacities, 1877–1920* (New York: Cambridge University Press, 1982), p. 68 and chap. 3 generally.

[35] Shefter, "Party, Bureaucracy and Political Change," p. 228.

[36] Skowronek, *Building a New American State*, pp. 68–69.

social programs designed to deal with its casualties. In addition, Progressive reformers were in the midst of battles against democratized "political corruption"; these overshadowed debates about social policies. At this point in American history, modern social-spending programs were neither governmentally feasible nor politically acceptable.

Workers' compensation legislation was the first modern welfare program to receive consideration in America, as it was across Europe, and it was substantially successful, achieving passage in thirty-eight states by 1919.[37] After the passage of workers' compensation laws, many European reformers had moved toward dealing with the situation of the aged poor, whose plight had helped to stimulate popular movements for pensions. As pensions were established, reformers and government officials were concerned to add a contributory element to programs designed to deal with unemployment, sickness, and dependency, and the political support for pensions was utilized in the service of social insurance. For example, in Britain, the problems of the aged served as a unifying focus for the political activities of reformers and some labor leaders, helping to cement a cross-class alliance in favor of new social-spending programs.[38] In contrast, in the United States, the problems associated with the aged—poverty, but also mismanaged Civil War pensions—served to drive apart groups who might otherwise have cooperated politically to push for a modern system of social protection. Thus, the trajectory of events in the United States was quite different from that in Europe, and the successful establishment of workers' compensation in many states was not followed by similar successes in instituting old-age pensions or social insurance.

Although they hesitated to press for new social-spending measures, Progressive reformers were not anti-statist in their orientation. On the contrary, they saw the state as having the potential to be an ethical agency, and this vision helped to inspire the movement for civil service reform. Therefore, it is important to be very specific about exactly what kind of cross-class coalitions were not possible in Progressive-Era America. Although middle-class reformers and organized labor were sometimes at odds over the issue of political "reform"—especially in Eastern cities where political machines had made inroads into working class constituencies—they did manage to cooperate on campaigns for workmen's compensation, labor standards legislation, and mothers' pensions. In general, middle-class reformers supported the expansion of the regulatory capacity of the government, which in fact kept pace with European developments.[39]

What can account for the American pattern of social reform legislation

---

[37] Brandeis, "Labor Legislation," pp. 575–77.
[38] Orloff, *The Politics of Pensions*, chap. 6.
[39] Irwin Yellowitz, *Labor and the Progressive Movement in New York State, 1897–1916* (Ithaca: Cornell University Press, 1965), p. 10.

in the years between the turn of the century and World War I? Why were social-spending initiatives so weakly supported by elites and ultimately unsuccessful? And why did other welfare innovations, such as workers' compensation and labor regulations, fare better?

Conventional historical portraits show Americans as culturally and ideologically opposed to new state welfare programs. The failure to enact new social insurance and pension programs is explained by invoking the strength of traditional U.S. liberalism among both educated elites and the population at large.[40] In fact, similar ideas were employed in support of the reform proposals in both Europe and America, as early social scientists demonstrated empirically the social causes of poverty and income insecurity, and politically active innovators grappled with the problem of integrating industrial workers into the polity.[41] In liberal-democratic countries such as Britain and the United States, support for new policy proposals came from a reworking of traditional liberal ideas away from pure self-help and distrust of state intervention toward "new liberal" or "progressive" conceptions.[42] Those inspired by "new liberal" ideas came to see that industrial society made people interdependent. Many noted that individual liberty could be thwarted as much by a lack of life's necessities as by the presence of governmental restrictions.[43] In modern society, argued new liberals, government could be an indispensable support for individual liberty, providing security against socially caused misfortunes and regulating competition to allow for individual initiatives. Thus, new state welfare activities could be—and were, on both sides of the Atlantic—advocated without violating the traditional liberal aim of enhancing individual freedom.[44]

[40] See, for one example among many, Gaston Rimlinger's *Welfare Policy and Industrialization in Europe, America and Russia* (New York: John Wiley, 1971).

[41] Among the better-known social-scientific surveys were, in the United States, Jacob Riis's *How the Other Half Lives* (New York: Charles Scribner's Sons, 1890), and, in Britain, Charles Booth's *Life and Labour of the People of London* (London: Williams and Norgate, 1889 and 1891) and *The Aged Poor in England and Wales* (New York and London: Macmillan, 1894). On the "social question"—that is, how to incorporate industrial workers into the democratic polity, see, for example, John Graham Brooks, *The Social Unrest* (New York: Macmillan, 1903), and J. A. Hobson, *The Crisis of Liberalism: New Issues of Democracy* (London: P. S. King and Son, 1909).

[42] On the British "New Liberals," see Michael Freeden, *The New Liberalism: An Ideology of Social Reform* (Oxford: Clarendon Press, 1978); P.F. Clarke, "The Progressive Movement in England," *Transactions of the Royal Historical Society* 24 (1974): 159–82; and Stefan Collini, *Liberalism and Sociology* (New York: Cambridge University Press, 1979). On their American counterparts, see Sidney Fine, *Laissez-Faire and the General Welfare State* (Ann Arbor: University of Michigan Press, 1965), and Robert Bremner, *From the Depths* (New York: New York University Press, 1956), chap. 8.

[43] See, e.g., Hobson, *The Crisis of Liberalism*, pp. 92–113.

[44] Orloff, *The Politics of Pensions*, chap. 3.; Collini, *Liberalism and Sociology*, p. 107;

What is more, turn-of-the-century American popular support for new welfare measures has been underestimated in conventional historical accounts. Consider the voting in the presidential election of 1912. The Progressive Party, led by former President Theodore Roosevelt, garnered the second-highest vote total, gaining four million votes to Democratic candidate Woodrow Wilson's six million, and edging out incumbent Republican President William Taft. The Progressives achieved this impressive vote total with a platform that endorsed "the protection of home life against the hazards of sickness, irregular employment, and old age through the adoption of a system of social insurance adapted to American use."[45] More precise and convincing evidence comes from Massachusetts, where eight cities held popular referenda on old age pensions in 1915 and 1916. Pensions were approved by Bay State voters by a margin of more than four to one, belying the notion that American popular values precluded this policy innovation.[46]

Organized labor in the United States prior to the New Deal also has been described as uniformly hostile to social welfare programs.[47] It is true that some national leaders of the American Federation of Labor (AFL)—most notably AFL President Samuel Gompers—opposed contributory social insurance, which would tax workers. Yet in the pre–New Deal era, most legislative activity on labor and welfare matters took place at the state and local levels, and it was here that labor unions and federations of labor exercised most of their political influence.[48] In the more industrialized states, where organized labor was relatively more weighty than in the United States as a whole, unions were often supportive of both pensions *and* contributory social insurance. During the Progressive Era, state labor federations endorsed a number of health and unemployment insurance bills, along with workers' compensation, mothers' pensions, and old-age pensions. The recession of 1914–15 induced reformers and labor organizations alike to support steps toward implementing unemployment insurance in California, Massachusetts, and New York.[49] By 1918, nine

Henderson, *Industrial Insurance*; Henry Seager, *Social Insurance* (New York: Macmillan, 1910), pp. 4–5, 148–50.

[45] Kirk Porter and Donald B. Johnson, eds., *National Party Platforms* (Urbana: University of Illinois Press, 1970), p. 177; U.S. Bureau of the Census, *Historical Statistics of the United States* (Washington, D.C.: Government Printing Office, 1960), p. 682.

[46] Massachusetts Special Commission on Social Insurance, *Report* (Massachusetts House No. 1850) (Boston: Wright and Potter, 1917), p. 57.

[47] See, for example, Rimlinger, *Welfare Policy and Industrialization*, pp. 80–84.

[48] Phillip Taft, *Organized Labor in American History* (New York: Harper and Row, 1964), p. 233; Gary Fink, *Labor's Search for Political Order: The Political Behavior of the Missouri Labor Movement, 1890–1940* (Columbia: University of Missouri Press, 1973), pp. 161–82.

[49] "Unemployment Survey," *American Labor Legislation Review* 5 (1915): 591–92;

state labor federations had endorsed unemployment benefits proposals.[50] Likewise, the labor federations from the industrialized states of Ohio, New Jersey, Pennsylvania, and Missouri, in addition to those from California, Massachusetts, and New York, endorsed health insurance proposals between 1915 and 1919.[51]

Interestingly, events in Britain (and elsewhere in Europe) reveal that it was not working-class groups who were responsible for the introduction of contributory social insurance. Instead, it was politicians and ministers who persuaded initially reluctant leaders of unions and other interest groups to go along with the new programs by negotiating about specific methods of implementing taxes and payments.[52] Since U.S. state and local unions were at least as willing as British labor groups to support social insurance programs, it is quite likely that comparable co-optive efforts directed at them by state-level elected or appointed officials would have succeeded. In the United States, government leaders did not make such efforts—and it was surely this lack, rather than lack of demands and political support from the unions, that explains why the social insurances failed in America.

In the case of old-age pensions, it is even clearer that the failure of this form of social provision in Progressive-Era America was not due to the failure of U.S. unions to support such measures. Leaders at all levels of the labor movement generally favored noncontributory old-age pensions. Even Samuel Gompers favored *noncontributory* old-age pensions, stating in 1916 that pensions "carry with them the conviction of their self-evident necessity and justice."[53] Moreover, national conventions of the AFL passed resolutions in favor of pensions in 1908, 1911, 1912, and 1913.[54]

Daniel Nelson, *Unemployment Insurance: The American Experience, 1915–1935* (Madison: University of Wisconsin Press, 1969), p. 18.

[50] Nelson, *Unemployment Insurance*, pp. 70–71.

[51] Ronald Numbers, *Almost Persuaded: American Physicians and Compulsory Health Insurance, 1912–1920* (Baltimore: Johns Hopkins University Press, 1978), p. 79; Paul Starr, *The Social Transformation of American Medicine* (New York: Basic Books, 1982), p. 250; Hace C. Tishler, *Self-Reliance and Social Security, 1870–1917* (Port Washington, N.Y.: Kennikat Press, 1971), p. 173: "Labor Getting Behind Health Insurance," *The Survey* 39 (1918): 708–9.

[52] On the British case, see C. L. Mowat, "Social Legislation in Britain and the United States in the Early Twentieth Century: A Problem in the History of Ideas," in J. C. Beckett, ed., *Historical Studies: Papers Read Before the Irish Conference of Historians* (New York: Barnes and Noble, 1969), pp. 81–96; Bentley Gilbert, *The Evolution of National Insurance in Great Britain* (London: Michael Joseph, 1966), chaps. 5–7; and Heclo, *Modern Social Politics*, pp. 78–90.

[53] Louis Reed, *The Labor Philosophy of Samuel Gompers* (New York: Columbia University Press, 1930), p. 117.

[54] American Federation of Labor, *History, Encyclopedia, Reference Book* (Washington, D.C.: American Federation of Labor, 1919), pp. 303–4.

Indeed, the first pension proposal introduced in the U.S. Congress came from former United Mine Workers leader William B. Wilson in 1909, and it was soon endorsed by the AFL and by many state and local labor leaders.[55] The Wilson bill borrowed from the positive symbolism of Civil War pensions by proposing to deal with poverty among the working-class aged through the creation of an "Old Home Guard," in which all Americans aged sixty-five or over were invited to enlist if their annual income fell below $240; their sole duty would be to report to the War Department on the state of patriotism in their communities, for which they would be paid $120 per year.[56]

During the Progressive Era, it was not working-class groups, but many social reformers—and the middle-class and professional strata from which they came and to whom they oriented their arguments—who were reluctant to accept, let alone champion, social-spending measures such as old-age pensions. These sorts of programs had been advocated by a cross-class alliance in Britain and elsewhere in Europe, but in the United States, such a coalition was not politically possible. This can be seen in the way that U.S. reformers dealt with the issue of old-age poverty—the issue that had brought together a cross-class coalition for social spending in Britain.

The first serious official investigation of old-age poverty occurred in Massachusetts in the wake of the introduction of several old-age pension bills in the state legislature from 1903 to 1906. The Massachusetts Commission on Old Age Pensions, Annuities, and Insurance was appointed in 1907 and issued its report in 1910. This investigatory commission, staffed predominantly with professionals and upper-class Bostonians, gathered data on the elderly poor in Massachusetts, considered various pension proposals, and reported that public pensions were neither necessary nor morally desirable. Given that Massachusetts had long been a pioneer in social and labor legislation, serving as a gateway to the United States for British social policy innovations and as an example to other states, the setback in the Bay State was critical to developments everywhere in America. Indeed, the report dealt a virtual death blow to what had previously been a promising movement toward old-age pensions in that state and elsewhere.[57]

[55] David Fischer, *Growing Old in America* (New York: Oxford University Press, 1978), p. 171.

[56] The text of the bill is reprinted in the *Report* of the Massachusetts Commission on Old Age Pensions, Annuities, and Insurance (Massachusetts House Document No. 1400) (Boston: Wright and Potter, 1910), pp. 339–40.

[57] On events in Massachusetts, see Alton Linford, *Old Age Assistance in Massachusetts* (Chicago: University of Chicago Press, 1949), chap. 1; Massachusetts Commission on Old Age Pensions, Annuities, and Insurance, *Report*; and Fischer, *Growing Old in America*, p. 161.

A labor representative, Arthur M. Huddell, expressed his disagreement
with the commission's recommendations and questioned their arguments
about the preferability of contributory pensions over noncontributory
pensions, citing Civil War pensions as a *favorable* precedent: "The pension to the veterans of the Civil War has built up the American family . . .
[and] the old veteran and his widow are made comfortable in their old
age . . . and have a feeling of independence that old people should
have."[58] But the willingness of Huddell and other reformers from labor's
ranks to endorse noncontributory pensions for the "veterans of industry"
was not complemented by a similar attitude on the part of elites in Massachusetts or in the rest of the United States.

Throughout Progressive-Era America, old-age pensions were down-
played even by the most socially progressive elites, such as the members
of the American Association for Labor Legislation (AALL). In 1913–14—
just as the AFL was solidifying its commitment to old-age pensions—the
AALL made the decision to promote health insurance rather than old-age
pensions as the "next great step" after workers' compensation in the "inevitable" progress toward a comprehensive program of modern social
protections in America.[59] Following the massive unemployment in the
recession of 1913–15, the AALL also advocated a model bill for unemployment insurance, along with other measures to help the jobless.[60] Yet
leaders of the AALL decided to forego a campaign for old-age pensions
after their successes in promoting workers' compensation and industrial
safety laws. Such a campaign assuredly would have appealed to organized
labor and to broader working-class electorate—as pensions did in Britain,
for example. A campaign for contributory social insurance was less able
to appeal to all segments of the labor movement, particularly since there
had been no momentum for new government social-spending programs
built up from prior reform activities on behalf of pensions. Yet pensions
were unappealing to many of the leaders and members of the AALL itself,
as well as to the broader middle-class political public.

Why did U.S. elites and middle-class people generally oppose new state
social-spending initiatives? And why were the capacities and character of
the U.S. state not conducive to the introduction of modern welfare measures? To understand these facts, we must turn to the institutional context
formed by the particular patterns of American state-building, and to the
ramifications this had for coalition-building and for the character of parties and the civil administration.

In Progressive-Era America, civil service reform made some headway,

[58] Massachusetts Commission on Old Age Pensions, Annuities, and Insurance, *Report*, p.
335.
[59] "Social Insurance," *American Labor Legislation Review* 4 (1914): 578–79.
[60] "Unemployment Survey," *American Labor Legislation Review* 5 (1915): 573–75.

though less at the national level than at the state and local levels.[61] The demand for reforms in government broadened from the very elite ranks of Mugwumpry to include the growing ranks of the educated, professionalizing middle class and, in many places, farmers and organized labor as well.[62] In the newly noncompetitive political situation ushered in by the realigning election of 1896, there was increased freedom for officials in the executive branch, especially the president himself, to move against patronage practices, and to establish bureaucratic organizations useful in augmenting executive power.[63]

Yet the legacies of nineteenth-century patronage democracy and the crisis it precipitated in the Progressive Era created a relatively unfavorable context for the enactment of social reforms such as old-age pensions and social insurance. At the most basic level, the civil administration of the early twentieth-century American state was quite weak, given the lack of an established state bureaucracy and the dispersion of authority inherent in U.S. federalism and division of powers. Civil service reform, which might have enhanced the capacities of American government for certain types of interventions in civil life, had still not achieved much progress by the early 1900s. In contrast to the situation in many European countries, there were in the United States no strategically placed officials to pave the way for new social welfare programs. Thus, reforms in this period did not have their source within the underdeveloped American bureaucracy. Instead, they were supported by broad coalitions of interest groups and pressed upon state legislatures.[64]

American political parties did not tend to be the vehicles of reform, either. They were not—as were many of their European counterparts—programmatic parties looking for new policies to attract newly enfranchised working-class voters. Rather, they were patronage parties with an already mobilized working-class following whose mode of operation was under attack as "corruption" by many reformers. The clear challenge for party leaders in the Progressive Era was to find ways to appeal to middle-class reformers and their organizations while not alienating their traditional, patronage-oriented supporters. New social-spending measures tended not to meet that challenge, for elites and middle-class groups were still not convinced that officials in control of the state administration had been sufficiently cleansed of "corruption" to be entrusted with such activities.

[61] Schiesl, *The Politics of Efficiency.*

[62] Robert Wiebe, *The Search for Order, 1877–1920* (New York: Hill and Wang, 1967), chap. 5; John D. Buenker, *Urban Liberalism and Progressive Reform* (New York: W. W. Norton, 1978), chap. 6.

[63] Skowronek, *Building a New American State*, chap. 6.

[64] Buenker, *Urban Liberalism.*

The possibility of continuing "political corruption" in new government interventions worried elites and middle-class groups. The struggle against the patronage system was far from complete, and the debate over new social welfare spending programs was additionally entangled by issues of administrative probity and competence. By contrast, in most European countries, where bureaucratization was effectively implemented prior to mass extension of the suffrage and the emergence of debates over workingmen's insurance, such entanglements were avoided. Thus, even as proposals for new social insurance or pension schemes were being debated, Civil War pensions continued to be a symbol of all that was wrong with mass patronage democracy and public policy. In 1911 and 1912, Charles Francis Adams, a well-known journalist and reformer, carried out an investigation of the abuses of the military pension system which was published in the reform magazine *World's Work*.[65] The series' title when reprinted as a book in 1912—*The Civil War Pension Lack-of-System, a four-thousand million dollar record of legislative incompetence tending to political corruption*—summarizes well the reformer's view of the link between patronage democracy and pensions.

Although worries about political corruption undermined cross-class coalitions for social spending, especially on old-age pensions, some important social-welfare innovations did occur in many states during the Progressive Era. Labor regulations were strengthened, especially for women and children, and mothers' pension legislation, which provided means-tested allowances to widows outside of the poor law, was also widely successful. Workers' compensation laws, too, were enacted by numbers of state legislatures.[66] Why was it possible for these to be enacted in a political climate so hostile to public initiatives that involved social spending? Regulatory activities, unlike social-spending programs, could address the new needs of industrial society—and appeal to both working- and middle-class voters—without adding to the potential for political "corruption" or overtaxing U.S. administrative capacities. The two new welfare programs that were successful in Progressive-Era America, workmen's compensation and mothers' pensions, represented the reworking of government functions already being carried out in the courts, and they did not significantly increase government spending. In Massachusetts and Wisconsin, reformers were able to overcome business op-

---

[65] See Charles Francis Adams, "Pensions—Worse and More of Them," *World's Work* 23 (1911–12): 188–92, 327–33, 385–98. *World's Work* carried many articles on pension abuse even as it championed various social, political, and labor reforms during the years between the turn of the century and the outbreak of World War I.

[66] Leff, "Consensus for Reform"; the entire third volume of *The History of Labor in the United States* by Lescohier and Brandeis chronicles the progress of workers' compensation and legislation regulating work conditions, wages, hours, and related topics in this era.

position to enact legislation establishing savings bank and government life insurance, programs that were not perceived to have a high potential for abuse.[67]

Progressive social reformism quickly lost its momentum with the entry of the United States into World War I. However, with the creation of centralized federal administrative agencies to mobilize American resources for the war effort, many reform-minded Americans expected that the new agencies could be reoriented to peacetime activities in the aftermath of the war. Of particular importance to reformers were the United States Employment Service (USES) and war risk insurance. The USES, set up as an independent agency in 1918, was operating over eight hundred field offices at its peak of operations in 1919. These offices provided some job referrals and also collected statistics on unemployment. Members of the AALL and others interested in problems of unemployment and labor market organization hoped that the USES would come to serve as the foundation for the administration of unemployment insurance, as had been the case in Britain, where the world's first unemployment insurance system (initiated in 1911) had soon followed the establishment of national labor exchanges (1909).[68] War risk insurance (established by law in 1917), explicitly designed to avoid the pitfalls associated with the post–Civil War pension system,[69] was also the cause for hopeful projections on the part of progressive reformers. Samuel McCune Lindsay, in his 1919 presidential address to the AALL, described soldiers' insurance as "so striking a forward step that it may almost be said to atone for our previous backwardness," and he called on "those who believe in social insurance . . . to see that our next step shall be to hold on to this gain" and to extend it to the civilian population.[70]

Yet reformers' hopes for extending wartime organizations and programs were dashed in the aftermath of the war. In Europe, the effect of national mobilization for war was to stimulate political trends favoring social insurance, but in the United States, the opposite happened. Congress—giving political expression to the opposition of state, local, and private interests to the extraordinary federal powers developed during the war—quickly dismantled the emergency war organizations, including the

[67] John Commons and John Andrews, *Principles of Labor Legislation* (New York: Harper and Brothers, 1927), p. 471; Lee Welling Squier, *Old Age Dependency in the United States* (New York: Macmillan, 1912), pp. 286–91.

[68] Roy Lubove, *The Struggle for Social Security, 1900–1935* (Cambridge: Harvard University Press, 1968), pp. 149–57; on British unemployment insurance, see José Harris, *Unemployment and Politics* (London: Oxford University Press, 1972).

[69] Glasson, *Federal Military Pensions*, p. 283.

[70] Samuel McCune Lindsay, "Next Steps in Social Insurance in the United States," *American Labor Legislation Review* 9 (1919): 111.

USES, after the Armistice. When Congress slashed the appropriations for USES in 1919, the agency was forced to disband its field offices and to depend for unemployment statistics on voluntary submissions of information from business, states, and localities.[71] Without sufficient funding and support for the USES, there was little immediate chance for the development of an unemployment insurance program. And in the postwar reaction against federal government intervention in civil society, public old-age, disability, and survivors' insurance for civilians was not to be built up from war risk insurance.

In essence, the postwar United States opted not to institute the modern public social provision considered during the Progressive Era, or to build upon and extend wartime government activities such as the USES or war risk insurance. Yet the Progressive-Era attempts to build new realms of public activity free from patronage were not without implications for the future of social policy. Two structural effects were the enhancement of the importance of sub-national governments and the intensification of administrative fragmentation inherent in a federal system. Partially because civil service reform had made most headway at the sub-national level, states were the locus of administration for successful labor and welfare innovations in the Progressive Era itself and into the 1920s, and interests in such state-level programs became institutionalized. When social reform again emerged on the policy agenda in the wake of the Great Depression, policymakers would have to contend with this Progressive state-building legacy as they designed new programs.

In the postwar years, reformers and political leaders, as well as many average Americans, believed that businessmen could and would look after the American economy and Americans' economic well-being. To the extent that the problems of income insecurity associated with industrial capitalism were given any attention at all, they were to be addressed through "welfare capitalism"—programs run by employers for their workers—or through private and local charity. Welfare capitalist schemes reached only a tiny proportion of the work force, but they were important in the 1920s as a cultural ideal in opposition to public social efforts.[72] The conservative Republican presidents of the 1920s were not at all interested in building a professionalized bureaucracy to administer social programs; rather, they embraced the vision of an anti-bureaucratic "as-

[71] Carroll Woody, The Growth of Federal Government, 1915–1932 (New York: McGraw Hill, 1934), pp. 371–72; I. W. Litchfield, "United States Employment Service and Demobilization," Annals of the American Academy of Political and Social Science 81 (1919): 19–27.

[72] David Brody, "The Rise and Decline of Welfare Capitalism," in Brody, Workers in Industrial America (New York: Oxford University Press, 1980), p. 61; see also Brandes, American Welfare Capitalism.

sociative state" developed by Herbert Hoover, who served as secretary of commerce for Presidents Warren Harding and Calvin Coolidge before becoming chief executive himself in 1928. Hoover worked in his capacity as a public servant to encourage research, planning, and cooperation on the part of private groups; these activities would help citizens, under the "enlightened" leadership of corporate capitalists, to "meet the needs of industrial democracy without the interference of government bureaucrats."[73] A striking example of the "associative state" approach to social problems was the 1921 President's Conference on Unemployment, organized by Hoover to gain backing from the invited politicians, labor leaders, and social policy experts (including some from the AALL) for plans—already largely formulated—to deal with the severe recession of that year. Harding and Hoover ruled out any kind of governmental action from the beginning, and the conference was left to recommend better coordination of private and local charitable efforts.[74]

Social reformers recognized that the 1920s were a remarkably unpropitious time for advocating public solutions to the problems of industrial capitalism.[75] Many—most importantly the members of the AALL—accommodated themselves to the new political climate by downplaying state initiatives and emphasizing the so-called "preventive approach" associated with the work of University of Wisconsin economist John R. Commons.[76] Commons and his disciples called for labor and social insurance legislation that would give individual businessmen tangible financial incentives for increasing workplace safety, stabilizing employment, and otherwise improving workers' and social welfare. Expert, coordinated administration of labor regulations at the state level was also an important part of the Commons approach to industrial relations.[77] It was in his home state of Wisconsin, with its unusually strong network of ties between state government and state research university, that this type of

[73] Joan Hoff Wilson, *Herbert Hoover: Forgotten Progressive* (Boston: Little, Brown, 1975), p. 89 and chap. 4 generally; Ellis Hawley, "Herbert Hoover, the Commerce Secretariat, and the Vision of an 'Associative State,' 1921–28," *Journal of American History* 61 (1974): 116–40.

[74] William Chenery, "Unemployment at Washington," *Survey* 37 (1921): 47; ibid., "The President's Conference and Unemployment in the United States," *International Labour Review* 5 (1922): 359–76; Carolyn Grin, "The Unemployment Conference of 1921: An Experiment in National Cooperative Planning," *Mid-America* 55 (1973): 83–107; Wilson, *Herbert Hoover*, pp. 90–93.

[75] Clarke Chambers, *Paul U. Kellogg and the Survey* (Minneapolis: University of Minnesota Press, 1971), p. 77.

[76] Lafayette Harter, *John R. Commons: His Assault on Laissez-Faire* (Corvallis: Oregon State University Press, 1962); Nelson, *Unemployment Insurance*, chap. 6; Lubove, *The Struggle for Social Security*, chap. 7.

[77] John R. Commons, *Labor and Administration* (New York: August Kelley, [1913] 1964); Commons and Andrews, *Principles of Labor Legislation*.

administration was best developed. The Wisconsin State Industrial Commission was staffed by labor economists schooled in the Commons philosophy. The commission engaged in research and was empowered by the legislature to enforce and adjust all the state's industrial regulations.[78] In the absence of other reform activity, the AALL became increasingly oriented to the experiences and policy ideas of the Wisconsin State Industrial Commission, where—almost alone among state government agencies in the 1920s—social reform–minded "experts" (albeit of the "preventive" stripe) were still in a position of political influence. Only in the state of Wisconsin was there continuing activity around proposed unemployment insurance legislation through the 1920s. In 1921, an unemployment insurance bill based on the preventive approach and including employers' incentives came close to passing in the state legislature. The reformers continued their campaign until a similar bill finally succeeded in 1932—the first in the United States.[79]

Outside Wisconsin, popular political activity for welfare reform in the 1920s consisted almost exclusively of state-level campaigns for noncontributory old-age pensions led by the Fraternal Order of Eagles, a predominantly working- and lower-middle-class, white fraternal order. At times, the Eagles worked in uneasy alliance with professional, middle-class reformers of the AALL or the newly formed American Association for Old Age Security (later the American Association for Social Security); a handful of progressive Republican and Northern Democratic politicians supported the pension cause as well.[80] But by 1928, the only fruits of the extensive campaigning for new public spending for old-age protection were six state-level pension laws, all of them "county-optional," meaning that counties were *allowed*, but not mandated, to pay pensions to some of their aged residents. As it turned out, not many counties exercised their option, and only about one thousand elderly people were receiving these pensions in 1928, fewer than those still collecting Civil War pensions![81]

[78] Lubove, *The Struggle for Social Security*, p. 33.

[79] Nelson, *Unemployment Insurance*, chap. 6.

[80] Louis Leotta, "Abraham Epstein and the Movement for Old Age Security," *Labor History* 16 (1975): 359–78; Jackson Putnam, *Old Age Politics in California* (Stanford, Calif.: Stanford University Press, 1970), pp. 18–24; Fraternal Order of Eagles, *The Fraternal Order of Eagles: What it Is, What it Does, What it Stands For* (Kansas City, Mo.: Organization Department, Fraternal Order of Eagles, 1929); Fischer, *Growing Old in America*, pp. 173–74.

[81] U.S. Bureau of the Census, *Historical Statistics of the U.S.*, p. 738; Fischer, *Growing Old in America*, pp. 173–74; Massachusetts Commission on Pensions, *Report on Old Age Pensions* (Boston: Wright and Potter, 1925), p. 37; U.S. Social Security Board, *Social Security in America: The Factual Background of the Social Security Act as Summarized from the Staff Reports to the Committee on Economic Security* (Washington, D.C.: Government Printing Office, 1937), p. 161.

From Welfare Capitalism to
the Welfare State

It was in the years of the Great Depression that the United States initiated nationwide programs of social protection through the passage of the Social Security Act of 1935. The economic crisis transformed the American political world as it had existed in the 1920s and set into motion political changes that allowed for the success of the New Deal social-welfare legislation. Nationally, the ideological and policy inheritance represented by welfare capitalism was utterly discredited. And American citizens, politically quiescent throughout the 1920s, became politically engaged on a mass scale. The social insurance and assistance legislation passed during the Depression era bears the imprint of these factors, but it was also shaped by institutional arrangements and policy feedbacks that were themselves the legacy of the struggles for civil service reform and social welfare innovation of the late-nineteenth and early-twentieth centuries.

THE ROLE OF POPULAR PRESSURES
IN NEW DEAL SOCIAL-WELFARE INITIATIVES

By the time of the 1932 election, close to four years of the Great Depression had shattered the ideas that businessmen could guarantee the economic and social well-being of Americans, and that limited private and local charity and corporate welfare programs could serve as a substitute for public social provision in times of economic downturn. President Hoover had responded to demonstrably increased need and to rising demands for federal relief within the framework of his voluntarist philosophy, in which the state's welfare role was limited to encouragement of private philanthropic efforts.[82] But with the persistence of the Depression, and the blatant failure of voluntary efforts to alleviate need, the demands for federal action to cope with the economic crisis mounted. Popular and expert interest again turned toward *public* policy solutions to economic and social problems.

Franklin Roosevelt's mandate was hardly definitive in terms of what national policies he would pursue to achieve economic recovery or to end economic insecurity; the 1932 platform of the Democrats pledged only old-age and unemployment insurance at the *state* level.[83] Yet Roosevelt was known as a reformer—when he served as governor of New York, he encouraged the initiation of public programs for old-age protection—and though he made no pledge as to what he would do beyond "bold experi-

[82] Wilson, *Herbert Hoover*, chap. 5.
[83] Porter and Johnson, eds., *National Party Platforms*, p. 331.

mentation," his campaign promised to involve the federal government actively in dealing with the problems caused by the economic crisis.[84] Frances Perkins, FDR's close advisor and labor secretary, later wrote that it was "basic in the appeal for votes that suffering would be relieved immediately" through federal action, a stance completely different from Hoover's.[85] In this way, popular support for a new political orientation toward problems of economic security, as expressed by the 1932 election, was critical in providing an opening for the Roosevelt administration or congressional Democrats to initiate new public social programs.

The democratic upsurge in American politics did more than sweep Roosevelt into office, of course. There was increased mass political activity throughout the decade—in addition to an increase in voting among new-stock urban dwellers, there were marches of the unemployed, sit-down strikes, and farmers' protests.[86] Of critical importance to New Deal social policy developments were the social movements that arose demanding extended government welfare activities and new public social spending: Huey Long's "Share Our Wealth" movement, Father Coughlin's National Union for Social Justice, and Dr. Francis Townsend's old-age pension movement.[87] Indeed, an explanation commonly offered for the New Deal social-welfare breakthroughs is that they resulted from popular pressures.[88] It is certainly true that such pressures played a critical role in the formation of the American system of social insurance and welfare, but it is not the case that the Social Security Act was a direct product of mass movements.

How, then, did popular demands for new state welfare activity affect the course of policy development? During the 1930s, the mass movements dedicated to expanded public social protection continued to press for state action—indeed, they made such action a political necessity.

[84] James Holt, "The New Deal and the American Anti-Statist Tradition," in John Braeman, Robert Bremner, and David Brody, eds., *The New Deal: The National Level* (Columbus: Ohio State University Press, 1975), p. 29; Daniel Fusfeld, *The Economic Thought of Franklin D. Roosevelt and the Origins of the New Deal* (New York: Columbia University Press, 1956), pp. 158–59. See also Frances Perkins, *The Roosevelt I Knew* (New York: Viking, [1946] 1964), pp. 166–67, 182.

[85] Perkins, *The Roosevelt I Knew*, p. 182.

[86] Two classics in a huge literature on the New Deal and the popular political upsurge include William Leuchtenberg, *Franklin D. Roosevelt and the New Deal* (New York: Harper and Row, 1963), and Arthur Schlesinger, Jr., *The Politics of Upheaval*, vol. 3 of *The Age of Roosevelt* (Boston: Houghton Mifflin, 1960).

[87] Abraham Holtzman, *The Townsend Movement* (New York: Bookman Associates, 1963); Alan Brinkley, *Voices of Protest: Huey Long, Father Coughlin and the Great Depression* (New York: Alfred A. Knopf, 1982).

[88] See, especially, the work of Frances Fox Piven and Richard Cloward, *Regulating the Poor* (New York: Random House, 1971), pt. 1, and ibid., *Poor People's Movements* (New York: Random House, 1977), pp. 30–31.

Without popular pressure, and the electoral incentive it represented to congressmen, the policy initiatives taken by the Roosevelt administration probably would not have been successful. Secretary of Labor Frances Perkins, a key policymaker for social security, saw popular political activity as creating a unique political opening for the enactment of social insurance programs.[89] She later recalled, in reference to the passage of old-age protections in the New Deal, that "without the Townsend Plan it is possible that the Old Age Insurance system would not have received the attention which it did at the hands of Congress."[90] Indeed, given the character of the American state structure in the 1930s, executive policy initiatives depended for their success on mass pressure being exerted on Congress. The divided authority of the American state meant that extremely broad coalitions had to come together to overcome the many potential vetoes and to achieve coordination among the various branches and levels of the government; this was especially the case in the New Deal period, before the emergence of the bureaucracy as a substantial factor in policymaking.[91]

Yet popular demands were not directly transmitted into the circles of policy formation. U.S. political parties were still far from being programmatic or committed to coherent social policies, and they were not organized to channel the policy proposals of groups to the elected and appointed officials who actually made policy, as did many European parties.[92] In fact, the very strength of mass movements pressing for the extension of state welfare activities had a somewhat paradoxical effect: it reinforced the fears of Roosevelt and his advisors that "unwise" legislation might be enacted, and thereby intensified their cautiousness on matters of social policy and their determination to exclude radical voices from policy discussions.[93]

[89] George Martin, *Madame Secretary: Frances Perkins* (Boston: Houghton Mifflin, 1976), p. 341.

[90] Perkins, *The Roosevelt I Knew*, p. vi.

[91] Christopher Leman, "Patterns of Policy-Development: Social Security in Canada and the United States," *Public Policy* 25 (1977): 264; ibid., *The Collapse of Welfare Reform: Political Institutions, Policy, and the Poor in Canada and the United States* (Cambridge: MIT Press, 1980), pp. 135, 165.

[92] The fact that U.S. parties had not completely given up patronage practices, or moved toward thoroughly programmatic electoral appeals, reflected the uneven and incomplete success of earlier attempts to reform the civil administration. Patronage politicians remained strong in many areas of the United States and coexisted with politicians making more issue-oriented appeals. On the character of American political parties, see Theodore Lowi, "Party, Policy, and Constitution in America," in W. Chambers and W. Burnham, eds., *The American Party Systems* (New York: Oxford University Press, 1967), pp. 238–76.

[93] This effect was reinforced by the fact that Roosevelt and his closest advisors had been influenced quite negatively by European experiences with unemployment insurance in the 1920s; there—at least partially in response to popular political pressure—benefits had lost

This cautious approach in response to mass pressure is perhaps best illustrated in the case of old-age protection. The Townsendites were the largest and politically best connected of the various organizations pressing for new state welfare activities. The movement consisted of thousands of elderly Americans, many of them middle-class, organized into "Townsend Clubs." The Townsend movement was especially influential in Congress, both because of the elderly's high propensity to vote and because of the organizational structure of the movement, with local clubs in almost every congressional district.[94] In contrast to the usual maximum monthly payments of about $30 under the state old-age assistance programs that had proliferated after 1929,[95] the Townsendites advocated a rather remarkable $200 monthly pension for all Americans aged sixty or more, given on the condition that they cease working and spend the pension payment within thirty days.[96] The Townsend Plan and others like it, though clearly popular with many Americans, were completely dismissed by the Roosevelt administration officials drafting the Social Security Act's old-age pension and insurance provisions.[97] Roosevelt insisted to his advisors that any program instituted be on a sound actuarial basis—as opposed to the "unsound" Townsend plan and other popular "panaceas." This meant some sort of contributory scheme, as opposed to one drawing exclusively on general revenues.[98] Noting that "Congress can't stand the pressure of the Townsend Plan unless we have a real old age insurance system," FDR resolved to take the initiative in the development of social programs, and to maintain careful control of the entire process of legislating social security.[99] Looking toward the future, Roosevelt was espe-

any connection to contributions and had become a "dole." Thus, Roosevelt noted in a 1934 address, "Let us profit by the mistakes of foreign countries and keep out of unemployment insurance every element which is actuarially unsound." See Franklin D. Roosevelt, "Addresses to the Advisory Council on Social Security" (November 14, 1934), in Samuel Rosenman, ed., *The Public Papers and Addresses of Franklin D. Roosevelt*, vol. 3 (New York: Random House, 1938), pp. 453–54. On the issue of the effects of popular pressures, see also Skocpol and Ikenberry, "The Political Formation of the American Welfare State," pp. 123–26.

[94] Irving Bernstein, *A Caring Society: The New Deal Confronts the Great Depression* (Boston: Houghton Mifflin, 1985), p. 66; Holtzman, *The Townsend Movement*, chaps. 1–6; W. Andrew Achenbaum, *Old Age in a New Land* (Baltimore: Johns Hopkins University Press, 1978), pp. 129, 132.

[95] While only six states had passed old-age pension legislation prior to 1929, twenty-eight states had initiated programs by the beginning of 1935, when the Roosevelt administration's draft social security legislation was introduced in Congress. See U.S. Social Security Board, *Social Security in America*, pp. 161, 166.

[96] Achenbaum, *Old Age in a New Land*, p. 129.

[97] Theron Schlabach, *Edwin E. Witte: Cautious Reformer* (Madison: State Historical Society of Wisconsin, 1969), pp. 109–10.

[98] Mark Leff, "Taxing the 'Forgotten Man': The Politics of Social Security Finance in the New Deal," *Journal of American History* 70 (1983): 359–81.

[99] Perkins, *The Roosevelt I Knew*, p. 294.

cially concerned to insulate his legislation from popular and political pressure for expansion by including contributions from beneficiaries.

Roosevelt's timing in introducing permanent as opposed to "emergency" measures also reflects the cautiousness of his approach. Planning for social insurance initiatives was undertaken immediately, but no legislation was proposed by the administration. In contrast, the president introduced federal emergency relief legislation almost immediately upon taking office, thus responding to the plight of the unemployed—and to the not inconsiderable protests of state and local welfare officials, whose agencies were overwhelmed financially by the proportions of need produced by the crisis.[100] By 1934, the year Roosevelt appointed the Committee on Economic Security (CES)—the group responsible for drafting the administration's proposed social security legislation—the most urgent demands for relief had been satisfied by public works and relief programs, so that the permanent program to be designed by these advisors could more easily be kept separate from the "dole" so abhorred by FDR, but so politically necessary in the first months of his administration.[101]

What, then, can be said of the role of mass pressures in stimulating the development of new state social-spending measures in the United States? Given the character of the U.S. state structure, popular pressures were critical in providing an opening for elite initiatives. Indeed, popular political activity encouraged policymakers in the Roosevelt administration to take initiatives, but, as we shall see below, they were largely able to insulate the process of formulating policy from popular demands. There is no doubt that some kind of social-welfare initiative was politically necessary, but the specific form it took was shaped by the institutional arrangements of the American state, the power of certain congressional groups, and the reaction of New Deal policymakers to the U.S. policy inheritance.

PRESIDENTIAL INITIATIVES FOR SOCIAL SECURITY

Roosevelt had long harbored political ambitions—for himself as well as for the Democratic party and the cause of progressive reform—and he eagerly worked to build and lead a cross-class coalition for social policy reform at the national level. There was substantial legislative activity on proposed pension and unemployment benefits legislation in Congress during 1933 and 1934, yet Roosevelt was interested in developing a comprehensive approach to social security, as well as in taking political credit for any legislation that did succeed. Roosevelt seized the initiative in formulating policy and was able to maintain control over the policymaking

---

[100] Bernstein, *A Caring Society*, chap. 1; Katz, *In the Shadow of the Poorhouse*, pp. 216–22; Piven and Cloward, *Regulating the Poor*, chap. 2.
[101] Perkins, *The Roosevelt I Knew*, p. 284.

process by setting up the CES.[102] This group of cabinet officers, established in early June of 1934, was chaired by Secretary of Labor and longtime social reform advocate Frances Perkins, who had come to Washington with Roosevelt from the position of Industrial Commissioner in his gubernatorial administration in New York.[103] The CES would study social insurance and assistance, aided by an expert staff, and have a legislative proposal ready for the start of the 1935 congressional session. The key position of executive director was filled by Edwin Witte, a former Commons student trained at the University of Wisconsin and a veteran of years of administrative service in Wisconsin with the State Industrial Commission and the Legislative Reference Library (another state agency with progressive origins).[104]

Roosevelt's choice of personnel for the important task of drafting the social security bill reflected his generally cautious approach to social policy. Roosevelt and the people he chose to be the architects of the Social Security Act came of age politically in the Progressive Era; as products of the progressive movement, they shared its concerns with "good government" and fiscal "responsibility." Moreover, they had received their political training and developed their distinctive outlook in the "expert," state-level administrative agencies dealing with labor and social legislation that were the enduring result of progressive state-building and social reform efforts. In particular, Roosevelt's social policymakers came from backgrounds that ensured their concern with fiscal "soundness." They would attempt to build programs able to withstand what they perceived as the ever-present danger of democratic pressure for expansion of government benefits into fiscally irresponsible and politically motivated "handouts."[105] Social policy experts who advocated more liberal policies were excluded from the inner circles of policy formulation, relegated to relatively powerless positions within advisory bodies, or left out of the official policy formation process altogether.[106]

THE DELIBERATIONS OF THE COMMITTEE ON ECONOMIC SECURITY

From the very outset of the deliberations of the CES, the tension between national standards and coordination and state-level autonomy and

---

[102] Bernstein, *A Caring Society*, pp. 41–42, 51–53; Edwin Witte, *The Development of the Social Security Act* (Madison: University of Wisconsin Press, 1962), pp. 4–7, 18.

[103] Martin, *Madame Secretary*, pp. 205–6.

[104] Schlabach, *Cautious Reformer*, chaps. 2, 3.

[105] Perkins, *The Roosevelt I Knew*, chap. 1, 2; Bernstein, *A Caring Society*, pp. 43–45; Schlabach, *Cautious Reformer*.

[106] Lubove, *The Struggle for Social Security*, p. 176; Skocpol and Ikenberry, "The Political Formation of the American Welfare State," pp. 127–28.

diversity was of overriding importance in debates over the character of the programs it would propose.[107] Although politics had acquired a more national focus in the 1930s, there were substantial obstacles to national uniformity and centralized administration. Policymakers faced the threat of any national social insurance programs they recommended being declared unconstitutional by the Supreme Court. In addition, they had to cope with the political exigencies represented by the distribution of power within the Democratic party, which favored the representatives of conservative and states'-rights viewpoints as much as or more than those of urban liberalism. In particular, the extraordinary political leverage of Southern representatives in Congress, out of proportion to the population and economic might of their states, was a fact that could never be ignored as FDR and the CES formulated the bill.[108] Moreover, the fact that states had been the principal actors in social policy until the mid-1930s meant that diverse programmatic and administrative interests in the various state programs were politically well entrenched and difficult to bypass by the time the CES began its work. Indeed, Roosevelt, Witte, and Perkins, all of whom had been involved in state-level labor and welfare administration, actually preferred to maintain the states as important administrative actors, even as they hoped to increase the uniformity and adequacy of social programs. Other politicians representing the interests of progressive Northern states, such as Senator Robert Wagner of New York, the Roosevelt administration's chief ally in the Senate, also took some stances which undercut nationalizing trends for programmatic uniformity in order to protect favored state legislation.[109]

One can see the working out of the tensions around national uniformity and state-level autonomy especially clearly in the struggles over the character of unemployment protection. Despite the many obstacles to national uniformity and administrative coordination, it is clear from these debates that important nationalizing tendencies coexisted with tendencies favoring decentralization of administration and lack of standardization. The policy options for unemployment insurance being debated by the CES and the U.S. community of social insurance experts included a purely national plan and a federal subsidy plan that would allow the federal government substantial control over standards, in addition to the favorite plan of Roosevelt, Perkins, and Witte—a federal-state tax-offset scheme, in which states would retain complete decision-making power over many

[107] Schlabach, *Cautious Reformer*, pp. 114–15.

[108] See Perkins, *The Roosevelt I Knew*, p. 291; Arthur Altmeyer, *The Formative Years of Social Security* (Madison: University of Wisconsin Press, 1968), pp. 14–15; and the paper by Jill Quadagno in this volume (Chapter 6).

[109] J. Joseph Huthmacher, *Senator Robert F. Wagner and the Rise of Urban Liberalism* (New York: Atheneum, 1968).

aspects of their unemployment programs.[110] Some sort of nationally standardized plan (either purely federal or a federal subsidy program that allowed substantial national control while addressing fears about constitutionality) was the overwhelming choice of policy experts, including those serving in technical positions within the CES.[111] Further, the more national approaches were favored by trade union leaders and the few businessmen who had not already rejected the New Deal, and social security along with it.[112] Despite this support for national standards, Roosevelt, Perkins, and Witte managed—after considerable resistance from their own technical staff, members of the official advisory council, and outside experts—to get the CES to recommend the tax-offset approach that preserved the most state-level autonomy.[113] The tax-offset plan left to the states the politically difficult decisions about merit rating, employee contributions, and pooled versus individual reserves. This meant the CES could avoid taking stands on these tense issues, and Witte in particular would not have to undermine the Wisconsin experiment in "preventive" unemployment legislation.[114]

In the area of old-age protection, the tension between nationalizing and decentralizing tendencies played itself out slightly differently, and the debate was complicated by the politically sensitive issue of whether to include contributions from future beneficiaries. Policymakers in the CES had to contend with the growing strength of Townsendism and other movements calling for noncontributory federal pensions, and with the fact that members of Congress were far more supportive of pensions than of contributory insurance for the aged. Roosevelt and Witte, reacting to a policy inheritance which dramatized the dangers of politically motivated expansion of benefits, were determined to keep the federal government out of the business of giving direct grants to citizens, and they never wavered from a commitment to contributory features for whatever permanent old-age program was settled on. The arguments of liberal New Dealers for a different approach found no favor. A vivid example of this intransigence came when Harry Hopkins, federal emergency relief administrator and member of the CES, eloquently argued for noncontributory old-age and unemployment benefits as a matter of right for citizens. Roosevelt saw

110 Altmeyer, *Formative Years*, pp. 17–25; Nelson, *Unemployment Insurance*, chap. 9; Witte, *The Development of the Social Security Act*.

111 Schlabach, *Cautious Reformer*, pp. 117–26; Bernstein, *A Caring Society*, p. 55.

112 Skocpol and Ikenberry, "The Political Formation of the American Welfare State," pp. 126–31; Nelson, *Unemployment Insurance*, pp. 192–97, 202–3.

113 Schlabach, *Cautious Reformer*, p. 129.

114 Although Witte himself did not believe the preventive approach was satisfactory, neither did he wish to interfere with the operation of Wisconsin's law. See Schlabach, *Cautious Reformer*, pp. 119–31.

this as being "the very thing he had been saying he was against for years—the dole," and he vetoed any such proposals.[115]

Roosevelt, Perkins, and Witte preferred to develop what they saw as the only reasonable and "fiscally sound" long-term solution to the problem of old-age dependency: a contributory program of old-age benefits, to be firmly distinguished from noncontributory social assistance. Even so, Witte and the members of the CES were willing to include a governmental contribution to the old-age insurance fund once payroll taxes and the contributory principle were well established; the draft bill used by the CES showed a subsidy from federal revenues beginning in 1965.[116] Yet Roosevelt, upon discovering at the last moment that the CES plan included a future subsidy from general revenues, demanded a redrafting of the proposed legislation so that it would always be self-sustaining from employer and beneficiary contributions alone. Even a governmental contribution to the social security fund was problematic for FDR, with his "prejudice about the 'dole.' "[117] In the end, Roosevelt's view prevailed, and the U.S. social insurance program for the aged received no financial input from federal coffers, a logical outcome of Roosevelt's concern to preserve a sharp distinction between social assistance and social insurance programs.

Given the preferences of the CES and FDR himself for state-level administration, it is worth explaining the fact that the contributory old-age insurance system was the only one of the several programs included in the Social Security Act that was administered completely at the federal level of government. To some extent this reflected the fact that Witte and Perkins were preoccupied with resolving the disputes about unemployment insurance, which by all accounts occasioned the most attention from the members of the CES and the policy experts who advised them.[118] The staff members in charge of developing the old-age security portions of the program were strongly in favor of establishing a national old-age insurance system; they and the CES actuaries were unanimous in advising that, given extensive labor mobility, a federal-state scheme involving contributions over workers' lifetimes would be unworkable from a technical point of view.[119] Moreover, old-age *insurance* was the only area of policy in which the states had not enacted legislation and, hence, the only one in which

[115] Perkins, *The Roosevelt I Knew*, p. 284.

[116] Schlabach, *Cautious Reformer*, pp. 127–28; Perkins, *The Roosevelt I Knew*, pp. 294–96.

[117] Perkins, The Roosevelt I Knew, p. 296; Leff, "Taxing the 'Forgotten Man.' "

[118] See, for example, Altmeyer, *Formative Years*, chap. 1; Witte, *The Development of the Social Security Act*; Perkins, *The Roosevelt I Knew*, chap. 23; and Schlabach, *Cautious Reformer*, chap. 6.

[119] Schlabach, *Cautious Reformer*, pp. 111–12; Altmeyer, *Formative Years*, pp. 25–26.

there were no state-level vested administrative and political interests to defend, as there were in the old-age assistance and unemployment programs.

Despite their strong commitment to establishing contributory old-age insurance, CES members believed that some sort of old-age assistance was needed to cope with existing poverty among the aged, at least until the contributory schemes matured.[120] The fact that four times as many elderly people were collecting benefits under federal relief programs as under state old-age assistance systems worried Roosevelt administration policymakers, who did not want to encourage Americans to continue looking to the federal government to take care of the needs of aged citizens directly through noncontributory programs.[121] State old-age assistance programs, with their inadequate financing and benefits, would have to be strengthened if the federal government was to be kept out of direct relief to the aged. The CES therefore recommended the enactment of the Old Age Assistance (OAA) program, a federal subsidy (of 50 percent) for state old-age assistance plans that met certain minimum requirements. Most importantly, the draft legislation required that plans be state-wide in operation, and that pensions be paid at a level that would ensure the "health and decency" of the elderly recipients.[122] Though not seen by CES members as a long-term solution to poverty among the aged, OAA would please congressional Democrats and allow the popular enthusiasm for public old-age protection to be harnessed to the Social Security Act as a whole.

The bill submitted to Congress by the CES also recommended that the federal government initiate a program of subsidies to state-level assistance schemes for fatherless families with dependent children—Aid to Dependent Children (ADC). These state programs would be modified versions of the mothers' pension systems that had been enacted in most states in the Progressive Era and into the 1920s. As had been the case with OAA, the CES did not want to bypass state-level administration of existing programs and was opposed to establishing permanent federal assistance. Likewise, the CES saw a need to provide stronger financial backing of these programs, which were completely inadequate in the face of the economic crisis. The CES recommended the broadening of eligibility requirements, so that all children of single mothers could be aided; many mothers' pension schemes had extremely restrictive provisions.[123]

---

[120] Achenbaum, *Old Age in a New Land*, p. 134; Committee on Economic Security, *Report to the President* (Washington, D.C.: Government Printing Office, 1935), pp. 4–5.

[121] Committee on Economic Security, *Report*, p. 27; Schlabach, *Cautious Reformer*, p. 110.

[122] Achenbaum, *Old Age in a New Land*, pp. 134–35.

[123] It is perhaps worth noting, in light of later developments, that policymakers deliberately designed this program to allow poor mothers to stay at home to care for their children,

Policymakers deliberately opted not to mandate assistance to all needy children regardless of family situation, a decision which has had far-reaching implications for the operations of and debates over public assistance to this day. In addition, the proportion of state expenses to be met by federal subsidy was substantially lower than that for OAA—one-third as opposed to one-half. Policymakers, noting the far greater interest of Congress in aid to the aged and the resistance of congressional conservatives to the bill as a whole, worried that more generous provisions would threaten passage of any program for poor children.[124]

The politically motivated decision to omit health insurance from the legislation the CES proposed obviously had important consequences for the future of American social provision. Roosevelt and his advisors on the CES looked on health insurance quite favorably, although they—along with most social insurance experts—saw unemployment and old-age provision as more pressing.[125] Roosevelt had directed the CES to study health insurance, and to develop a legislative proposal. But even the decision merely to consider publicly run health insurance drew massive opposition from the medical profession. Although there was a brief moment in 1934 when Witte was "unsure that health insurance is out of the question"— because the American Medical Association (AMA) had been silenced temporarily by some concessions from the CES and by a desire to overcome internal dissension—FDR and the members of the CES ultimately decided that including health insurance in the proposed Economic Security Act was politically impossible.[126] Witte wrote that he believed the inclusion of health insurance "would spell defeat for the entire bill." Roosevelt was of the same opinion, and he would not authorize a health insurance title for the administration bill, or even the publication of a CES report favoring health insurance.[127] The hope of members of the CES and of FDR himself that health insurance would be introduced at a later date went unfulfilled as the conservative coalition in Congress gained ground in the years following the passage of the Social Security Act.[128]

---

just as better-off mothers were expected to do. See U.S. Social Security Board, *Social Security in America*, p. 233, and Irwin Garfinkel and Sara S. McLanahan, *Single Mothers and Their Children: A New American Dilemma* (Washington, D.C.: The Urban Institute, 1986), pp. 101–5.

[124] Witte, *The Development of the Social Security Act*, pp. 163–65; Winifred Bell, *Aid to Dependent Children* (New York: Columbia University Press, 1965), pp. 27–28.

[125] Witte, *The Development of the Social Security Act*, p. 187; Schlabach, *Cautious Reformer*, pp. 108, 112; Perkins, *The Roosevelt I Knew*, chap. 13.

[126] Schlabach, *Cautious Reformer*, pp. 112–14; Starr, *The Social Transformation of American Medicine*, pp. 266–69.

[127] Witte, *The Development of the Social Security Act*, p. 188.

[128] James T. Patterson, *Congressional Conservatism and the New Deal* (Lexington: University of Kentucky Press, 1967).

The adoption of universal national health insurance during the New Deal was ultimately precluded by the failure of social insurance in the Progressive Era. After the health insurance campaign of 1915–20 ended in failure, the field was left open for the foes of health insurance, principally the medical profession, to consolidate their position.[129] The AMA became virtually unopposable, given their capacity to pressure congressmen, especially in the absence of any significant and politically well-situated popular movement for health insurance (such as existed in the case of old-age protection). Thus, when the possibilities for social reform generally opened again in the 1930s, and despite public opinion favorable to new public health protections,[130] even so popular and powerful a politician as Franklin Roosevelt was unwilling to risk the passage of his other proposed programs by including health insurance in the package.

The fact that patronage practices continued unabated in many states, and had not been completely eradicated even from the federal government, meant that the CES faced a challenge in constructing realms of administration that could manage the new programs while avoiding entanglements in patronage politics. That it was willing to face the challenge, rather than await the development of a public administration more suited to its preferences, is testament to the crisis atmosphere produced by the Great Depression and to its conviction that the continuing popular pressure for some kind of federal action on the social welfare front would produce "unwise" legislation if it did not act. Yet the CES carefully included as many guarantees against corruption, patronage, and mismanagement as possible in its proposed permanent social security legislation, and it tried to design programs capable of withstanding periodic democratic onslaughts demanding "unwarranted" expansion.

THE SOCIAL SECURITY ACT:
CHARTER LEGISLATION OF AMERICA'S WELFARE STATE

The legislative recommendations of the CES included a federal-state contributory unemployment system; federal subsidies to state programs for the needy aged, dependent children, and the blind; and a purely federal contributory old-age benefits program.[131] The pragmatic formulators

---

[129] Lubove, *The Struggle for Social Security*, p. 89.

[130] U.S. Department of Health, Education, and Welfare, Social Security Administration, Office of Research and Statistics, *Public Attitudes Toward Social Security, 1935–1965*, by Michael E. Schlitz, Research Report No. 33 (Washington, D.C.: Government Printing Office, 1970), pp. 128–29.

[131] To deal with concerns about the constitutionality of the fully national old-age insurance program, separate titles were used to establish taxes and benefits; the CES was depending on the taxing power of the federal government to ensure the plan's constitutionality. See Achenbaum, *Old Age in a New Land*, pp. 136–37.

of the CES social security proposals had opted for substantial state-level autonomy in most of the programs they recommended. Yet the *Report to the President of the Committee on Economic Security* also recommended the establishment of minimum national standards, such as the "health and decency" requirement for old-age assistance benefit levels, and practices that would lead to administrative regularity, such as the recommendation for merit personnel systems in state-level administration of the programs. Moreover, the CES hoped to see all social insurance administration united within a single social insurance board located in the Department of Labor, with the social assistance programs grouped together under the aegis of the Federal Emergency Relief Administration. Finally, the CES recommended continuing research and planning for national coordination of the new social welfare activities, endorsing the establishment of a national planning board.[132]

The CES proposal had been designed to propitiate important congressional interests, of course, especially those representing the South. These had largely determined that an approach favoring state-level autonomy would be taken. But even more concessions were wrested from the congressional sponsors of the administration bill by Southern lawmakers and other conservatives.[133] Federal standards in general came under fire, and the CES proposal that state programs be administered along merit system lines had to be dropped. In addition, the administration of the insurance programs was taken away from the Department of Labor and grouped with the assistance programs in an independent administrative agency, the Social Security Board.[134] The CES recommendation that all employed persons be included in the unemployment and old-age insurance systems was not accepted by Congress, with the result that agricultural and domestic workers were excluded from coverage.[135] This meant that the insurance programs of the Social Security Act would not reach most American blacks, who were still overwhelmingly concentrated in rural, agricultural regions of the South.[136] Southern senators and congressmen led the fight for "states' rights" and against national standards

---

[132] Committee on Economic Security, *Report*, p. 9.

[133] On getting the Social Security Act through Congress, and the changes this necessitated, see Witte, *The Development of the Social Security Act*; Perkins, *The Roosevelt I Knew*, pp. 296–301; Achenbaum, *Old Age in a New Land*, pp. 134–35; Altmeyer, *Formative Years*, p. 35; and the papers by Kenneth Finegold and Jill Quadagno in this volume (Chapters 5 and 6, respectively).

[134] Witte, *The Development of the Social Security Act*, pp. 101, 144-45.

[135] Witte, *The Development of the Social Security Act*, pp. 131, 152–53. On Roosevelt's preference for universal insurance coverage, see Perkins, *The Roosevelt I Knew*, pp. 282–83.

[136] Nancy J. Weiss, *Farewell to the Party of Lincoln: Black Politics in the Age of FDR* (Princeton, N.J.: Princeton University Press, 1983), 166–68.

and universal coverage. They especially attacked the provision of OAA that mandated that states pay pensions sufficient to provide, "when added to the income of the aged recipient, a reasonable subsistence compatible with decency and health," fearing it would represent an entering wedge for federal interference in their states' system of segregation and discrimination. In the end, the Southern-led bloc won on that fight and the requirement was dropped.[137]

After the compromises, the Social Security Act was finally signed into law in August of 1935. States soon acted to pass legislation establishing programs under the act, and by 1937, the programs were nationwide in operation. Also in 1937, the act was declared constitutional by the Supreme Court, and the first payroll taxes were taken out of covered employees' paychecks, though benefits under the old-age insurance program were not scheduled to begin until 1942. Yet before the first benefit check was ever mailed, important changes were made in the contributory old-age benefits part of social security. A new advisory council began discussions in 1937 on certain controversial aspects of the social security program.[138] In addition to dissatisfactions with some of the more technical aspects of the law, there was widespread support for adding survivors' benefits. As a result of the council's recommendations and new negotiations in Congress, the 1939 amendments to the Social Security Act were passed. The most notable changes included a shift from full reserves to a modified pay-as-you-go system, and, in an early demonstration of the potential for expansion that even contributory social insurance systems can have in the United States, benefit payments became payable two years earlier (in 1940), payroll tax increases were delayed, and benefits for wage-earners' dependents and survivors were added.[139] Whatever its shortcomings as a system of social protection, it was already clear that social security represented an expandable set of social programs, despite the intentions of its formulators.

While the 1939 amendments to the Social Security Act showed the channels along which the nascent U.S. welfare state might be expanded, other events in the late 1930s undermined the capacity of social security programs to ensure Americans' economic well-being. The CES had believed that the success of their package of social programs in guaranteeing social security for the American people depended upon "employment assurance"—the government's provision of suitable jobs for all who wanted to work.[140] As the *Report* of the CES pointed out:

[137] Witte, *The Development of the Social Security Act*, pp. 144–45.

[138] Schlabach, *Cautious Reformer*, chap. 8.

[139] Achenbaum, *Old Age in a New Land*, pp. 136–37; Altmeyer, *Formative Years*, chap. 3.

[140] Committee on Economic Security, *Report*, pp. 3–4, 7–10.

Any program for economic security that is devised must be more comprehensive than unemployment compensation, which of necessity can be given only for a limited period. In proposing unemployment compensation we recognize that it is but a complementary part of an adequate program for protection against the hazards of unemployment, in which stimulation of private employment and provision of public employment . . . are the other major elements.[141]

The CES expected that employment assurance would come through the institutionalization of the New Deal public employment programs; as the papers by Margaret Weir and Theda Skocpol in this volume detail, however, this did not happen, and social insurance and assistance programs—however inadequate to the task—were left to deal with problems of economic and social insecurity.[142] 1935 turned out to have been the highpoint of congressional willingness to go along with Roosevelt's social reform initiatives, as a coalition of congressional conservatives gained strength in the late 1930s.[143] During this period, FDR was thwarted in his attempts at administrative and judicial reform—which likely would have enhanced the capacity of the American state to undertake economic and social interventions—and new social reforms were turned back as well.[144] It would be many years before Americans again enjoyed an era hospitable to social reform.

The Social Security Act represented one of the most important of all the New Deal reforms of American social and political life. Along with such legislation as the National Labor Relations (Wagner) Act and the Fair Labor Standards Act, it established critical social rights for American citizens. Yet these rights were compromised by uneven national standards, the sharp distinction between assistance and insurance, and the omissions of health insurance, employment assurance, and allowances for all needy children. This largely reflected the inability of the New Deal social reform coalition, led by the Roosevelt administration, to overcome the deep resistance of congressional conservatives and some congressional constituencies to the changes they wanted to effect in American social policy, but the policymakers themselves were responsible for some of the choices that left the U.S. welfare system incomplete. Ultimately, it was the larger obstacles produced by the legacies of U.S. state-building, state structure, and past policy that prevented the achievement of a more complete welfare state in New Deal America.

---

[141] Committee on Economic Security, *Report*, pp. 7–8.

[142] See also Katz, *In the Shadow of the Poorhouse*, pp. 227–33, on the problems of institutionalizing work relief in the New Deal United States.

[143] Patterson, *Congressional Conservatism and the New Deal*.

[144] Richard Polenberg, "The Decline of the New Deal, 1937–1940," in Braeman, Bremner, and Brody, eds., *The New Deal*, pp. 246–66.

From Civil War Pensions to a Belated Welfare State: The Fate of Social Policy in America

We have seen that throughout the history of American social policy, the possibilities for reform have been constrained by the legacies of state-building as well as by the characteristics of the American state structure. The fragmentation of authority encouraged by federalism and the division of powers has consistently undermined coordinated national welfare initiatives, even in the periods most hospitable to reform. The patronage practices initially encouraged by early mass democracy and the lack of bureaucratic state-building in America deprived reformers of readily available institutional capacities for carrying out new social-spending activities. Successful reforms have had to work around the obstacles represented by America's institutional and policy legacies, and they have built the bureaucratic capacity for social intervention slowly when it has been possible to build it at all. We have seen as well that American policy innovators and reformers have developed policy preferences in response to earlier state social interventions and policies, from the Progressives' reactions against the excesses of the Civil War pension system and patronage democracy to the New Dealers' preference for contributory social insurance. Moreover, the historically varying possibilities for cross-class coalitions—joining elite, middle-class, and working-class interests—have been critical to explanations of the fates of failed and successful social-spending programs. In the Progressive Era, it proved impossible to unite these interests around new social-spending programs, but during the New Deal, a cross-class coalition was able to form around the Social Security Act. Again today, the feedback from the programs established by the Social Security Act has shaped the possibilities for joining interests around alternative futures for social policy.

If I have made some sense here of the origins of America's belated welfare state, perhaps the insights derived from such an institutional-political process approach will be of use to both academics and those active in today's policy debates. Policy options are always constrained by the legacies of existing policy, politics, and administration, and our choices today are burdened by our past—not least by the legacies of the initial legislation of America's incomplete welfare state, the Social Security Act—and we will do well to understand the limits to our alternatives. Yet the past development of American social policy shows as well that alternatives did exist. In the 1980s, we again find ourselves faced with alternative futures for American social provision. I conclude with the hope that these lessons about our past will serve to enhance the possibilities for more generous public social provision in America.

2

Redefining the New Deal: World War II and the Development of Social Provision in the United States

EDWIN AMENTA AND THEDA SKOCPOL

Accounts of the development of public social provision in the United States often focus on major periods of domestic reform, in particular the New Deal of the 1930s and the Great Society of the 1960s. By comparison, the period during and immediately after World War II seems inconsequential. When the wartime period is discussed, students of social policy frequently claim that it consolidated the changes wrought by the New Deal.[1] Yet this time brought some new departures and also saw the failure of bold plans to extend the social policies of the 1930s. The welfare aspirations of the New Deal were not realized as a result of the impact of war; they were redefined.

A comparison of the U.S. experience with that of Great Britain indicates that World War II could spur comprehensive innovations, for there the war catalyzed the reorganization and extension of social benefits and

For constructive criticism and comments, we thank James Cronin, Alfred Darnell, Jennifer Hochschild, Michael Katz, Barbara Laslett, Mark Leff, Sunita Parikh, Craig Reinarman, the members of the brown bag workshop at the Center for the Study of Industrial Societies at the University of Chicago, and the members of the 1986–87 Colloquium on American Society and Politics, held in Cambridge, Massachusetts.

[1] See, for instance, Richard E. Neustadt, "Congress and the Fair Deal: A Legislative Balance Sheet," in Carl Friedrich and John Kenneth Galbraith, eds., *Public Policy*, vol. 5, pp. 351–81; David Brody, "The New Deal and World War II," in John Braeman, Robert H. Bremner, and David Brody, eds., *The New Deal: The National Level* (Columbus, Ohio: Ohio State University Press, 1975), pp. 267–309; and Richard O. Davies, "Social Welfare Policies," in Richard S. Kirkendall, ed., *The Truman Period as a Research Field* (Columbia: University of Missouri Press, 1967), pp. 149–86. For different views, see Mary Hedge Hinchey, "The Frustration of the New Deal Revival, 1944–1946," (Ph.D. diss., University of Missouri, 1965), and Barton J. Bernstein, "America in War and Peace: The Test of Liberalism," in Barton J. Bernstein, ed., *Towards a New Past* (New York: Random House, 1967).

services. The British changes were largely mapped out in the Beveridge Report of December 1942 and put into effect between 1944 and 1949, as specified by White Papers sponsored by the wartime coalition government and a series of parliamentary acts passed by the postwar Labour government. The new and extended social policies were intended to protect all British citizens from want due to sickness, unemployment, disability, old age, family obligations, or lack of income. The sum of these innovations was called "the welfare state," a phrase coined to contrast the aspirations of Britain with the horrors of the Nazi "warfare state."[2]

Planning for a postwar American welfare state was detailed in various reports—most notably *Security, Work, and Relief Policies* (the "American Beveridge Plan"), released in March 1943. In it, the National Resources Planning Board (NRPB) proposed major reorganizations and extensions of U.S. social policies that would accompany measures to sustain a full-employment economy. With the Democrats in nominal control of Congress and President Roosevelt in office, reformers hoped to use the war to complete the New Deal. But their aims were not to be realized. New Deal public employment agencies were phased out, and the comprehensive plans of the National Resources Planning Board were thwarted.

Still, the World War II period in the United States was not entirely a missed opportunity, for some significant innovations were made. A new set of benefits for individuals was included in the 1944 GI bill, and other legislation for veterans followed. Like the reforms unsuccessfully advocated by the NRPB, the measures for veterans were comprehensive; they covered needs ranging from physical rehabilitation to employment assistance and health care, and offered grants or loans for education, for home ownership, and for starting a new business. This American welfare state for veterans and their families was administered primarily by the Veterans Administration. Although Congress dismissed comprehensive proposals for changes in employment policy and income transfers, the war brought a broadening of the base of the federal income tax and an increase in its progressiveness. The enhanced fiscal capacity of the national government enabled it to fund postwar veterans' benefits, as well as to spend higher sums for defense. Also funded were new domestic policies that indirectly met social welfare needs. Such measures as federal subsidies for housing and hospital construction signaled the beginning of a trend; until the 1960s U.S. social provision would rely heavily on federal funds channeled through states, localities, and businesses.

In short, a war that had brought comprehensive, nationalizing reforms of social policy to Great Britain furthered the development of indirect and

2 Peter Flora and Arnold J. Heidenheimer, "The Historical Core and Changing Boundaries of the Welfare State, in Peter Flora and Arnold J. Heidenheimer, eds., *The Development of the Welfare State in Europe and America* (New Brunswick, N.J.: Transaction Books, 1982), p. 19.

disjointed forms of public social provision in the United States. To understand why, we probe the gaps between the plans put forward in the United States during the war and the new legislation that survived the battles of wartime domestic politics. In the next two sections, we present an overview of American social policies as they stood in 1939 and a description of wartime plans and changes in social policies made during the 1940s. In an attempt to determine why events followed the course they did, we examine British policy changes and some theories about war and the welfare state that were inspired by the British example. Because we find these theories inadequate, we offer explanatory arguments of our own. By analyzing the impact of America's mode of mobilization on the evolving capacities of the national government, on the options available to business and industrial labor, and on the political alliances that vigorously debated the various social policy proposals, we attempt to explain why the United States did not fashion a comprehensive welfare state out of the crucible of war, as Britain did. Our analysis also reveals the ways in which the war and its immediate aftermath redirected the social policies of the New Deal.

U.S. Social Policy at the End of the New Deal

At the end of the 1930s, social policy in the United States consisted of a wide assortment of programs. In addition to veterans' benefits carried over from previous wars and state workers' compensation laws passed in the Progressive Era, there were job programs offering publicly funded employment, public works projects, a federal-state employment service, two newly established contributory social insurance programs, state-level public assistance programs (some of which were supplemented by federal funds), and housing programs, including subsidies for home building and a modest program for slum clearance and the erection of public housing. Most of these programs either had been created or were substantially altered during the first two administrations of President Franklin Delano Roosevelt.

By far the most important national welfare effort in 1939 was public employment, although it covered only approximately 3 million of the nearly 10 million out of work in that year. About 0.8 million young Americans were working for the National Youth Administration and the Civilian Conservation Corps (CCC); some 2.3 million workers were on the rolls of the Work Projects Administration (WPA), which was created in 1935 and made an independent agency in 1939. The WPA administered labor-intensive projects, such as the construction or rehabilitation of highways, streets, and public buildings. Congress provided financial resources and state and local governments sponsored the projects; the WPA decided which ones to fund and ran them. The cost of all these public employment programs was approximately $1.9 billion, which represented more than 20 percent of total federal expenditures and about 47 percent of federal social welfare expenditures in 1939.[3]

More people were receiving public assistance, but it was transmitted primarily through the states and localities. In 1933, the Federal Emergency Relief Administration (FERA) was established to provide financial relief to the unemployed. After the 1934 elections, the president decided to "quit this business of relief" and changed the focus to public employment. When FERA wound up its operations at the end of 1935, general assistance was back under the control of states and localities, with no federal controls or standards. To some extent, the 1935 Social Security Act brought the federal government back into the relief business. Washington would match state and local government expenditures up to specified maximums for means-tested old-age assistance and aid to the blind, and would provide one-third of payments for aid to dependent children. The Social Security Act amendments of 1939 increased the federal share of ADC to one-half. In that year approximately 1.9 million were receiving OAA, approximately 1 million were receiving ADC, and 1.7 million were still receiving general assistance.[4]

The Social Security Act also established old-age and unemployment insurance, with payments to begin in 1942. For unemployment insurance, a federal tax (that reached 3 percent in 1937) was levied on employers' payrolls. The law provided that this tax could be credited to the employer if the state in which the employer operated passed a suitable unemployment compensation law. By the middle of 1937, all states had passed such legislation; the result was a variety of benefit provisions, levels of taxation, and forms of administration. State unemployment insurance funds were intended to be sufficient without drawing on state revenues or federal general revenues.[5] For old-age insurance under the Social Security Act, a 1 percent payroll tax on a maximum wage base of $3,000 was levied on employers and employees. The tax was to begin in 1937 and was scheduled to increase in steps until 1949, when both employers and employees were to be taxed at a rate of 3 percent. Old-age insurance was

[3] Committee on Long-Range Work and Relief Policies, *Security, Work, and Relief Policies* (Washington, D.C.: Government Printing Office, 1942), p. 604 (hereafter referred to as Committee, *Security*); Donald S. Howard, *The WPA and Relief Policy* (New York: Sage, 1943), chap. 4, pp. 854–57; *Historical Statistics of the United States from Colonial Times to 1976* (Washington, D.C.: Government Printing Office, 1976), p. 357.

[4] Searle F. Charles, *Minister of Relief: Harry Hopkins and the Depression* (Syracuse, N.Y.: Syracuse University Press, 1963), chap. 2; Howard, *The WPA and Relief Policy*, chap. 1; Josephine Brown, *Public Relief, 1929–1939* (New York: Henry Holt, 1940), chaps. 7, 13, 14; *Historical Statistics*, p. 356.

[5] Daniel Nelson, *Unemployment Insurance: The American Experience, 1915–1935* (Madison: University of Wisconsin Press, 1969), chap. 9.

to be paid according to recipients' previous earnings and was to be financed solely with funds accruing from the payroll tax. The 1939 amendments added benefits for survivors and allowed payments to begin in 1940 rather than 1942. The amended legislation also postponed until 1943 a tax increase that was to have taken effect in 1940; according to 1939 projections, the tax postponement and the increased benefits would require the fund to be heavily supplemented by general revenues in later years.[6]

Reformers considered other New Deal social policy innovations as preliminary steps toward a comprehensive public policy. In the area of employment policy, an important new agency, the United States Employment Service, was established in 1933. The federal government provided grants-in-aid for states to set up employment offices, and the USES attempted to coordinate their efforts. In the area of housing policy, the first problem addressed by New Deal reformers was the foreclosure of mortgages; the National Housing Act of 1934 created the Federal Housing Administration, which insured individual home mortgages. By 1938, the emphasis had changed; legislation now provided modest funding for public housing and slum clearance. Also in that year, an administration-sponsored report called for, among other things, national hospitalization insurance. Roosevelt limited his health initiatives in 1939, however, to a bill for a WPA hospital construction project, which failed to pass Congress.[7]

The New Dealers attempted to cut back one category of social expenditures: benefits for military veterans. They believed that the needs of ex-soldiers should be met chiefly by programs directed at the entire population. In the 1920s, Congress had passed several laws to aid World War I veterans and made the Veterans' Bureau responsible for the administration of all such programs. The most expensive program was compensation to the disabled; in 1933 nearly 750,000 were receiving benefits for service- and nonservice-connected disabilities. The National Economy Act of 1933 gave Roosevelt the power (for two years) to issue executive orders to regulate veterans' benefits. Under this economy regime, the primary savings came from a reduction in compensation for veterans with service-connected disabilities, and the removal from pension rolls of the vast majority having nonservice-connected disabilities.[8] Moreover, like

[6] On the payroll tax, see Mark H. Leff, *The Limits of Symbolic Reform: The New Deal and Taxation, 1933–1939* (New York: Cambridge University Press, 1984), chap. 1.

[7] J. Joseph Huthmacher, *Senator Robert F. Wagner and the Rise of Urban Liberalism* (New York: Atheneum, 1968); Monte M. Poen, *Harry S. Truman versus the Medical Lobby: The Genesis of Medicare* (Columbia: University of Missouri Press, 1979); Richard O. Davies, *Housing Reform during the Truman Administration* (Columbia: University of Missouri Press, 1966).

[8] William P. Dillingham, *Federal Aid to Veterans, 1917–1941* (Gainesville: University of

his predecessor (though FDR did not use the Army against protesting veterans as President Herbert Hoover had done in 1932), Roosevelt attempted to stop the movement to redeem adjusted compensation certificates. These so-called bonuses, granted by Congress in 1924, were not to
mature until 1945. But in 1935 Congress passed a measure allowing immediate redemption of the certificates and, in 1936, overrode Roosevelt's
veto and disbursed or credited $3.2 billion to veterans. Nevertheless, by
1939 New Deal reformers had managed to slow special benefits to military veterans; the federal government was spending $606 million, mainly
for disability pensions, compared with $825 million in 1932.[9]

Following its failure in 1938 to get comprehensive executive reorganization measures through Congress, the Roosevelt administration made a
more modest and ultimately successful effort to coordinate social policies—specifically, to improve coordination of social-spending programs
with employment programs and enhance the executive's ability to plan
and reform social policies. The 1939 executive reorganization legislation
incorporated the Work Projects Administration and the Public Works
Administration into a newly created Federal Works Agency, underscoring
the administration's commitment to employment. The USES was placed
under the Social Security Board (SSB), which controlled old-age insurance, unemployment insurance, and special assistance programs. The
board itself was placed under the new Federal Security Agency. The Veterans Administration remained in control of veterans' programs, including hospitals. Although the administration hoped that spending for veterans would decrease and eventually end as World War I veterans died,
there was no merger of programs for veterans with the nationwide programs for all citizens before the outbreak of World War II.[10]

U.S. Social Policy in the 1940s:
Plans and Accomplishments

When Franklin Roosevelt was reelected for a third presidential term in
1940, the United States was already informally involved in World War II

Florida Press, 1952); Davis R. B. Ross, *Preparing for Ulysses: Politics and Veterans during
World War II* (New York: Columbia University Press, 1969), chap. 1; *Historical Statistics*,
pp. 1147–50.

[9] Irving Bernstein, *The Lean Years: A History of the American Worker, 1920–1933* (Boston: Houghton Mifflin, 1960), chap. 13; Dillingham, *Federal Aid to Veterans*; Ross, *Preparing for Ulysses*, chap. 1.

[10] Richard Polenberg, *Reorganizing Roosevelt's Government, 1936–1939: The Controversy over Executive Reorganization* (Cambridge: Harvard University Press, 1966); William E. Pemberton, *Bureaucratic Politics: Executive Reorganization during the Truman
Administration* (Columbia: University of Missouri Press, 1979), pp. 11–14; Committee,
Security, p. 33.

as a result of its ties with Great Britain. Plans and partial measures for wartime mobilization of the economy had been discussed for many months before the Japanese attack on Pearl Harbor on December 7, 1941.[11] Early on, Roosevelt's New Deal reforms also set the stage for postwar developments. In November 1940, he instructed the National Resources Planning Board (NRPB), a nonadministrative agency located in the Executive Office of the President, to refrain from direct involvement in war mobilization and to concentrate on formulating national social and economic policies for the postwar period. In response, the NRPB sponsored a series of investigations concerning employment, relief, social insurance, housing and urban development, and benefits for World War II veterans. The resulting reports reveal the outlines of an American full-employment welfare state that might have emerged after World War II, had the New Deal planners achieved their aims. Before considering why they failed, let us examine the recommendations developed by the groups sponsored or otherwise supported by the NRPB.

The most important of these reports on social policy was *Security, Work, and Relief Policies*, submitted by the Committee on Long-Range Work and Relief Policies. Appointed by the NRPB at the end of 1939, this committee was chaired by William Haber, professor of economics at the University of Michigan; the director of research was Eveline Burns of the Economics Department of Columbia University. The committee included representatives from the Work Projects Administration, the Federal Security Administration, the Children's Bureau, and the Farm Security Administration, as well as leaders of private social work associations. It was charged with surveying all existing work and income-maintenance programs and designing ways to restructure them, and it proceeded without interference from the president or Cabinet members.[12] *Security, Work, and Relief Policies* was submitted three days before the attack on Pearl Harbor. The report was intended to be a comprehensive study of U.S. social policy, and 50 of its 640 pages were devoted to recommendations for policy innovations.

In the report, relief, social insurance, and public employment programs

[11] Harold G. Vatter, *The U.S. Economy in World War II* (New York: Columbia University Press, 1985), chap. 1.

[12] Marion Clawson, *New Deal Planning: The National Resources Planning Board* (Baltimore: Johns Hopkins University Press, 1981), pp. 136–40; Philip W. Warken, *A History of the National Resources Planning Board* (New York: Garland, 1979), pp. 224–26. The NRPB added a 4-page introduction to the 640 oversized pages of the committee's report in which it endorsed the group's work and recommendations but made a stronger pitch for a national guarantee of work and emphasized the need for immediate action. The board also referred to matters not mentioned in the report, such as international trade, labor relations, and antitrust policies. See Committee, *Security*, pp. 1–4.

were discussed together under the rubric of "public aid."[13] Echoing the sentiments of the Committee on Economic Security, the NRPB committee called for the assurance of an "American standard" of economic security as a *right* of every citizen. Through one or another of the programs of public aid a citizen should, the NRPB committee felt, receive at least the minimum wage as specified by the 1938 Fair Labor Standards Act.[14] Although it retained the distinction between "social insurance" and "public assistance" programs, the committee did not want insurance to gain at the expense of assistance; thus it proposed nationalization of public assistance as well as new social insurance policies to fill gaps in the Social Security Act. Measures to ensure full employment were a primary concern of the committee. Like most other observers of the American economy at that time, committee members expected high postwar unemployment. Like many other products of NRPB research, both the NRPB's introduction to the report and the committee's recommendations were couched in the rhetoric of Alvin Hansen's "stagnationist" version of Keynesianism, which presumed that private business activities alone would be insufficient to maintain full employment in the postwar era.[15]

The NRPB, like previous New Dealers, regarded public works and public employment as the solutions to the unemployment problem. For those in need of steady work that the private economy could not provide, the federal government should provide a job. The NRPB committee sought something as flexible as, yet more powerful than, the WPA, which at its peak of operations employed less than 40 percent of the unemployed. The committee proposed the permanent planning of projects, both the labor-intensive WPA kind of project and the capital-intensive PWA kind. Project work would be provided without a means test and would be similar to private employment in hours, wages, and conditions of employment; the prevailing wage would be paid where wages were high, and the security or minimum wage would be paid elsewhere.[16] The committee emphasized the value of the nation's youth. It proposed to keep those between sixteen and twenty-one years of age out of the labor force and in school; job programs for youths would supplement educational aid.[17] To guarantee employment would require organizational change. Because of the need to

---

[13] Committee, *Security*, p. 9.

[14] Ibid., pp. 514–15.

[15] Ibid., pp. 1–4, 502–3.

[16] The WPA at first compromised between the two and paid an hourly "prevailing" wage until a monthly "security" level of payments had been reached. The skilled worker did not have to work as many hours as the unskilled worker to get the full benefit. In 1939 Congress forced all WPA workers to work a certain number of hours per month, in effect legislating the security wage. See Charles, *Harry Hopkins*, pp. 150–52.

[17] Committee, *Security*, pp. 504–11.

gather detailed information about employment and employment trends, a national employment service was deemed essential.[18] The committee wanted such a service to administer all work and training programs, as well as unemployment compensation.[19]

Because of the strong emphasis placed by the NRPB committee on public programs to combat unemployment, the failure of all such efforts during the 1940s represents the widest gap between social policy plans and accomplishments. The termination of public employment programs began in 1942 when Congress ended the Civilian Conservation Corps. Shortly after the 1942 elections, Roosevelt called for the end of the WPA; Congress abolished the National Youth Administration the following summer. In June 1943 Congress appropriated only enough funds for the NRPB to allow it to phase itself out of existence. This left the Bureau of the Budget as the only nonemergency department in the Executive Office of the President. Thereafter, no public employment or planning agencies were reestablished; federally financed projects were considered on their own political merits and were not incorporated into any national employment program.[20]

The full employment bill of 1945 would not have brought back public employment; at best the bill might have revived some of the NRPB's functions through the creation of certain executive budgeting procedures. But even this bill was watered down to specify that economists, who were not required to adhere to Keynesian principles, were to serve in a purely advisory capacity.[21] Perhaps more important, plans to permanently strengthen the United States Employment Service failed. Although the service was nationalized soon after Pearl Harbor, Congress gave responsibility for public employment offices back to the states at the end of the war.[22]

[18] The employment offices would be expected to construct detailed work histories to classify applicants. Ibid., pp. 507, 513–14, 536.

[19] Ibid., pp. 523–24.

[20] Barry D. Karl, *Charles E. Merriam and the Study of Politics* (Chicago: University of Chicago Press, 1974), chap. 12; Clawson, *New Deal Planning*, chaps. 15–19; Warken, *National Resources Planning Board*, pp. 237–45; Richard Polenberg, *War and Society: The United States, 1941–1945* (Philadelphia: J. B. Lippincott, 1972), pp. 80–82.

[21] Stephen Kemp Bailey, *Congress Makes a Law: The Story behind the Employment Act of 1946* (New York: Columbia University Press, 1950). For the view that the full employment bill did not require the government to spend, see "What the Bill Proposes," in *The Road to Freedom: Full Employment*, special section of *The New Republic* (September 24, 1945): 396–97. The articles in this special section were written by Heinz Eulau, Alvin H. Hansen, Mordecai Ezekiel, James Loeb, Jr., and George Soule. No byline preceded any article, yet the various authors were not collectively responsible for the articles. This article clearly could not have been written by Hansen.

[22] Leonard P. Adams, *The Public Employment Service in Transition, 1933–1968: Evolution of a Placement Service into a Manpower Agency* (Ithaca, N.Y.: New York State

In the area of public assistance, or "relief" for the poor, the NRPB committee was strongly committed to general assistance and the setting of national standards, rather than continued reliance on special-category programs such as aid to dependent children and old-age assistance. Some things should remain as they were, in the committee's view: states would continue to contribute fiscally and to administer programs along with local authorities; means tests would continue to be used. But the committee wanted general public assistance to be a top priority and called for increased federal funding and strict controls.[23] Specifically, it proposed that all public assistance programs be administered by one agency in each state and that the federal government administer general public assistance according to national standards until every state had demonstrated the ability to do so independently.[24]

In its report, the NRPB Committee on Long-Range Work and Relief Policies adopted the term "social insurance," yet refused to embrace an analogy to private insurance. The committee did not want *only* unemployment and old-age benefits to be provided as a right. What is more, it opposed the way such programs were being funded: it considered the trust fund a drag on aggregate consumption (according to Keynesian theory), and it considered the payroll tax regressive. Although it preferred to see the tax eclipsed by general revenues, it suggested the continuation of the payroll tax, in a reduced form, chiefly for the sake of appearances.[25] The uncoupling of accrued taxes and payments would result in more generous benefits financed mainly through general revenues. The NRPB committee sought to improve unemployment insurance by nationalizing the program and extending benefits to twenty-six weeks. In addition, domestic, agricultural, and other formerly excluded workers were to be covered by contributory insurance programs, and social insurance was to cover both temporary and permanent disability.[26]

National health insurance had been omitted from the Social Security

---

School of Industrial and Labor Relations, 1969), chap. 3; Hinchey, "New Deal Revival," chap. 6.

[23] The committee rejected the 1935 recommendations of the CES regarding relief and sided with the CES Advisory Committee on Public Employment and Relief, which was dominated by social workers and others concerned with public welfare. The NRPB committee proposed that all relief programs adhere to national standards of adequacy. Specifically, aid to dependent children should go to mothers and should be as adequate as aid to the aged and the blind. The report indicated that ADC benefit levels were significantly lower than those of other aid programs. For the views of the advisory committee, see J. Brown, *Public Relief*, pp. 304–6, and Committee, *Security*, pp. 518–20.

[24] In 1939, only a few states had control over general assistance.

[25] Committee, *Security*, pp. 522–28.

[26] Ibid., pp. 515–17.

Act of 1935, and the NRPB committee spent little time on health issues.[27] The NRPB endorsed health insurance, however, and undoubtedly supported many of the recommendations of the Roosevelt administration's Interdepartmental Committee to Coordinate Health and Welfare Activities, which in the late 1930s had called for increases in federal public health expenditures; expansion of maternal and child health services; federal grants to expand hospital facilities; federal aid to state programs for the medically needy; grants-in-aid to establish state-level temporary disability insurance; and a general program of publicly supported medical care.[28]

Wide-ranging as the NRPB committee's proposals were, few changes were made in U.S. public assistance and social insurance during and immediately after the war. The proposed reforms of public assistance had little impact on wartime political debates. The Wagner-Murray-Dingell bills of 1943 and 1945 did not provide for the federal reorganization of state assistance systems, but called for grants-in-aid for all the needy without respect to special assistance categories, eliminated the maximums on matching payments, and changed the matching formula to increase aid to poorer states. Such provisions might have increased the benefits provided under the public assistance system in some states to a level approximating those provided by national social insurance for the elderly, and preempted the expansion of other social insurance programs. But the Wagner-Murray-Dingell bills failed to pass, and Congress also refused to expand federal grants-in-aid to include another form of special assistance for unemployable adults. The main achievement was the creation of a new special assistance program for permanent disability, a risk that the NRPB committee had thought should be covered by social insurance.[29]

The social insurance reforms fared better in the bills brought before Congress, but the legislative gains were minimal. Proposals to make so-

[27] Unlike employment and income maintenance programs, health services were given little attention. The committee nodded toward national health insurance but said little about it (about one-half page). It was more specific about two other services: school lunches (it called for free lunches for all) and surplus commodity distribution (it recommended replacement by the food stamp plan and elimination of the means test for it). Ibid., pp. 520–22, 528–39.

[28] Soon after the interdepartmental committee met, Senator Robert Wagner of New York introduced what would be an ill-fated bill that was consistent with its report. The bill's medical care provision included a *grant-in-aid* to states for health insurance and for expansion of medical services to the poor and public health programs. See Huthmacher, *Senator Robert F. Wagner*, pp. 263–67; Poen, *Truman versus the Medical Lobby*, pp. 19–24.

[29] Wilbur J. Cohen and Robert J. Myers, "Social Security Act Amendments of 1950: A Summary and Legislative History," *Social Security Bulletin* 13 (October 1950): 3–14. Jerry Cates argues that generous state-administered old-age assistance would have constituted a threat to old-age insurance; see *Insuring Inequality: Administrative Leadership in Social Security, 1935–54* (Ann Arbor: University of Michigan Press, 1983), chap. 5.

cial insurance more comprehensive were the key provisions of the unsuccessful Wagner-Murray-Dingell bills, which emphasized the creation of
health insurance and the nationalization of unemployment insurance. But
rather than increasing social insurance without reliance on payroll taxes,
which was the hope of the NRPB committee, the proposed bills called for
stiff increases in payroll taxes. Later attempts to pass legislation establishing national health insurance also failed. Hard as the Truman administration pushed for such a program in 1946 and 1949, all it had to show for
the effort were grants-in-aid for the building of hospitals, expansion of
state public health systems, and medical research.[30] In the end, the only
successful social insurance reform was that of old-age and survivors' insurance, whose eligibility, coverage, and benefits were expanded in
1950.[31]

    In the area of urban reform, the NRPB had a radical viewpoint. The
"right to shelter" was included in its 1942 New Bill of Rights, which
President Roosevelt cited in his 1944 reelection campaign. The NRPB was
more concerned with comprehensive urban planning than with public
housing and slum clearance.[32] It called for the coordination of national
and local planning for slum clearance and public housing, but saw no
organic connection between the two. Instead, the board wanted both
kinds of projects incorporated in a comprehensive urban redevelopment
program. The NRPB was concerned with the timing of public housing
projects, for they were to be included in the approved public works for
which it would be responsible.[33]

[30] Authorship of the 1943 Wagner-Murray-Dingell bill has been variously attributed.
Wagner's biographer, J. Joseph Huthmacher, sees the bill as mainly the work of Wagner,
who was influenced by many, including the NRPB. See *Senator Robert F. Wagner*, pp. 292–
93. Martha Derthick claims that it was written almost entirely by Wilbur Cohen and I. S.
Falk of the Social Security Board. See Derthick, *Policymaking for Social Security* (Washing-
ton, D.C.: The Brookings Institution, 1979), pp. 111, 114. For the bill, see *Congressional
Record*, 78th Cong., 1st sess., June 3, 1943, pp. 5260–62. On Truman's battles over national health insurance, see Poen, *Truman versus the Medical Lobby*, chap. 6, and Donald
E. Spritzer, *Senator James E. Murray and the Limits of Post-War Liberalism* (New York:
Garland, 1985), pp. 133–35.

[31] On the 1950 amendments, see Arthur Altmeyer, *The Formative Years of Social Security*
(Madison: University of Wisconsin Press, 1966), pp. 182–86. See also Cohen and Myers,
"Social Security Act Amendments of 1950."

[32] In 1940, the NRPB contracted for and published a report entitled *Housing: The Continuing Problem*, but it did not endorse any of its conclusions.

[33] Phillip J. Funigiello, *The Challenge to Urban Liberalism: Federal-City Relations during
World War II* (Knoxville: University of Tennessee Press, 1978), chap. 5; Clawson, *New
Deal Planning*, p. 132. The most important report on urban planning sponsored by the
NRPB was Charles S. Ascher, *Better Cities* (Washington, D.C.: Government Printing Office,
1942). See also NRPB, *National Resources Development, Report for 1943* (Washington,
D.C.: Government Printing Office, 1943), pp. 14–16.

In different ways, both urban planning and public housing failed in the United States, however. The urban planners lost their bid to gain influence over reform efforts in 1943, with the abolition of the NRPB and the defeat of bills providing federal aid for state and local planning and redevelopment. Public housing proponents, who cared little about urban planning, eventually won their battle, but without a comprehensive program. Truman's public housing legislation did not pass until 1949, and by the end of his term only 60,000 dwelling units of public housing had been built. Moreover, Truman's policy to encourage home construction owed its limited success to subsidies for private builders and homeowners. In the absence of public planning, FHA insurance and "yield insurance" for builders of middle-class homes and apartment buildings facilitated a private construction boom; five million such housing units were built between 1946 and 1950.[34]

Not until late in the game did the National Resources Planning Board become concerned specifically with the problems of veterans. The NRPB committee did not include veterans' programs in its definition of "public aid," for instance. To coordinate planning aimed at meeting the readjustment needs of soldiers and war workers with long-range social planning, the NRPB organized the Postwar Manpower Conference, which met for the first time in July 1942 and included representatives from the NRPB; the Departments of Agriculture, Labor, Navy, and War; the Federal Security Agency; the War Manpower Commission; the Selective Service System; and the Veterans Administration. The NRPB representatives wanted to ensure that the emergency postwar provision for veterans would mesh with comprehensive plans to achieve full employment and to revamp the social security system. If possible, soldiers and war workers should be included in the same legislation; if not, special legislation for veterans was acceptable so long as it did not establish an administratively separate scheme of superior benefits and employment arrangements, thus undermining proposals for more comprehensive measures.

The recommendations of the conference's report of June 1943 were consistent with NRPB preferences, although most of its proposals pertained to short-term issues concerning munitions workers and the demobilization of veterans. The main proposals with regard to soldiers included three months' furlough pay at a maximum of $100 per month; provision of unemployment insurance administered by the USES for up to twenty-six more weeks; aid for education; and credit toward old-age and survivors' insurance for time spent in the armed services. These proposals underlined the concern of conference members and the NRPB with mitigating the high postwar unemployment that everyone expected. Pro-

---

[34] See Davies, *Housing Reform*; Funigiello, *The Challenge to Urban Liberalism*, chap. 7.

viding educational opportunities for veterans was also consistent with the NRPB committee's proposal to use educational opportunities to keep young people out of the labor market.[35]

To some extent, the new wartime laws providing veterans' benefits corresponded with the ideas of the NRPB. The GI bill of 1944 did not include large bonuses for able-bodied veterans but instead offered "readjustment allowances," a type of unemployment compensation. The benefits offered for vocational or college study were considerably more generous than those the conference members had originally proposed.[36] These programs were supplemented by veterans' benefits that undercut demands for more comprehensive social programs for all citizens, however, especially in the areas of health and housing. The GIs could not be denied the benefits of World War I veterans; therefore, in the absence of national health and disability insurance, veterans with war-related injuries were granted free medical care and generous disability pensions. The GI bill also included incentives for able-bodied veterans to purchase homes, and, during the Truman administration, veterans were provided mortgage subsidies and insurance for the construction of cooperative housing.[37]

In sum, although the NRPB and like-minded planners pointed the way toward a national and comprehensive full-employment welfare state for the United States, and even though congressional liberals and the Truman administration were able to translate some of the plans into legislation, the social policy changes achieved during and after World War II were minor, except where veterans were concerned. They and their families now enjoyed a comprehensive set of benefits and services. Americans in general benefited primarily from extensions of OASI and from modest federal subsidies for home and hospital construction; but the unemployed could no longer depend on public jobs programs. Hence the war brought what the New Deal reformers had hoped to avoid: a special welfare state for a substantial sector of the population deemed especially deserving. The social reformism of the New Deal had been channeled into expanded public provision for veterans, making it henceforth less likely that establishment of a national welfare state could be completed along the lines envisaged by the Committee on Economic Security or by the NRPB committee.

[35] National Resources Planning Board, *Demobilization and Readjustment: Report of the Conference on Postwar Readjustment of Civilian and Military Personnel* (Washington, D.C.: Government Printing Office, 1943).

[36] Ross, *Preparing for Ulysses*, chap. 4; Keith W. Olson, *The G.I. Bill, the Veterans, and the Colleges* (Lexington: University Press of Kentucky, 1974), pp. 10–15.

[37] President's Commission on Veterans' Pensions, *The Historical Development of Veterans' Benefits in the United States* (Washington, D.C.: Government Printing Office, 1956); Ross, *Preparing for Ulysses*, chap. 8; Davies, *Housing Reform*, pp. 41–47, 50–57.

Counterpoint: War and the Welfare State
in Great Britain

In Britain, wartime planners had much greater success. The NRPB Committee on Long-Range Work and Relief Policies had its British counterpart in William Beveridge. A student of policy and former civil servant who had been involved with British social insurance since its inception, Beveridge was commissioned in June 1941 to study and make recommendations with regard to British social policy. His mandate came from Arthur Greenwood, the minister without portfolio in charge of reconstruction and a member of the coalition government's wartime Cabinet. Beveridge was to work with a committee of civil servants from the ministries involved in social policy. The Beveridge Report, *Social Insurance and Allied Services*, was released in December 1942 to widespread public acclaim. In sharp contrast to the influence of the NRPB's plans in the United States, the Beveridge Report, although it was not immediately adopted by the government, set the tone of comprehensive social policy changes in Britain.

Aside from the Beveridge Report, responsibility for reconstruction planning was at first scattered among the ministries of the wartime coalition government. Notably, the president of the Board of Trade, Hugh Dalton of the Labour party, formed his own reconstruction team. The government as a whole concerned itself with reconstruction in November 1943 when Prime Minister Winston Churchill appointed a minister of reconstruction. The Reconstruction Committee became the key standing committee, its ten members were divided equally among Conservative and Labour ministers. Churchill paid little attention and established the principle that no measures requiring Treasury funds would be passed until after a postwar general election. The compromises of this committee and its many subcommittees were embodied in a series of White Papers, issued in 1944, dealing with social insurance, health, and employment policy.[38] The first of these, *Social Insurance*, was largely consistent with the Beveridge Report.

Like *Security, Work, and Relief Policies*, the Beveridge Report ranged across many realms of social policy. Although the report was couched in visionary rhetoric, Beveridge's main recommendation was merely to reorganize and revamp social insurance, including workmen's compensation. All programs would provide similar flat subsistence benefits and

---

[38] J. M. Lee, *The Churchill Coalition, 1940–1945* (Hamden, Conn.: Archon Books, 1980), pp. 127–38; Ben Pimlott, *Hugh Dalton* (London: Jonathan Cape, 1985), chap. 13. For the view that postwar social policy developments were mainly due to the policies and actions of the coalition government, see Paul Addison, *The Road to 1945* (London: Jonathan Cape, 1975).

would be financed by equal, flat contributions from employer and employee, with the final third provided by the state, as in the original 1911 social insurance programs. Unlike the NRPB committee, Beveridge did not call for a high level of benefits and was not concerned about the incidence of taxation. He called for the end of the Assistance Board (which administered public assistance) as a separate entity, and expected that the scope of public assistance would be substantially reduced. He wanted all programs to be combined under one social insurance ministry. Finally, the nuts-and-bolts treatment of social insurance was annexed to three sweeping assumptions about postwar social policy: that it would include the introduction of family allowances, the creation of a national health service, and a commitment to maintain full employment.[39]

Beveridge's assumption regarding the creation of a national health service had been foreshadowed by wartime developments. In 1939 the Emergency Medical Service was organized, partly because of fears that bombings would leave large numbers of citizens in need of medical care. Under the emergency program, voluntary and local hospitals provided free treatment for an increasing number of patients, including servicemen, war workers, and those injured in bombing raids. In 1944, the coalition government's White Paper, written under the direction of the Conservative Henry Willink, the minister of health, called for a free national health system financed mainly by the Treasury, but also with a small payroll tax. The system would be administered by the national government and by local authorities, who would retain considerable authority. Voluntary hospitals would be coordinated with the system, but would remain private. Doctors connected to health centers would derive their income from salaries and capitation fees.[40]

After completing his report on social insurance, Beveridge turned to the study of employment policy, but this time the government beat him to the presses. His *Full Employment in a Free Society* was preceded by the 1944 White Paper, entitled *Employment Policy*, which called for the government to accept responsibility for ensuring high and stable employment. For short-run aims, the White Paper drew upon the 1940 Barlow Report, issued before formation of the coalition government. To move new in-

[39] William Beveridge, *Social Insurance and Allied Services* (New York: Macmillan, 1942). Beveridge did not care that the flat rates of contributions for workers would take a larger proportion of the incomes of poor workers—even without consideration of employer contributions. See José Harris, *William Beveridge: A Biography* (Oxford: Clarendon Press, 1977), chap. 16.

[40] Almont Lindsey, *Socialized Medicine in England and Wales: The National Health Service, 1948–1961* (Chapel Hill: University of North Carolina Press, 1962), pp. 32–39; Roger Eatwell, *The 1945–1951 Labour Governments* (London: Batsford Academic, 1979), pp. 62–63; Henry Pelling, *The Labour Governments, 1945–51* (New York: St. Martin's Press, 1984), pp. 151–64; Derek Fraser, *The Evolution of the British Welfare State* (London: Macmillan, 1973), p. 214.

dustries to declining areas, the paper proposed to maintain munitions fac-
tories in depressed areas. It suggested that licenses, government contracts,
and financial assistance be used to achieve this result, and that this industrial policy be coordinated by the Board of Trade.[41] With regard to long-
run aims, *Employment Policy* called for the use of Keynesian spending
categories to analyze economic trends and the use of public works projects to offset declines in private capital expenditure. The paper also included Keynesian proposals for the use of varying tax rates to regulate
contributions for social insurance. In the matter of public works, local
authorities were expected to submit five-year plans for public improvements and the national government was to use loans to speed or slow
such projects.[42] The White Paper did not propose that the government
fund the projects or development of the five-year plans, however. Nor
were public employment programs suggested for postwar Britain.

Both American and British planners of social policy in the postwar period devised comprehensive sets of reforms, aiming to fill programmatic
gaps, to merge social insurance and relief programs, and to further national economic growth—specifically, to achieve full employment. Yet the
emphases of postwar planning efforts in the two nations differed considerably. The American plans dealt mainly with work and relief, and called
for the creation of brand new social insurance programs along with the
centralized administration of federal unemployment insurance. The British plans concentrated on the rationalization and extension of existing
social insurance. The new British proposals for family allowances and for
creation of a national health service had nothing to do with unemployment and economic depression, and relief reform seems to have been an
afterthought. Moreover, the British plans for preventing postwar unemployment were conspicuously undeveloped compared with the elaborate
American proposals for public works and public employment.

The achievements of American and British planners also differed
sharply. In the area of social insurance, the Labour government adopted
the Beveridge reforms in 1946, revamping old-age insurance, unemployment insurance, disability insurance, and workers' compensation. As to
the related area of relief, Beveridge had called for the end of the locally
rooted poor law, and in 1948 the Labour government nationalized public
assistance. In establishing the new British National Health Service, the
government followed the controversial recommendations for universal
and free medical care specified in the coalition government's 1944 White
Paper—and went beyond them. In 1946, the Labour government passed

[41] Ministry of Reconstruction, *Employment Policy* (New York: Macmillan, 1945), pp.
10–15; Kenneth O. Morgan, *Labour in Power, 1945–51* (Oxford: Clarendon Press, 1984),
pp. 182–83.
[42] *Employment Policy*, pp. 20–24.

legislation nationalizing the hospitals, and induced the reluctant medical profession to join the system when the law took effect in 1948.[43]

Unambitious as they were, Britain's wartime plans for a postwar employment policy were also largely carried out. For the short run, the British planned to manipulate industrial policy to direct development to depressed areas. Under the Labour government, however, the use of Keynesian demand management was limited, partly because of Labour's preference for direct industrial controls and partly because of postwar inflation and high employment.[44]

British urban and housing planners achieved what their U.S. counterparts could only dream about. Although the coalition government could not agree on the compulsory purchase of land, the Town and Country Act of 1947 empowered planners to purchase sites for renewal and other projects. There was little coalition government planning with regard to public housing.[45] Yet postwar British housing policy provided for the construction of locally controlled and planned public housing. About 80 percent of the one million permanent housing units built from 1945 to 1951 were publicly owned.[46]

British Theories about War and Social Policy

Major reforms of British social policy were planned during World War II and were quickly put into effect after the war; social theory lagged only

[43] On social insurance, see Pelling, *The Labour Governments*, p. 98; Morgan, *Labour in Power*, p. 143; and Fraser, *British Welfare State*, p. 220. On public assistance legislation, see Pelling, *The Labour Governments*, p. 101; Morgan, *Labour in Power*, p. 173; and Fraser, *British Welfare State*, pp. 212–13. On family allowances, see John Macnicol, *The Movement for Family Allowances, 1918–1945: A Study in Social Policy Development* (London: Heinemann, 1980), chap. 7. On the national health service, see Lindsey, *Socialized Medicine in England and Wales*, pp. 43–46; Pelling, *The Labour Governments*, pp. 102–8; and Morgan, *Labour in Power*, pp. 151–64.

[44] Alan Booth, "The 'Keynesian Revolution' in Economic Policymaking," *Economic History Review* 36 (1983): 103–23; Margaret Gowing, "The Organization of Manpower in Britain during the Second World War," *Journal of Contemporary History* 7 (1972): 147–67; Pimlott, *Hugh Dalton*, chap. 16.

[45] During the war, British urban planners urged that national legislation create sanctions whose effect would be to encourage comprehensive local land-use planning and redevelopment. The Uthwatt Report, which was commissioned by the Minister of Works and Buildings, called for government planning authorities to purchase land for redevelopment sites. The coalition government split over the issue of compulsory purchase of land, however, and did not issue a White Paper on postwar planning. Nor was the question of public housing covered in any White Paper. See J. M. Lee, *The Churchill Coalition*, p. 137, and Funigiello, *The Challenge to Urban Liberalism*, pp. 189–95.

[46] J. B. Cullingworth, *Town and Country Planning in Britain* (London: George Allen and Unwin), pp. 15–23; Pelling, *The Labour Governments*, pp. 110–13; Morgan, *Labour in Power*, pp. 163–70.

slightly behind. In 1955 at King's College in London, Richard Titmuss delivered a lecture on "War and Social Policy" in which he outlined a thesis about the positive relationship between modern "total" warfare and the development of the welfare state. Echoing Max Weber's dictum that "the discipline of the army gives birth to all discipline," and pointing out that modern wars rely on conscripts and civilians as well as special-ized military castes, Titmuss concluded that "the waging of modern war presupposes and imposes a great increase in social discipline . . . [and] this discipline is tolerable if—and only if—social inequalities are not intoler-able."[47] Titmuss also agreed with Arthur Marwick that the impact of modern wars on civilians must be taken into account.[48] The more civil-ians who are involved in wartime efforts, Titmuss concluded, the greater the equalizing effects achieved by new social policies and reforms of ex-isting ones; the reforms should be universal, benefiting civilians as well as soldiers.

Provocative as Titmuss's arguments are, they constitute only a starting point for analysis, for comparative evidence indicates that the causal links are not as simple as Titmuss suggests. In neither Great Britain nor the United States did the first modern pension and social insurance policies *originate* during or right after the world wars. The Liberal party launched the major British social policies from 1906 to 1911. American progres-sives failed to gain passage of social insurance legislation before World War I; congressional Democrats gained passage of the social security bill in 1935. An analysis of the *expansion* of social programs and expendi-tures reveals that in the United States, both world wars culminated in periods of conservative retrenchment and the frustration of virtually all

[47] Richard M. Titmuss, "War and Social Policy," in *Essays on the "Welfare State"* (Bos-ton: Beacon Press, 1969), p. 85. Titmuss acknowledged that his formulation was similar to Stanislav Andreski's military participation ratio. See Andreski, *Military Organization and Society* (London: Routledge and Kegan Paul, 1954).

[48] Arthur Marwick, *War and Social Change in the Twentieth Century: A Comparative Study of Britain, France, Germany, Russia, and the United States* (New York: Macmillan, 1974). With the emergence of the small war in the second half of the twentieth century, scholars began to perceive a negative relationship between war and social policy. The result was a sort of academic consensus that large or total wars such as World War I and World War II help to strengthen and universalize social policy, whereas small wars and large stand-ing forces tend to fragment social policy and drain resources away from it. For the most explicit statement of this view, see Harold L. Wilensky, *The Welfare State and Equality: Structural and Ideological Roots of Public Expenditures* (Berkeley: University of California Press, 1975), chap. 4. The evidence is sketchy, however. Wilensky's analysis of twenty-two industrialized nations shows that military spending between 1950 and 1952 is negatively correlated with social spending as a percentage of the GNP in 1966. Arthur Stein examines the four wars of the twentieth century in which the United States has participated and finds no evidence to support his hypothesis that mobilization leads to equality by way of social spending. See Stein, *The Nation at War* (Baltimore: Johns Hopkins University Press, 1978), chaps. 3, 7.

wartime reform hopes for expanded federal social interventions, except those aimed at veterans. In Britain, by contrast, social insurance expanded rapidly right after World War I, to encompass veterans and civilian workers alike,[49] and all social policies were reorganized and extended soon after World War II. Even so, the British experience in that war does not bear out the Titmuss conclusion as to the influence of war on equality. The World War II effort put a premium on the participation and morale of British civilians as well as soldiers and, according to Titmuss's reasoning, should have led to policies funded by a more progressive income tax structure. Instead, the Beveridge reforms relied heavily on a regressive, flat payroll tax to finance the extension of flat benefits.

To give Titmuss his due, the destruction of World War II did affect British *civilians* more than their U.S. counterparts. In the United States there were only brief and false scares about Japanese attacks on the West Coast following Pearl Harbor. But British civilians were bombed by the Nazis; civilian deaths numbered 60,000.[50] This may help to explain the establishment of war-related health programs for British civilians. The Emergency Medical Service covered many civilians along with servicemen, and its formation was the basis of Beveridge's assumption that a national health service would be created.[51] In other policy areas, however, the differential impact of the war on the two civilian populations had little effect on public policy. For instance, the wartime boom in the U.S. domestic economy brought a mass migration of American workers from rural to urban areas and across regions. Had social policies been changed to reflect this situation, they would have included more generous and nationally uniform disability insurance, unemployment insurance, and family support measures. But U.S. proposals for such policy changes failed, whereas similar British proposals were more successful, even though the uprooting of British workers was less dramatic.

Another British theory of war and the welfare state is the fiscal argu-

[49] See Bentley B. Gilbert, *British Social Policy, 1914–1939* (Ithaca, N.Y.: Cornell University Press, 1970), pp. 54–61.

[50] Marwick, *War and Social Change*, p. 155. In other ways, the U.S. and British experiences in World War II were similar. Both nations were winners, and both escaped occupation. In terms of casualties, the two countries did not differ much. The percentage of the British population killed during the war was 0.97; the percentage of Americans was 0.23. The British figure is larger, but much closer to the U.S. percentage than the percentages for Germany (6.42), Poland (9.66), or Yugoslavia (11.14). The British figure is also smaller than those for some other Western European countries, such as the Netherlands (2.44) and Finland (2.34). These data are from John Dryzek and Robert E. Goodin, "Risk-Sharing and Social Justice: The Motivational Foundations of the Post-War Welfare State," *British Journal of Political Science* 16:1–34.

[51] Richard Titmuss, *Problems of Social Policy* (London: His Majesty's Stationery Office, 1950), chaps. 11, 22–24.

ment developed by Alan Peacock and Jack Wiseman.[52] Like Titmuss, these authors posit that wars lead to advances in social policy, but they emphasize a different causal mechanism: increases in the state's fiscal capacities through the "displacement effect." To prosecute a war, their argument goes, the state must raise taxes, and this is easier to do during national emergencies. When the crisis ends, the level of taxation remains higher than before, because the populace has grown accustomed to higher taxes. This situation facilitates new social policy initiatives or expansion of existing programs, for people always want higher public expenditures than they are willing to cover with increased taxes. In short, any crisis that loosens fiscal constraints will quickly lead to increased social expenditures.

Peacock and Wiseman's argument does not explain the differences in the two nations' social policy development. If this fiscal perspective were valid, the United States would have been able to achieve greater advances in social policy more rapidly than did Britain, for the United States benefited economically from the war whereas Britain was decimated. Indeed, Britain was forced to turn to the United States for loans immediately after the war. The United States ended the generous Lend-Lease Program in 1945 but in 1947 began to provide grants to Britain under the Marshall Plan. In effect, the United States helped to finance a series of nationalizing reforms of British social policy, while comparable reforms were rejected at home.[53]

Why did a more dramatic "displacement effect" not occur in the United States? A close look at tax politics and its relation to changes in social policy casts doubt on the applicability of Peacock and Wiseman's reasoning to the U.S. case. Their theory predicts tax increases throughout the war and no large tax cuts after the war. At first, the war did lead to tax increases. To pay for the war, Congress passed the U.S. Revenue Acts of 1941 and 1942, which broadened the base of the personal income tax and thus added 20 million people to the rolls, mainly by lowering exemptions. The income tax structure was also made more progressive.[54] In addition, these early tax acts established a "victory tax" surcharge and increased the corporate income tax and the excess profits taxes; altogether

[52] Alan T. Peacock and Jack Wiseman, *The Growth of Public Expenditure in the United Kingdom* (Princeton, N.J.: Princeton University Press, 1961).

[53] Morgan, *Labour in Power*, pp. 143–51. On the British tax system during the war, see B.E.V. Sabine, *A History of Income Tax* (London: George Allen and Unwin, 1966), chaps. 12, 13. For a comparison of changes in U.S. and British income taxes during World War II, see Carolyn Webber and Aaron Wildavsky, *A History of Taxation and Expenditure in the Western World* (New York: Simon and Schuster, 1986), pp. 472–76.

[54] The income tax structure was not made as progressive as the Roosevelt administration would have liked, however. See John F. Witte, *The Politics and Development of the Federal Income Tax* (Madison: University of Wisconsin Press, 1985), pp. 114–19.

these revenues met about 45 percent of the costs of the war. All U.S. taxes did not increase throughout the war, however. Notably, previously scheduled increases in the payroll tax for old-age and survivors' insurance were consistently delayed.

The Roosevelt administration failed to gain much support for its tax proposals after 1942. Overriding Roosevelt's veto, Congress passed the Revenue Act of 1944, which yielded much less revenue than Roosevelt had demanded. Soon after the war, Congress passed a $5 billion tax cut that mainly affected the victory and excess profits taxes. In 1948, Congress passed, over Truman's veto, another $5 billion tax cut, this time affecting the personal income tax. It nearly erased an $8.8 billion surplus in fiscal 1948, although the 1941 and 1942 changes in the structure of the personal income tax largely remained on the books.[55] In sum, Peacock and Wiseman's theory is borne out in that the income tax system was strengthened during the war and was not severely weakened afterward, but the increased revenues were not automatically channeled into social spending, and previously scheduled increases in the OASI payroll tax were not made during the war.

Peacock and Wiseman also expect war to promote the permanent centralization of government functions.[56] The postwar fiscal predominance of the U.S. federal government would appear to be consistent with their thesis. In 1939, federal revenues were 7.4 percent of GNP, and state and local revenues were 10.6 percent. In 1946, the tables were turned: federal revenues amounted to 18.7 percent of GNP, and state and local revenues constituted 6.2 percent.[57] But in terms of social policy, centralizing reforms failed; states and localities gained greater control over existing social programs. Moreover, the additional federal revenues brought by wartime tax increases (and not rolled back by postwar tax cuts) were used to fund veterans' benefits and grants-in-aid to states and localities, rather than national social programs covering all citizens. Why are Peacock and Wiseman's expectations incorrect?

The war had an ironic effect on the relative fiscal capacities of the various levels of government. In the early New Deal period, the initial impetus toward federal control over relief policy had been the fiscal crisis of the states and localities, both of which had relied heavily on property

[55] Ibid., pp. 132–37. See also Roland Young, *Congressional Politics in the Second World War* (New York: Da Capo Press, 1972), pp. 128–30, and Herbert Stein, *The Fiscal Revolution in America* (Chicago: University of Chicago Press, 1969), pp. 206–10.

[56] Peacock and Wiseman, *Public Expenditure in the United Kingdom*, chap. 6. On the centralization of American government in wartime, see A. Stein, *The Nation at War*, pp. 55–63.

[57] *Economic Report of the President, 1980* (Washington, D.C.: U.S. Government Printing Office, 1980), pp. 203, 288.

taxes. When all levels of government were fiscally hurt by the Depression, the federal government gained a relative advantage because of its greater ability to tolerate deficits.[58] During the war, although the absolute and relative size of federal revenues greatly increased, the high employment rate ended the fiscal crises of the states and localities.

In ways not revealed by the highly aggregate approach of Peacock and Wiseman, preexisting U.S. social policies and their associated fiscal instruments discouraged the channeling of wartime federal revenues toward more generous citizen benefits. Overall, because national social programs relying on payroll taxes were not fully developed before the war, it was difficult to expand them through fiscal sleights of hand during and right after the war. An almost politically costless way to extend social insurance programs is to spend the unexpected surpluses in earmarked trust funds. In Britain the prior, long-term existence of payroll taxes that funded a number of national social insurance programs doubtless made it easier for the wartime coalition government to agree on their expansion and rationalization, and to put into effect the concrete proposals of the Beveridge Report beginning in 1944. In the United States, however, unemployment insurance was not nationalized, and there were no national programs for health and disability insurance. Only old-age and survivors' insurance benefited from the fiscal dividends of the increased employment and higher wages brought about by the war. Although Congress rejected scheduled OASI tax increases during the war, by 1949 the program's financial prospects were so favorable that Congress could increase benefits and extend coverage with only a slight increase in the payroll tax (and without projecting any use of general revenues).[59]

In sum, neither the ideas of Titmuss about the impact of war on a population, nor the argument of Peacock and Wiseman about the effects of war mobilization on the state's aggregate fiscal capacities, can explain the differences between American and British development of social policy during and after World War II. Such theories, based on what apparently happened in Britain, do not explain why the United States failed to forge a national welfare state despite the renewed solidarities and increases in federal fiscal capacity brought about by the war. In the following section,

[58] States now rely primarily on sales and income taxes, not property taxes, which are still the main source of revenue for local governments. See James A. Maxwell and J. Richard Aronson, *Financing State and Local Governments*, 3d ed. (Washington, D.C.: The Brookings Institution, 1977), pp. 18–21; Joseph A. Pechman, *Federal Tax Policy*, 3d ed. (Washington, D.C.: The Brookings Institution, 1977), chap. 9; Henry J. Bitterman, *State and Federal Grants-in-Aid* (New York: Mentzer, Bush, 1938), chap. 1; and I. Bernstein, *The Lean Years*, chap. 7.

[59] Derthick claims that conservative actuarial estimates regarding the OASI program facilitated its expansion throughout the postwar period. See *Policymaking for Social Security*, chap. 17.

we explore the impact of specifically political processes on social policy outcomes in the two countries.

Explaining The Impact of World War II on Social Policy in the United States and Great Britain

Wars are not fought by "the state" in the abstract, but by particular states with different institutional structures, prior policies, and contending political coalitions. Preexisting institutional structures and political coalitions influence the choices national leaders make about how to plan for the postwar period and how to mobilize the nation for war. The exigencies of war and the mode of mobilization reinforce some political forces and undermine others, in part by changing the agenda of problems discussed by the nation's politicians and in part by changing the goals and capacities of politically active groups.

Taking this approach, we compare the impact of World War II on social policy plans and outcomes in the United States and in Great Britain. First, we examine the effects of prior social policies on the content of new policy proposals and on the ability of planners to translate them into proposed legislation during the war. Next, we analyze the different strategies used to mobilize the people and the economies for war. The modes of mobilization in Britain and the United States influenced social policy agendas, support for political parties, and possibilities for extending wartime controls into postwar reforms. Finally, we discuss political coalitions and the role of industrial labor in them during and right after the war, examining how mobilization strengthened the position of those advocating certain policy alternatives and weakened the position of others at critical moments.

The comparisons in this section clarify why World War II affected social policy outcomes differently in the United States and in Britain. In brief, the administrative and political forces strengthened by America's participation in World War II worked against the extension and nationalization of many social policies and their coordination with planning to achieve full employment. The national role in the formulation and administration of social policy began to expand during the New Deal but was redefined during the 1940s. Thereafter the trend was away from public assistance and employment programs, and toward national social provision primarily for veterans and the elderly.

PRIOR SOCIAL POLICIES AND WARTIME PLANNING

As has been noted, sweeping social policy reforms were proposed in both Britain and the United States. The heightened sense of public purpose in wartime encouraged national planning, and the projections of Beveridge and the NRPB were released within a few months of one another, in December 1942 and March 1943. Yet the central emphases of the Beveridge Report and the NRPB's *Security, Work, and Relief Policies* differed considerably. The latter called for the use of progressive general revenues to improve public employment, public assistance, and public works, as well as for nationalized and more generous unemployment insurance; the former recommended rationalizing social insurance and establishing family allowances and a national health service. The plans fared differently in the two countries. The characteristics of the British reform plan helped it to gain a favorable public and administrative reception. By contrast, the NRPB proposals seemed irrelevant to American problems after 1942, and fell prey to bureaucratic rivalries within the executive branch.

American planners relied more heavily than the British on Depression era tools to fight unemployment, and this difference of approach reflected overall differences in the prior social policies of the two countries. The U.S. policies were of more recent origin; most nationwide social policies had been created in the 1930s. British social policies had been in existence since the 1910s and 1920s. Moreover, the two nations had previously coped in contrasting ways with economic crisis, including mass unemployment. During the 1920s and 1930s, the British government had avoided public works and jobs programs and had provided relief to the unemployed through extensions of social insurance programs that had always been financed by contributions from general public revenues as well as payroll taxes. The United States government, however, stressed emergency public relief and employment programs to help the unemployed during the Depression, and kept its new contributory social insurance programs separately based on payroll taxes without immediate contributions from general revenues.

When they turned to postwar planning, British and American reformers built on what they considered the best of their respective systems. The Beveridge Report did not include public works or employment programs, leaving for later consideration what appeared to be less pressing questions about full employment. Because the British had long experience with nationally organized social insurance, Beveridge could assess the previous performance of various programs and suggest what appeared to be adjustments, extensions, and rationalizations of existing social insurance policies, accomplished by tripartite financing.[60] The Committee on Long-Range Work and Relief Policies, however, considered all New Deal programs experimental and held no financing technique sacred. It saw no major distinction between supposedly emergency programs such as the

[60] Fraser, *British Welfare State*, pp. 185–97; B. Gilbert, *British Social Policy*, pp. 180–92.

WPA and the supposedly permanent programs of the Social Security Act.[61] Moreover, in the late 1930s and early 1940s, providing adequate benefits to the needy and work for the unemployed seemed more important than preserving and extending strict contributory financing by imposing taxes on employers and employees. Unlike British reformers, who had experienced the 1930s as a period of conservative muddling through, New Deal planners hoped to use the wartime period to realize their aims by adding new programs and nationalizing old ones, mainly along the lines projected by the 1934–35 Committee on Economic Security.

But the impact of wartime realities on the projections of the planners shattered the hopes only of the Americans. Although the unemployment crisis of the Depression came to an end in both countries, the wartime surge of full employment had different effects on their plans for postwar social policies. In Britain, social insurance, the central concern of the Beveridge Report, remained important throughout the war, and this helped to overcome the initial reluctance of the coalition government to enact its provisions.[62] Because the American plans for social policy reform were grounded in late-1930s thinking, they were soon undercut by the skyrocketing wartime employment rates, which minimized the importance of the employment and relief programs stressed by the NRPB committee. Probably for these reasons, a lack of enthusiasm for *Security, Work, and Relief Policies* was registered in public opinion polls taken soon after its release in early 1943. Surveys found that 76 percent of the public approved of the principles in the report, but 58 percent thought its proposals would not affect them personally.[63]

In other ways, British and American experiences with preexisting social policies helped Beveridge's proposals and hurt the NRPB's plans. The Brit-

[61] Warken, *National Resources Planning Board*, p. 229.

[62] The coalition government supported the Beveridge reforms only in principle. In February 1943, when the House of Commons began to consider the report, 121 Labour backbenchers supported an amendment calling for immediate implementation of the plan, the first time since formation of the coalition that Labour had taken issue with the coalition government. See Henry Pelling, *Britain and the Second World War* (Glasgow: Collins, 1970), pp. 168–73.

[63] A week after *Security* was transmitted to Congress, 58 percent of a random sample of the public had heard of the plan. Only 34 percent felt that it would help them personally. See Jerome Bruner, *Mandate from the People* (New York: Duell, Sloan and Pierce, 1944), chap. 8. The lack of enthusiasm was not due to the committee's rejection of conventional social insurance. According to survey data compiled by Michael E. Schiltz, public approval ratings of old-age insurance and old-age pensions in the middle 1930s were similar; ratings for old-age pensions were perhaps higher. For instance, 89 percent of respondents approved pensions for the needy (December 1935), whereas polls of different samples revealed that 68 percent (September and November 1936) and 77 percent (January 1937) approved of old-age insurance. In 1941, 93 percent approved of old-age pensions; in 1943, 97 percent approved of old-age insurance. See Schiltz, *Public Attitudes toward Social Security, 1933–1965* (Washington, D.C.: Government Printing Office, 1970), p. 36.

ish plan employed visionary rhetoric, yet what was envisioned did not differ significantly from existing administrative and fiscal arrangements. The American plans were comprehensive and visionary only because they did not build upon and elaborate the undeveloped fiscal and administrative arrangements specified by existing U.S. social policies, with the exception of those pertaining to employment. Although ultimately answerable to himself, Beveridge met with an interdepartmental committee of administrators familiar with the details of each area of social policy, and his report coincided sufficiently with their views to make its proposals seem practicable to the British government.[64] In contrast, the NRPB committee was heavily weighted with academicians and leaders in the field of social work. Because there was less long-term administrative experience to draw upon in formulating social policy, U.S. planners had no solid base within the executive branch, and their proposals were vulnerable to bureaucratic rivalries.

One rivalry was with the newly established Social Security Board (SSB). The thinking of the NRPB Committee on Long-Range Work and Relief Policies partially clashed with the postwar plans of the SSB, the agency established in 1935 to administer the Social Security Act's provisions. This disagreement led to a battle over proposed legislation. Although the SSB and the NRPB committee shared many goals, including permanent nationalization of the United States Employment Service and unemployment insurance and the creation of disability and health insurance, the SSB's reception of *Security, Work, and Relief Policies* was lukewarm. A firm supporter of contributory insurance based on payroll taxes, the SSB objected to the NRPB committee's criticism of payroll taxes and its attempts to uncouple benefits from contributions. The SSB was not opposed to some contribution to social insurance from general revenues, but it wanted payroll taxes to provide most of the funding, and considered the adequacy of benefits strictly a secondary goal. Although the SSB was in favor of a new federal grant-in-aid as a form of general assistance to the states, it could not agree to the extension and partial nationalization of general assistance, for this might transform the aid into a sort of guaranteed income, displacing contributory social insurance.[65] If results are

[64] José Harris, "Some Aspects of Social Policy in Britain during the Second World War," in W. J. Mommsen, ed., *The Emergence of the Welfare State in Great Britain and Germany* (London: Croom Helm, 1981), pp. 247–62.

[65] The debate between Eveline M. Burns and Edwin E. Witte over the future of social security reflects the debate between the NRPB and the SSB. See Burns, "Social Insurance in Evolution," *American Economic Review* 34, no. 1 (supplement): 199–211; Witte, "What to Expect of Social Security," *American Economic Review* 34, no. 1 (supplement): 212–21. See also Edwin E. Witte, "American Post-War Social Security Proposals," *American Economic Review* 33 (December 1943): 825–38. For the views of the SSB and of people associated with it, see Arthur Altmeyer, "War and Post-War Problems," in Wilbert Cohen, ed., *War and Post-War Social Security: The Outlines of an Expanded Program* (Washington,

judged in terms of legislation passed in the mid-1940s, neither the SSB nor the NRPB committee realized anything close to their policy goals. But in terms of proposed legislation the SSB outmaneuvered the committee; the Wagner-Murray-Dingell bills called for large payroll tax increases, to be channeled into a single trust fund.

The National Resources Planning Board also had to contend with the Veterans Administration, another autonomous organization in the federal bureaucracy with authority over matters central to postwar social policy. The NRPB got what it wanted only insofar as its ideas did not conflict with VA-supported programs for veterans. After the NRPB organized the Postwar Manpower Conference, it achieved some of its goals through the GI bill: veterans received readjustment allowances, improved unemployment benefits, and educational subsidies, rather than bonuses. But in matters such as health insurance and disability programs, the jealous control maintained by the VA over national programs for veterans prevented the NRPB from realizing its vision of national programs for all citizens, even in areas where the SSB favored the NRPB's ideas.[66] In Britain, the increase in the number of World War II veterans who were covered by existing national health programs increased the possibility that a comprehensive national health service would be established.

To summarize, in wartime Britain, Beveridge presented a vision of welfare state reforms grounded in previously well developed social insurance measures. In the United States, NRPB planners did not have well-developed social policies upon which to build, and, in the spirit of 1930s reformism, they tried to expand the New Deal employment and public assistance programs during the wartime employment boom. Inside the executive branch, the Social Security Board and the Veterans Administration promoted their visions of social policy at the expense of key NRPB plans. In contrast to the Beveridge Report, the NRPB's *Security, Work, and Relief Policies* had neither public enthusiasm nor bureaucratic backing.

STATE CAPACITIES, POLITICAL SYSTEMS, AND NATIONAL MOBILIZATION FOR WAR

During World War II, the United States and British governments had to mobilize people and economies. Yet the mobilization effort was man-

---

D.C.: American Council on Public Affairs, 1942), pp. 20–30; Arthur Altmeyer, "Desirability of Expanding the Social Insurance Program Now," *Social Security Bulletin* 5, no. 11 (November, 1942): 5–9; and George E. Bigge, "Social Security and Post-War Planning," *Social Security Bulletin* 5, no. 12 (December 1942): 4–10. For the SSB's view of Committee, *Security*, see "Social Security in Review," *Social Security Bulletin* 6, no. 3 (March 1943): 1–2.

[66] On the operation of the separate veterans' social policy system, see Sar A. Levitan and Karen A. Cleary, *Old Wars Remain Unfinished: The Veteran Benefits System* (Baltimore: Johns Hopkins University Press, 1973).

aged quite differently in the two nations, in part because of their different political systems and state structures. The British government was run politically by a formal coalition, and the imposition of strong controls over the wartime economy was facilitated by the greater capacities of the British state. In the United States, the wartime political coalition was informal, and federal control over the economy was weak. As we show in this section, these differences in mobilization help to explain why the postwar expansion of social policies was accomplished more easily in Britain than in the United States.

The British parliamentary system of government allows the creation of formal governing coalitions, and a Conservative-dominated bipartisan coalition directed British participation in the war. The formalization of a bipartisan coalition opened the Conservatives to reforming influences. Labour party leaders were brought into the wartime Cabinet and, more important, were placed in key ministerial positions. Arthur Greenwood commissioned the Beveridge Report in his capacity as minister without portfolio; trade union leader Ernest Bevin was given responsibility for the Ministry of Labour and Hugh Dalton was put in charge of the Board of Trade. Throughout the war, these ministers were able to use their positions to advance reform. Equally important, formalization of the coalition promoted the explicit agreement concerning postwar health and social insurance reforms embodied in the White Papers of 1944.[67]

The British coalition government imposed comprehensive public controls that were administered by the permanent ministries of the long established national civil service. Soon after its inauguration in May 1940, the British coalition government obtained passage of the Emergency Powers Act, which required conscription of property, control of labor, and rationing of food. Every year the controls were extended, and in 1944 the Conservative and Labour parties agreed to continue them for two years after the war. Moreover, the relative importance of British ministries changed during the war. The Ministry of Labour, which was historically identified with social policy improvements, played an important role in British war mobilization.[68] The use of manpower budgeting had come into its own by 1943, allowing the role of the Ministry of Labour to eclipse that of the Treasury, with its long history of thwarting social re-

[67] J. M. Lee, *The Churchill Coalition*, chap. 5.

[68] W. K. Hancock and M. M. Gowing, *British War Economy* (London: His Majesty's Stationery Office, 1949). On the role of the Treasury, see Henry Roseveare, *The Treasury: The Evolution of a British Institution* (New York: Columbia University Press, 1969); Robert Skidelsky, "Keynes and the Treasury View: The Case For and Against an Active Employment Policy," in Mommsen, ed., *Emergence of the Welfare State*, pp. 167–87, and James E. Cronin, "The Resistance to State Expansion in Twentieth Century Britain," Center for the Study of Industrial Societies Occasional Paper no. 24 (Chicago: University of Chicago, 1986).

forms.[69] For British social policy making, there were direct advantages to be gained from the strong role the government played in war mobilization. The wartime controls were crucial to the establishment of planning for industrial location and housing, and the continuation of controls into the postwar period allowed the Labour party to follow the wartime reforms in planning and employment with vigorous new programs for public housing and industrial location.[70]

In contrast to the British parliamentary system, the U.S. governmental system ensured that wartime cooperation between the Republicans and Democrats would be merely informal. President Roosevelt named Henry Stimson secretary of war and appointed many Republican-leaning businessmen, or at least businessmen acceptable to Republicans, to the planning bureaus in charge of wartime production. But Roosevelt received no explicit promise of support in return; Republicans remained free to attack the administration whenever there was an opportunity. The same was true of Southern Democrats, who generally supported the president on war matters, but not on the continuation of New Deal programs or social initiatives.[71]

The fact that U.S. wartime bipartisanship was tacit and limited to immediate war issues helped, in the course of the war, to undermine Roosevelt's base of power in Congress. Partisan electoral politics could not and did not cease in the United States, whereas British elections were suspended. In both countries, the unpopularity of various aspects of the war reflected on the party in power. Thus public support for the British Conservatives was low at the time of the 1942 U.S. elections, and the Conservatives lost a few by-elections in the first half of 1942. In June 1943, about one-half year *after* the war had started to go in the Allies' favor, a Gallup poll found that if British elections were held, 38 percent would vote for the Labour party as opposed to 31 percent for the Conservatives.[72] But the British did not hold midwar elections. In the United States the electorate had a chance to act on its grievances. Congressional elections came as usual in November 1942—soon after Allied armed forces had suffered loss after loss in the Pacific theater, and after Americans at home had been covered by a crazy quilt of controls. The U.S. electoral result was about twice as bad for the presidential party as that of the typical off-year election; the Democrats lost 50 seats in the House. Because almost all of the

[69] Gowing, "Organization of Manpower in Britain," p. 155.

[70] On British housing and planning policies, see note 46 to this paper.

[71] V. O. Key, *Southern Politics in State and Nation* (New York: Knopf, 1949), chaps. 16, 17.

[72] Paul Addison, "By-Elections of the Second World War," in Chris Cook and John Ramsden, eds., *By-Elections in British Politics* (London: Macmillan, 1973), pp. 165–90; *The Gallup Poll in Britain, 1935–1951*, p. 73.

losses were non-Southern Democrats, the midwar election weakened the reform element of the Democratic party, and at a crucial point.[73]

In the United States, the existence of a nonparliamentary system and the division of sovereignty within the federal government also hurt the prospects for enacting social policy reforms. Policy struggles between Democrats and Republicans took place both outside and inside Congress. When Roosevelt put the New Deal on the back burner so that he would have a freer hand to run the war, struggles over social policy did not end. Instead, liberals in Congress, not in the administration, took the initiative and constructed their own postwar reform plans, with the help of appropriate administrative agencies. For instance, the Wagner-Murray-Dingell bills were influenced by the Social Security Board, and Senator James Murray relied on the Bureau of the Budget in formulating the 1945 full employment bill. Congressmen working with the Veterans Administration and military agencies were key proponents of veterans' legislation. Despite such liberal initiatives, however, U.S. social policy initiatives could progress no further than Congress would move them.

This situation resulted in the removal of many administration proposals from the postwar social policy agenda. After the 1942 elections, the conservatives in Congress were strong enough to roll back the New Deal, first by eliminating public employment agencies. By 1943, moreover, Congress had claimed the initiative in questions of reconstruction; it made postwar planning the province of congressional committees and abolished executive planning agencies, including the NRPB. Congressional planning committees were so weighted by conservatives that a Republican, Robert Taft, was named to head one key Senate subcommittee.[74] Accordingly, by the time Harry Truman became president in April 1945, Congress had already reached unfavorable decisions on several questions important to the liberal social policy planners of the late New Deal and early war periods.

In the United States, the weakness of most federal controls over the wartime economy made it likely that controls would not be converted into postwar reforms. As in Britain, economic mobilization for war meant centralization, but in the United States centralization was accomplished mainly by temporary bureaucratic agencies intended to coordinate the activities of industries and government, or to coordinate federal activities with those of the state and local governments. Roosevelt relied heavily on

[73] Hadley Cantril and John Harding, "The 1942 Elections: A Case Study in Political Psychology." The authors argue that the Democratic loss can be explained by a low Democratic voter turnout. They suggest that the reason for their political indifference is that these voters had grown more comfortable as a result of high war employment, but they were also apathetic because of the lackluster running of the war.

[74] Young, Congressional Politics in the Second World War, chap. 8.

businessmen to staff these emergency agencies, partly because the U.S. state lacked sufficient administrative capacities and partly because he wished to avoid re-creating the political divisions of the late 1930s. Military agencies retained control over much of the weapons procurement process and over the flow of some key materials.

At the apex of the U.S. war-time government, several oversight agencies were created within the Office of Emergency Management, a temporary division of the Executive Office of the President. Notably, however, the National Resources Planning Board was kept out of the war mobilization effort, as was the Bureau of the Budget. Had the NRPB been involved, it would have at least outlived the war and might have been in a better position to gain support for some postwar social policy reforms.[75] In short, the Roosevelt administration never achieved the degree of control over the wartime economy that the British coalition government did. In the United States, direct controls were imposed on profits, prices, and raw materials; secondary controls were placed on wages; but there was almost no control over costs.[76] And the administration had no instrumentalities such as a national service or manpower controls by which to manage industrial labor.

Because, politically and administratively, Britain and the United States managed their mobilization effort in different ways, plans for postwar social policy improvements were formulated throughout the war in Britain and protected from backlashes, whereas in America they were not. Although the British Conservatives did not agree to many left-wing positions on postwar social policies, the makeup of the coalition and the British approach to economic mobilization ensured that some agreements would be reached and that some plans could be put "on hold" for possible postwar enactment. Furthermore, the continuation of strong governmental controls into the postwar period facilitated a number of British reforms.

In the United States, however, there were few such controls to continue, and the informality of the wartime coalition hurt liberal Democrats. War spurred visionary social planning in America, but the political system allowed no bureaucratic continuity for, or moratorium on, the social policy plans that had been devised early in the war. After the effective authority in postwar planning was appropriated by Congress, congressional liber-

[75] On the reform potential of U.S. wartime controls, see Brody, "The New Deal and the Second World War"; Herman Miles Somers, *Presidential Agency: OWMR, The Office of War Mobilization and Reconversion* (New York: Greenwood Press, 1950), pp. 76–80; and Edward Berkowitz and Kim McQuaid, *Creating the Welfare State: The Political Economy of Twentieth-Century Reform* (New York: Praeger, 1980), chap. 7.

[76] See John Morton Blum, *V Was for Victory* (San Diego: Harcourt Brace Jovanovich, 1976), chap. 4; Vatter, *The U.S. Economy in World War II*, chap. 4.

als incorporated only a few aspects of the plans, in watered-down forms, in their legislative proposals. This ensured that many ideas of the NRPB would not survive the war in their original form, if they survived at all.

But even the ability of plans to survive the war and the existence of strong wartime controls would not have been enough to bring about post-war reforms. After all, the federal government had managed to nationalize the employment service during the war, yet was forced to return control to the states afterward. In addition to the conditions discussed in this section, social policy changes in the United States depended on the congressional coalitions that could be constructed to pass or obstruct bills. By influencing such coalitions, as some theories of the welfare state suggest, industrial labor and its champions could significantly affect social policy innovations. What, specifically, was the role of the American labor movement in the wartime and postwar struggles over social policies?

LABOR, POLITICAL COALITIONS, AND SOCIAL POLICIES

In the social science literature on modern welfare states, theories about how industrial labor can influence social policy are of two general types.[77] According to arguments in the first category, if labor has a strong or increasingly strong societal presence in relation to capital—as evidenced by the growth of unions or the launching of strikes, for instance—whatever party happens to be in power must take this strength into account and respond with prolabor social policies. According to the second type of argument, social policy innovations are likely only when a political party that represents or is allied with the labor movement is in a position to rule. We find that the relevant experiences of the United States and Britain during World War II do not entirely support either argument. Rather, the different modes of wartime mobilization determined the influence of social groups and political coalitions on social policy.

To some extent, what happened in America compared with what happened in Britain was inconsistent with the first argument, which stresses labor organization and strikes. The organized labor movements in Britain and the United States were growing at similar paces, but labor's organizational power was increasing more rapidly in the United States. Union density, or the percentage of the labor force belonging to unions, increased by 49.4 percent between 1939 and 1946 in the United States, while in Britain the growth was 36.1 percent.[78] As far as strikes are con-

[77] For a discussion of these two approaches, see Francis G. Castles, *The Working Class and Welfare: Reflections on the Political Development of the Welfare State in Australia and New Zealand, 1890–1980* (Wellington: Allen and Unwin, 1985).

[78] In the United States, union density increased from 15.8 percent in 1939 to 21.9 percent in 1945 to 23.6 percent in 1946. In Great Britain, union density increased from 31.6 percent

cerned, from 1939 to 1945 American labor was on the offensive much more than British labor. The volume of strikes—the average number of man-days lost (times 1,000) as a percentage of the labor force—was almost three times as large in the United States as in Britain.[79]

More important than organizational gains or collective action was how American and British labor were incorporated into wartime mobilization effort and the politically structured compromises between capital and labor. American labor was not as influential in the mobilization effort as British labor, and the way American labor was incorporated into the wartime administrative machinery worked against attempts at social reform. Strikes in the United States were provoked by weak wartime controls, and U.S. strike activity worked *against* the possibility of passing social policy legislation. Democratic administrations were forced to turn their attention to the management of labor unrest. Wartime strikes tended to decrease public support for labor and to harm chances for the passage of social policy legislation.

Government controls over labor were strong in Britain, but they were administered by a friendly leadership. Ernest Bevin, the leader of Britain's major trade union and an official of the Labour party, was made minister of labour in 1940 and added the national service to his portfolio. He strove to treat servicemen and war workers equally and had the power to direct labor. In 1941, Bevin froze the number of workers in war-related jobs (but only if he found their wages and working conditions to be satisfactory) and established worker and management production boards. He allowed collective bargaining to continue and relied on the moderation of demands for increases in wages rather than an incomes policy.[80]

In contrast, American organized labor had little say as to the administration of war production. Although labor was well represented on the Office of Production Management (OPM), which was established in January 1941 and was the first of many such coordinating bodies, the OPM

---

in 1939 to 38.6 percent in 1945 to 43.0 percent in 1946. The data for the United States are from *Historical Statistics*, p. 178. The data for Britain are from James E. Cronin, *Labour and Society in Britain, 1918–1979* (New York: Schocken Books, 1984), pp. 241–42.

[79] In the years 1939 to 1945, the strike volume in the United States was 261.5. In Great Britain the strike volume in the same period was 93.7. In 1946, the strike volume in the United States was 1901.8, compared with 105.4 in Britain. Calculated from data in *Historical Statistics*, pp. 178–79, and Cronin, *Labour and Society in Britain*, pp. 241–42. On the influence of the postwar strike wave in the United States on antilabor legislation, see R. Alton Lee, *Truman and Taft-Hartley: A Question of Mandate* (Lexington: University of Kentucky Press, 1966), and Arthur F. McClure, *The Truman Administration and the Problems of Post-War Labor, 1945–1948* (Cranbury, N.J.: Associated University Press, 1969).

[80] Alan Bullock, *The Life and Times of Ernest Bevin*, vol. 2, *Minister of Labour, 1940–1945* (London: Heinemann, 1967); Gowing, "Organization of Manpower in Britain," pp. 160–66.

did not create the sort of management-labor production committees prevalent in Britain. Moreover, labor was not well represented on the OPM's successor, the War Production Board (established in January 1942), which was dominated by businessmen. To some extent, organized labor was consulted on manpower questions. The War Manpower Commission was in charge of manpower mobilization, and representatives of organized labor and business and farm associations formed the Management-Labor Policy Committee to advise it. The management and labor representatives joined forces to help defeat the selective service legislation supported by the president, however.[81]

In the United States, the compromise between capital and labor on unionization and wages was less favorable to labor than that reached in Britain. After Pearl Harbor, organized labor gave Roosevelt a no-strike pledge. The National War Labor Board (NWLB) was established in January 1942 to aid in the settling of industrial disputes. It included four labor representatives, four industry representatives and four persons presumed to represent the public. The key compromise called for organized labor to receive "maintenance of membership" guarantees (unionized workers had to remain in unions or forfeit their jobs) in return for wage restraint. According to the so-called Little Steel formula, workers were allowed 15 percent cost-of-living raises. Roosevelt's hold-the-line order, issued in April 1943, prevented wage increases beyond this level. On wages and unionization, capital and labor did not agree; these decisions were made by the public members, who sided with capital on wages and with labor on maintenance of membership. This quasi-corporatism did not extend to other realms, such as social policy, because the NWLB had little authority beyond the mediation of industrial disputes. To the extent that the wage freeze had an effect on social policy issues, it encouraged agreements on private fringe benefits for workers in a favorable bargaining position.[82]

Federal labor policies also encouraged disputes—and the strikes helped to undermine the chances that Congress would accept social policy proposals. For instance, organized labor sponsored the Wagner-Dingell-Murray bills of 1943 and 1945, but, as mentioned, wartime strikes turned the attention of Congress away from social policy to antilabor legislation. Large-scale strike activity took place after the 1943 hold-the-line order, and again after the war when the no-strike pledge was no longer in ef-

---

[81] Mathew Josephson, *Sidney Hillman: Statesman of American Labor* (Garden City, N.Y.: Doubleday, 1952); Brody, "New Deal and the Second World War."

[82] Joel Seidman, *American Labor from Defense to Reconversion* (Chicago: University of Chicago Press, 1953), chaps. 6–7.

fect.[83] Congress passed, over Roosevelt's veto, the antistrike Smith-Con-
nally bill in June 1943, after strikes had begun in the coal mining industry. The strike wave that began at the end of 1945 provoked Truman to
propose antistrike legislation and led Congress to pass, over Truman's
veto, the 1947 Taft-Hartley bill limiting the power of the 1935 National
Labor Relations Act.

With respect to the second theoretical argument, about how labor can
influence social policy, which focuses on the importance of the rule of
parties allied to labor, we find that war and the mobilization for war mediated the effect on social policy of dominant political parties supported
by labor. According to this view, the political makeup of the U.S. wartime
government should have led to greater gains in social policy than were
achieved in Britain. In America, a reformist Democrat occupied the presidency and enjoyed a Democratic majority in Congress. The British wartime coalition government was voluntary on the part of the dominant
Conservatives; when Britain entered the war, the Conservatives had a
more than 200-vote margin in the House of Commons. The British partnership furthered the possibility of successful social policy reform during
the war, however.

The prospects of the British Labour party were not adversely affected
by the wartime predominance of the Conservatives and the agreement to
postpone elections, because of the influence over social policy that wartime coalitions tend to give to the minority partner. The preoccupation of
the dominant party with war and world issues means that its leaders pay
less attention to domestic concerns. In the United States, "Dr. New Deal"
became "Dr. Win the War," as Roosevelt's post-1939 administrations put
social policy aside. Similarly, Churchill, who was minister of defense as
well as prime minister, was chiefly concerned with the war and left reconstruction questions to others. The British Standing Committee on Reconstruction and its subcommittees were much more heavily weighted toward Labour than either the party's parliamentary delegation or its
ministerial representation.[84] They could make and officially protect plans
for the postwar period.

During the immediate postwar period in Britain, the direct rule of a
party directly allied with organized labor proved important. The Labour
party's 1945 victory (a majority of 146) ensured that legislation resembling all of the coalition government's White Papers on social policy
would pass. Yet, to some extent this was also constraining, for the Labour

[83] For a summary of arguments concerning the positive effect of strikes and civil unrest
on social policy and cross-national evidence that opposes these arguments with respect to
the quality of old-age pensions, see John Myles, *Old Age in the Welfare State: The Political
Economy of Public Pensions* (Boston: Little, Brown, 1984), pp. 89–91, 96.

[84] A.J.P. Taylor, "1932–1945," in David Butler, ed., *Coalitions in British Politics* (New
York: St. Martin's Press, 1978), pp. 74–94; J. M. Lee, *The Churchill Coalition*, chap. 5.

government was forced to accept the fairly conservative Beveridge plan. If it had considered social policies on its own, the postwar Labour government might have opted for a progressive tax system, such as the one it chose for the creation of the National Health Service. The Labour victory ensured continuation of the National Health Service, and it also won the day for advocates of local planning. The 1945 election may have doomed Keynesian full-employment planning, however, for Labour had a whole-hearted commitment to the direct controls used during the war and an indifferent commitment to Keynesianism. These controls could influence the location of new industry, but they were no basis for achieving full employment in the long run.

In the United States, throughout the war and into the postwar period, Democrats, including reformist presidents, were reelected. But even though the Democratic party was heavily subsidized by organized labor in the electoral campaigns of 1940, 1944, and 1948, the Democrats were not a functional equivalent of the Labour party. To achieve a balance that would be even close to the Labour majority of 1945, Americans would have had to elect a left-wing Democratic president and a majority of *urban* Democrats to Congress.[85] In the 1940s, there was a split between urban and rural constituencies and between Republicans and Democrats over prolabor social policies. Congressional Republicans and rural Democrats were especially opposed to policies advocating centralized controls, such as presented in the NRPB proposals and the liberal bills based partly on them. Democrats won the 1944 election and won again in 1948, but in neither case was there sufficient liberal strength in Congress to legislate general social reform.

The main problem was that the House, which was weighted in favor of rural areas, killed almost all of the reform bills that survived consideration by the Senate. Although Roosevelt's reelection in 1944 brought with it a 52-seat Democratic majority in the House, it was not close to the 106-seat majority he had brought with him after his reelection in 1940, or even to the 97-seat majority returned in the 1938 congressional elections, which were considered a disaster for the Democrats.[86] Truman picked up 74 seats in the House when he was elected in 1948. This victory gave him a 91-vote majority overall, a margin comparable to Roosevelt's in 1938.

[85] For an analysis of organized labor's influence on U.S. farm policy in which urban Democrats are seen as the allies of labor, see Karen Orren, "Union Politics and Postwar Liberalism in the United States, 1946–1979," in Karen Orren and Stephen Skowronek, eds., *Studies in American Political Development*, vol. 1 (New Haven, Conn.: Yale University Press, 1986), pp. 215–52.

[86] On the decline of congressional support for the New Deal reforms, see David L. Porter, *Congress and the Waning of the New Deal* (Port Washington, N.Y.: Kennikat Press, 1980), and James T. Patterson, *Congressional Conservatism and the New Deal: The Growth of the Conservative Coalition in Congress, 1933–1939* (Lexington: University Press of Kentucky, 1967).

Moreover, in every House throughout the 1940s, 105 Democrats came from the former states of the Confederacy, whose representatives had always tended to oppose national standards and centralized social policies. To achieve the kind of majority that the Labour party received in 1945, the Democrats needed to win almost all of the House districts dominated by urbanites or labor, for, in the 1940s, there were fewer than 240 of these. The Democrats did not even come close to succeeding.[87]

Even had the House had a majority of urban Democrats in 1944, not all the proposals of the New Deal planners would have been enacted, because many of their recommendations had been removed from the political agenda by then. Had there been such a majority, the second Wagner-Murray-Dingell bill would have passed, giving America a comprehensive system of social insurance financed by payroll taxes. All of the improvements in public assistance and the financing changes for social insurance envisaged by the Committee on Long-Range Work and Relief Policies still would not have been achieved, however. Although the full employment bill of 1945 would also have been passed, it seems unlikely that Congress would have reestablished the NRPB or the WPA, both necessary to the committee's plans, unless there were double-digit unemployment. Moreover, after 1944 no one could have demanded the return of benefits already voted for veterans.

The American system of political representation and the composition of political coalitions after the end of the New Deal thus made it difficult for post-1942 Democratic victories to be translated into majorities that would demand new social benefits, except those aimed at veterans. Conservative coalitions that opposed other strong federal measures collapsed on the issue of generosity toward veterans. Conservatives were mollified by the fact that the Veterans Administration would administer the programs, and they could not resist veterans' lobbying groups, especially the American Legion, which was locally organized throughout the nation and actively appealed to wartime sentiments favoring soldiers.[88]

The narrow margin of the Democratic victory in 1948 meant that President Truman could obtain passage of only part of what was left of the wartime social policy agenda. By then, many issues had receded from prominence. Truman could have gained passage of the new health and disability insurance measures only if there had been a larger urban-liberal majority in Congress. In the end he could get only small funding for public housing, without national controls, and accompanied by measures that appealed to private home builders. The period did bring one success-

---

[87] David R. Mayhew, *Party Loyalty among Congressmen: The Difference between Democrats and Republicans, 1947–1962* (Cambridge: Harvard University Press), chap. 1; Key, *Southern Politics.*

[88] Ross, *Preparing for Ulysses*, pp. 283–86.

ful nationalizing reform of social insurance: the revamping of OASI to include more contributors and beneficiaries. This change, however, was an improvement of an already existing program championed by the Social Security Board. To these reforms, Congress attached a new grant-in-aid for public assistance to the permanently disabled; this legislation contradicted wartime proposals to include benefits for the disabled in social insurance.[89]

In sum, the different positions of labor in Britain and the United States during and right after the war resulted in different governmental approaches to social policy making. In most cases, however, the results were not those predicted by the two most prevalent theories about the influence of labor on social policy. American labor was organizing at a more rapid pace and was more militant during the war than was British labor. Nevertheless, the way labor was incorporated into wartime mobilization was more important. The U.S. government's weak controls provoked labor militancy, and this militancy undercut the support of labor in American public opinion and made more likely the defeat of social policy legislation supported by labor.

The American wartime political coalition was dominated by a reform Democrat and the British coalition was dominated by Conservatives. Yet the war ensured that these partisan configurations would have an effect on social policy different from that predicted by existing theories. In Britain, the minority coalition partner had a stronger influence on social policy, for questions of postwar reconstruction were decided in executive committees weighted to the advantage of the Labour party. In 1945, a strong Labour government inherited these plans and put them into effect, creating the British welfare state. Postwar American elections returned reformist presidents, but the political system ensured that no majority urban-liberal coalition would be formed in Congress. Except for policies benefiting veterans, Congress would not channel income tax revenues into establishment of a more national and comprehensive welfare state for all Americans. Instead, it preferred to preserve or initiate domestic policies that were under the control of states, localities, and private enterprises. In addition, it pledged much of the nation's postwar public wealth to American military power and global economic influence.

Conclusion: Redefining the New Deal

In the United States, World War II and its aftermath did not bring consolidation of the New Deal, but rather its failure and redefinition. Various liberal plans for completing New Deal socioeconomic reforms were

---

[89] Cohen and Myers, "Social Security Act Amendments of 1950."

thwarted; health insurance failed; and public assistance was not nation-alized. The federal government quit the business of administering public employment programs; even the less ambitious Keynesian public works projects of the NRPB failed to become institutionalized.

At the same time, American social policy developed different emphases. Although the original aim of New Deal social policy was to provide em-ployment and relief, old-age insurance became the centerpiece of U.S. so-cial policy. And although the New Dealers had attempted to downplay separate veterans' programs, after the war the Americans benefiting most from public social provision were veterans and their families. They were eligible for housing, health, and educational benefits that made the civil-ian welfare state conspicuous by its absence. The principle of treating vet-erans much better than other citizens, which originated immediately after the Civil War, was reestablished.

If the politics of the New Deal did not resemble the politics of the war-time period, it is partly because there were profound differences between the Depression and World War II as national crises. During the Depres-sion, nationalizing social reforms were promoted by the fiscal crises of the states and localities. But during and after the war, even though the na-tional government put itself on a relatively stronger fiscal footing with the expanded income tax, the states and localities were no longer financially insecure; moreover, local interests could work through Congress in an attempt to ensure that new domestic policies would have decentralized controls. The Depression forced the Roosevelt administration to give so-cial policy its undivided attention, whereas during the war the same pres-ident focused on foreign policy. The Allied victory ensured that foreign policy would remain a central concern of all postwar U.S. presidents.

The decline of presidential interest in social policy was accompanied by the resurgence of congressional strength and the lack of coordination of the agencies in charge of social policies. The reassertion by Congress had begun before the war, with Roosevelt's post-1936 battle to reorganize the executive branch and the increasing restrictions placed on the WPA; there-after, the administration's concern with the war reinforced the process. The assumption of control by congressional committees and individual senators over the planning of postwar social legislation led to scrambling among agencies and bureaus of the executive branch. No longer under the close control of the administration, these agencies found that they could increase their influence over delimited realms of policy—*if* they could make themselves useful to congressmen.

The only national civilian program strengthened during the immediate postwar period, Old Age and Survivors' Insurance, predicted the future of American social policy. In a number of ways, the war aided the bu-reaucratic fortunes of the Social Security Board and set the stage for OASI to become the keystone of postwar U.S. public social provision. The reluctance of the executive branch to introduce new social policy legislation during the war gave the SSB room to maneuver in Congress. Through its Bureau of Research and Statistics, the SSB supplied "technical help" to those formulating the Wagner-Murray-Dingell bills, in the process influencing their provisions to protect the payroll tax. The demise of the National Resources Planning Board also contributed to the program's strength, for it was the only governmental body to sponsor expert criticisms of the SSB's priorities.[90] Finally, the high employment rates of the war and its aftermath aided the OASI program. According to the 1939 Social Security Act amendments, the tax should have reached 6 percent in 1949, but instead remained at 2 percent. Yet the many delays in the increase of the payroll tax became less significant when employment and wage rates turned out to be much higher than had been projected in 1939.

After the war, the Social Security Board formed ties to the congressional taxing committees; it provided technical assistance to a Senate Advisory Council on Social Security and was able to influence the direction of its recommendations. The Democratic majority swept in with Truman in 1948 provided just enough strength to gain passage of some extensions of the OASI program. The 1950 legislation extended coverage to domestic workers and some categories of agricultural workers and increased benefits to keep up with inflation. Although nationalized unemployment insurance and temporary disability insurance were lost for good, OASI survived despite the wartime delays of its tax increases and gained new life in 1950. Afterward, the (now renamed) Social Security Administration found it easiest to pursue the goal of comprehensive social insurance by making improvements in the OASI program. Its sights were set on permanent disability insurance and health insurance for the retired.

At the end of a decade of war and reconversion, a comprehensive national welfare state had been created in Great Britain; meanwhile, the United States had settled into other patterns. Despite the dreams of New Deal and early wartime planners for a distinctively American full-employment welfare state, nearly all possibilities for nationalized social policy had been eliminated from the agenda of mainstream politics by the beginning of the 1950s. Thereafter, for civilians, national public social provision would be restricted to those contributory social insurance programs that the Social Security Administration already managed, or would devise, primarily for elderly retired workers. A postwar American welfare state of sorts would be established for the elderly veterans of industry,

[90] Derthick notes that one reason for the success of the SSB was that it was rarely confronted by the criticism of experts, which the NRPB undoubtedly would have continued to provide. See *Policymaking for Social Security*, chap. 7.

comparable to the one already established for the veterans of war. But the New Deal dream of national social and economic policies to meet the many needs of all Americans had been dissolved by the domestic politics of the war years. The dream would not soon reappear, and never again in the same way.

3

Blurring the Boundaries:
How the Federal Government Has
Influenced Welfare Benefits
in the Private Sector

BETH STEVENS

The half century since the New Deal has witnessed a deepening commitment by the federal government to the maintenance of individual economic security. This commitment has taken the form of an ever-longer
parade of government efforts to minimize the impact of the market economy on the financial fortunes of its citizens through such programs as
farm price supports and unemployment insurance. Other programs, primarily Social Security and Medicare, have been intended to protect Americans from the financial problems associated with old age, illness, and
death.

Much of American politics since the New Deal has swirled around diverse visions of the consequences and future of such governmental commitments. This debate over the growth of the American welfare state has
diverted attention from the equally dramatic growth of similar types of
programs in the private sector. This private welfare state, in which corporations offer social welfare programs to workers and their dependents,
has developed simultaneously with the more visible public welfare states.
Although less noticed, these employee benefits—such as pensions and
various forms of life, health, and disability insurance—have become a
major source of social welfare for most Americans. By the 1970s, over
one-quarter of the welfare expenditures in the United States were those
of nonpublic institutions.[1] In the 1980s, corporate-sponsored health in-

I am grateful to Kevin Dougherty and Rachel Lowder for their comments on an earlier
version of this paper, which was published as Working Paper no. 3 by the Project on the
Federal Social Role, Washington, D.C.
[1] Alfred Skolnick and Sophie Dales, "Social Welfare Expenditures, 1950–1975," *Social
Security Bulletin* 39 (1976): 3–20.

surance constitutes the bulk of consumer expenditures for health care; private long-term disability benefits supplement the income of nearly one-half of the recipients of public-sector disability benefits; and private pension plans distribute stipends to one-fifth of aged Americans.[2] Despite their extent and number, private-sector benefits have only been acknowledged by both the public and the policymakers since the late 1970s as important in the maintenance of individual economic security.

The development of employee benefits poses a problem for traditional theories concerning the rise of the welfare state in modern industrialized societies. Such theories have explained their development as a state[3] response to one of three principal pressures: the social and economic dislocations brought on by industrialization; the demands by politically mobilized working classes and left-wing political parties; or the pleas of the beleaguered capitalist class to maintain labor peace.[4] These theories do

[2] Robert M. Gibson and Daniel Waldo, "National Health Expenditures, 1980," *Health Care Financing Review* 3 (1981): 1–54; L. Scott Muller, "Receipt of Multiple Benefits by Disabled Worker Beneficiaries," *Social Security Bulletin* 43 (1980): 3–19; Susan Grad, *Income of the Population 55 and Over, 1980* (Washington, D.C.: Department of Health and Human Services, Social Security Administration, Office of Research and Statistics, 1983), publication no. 13–11871.

[3] In this paper the "state" refers to the government, particularly the federal government.

[4] These three explanations are found in a diverse set of scholarly works; most of them tend to emphasize one explanation over the others, but some test or compare all three explanations. For examples of works that emphasize the effect of industrialization, see Harold Wilensky, *The Welfare State and Equality* (Berkeley: University of California Press, 1975), and Phillips Cutright, "Political Structure, Economic Development, and National Social Security Programs," *American Journal of Sociology* 70 (1965): 537–50. Studies that emphasize the role played by leftist reformist political parties and trade unions include John Stephens, *The Transition From Capitalism to Socialism* (London: Macmillan, 1979); Ian Gough, *The Political Economy of the Welfare State* (New York: Macmillan, 1979); Peter Flora and Jens Alber, "Modernization, Democratization, and the Development of Welfare States in Western Europe," in Peter Flora and Arnold Heidenheimer, eds., *The Development of Welfare States in Europe and America* (New Brunswick, N.J.: Transaction Press, 1981); and Walter Korpi, *The Working Class in Welfare Capitalism* (London: Routledge and Kegan Paul, 1978). For an excellent review of this body of literature, see Michael Shalev, "The Social Democratic Model and Beyond," *Comparative Social Research*, Volume 6 (Greenwich, Conn.: J.A.I. Press, 1983). For studies that emphasize business pressure as a source of welfare state programs, see James Weinstein, *The Corporate Ideal in the Liberal State* (Boston: Beacon, 1968), and Edward Berkowitz and Kim McQuaid, *Creating the Welfare State: The Political Economy of Twentieth-Century Reform* (New York: Praeger, 1980). Scholars who accept all these three factors as contributing to the rise of the welfare state concentrate on the factors that shape its timing and eventual structure. See, for example, Ann Shola Orloff and Theda Skocpol, "Why Not Equal Protection? Explaining the Politics of Public Social Welfare in Britain, 1900–1911 and the United States, 1880–1920," *American Sociological Review* 49 (1984): 726–50. They emphasize the influence of the structure of the state itself on the form and timing of the development of social policies. Gaston Rimlinger, in *Welfare Policy and Industrialization in Europe, America and Russia* (New York: John Wiley, 1971), focuses on the influence of ideology on the development of welfare programs.

not, however, adequately explain the development of employee benefits. The majority of these explanations tend to make two assumptions: (1) that the response of governments to these pressures is the expansion of *state* institutions or activities; and (2) that the various groups demanding welfare state programs are pressing for *public* programs.[5] Both assumptions are not so much mistaken as they are overly restrictive. Governments can cope not only by expanding their own programs but also by fostering the development of government-regulated social programs in other sectors. Furthermore, various groups can exert, and have exerted, political pressure for the development of *private*-sector social welfare programs as well as public-sector programs.

The provision of employee benefits in the United States is an example of the second type of development. The federal government has stimulated the expansion of private-sector social welfare programs in the form of employee benefits. Moreover, the federal government did so in response to labor movement pressure for *private* benefits. Those who advance the traditional theories of welfare state development fail to consider that the political pressure exerted by the American labor movement was, in part, a demand for a private alternative to state-run welfare programs. Clearly, theories of the development of welfare states should incorporate an understanding of the conditions under which states and labor/reform movements choose alternative, private paths of development.

In this paper I explore the federal role in the development of private-sector employee benefits. The discussion focuses on two questions: Why and how did the federal government come to encourage such welfare benefits? How has the development of this alternative benefits system affected the political dynamics surrounding the formulation of social welfare policy?

The development of employer-sponsored benefits plans, I will argue, was the result of a combination of inadvertent and intentional actions by the federal government from the late 1920s through the 1940s.[6] Initially,

---

[5] There are a few exceptions to this statement; not all scholars limit their focus to the expansion of state activities or believe that political pressure has been a demand for *public* provision of social welfare. Richard Titmuss, in "The Social Division of Labor," recognizes the possibility of "occupational" welfare. See *Essays on the "Welfare State"* (London: George Allen and Unwin, 1958). Those who recognize alternate explanations include Peter Flora and Jens Alber, "Modernization, Democratization, and the Development of the Welfare State in Western Europe," in Flora and Heidenheimer, eds., *Welfare States in Europe and America*; Harold Wilensky, *The "New Corporatism": Centralization and the Welfare State* (Beverly Hills, Calif.: Sage, 1976); and Martin Rein and Lee Rainwater, *From Welfare State to Welfare Society: Some Unresolved Issues in Assessment*, Working Paper no. 69 (Cambridge: Joint Center for Urban Studies of the Massachusetts Institute of Technology and Harvard University, 1981).

[6] I focus on this specific period because it saw the establishment of the modern private-

federal influence was inadvertent; the government's stimulation of the private expansion of employee benefits was an unintended byproduct of its wartime efforts to standardize tax policies and regulate wages. By the late 1940s, with a significant number of private benefits programs in existence, the federal government moved to rationalize and institutionalize the private welfare state. This federal decision stemmed from the realization that private benefits were useful in maintaining labor peace and reducing union pressure for *public* programs. These federal government policies legitimated and encouraged the adoption of private-sector social welfare.

The development of this sizable private-sector social welfare system has altered the nature and scope of American social welfare politics. I will argue that this development has had five major consequences. First, the growth of employer-sponsored benefits has narrowed the national political agenda by placing an important set of welfare issues within labor market, rather than political, institutions. Second, the distribution of welfare by the private sector bolsters public loyalty to the corporate community rather than fostering popular support for the state, thus shifting the balance between business and government, both of which make ideological claims for jurisdiction over general welfare.[7] The third consequence has been the creation of a viable alternative to public programs. The political decisions concerning social welfare have become increasingly subject to debate as *private*-sector programs have been increasingly revealed as conceivable solutions to social problems. This, in turn, has led to a fourth consequence—a considerable change in the dynamics of welfare policy making. The growth of employer-sponsored programs has meant that the public and the private sectors have exerted influence on each other's welfare policies. Fifth, employee benefits programs have changed the nature of social welfare politics as the goals of reform groups have changed, or have been redirected to new targets and new tactics. As a group, these consequences have altered the development of the American welfare state.

The development of this private welfare state spanned two decades of depression, war, and a return to prosperity. The following discussion is organized chronologically so that we can clearly see the actions of labor,

---

sector social welfare programs. After 1950, employee benefits continued to expand, and federal policy continued to evolve. These later developments, however, raise issues of the *regulation* of existing benefits rather than their creation and will not be discussed here. For more information on the expansion of benefits since the 1950s, see Beth Stevens, "In the Shadow of the Welfare State: Corporate and Union Development of Employee Benefits" (Ph.D. diss., Harvard University, 1984).

[7] For a detailed discussion of past corporate and union attitudes toward welfare benefits, see Beth Stevens, "New Ties That Bind: The Development of Employer-Sponsored Welfare Benefits," paper delivered at the meetings of the American Sociological Association, San Antonio, Texas, August 1984.

employers, and the state as they respond to the flow of events. In the concluding section, I explore the implications of the events described.

Private-Sector Benefits before
Federal Involvement

Private-sector social welfare benefits were first provided in the late 1800s, as many corporations and labor unions embarked on separate campaigns to improve the fortunes of workers. Some unions established welfare funds for a range of crises—sickness, unemployment, and the death of the wage earner. Other unions, rather than providing stipends, built retirement homes and tuberculosis sanitariums, or established banks, home loan associations, and investment consulting services. Because most of these labor efforts drained rather than increased union strength, they had declined by the early twentieth century.

Corporate social welfare benefits have a more lasting history. This tradition, known as "welfare capitalism," includes such practices as the company town, in which companies established schools, housing, and even churches for employees. Small firms, unable to afford large-scale programs, provided lunchrooms, libraries, and hygiene classes.[8] Such direct provision of services was quite costly and proved to be administratively difficult. As a result, welfare capitalism gave way to programs that simply provided payment for financial support during crises such as illness or death. These programs are now known as employee benefits.

Group insurance plans are the most common form of private-sector benefits. Life insurance was introduced in 1911, and accident and sickness insurance and group pension annuities were created soon thereafter. Many employers adopted group insurance because of the convenience of this prepackaged format. By 1930, 10 million workers were covered by employer-purchased life insurance policies, and nearly as many were covered by accident and sickness insurance.[9] Furthermore, over 400 corporations had established formal pension plans, paying stipends to 90,000 retirees.[10]

[8] Stuart Brandes, *American Welfare Capitalism, 1880–1940* (Chicago: University of Chicago Press, 1976); Bureau of Labor Statistics, *Bulletin 123: Employers' Welfare Work* (Washington, D.C.: Department of Labor, 1913); Bureau of Labor Statistics, *Bulletin 250: Welfare Work for Employees in Industrial Establishments in the U.S.* (Washington, D.C.: Department of Labor, 1919); Bureau of Labor Statistics, *Bulletin 458: Health and Recreation Activities in Industrial Establishments, 1926* (Washington, D.C.: Department of Labor, 1928). (Hereafter, the Bureau of Labor Statistics will be referred to as B.L.S.)

[9] Louise Ilse, *Group Insurance and Employee Retirement Plans* (New York: Prentice-Hall, 1953).

[10] Murray Latimer, *Industrial Pension Systems in the United States and Canada*, vol. 1 (New York: Industrial Relations Counselors, 1932).

Federal Influence on the Development
of Private-Sector Benefits

Federal influence on private-sector benefits dates from the mid-1920s, the period when many large American corporations first adopted insurance plans. The Revenue Act of 1926, which amended the Internal Revenue Code, was the government's first major attempt to exert such influence.[11] It exempted from taxation employer contributions to pension trusts and postponed taxes on the benefits of those trusts until they had been received by the employees. The premise was that such a tax exemption would lead employers to regard pensions as a mechanism for lowering their tax bills, as well as for ensuring the welfare of their older workers. Workers would also have reason to request pensions, since the funds contributed to the pension trust would not be considered taxable income for them until retirement.

Despite their persuasive logic, these federal tax incentives did not prove very powerful; most employers were indifferent to the tax advantages. As late as the 1930s annuity salesmen, accountants, and pension counselors were finding that many employers were slow to see the advantages of pensions.[12] Furthermore, many plans relating to the pension trusts set up prior to the 1940s covered only small groups of officers in high-income brackets.[13] (This was perhaps encouraged, as we will see, by the Social Security Act of 1935, which provided public pensions for low-income workers.) Private pension trusts thus served primarily as mechanisms for evading taxes rather than as substantive components of social welfare programs. The mild social policy aspirations that had inspired establishment of the pension provisions in 1926 seem to have had little impact on the expansion of benefits.

THE NEW DEAL YEARS

During the 1930s, private-sector benefits declined; few companies added benefits, and most dropped the few programs they had adopted.[14]

[11] The relevant section of the act is Section 219(f). The 1926 legislation formalized a practice that had been followed since 1921: the granting of tax-exempt status to profit-sharing plans. Before 1921, payments for pension trusts had been deducted from taxes as regular business expenses; such deductions did not have the financial advantages of later tax exemptions. Group insurance premiums had been tax-deductible since 1920; see Internal Revenue Service Regulations 45, Article 33, as cited by Hugh Macaulay, *Fringe Benefits and Their Federal Tax Treatment* (New York: Columbia University Press, 1959).

[12] Rainard Robbins, *Impact of Taxes on Industrial Pension Plans*, monograph no. 14 (New York: Industrial Relations Counselors, 1949).

[13] Charles Dearing, *Industrial Pensions* (Washington, D.C.: The Brookings Institution, 1954).

[14] Ilse, *Group Insurance*.

Corporations were more concerned with maintaining employment and wage rates than with preventing individual financial disasters. The New Deal reforms not only failed to stop the decline but had a negative effect on the expansion of private-sector welfare benefits.

The 1930s saw the passage of two pieces of federal legislation that actually reduced private-sector programs. In 1934, the federal government took over the the the largest group of private benefits—the pension plans of the railroad companies—in an attempt to speed the nation's economic recovery.[15] The government financed the retirement of older workers so that the railroads would not have to lay off thousands of younger railroad workers who had been forced out by the seniority system.[16] Then, in 1935, Congress passed the Social Security Act, which established a wide range of social welfare programs. Private-sector employers reacted to passage of the act by either eliminating or reducing their own pension plans. They argued that they would be paying for the public benefits in the form of payroll taxes and therefore did not need to provide private pension benefits that duplicated the public Social Security benefits. This possible duplication was particularly true of the benefits of workers who earned less than $3,000 per year, since this was the salary limit for employer payroll contributions to the Social Security trust fund. Many employers either restricted their pension plans to those employees earning more than $3,000, or integrated their pension plans with Social Security, reducing their benefits by the amount of the Social Security stipend given to the retired worker. Since half of all families in 1930 had an annual income of less than $2,000, few workers received private pensions.[17] Thus a result of passage of the Social Security Act was that the private sector ceded responsibility for the support of low-income retirees to the federal government.[18]

[15] The 1934 legislation was declared unconstitutional, but the takeover was included in the 1937 Railroad Retirement Act, which passed the test of constitutionality.

[16] Dearing, *Industrial Pensions*.

[17] Internal Revenue Service, *Statistics of Income for 1930* (Washington, D.C.: Treasury Department, 1932). A similar phenomenon occurred in the late 1960s, for after Congress created the Medicare program in 1965, many employers who had been providing health insurance to their older employees or retirees reduced their coverage to policies that supplemented the federal coverage (Stevens, "In the Shadow of the Welfare State").

[18] During the debate over the Social Security Act, the private sector had the chance to establish its private pension plan as a legal substitute for Social Security. Yet it did not succeed. When Congress was debating the Social Security bill in 1935, it considered the Clark amendment, which would have exempted from participation in federal old-age programs any employers and workers who had a private pension plan that provided a stipend as large as that provided under Social Security. The amendment passed the Senate but was eliminated from debate after a two-month stalemate in the House-Senate Conference Committee and the threat of a presidential veto. Surprisingly, the amendment was only marginally supported by employers; see Paul Douglas, *Social Security in the United States*, 2d ed.

The War Years

The effect of wartime legislation, unlike earlier federal policies, was to increase provision of benefits by the private sector. The first federal intervention was another tax law, the Revenue Act of 1942. Designed primarily to raise taxes to fund the war mobilization, it had two fairly obscure provisions that encouraged the adoption of pensions. The first was a change in the 1926 rules governing pension trust exemptions. Arguing that "the tax avoidance potentialities of pension trusts are well known," the secretary of the Treasury sponsored the requirement that pension plans cover at least 70 percent of employees in order for employers to receive tax exemption for corporate contributions to their pension trusts.[19] In addition, the provision required that the formulas both for eligibility and for the amount of benefits must not discriminate in favor of highly paid employees.[20] These requirements were intended to prevent employers from using pensions as tax dodges and to encourage them to provide security for retired workers.[21]

The second, and arguably more important, provision of the 1942 Revenue Act was the introduction of an excess profits tax on corporate earnings. Corporate profits above prewar profit levels were to be taxed at a rate of approximately 80 to 90 percent, thereby encouraging employers to lower their pretax profits by depositing earnings in exempt pension trusts rather than have them taxed.[22] As a result of the new law, employer

---

(New York: Whittlesey House, McGraw-Hill, 1939), and Edmund Witte, *The Development of the Social Security Act* (Madison: University of Wisconsin Press, 1962). Its main proponents were insurance brokers, who would have gained business from an expanded private welfare sector. One possible explanation for this lack of interest is that employers focused most of their efforts on completely defeating the public program. But this could not be the entire explanation, since employers had the opportunity, *after* the passage of the act, to revive the Clark amendment in the next Congress. This was a condition of the House-Senate Conference Committee. Yet employers did not press for its revival. They were perhaps not enthusiastic about the possibility of an exempted private pension system because the amendment would have forced companies to upgrade their pension plans to Social Security benefit levels. Most of the private sector seemingly preferred a public retirement system to one that placed increased financial obligations on their shoulders just when they were least able to support them.

[19] House Committee on Ways and Means, *Revenue Revision of 1942, Hearings before the Committee on Ways and Means*, 77th Cong., 2d sess. (Washington, D.C.: Government Printing Office, 1942), p. 87.

[20] Revenue Act of 1942, Secs. 165(a) and 23(p). The Internal Revenue Service set similar standards for insured benefits by one year later in order to standardize its treatment of employee benefits (Macaulay, *Fringe Benefits*).

[21] House, *Revenue Revision of 1942*; Senate Committee on Finance, *The Revenue Bill of 1942, Report 1631*, 77th Cong., 2d sess. (Washington, D.C.: Government Printing Office, 1942).

[22] Ilse, *Group Insurance*; Paul Harbrecht, *Pension Funds and Economic Power* (New

contributions to pension trusts quintupled, soaring from $171 million in 1941 to $857 million in 1945.[23] Federal wartime policies had the unintended result of prompting corporations to adopt pension plans.

The changes wrought by passage of the Revenue Act of 1942 were primarily inspired by *public*-sector, not private-sector interests. Neither employers nor unions seemed to have a strong desire to involve the government in the development of private benefits. Neither was responsible for the specific pension provisions of the 1942 act. A careful reading of the record of the hearings reveals that members of the Treasury Department staff met with employers *after* the proposals had been put forward by the government in the first days of testimony.[24] In the more than 2,000 pages of testimony on the Revenue Act, few employer or labor representatives spoke about the proposed changes in the pension regulations; most of the attention was focused on other parts of the bill. Those who did testify on the issue accepted the government proposal for 70 percent coverage with few objections.[25]

The labor movement was also indifferent to the proposed changes in the tax code. In its only comment on pensions, the American Federation of Labor (AFL) *supported* employers who opposed raising funding standards.[26] The Congress of Industrial Organizations (CIO) paid no attention

York: Twentieth Century Fund, 1959); Macaulay, *Fringe Benefits*; and Robbins, *Impact of Taxes*.

[23] Dearing, *Industrial Pensions*.

[24] House, *Revenue Revision of 1942*; Senate, *The Revenue Bill of 1942*.

[25] Employers probably did not object to the increased eligibility requirements because eligibility did not (and still does not) mean that those eligible actually would receive pensions when they retired. In 1979, only 48 percent of those eligible qualified for pensions; see Gayle Thompson Rogers, *Pension Coverage and Vesting among Private Wage and Salary Workers, 1979*, Office of Research and Statistics Working Paper no. 16 (Washington, D.C.: Social Security Administration, 1980). Figures are not available for the 1940s but would probably be even lower because qualification levels then were more stringent.

Most employers who testified seem to have saved their disapproval for a related proposed change in pension regulations—the Treasury Department proposal that the contributions to a pension trust made on behalf of an individual employee should be fully vested after a certain number of years. By "vesting," the Treasury meant that workers would be entitled to receive those moneys if they left the employer's employ before retirement. Employers argued that such a requirement would destabilize or destroy their trust funds. They were unenthusiastic about government regulations that would force them to upgrade their benefits. After a letter-writing campaign, the Treasury withdrew the proposal, not wishing to "adversely affect the stability" of existing plans (House, *Revenue Revision of 1942*, p. 2406). Since the government was not primarily interested in pension reform but instead wanted tax reform, it did not press the issue.

[26] House, *Revenue Revision of 1942*, p. 2504. The AFL favored raising standards in principle but feared the possible practical consequences at this time. The federation supported the employers' objection to vesting because it would possibly destabilize existing corporate pensions.

to the pension reforms, preferring to focus on other tax provisions.[27] Unions clearly did not place private pensions high on their list of priorities. Since few low-income workers were eligible for private pensions because they were now eligible for Social Security, this is not surprising.

Both pension-related provisions in the Revenue Act of 1942 were inspired by the government's desire simultaneously to (1) generate revenue to finance the mobilization by reducing the opportunities for tax avoidance, and (2) raise popular morale during the war by removing inequities in the tax code. The Treasury Department argued: "There are in our tax system certain provisions which grant relatively few of our people special advantages and privileges at the expense of the great mass who must pay what is thereby lost. . . . They are bad enough in time of peace—they are intolerable in time of war."[28] American soldiers were not to fight knowing that the private-sector pension system favored the few, but were to be inspired by the knowledge that the system back home was equitable.

The equity motive for imposition of the excess profits tax was even stronger. Again the Treasury Department insisted that the legislation remove the privileges specified in the tax code: "The country will not tolerate the retention of undue profits at a time like this, when millions are pledging their very lives to save and perpetuate our freedom."[29] Employee benefits were to be part of the government's campaign to legitimize the pension system at a time when Americans needed to know what they were sacrificing for.

Wartime wage control policies also encouraged the development of employee benefits. By imposing a freeze on wages, the National War Labor Board (NWLB) inadvertently encouraged employers to adopt welfare plans. By 1942, government economists had become aware of two serious threats to the war effort: inflation, which would distort the economy by decreasing the purchasing power, and thus the morale, of the civilian population; and strikes, which would disrupt war production. Both threats would cause instability at home at a time when the government was organizing Americans to fight instability abroad. The federal government's creation of the NWLB in 1942, in reaction to these dangers, was a critical turning point in the development of employee benefits.[30]

The NWLB was given the task of stabilizing wages and reducing inflation. Empowered to impose wage controls on all agreements between labor and management, the Board quickly limited wage increases to 15 per-

---

[27] House, *Revenue Revision of 1942*; Senate, *The Revenue Bill of 1942*.

[28] House, *Revenue Revision of 1942*, p. 7.

[29] Ibid., p. 3.

[30] Allan Richards, *War Labor Boards in the Field* (Chapel Hill: University of North Carolina Press, 1953).

cent above the wages in effect in January 1941.[31] This cap was not completely successful, however, since pressure for wage increases continued. American workers were starved for the pay raises that they had not received during the Depression. Organized labor, meanwhile, never wholeheartedly supported the wage freeze because it felt that the parallel freeze on prices was not as uniform and would not be as effective as a limit on the income of workers.[32] Thus, wages would stay low, while prices would rise. Moreover, unemployment was low (it remained at less than 2 percent during most of the war).[33] All of these factors resulted in substantial upward pressure on wages.

In an attempt to reduce the demands for higher wages, the board ruled in 1943 that employer contributions to insurance and pension plans would not be counted as "wages" during the freeze.[34] This move, of course, opened the floodgates to the institution of employee benefits programs as unions and management sought wage increases under the guise of "fringe adjustments."[35]

As with the tax reforms, federal actions had not been expressly intended to stimulate provision of benefits by the private sector. The federal interest in maintaining economic stability was paramount. E. Robert Livernash, a member of the NWLB, explained the rationale behind this policy: "The problem though was that we had to keep down inflation. So we agreed to allow increases in various benefits that we felt would not be inflationary—vacations, insurance and so on."[36] That the policy was primarily intended to be an anti-inflationary policy is confirmed by the fact that in 1944, when increases in employee benefits plans seemingly began to worsen inflation, the NWLB made several (unsuccessful) attempts to curb benefits increases.[37]

The NWLB policy was not a disguised attempt to force the development of private-sector benefits plans that could substitute for public welfare programs. Had the government wanted to do this, it would not have refused to order the adoption of plans when labor unions petitioned for them. Instead, the NWLB approved introduction of such plans only when

[31] B.L.S., *Bulletin 1009: Problems and Policies of Dispute Settlement and Wage Stabilization during World War II* (Washington, D.C.: Department of Labor, 1950).

[32] Congress of Industrial Organizations, *Economic Outlook* (Washington, D.C.: CIO), vol. 2, no. 12 (1941), and vol. 3, nos. 4–8 (1942).

[33] Bureau of the Census, *Historical Statistics of the United States: Colonial Times to 1970* (Washington, D.C.: Government Printing Office, 1974), p. 135.

[34] National War Labor Board, *The Termination Report of the National War Labor Board*, vol. 2 (Washington, D.C.: Government Printing Office, 1948).

[35] Richards, *War Labor Boards*, p. 143.

[36] E. Robert Livernash, interview with author, Cambridge, Mass., fall 1981.

[37] Richards, *War Labor Boards*.

both management and labor agreed or when a company voluntarily instituted a plan of its own.[38]

Although they had other basic objections, the tax changes and the wage freeze spurred the development of private-sector benefits. Before the war, only a small proportion of corporations had offered comprehensive welfare protection to their workers. By the end of the war, health insurance coverage had tripled, and pension coverage had increased by a third.[39] Employers were allocating increasing amounts to employee benefits, spending $21.00 per worker in 1945, whereas they had spent only one-third of that five years earlier.[40]

THE POSTWAR YEARS

At the end of the war, federal influence on the development of private-sector benefits entered its most direct phase. From 1946 to 1949, the federal government aimed its policies more directly toward supporting such benefits. Pressed by the labor movement and by autonomous interests to maintain social order and economic stability, the government ultimately institutionalized private benefits within the collective bargaining framework. Two different developments explain the increasingly deliberate government support of private benefits.

The first development consisted of a distinct change in the attitude of the labor movement toward winning better social welfare protection for their members. Unions had always considered employer-sponsored benefits as merely a cheap substitute for wages.[41] From the 1930's on they were committed to obtaining welfare benefits through the public sector. But in 1945, unions began to change their views. The first indication of their change in attitude came in 1945, when three members of the CIO—the United Mine Workers, the United Automobile Workers, and the Amalgamated Clothing Workers—launched campaigns to obtain retirement plans from employers. In 1946 the AFL passed a resolution support-

[38] There is scattered evidence that the NWLB did, in rare cases, order employers to improve an already existing plan. Sidney Podolsky, *Guide to National War Labor Board Policy* (Washington, D.C.: Bureau of National Affairs, 1944); Nathaniel Minkoff, "Trade Union Welfare Programs," in B.L.S., *Bulletin 900: Union Health and Welfare Plans, 1947* (Washington, D.C.: Bureau of Labor Statistics, 1948); National War Labor Board, *The Termination Report*.

[39] Louis Reed, "Private Health Insurance: Coverage and Financial Experience," *Social Security Bulletin* 30 (1967): 3–22; Alfred Skolnick, "Private Pension Plans, 1950–1974," *Social Security Bulletin* 39 (1976): 3–17.

[40] Bureau of the Census, *Historical Statistics*.

[41] American Federation of Labor, *Convention Proceedings, 44th Annual Convention* (Washington, D.C., 1924).

ing the establishment of private pension plans.[42] But it was the CIO unions that spearheaded the campaign.[43]

What had happened to induce this collective change of heart? First unions felt pressured to obtain better welfare benefits from either the private or the public sector. Although the level of worker mobilization was the highest that unions had ever achieved (23 percent of the labor force),[44] unions were also being subjected to some of the most severe attacks that they had ever experienced. They were aware of their increasing strength and simultaneously of the growing need to demonstrate success in the face of the campaign against them. Second, workers began to value employee benefits more highly because they recognized that employers were using welfare benefits with increasing success to edge unions out of the workplace.[45] Third, by the mid-1940s, the wage increases that many union members had received were large enough to make them liable for income taxes for the first time. As a result, labor leaders had an incentive to push for private benefits and their consequent tax exemptions.[46] But the change that most increased union enthusiasm for employer-sponsored employee benefits was the unions' realization that the public-sector welfare programs they had long championed were not likely to meet the security needs of workers because the public sector had failed to expand its own programs. This failure was one of the most significant ways in which the federal government influenced the expansion of private-sector welfare programs.

By the mid-1940s, unions were growing impatient with the lack of progress toward expansion of public social welfare programs. Despite strong labor pressure, the federal government had continually failed to improve its social welfare system. Unions had seen Congress stubbornly refuse to establish a national health insurance program and fail to extend Social Security to permanently disabled workers, despite the introduction of such bills yearly from 1945 to 1948. Even the public social insurance programs that had been achieved were not living up to their early prom-

[42] American Federation of Labor, *Convention Proceedings, 65th Annual Convention* (Washington, D.C., 1946).

[43] These unions—the autoworkers, steelworkers, and mineworkers—were predominantly based in industries that had made some of the largest profits of the war. Moreover, these unions faced employers that were larger and thus more likely to be able to afford benefits plans. The AFL faced smaller and sometimes less prosperous employers who were less likely to be able or willing to provide employee benefits.

[44] B.L.S., *Handbook of Labor Statistics* (Washington, D.C.: Government Printing Office, 1980), p. 412.

[45] Richard Lester, *Labor and Industrial Relations* (New York: Macmillan, 1951); Minkoff, "Trade Union Welfare Programs."

[46] Bruno Stein, "Rise of Pensions and Social Security Created Alternating Goals for Unions," *Monthly Labor Review* 103, no. 8 (1980): 26.

ises to provide security. Throughout the war, Congress had repeatedly postponed scheduled increases in employer and employee contributions, thereby restricting the growth of the Social Security trust funds. In 1948, Congress actually narrowed the definition of employee, thereby reducing the number of people eligible for benefits. Moreover, Social Security stipends remained at their initial 1937 levels. By the late 1940s, not surprisingly, labor was frequently complaining about the inadequacy of the retirement benefits.[47]

The reasons for this federal paralysis are varied. Social Security administrators insisted that the social programs were put on the back burner to allow the government to devote its attention to the war. Others argued that the New Deal reforms had begun to wane as early as 1938.[48] Still others pointed to legislative defeats resulting from the combination of an increasingly conservative Congress and the renewed opposition of interest groups, notably the medical profession.[49]

The blocking of social reforms was not new; indeed, federal inaction in social policy was a common occurrence. What was new was that federal inaction had different implications now. In previous years, labor had been forced to retreat after a defeat, reorganize its campaign, and then try again. But by 1946, private-sector social welfare programs had developed to the point that they were a reasonable alternative to public programs. Unions could change tactics and obtain supplementary benefits from the private sector. The CIO recognized this opportunity:

> The CIO has unequivocally stated that it is the responsibility of the federal government to provide all these types of benefits. . . . However, political pressures over the past dozen or so years by the CIO and other groups interested in improving federal legislation in this field have not been successful. . . . The American worker was, therefore, faced with the question of awaiting Congressional action or attempting to win some of these benefits through collective bargaining.[50]

[47] Arthur Altmeyer, *The Formative Years of Social Security* (Madison: University of Wisconsin Press, 1966); American Federation of Labor, "Issues in Social Security," *American Federationist* 56, no. 2 (1947): 26–28; Congress of Industrial Organizations, *Economic Outlook*, vol. 9, no. 8 (1948).

[48] Altmeyer, *The Formative Years*; Richard Polenberg, *War and Society: The United States, 1941–1945* (Philadelphia: J. P. Lippincott, 1972).

[49] Eric Goldman, *Rendezvous with Destiny*, 25th Anniversary Edition (New York: Vintage Books, Random House, 1977); Theodore Marmor, *The Politics of Medicare* (Chicago: Aldine, 1970); Paul Starr, *The Social Transformation of American Medicine* (New York: Basic Books, 1982).

[50] Congress of Industrial Organizations, "CIO Pension Gains Mean Victory for All," *Economic Outlook*, vol. 9, no. 12 (1949).

The AFL, more reluctantly, sounded the same note. In testimony before Congress, William Green, president of the AFL, warned the legislators that if they failed to expand Social Security, labor "will have no other recourse than to demand private welfare plans from private employers."[51]

Union leaders argued that they were demanding private-sector benefits in order to pressure employers to join them in campaigns for *public* programs. In December 1949, CIO leaders asserted:

> One of the basic contributions, therefore, which the trade union movement has made in this whole social security field may well be the stimulation of *employer* groups to fight for improved old age pension programs . . . not because they believe in them, as such, but because they are interested in reducing their own costs (emphasis added).[52]

Corporations were expected to provide the political leverage that Congress would not, and the unions could not, provide.

This dramatic shift by unions was not well received by the business community. Employers wanted employee benefits plans to remain a voluntary form of compensation that was under their complete control so that they might enjoy the loyalty that can result from voluntarily providing extra compensation and retain the freedom to administer their benefits programs as they saw fit. They did not want to share the credit with the unions. This clash of interests resulted in a wave of strikes because the major unions tried to induce corporations to negotiate benefits. Ultimately, the labor unrest would further involve the federal government in the expansion of private benefits when it tried to resolve the disputes. This leads us to the second development that drew the government into more direct involvement with private-sector benefits.

This second development also proceeded from increased labor activity, but in this case, unions were oriented toward both combating employers and fighting the antilabor legislation of an increasingly conservative Congress. The period 1946–49 was one of increasing tension between labor and management, which led to a dramatic increase in the number of strikes, as unions sought to repair the ravages of a wage freeze combined with inflation. The years 1945 and 1946 were the most strike-filled in

---

[51] American Federation of Labor, "AFL Day of Social Security," *American Federationist* 56, no. 5 (1949): 20–21. Despite Green's challenge, however, the burden of the drive for private-sector benefits was shouldered by the CIO. The AFL preferred to continue pressing for increased public-sector programs. It permitted member unions to obtain employer-sponsored benefits but put little effort into a campaign to obtain private benefits on a large scale. The CIO, in contrast, was a vigorous promoter of the two-tiered system of welfare. See Ilse, *Group Insurance.*

[52] Congress of Industrial Organizations, "CIO Pension Gains."

American history. The proportion of employed workers involved in work stoppages reached 8 percent in 1945 and 10 percent in 1946, double the percentages in the years before and after this two-year period.[53] Compensation increases were one of the less radical union demands, however. Many unions, particularly those belonging to the CIO, sought to open discussions of broad economic issues by proposing programs to establish industrial councils, national planning agencies, and guarantees of full employment. Within the framework of collective bargaining, unions demanded a voice in the making of rules such as those regarding promotion, layoffs, bonuses, and job assignments. These issues went far beyond the limited scope of bargaining over wage and work rules, to which many employers had only recently resigned themselves. The reaction of employers was predictably hostile: they refused to negotiate such matters, asserting that labor was overstepping the traditional boundaries between management and labor.[54] The tension between labor and management relations was further intensified; increased labor unrest was again the result.

Suddenly the federal government found itself confronted by two distinct conflicts between the business community and organized labor: disagreement over who would control private-sector welfare, and a battle over who would organize the workplace. These major disputes threatened to further destabilize an already shaky economy undergoing the dislocations associated with demobilization and pent-up consumer demand. The government had to take prompt action to ensure continued economic growth. The labor policies that resulted involved the federal government even more deeply in the expansion of private-sector benefits.

In dealing with labor unrest, the federal government was not, however, one actor, unified in its interests and purposes. Rather, there were two actors with two different strategies for dealing with the problem: Congress and the executive branch. The strategy of the Republican-dominated Congress for dealing with the disputes between labor and management was to reduce the power of the unions. The legislators believed that economic stability could be achieved by establishing more restrictive rules governing labor-management relations.

In 1946, newly elected Republican members of Congress were eager to reverse the prolabor policies that had been implemented during the long period when their party was in the minority. Seventeen bills to amend the Wagner Act or otherwise pertaining to unions or collective bargaining were introduced in the House of Representatives on the first day Congress

[53] Bureau of the Census, *Historical Statistics*, p. 179.
[54] David Brody, *Workers in Industrial America* (New York: Oxford University Press, 1980).

was in session in 1946. A mere two months later there were a total of sixty-five such bills.[55] This parade of bills culminated in 1947 with passage of the Taft-Hartley Act, which limited or terminated many of the key rights labor had won under the Wagner Act. Taft-Hartley eliminated union rights to a closed shop, made it easier for workers to carve out their own bargaining units (thereby weakening the industrial unions of the CIO), and imposed severe penalties for staging unauthorized strikes.[56] Among its numerous provisions were restrictions on private-sector welfare benefits, including a ban on union control over welfare funds that were financed by employers. There can be little doubt that the act was a direct slap at the labor movement. One congressman expressed congressional sentiment clearly: "It is not in the national interest for union leaders to control these great, unregulated, untaxed funds derived from exactions upon employers. The clause forbids employers to conspire with unions to mulct employees, without their consent, of huge amounts that ought to go into the workers' wages."[57] This prohibition was a critical change in federal policy concerning employee benefits because it precluded a union strategy for developing new forms of *union-based* welfare benefits. Congress thus forced unions to choose between public and corporate welfare benefits.

The ban on union-controlled funds did not necessarily mean unqualified endorsement of employer-sponsored benefits. The hearings and debate over Taft-Hartley evidence a widespread reluctance to support employee benefits by placing them under the protection of national labor law. Congress had twice defeated proposed amendments to legislation that specifically included employee benefits in the list of subjects to be discussed in negotiations. Employee benefits had, by them, become identified in many eyes with the radical demands made by aggressive unions. A vote in favor of private benefits, even simply to place them within the collective bargaining framework, seemed a vote in favor of unions and their radical demands. Few in the conservative Congress of 1946 were likely to cast such a vote.

This act of Congress had three important impacts. It increased the pressure on unions to achieve some success, if only to show that the legislation had not injured them. It prompted unions to turn to employer-sponsored benefits, since it eliminated the possibility of reviving their own programs.

[55] John Fitch, "The New Congress and the Unions," *Survey Graphic* (April 1947), cited by Arthur McClure, *The Truman Administration and the Problems of Post-War Labor, 1945–1948* (Rutherford, N.J.: Fairleigh Dickinson University Press, 1969).

[56] Sumner Slichter, James Healy, and E. Robert Livernash, *The Impact of Collective Bargaining on Management* (Washington, D.C.: The Brookings Institution, 1960).

[57] National Labor Relations Board, *Legislative History of the Labor-Management Relations Act, 1947*, 2 vols. (Washington, D.C., 1948), p. 321.

And its failure to specify whether employers had to bargain over benefits left employers with a welcome escape clause, which they subsequently used to avoid sharing control over benefits with the unions. Although the act was intended to reduce labor unrest, this last impact only increased the conflict. Ironically, this increased conflict involved the other governmental actor, the executive branch (including the president) and its appointees, in direct regulation of private benefits.

In contrast to the conservative Congress, the president often sided with labor leaders on social policy matters and chose to negotiate with labor rather than attempt to weaken it directly. His electoral future depended on continuation of the traditional Democratic alliance with labor. Truman's response to the increased labor activism was to try to restore order and maintain economic stability, but he did so by breaking the deadlocked negotiations between management and labor and either negotiating with the union himself or creating a fact-finding board to arbitrate the matter. This actor had decided that private benefits were not to be restricted along with unions, but were instead to be used as a form of compromise.

Truman's first intervention was to end the 1946 mineworkers' strike, which had been called to pressure mine owners to set up a welfare fund. Citing the strike's adverse economic consequences, the president nationalized the mines and negotiated an agreement with the union, stating that employers were to contribute to a welfare fund for the miners. This groundbreaking agreement showed for the first time that the federal government was willing to force the establishment of welfare benefits by collective bargaining.

The conflict over collective bargaining with regard to employee benefits came to a head in 1948 in a landmark case that was decided by the National Labor Relations Board (NLRB). The steelworkers had sought to bargain with the Inland Steel Company over its policy of compulsory retirement. The company refused to bargain, arguing that the policy was contained in a provision of its pension plan and therefore not subject to collective bargaining.[58] In April 1948, the NLRB ruled against Inland Steel, stating that the Taft-Hartley Act required employers to bargain over pensions. Pensions, it held, came within the meaning of the term "conditions of employment" that the legislation had identified as an appropriate topic for bargaining.[59] Two months later, in the *W. W. Cross* case, the board

[58] Vernon Jensen, "Pensions and Retirement Plans as a Subject of Collective Bargaining," *Industrial and Labor Relations Review* 2 (1948): 227–36.

[59] *Inland Steel Company* v. *United Steel Workers of America (CIO)*, 77 NLRB 4 (1948). The United States Supreme Court upheld the NLRB in April 1949. The full opinion can be found in the U.S. Court of Appeals decision; the Supreme Court merely reaffirmed the lower

extended its ruling to group insurance. In early 1949 it ruled that General Motors could not institute a group insurance plan without first consulting with the union.[60] The Truman administration and the New Deal survivor, the NLRB, had thus dealt with the hostility between labor and management by institutionalizing one of the chief causes of acrimony—private-sector welfare benefits—within the legal framework designed to regulate relations between labor and management.

Still unwilling to share control with labor, many major employers delayed compliance with the NLRB decisions. The result was a series of strikes, by which the unions attempted to force the inclusion of employee benefits in their contracts. Fifty-five percent of the strikes in 1949 and 70 percent of the strikes in the first half of 1950 were over health and welfare issues in labor contracts.[61]

The steelworkers' strike in 1949 finally settled the issue. In that year the steelworkers requested renegotiation of their contract in order to discuss the establishment of insurance benefits. The steel companies reopened negotiations but held that welfare provisions were not bargainable under the reopening clause. President Truman, faced with work stoppage in yet another crucial industry, appointed a fact-finding board in an attempt to settle the matter. The board supported the union position on the necessity of welfare benefits, finding that industry has a social obligation "to provide insurance against the economic hazards of modern life . . . as supplementary to the amount of security furnished by Government."[62] The company rejected the board's findings, and an industrywide strike began. The Bethlehem Steel Company was the first to concede, in October 1949. This broke the stalemate and encouraged the inclusion of employee benefits in contracts by all employers, not only those in the steel industry. Two-fifths of the employers that had bowed to the NLRB's *Inland Steel* ruling in 1949 did so after settlement of the strike in the steel

---

court's ruling. See *Inland Co. v. NLRB*, U.S. Court of Appeals for the 7th Circuit, September 23, 1948, cited in *Labor Relations Reference Manual* 22:2506–13.

[60] Fred Slavick, "The Provision of Disability and Medical Care Insurance through Collective Bargaining: An Analysis of Ten Programs," Ph.D. diss., Princeton University, 1953. The board had signaled its approach to employee benefits in 1942 with decisions in two cases that slipped by almost unnoticed. In the *Stackpole Carbon Company* case, it ruled that insurance rights were part of employees' wages. Later that year, in a case involving the Aluminium Ore Company (Harbrecht, *Pension Funds*), it ruled that it was the duty of the employer to provide sufficient information to a union to allow it to bargain about pensions. But the implications of these decisions were not exploited by the unions until the mid-1940s, when they had become determined to obtain welfare benefits by means of collective bargaining.

[61] B.L.S., *Bulletin 1017: Employee Benefits Plans under Collective Bargaining, Mid-1950* (Washington, D.C.: Department of Labor, 1951).

[62] Representative of Steel Industry Board, quoted by Dearing, *Industrial Pensions*.

industry.[63] In this instance it was a union, not the federal government, that forced the issue, but it did so with federal approval.

Although they had different motives, both the conservative Republican and liberal Democratic wings of the government pressured the government to deal specifically with private-sector welfare benefits, even though the Republican Congress had sought to keep the government from intervening with regard to the issue of benefits. In its zeal to restrict unions, Congress inadvertently channeled labor's energies into attacks on the corporations for benefits programs. The Democratic administration's efforts were more direct. It used the least controversial issue, benefits, as a ground for achieving compromise in a tense, volatile situation.

Resistance to welfare benefits essentially disappeared with the settlement of the strike in the steel industry. In the following decade, private benefits became a standard offering of the majority of American employers and a major economic security resource for large segments of the labor force.

The Political Basis of Federal Action

Federal involvement in the development of private-sector benefits had two distinct stages. In the first stage, from the late 1920s to the end of World War II, federal influence on private welfare was mostly indirect. Efforts to encourage provision of benefits were primarily a byproduct of federal policies that had other purposes, such as eliminating tax loopholes, restricting war profiteering, and minimizing inflation. In the second stage, from 1946 to 1949, private benefits became a policy consideration in and of themselves. Congress directly outlawed certain types of benefits, the president negotiated regarding benefits with the mineworkers, and the NLRB ordered bargaining over benefits.

INDIRECT FEDERAL INFLUENCE

One reason why the federal government did not directly promote the development of private benefits before World War II is that neither employers nor unions pressed the state to take a more active role. Most employers preferred that provision of employee benefits continue to be voluntary. Some found them useful in reducing turnover and winning the loyalty of workers away from the unions, although others found them unnecessary or too expensive. Employers wanted to keep their options open. The flexibility afforded by voluntary plans could enable them to ride out the ups and downs of the business cycle. The only employers who

[63] Slavick, "Provision of Disability."

urged the adoption of benefits plans, or even vaguely suggested that government encourage their adoption, were a few liberal corporations that were the only firms in their industries to offer benefits. Because they thought all of their competitors should be required to offer similarly expensive benefits, corporate leaders in this category urged federal oversight of provision of private benefits under the National Industry Recovery Act of 1933.[64] It was not until after the war that a large number of corporations offered benefits; not until then did they have any interest in federal policy regarding employee benefits.

Nor did unions press the federal government for incentives to provide employee benefits until the 1940s. They deemed public social welfare programs more comprehensive than individual company plans.[65] Moreover, they devoted their energies to achieving legal recognition. Negotiations with corporations over welfare benefits were not their highest priority.

The government itself did not have an interest in the promotion of private benefits until World War II. Before the war, the government had no particular problem for which private benefits were a solution. Even if government planners had considered satisfying demands for public programs by pushing for private-sector benefits (and there is no evidence that this was seriously contemplated), their prospects were poor. During the Depression, corporations were not financially able to support welfare programs.

DIRECT FEDERAL INFLUENCE

After the war, the federal government more directly supported private-sector benefits. The two stages also differ in terms of the number of private programs. After the war, private benefits programs were no longer the orphans of the social welfare field. A critical mass of companies had begun to offer benefits, making employer-sponsored benefits a reasonable alternative to public programs. This altered the interests of the government, the labor movement, and even the business community toward federal policies concerning benefits. Frustrated unions could now turn to the private sector to obtain welfare programs for their members. No longer willing to let the federal government remain indifferent toward private benefits programs, unions forced the state to ally with them against the recalcitrant employers, first by striking over the issue of negotiating benefits and then by appealing to the NLRB.

[64] Jill Quadagno, "Welfare Capitalism and the Social Security Act of 1935," *American Sociological Review* 49 (1984): 632–47.

[65] American Federation of Labor, *Convention Proceedings, 67th Annual Meeting, Cincinnati, Ohio* (Washington, D.C., 1948); Congress of Industrial Organizations, *Economic Outlook*, vol. 6, no. 4 (1945), and vol. 7, no. 4 (1946).

The subsequent federal decision to require negotiation over private benefits represented the path of least resistance. Government policies are most likely to be ones that require the smallest structural change, and thus, the least controversy. Federal enforcement of the union right to bargain over benefits served the interests of the government, the unions, and the workers, and entailed the least strife.

The unions were the most obvious beneficiaries of the federal decision because it increased their prestige. After years of trying, and failing, to obtain social welfare programs through the federal government, they had at last won the right to seek them from the private sector. This increased their chances of maintaining and even expanding their membership. Moreover, federal support of the union position meant that the unions had gained something from the government after the resounding defeat represented by passage of the Taft-Hartley Act.

The federal government benefited because by forcing employers to negotiate, the government mitigated labor's increasing rancor and thus reduced a very real threat to economic stability. As mentioned, the number of work stoppages in 1945 and 1946 was the highest in history. The Truman administration gained the needed electoral support of the labor movement in return for the federal decision. Conservative politicians, especially Republican congressmen, gained the possibility that labor would be less intent on obtaining social insurance programs from the public sector. This reduced pressure on Congress to improve Social Security programs.

Even the business community gained from the federal policy of forcing negotiations over their benefits programs. First, the more liberal or vulnerable employers profited because *all* employers would be subject to the same pressure for benefits. Second, the business community was far more willing to bargain over benefits programs than over profit rates, promotion rules, and some of the more radical union demands. The federal decision created the possibility that unions would be diverted from pursuing those demands. Third, Congress framed the employer concessions to be in the larger business interest. The provision of welfare benefits was based not on legal mandate but on the strength of the union versus the vulnerability of the employers. Employers were forced only to *bargain* over benefits; they were not required to *offer* them. The government did not require certain types of benefits, set standards, or encourage provision of other types of private-sector welfare benefits to compete with employer-sponsored benefits. In fact, the federal government specifically prohibited employer-funded, but union-operated, benefits programs.[66]

[66] In practice, although most benefit plans subject to collective bargaining are controlled by employers, unions occasionally do control benefits programs. These few exceptions fall

By enforcing the right of labor unions to press for welfare benefits at the bargaining tables of corporations, the federal government essentially settled a crisis of its own making. Having first stimulated the adoption of private plans, albeit indirectly, and then having failed to upgrade its own welfare programs, the government set the agenda for a new conflict between business and labor. The state's action in requiring negotiations was a response to an anticipated economic crisis. In the end, private-sector welfare benefits were institutionalized as much out of political considerations as to satisfy the needs of workers.

The Impact of Private-Sector Benefits on Federal Policy

Unlike the use of force or the regulation of currency, social welfare has never been the exclusive province of the state. The state has usually shared the provision of security with all types of charitable, family, and market-based institutions. The key issue has always been where to draw the line between these institutions. Who gets the lion's share of responsibility? Who gets to go scot-free? Which sector gains the credit and draws the loyalty?

The development of a viable set of private-sector welfare programs as an alternative to public social welfare programs has had far-reaching consequences for the politics of social welfare in the United States. The dual nature of social welfare, because of its public and private sponsors, has changed the content of policy debate, caused shifts in political loyalties, and complicated the social policy process. In this concluding section I discuss five of these consequences.

First, the division of responsibility for social welfare programs between the public and private sectors has reduced the power of both individual citizens and organized interest groups to influence social welfare decisions regarding whether important issues should be regarded as economic rather than political. Countless decisions about the needs of Americans, the amount of social and economic resources that should be devoted to alleviating these needs, and the circumstances under which such support will be distributed are made by private-sector institutions, not those in the public sector. Decision making on such issues by the private sector removes those decisions from the ballot and from congressional legislation.

The distribution of social welfare benefits by the private sector fosters

into two categories: (1) the few unions whose benefit programs were in existence before passage of the Taft-Hartley Act, and (2) unions that represent workers in certain industries, such as the garment industry, where most employers are small firms and the union is the main institution organizing the labor market.

loyalty to the corporate community and decreases loyalty to the state. Since welfare benefits protect individuals during times of crisis, the sponsor of such benefits is the recipient of considerable respect. Thus when the business community assumes the mantle of benefactor, it gains legitimacy as an arbiter of social life. In a society where the common theme of political debate is the preferability of the private sector over the public sector in the supervision of most social welfare activities, the provision of welfare benefits according to market forces rather than by political institutions gives the private sector increased prestige and power, and enables it to make a stronger claim for a greater role in social welfare policy making.

Third, the existence of a private welfare system has changed the political landscape in that it has changed both the goals and the tactics of important reform groups. Employer-sponsored benefits have to some extent redirected the goal of the labor movement, from an emphasis on structural change of the economic order to a search for pragmatic economic rewards. Thus the existence of private benefits has (1) strengthened the tendency toward "business" rather than "political" unionism and (2) divided the working class—the traditional supporters of an expanded welfare state—into those whose employers can afford the substantial expenditures for employee benefits and those whose employers cannot.[67] The former group has less interest in the development of public programs and more interest in the continued support of private programs. A change in tactics has accompanied this change in goals. Different types of political mobilization are needed to effect change in the private and public sectors. To effect change in public welfare programs requires media campaigns and legislative lobbying; causing change in the private sector requires knowledge of strategies to use in collective bargaining and passage of labor relations laws favorable to the labor movement. Moreover, obtaining welfare benefits from employers has required union leaders who are comfortable with the planning and administration of complex financial instruments rather than those eager to stand at the barricades.[68]

Fourth, the creation of an alternative to public programs has vastly complicated the social policy making process. Private programs have increasingly been recognized as viable solutions to social problems. As insurance companies have gained experience in developing and administering programs, they have introduced programs to cover personal crises and social welfare problems not covered by private-sector programs.

[67] James O'Connor, *The Fiscal Crisis of the State* (New York: St. Martin's Press, 1973).
[68] Stanley Aronowitz, *Working Class Hero: A New Strategy for Labor* (New York: Pilgrim Press, 1983).

They have been joined by a host of brokers and consultants who advise, educate, and develop welfare programs for their corporate and labor clients. Such providers and promoters of benefits constitute an interest group committed to the continuation and perhaps expansion of the private alternative. Thus the content of policy debates has changed; no longer do politicians or the public now debate whether or not some social problem should be addressed, but additionally whether the state or the corporate community should do so.

Fifth, the public and private sectors now exert mutual influence on each other. In one sense, public and private programs have served as pressure valves for the other. The establishment of a welfare program by one sector, has reduced the pressure on the other sector to satisfy certain needs. The establishment of Social Security relieved private corporations of the responsibility for providing pensions for poorly paid workers, and the development of private health insurance reduced the pressure for national health insurance. In such a process inaction, not just action, is critical. The failure of one sector to develop a program increases pressure on the other sector because neglected groups turn to the alternative program. For example, unions turned to corporations for pension plans when Social Security proved inadequate.

The existence of two social welfare systems has divided the population into those served by private-sector plans and those served by public programs. The beneficiaries of private plans are corporate employees and their dependents. Corporations in effect "adopt" the healthiest and most easily serviced segment of the population: the able-bodied, full-time members of the labor force. The government provides benefits to the remainder: the disabled, the elderly, and the unemployed.

The existence of two systems will continue to have important implications for the division of responsibilities between the public and private sectors. Because public programs serve marginal groups whose needs are greater and more intractable, they are less likely to appear to be effective. For example, it is much more costly and difficult to provide medical care for the elderly than for young workers and their families. Thus, the reputation of the public sector as a sponsor of social programs suffers, while that of the private sector improves. This problem is exacerbated by the fact that the costs of public programs are more visible than those of private programs, especially in an era of rising social welfare expenditures. Since public programs are funded through taxation, their costs are directly perceived by the general public. Private programs are only indirectly funded by higher labor costs and are perhaps more costly. Given the different degrees of both success and visibility, over the long run pri-

vate-sector programs tend to be given greater credence and larger responsibilities. Unless the current division of responsibilities is altered, this
tendency will increase. The federal decision to encourage development of
private welfare programs may ultimately have made the provision of adequate public welfare programs even more difficult.

4

The Federal Government and Unemployment: The Frustration of Policy Innovation from the New Deal to the Great Society

MARGARET WEIR

Devising a national strategy to cope with unemployment is one of the most complex tasks faced by modern governments. The range of public actions that affect employment directly and indirectly is vast, and the variety of tools that governments can bring to bear on unemployment is wide. The choice of tools is critical because of the far-reaching ramifications of government action in this realm. Employment strategies affect other important national goals including price stability, balance of payments, economic growth, and social welfare broadly defined.

Since World War II, governments of advanced industrial societies have responded to unemployment with three broad types of policy: macroeconomic measures, selective economic intervention, and income maintenance programs. Macroeconomic measures aimed at general economic stimulation via tax cuts or government spending have been the hallmark of this "Keynesian" era. Such economic stimulation, say proponents of this approach, should lead to a sufficient increase in the number of jobs so that unemployment would be substantially alleviated. This aggregate approach has been supplemented by more selected interventions designed to alter the supply or characteristics of labor, the demand for labor, or the functioning of labor markets. Selective economic interventions include such measures as training and retraining programs, placement services, and assisted migration as well as public investment and public employment programs.[1] When efforts to increase employment have fallen

I would like to thank Richard Bensel, Peter Hall, Mark Peterson, and Theda Skocpol for helpful comments, and Matthew Dickinson for research assistance.
[1] See Eveline M. Burns, "The Determinants of Policy," in Joseph M. Becker, ed., *In Aid*

short, governments have relied on various income maintenance programs, including unemployment insurance and noninsurance forms of
transfer payments.

Of this array of choices, the American government has, since the 1930s,
most consistently relied on nonspending versions of macroeconomic
management supplemented by a sharply stratified system of income maintenance. The dominant approach to alleviating unemployment has centered on passive macroeconomic measures including automatic stabilizers
and tax cuts, both intended to stimulate economic growth by boosting
aggregate demand.[2] Unemployment that does not respond to macroeconomic intervention is dealt with primarily through temporary unemployment insurance for those who are eligible and less generous "welfare"
payments for those not covered or deemed unemployable. Benefits are not
guaranteed for those classified as employable but ineligible for unemployment insurance.[3]

This approach to unemployment has meant that government spending
for public goals has never been a primary component of fiscal stimulus in
the United States. Rather, federal spending has grown mainly in response
to political pressures; the link between economic and social policy has
thus been largely coincidental. The dominance of the macroeconomic approach to unemployment has also influenced the use of selective intervention in the United States. Although public employment and training programs were instituted in the 1930s and again in the 1960s and 1970s,
they never laid the basis for a comprehensive active labor market policy.
Public employment programs were viewed as temporary expedients in
both periods; training programs were kept small and were limited by targeting those at the end of the job queue. With little capacity to alter patterns of private activity, selective interventions in employment had little
to do with American economic policy; they became viewed as welfare
policies that offered minimal services to the poorest citizens.

This pattern stands in contrast to that in the majority of industrialized
welfare states in Western Europe, which have used public spending to
reach macroeconomic goals and have made extensive use of a variety of
selective measures to help reduce unemployment, often coordinating such

of the Unemployed (Baltimore: Johns Hopkins University Press, 1965), p. 275; Robert
Aaron Gordon, *The Goal of Full Employment* (New York: Wiley, 1967), pp. 178–81.

[2] Herbert Stein, *The Fiscal Revolution in America* (Chicago: University of Chicago Press,
1969), chaps. 15–17; Robert M. Collins, *The Business Response to Keynes, 1929–1964*
(New York: Columbia University Press, 1981), chaps. 6, 7; Robert Lekachman, *The Age of
Keynes* (New York: McGraw-Hill, 1975), pp. 194–202.

[3] Robert J. Lampman, "Employment versus Income Maintenance," in *Jobs for Americans*
(Englewood Cliffs, N.J.: Prentice-Hall, 1976), pp. 174–77.

interventions with measures to achieve macroeconomic goals. Sweden, the prototype, has based its employment efforts on an active labor market policy, including extensive worker retraining, placement, worker relocation, and targeted job creation.[4] West Germany, the Netherlands, and France have all relied on extensive training and retraining programs to cushion labor market adjustment.[5] The Netherlands and Great Britain have designed local development programs for areas of industrial decline.[6] Since the mid-1970s, many West European countries have also made use of wage subsidies.[7] West Germany, Sweden, the Netherlands, and Great Britain have well-organized public employment agencies charged with coordinating and implementing many aspects of selective employment policies.[8]

Why did the United States reject macroeconomic management tied to public spending and how can we explain the federal government's failure to develop selective intervention techniques as a central component of national efforts to cope with unemployment? In this paper, I answer these questions by examining the fate of proposed employment policy innovations in the 1930s and the 1960s. For each period, I first explore how such proposals made their way into deliberations over national policy. I then examine two recurring problems that have worked in tandem to marginalize such proposals. The first is the difficulty of constructing coalitions of social and economic interests potentially supportive of diverse employment policies in the context of the American party system. The second is the failure to change the national administrative structure to increase the government's capacity to administer complex employment

[4] Per Holmberg, "Active Manpower Policy in Sweden," in U.S. Congress, Senate Subcommittee on Employment and Manpower, Selected Readings in Manpower, vol. 9, 1965, pp. 277–90; Ingeman Stahl, "From Job Mobility to Job Preservation: The Development of Swedish Manpower Policies, 1973–1978," in European Labor Market Policies, Special Report no. 27 of the National Commission for Manpower Policy (September 1978), pp. 27–60.

[5] Beatrice G. Reubens, The Hard-to-Employ: European Programs (New York: Columbia University Press, 1970), chap. 4; Margaret S. Gordon, Retraining and Labor Market Adjustment in Western Europe (Washington, D.C.: Department of Labor, Office of Manpower, Automation, and Training, 1965); U.S. National Commission for Manpower Policy, Recent European Policy Initiatives, Special Report no. 3 (November 1975), pp. 28–29.

[6] L.D.A. Baron, "Active Manpower Policy in the U.K.," in Senate, Selected Readings, pp. 180–191; R. Nolen, "Active Manpower Policy in the Netherlands," ibid., pp. 247–60.

[7] U.S. National Commission for Manpower Policy, Recent European Policy Initiatives (November 1975), pp. 24–27; Daniel S. Hamermesh, "Subsidies for Jobs in the Private Sector," in John L. Palmer, ed., Creating Jobs: Public Employment Programs and Wage Subsidies (Washington, D.C.: The Brookings Institution, 1978), pp. 88–93.

[8] Alfred Green, Manpower and the Public Employment Service in Europe (Washington, D.C.: Department of Labor, Office of Manpower Policy, Evaluation, and Research, December 1966).

policies. I conclude by analyzing the limits that America's distinctive party system and its decentralized national institutional structure place on policy innovation in the area of employment.

In both the 1930s and the 1960s, the normal operation of the party system and the fragmented national state served to reinforce the power of local business and agricultural elites who did not want the government meddling in matters that could affect the price and availability of labor. At the same time, the fragmentation of the American state made the task confronting proponents of a national policy that would promote full employment all the more difficult. Even when such jolts as economic depression, political mobilization of new constituencies, or the emergence of innovative ideas about economic policy created possibilities for policy departures, the practical difficulties of cementing supportive political coalitions and increasing the government's capacity to administer new policies proved insurmountable.

The New Deal, World War II, and
Keynesian Economic Proposals

The Great Depression struck the United States with a force that shook the foundations of long-established political and economic relationships. The profound disruption of normal life, after several years of quiesence under Hoover, increasingly raised doubts about the efficacy and justice of American government. As the ranks of unemployed swelled, and demands for government action mounted, rare opportunities for reorganizing national political institutions and forming new political alliances presented themselves to political leaders. As the party out of power, the Democrats were best positioned to take advantage of the electoral disarray that accompanied the Depression.

Yet, any effective consolidation of power required meeting the chief policy challenge of the decade—the massive unemployment that had idled over a quarter of the work force. As new proposals, based on Keynesian ideas, gathered support within the executive branch, possibilities emerged for carving out an altogether new role for the federal government in solving the problem of unemployment. As we shall see, the fate of these proposals rested on the executive's ability to reshape the political coalitions that had taken form during the first half of the New Deal and to assert control over the burgeoning bureaucratic apparatus spawned by the economic emergency. Even in this period of flux, political actors could not at once alter political alliances or government capacities. Established patterns of policy and politics facilitated the introduction of some policy innovations in response to the Depression and blocked the introduction of others.

KEYNESIAN PROPOSALS IN THE EXECUTIVE BRANCH

Although the notion that public works could be used in a countercyclical fashion had become a part of the "conventional wisdom of the 1920s," the early New Deal recovery strategy eschewed a spending approach in favor of the regulatory measures authorized by the National Industrial Recovery Act (NIRA) and the Agricultural Adjustment Act (AAA).[9] Relief spending and public works programs accompanied these regulatory measures, but as Roosevelt repeatedly stressed, they were only temporary expedients to cope with the human misery created by the Depression. Proponents of public works within the administration, including Harry Hopkins, Harold Ickes, and Francis Perkins, did succeed in attaching provisions for public works to the NIRA and persuaded Roosevelt to launch a major public employment program, the Civil Works Administration (CWA), in the winter of 1933–1934.[10] Yet spending on these programs was not guided by economic objectives: the CWA was disbanded as spring approached. Ickes was so stringent in approving public works that "he practically spent money through a medicine dropper."[11] Likewise, the new public works program launched in 1935 under the Works Progress Administration (WPA) was not conceived or administered to meet any macroeconomic objectives.

By the late 1930s, the corporatist experiment authorized by the NIRA had clearly failed to revive the national economy. Public spending tied to macroeconomic objectives and permanent public employment programs emerged as major proposals for alleviating the massive unemployment of the Great Depression.[12] Within the administration, the advocates of spending, including Hopkins, Ickes, and Perkins, argued that the federal government should establish permanent public spending and public employment programs. Their reasoning led the president to appoint the Committee on Economic Security, which formulated the proposals for

[9] Stein, *Fiscal Revolution in America*, p. 10; see also U.S. Congress, House Committee on the Judiciary, *Unemployment in the U.S.*, 71st Cong., 2d sess., June 11, 12, 1930, pp. 59, 90–92.

[10] Forrest A. Walker, *The Civil Works Administration: An Experiment in Federal Work Relief, 1933–1934* (New York: Garland, 1979), pp. 26–36; U.S. Congress, House Committee on Appropriations, *Federal Emergency Relief and Civil Works Program, Hearings on H.R. 7527*, 73d Cong., 2d sess., 1934, pp. 1–24.

[11] John Morton Blum, *Roosevelt and Morgenthau* (Boston: Houghton Mifflin, 1970), p. 114.

[12] See Ellis W. Hawley, *The New Deal and the Problem of Monopoly* (Princeton, N.J.: Princeton University Press, 1966), chap. 6, for a discussion of the failure of the NIRA.

social security. The committee advocated that both income security for those who could not work and public employment projects become the "permanent policy of the government."[13]

Federal Reserve Board Chairman Marriner Eccles joined these heads of spending agencies in urging increased public expenditures. Unlike his colleagues in the Cabinet, however, the former Utah banker viewed compensatory deficit spending as a measure designed to bring about economic recovery.[14] Later dubbed an "unconscious Keynesian," Eccles built a network of advocates of deficit spending as a recovery measure both within the federal executive and among sympathetic liberal businessmen, most notably Beardsley Ruml.[15] These men were well positioned to influence Roosevelt regarding possible alternatives when the routes to economic recovery appeared to have been exhausted.[16]

Developments since the beginning of the New Deal suggested that the recovery path Eccles and his allies advocated would be attractive to the president. The government's capacity to implement spending and public employment programs had been greatly enhanced. The Public Works Administration (PWA) under Ickes, which had been in operation since 1933, and the massive public employment programs administered by the Work Progress Administration had laid the institutional groundwork for implementing a public employment strategy.[17] The situation in Congress seemed to indicate that it would not be difficult to assemble a majority in support of increased government spending and public employment. Since 1936, when the AAA and the processing tax that funded it were declared illegal, conservative rural interests had become dependent on Congress for the parity payments to which they had become accustomed. Although their willingness to support ongoing government spending programs had diminished by the late 1930s, these rural interests were forced to cooperate with urban liberals to secure implementation of their own programs.[18]

The most immediate impetus for moving in the direction of public

[13] U.S. Congress, House, *Message of the President Recommending Legislation on Economic Security*, House Document no. 81, 74th Cong., 1st sess., 1935.

[14] Dean May, *From New Deal to New Economics: The American Liberal Response to the Recession of 1937* (New York: Garland, 1981), pp. 40–52.

[15] The label "unconscious Keynesian" is that of Rexford Guy Tugwell; see Stein, *Fiscal Revolution in America*, p. 148.

[16] May, *From New Deal to New Economics*, pp. 53–66.

[17] Arthur W. MacMahon, John D. Millett, and Gladys Ogden, *The Administration of Federal Work Relief* (Chicago: Public Administration Service, 1941); Arthur E. Burns and Edward A. Williams, *Federal Work, Security, and Relief Programs* by Works Progress Administration, Research Monograph 24 (Washington, D.C.: Government Printing Office, 1941); Stein, *Fiscal Revolution in America*, p. 106.

[18] Christina McFadyen Campbell, *The Farm Bureau and the New Deal: A Study of National Farm Policy, 1933–40* (Urbana: University of Illinois Press, 1962), pp. 105–21.

spending and public employment programs was the sharp economic downturn of 1937–1938, precipitated by Roosevelt's decision to balance the budget in 1937.[19] The lack of realistic alternatives, combined with the concerted efforts of Hopkins, in particular, finally convinced Roosevelt to embrace a spending approach to economic recovery. In 1938 the president proposed a $6.5 billion program including $1.55 billion for the WPA and other relief programs and $1.5 billion for the PWA.[20] Congress passed the package relatively quickly because of the continuing pressure of the economic slump.[21] The administration reaffirmed its commitment to this new economic strategy the following year when it proposed another major fiscal stimulus measure in the form of a revolving fund for public projects.[22]

Further endorsement of public spending to stimulate the economy came from a newly emerging American school of left-wing Keynesianism led by Alvin Hansen of Harvard.[23] According to the "stagnationist" analysis it formulated, the American economy had reached a stage of maturity in which it could not be revitalized by private activity alone. A continuous program of public investment would be required to ensure adequate levels of total investment. By 1939, these Keynesian economists had begun to staff several government agencies including the Department of Commerce and the Budget Bureau.[24] Although the war put consideration of their agenda on hold, the advocates of public investment and public employment programs continued to elaborate their ideas from their positions in federal agencies, the most important of which was the National Resources Planning Board (NRPB), a central meeting ground for planners and Keynesian economists.[25] In its 1942 report, *Security, Work and Relief Policies*, it endorsed the reforms of the late New Deal period and argued for greater coordination and advanced planning to implement major social spending programs.[26]

As the war drew to a close, fear that peace would bring widespread

[19] Blum, *Roosevelt and Morgenthau*, pp. 137, 145; Stein, *Fiscal Revolution in America*, pp. 95–102.

[20] Collins, *Business Response to Keynes*, p. 43.

[21] James T. Patterson, *Congressional Conservatism and the New Deal: The Growth of the Conservative Coalition in Congress, 1933–1939* (Lexington: University Press of Kentucky 1967), pp. 233–42.

[22] Collins, *Business Response to Keynes*, pp. 46–47.

[23] Stein, *Fiscal Revolution in America*, pp. 163–68; Collins, *Business Response to Keynes*, pp. 10–11; James Tobin, "Hansen and Public Policy," *Quarterly Journal of Economics* 90 (February 1976): 32–37.

[24] Stein, *Fiscal Revolution in America*, p. 168.

[25] Collins, *Business Response to Keynes*, pp. 13–14.

[26] National Resources Planning Board, *Security, Work, and Relief Policies* (Washington, D.C.: Government Printing Office, 1942).

joblessness generated numerous proposals for ensuring adequate employment.[27] In Congress, debate centered on the Full Employment Bill of 1945, which was aimed at establishing a permanent and substantial role for the federal government in managing the economy; it called on the government to make up any shortfall in investment needed to reach full employment.[28] Crafted in accordance with the theoretical perspectives of the stagnationist Keynesians, the bill represented an attempt to institutionalize the liberal agenda that had been elaborated at the end of the New Deal.

The defeat of the Full Employment Bill in Congress, and the passage of the much more modest Employment Act of 1946, marked a major setback for proponents of full employment guaranteed by government spending. The act endorsed "maximum" rather than "full" employment and eliminated the "National Production and Employment Budget" in favor of an annual economic report by the president.[29] In so doing, it eliminated the chief mechanism that would have facilitated coordinated planning to attain employment objectives as well as the endorsement of public spending built into the 1945 bill.[30] The central new mechanism that the act established was the Council of Economic Advisers, which had no authority or mandate other than to advise the president. Thus, at the beginning of the postwar period, little was left of the public spending and employment strategy that had been developed during the New Deal and the war years.

THE FAILURE TO UNITE LABOR AND AGRICULTURE

In the decades preceding the Great Depression, national politics in America was controlled by a Republican, business-dominated alliance that favored the Northeast, leaving the South and the West on the periphery of national power.[31] Local party organizations exercised substantial power in this highly sectional political alignment. But this pattern of politics collapsed with the onset of the Depression, and new possibilities for establishing national Democratic dominance were created. The wide-

[27] Collins, *Business Response to Keynes*, pp. 99–100; Stephen Kemp Bailey, *Congress Makes a Law* (New York: Vintage Books, 1950), pp. 9–11.

[28] See Bailey, *Congress Makes a Law*; Collins, *Business Response to Keynes*, pp. 99–100; Stein, *Fiscal Revolution in America*, pp. 197–206.

[29] Collins, *Business Response to Keynes*, pp. 107–8; Bailey, *Congress Makes a Law*, chap. 11.

[30] Collins, *Business Response to Keynes*, p. 109.

[31] On the structure of national politics before the New Deal, see Walter Dean Burnham, "Party Systems and the Political Process," in William Nisbet Chambers and Walter Dean Burnham, eds., *The American Party Systems: Stages of Political Development* (New York: Oxford University Press, 1967), pp. 298–302.

spread unemployment among urban workers, combined with the prolonged depression in agriculture, made these two sectors the most plausible bases for making the Democratic party a national force. In other Western nations, Social Democratic governments dedicated to full employment based precisely on such farmer-labor coalitions were gaining strength in the 1930s.[32] Yet, we shall see, both the structure of American parties and prior policy initiatives undercut possibilities for joining these interests in support of a national employment policy.

The massive electoral victory of the Democrats in 1932 created a Congress with lopsided Democratic majorities in both chambers. With opposition Republicans and conservative Democrats disorganized and demoralized, Roosevelt enjoyed what James Patterson has called a "tractable Congress."[33] Indeed, the new Congress had granted Roosevelt wide emergency powers and eagerly backed numerous spending programs. Yet, if such a general victory, won in an atmosphere of crisis, was to be consolidated, bases of cooperation and coalition needed to be more clearly defined.

The 1932 presidential campaign and the central policy measures of the early New Deal reflected Roosevelt's preoccupation with consolidating rural support and appeasing business interests.[34] The potential electoral importance of urban workers had not yet been recognized. But early New Deal policies guaranteeing workers' rights to organize and bargain collectively with employers helped to mobilize industrial working-class voters in favor of the Democratic party. The congressional elections of 1934 confirmed that urban workers and urban liberals would henceforth play a major role in increasing Democratic electoral strength.[35] Growing business disenchantment with the National Recovery Administration (NRA), the eruption of bitter strife between workers and corporations over union recognition, and the Supreme Court's 1935 decision declaring the NRA unconstitutional all signaled the failure of the political strategy that had guided the first Roosevelt administration.

The spending and security measures that Roosevelt backed in 1935 indicated the president's desire to increase his political appeal to urban workers. The overwhelming Democratic victory in 1936 confirmed the

---

[32] On Social Democratic coalitions, see Gøsta Esping-Andersen, *Politics against Markets: The Social Democratic Road to Power* (Princeton, N.J.: Princeton University Press, 1985), esp. chap. 2.

[33] Patterson, *Congressional Conservatism*, chap. 1.

[34] John M. Allswang, *The New Deal and American Politics* (New York: Wiley, 1978), chap. 2.

[35] See Kristi Andersen, *The Creation of a Democratic Majority, 1928–1936* (Chicago: University of Chicago Press, 1979); J. Joseph Huthmacher, *Senator Robert F. Wagner and the Rise of Urban Liberalism* (New York: Atheneum, 1971), chap. 11.

political wisdom of this strategy—Roosevelt had mobilized urban industrial workers without losing his rural support.[36] The invalidation of the
AAA and the processing tax increased the prospects for rural-urban political cooperation. Agriculture's subsequent dependence on Congress for
parity payments in effect required that farm interests work with urban
workers' representatives in Congress to gain passage of spending measures. Several of the most significant measures allocating federal resources
to employment programs owed their passage to such urban-rural cooperation.[37]

Welding these diverse elements into an enduring coalition that would
support full employment was not easily accomplished, however. Agricultural interests increasingly perceived federal efforts to ensure social and
economic security as a threat. The American Farm Bureau Federation, the
major organization representing farm interests, opposed unionization,
fearing that it would lead to upward pressure on the wages of agricultural
workers. The farm bureau also resisted generous social welfare measures
that could decrease the supply of farm labor or increase costs to agricultural producers.[38] These representatives of rural interests fought equally
hard to defeat proposals that would increase the administrative discretion
of the federal government, which had, by establishing such agencies as
the Farm Security Administration, demonstrated an insensitivity to local
power relationships.

Particularly in the South, opposition both to federal control and to the
substance of federal programs began to outweigh interest in the benefits
to be derived from social spending. Many of the New Deal programs introduced after 1934, especially the WPA and the Farm Security Administration, allowed the federal government to encroach on jealously guarded
local terrain. In so doing they threatened to disrupt the caste system of
race relations upon which Southern economic and political arrangements
were based. Challenges to that system directly threatened the planter elite
that had dominated the region's political and economic life for over half
a century. Drawing on their close ties in Congress, this elite sought to
defeat proposals that would expand the purview of the central government or transfer local functions to Washington.[39] As the upheaval in industrial relations spread throughout the nation, Southern leaders sought

[36] Andersen, *Creation of a Democratic Majority*; Campbell, *Farm Bureau and the New Deal*, chap. 7.

[37] Campbell, *Farm Bureau and the New Deal*, chap. 3.

[38] Theodore Saloutos, "The American Farm Bureau Federation and Farm Policy: 1933–1945," *Southwestern Social Science Quarterly* 28 (March 1948): 235–36.

[39] Campbell, *Farm Bureau and the New Deal*, pp. 167–68; Patterson, *Congressional Conservatism*, pp. 334–35; Grant McConnell, *The Decline of Agrarian Democracy* (New York: Atheneum, 1969), chaps. 8–10.

to protect themselves from the actions and policies of the Roosevelt administration, which they held responsible for the growth in union power.[40] Thus, it was to preserve both local political autonomy and local social and economic relationships—most fundamentally, the laws and customs governing the low-wage, racially segmented labor force—that Southern Democrats turned their backs on the social and economic programs that would expand federal power.

The ability of agricultural interests to secure implementation of their programs and to block policies to which they objected was itself a product of the New Deal. Before the 1930s, representatives of agricultural interests, including the export-oriented Southern cotton producers and the domestically oriented hog and corn farmers of the Midwest, had cooperated in Congress, but their ties were often attenuated by their conflicting interests in the realm of international trade. The AAA helped to reconcile these differences by bringing Southern and Midwestern farmers together on grounds of mutual interest in the parity system, which favored large commercial farmers regardless of their international trade orientation.[41] With the South and the Midwest united across sectional lines by the district-level organization of the American Farm Bureau Federation (AFBF), agricultural interests were well positioned to exercise substantial influence in Congress.[42]

After 1936 the AFBF used that power, whenever possible, to restrict or block New Deal proposals that authorized spending for social welfare programs or guaranteed the rights of labor.[43] Although rural interests were not strong enough to defeat major New Deal initiatives in the mid- and late 1930s, they were able to resist permanent compromise with the liberal wing of the Democratic party. Congressional policy making based on legislative trade-offs on particular issues, together with the control that the seniority system gave rural and Southern committee chairmen, gave agricultural interests substantial leverage. Agricultural opponents of social spending measures and federal government expansion bided their time, striking ad hoc deals over particular spending initiatives while they looked for a more permanent means to ensure support for agricultural programs.

Recognizing the danger these outspoken foes of his social and economic programs posed to the New Deal, Roosevelt attempted to increase

[40] This antagonism was especially evident in the fight over the Labor Standards Bill in 1937–1938. See Patterson, *Congressional Conservatism*, pp. 178–82; see also Richard Bensel, *Sectionalism and American Political Development, 1880–1980* (Madison: University of Wisconsin Press, 1984), pp. 152–68.

[41] Campbell, *Farm Bureau and the New Deal*, chap. 3.

[42] Ibid., chap. 2.

[43] Patterson, *Congressional Conservatism*, pp. 193–245.

the programmatic coherence of the Democratic party by eliminating his most vocal opponents from the party during the 1938 primary.[44] His total failure attested to the durability of local party organization and the impossibility of constructing a coherent policy coalition of rural and urban interests, given the structure of American parties.

The failed purge only strengthened the determination of the targeted Democrats and, in mobilizing to block Roosevelt's programs, they contributed to a general electoral disillusionment with the president. The defeat of many liberal Democrats in the 1938 congressional elections indicated that attempts to gain support for innovative social and economic programs and to increase federal government authority had reached a dead end politically.[45] As rural Democrats deserted the president and Republicans made modest gains in Congress, New Deal policy innovations ended in stalemate.[46] The guarantee of 85 percent parity prices included in the Bankhead Mandatory Loan Act of 1941 freed representatives of agricultural interests from the need to cooperate with urban legislators in the annual appropriations process.[47]

When the final act of the New Deal was played out in 1945 in the fight over the Full Employment Bill, the positioning and strength of the interests in Congress reflected the legacies of both the New Deal and the war. The revival of business influence during the war meant that business interests would influence congressional activity much more than they had during the New Deal. The conservative coalition in Congress that joined agricultural interests with business-oriented interests was able to defeat initiatives aimed at increasing federal control of spending and governmental intervention. The Chamber of Commerce and the Farm Bureau were both involved in the struggle against the Full Employment Bill. Their representatives lobbied intensively to stress the interest that farmers and business shared in keeping government from undertaking any action that might increase the cost of labor.[48]

The fight over the Full Employment Bill made clear that, unless agriculture's opposition to the administration's employment policy could be neutralized, friends of urban labor in Congress could expect little improvement in the political prospects of employment policies. Although

[44] William Leuchtenberg, *Franklin D. Roosevelt and the New Deal* (New York: Harper and Row, 1963), pp. 266–80.

[45] Leuchtenberg, *Roosevelt and the New Deal*, p. 271; E. Cox, *State and National Voting* (Hamden, Conn.: Archon, 1972), pp. 254–55.

[46] Patterson, *Congressional Conservatism*, pp. 318–22; Collins, *Business Response to Keynes*, pp. 46–47.

[47] Campbell, *Farm Bureau and the New Deal*, pp. 137–38.

[48] Bailey, *Congress Makes a Law*, chap. 7; Collins, *Business Response to Keynes*, pp. 102–9.

organized labor had made tremendous gains during the war, the resurgence of congressional conservatism late in the New Deal period and especially during the war restricted labor's influence to the North and the West. Passage of the Taft-Hartley Act and labor's abandonment of the campaign to organize the South meant that labor would have to cooperate with some segment of agriculture if the social and economic programs that Roosevelt had launched during the New Deal were to be expanded.

In 1949, following an electoral victory that was due in part to unexpected support in the rural Midwest, the Democrats made a last-ditch effort to join the interests of agriculture with those of urban labor.[49] In the face of sliding farm prices and mounting program costs, Truman's secretary of agriculture, Charles Brannan, a New Dealer who had worked in the Farm Security Administration, proposed to replace the current price support system with a plan that combined maintenance of market prices with direct subsidies to farmers. Liberal Democrats seized the Brannan Plan as a means of creating a common interest between smaller farmers and urban labor.[50] Low prices for the consumer and guaranteed levels of income for farmers, presented in a framework that made farm subsidies far more visible than were the price support mechanisms, appeared to offer a basis for reviving the urban-rural cooperation that had occurred briefly during the New Deal.[51]

Although liberal Democrats, and their allies in organized labor and among small farmers, enthusiastically endorsed the plan, large commercial farmers, the Farm Bureau, and the Republican party mounted a vigorous campaign against it. Republicans feared that "if the Democrats get [the Brannan Plan] through they are in for life."[52] Many of the most powerful farm organizations were arrayed against the plan, and the liberal wing of the Democratic party was its most vocal proponent; support for the plan diminished as the debate between them proceeded. The increase in farm prosperity that accompanied the Korean War eliminated the possibility that the nation's politicians would reformulate farm policy.

[49] Matusow attributes the unexpected Democratic gains among Midwestern farmers to their assumption that the actions of the Republican Congress were responsible for falling prices; see Allen J. Matusow, *Farm Policies and Politics in the Truman Years* (New York: Atheneum, 1970), pp. 178–88.

[50] The plan benefited smaller farmers more than large commercial farmers because it established an arbitrary upper-income level above which prices would decline. See Reo Christenson, *The Brannan Plan* (Ann Arbor: University of Michigan Press, 1959), pp. 39–40.

[51] For evidence that liberals saw the Brannan Plan as a means of reviving such cooperation, see Alonso Hamby, *Beyond the New Deal: Harry S. Truman and American Liberalism* (New York: Columbia University Press, 1973), pp. 303–9; Charles F. Brannan, "The Economics of Agriculture," in Francis H. Heller, ed., *Economics and the Truman Administration* (Lawrence: Regents Press of Kansas, 1981), pp. 54–57.

[52] Matusow, *Farm Policies and Politics*, pp. 200–201.

The glimmerings of hope in the late 1930s that the United States would embark on a fundamentally new policy by which the federal government would undertake a range of new activities to reduce unemployment had been obliterated by the end of the war. Although the flux of the 1930s had presented opportunities for joining the interests of labor and agriculture, the Democratic party was ill-equipped to take advantage of them. The chaotic groping that characterized New Deal policy making, as the administration shifted strategies and experimented with new approaches, combined with the Democratic party's decentralization and lack of policy orientation, made it unlikely that the party would emerge as a programmatic party aligned with organized labor and agricultural interests in support of a liberal social and economic agenda of programs administered by a strong federal government. Not until the late 1930s did Roosevelt make an effort to establish some programmatic unity in the party. By then, however, it was too late. By implementing policies that revitalized local centers of power and created common grounds of interest among formerly competing groups, the New Dealers had contributed to the formation of a conservative coalition that would block further social and economic initiatives—particularly after the war, when business had regained its influence over the policy-making process. After 1938, this alliance between agriculture and business amassed enough strength in Congress to oppose liberal proponents of strengthened federal authority. It is to these struggles over reorganizing national institutions that we now turn.

Reorganizing National Political Institutions

Before 1933 the national government had never attempted to solve the problem of unemployment. During previous periods of extreme distress, local officials had taken on limited public responsibility, providing relief and, in some cases, public employment to those out of work.[53] Not only was the federal government inexperienced in coping with mass joblessness, it also lacked institutions that could be readily converted to implement a national employment policy. The only kind of activity that the federal government had undertaken with any consistency was regulation. If Roosevelt was to devise an unemployment policy that did not rely on regulation, he would have to create qualitatively new governmental capacities to monitor the economy and to affect the operation of labor mar-

[53] On unemployment policies prior to the New Deal, see Leah H. Feder, *Unemployment Relief in Periods of Depression* (New York: Russell Sage Foundation, 1936); E. Jay Howenstein, Jr., "Public Works Policy in the Twenties," *Social Research* 13 (December 1946): 479–500.

kets. This would necessarily increase federal authority over states and localities.

Yet, in a decentralized polity such as the United States, new national
institutions are not easily put into place. Threatened with loss of power,
both local political officials and business and agricultural interests
staunchly resisted efforts to create a strong national government. Foes of
the administration's employment policy viewed creation of new institutional channels as an issue that could attract a broad range of supporters
who opposed altering government structure for a range of reasons. During the New Deal and immediate postwar periods, supporters of the
administration's employment policy lost four battles: the attempts to reorganize the executive branch, strengthen the National Resources Planning Board, enact the Full Employment Bill, and federalize the Employment Service.

When Roosevelt took office in 1933, several proposals for governmental reorganization left over from the Hoover administration were awaiting action.[54] The Economy Act of 1933 had granted the new president
the power to reorganize the executive branch, but the administration
took no action within the two-year period stipulated. Roosevelt blamed
the lack of action on the Depression emergency, which overshadowed the
need for executive reorganization.[55] But there is a more fundamental reason why reorganization did not command priority at the beginning of the
New Deal. Roosevelt's preferred plan for pulling the nation out of depression and maintaining prosperity thereafter centered on the new ties that
the NRA created between government and industry and between industries.

This strategy had important consequences for the organization of the
earliest New Deal spending programs. Rather than taking advantage of
the financial crisis of state and local authorities to increase federal control, the administration implemented programs that utilized old federal
channels for the funneling of funds and left discretion to local authorities.
Even when some functions were federalized, as the labor exchanges were
in order to get the public works programs into operation quickly, the
federal government evinced little interest in maintaining control, and
shifted authority back to the states.[56] The new agencies and programs,
considered emergency measures whose permanency was not envisioned,

[54] Richard Polenberg, *Reorganizing Roosevelt's Government: The Controversy over Executive Reorganization, 1936–1939* (Cambridge: Harvard University Press, 1966), pp. 8–
11.

[55] Ibid.

[56] Raymond C. Atkinson, Louise C. Odencrantz, and Ben Deming, *Public Employment
Service in the United States* (Chicago: Public Administration Service, 1938), pp. 24–28.

were allowed to proliferate with little coordination or control from the center.

In 1935, however, Roosevelt began to take a greater interest in executive reorganization. The NRA had been declared unconstitutional and the consensus on the regulatory approach it embodied was collapsing; thus he increasingly turned, as we have seen, to spending initiatives. In late 1935, after most of the legislation of the "second" New Deal had been introduced, Roosevelt indicated his desire to reorganize federal agencies so as to place the new programs under the control of regular departments.[57] After his 1936 electoral triumph appeared to signify a popular mandate for the spending programs, Roosevelt embraced a sweeping reorganization proposal that had been presented to him by a committee of leading progressive students of public administration—Louis Brownlow, Charles A. Merriam, and Luther Gulick—that he had appointed to study the matter.[58] The proposal was aimed at creating a powerful presidency "equipped with the personnel, planning, and fiscal control necessary to implement [its] . . . social program."[59]

Yet in 1937, executive reorganization, which Congress had approved in principle in 1933, precipitated a storm of controversy because it was now interpreted as a presidential power grab. Under any circumstances, reorganization would likely invite some opposition since such changes threaten established relations. Because individual congressmen's power was increasingly tied to carefully cultivated relationships with particular federal administrative agencies and interest groups, any threat to established patterns of interaction could be viewed as a challenge to Congress. In 1937, executive proposals for reorganization were especially vulnerable. The sense of emergency that was prevalent during Roosevelt's first years in office had dissipated, and the paralysis the Depression had caused in many local centers of power had ended. Moreover, Roosevelt had accumulated political enemies during his first term.[60] Most significant, however, was his decision simultaneously to wage a battle against the Supreme Court, which had declared unconstitutional numerous key measures of the "first" New Deal.[61]

In the context of the Court battle, reorganization took on a more sinister cast, and as Congress mobilized against Court packing, it also moved

[57] Polenberg, *Reorganizing Roosevelt's Government*, p. 13.

[58] Ibid., pp. 11–20; Barry Karl, *Executive Reorganization and Reform in the New Deal* (Cambridge: Harvard University Press, 1963).

[59] Polenberg, *Reorganizing Roosevelt's Goverment*, p. 26.

[60] See, for example, the account of Roosevelt's relationship with Burton K. Wheeler, Democratic senator from Montana, leader of the fight against reorganization, in Patterson, *Congressional Conservatism*, pp. 220–22.

[61] Ibid., pp. 85–127.

to defeat the reorganization plan. On this issue, urban liberals who generally supported Roosevelt's programs joined conservative opponents to block what they both viewed as a potential menace to congressional authority.[62] The boldest features of the reorganization plan were defeated; the modifications introduced in the Reorganization Bill that finally did pass in 1939 were far less sweeping. Without the kind of central authority and coordinating capacities that the original reorganization plan would have given the federal government, spending programs designed to cope with unemployment could not be coordinated with Keynesian macroeconomic management objectives. Many new federal agencies had been established unsystematically during the New Deal, and in the absence of administrative reform such as that embodied in the original reorganization plan, they remained ill-suited to creating national policy.

One of the more controversial aspects of the reorganization plan was the proposal to enhance the authority of the NRPB. Set up in 1933, the board was charged with a wide variety of duties including publication of comprehensive studies on population, land use, industry, housing, and social and economic issues that might impinge on development projects. It later assumed responsibility for long-range planning for the use of natural as well as social and economic resources.[63] The board's supporters saw such a national planning authority as a prerequisite to coherent, rationally formulated public policy. But members of Congress, particularly in the South and the West, viewed the NRPB as a challenge to local authority. Congressional misgivings about the board had been apparent since its creation. Of special concern was its potential to interfere with local development projects already being overseen by the Army Corps of Engineers. Southern representatives in particular feared that the board's broad mandate would allow it to "go into the entire question of tenancy, share-cropping, and the effect of tenancy upon human nature."[64]

The far more modest Reorganization Act of 1939 placed the NRPB under the newly created Executive Office of the President, but restricted its authority. Nonetheless, congressional critics continued to view the agency with suspicion, for they considered it a beachhead for proponents of expanded federal authority. Suspicion led to outright attack when the agency, in accordance with the president's request, began to articulate its postwar vision for America. Invigorated by the participation of leading Keynesians, the board responded to its new mandate by publishing a number of reports that called for greatly increased coordination of national social and economic policy, and urged that national institutions be

[62] Ibid., pp. 226–29; Huthmacher, *Senator Robert F. Wagner*, pp. 243–45.

[63] Marion Clawson, *New Deal Planning: The National Resources Planning Board* (Baltimore: Johns Hopkins University Press, 1981), pp. 44–45.

[64] Polenberg, *Reorganizing Roosevelt's Government*, pp. 134–35.

reformed so that they could oversee implementation of such policies.[65] Congressional response was swift and harsh. In 1943, conservative Democrats joined the growing ranks of Republicans in Congress who sought to cut off funding for the NRPB. Postwar planning continued, but under the guidance of Senator Walter George (D., Ga.), one of the targets of Roosevelt's failed purge, planning would proceed "with the minimum amount of Government ownership and the minimum amount of regulation."[66]

The struggle over the fate of the NRPB was a rehearsal for postwar conflicts over the shape of the American state. The most significant of these battles was fought over the Full Employment Bill, which required that federal spending be consistent with national economic objectives and also greatly augmented executive power by granting the executive the authority to decide the timing and size of public investment. Both business and commercial agriculture feared the consequences of such a substantial increase in federal authority.

Similar concerns lay behind the decision to defederalize the Employment Service, which had been established as a federal-state agency in 1933. The Social Security Act of 1935 had made the Employment Service responsible for administering the state-run unemployment insurance program, but in 1941 the agency was federalized to facilitate the war effort. Labor market economists and progressive public administrators had urged, even before the war, that the system be nationalized to overcome administrative fragmentation and to facilitate implementation of a truly national labor market policy.[67] After the war ended, they were joined by representatives of organized labor, who argued that federalization was the only way to make the Employment Service an essential component of a national employment policy.[68] The Truman administration indicated little willingness to do battle on this issue, however; the labor exchange function was of marginal importance to Keynesian economic management, which was the dominant concern of liberal economists in the administration. In the face of resistance by state unemployment insurance administrators, and lacking the support of the administration, the pro-

---

[65] The most comprehensive publication was National Resources Planning Board, *Security, Work, and Relief Policies*. See also Alvin Hansen, *After the War: Full Employment*, rev. ed. (Washington, D.C.: Government Printing Office, February 1943).

[66] The quote is from Senator Millard E. Tydings's (D., Md.) description of his objectives for the postwar planning committee; see *Congressional Record*, May 27, 1943, p. 4964.

[67] Oscar Weigert, "Administrative Problems of Employment Services in Eight States," publication no. 72 (Chicago: Public Administration Service, 1940); William Haber, "Proposals for Reorganization of Unemployment Compensation and the Employment Service," *Social Service Review* 16 (March 1942): 37–56.

[68] "A National Employment Service: A Report of the Labor Committee of the National Planning Association" (Washington, D.C.: National Planning Association, 1945).

ponents of a national system stood little chance. In 1946 the service quietly resumed its prewar status as a federal-state organization.

Each of these failures to enhance national authority had far-reaching ramifications for the range of employment policies that would be possible in the future. The inability of the executive branch to plan and to coordinate social policy is a problem that has been faced by every activist administration since Truman. In the absence of the NRPB, the Bureau of the Budget took over the role of policy planner and coordinator. As guardian of the national budget, the bureau tended to be skeptical of expenditures, and thus was unlikely to be attracted to major expenditure programs. In addition, its planning capabilities were both skewed and sharply limited:[69] multiyear projections were rare, and programs tended to be considered individually rather than in relation to one another. Nor was the Council of Economic Advisers (CEA), created by the Employment Act, able to fulfill the role of planner and coordinator of economic policy. As a small, nonoperational agency, the CEA's main task was to provide the executive with information on changes in macroeconomic variables. Because the council was not capable of gathering sector-level information, its reports called for manipulating aggregate-level variables. Finally, the state-based organization of the Employment Service made it impossible to link unemployment insurance with economic policy and made the job placement function a peripheral activity of local agencies.

Each of the proposed innovations would have equipped the federal government with new tools for combating unemployment. But each was predicated on the creation of a national capacity that had no precedent in the United States. Conflicts about the creation of such capacity intensified disagreements over the policies themselves. Moreover, the decentralized institutions that did exist provided opponents of national employment policy with an additional source of strength, for they allied with such groups as the Army Corps of Engineers and the Employment Service administrators to block proposed nationalizing reforms. Over time, such ties were strengthened as coalitions of interest developed from the earlier alliances. Employment issues would again be placed on the national agenda in the 1960s, but the failure to create a national capacity in the

[69] On the Budget Bureau's emergence as planner of the president's program, see Richard Neustadt, "Presidency and Legislation: Planning the President's Program," *American Political Science Review* 49 (December 1955): 980–1021; see also Larry Berman, *The Office of Management and Budget and the Presidency"* (Princeton, N.J.: Princeton University Press, 1979), chap. 2. In the debates over the Full Employment Bill, Luther Gulick, a leading progressive public administration expert and a member of Roosevelt's reorganization committee, had urged that the Budget Bureau not be placed in charge of developing a budget for achieving full employment; see Bertram R. Gross, "The Employment Act of 1946, in Heller, ed., *Economics and the Truman Administration*, p. 103.

1930s and 1940s would sharply restrict the range of policies seriously considered and would even more sharply constrain what could actually be implemented.

Macroeconomic Management and Manpower Policy: Employment Policies in the 1960s

Although no economic disruption comparable to the Great Depression took place during the Kennedy and Johnson administrations, there were pressures and opportunities to reshape federal social and economic policy. Throughout Eisenhower's second term, unemployment hovered at a rate of 6–7 percent, high by comparison with the 2–3 percent that had prevailed during the early 1950s. With the return of the Democrats to power, proponents of Keynesian macroeconomic management tied to spending programs once again argued for their approach to combating unemployment, and were joined this time by proponents of active labor market policies. To make sense of the configuration of policy that actually emerged in the 1960s we must look, as we did for the 1930s, at the failure to unite potential allies of employment policy and to create a new national capacity.

KEYNESIANISM AND ACTIVE MANPOWER POLICY

Not until Kennedy's election in 1960 did the problem of unemployment again occupy a central position on the national agenda. The stagnationist reading of Keynes that had been so influential in the 1930s had been eclipsed by the evident vitality of the postwar economy. It was obvious that the American economy was not doomed to stagnation in the absence of government investment. Nonetheless, unemployment had not been eliminated. In fact, the tendency for the rate of unemployment to remain at higher levels after each recession during the 1950s stimulated speculation about the ability of the current passive economic approach to produce sustained high employment.[70] These apprehensions, together with new concerns about the quality of American life, prompted calls for major modifications of the federal government's approach to unemployment.

The most far-reaching of these criticisms was elaborated by Harvard economist John Kenneth Galbraith. Both in the political arena and in his widely read books, he pressed for increases in public spending. Arguing that many unfulfilled public needs could be met only by government spending, Galbraith derided the waste inherent in private consumption

[70] Stein, *Fiscal Revolution in America*, pp. 372–73.

because consumer wants, he maintained, were created by corporate activity.[71] During the 1950s, Galbraith had been active in Democratic party politics, advocating greater party commitment to social programs.[72] As a long-time acquaintance of John Kennedy, the economist tirelessly sought to persuade the new president that fiscal stimulation achieved through public spending would be superior both politically and economically to the tax cut route. Although his main emphasis was on the need for public services to improve the quality of life, he also maintained that "direct assistance or employment" would be welcomed by the unemployed more than would "cutting someone else's taxes."[73]

Galbraith's views received some support from old-line Keynesian Seymour Harris, in the Treasury, but it was the Labor Department that argued most forcefully for an increase in public spending to attack unemployment.[74] In the first months of the new administration, Labor Secretary Arthur Goldberg presented the president's advisers with a proposal for a "Full Employment Act of 1961."[75] The Labor Department unambiguously declared that "full employment" would be the "paramount criterion for judging the success of national economic policy under the Employment Act of 1946."[76] To that end the proposal authorized substantial expenditures for a permanent public works program to be administered by a newly created Public Facilities Administration.[77] The economy would also be stimulated by a long-term commitment to housing rehabilitation and to the construction of low-income public housing. The bill called for the creation of a Central Mortgage Bank to facilitate expenditures for these purposes.[78]

The proposed act also included provisions for job training, an approach to unemployment that had attracted growing interest in the 1950s.[79] The increase in unemployment, coinciding with relative eco-

[71] John Kenneth Galbraith, *The Affluent Society* (New York: New American Library, 1973).

[72] Herbert Parmet, *The Democrats* (New York: Oxford University Press, 1970), p. 158.

[73] John Kenneth Galbraith to John F. Kennedy, August 20, 1962; "Tax Reduction, Tax Reform, and the Problems in this Path," memorandum from John Kenneth Galbraith to John F. Kennedy, n.d., in John Kenneth Galbraith Papers, John F. Kennedy Library, Boston.

[74] On Harris, see Seymour Harris, *Economics of the Kennedy Years and a Look Ahead* (New York: Harper and Row, 1964), p. 237.

[75] "Discussion Paper Prepared by the Department of Labor, April 13, 1961: An Act to Implement the Employment Act of 1946," White House Files, President, Department of Labor, RG 174, National Archives, Washington, D.C.

[76] "Discussion Paper," p. 2.

[77] "A Program of Public Works," LL-2 National Legislation (April 1–13) Files, Department of Labor, RG 174, National Archives, Washington, D.C.

[78] "A Housing Program, Summary and Recommendations," Files of Undersecretary Millard Cass, Reel 49, John F. Kennedy Library, Boston.

[79] "Discussion Paper," p. 9.

nomic prosperity, had aroused fears that automation was leaving many workers unprepared for the modern job market. This interest in raising skill levels to help reduce unemployment had been prompted by an increasing concern that the work force was inadequately skilled to meet the national defense needs of the nation in this era of cold war.

The National Manpower Council, a private group established in the heat of the Korean War and funded by the Ford Foundation, served as a lightning rod for these concerns.[80] The council's activities were inspired by the belief that long-term planning was needed if the nation was to utilize its manpower adequately. Led by Eli Ginzberg of Columbia University, the growing group of manpower economists within the council established close ties with the Labor Department.[81] By the end of the second Eisenhower administration, there was a substantial group of manpower training supporters within the Labor Department who were convinced that a better match between workers and available jobs would help to reduce the unemployment rate.[82] Their interest in such selective measures was echoed in Congress, where representatives of "depressed areas"—regions with high unemployment rates—were backing proposals to direct federal aid to such distressed regions. Depressed areas legislation, whose chief advocate was Senator Paul Douglas of Illinois, called for job training, public works, extension of unemployment insurance, and credit to industries moving to such areas.[83] By the end of Eisenhower's second term, the legislation had managed to attract bipartisan support in Congress.

During the Kennedy administration, the Labor Department became the institutional home for supporters of the notion that the targeted intervention made possible by an active manpower policy was a vital adjunct to macroeconomic policy. Particularly after 1962, when Willard Wirtz took over as Labor Secretary and Congress expressed its approval of training by passing the Manpower Development and Training Act of 1962, selective, targeted intervention appeared to be an essential component of the

[80] See Henry David, *Manpower Policies for a Democratic Society: The Final Statement of the Council* (New York: Columbia University Press, 1965).

[81] Gladys Roth Kremen, "The Origins of the Manpower Development and Training Act of 1962" (unpublished manuscript, Historian's Office, Department of Labor, Manpower Adminstration, 1974), pp. 10–13.

[82] Garth Mangum, *MDTA: Foundation of Federal Manpower Policy* (Baltimore: Johns Hopkins University Press, 1968), p. 11; Kremen, "Manpower Development and Training Act," pp. 13–17.

[83] Sar A. Levitan, *Federal Aid to Depressed Areas: An Evaluation of the Area Redevelopment Administration* (Baltimore: Johns Hopkins University Press, 1964), chaps. 2, 3; Roger H. Davidson, *Coalition-Building for Depressed Areas Bills: 1955–1965* (Indianapolis: Bobbs-Merrill, 1966), p. 4.

administration's efforts to cope with unemployment.[84] Wirtz hailed the passage of the act and the annual Manpower Report that it mandated as signaling "the emergence of a national full employment program."[85] Convinced that fiscal measures alone were not sufficient to solve the unemployment problems created by adjustment to technological change, the secretary became a major force within the administration pushing for increased federal support for selective interventions to boost employment.[86]

Despite these proposals for macroeconomic management based on public spending and public employment, and despite the growing number of arguments favoring selective intervention policies to supplement fiscal measures, the United States emerged from the 1960s with a two-track employment policy that included neither. The primary thrust of intervention centered on macroeconomic measures, which took the form of what Robert Lekachman has called "commercial Keynesianism"—tax cuts aimed at stimulating the economy with a minimum of government direction.[87] Supplementing this approach was a pastiche of uncoordinated, constituency-focused training measures that were either rapidly evolving into income maintenance programs or being shifted to the private sector.

DEVISING MACROECONOMIC STRATEGIES AND LABOR MARKET POLICIES

In order to see why "commercial Keynesianism" became the dominant economic strategy of the 1960s, we must examine how the political viability of this approach was enhanced by the structure of American economic policy-making institutions inherited from the 1940s. The hierarchy of these institutions and the federal government's limited capacity to formulate and oversee economic policy were critical in making commercial Keynesianism the centerpiece of Democratic employment policy in the 1960s.

In contrast to the 1930s, Keynesian ideas about macroeconomic management reached the centers of policy making in the Kennedy administration even before the new president took office. By the 1960s, Keynesianism was a major stream of thought, widely accepted by many academic

[84] On the passage of the MDTA, see Mangum, *MDTA*, chap. 2, and David Brian Robertson, "Politics and Labor Markets: Toward an Explanation of the Formation and Adoption of U.S. Labor Market Policy" (Ph.D. diss., Indiana University, 1981), chap. 5.

[85] "Secretary Wirtz before the Midwestern Governors Conf.—Chicago, Ill., 12/13/62," Speeches File, Department of Labor, RG 174, National Archives, Washington, D.C., p. 5.

[86] N. J. Simler, "Memorandum to the Council Re: Secretary Wirtz and that Four Percent Figure," November 21, 1962, Council of Economic Advisers File, Department of Labor, RG 174, National Archives, Washington, D.C.

[87] Lekachman, *The Age of Keynes*, p. 287.

economists. However, the face of Keynesianism had been modified since
the 1930s and 1940s. Not only had the stagnationist analysis been discredited, but macroeconomic management no longer necessarily entailed
public spending as it had in the 1930s.[88] In the intervening years, the introduction of the withholding system for the collection of federal income
taxes and the widening of the tax base, combined with the wartime legacy
of large federal budgets, made the tax reduction strategy a powerful alternative to government spending. During the war, in fact, the Committee
for Economic Development (CED), a group of economists assembled under the auspices of the Business Advisory Council, had formulated the tax
reduction approach for coping with economic downturns.[89]

Kennedy's choice of members for his Council of Economic Advisers
signaled from the start that the highly interventionist approach championed by Galbraith was beyond the pale. Although Kennedy had been
friendly with the economist since his Harvard days, the new president did
not select Galbraith to serve on the CEA.[90] The three men he chose were
highly qualified academic Keynesians whose approach reflected the mainstream of Keynesianism embodied in the "neoclassical synthesis," and
who thus did not join economic objectives with collective public goals in
the explicit way that Galbraith did.[91] The new chairman, Walter Heller,
and his colleagues were above all concerned with the need to achieve aggregate economic objectives—particularly to increase the rate of economic growth.

Although guided by an economic theory that was neutral between
spending and tax cuts, these advisers ultimately came to favor tax cuts as
the simpler and more efficient of the two strategies. In the first year of the
Kennedy administration, the council had backed Senator Joseph Clark's
(D., Pa.) proposal for increases in public works, only to be rebuffed by
the president.[92] The conservative cast of Congress kept major spending

[88] Stein, *Fiscal Revolution in America*, pp. 178–84; Collins, *Business Response to Keynes*,
pp. 17, 144–47.

[89] Collins, *Business Response to Keynes*, pp. 81–84, 138–40.

[90] "John Kenneth Galbraith: Economist as Social Critic," in William Breit and Roger L.
Ransom, eds., *The Academic Scribblers* (New York: Dryden Press, 1982), p. 164.

[91] See Edward S. Flash, Jr., *Economic Advice and Presidential Leadership: The Council
of Economic Advisers* (New York: Columbia University Press, 1965), pp. 175–78, for background on Kennedy's Council of Economic Advisers; see also Hugh S. Norton, *The Employment Act and the Council of Economic Advisers* (Columbia: University of South Carolina Press, 1977), chap. 6.

[92] Arthur M. Schlesinger, Jr., *A Thousand Days: John F. Kennedy in the White House*
(Boston: Houghton Mifflin, 1965), pp. 629–30, 648–49. See also Walter W. Heller, "Mem-
orandum for the President Re: Possible Second-Stage Measures for Economic Recovery,"
March 21, 1961, Walter Heller Papers (3/16/61–3/31/61) File, John F. Kennedy Library,
Boston.

initiatives and tax cut proposals off the national agenda during Kennedy's first year, but the cumbersome process of implementing the few spending measures that did pass convinced Heller and his colleagues that tax cuts would be the most efficient means of achieving their aggregate objectives.[93] In the absence of institutions through which public spending could be funneled and with Congress split along party and sectional lines, the prospects for reaching agreement on large new spending programs were dim.[94]

In 1962, the CEA won Kennedy over to the cause of tax cuts. Its success can be attributed in part to council members' substantial access to the president and their unmatched economic expertise within the administration.[95] Certainly, advocates of spending programs in the understaffed Labor Department could not compete with the CEA in offering sound economic advice during this period. Moreover, important elements within the business community, influenced by the strategy of the CED, now favored tax cuts.[96] This was important to Kennedy, who had already been labeled "anti-business."[97] Yet it would be incorrect to cite business pressure as the determining factor behind the decision to adopt the tax cut strategy rather than public spending: spending had already been rejected for reasons that had little to do with direct business pressure on the administration.

The triumph of the CEA's tax cut strategy had several consequences for both the intellectual and programmatic approaches to unemployment. In winning support for the aggregate measures, the CEA had battled against an alternative explanation for unemployment—that it was caused by structural problems of the labor market and automation.[98] This view was

[93] See "Recap of Issues on Tax Cuts and the Expenditure Alternative," December 16, 1962, Council of Economic Advisers File, Department of Labor, RG 174, National Archives, Washington, D.C.

[94] See *Congressional Quarterly Almanac 1961*, pp. 642–45, on the strength of the conservative coalition in Congress. See "Memorandum for Lawrence F. O'Brien," 7/9/62, Congress File, Theodore Sorensen Papers, John F. Kennedy Library, Boston, for the Kennedy administration's view regarding conservative southern opposition in Congress.

[95] See Roger B. Porter, "Economic Advice to the President: From Eisenhower to Reagan," *Political Science Quarterly* 98 (Fall 1983): 403–26, and Hobart Rowen, *The Free Enterprisers: Kennedy, Johnson, and the Business Establishment* (New York: Putnam, 1964), pp. 166–67.

[96] Collins, *Business Response to Keynes*, pp. 180–83.

[97] Rowen, *The Free Enterprisers*, chap. 1.

[98] On the structural versus aggregate demand debate, see James L. Sundquist, *Politics and Policy: The Eisenhower, Kennedy, and Johnson Years* (Washington, D.C.: The Brookings Institution, 1968), pp. 57–58; Henry Aaron, *Politics and the Professors: The Great Society in Perspective* (Washington, D.C.: The Brookings Institution, 1978), pp. 113–16; Eleanor G. Gilpatrick, *Structural Unemployment and Aggregate Demand: A Study of Employment*

espoused by a diverse group that included Federal Reserve Board Chairman William McChesney Martin, numerous labor market economists, and Labor Department officials.[99] Although these explanations were not necessarily mutually exclusive, in the debate over the two approaches they became viewed as opposing strategies, mainly because many of the most vocal advocates of the structural approach, such as Martin, viewed it as a way of avoiding macroeconomic intervention.[100]

As this debate polarized, the Labor Department position, that the structural and aggregate approaches were complementary, was ignored.[101] Those experts favoring interventionist strategies belonged to operational agencies; their arguments for more spending on selective intervention could thus be dismissed as agency or constituency bias. The result was a division of experts in the field of employment into a two-tiered hierarchy, with noninterventionist macroeconomists at the top, in operational agencies, and more programmatically minded labor market economists relegated to much less influential administrative agencies.

The budgetary impact of the tax cuts, together with the legacy of the aggregate measures versus structural unemployment debate, limited the scale of the few selective employment programs that were adopted. The tax cuts made it impossible to allot substantial revenues for alleviating unemployment that did not respond to aggregate measures. Although both the Kennedy and Johnson administrations tried to avoid choosing sides in the debate—maintaining that the unemployment was a little bit of both—they effectively cast their lot with the aggregate explanation.[102] And as Hobart Rowen has remarked, the strategy they chose "set the outer limits of national government policy—more than its originators realized when they started."[103]

If labor market policy was to be a central element of American employment policy, major new national capacities would have to be created.

---

and Unemployment in the United States, 1948–1964 (Baltimore: Johns Hopkins University Press, 1964), pp. 10–14.

[99] See Martin's testimony before the Joint Economic Committee, March 7, 1961, in Economic Report of the President and the Economic Situation and Outlook, 87th Cong., 1st sess. (Washington, D.C.: Government Printing Office, 1961), pp. 470–71, and the testimony of labor market specialist Charles Killingsworth in Unemployment Problems, pt. 3 of Hearings before the Senate Special Subcommittee on Unemployment Problems, 86th Cong., 1st sess. (Washington, D.C.: Government Printing Office, 1960), pp. 1144–54.

[100] See Lloyd Ulman, "The Uses and Limits of Manpower Policy," The Public Interest no. 34 (Winter 1974): 87.

[101] See "Press Conference of Honorable W. Willard Wirtz, 10/10/63," President's Office Files, Departments and Agencies/Labor (3/62–4/62) File, John F. Kennedy Library, Boston.

[102] See Kennedy's remarks at his news conference of March 15, 1961, in Public Papers of the Presidents of the United States (Washington, D.C.: Government Printing Office, 1962), pp. 187–88; Lekachman, The Age of Keynes, pp. 242–43.

[103] Rowen, The Free Enterprisers, p. 252.

Throughout the 1960s, the Labor Department fought to make itself the organizer and overseer of a policy aimed at improving the operation of local labor market intermediaries and bringing them into harmony with national employment objectives. However, the department's ability to preside over implementation of such a policy was severely hampered by its own institutional incoherence and the existence of several competing state-based agencies and their allies in Congress. Defense of these local centers of power, combined with presidential indifference, made the Labor Department's quest a futile one; efforts to establish national standards and federal government accountability were repeatedly defeated. The evolution of two key selective employment measures passed early in the Kennedy administration—the Area Redevelopment Act of 1961 (ARA) and the Manpower Development and Training Act of 1962 (MDTA)—clearly reveals the obstacles that decentralized political institutions posed to a national employment policy.[104]

Much like the regional development measures widely used in Europe, the ARA introduced by Senator Paul Douglas in 1955 intended to pour federal resources into a few selected areas suffering from industrial decline.[105] By 1961, congressional bargaining to obtain bipartisan and sectional agreement had so widely extended eligibility that the funds allocated did not have a substantial effect on any one area.[106] The relatively low level of funding severely compounded this limitation.[107] Moreover, provisions for relocation assistance, which labor market economists viewed as an important adjunct to economic development funds, were eliminated by congressional members unwilling to pay for the relocation of their own constituents.[108] Because little central control was exercised by the Commerce Department, which was responsible for its implementation, the ARA soon fell into a pattern of pork-barrel spending. However, because the ARA's industrial aid could potentially favor some areas of the country at the expense of others, the program was fraught with conflict uncharacteristic of pork-barrel spending. Congressional consensus collapsed in 1965 and the program was replaced by a much more straightforward public works measure.[109]

---

[104] On the ARA, see Davidson, *Coalition-Building for Depressed Areas*, and Levitan, *Federal Aid to Depressed Areas*. On the MDTA, see Mangum, *MDTA*, and Robertson, "Politics and Labor Markets," chap. 6.

[105] Davidson, *Coalition-Building for Depressed Areas*, p. 4.

[106] Ibid., pp. 28–29; Levitan, *Federal Aid to Depressed Areas*, p. 250.

[107] Randall B. Ripley, *The Politics of Economic and Human Resource Development* (Indianapolis: Bobbs-Merrill, 1972), pp. 26–27.

[108] Aaron, *Politics and the Professors*, p. 114; Levitan, *Federal Aid to Depressed Areas*, pp. 239–41.

[109] This new measure was the Public Works and Economic Development Act of 1965; see Ripley, *Economic and Human Resource Development*, chap. 2.

The MDTA likewise was a poorly coordinated program despite the efforts of the Labor Department to establish coherence. Senator Clark had borrowed the concept of retraining unemployed workers from a Pennsylvania program run by the state's vocational educators.[110] The initial bill, which provided that the training programs be implemented by the state-based vocational administrations, was actually written by vocational educators, who stood to gain from the initiation of a federal program.[111] Prodded by the Bureau of the Budget, the Labor Department challenged the vocational educators and attempted to gain control of the new program. They charged that the vocational education establishment—which divided its programs into industrial arts, homemaking, and agriculture— was hopelessly out of touch with the labor market, and argued that on-the-job training would be superior to institutional training.[112] However, these federal officials were no match for the vocational educators, who had benefited from federal funds since 1917 and had formed a strong, state-based interest association whose chief lobbyist was reputed to be the most successful in Washington.[113] In its final version, the bill gave vocational educators a major role, for it assured that their state-based organizational hierarchy would be retained under the new program and that responsibility at the federal level would be split between the Department of Health, Education, and Welfare, and the Department of Labor.

The administrative structure of the Labor Department in the early 1960s also vitiated possibilities for coherent central direction.[114] Characterized as "a conglomeration of autonomous enclaves," the department comprised several agencies that enjoyed significant sources of independent funding and political support. Responsibility for implementing the MDTA was initially split between the Bureau of Apprentice Training, which was tied to organized labor; the United States Employment Service, funded largely under the Social Security Act and supported by the Interstate Conference of Employment Security Agencies, a state-based organization with close ties to the House Appropriations Committee; and the newly created Office of Manpower, Automation, and Training, a federal agency that had the secretary's support but did not have the local administrative capacity of the Employment Service and also lacked the inde-

[110] Sundquist, *Politics and Policy*, pp. 76–77.

[111] Mangum, *MDTA*, p. 13.

[112] Ibid., pp. 14–19; Sundquist, *Politics and Policy*, pp. 87–91; Millard Cass, "Memorandum to the Secretary Re: Position to Be Taken with Respect to Senator Clark's Vocational Training Act, S.987," March 17, 1961, Department of Labor, Reel 50, John F. Kennedy Library, Boston. On the problems with vocational education, see Garth L. Mangum, *Reorienting Vocational Education*, Policy Papers in Human Resources and Industrial Relations no. 7 (Ann Arbor, Mich.: Institute of Labor and Industrial Relations, May 1968), pp. 2–4.

[113] See Sundquist, *Politics and Policy*, p. 88.

[114] This paragraph relies on Mangum, *MDTA*, pp. 44–47.

pendent political constituency that supported both of the other bureaus. The new legislation thus set off a prolonged power struggle within the Labor Department between old-line constituency-based and locally based agencies and the new central agency.

As the decade progressed, the Labor Department sought to centralize authority and to augment its capacity to plan and to administer a comprehensive employment policy based on selective interventionist programs. Secretary Wirtz created the Manpower Administration within the department in 1964, and attempted in the years that followed to establish it as the central authority in charge of training and work experience programs within the department.[115] The Labor Department also sought to strengthen its own capacity for independent planning by requesting, in 1962, funds for an Office of Policy Planning and Development. It drew on Title I of the MDTA (written by Labor Department staffers), which allotted funds for manpower research. By distributing the grant money to manpower experts in universities around the nation, the department helped to build a community of expertise concerning the problems of manpower policy.[116] In the Kennedy and Johnson administrations, Labor Department officials were the strongest advocates for increasing federal efforts aimed at unemployment and continually reminded administration members that the CEA's definition of full employment (4 percent unemployment) should not be interpreted as the goal of all federal employment efforts.[117]

Without the strong support of the president, however, the Labor Department's attempts both to control existing labor market policies and to make its voice heard within the administration were doomed to frustration. Johnson's constituency-focused approach to policy making, together with the two-tiered organization of economic expertise within the administration, not only failed to support the Labor Department's position but actually undercut the department's efforts. The design of the War on Poverty, initiated by the CEA at Kennedy's request, clearly reflected

[115] Ibid., pp. 47–49.

[116] On Title I, see ibid., pp. 138–45. For a summary of Department of Labor research under Title I (and later), see Department of Labor, Employment and Training Administration, *Research and Development: A 16-Year Compendium, 1963–1978* (Washington, D.C.: Government Printing Office, 1979). For an evaluation of that research, see National Research Council, Committee on Department of Labor Manpower Research and Development, *Knowledge and Policy in Manpower: A Study of the Manpower Research and Development Program in the Department of Labor* (Washington, D.C.: National Academy of Sciences, 1975).

[117] See Simler, "Memorandum to the Council," and W. Willard Wirtz, "Memorandum to Walter Heller," January 2, 1963, protesting the 4 percent figure as the goal, in a draft of the Economic Report of the President, Department of Labor, RG 174, National Archives, Washington, D.C.

that body's rejection of the structural unemployment thesis. The CEA's efforts to carry out the program were circumscribed by the budgetary limitations imposed by the tax cut strategy it had advocated.[118] Wirtz had argued bitterly with the War on Poverty planners to make adult employment the centerpiece of their program but was defeated.[119] Instead, the policy planners sought to devise a modest program that would get around the limitations of the MDTA and of some vocational education programs, which had been accused of "creaming" and not really reaching the "hardcore" unemployed.[120]

Because it was guided by the underlying assumption that unemployment would gradually disappear with sufficient aggregate economic stimulation, the poverty committee viewed these new programs simply as supplemental boosts to get the "disadvantaged" into the labor market. The committee did not envision its proposals as part of a permanent employment policy that would complement, and therefore need to be coordinated with, macroeconomic interventions. The War on Poverty, as ultimately formulated, was both substantively and organizationally at odds with the early efforts of the Labor Department to create an active labor market policy.

Lyndon Johnson had little interest in the kind of state building in which the Labor Department was engaged. After the stalemating of the New Deal, the Democrats had elaborated a constituency-focused policy that had no room for nationalizing reforms that could disaffect some constituencies. In this context the president's role was to keep distinct groups of Democrats happy by pursuing policies that would cater to each faction of the party without antagonizing others. Johnson was quite comfortable presiding over implementation of the welter of competing programs that made up manpower policy in the 1960s. The approach used in the War on Poverty—avoiding open challenges to the administrators of existing

---

[118] Gardner Ackley, "Troika Meeting with President Johnson, Monday 11/25/63," Walter Heller Papers (11/16/63–11/30/63) File, John F. Kennedy Library, Boston. See also Richard Blumenthal, "The Bureaucracy: Anti-Poverty and the Community Action Program," in Alan Sindler, ed., *American Political Institutions and Public Policy* (Boston: Little, Brown, 1969), pp. 151–52.

[119] See Willard Wirtz's memos on the subject: "Memorandum to Honorable Theodore Sorensen," January 23, 1964, White House General Files; "Memorandum for Honorable Kermit Gordon from the Secretary of Labor," February 27, 1964, LL2-3 War on Poverty File, Department of Labor, RG 174, National Archives, Washington, D.C.

[120] Blumenthal, "The Bureaucracy," pp. 137–42. See also Garth Mangum, *The Emergence of Manpower Policy* (New York: Holt, Rinehart, and Winston, 1969), p. 50, and Frances Fox Piven and Richard Cloward, *Regulating the Poor: The Functions of Public Welfare* (New York: Vintage Books, 1971), pp. 256–68. Labor Secretary Wirtz acknowledged the need to bypass existing agencies; see Robert A. Levine, *The Poor Ye Need Not Have with You: Lessons from the War on Poverty* (Cambridge: MIT Press, 1970), pp. 231–32.

programs and their allies simply by bypassing congressional and local channels—appeared to be the best way to extend the political reach of the Democratic administration without alienating established constituencies.

Johnson's lack of interest in state building became clear in 1968, when the Labor Department sought to implement its long-planned reorganization of the Manpower Administration.[121] Designed to increase the Labor Department's control over local manpower programs, the plan called for abolishing the Bureau of Work and Training Programs and the Bureau of Employment Security, of which the United States Employment Service was a part, and assigning their responsibilities to the Manpower Administration. The reorganization would enhance federal control at the expense of the state-based employment service. When some of those attending the National Governors Conference loudly protested the reorganization, Johnson demanded that Wirtz rescind the order. After a bitter confrontation, the Labor Department backed down.[122]

Thus in the 1960s, as in the 1930s, efforts to create new tools to cope with unemployment had first to confront the decentralization and fragmentation of national policy-making institutions. The intense jurisdictional disputes that were set off with each effort to nationalize employment policies prevented the implementation of national standards for training and placement programs. They also gave employment programs a decidedly localistic character, and prevented the gathering and use of information about regional and national labor markets that might have increased the options of the unemployed. Jurisdictional disputes were even more detrimental in that they undermined labor market policy politically. As Johnson's term neared its end, the federal government began to pare down its involvement in employment programs, turning instead to encouragement of private-sector initiatives, such as the Job Opportunities in the Business Sector (JOBS) Program.[123] The retreat from labor market policy was made easier by the War on Poverty's targeting of blacks. As we shall see, the job training approach of the War on Poverty

---

[121] See Mangum, *Reorienting Vocational Education*, pp. 47–49, and Willard Wirtz, "Statement by Secretary of Labor," November 21, 1968, MA-1 Summary Plans and Reports File, Department of Labor, RG 174, National Archives, Washington, D.C.

[122] Jonathan Grossman, *The Department of Labor* (New York: Praeger, 1973), pp. 80–82; Buford Ellington, chairman, National Governors Conference, telegram to the president, October 23, 1968, MA-1 Summary Plans and Reports File, Department of Labor, RG 174, National Archives, Washington, D.C.

[123] For information on and evaluation of the JOBS Program, see Henry Levin, "A Decade of Policy Developments in Improving Education and Training for Low-Income Populations," in Robert H. Haveman, ed., *A Decade of Federal Anti-Poverty Programs: Achievements, Failures, and Lessons* (New York: Academic Press, 1977), p. 145; *Manpower Report of the President, 1969* (Washington, D.C.: Government Printing Office), pp. 93–94; and Hamermesh, "Subsidies for Jobs," p. 94.

undercut possibilities for building broad-based support for this new federal activity.

DIVISIONS AMONG URBAN DEMOCRATS: THE POLITICS OF BACKLASH

In the 1960s, new opportunities emerged to redefine the social bases of the Democratic party in order to increase support for interventionist employment policies. Organized labor had consolidated in 1955 and expanded its organizational capacity to mobilize Democratic support at the local level. In the late 1950s, labor made the growing rate of unemployment one of its key issues. The 1960s also witnessed the entrance of blacks into national politics. The potential political impact of black mobilization electorally, and as an interest group in the national arena, was unknown. But as a group whose unemployment rate exceeded that of whites by two to one, blacks could be expected to have a substantial interest in federal employment policies.[124] Democrats, however, made no attempts to join these groups by devising an approach to unemployment that would benefit both of them. Instead, the administration's labor market policy became a constituent-based program largely targeted at blacks. As in the 1930s, government policies reinforced divergent interests, hindering the development of a potential coalition of support for employment policy.

With the merger of the AFL and the CIO in 1955, organized labor proved to be an important source of organizational support for the Democratic party. David Greenstone has documented the ways in which organized labor formed close ties with local Democrats, resulting in an organizational infrastructure vital to Democratic electoral strength.[125] Organized labor also exerted the most consistent pressure within the party for liberal social welfare legislation.[126] In the late 1950s, the AFL-CIO made unemployment a target issue and scheduled a march on Washington in 1959 to protest Eisenhower's inaction in the face of continuing unemployment. Although many of the proposals that labor favored were for programs that would benefit unionized workers, such as public works, unions also backed more general measures. They called for macroeconomic stimulation in the 1950s and, later, urged Kennedy to stimulate the economy with more spending rather than with tax cuts,

---

[124] Charles C. Killingsworth, *Jobs and Income for Negroes*, Policy Paper in Human Resources and Industrial Relations no. 6 (Ann Arbor, Mich.: Institute of Labor and Industrial Relations, 1968), pp. 20–28.

[125] David Greenstone, *Labor in American Politics* (Chicago: University of Chicago Press, 1969), esp. chaps, 8, 9.

[126] Ibid., chap. 10.

which they viewed as benefiting only the wealthy.[127] Moreover, organized labor favored extending federal government control in new areas of policy. Labor representatives testified in favor of the MDTA but argued that federal authority would be superior to state control, since the result of a division of responsibility might be control of labor markets by different administrative authorities.[128]

The 1950s also witnessed the emergence of blacks as political actors of national importance. Supreme Court rulings on school integration and attempts to pass federal civil rights legislation focused national attention on issues of concern to blacks, thus helping to build a core of Northern Democratic support for the agenda of civil rights groups.[129] The importance of blacks in national electoral contests, particularly in determining Democratic electoral fortunes, had grown substantially as blacks migrated North during World War II and in the postwar era. The impact of their numbers was magnified by their concentration in major cities that could exercise decisive influence in national elections.[130] Although the activity of most blacks in the late 1950s and early 1960s was focused on the acquisition of civil rights in the South, national action on the problem of unemployment could be expected to concern the black community, particularly in the North where wartime prosperity had resulted in high unemployment rates for blacks.[131]

What is perhaps most significant for the prospects of this potential coalition between blacks and organized labor under the auspices of the Democratic party is that their national organizations cooperated on issues of mutual concern. In particular, labor put its organizational weight behind the effort to secure civil rights for blacks, attempting to hasten a realignment of the Democratic party by refusing to support conservative

[127] See Oral History Interview with Stanley Ruttenberg by Gladys Kremen, July 19, 1974, Historian's Office, Department of Labor, esp. pp. 11–12; Douglas Dillon, "Memorandum for the President Re: My Talk with AFL-CIO Leaders and Possible Modification of Emergency Public Works Bill," March 12, 1962, President's Office Files, Departments and Agencies/Labor (3/62–4/62) File, John F. Kennedy Library, Boston; Myron Joseph, "Memorandum to the Council Re: Background Material for Meeting with Walter Reuther and Nat Goldfinger," December 4, 1963, Walter Reuther (12/5/63) File, Walter Heller Papers, John F. Kennedy Library, Boston.

[128] U.S. Congress, Senate, *Training of the Unemployed, Hearings before the Subcommittee on Labor and Public Welfare*, 87th Cong., 1st sess., March 20, 1961, pp. 18–21.

[129] Sundquist, *Politics and Policy*, chap. 6.

[130] John R. Petrocik, *Party Coalitions: Realignments and the Decline of the New Deal Party System* (Chicago: University of Chicago Press, 1981), pp. 88–89; Piven and Cloward, *Regulating the Poor*, pp. 250–56.

[131] Killingsworth, *Jobs and Income for Negroes*, pp. 20–28; August Meier, "Civil Rights Strategies for Negro Employment," in Arthur Ross, ed., *Employment, Race, and Poverty* (New York: Harcourt Brace and World, 1967), pp. 198–201.

Southern Democrats.[132] In Northern cities, organized labor assumed what Greenstone has called an "aggregating posture": it mobilized minorities into party politics and encouraged them to support the liberal social agenda favored by labor.[133] Thus despite the potential for economic conflict between blacks and organized labor over such issues as equal employment, substantial grounds for cooperation existed between the Democrats' organized black and labor constituencies.

The Democratic party, however, proved unable to take advantage of these developments to build a lasting coalition in support of employment programs that required macroeconomic spending and selective intervention. The conservative coalition of Southern Democrats and Republicans that had blocked liberal employment measures since the New Deal continued to claim a majority in Congress during the Kennedy administration.[134] By the time of Johnson's landslide victory in 1964, which brought a majority of Northern Democrats to Congress, the fundamental course of employment policy had already been charted. Employment policy now meant creating jobs via macroeconomic measures based on tax cuts and creating an adequately skilled work force with training programs such as those authorized by the MDTA and the War on Poverty.

In accordance with the national Democratic party's desire to provide benefits for blacks and its perception of this issue as one of increasing importance in Democratic electoral politics, these manpower programs were now targeted primarily at "the disadvantaged" (largely urban blacks). The policies were to be implemented by a variety of agencies, many of which sought to bypass established bureaucratic and institutional channels.[135] This policy package—macroeconomic policy based on tax cuts, and fragmented, narrow, constituency-targeted training programs—had far-reaching political ramifications that helped to undercut the potential for an effective coalition of blacks and labor within the Democratic party in support of federal employment policies.

This particular package of policies, representing the American approach to unemployment, was the product of both economic and political constraints. The inability of Congress to agree on spending programs early in the Kennedy administration, together with the preference of the CEA, dictated the choice of tax cuts as the macroeconomic policy. This strategy imposed budgetary limitations on selective interventionist employment programs, since restraint of national spending had been an ex-

[132] Greenstone, *Labor in American Politics*, pp. 248–61; Sundquist, *Politics and Policy*, chap. 6.

[133] Greenstone, *Labor in American Politics*, pp. 248–61.

[134] *Congressional Quarterly Almanac, 1961*, pp. 642–45.

[135] Mangum, *The Emergence of Manpower Policy*, p. 50; Levine, *Lessons from the War on Poverty*, pp. 231–32.

plicit quid pro quo in gaining approval for the tax cut. The constraint on spending was a major factor behind the adoption of the War on Poverty strategy of small, targeted training programs and the rejection of public employment programs.[136]

The administrative structure of the new interventionist programs reflected the inability of both the federal government and the Democratic party to target racial groups at the local level. The New Deal legacy of fragmented, semiautonomous centers of bureaucratic power meant that efforts to redirect the course of federal policy would face substantial barriers on the local level, reinforced by the inability of the party to impose its will in localities. In the 1960s, the Democratic party continued to be a loose aggregation of local organizations that constituents were mobilized to join often on quite different bases. The War on Poverty sought to increase the federal government's ability to achieve its own objectives by creating administrative structures that could bypass and challenge existing bureaucratic and political authorities.[137]

This policy package decreased the potential for building a social coalition of blacks and labor ready to support a federally directed activist employment strategy. Both the way that the War on Poverty programs mobilized blacks into national politics and the backlash effect that it prompted among labor's white members helped to create strains that would drive these two groups apart. By emphasizing group-specific benefits, the Great Society's employment programs undermined the bases for intergroup cooperation necessary to create more universal approaches in this policy area.

The War on Poverty helped to mobilize blacks into interest-group politics in a manner characteristic of American politics—by offering them control over a host of programs aimed at benefiting them.[138] Training and employment programs occupied a central place in the package of benefits for this group, which suffered from substantial unemployment. However, in offering particularistic benefits, the War on Poverty reinforced incentives for black leaders to seek race-specific policies. Universal approaches to unemployment, such as Bayard Rustin's Freedom Budget or the vision Martin Luther King articulated near the end of his life, were still only

[136] Ackley, "Troika Meeting with President Johnson"; Sundquist, *Politics and Policy*, pp. 141–42; Aaron, *Politics and the Professors*, p. 28; Stanley H. Ruttenberg and Jocelyn Gutchess, *Manpower Challenge of the 1970s: Institutions and Social Change* (Baltimore: Johns Hopkins University Press, 1970), pp. 24–25.

[137] Mangum, *The Emergence of Manpower Policy*, p. 50; Levine, *Lessons from the War on Poverty*, pp. 231–32; Ulman, "Uses and Limits of Manpower Policy," pp. 93–95.

[138] See Theodore Lowi, *The End of Liberalism: Ideology, Policy, and the Crisis of Public Authority* (New York: Norton, 1969), chap. 8; Charles V. Hamilton, "Blacks and the Crisis in Political Participation," *The Public Interest*, no. 34 (Winter 1974), pp. 207–8.

dreams.[139] Practical politics dictated that black leaders and black program administrators frame their demands in group-specific terms. The importance of defending the right to control these resources outweighed considerations about their ability to address the problems of black unemployment. This pattern of policy undercut the incentives of black administrators of such programs to seek bases of cooperation with other social interests in order to construct more universal programs.[140] Instead, the particularistic design of the War on Poverty helped to foster demands for community control despite the lack of evidence to suggest that such a strategy would provide an effective approach to the employment problems of the black community.[141]

The racial targeting of the War on Poverty helped to create the conditions for a powerful backlash that would severely damage prospects for meaningful cooperation between blacks and labor in support of employment programs. Because they were part of the resources that blacks used to challenge local political structures, poverty employment programs became identified with the contentious process of black political incorporation, which threatened to upset local political arrangements. Mayors whose authority had been challenged by the new black organizations were anxious to strip them of the federal resources that had bolstered their activities.[142] The white working class resented the "special privileges" offered to blacks. Moreover, because workers were mobilized into local politics through local political organizations and not through their labor unions, rank-and-file labor viewed black political incorporation as

[139] The Freedom Budget is printed in U.S. Congress, Senate Subcommittee on Employment, Manpower and Poverty, *Examination of the War on Poverty*, Part I, 90th Cong., 1st. sess., 1967, pp. 407–504. For Martin Luther King's vision of a low-income coalition across racial lines, see Martin Luther King, *Where Do We Go from Here: Chaos or Community?* (Boston: Beacon Press, 1967). See also Bayard Rustin, *Down the Line: The Collected Writings of Bayard Rustin* (Chicago: Quadrangle Books, 1971), and Charles V. Hamilton and Dona C. Hamilton, "Social Policies, Civil Rights, and Poverty," in Sheldon H. Danziger and Daniel H. Weinberg, eds., *Fighting Poverty: What Works and What Doesn't* (Cambridge: Harvard University Press, 1986), pp. 296–303.

[140] Michael K. Brown and Steven P. Erie, "Blacks and the Legacy of the Great Society: The Economic and Political Impact of Federal Social Policy," *Public Policy* 29 (Summer 1981): 322–24; Roger Friedland, "Class Power and Social Control: The War on Poverty," *Politics and Society* 6 (1976): 466–68.

[141] Brown and Erie, "Blacks and the Legacy," p. 317; Hamilton, "Blacks and the Crisis," pp. 207–8.

[142] William E. Selover, "The View from Capitol Hill: Harassment and Survival," in James Sundquist, ed., *On Fighting Poverty* (New York: Basic Books, 1969), p. 181; Paul E. Peterson and J. David Greenstone, "Racial Change and Citizen Participation: The Mobilization of Low-Income Communities through Community Action," in Haveman, *A Decade of Federal Anti-Poverty Programs*, p. 266; Bernard J. Frieden and Marshall Kaplan, *The Politics of Neglect: Urban Aid from Model Cities to Revenue Sharing* (Cambridge: MIT Press, 1975), pp. 82–84.

a threat to local social and political arrangements, not as a process that would further labor's broad national interests.[143]

Thus, the design of the War on Poverty created rifts in local Democratic coalitions by providing meager resources that became the focus of contention, rather than building cooperation and emphasizing the mutual interests of the diverse groups composing the Democratic constituency by establishing more universal employment policies. By 1966, the backlash against "black" programs prompted Congress to impose increasingly severe restrictions on their operations and eroded the bases of support for such social spending. The result of this division was apparent in 1968, when many white workers left the Democratic party to vote for Wallace and Nixon.[144]

The implementation of structural employment programs in the fragmented and particularistic fashion of the Great Society also tended to undermine the credibility of the structural analysis of unemployment and the structuralist solutions. The failure of such programs to solve the problem of unemployment in urban ghettos made them, as Brown and Erie have pointed out, "de facto income maintenance programs."[145] Some of these programs, including the largest, the National Youth Corps, were not designed to move participants into the labor market. They offered menial employment whose primary aim was temporarily to increase the income of the participants and to offer cities summer "riot insurance."[146] The Community Action Programs provided a useful way of challenging the local power structure in many cities, but they were ill-equipped to administer job training and placement programs. Nonetheless, they were given authority over several job training programs aimed at black ghetto residents. For example, in 1967 Community Action Programs were assigned operating responsibility for the newly created Concentrated Employment Program, designed to assist ghetto residents whose unemployment rates remained high despite the nationwide drop in unemployment that had occurred by that time. Yet the administrators of Community Action Programs had little experience or capacity to create jobs and had little sway over employers, whose cooperation would have been essential to the programs' success.[147]

[143] See Ira Katznelson, *City Trenches* (New York: Pantheon, 1981), chap. 3, for a discussion of the splits between community politics and labor policies in America.

[144] Walter Dean Burnham, *Critical Elections and the Mainsprings of American Politics* (New York: Norton, 1970), pp. 143–59, and Walter Dean Burnham, "The 1976 Election: Has the Crisis Been Adjourned?" in Walter Dean Burnham, *The Current Crisis in American Politics* (New York: Oxford University Press, 1982), p. 231.

[145] Brown and Erie, "Blacks and the Legacy," p. 315.

[146] Eli Ginzberg, "Manpower Training: Boon, Not Boondoggle," *Challenge* 16 (September/October 1973): 55.

[147] Ruttenberg and Gutchess, *Manpower Challenge of the 1970s*, pp. 64–71; Mangum, *The Emergence of Manpower Policy*, pp. 88–90.

The triumph of the aggregate approach to unemployment during the Kennedy administration put the entire burden of job creation on macroeconomic policy; programmatic intervention was restricted to training. With the advent of the War on Poverty, the concern about structural unemployment was supplanted by concern about poverty. The focus of attention shifted from the structure of the economy to the characteristics of the individual, characteristics that training was supposed to modify. The widespread support training programs had enjoyed less than a decade earlier had been undermined by their apparent failure to remedy the problems of structural unemployment in the nation's ghettos, as well as by the political divisions their implementation had helped to foster.

Explaining Federal Employment Policies

In these two periods of policy innovation, the recurrent failure to construct supportive social and political coalitions and the repeated collapse of efforts to transform national policy-making capacities limited the scope and effectiveness of national intervention in the area of employment. We can make sense of this pattern of failure in the political and institutional realms by looking at the way two features of American national political structure have influenced the politics and policy initiatives that affected employment. The first is what Lowi calls the "constituent"—or nonprogrammatic—nature of American political parties.[148] The second is the fragmented and decentralized organization of the national institutions concerned with formulating and administering economic policy. These two features, in combination, have limited the range of tools used to cope with unemployment and have prevented formation of coalitions that might have supported alternative policy configurations. Moreover, the policy legacies of the 1930s created institutions and interests that further limited the range of acceptable employment policies that might have been available in the 1960s.

Because political parties provide a critical link between society and politics, possibilities for joining diverse interests in support of national policies are contingent on the ability of parties to translate electoral victories into policy. American parties, however, have rarely performed such policy-making functions. Serving primarily as mechanisms for organizing elections and succession in office, parties have only occasionally sought to promote policy consensus among their diverse constituencies. Policy outcomes in the United States thus reflect accommodations and trade-offs among the many conflicting interests represented in Congress. Institution-

---

[148] Theodore J. Lowi, "Party, Policy, and Constitution in America," in Chambers and Burnham, eds., *The American Party Systems*, pp. 238–76.

alized in the norms of reciprocity of the congressional committee system, policy trade-offs have provided a mechanism for making national policy since the New Deal.[149] Efforts to break this decentralized pattern of brokered policy have led to struggles between would-be nationalizers—generally in the executive branch—and congressional defenders of local prerogatives.[150] Although the outcomes of such struggles are not predetermined, congressional foes of executive policy initiatives possess formidable resources to block proposals that they oppose. Both interest groups and members of Congress have generally been able to shape policy through decentralized legislative procedures and to influence bureaucratic implementation procedures.

The structure of American parties has had a particularly adverse effect on the possibilities for assembling coalitions that support employment policies. Deep regional and economic differences pose formidable barriers to agreement on a national approach to dealing with unemployment. In other industrial countries, party structures have more readily united interests around national policies to fight unemployment.[151] The political incentives built into the American party system, however, have undermined possibilities for forming coalitions that might support an active federal employment policy. Potential grounds for broad-based cooperation are whittled away as groups obtain more narrowly drawn benefits as a result of congressional trade-offs. Moreover, narrow policies, once implemented, often create new cleavages among social groups.

Thus, two fundamental cleavages in American society—the distinctive economic and political arrangements of the South, and racial distinctions—have been magnified by the normal operation of party politics. The ramifications for employment policy have been enormous. The ability of Southern congressional representatives to secure passage of their favored agricultural legislation after 1938 without cooperating with Northern Democrats doomed efforts to devise a national employment policy in the 1940s. Similarly, Democratic efforts to address the problems of blacks with highly visible, targeted policies undercut the possibilities for assembling a broad employment coalition in the 1960s. In each instance, the party system and congressional brokering of policy reduced

---

[149] Bensel, *Sectionalism and American Political Development*, chap. 7.

[150] See Morris Fiorina, *Congress: Keystone of the Washington Establishment* (New Haven, Conn.: Yale University Press, 1977), for an analysis of this pattern in the post–New Deal era.

[151] See Gosta Esping-Andersen, *Politics against Markets* (Princeton, N.J.: Princeton University Press, 1985); Francis G. Castles, *The Social Democratic Image of Society* (London: Routledge and Kegan Paul, 1978); and Francis G. Castles, "The Impact of Parties on Public Expenditure," in Francis G. Castles, ed., *The Impact of Parties* (Beverly Hills, Calif.: Sage, 1982), pp. 21–96.

the potential for forming cross-group coalitions. At the same time, these processes of congressional policy making eased the task of opponents of employment policy; with minimal bases of agreement, they were able to challenge broad national programs.

In addition to weakening political support for public action on employment issues, the structure of American parties has tended to limit the range of tools available for coping with unemployment. By securing the power of local elites, decentralized, patronage-oriented parties helped to perpetuate regional differences, undermining the movement toward nationalization of American politics and policy. The persistence of local power has had particularly significant consequences for employment policies. It has meant that approaches to unemployment that challenged regional autonomy were unlikely to survive congressional scrutiny. Thus, job creation and labor market policies that might have disrupted local economic and political arrangements have repeatedly been defeated in Congress. Only approaches that preserved local control of federal resources were likely to receive a sympathetic hearing.

The fragmented, decentralized organization of the national institutions concerned with economic policy making and administration is the second feature that has placed limits on American employment policies.[152] By circumscribing administrative capacity, and by channeling research and the development of expertise in particular directions, the institutional structure of the national government has made some approaches to unemployment far more feasible than others. In the 1930s, when the federal government sought for the first time to devise a national response to unemployment, no national institutions were available to plan or administer such a policy. The need to create institutions and centers of federal authority gave rise to struggles over such extensions of federal power. Thus fights over employment policy were not only about what should be done to deal with unemployment but also about the desirability of expanding federal authority.

Resistance to increasing federal authority did not entirely block the creation of new institutions to cope with unemployment in the 1930s and 1940s, but it did prevent the emergence of major centers of federal power equipped to shape unemployment policy. The inability of national institutions to oversee policy implementation meant that attempts to enforce nationally determined objectives ignited major jurisdictional disputes. The failure to create strong national institutions to cope with unemployment restricted the scope of future policy possibilities. As policy-relevant

---

[152] On the structure of the American state at the end of the Progressive Era, see Stephen Skowronek, *Building a New American State: The Expansion of National Administrative Capacities, 1877–1920* (New York: Cambridge University Press, 1982).

expertise became segmented and narrowed to reflect the institutional structure in which it developed, the range of plausible policies was narrowed. These arrangements discouraged the development of policies that crossed departmental lines or required close cooperation among different agencies. Notions of what policy options were possible and reasonable were thus powerfully influenced by the course of institutional development, for it marginalized solutions that called for a range of tools that could be deployed by the federal government.

The failure to create strong national institutions to cope with unemployment also limited the possibilities for amassing political support for employment policies. Decentralized institutional structures gave local opponents of vigorous employment policies increased leverage to block policies that might challenge their power. Decentralized bureaucracies became the natural allies of local elites who sought to block the expansion of public authority in the area of employment. Moreover, the limited number of policies that were possible, given the institutional framework of national economic policy making, encouraged policies that were targeted at politically significant groups. Such narrow policies did little to create a common interest in employment policies.

Clearly, the operation of American political parties and the national institutional structure had the joint effect, over time, of limiting the kinds of solutions to unemployment that would be acceptable in the United States. As the triumph of conservative opponents of interventionist employment policies became institutionalized in the immediate postwar period, both the group demands and the options debated by policy experts were transformed into more narrow proposals. The sweeping approaches advocated in the late New Deal period had been removed from the national agenda by the 1950s; after that time proponents of social spending directed by national planning became politically marginal. "Practical" demands and proposals rarely diverged from the nondirective form of Keynesianism embodied in tax cuts. More direct sorts of intervention were tolerated only when they were targeted at a group that could attract political sympathy or were the result of pork-barrel politics.

The failure and frustration of employment policy made politically convincing new arguments that government can do little to affect employment and that its efforts in this area are in fact detrimental to the health of the economy. The federal government could not intervene, in administratively and technically complex ways, in the area of employment, and proved ill-equipped to cope with the inflation that was the overriding concern of the 1970s. Manpower programs, too, proved badly suited to meet the economic challenges of the 1970s: both welfare programs for the poor and pork-barrel rewards for politicians were increasingly difficult to defend on economic grounds. The possibilities that were opened during the

Great Depression, to form enduring political coalitions or to establish an administrative-intellectual network with the strength and credibility necessary to defend a public role in the area of employment, had not been utilized. With the advent of the Reagan administration, most of the employment policy that remained was easily dismantled.

II

**TRANSFORMATIONS WITHIN
THE NEW DEAL SYSTEM**

The political coalitions and conflicts that have shaped modern American social provision figure centrally in this second part as they did in the first. Yet here "the politics of social policy" is approached with a different method—similarly historical but more microscopic. The earlier chapters connected U.S. state formation to broad configurations of social and economic policy, dealing as much with absent developments and with failed attempts at policy innovation as with the origins and shape of policies actually instituted. Taking off from the New Deal's social policy accomplishments, the chapters of this part trace legislative changes in particular programs over several decades into the 1970s.

Two of the Social Security Act's major programs are discussed by all three authors, Kenneth Finegold, Jill Quadagno, and John Myles. The first is national Old Age Insurance, which became Old Age and Survivors' Insurance in 1939 and Old Age, Survivors' and Disability Insurance in 1956. The second is Old Age Assistance, a federal program eventually nationalized as Supplemental Security Income in 1972. In addition, Finegold discusses the agricultural commodity and food stamps programs first established in the New Deal, and their connections to the significantly different Food Stamps programs of the 1960s and 1970s. Additional programs could have been discussed in this part, including Aid to Dependent Children (later Aid to Families with Dependent Children) and Unemployment Insurance, the other major parts of the 1935 Social Security Act. In fact, in their chapter in Part I, Edwin Amenta and Theda Skocpol analyzed failed attempts to nationalize unemployment insurance in the 1940s; and in an article published elsewhere, Edward Harpham explores developments in federal unemployment insurance. His analysis parallels Margaret Weir's earlier discussion of federal employment policies, underlining the limited success of attempted postwar reforms.[1] As a complement to such perspectives on "the frustration of policy innovation" in the employment area, these chapters focus on more successful and substantial innovations in old-age benefits and food assistance.

By virtue of their periodic revisions, old-age insurance, old-age assistance, and food assistance programs serve as excellent prisms through which we can see shifts in Congress and the federal executive, and complementary changes in the political and socioeconomic relations of the nation as a whole. Transformations after the New Deal and World War II—such as the accumulating capacities of the Social Security Administra-

[1] Edward J. Harpham, "Federalism, Keynesianism, and the Transformation of Unemployment Insurance in the United States," in Douglas Ashford and E. W. Kelley, eds., *Nationalizing Social Security in Europe and America* (Greenwich, Conn.: JAI Press, 1986), pp. 155–79.

tion, the changing economic interests of Southerners, and alterations in
the leverage of agricultural groups in Congress and the Democratic
party—were essential to the extension and upgrading of benefits for the
elderly and disabled and of food-aid programs for the poor. These improvements in benefits were, moreover, the most important to occur in
postwar U.S. social provision.

In their examinations of Social Security's provisions for benefits to the
elderly, Finegold and Quadagno offer arguments with different analytic
emphases, but also many overlaps and complementarities. To explain the
initial exclusion of agricultural workers from contributory old age insurance and the defeat of early proposals for national standards in old-age
assistance, both highlight the concern of Southern planters to keep blacks
at work in a low-wage, paternalist, and racialist system of agricultural
production. Both authors also emphasize the importance in the Democratic party of the nondemocratic, one-party South, and the way congressional committees helped Southern representatives with seniority to make
trade-offs on their own terms with urban-liberal northern Democrats.

Where Finegold and Quadagno diverge is in their accounts of subsequent programmatic developments. Drawing on previously published
works by Martha Derthick and Jerry Cates,[2] Finegold stresses the capacities of the Social Security Board/Administration to manage expertise,
manipulate outside interest groups, and eventually persuade Congress to
include agricultural workers in contributory insurance. Quadagno looks
primarily at changes in old-age assistance. She agrees with Cates that the
Social Security administrators originally worked to restrict the program
while expanding contributory insurance. Yet policy developments must
also be explained in broader social terms, she maintains. In Quadagno's
argument, shifting economic and political interests in the plantation
South accounted first for federal decentralization in old-age assistance
and the very restricted and racially differentiated benefits offered in the
South; then for growing pressures for differential federal subsidies favoring poor states; and finally for the relatively easy enactment of nationally
standardized Supplemental Security Income in 1972.

The differences between the analytic approaches of Finegold and
Quadagno are worth underlining. The former emphasizes the ways in
which governmental institutions and political parties select (as well as
channel) the social interests that become embodied in public policies,
while the latter emphasizes the ways major socioeconomic groups with
changing class interests use available levers of political power to achieve

[2] Martha Derthick, *Policymaking for Social Security* (Washington, D.C.: The Brookings
Institution, 1979); Jerry R. Cates, *Insuring Inequality: Administrative Leadership in Social
Security, 1935–54* (Ann Arbor: University of Michigan Press, 1983).

their ends. Finegold is more skeptical about how often dominant economic interests can use government to achieve their ends—unless the representative institutions help them to enter into broader political coalitions. Thus, Finegold points out, aided by the workings of Congress and the Democratic party in the 1960s and early 1970s, welfare reformers and commercial farmers could temporarily coalesce in support of Food Stamps; but "automobile stamps" remained out of the question, no matter how much appeal the notion might have had for both welfare reformers and the Big Three auto manufacturers.

Nevertheless, class relations and political structures intersect in both Finegold's and Quadagno's explanatory accounts of the origins and development of social programs. in this respect, they stand together in clear contrast to other major analysts of American social politics. Finegold and Quadagno deal primarily with dominant groups, rather than with the popular protesters so prominently discussed by Frances Fox Piven and Richard Cloward.[3] At the same time, the arguments of Finegold and Quadagno do not focus so exclusively as those of Derthick and Cates on the "bureaucratic politics" of particular federal agencies. To be sure, for one strand of his explanation Finegold traces the Social Security Board's effects on old-age insurance and the U.S. Department of Agriculture's influence on food programs. But he also connects bureaucratic initiatives with broader political processes, including those expressing class conflicts.

Formulated in the same broad analytic terms, the chapter by John Myles adds to our understanding of the changes American old-age provision has gone through since the 1930s, and he locates those changes in cross-national terms. According to Myles, a fully modern system of public provision for the elderly has two features, universality and adequacy of income-replacement in relation to pre-retirement earnings. In legal principle, the U.S. old-age insurance system graduated benefits in relation to earnings (and contributions) right from the start—unlike certain European flat-rate systems that achieved early universality but required major modifications later to enshrine any approximation to income-replacement for higher earners. The American system moved gradually toward near-universality of coverage without any need to add graduated benefits. But it was not until the reforms of 1969–72 under President Richard Nixon that the graduated benefits became sufficiently inflation-proof, and generous in relation to previous earnings, to offer a fairly continuous standard of living to working and middle-class Americans after retirement.

[3] See especially Frances Fox Piven and Richard Cloward, *Poor People's Movements: Why They Succeed and How They Fail* (New York: Pantheon Books, 1977).

Myles points out that this policy transition—toward an adequate "modern welfare state," even by international standards, for the formerly employed elderly—occurred at a point in the development of the postwar U.S. political economy when the president was looking for a way to make wage controls more palatable through the "deferred income" promised in indexed retirement benefits. Myles does not gainsay that, as Derthick and others would have it, the Social Security administrators had long laid plans for improved benefits within the graduated benefit framework that had been there from the start in 1935. Nor does he doubt that the political processes through which policy change came in the United States were unique. But Myles does underline the similarities between the trade-off of wages for retirement benefits achieved by workers in postwar European "corporatist" bargains and those achieved in the U.S. Nixon-era reforms.

Before long, Myles points out, business interests and conservative intellectuals in the United States launched an intense propaganda barrage against the most generous social security system fashioned in the 1970s. But so far, even in the fiscally retrenchment-minded atmosphere of the 1980s, the broad popularity of these benefits has made congressional representatives and other politicians, including Ronald Reagan, wary of proposing any significant cutbacks for pensioners in the present or near future. The nearly universal political coalition behind "social security" in the United States can frustrate frontal attacks on the system, even though American capitalists operate in a polity without a social democratic party or a strong organized labor movement. As Myles concludes, those who would roll back social security must now use more subtle tactics of chipping away at expectations of the system in the future.

Social security has not helped all the elderly equally well, however. Because of sharp income-gradations, Myles points out, the elderly poor have remained relatively badly off even after the 1969–72 insurance reforms and the nationalization of old-age assistance. These distributional facts allow Myles to stress the overall double meaning of the "welfare state" concept as applied to American realities. On the one hand, the United States may have for the elderly who formerly were steadily employed an approximation to European-style "welfare state" benefits, where welfare positively connotes something close to adequate, income-replacing benefits in a universal system. But on the other hand, American universal programs are not very redistributive, and many targeted "welfare" programs continue to provide ungenerous benefits for the poor alone.

This theme of the persistent bifurcations built into American social provision figures in Finegold and Quadagno as well. Perhaps most tellingly Finegold shows that even when Food Stamps became relatively generous and universal for low-income citizens, the program still remained a visible, somewhat stigmatizing "welfare" alternative to, say, a guaranteed national income that would incorporate poor and non-poor alike into the same routines of federal taxation and rebates. Thus, at the same time that they trace major changes in U.S. social programs since the 1930s, the chapters of this part dramatize the durability of the overall programmatic configuration established by the New Deal and confirmed in the 1940s. The policy changes analyzed in this part truly are "transformations *within* the New Deal system," not transformations of it.

5

Agriculture and the Politics of U.S. Social Provision: Social Insurance and Food Stamps

KENNETH FINEGOLD

"Today a hope of many years' standing is in large part fulfilled," began the statement issued when President Franklin Roosevelt signed the Social Security Act of 1935. "The civilization of the past hundred years, with its startling industrial changes, has tended more and more to make life insecure. Young people have come to wonder what would be their lot when they came to old age. The man with a job has wondered how long the job would last."[1] This view of social insurance as a solution to the new needs created by the "startling changes" of industrialization had long been expressed by such advocates as I. M. Rubinow and Abraham Epstein.[2] And more recent social scientists have also drawn connections between industrialization and the development of the welfare state. Some emphasize economic growth and its effects on social structure, demography, or ideology.[3] Others identify industrial capitalists or industrial workers as key political actors in shaping the development of social policy.[4]

Michael Nelson and Richard Valelly were helpful sounding boards as I began writing this paper. David Menefee-Libey, Benjamin Walter, the editors, and Princeton University Press's anonymous reader prepared incisive comments. I also benefited from discussions sponsored by the Center for Industrial Societies and by the History and Politics Group of the Vanderbilt Institute for Public Policy Studies. Gregory Siskind assisted with research. Marva Younger of the Food and Nutrition Service provided updated statistics on the Food Stamp Program.

[1] "Presidential Statement Signing the Social Security Act. August 14, 1935." Reprinted in *The Report of the Committee on Economic Security of 1935*, 50th Anniversary Edition (Washington, D.C.: National Conference on Social Welfare, 1985), p. 145.

[2] Carolyn L. Weaver, *The Crisis in Social Security: Economic and Political Origins* (Durham, N.C.: Duke University Press, 1982), p. 38; Roy Lubove, *The Struggle for Social Security, 1900–1935* (Cambridge: Harvard University Press, 1968), pp. 114–15.

[3] See, for example, Harold L. Wilensky, *The Welfare State and Equality: Structural and*

Yet to understand the development of many welfare states, and especially to understand public social provision in the United States, we must analyze the role of agriculture as well as that of industry. This analysis is both economic and political. Like other capitalists, commercial farmers seek control over markets and labor. Yet the economic effects on farmers of policy proposals will vary by farm size, crops, and region. Policy outcomes, however, do not directly reflect the economic situation of agricultural interests. Farmers rarely speak directly for themselves. Instead, their concerns are often interpreted by competing interest organizations that may have sharply alternative conceptions of what farmers want and need. How organizationally mediated farm demands are translated in turn into actual policies depends on the institutional structure of the state and the operations of political party systems. Within the state structure, representational and administrative arrangements both matter.

Representational arrangements may determine which farm groups' interpretations of socioeconomic demands become salient, and what alliances are formed between these organizations and other socioeconomic interests. Party systems, durable patterns of electoral competition, aggregate interests as well as individual voters. They thus set patterns for coalitions between groups. Exchange within these coalitions is not always equal: skill or strategic location within government may give one partner special advantages. Within the American national government, the structure of Congress has been an important source of these advantages. Though leadership and caucuses have sometimes been dominant in the structure of Congress, for much of the twentieth century the key element of congressional structure has been the committee system.

Administrative arrangements may allow bureaucrats and experts to promote policies not directly demanded by farm groups. "Governments that have, or can quickly assemble, their own knowledgeable administrative organizations," Theda Skocpol and I have argued, "are better able to

Ideological Roots of Public Expenditures (Berkeley: University of California Press, 1975), chap. 2, and Gaston V. Rimlinger, *Welfare Policy and Industrialization in Europe, America, and Russia* (New York: John Wiley and Sons, 1971), pp. 8–9, 334–41.

[4] See, for example, Jill S. Quadagno, "Welfare Capitalism and the Social Security Act of 1935," *American Sociological Review* 49, no. 5 (October 1984): 632–47; Thomas Ferguson, "From Normalcy to New Deal: Industrial Structure, Party Competition, and American Public Policy in the Great Depression," *International Organization* 38, no. 1 (Winter 1984): 85–92; James O'Connor, *The Fiscal Crisis of the State* (New York: St. Martin's Press, 1973), chaps. 1, 6; James Weinstein, *The Corporate Ideal in the Liberal State: 1900–1918* (Boston: Beacon Press, 1968), chaps. 1–2, 6–7; Karen Orren, "Liberalism, Money, and the Situation of Organized Labor," in J. David Greenstone, ed., *Public Values & Private Power in American Politics* (Chicago: University of Chicago Press, 1982), pp. 192–93; and Karen Orren, "Union Politics and Post-War Liberalism, 1946–1979" (unpublished ms., 1984), pp. 29–31.

carry through interventionist policies than are governments that must rely on extragovernmental experts and organizations."[5] In the United States, preexisting networks of policy specialists, positioned between the national government and business in think tanks, universities, or the states, have sometimes served as the basis for the construction of unusually efficacious administrative organizations.

These analytical pointers about the joint socioeconomic and political bases of agricultural influence on policymaking can inform our understanding of specific U.S. social policy outcomes in the New Deal and afterwards. During the New Deal, the American national state was partially restructured and the system of electoral competition between the political parties was partially realigned. Within the New Deal executive, the Department of Agriculture (USDA) was an unusually capable administrative organization that took an active role in economic and social policy innovation. Within the party system, Southern Democrats came to occupy a pivotal position. The next section of this essay examines these basic transformations in the U.S. polity and their implications for New Deal agricultural policy. We shall then analyze how the new agricultural policy system shaped the Social Security Act and the original food stamps program, each of which was also a product of the New Deal. Transformations in the U.S. state and party system after the New Deal altered the impact of agricultural interests on policy in both areas of social provision. Thus, we shall examine changes in social security's contributory old-age insurance system through 1954 and changes in the food stamps program from the 1930s to the present.

The New Deal and Agricultural Politics

Before the New Deal, agricultural policy was made in the interests of Eastern finance and industry. But with Franklin Roosevelt, a political realignment occurred between and within the parties, bringing agricultural groups into new alliances. Within Roosevelt's administration, moreover, planners in the Department of Agriculture took the lead in making farm policy. From the New Deal on, then, agricultural policy would be made in the interests of commercial farmers, but as those interests were perceived by a capable and cohesive Department of Agriculture.[6]

[5] Theda Skocpol and Kenneth Finegold, "State Capacity and Economic Organization in the Early New Deal," *Political Science Quarterly* 97, no. 2 (Summer 1982): 260–61.

[6] This section draws on arguments presented in Skocpol and Finegold, "State Capacity and Economic Organization"; Kenneth Finegold, "From Agrarianism to Adjustment: The Political Origins of New Deal Agricultural Policy," *Politics & Society* 11, no. 1 (1982); Kenneth Finegold, "Agriculture, State, Party, and Economic Crisis: American Farm Policy and the Great Depression," paper presented to the Conference on the Political Economy of

During the Republican Harding, Coolidge, and Hoover administrations of the 1920s, farmers were divided between the parties. Under the party system in place since the election of 1896, Republicans controlled both Congress and the presidency with electoral support from every section except the South. The dominance of Eastern capital within the Republican party was symbolized by Andrew Mellon, who served as treasury secretary for all three presidents. Midwestern farmers were represented within the Republican party by frustrated insurgents like Robert La Follette and George Norris. The Democratic minority was split between two ethnocultural blocs: a wet, foreign-stock, urban wing led by Al Smith and a dry, native-stock, rural wing led by William McAdoo. In 1924, the party convention was deadlocked for 103 ballots; in 1928, Smith won the nomination, but many McAdoo adherents defected to Hoover. Besides ensuring that the Democrats would continue to lose national elections, this internal division meant that the party would not address farmers' economic concerns. The McAdoo bloc did not appeal to them as producers, but it did appeal to them as Protestants or prohibitionists. The Smith bloc was more interested in the needs of its supporters in the cities.

Because Eastern capital had great influence on the Republican party that controlled the national government of the 1920s, that government would do little to ease the long agricultural depression that followed World War I. Low farm prices meant cheap food, and cheap food meant low wages for industrial workers, which Eastern business interests wanted to maintain. Experts in the Department of Agriculture were subordinated to the leadership of Herbert Hoover as secretary of commerce and then as president.

With the Republican majority, the Democratic minority, and the Department of Agriculture all indifferent or hostile toward them, farmers depended on the agricultural peak associations—the American Farm Bureau Federation (AFBF), the National Grange, and the National Farmers' Union—to develop proposals for raising farm prices. By 1927, the three groups had united in support of the McNary-Haugen plan to "make the tariff effective for agriculture." This plan would have created a corporation to buy the domestic farm surplus at a high domestic price and dump

Food and Agriculture in Advanced Industrial Societies, Rural Sociological Society Annual Meeting, Guelph, Ontario, August 1981; and Kenneth Finegold and Theda Skocpol, "Capitalists, Farmers, and Workers in the New Deal—The Ironies of Government Intervention: A Comparison of the Agricultural Adjustment Act and the National Industrial Recovery Act," paper presented to the Conference Group on the Political Economy of Advanced Industrial Societies, American Political Science Association Annual Meeting, Washington, D.C., August 1980. These essays contain more numerous references to sources on agricultural policy than are present here.

it abroad at a low world price. For Eastern capital, McNary-Haugen was doubly bad: not only would it raise domestic prices, and thus wages, but also it would subsidize European competitors by providing cheap food for their workers. In 1927 and again in 1928, a coalition of Midwestern Republicans and Southern Democrats ("corn and cotton") approved versions of the plan.[7] Each time, President Coolidge vetoed the bill with scathing comments written mostly by Secretary of Commerce Hoover and Secretary of Agriculture William Jardine.

The general economic crisis after 1929 led some industrialists to modify their opposition to agricultural recovery. Yet the transformation in agricultural policy also required a transformation of the party system. In 1932, Franklin Roosevelt overcame the ethnocultural divisions within the Democratic party by mobilizing farmers as an economic group and combining their support with that of urban workers. This electoral response to the stubborn Depression allowed the Democrats under Roosevelt to win overwhelmingly in the general election of 1932. Roosevelt's campaign promises had been vague enough to convince the leaders of the major farm organizations that he favored McNary-Haugen or other pet proposals of theirs. Instead, however, Roosevelt installed a system of production controls and subsidy payments under the Agricultural Adjustment Administration (AAA).

Production control was disliked by farmers, who wanted to produce more, not less; by consumers, who had to pay higher prices; and by middlemen, whose processing tax initially financed the program.[8] Whose policy was this, then? The new approach to agricultural woes was in fact proposed, initiated, and implemented by agricultural experts drawn from a longstanding network connecting the Department of Agriculture, particularly the Bureau of Agricultural Economics, with the land-grant colleges.[9] M. L. Wilson, Howard Tolley, and Mordecai Ezekiel, among others, had campaigned for production control since the 1920s. Rexford Tugwell brought these agricultural economists into Franklin Roosevelt's 1932 campaign. After the election, the Agricultural Department experts cajoled and argued the leaders of the farm organizations into accepting

[7] Sectional voting patterns are traced in Richard Franklin Bensel, *Sectionalism and American Political Development, 1880–1980* (Madison: University of Wisconsin Press, 1984), pp. 139–47, and in Christiana McFadyen Campbell, *The Farm Bureau and the New Deal: A Study of the Making of National Farm Policy, 1933–40* (Urbana: University of Illinois Press, 1962), pp. 36–40.

[8] Janet Poppendieck, *Breadlines Knee-Deep in Wheat: Food Assistance in the Great Depression* (New Brunswick, N.J.: Rutgers University Press, 1986), pp. 95–96, 109, 115–21; Gilbert C. Fite, "Farmer Opinion and the Agricultural Adjustment Act," *Mississippi Valley Historical Review* 48, no. 4 (March 1962).

[9] Richard S. Kirkendall, *Social Scientists and Farm Politics in the Age of Roosevelt* (Columbia: University of Missouri Press, 1966).

production controls, along with other policies made possible under the Agricultural Adjustment Act of 1933. The agricultural economists were then appointed to key positions within the new AAA.

With the support of Secretary of Agriculture Henry Wallace, these experts carried out the planning tasks necessary for implementing production controls and won the internal struggle to make production control the primary focus of the AAA. Roosevelt's campaign statements, the Agricultural Adjustment Act, and the AAA's organizational structure each seemed to encompass so many different approaches that outside interest groups and administrative factions within the AAA all believed New Deal farm policy would follow their prescriptions for relief. George N. Peek, coauthor of the McNary-Haugen Plan, was appointed as the AAA's first administrator and continued to stress marketing; he later wrote that "through all my life I have been steadfastly against the promotion of planned scarcity." In December 1933, however, Peek resigned to become a special advisor to Roosevelt on foreign trade. Chester C. Davis, his successor, was more closely aligned with Wallace and the agricultural economists.[10]

The support of the farm organizations, particularly the Farm Bureau, legitimized the production control program and convinced individual farmers to cooperate and to join the local production control committees that allocated quotas and checked compliance. The state extension services helped coordinate this "economic democracy"; reliance on their preexisting organizational capacity enabled the AAA to act quickly, as was required by both the severity of the crisis and the calendar of agricultural production.[11] Large farmers dominated the local committees and had the closest relations with the extension services. Experts in the AAA who trained in the USDA and the land-grant colleges also thought in terms of the needs of successful farmers, not of small farmers, tenants, sharecroppers, and laborers. As Theodore Saloutos notes, "Agricultural thinking, research, teaching, and extension work through the years prior to the New Deal had been concentrated almost exclusively on the well-managed farm, and this approach strongly influenced the AAA."[12]

During the early years of the New Deal interventions in agriculture, a series of related developments inside the Department of Agriculture and at the interstices of the federal government and local farm communities

[10] Theodore Saloutos, *The American Farmer and the New Deal* (Ames: Iowa State University Press, 1982), chaps. 4, 6 (Peek quote, p. 54); Finegold, "From Agrarianism to Adjustment," pp. 17–22.

[11] Edwin G. Nourse, Joseph S. David, and John D. Black, *Three Years of the Agricultural Adjustment Administration* (Washington, D.C.: The Brookings Institution, 1937), pp. 68–86, 255–66; Campbell, *Farm Bureau and the New Deal*, chaps. 4, 6.

[12] Saloutos, *American Farmer*, pp. 261–62.

strengthened conservative agricultural interests. The basic orientation of the agricultural economists from the USDA–land-grant network—on orientation toward planning in the interests of commercial farmers—was challenged within the AAA by urban liberals in the Legal Division and the Consumers' Counsel Division. The AAA liberals sought to ensure that tenant farmers and sharecroppers gained their share of AAA subsidies and were protected against evictions. They also tried to prevent food price increases for urban consumers. In February 1935, however, the liberals were "purged" from the AAA after a dispute over the interpretation of tenancy provisions in the cotton contracts. Secretary of Agriculture Wallace, although sympathetic to the liberals' ideas, feared that if he did not end the conflict, indispensable AAA officials might resign. Chester Davis, Wallace wrote in his diary, "more nearly has the necessary experience and grasp of all details of the agricultural situation than anyone else who could be used at this time to run the AAA"; Oscar Johnston, manager of the nation's largest cotton plantation, was perhaps the only one who could master the complicated legal and financial operations of the Cotton Pool. "So many of the people in the legal section," in contrast, "had no agricultural background whatever."[13]

Later in the New Deal, the Farm Security Administration (FSA), established outside the Department of Agriculture, would fight other battles for the rural poor. The result was similar: the FSA was restricted and finally abolished by a congressional coalition of Southern Democrats and Midwestern Republicans.[14]

By the early New Deal, then, a new agricultural policy system had come into being. Large commercial farmers, formerly isolated from national policymaking, were now a key component of the New Deal Democratic majority. Experts from the USDA–land-grant network proved willing and able to carry out the AAA's complex agricultural planning tasks. Estab-

---

[13] Richard Lowitt, "Henry Wallace and the 1935 Purge in the Department of Agriculture," *Agricultural History* 53, no. 3 (July 1979): 619, 614 (Wallace quotes); Lawrence J. Nelson, "The Art of the Possible: Another Look at the 'Purge' of the AAA Liberals in 1935," *Agricultural History* 57, no. 4 (October 1983): 418, 425–26, 433; Poppendieck, *Breadlines*, pp. 100–102, 187–89; Nourse et al., *Three Years of the AAA*, pp. 341–49; David Eugene Conrad, *The Forgotten Farmers: The Story of Sharecroppers in the New Deal* (Urbana: University of Illinois Press, 1965); Donald H. Grubbs, *Cry from the Cotton: The Southern Tenant Farmers' Union* (Chapel Hill: University of North Carolina Press, 1971). The AAA liberals included Jerome Frank, Frederic C. Howe, Gardner Jackson, Alger Hiss, and Lee Pressman.

[14] Sidney Baldwin, *Poverty and Politics: The Rise and Decline of the Farm Security Administration* (Chapel Hill: University of North Carolina Press, 1968); Lee J. Alston and Joseph P. Ferrie, "Resisting the Welfare State: Southern Opposition to the Farm Security Administration," in Robert Higgs, ed., *The Emergence of the Modern Political Economy* (Greenwich, Conn.: JAI Press, 1985), pp. 91–114.

lished farm groups, once enemies of the state, now mobilized support for its initiatives.[15] State capacity in agriculture would serve the interests of large commercial farmers. Farm interests, however, would be interpreted by agricultural experts, not by the farmers themselves. This new system would shape future agricultural policy. It would also lay the basis for the participation of agricultural interests in broader realms of New Deal social policymaking. To the extent that welfare policies came within the purview of the agricultural state, they would reflect the orientation of experts trained in the Department of Agriculture and the land-grant colleges.

As the AAA purge of liberals and the FSA's demise suggest, the agricultural policy system of the early New Deal functioned to strengthen the leverage of conservative Southern Democrats. This outcome was *not* foreordained. In January 1935, the *San Francisco Chronicle* characterized most Southern Democrats as "politically, economically, and traditionally conservative, often reactionary. They swallowed most of the New Deal because of its Democratic label, but the South has always stood against social legislation. It has its own peculiar problem."[16] Yet as the *Chronicle* admitted, there were exceptions; only on their "own peculiar problem" of race were Southern members of Congress united. Huey Long, whose "Share Our Wealth Plan" to finance pensions through confiscatory taxation was a popular alternative to Roosevelt's social insurance proposals, was from Louisiana.[17] Senator Theodore Bilbo of Mississippi, though notorious as a racist demagogue, was a loyal New Dealer on economic issues. During the later New Deal, Alabama Senators Lister Hill and Hugo Black, Florida's Claude Pepper, then in the Senate, and Texas Representative Maury Maverick, head of the "Maverick bloc," were downright progressive.[18] Thus, the universe of Southern politicians was broader

[15] The Farmers' Holiday Association, an Iowa-based offshoot of the Farmers' Union, and various Communist-affiliated farm groups continued to demand more radical federal action. Though they were able, at the state and local levels, to block foreclosures and obtain more favorable arrangements with distributors, their protests had little impact on national farm policy. See John L Shover, *Cornbelt Rebellion: The Farmers' Holiday Association* (Urbana: University of Illinois Press, 1965), and Finegold, "From Agrarianism to Adjustment," pp. 24–25.

[16] Reprinted in the *New York Times*, January 13, 1935.

[17] The details of the Share Our Wealth Plan are discussed in Alan Brinkley, *Voices of Protest: Huey Long, Father Coughlin, and the Great Depression* (New York: Knopf, 1982), pp. 72–73, and in T. Harry Williams, *Huey Long* (New York: Knopf, 1969), pp. 692–96.

[18] V. O. Key, Jr., *Southern Politics in State and Nation* (New York: Knopf, 1949), pp. 359–68; James T. Patterson, *Congressional Conservatism and the New Deal: The Growth of the Conservative Coalition in Congress, 1933–1939* (Lexington: University Press of Kentucky, 1967), pp. 325–27; James McGregor Burns, *Congress on Trial* (New York: Harper Brothers, 1949), p. 81; Stuart C. Weiss, "Maury Maverick and the Liberal Block," *Journal of American History* 57, no. 4 (March 1971): 880–95.

than the caricature of "a frock-coated, long-maned, and long-winded statesman of the old school, who conspires in the cloakroom with Republicans to grind down the common man."[19]

The AAA worked against the liberal alternatives, however. The purge of the AAA liberals in early 1935 ensured that landlords would continue to appropriate subsidies intended for tenants and sharecroppers, that they would continue to meet reduced allotments by removing tenants from the land, and that the efforts of the Southern Tenant Farmers' Union to organize against these abuses would fail. Since allotments were issued by acreage, not output, they also encouraged mechanization. Tenants and sharecroppers became landless laborers; many, black and white, eventually headed north.[20] Moreover, the AFBF, the most conservative of the three agricultural peak associations, was better able than its rivals to use local and state AAA committees as the nuclei for its own membership drives. This tactic was particularly successful in the South, where the Farm Bureau had previously been weak.[21] Both the economic and the political effects of the AAA, in sum, hurt Southern insurgents and strengthened their conservative opponents. From the mid-1930s onward, in turn, most Southern Democrats in Congress would use their influence over welfare policy on behalf of the large farmers with whom they were allied. Moreover, through the AFBF, Southern planters enjoyed strengthened associational ties to commercial farmers in other regions, especially the Midwest.[22]

Since Southern Democrats did not control a congressional majority, they needed to form coalitions to pass favorable legislation or block unwanted executive initiatives.[23] By 1939, a conservative coalition linking Southern Democrats with Republicans who often represented other agricultural areas had defeated President Roosevelt and Northern, pro-labor Democrats on many issues, including the FSA, court-packing, executive

---

[19] Key, *Southern Politics*, p. 355.

[20] See the sources cited in note 13, and Gilbert C. Fite, *Cotton Fields No More: Southern Agriculture, 1865–1980* (Lexington: University Press of Kentucky, 1984), pp. 139–43, 170, 208–10.

[21] Campbell, *Farm Bureau and the New Deal*, pp. 88–89, 95, 100, 102; Nourse et al., *Three Years of the AAA*, p. 266.

[22] This point is made by Margaret Weir and Theda Skocpol, "State Structures and the Possibilities for 'Keynesian' Responses to the Great Depression in Sweden, Great Britain, and the United States," in Peter B. Evans, Dietrich Rueschemeyer, and Theda Skocpol, eds., *Bringing the State Back In* (New York: Cambridge University Press, 1985), pp. 143–44.

[23] The next two paragraphs draw on Patterson, *Conservative Coalition*, chaps. 6–10; Baldwin, *Poverty and Politics*; Weir and Skocpol, "State Structures and the Possibilities for 'Keynesian' Responses," pp. 138, 145; Campbell, *Farm Bureau and the New Deal*, pp. 115–19, 186; Bensel, *Sectionalism*, pp. 214–16; and Key, *Southern Politics*, pp. 355–59, 374–78.

reorganization, and public works spending. On farm subsidy issues, however, the usual "conservative coalition" could not be maintained. Southern cotton, tobacco, and peanut farmers favored high, fixed price supports, while Midwestern corn-hog farmers favored low, flexible supports. The result was that Southern Democrats sometimes allied themselves with urban-liberal Democrats rather than with Midwestern Republicans.

The original Agricultural Adjustment Act, financed by a processing tax, did not require specific appropriations. But the invalidation of the 1933 act by the Supreme Court, and its replacement by the Soil Conservation and Domestic Allotment Act of 1936, financed by appropriations from general revenues, forced Southern Democrats to form coalitions with the Northern wing of their party. Northern Democrats accepted farm legislation that raised the cost of food and clothing for their constituents. In return, Southern Democrats selectively supported liberal labor and social welfare legislation. In 1939, for example, urban Democrats switched their votes to save the farm parity appropriation; their price was House rejection of a $50,000 limit placed on Works Progress Administration projects.

Coalitions between Southern and Northern Democrats were brokered by the congressional committees.[24] But these brokers were not neutral, because the committees were dominated by chairmen chosen under the seniority system. Since the South was less electorally competitive, and had been Democratic before the New Deal realignment, Southern members were much more likely to control congressional committees. As a result, coalitions tended to favor the Southern side. Northern Democrats did best when their Labor committees were involved in the exchange. Even then, Southerners could cheat: in 1938, after Northern votes had helped pass the farm bill, Southerners reneged by renewing their opposition to the wages and hours bill.[25] To continue farm subsidies, then, Southerners had to trade with Northern Democrats on labor and welfare bills, but the Southerners controlled most of the trading posts. Southern Democratic control of key committees made it difficult for urban Democrats to negotiate an alternative coalition with Midwestern Republicans against high farm subsidies. Such a coalition also would have threatened the Democratic electoral majority, maintenance of which helped both wings of the party.

These changes in the U.S. federal state and party system, changes associated with the reconstruction of the agricultural policy system around the New Deal's newly activated AAA, in turn helped to shape both social security and food stamps. Southern Democrats, representing the interests of commercial farmers, sought to exclude farm workers from social in-

[24] This paragraph draws heavily on Bensel, *Sectionalism*, pp. 26–27, 173, 216–22.
[25] Burns, *Congress on Trial*, pp. 75–77.

surance, and to use nutrition programs to dispose of their own surpluses. The Department of Agriculture administered the food stamp program and weighed its nutritional goals against its agricultural goals. Social security, however, was administered by a new agency that, like the AAA, drew upon a preexisting expert network to create another locus of state capacity. The Social Security Board (later, the Social Security Administration) could thus extend coverage in accordance with the broader, national conception of social insurance developed by its own experts.

Agriculture and the Social Security Act: Inclusion or Exclusion?

Industrial workers have been covered by the contributory old-age insurance program established in the Social Security Act of 1935 since the law was enacted. The policy specialists who developed the contributory old-age insurance proposals conceived of them as solutions to the insecurities of industrial life. Urban liberals in Congress, particularly Senator Robert Wagner of New York, provided effective representation for their industrial constituents. And some "corporate liberal" capitalists also favored contributory social insurance for their employees.[26] Though the experts responsible for the Social Security Act also favored inclusion for workers in agriculture, the representatives and employers of these workers opposed their coverage. Disfranchised and disorganized, agricultural workers had little power over either members of Congress or landowners. From 1934 to 1954, therefore, Southern Democrats responsive to the interests of landowners kept farm operators, laborers, tenants, and sharecroppers outside the contributory old-age insurance program established under the Social Security Act.

Opponents of extending contributory social insurance stressed its administrative difficulties, but their arguments should not be taken at face value: they showed little interest in exploring ways to address the practical problems, as had already been done in other countries, and would eventually be done rather easily in the United States. Inclusion was opposed because it was contrary to the economic interests of large landowners, who benefited from the economic insecurity of their agricultural workers and tenants. Even a minimal social insurance program might reduce compulsion to work for low wages, and the taxes for social insurance would increase the costs of farm operations. Incorporation of agricultural workers into a national system of social insurance, moreover,

[26] Theda Skocpol and John Ikenberry, "The Political Formation of the American Welfare State in Historical and Comparative Perspective," paper presented to the American Sociological Association Annual Meeting, San Francisco, September 1982, pp. 56–82; Quadagno, "Welfare Capitalism," pp. 639–41.

would erode longstanding patterns of paternalism, which had proven economically efficient for Southern plantation operators. In contrast, means-tested relief, subsidized by the federal government through the Social Security Act's public assistance provisions, could be adjusted (by landowner-dominated state and local governments) to landowners' needs, expanded in winter and contracted when labor was needed, offered to docile workers and denied to troublemakers.[27]

During the 1930s and 1940s, conservative agricultural interests managed to keep farmers, tenants, and farm workers out of the contributory social insurance program. Proposals to include these groups were rejected by the House Ways and Means Committee, which was responsible for social security legislation and was controlled by Southern Democrats. But eventually, by 1954, old-age insurance coverage was extended to agricultural groups; this extension in coverage was due to the Social Security Administration's determination to achieve universal coverage, and to its fear of flat-plan alternatives to contributory social insurance.

The legislative history of the American social security system began with Executive Order No. 6757, signed by President Roosevelt on June 29, 1934. This order established a Committee on Economic Security (CES), along with a technical board and an advisory council to assist it. Representing farm interests, Secretary of Agriculture Wallace served on the CES and Louis Taber of the Grange was on the advisory council. Two Department of Agriculture economists, Howard Tolley and Victor N. Valgren, were on the technical board.[28]

The original proposal for contributory old-age insurance drafted by the technical board covered only industrial workers. But coverage for agricultural workers under both unemployment insurance and contributory old-age insurance programs was suggested in six preliminary surveys, directed by Louis H. Bean, of the security problems of workers in agriculture. The CES recommended coverage for all employed persons. This broader insurance program, embodied in the administration's initial economic security bill, fit the conception of Roosevelt, who had told Secretary of Labor Frances Perkins: "And there is no reason why just the industrial workers should get the benefit of this. Everybody ought to be in on it—the farmer and his wife and his family." Perkins and Harry Hopkins, Federal Emergency Relief Administrator, were the strongest supporters in the administration of universal coverage.[29]

[27] Ibid., pp. 635, 643; Poppendieck, *Breadlines*, pp. 229–30; Lee J. Alston and Joseph P. Ferrie, "Labor Costs, Paternalism, and Loyalty in Southern Agriculture: A Constraint on the Growth of the Welfare State," *Journal of Economic History* 45, no. 1 (March 1985): 98–104, 113 n. 61; Alston and Ferrie, "Resisting the Welfare State," pp. 84–90.

[28] U.S. Congress, House Committee on Ways and Means, *Economic Security Act*, 74th Cong., 1st sess., 1935, pp. 60–61.

[29] Frances Perkins, *The Roosevelt I Knew* (New York: Viking Press, 1946), p. 283 (Roo-

Considerable congressional conflict over the Roosevelt administration's bill focused on the provisions for noncontributory old-age assistance payments. The CES proposed a federal program of old-age assistance, with the national government providing 50 percent of the states' costs; contributory insurance, in contrast, was to be purely national. Southern Democrats, led by Senator Harry Byrd of Virginia, won important changes in the old-age assistance provisions, eliminating national minimum standards that might have provided blacks adequate support, and allowing states to impose eligibility requirements stricter than the statutory criteria. As Quadagno concludes, old-age assistance could "continue to function as a traditional form of labor control," with the national government now paying half the bill.[30]

The broad old-age insurance coverage proposed by the administration was also modified by Congress. Edwin Witte, executive director of the CES, admitted in the House hearings that exclusion of agricultural workers and farmers would make initial administration easier, but "if you wish to solve the problem permanently, you will probably bring them in at some later date." He estimated that the cost of the system would not vary much either way.[31] But Henry Morgenthau, the secretary of the Treasury, argued strongly against inclusion before the House Ways and Means Committee. Though Morgenthau had been a member of the CES, which had proposed a universal bill, he now argued upon the recommendations of Treasury officials that it would not be "feasible" for the Internal Revenue Service to collect payroll taxes for agricultural workers, domestic servants, and casual laborers. Questioning by Committee Chairman Robert Doughton of North Carolina and by Congressman Fred Vinson of Kentucky brought out Morgenthau's views, though Congressman John McCormack, a Massachusetts Democrat, challenged the exclusion of agricultural workers from contributory old-age social insurance. As Perkins recalled, Morgenthau's testimony "was a blow. The matter had been discussed in the Committee on Economic Security, and universal coverage had been agreed upon almost from the outset. One could concede that it

---

sevelt quote); Edwin E. Witte, *The Development of the Social Security Act* (Madison: University of Wisconsin Press, 1962), pp. 28, 32; Arthur J. Altmeyer, *The Formative Years of Social Security* (Madison: University of Wisconsin Press, 1966), p. 7; *New York Times*, September 4, 1934, February 26, 1935, March 25, 1935; Alston and Ferrie, "Labor Costs, Paternalism, and Loyalty," pp. 107–11.

[30] Quadagno, "Welfare Capitalism," p. 643; Witte, *Development*, pp. 143–45; Alston and Ferrie, "Labor Costs, Paternalism, and Loyalty," pp. 114–15. Old-age assistance was finally nationalized in 1972, with the creation of the Supplemental Security Income (SSI) program for providing cash grants to the needy aged, blind, and disabled. This change was a largely unnoticed byproduct of the controversy over the Family Assistance Plan proposed by the Nixon administration. See Vincent J. and Vee Burke, *Nixon's Good Deed: Welfare Reform* (New York: Columbia University Press, 1974), chap. 9.

[31] House, *Economic Security Act*, p. 113.

would be difficult for the Treasury to collect these taxes. But the whole administration of the act was going to be difficult."[32]

After Morgenthau's testimony, Henry I. Harriman of the U.S. Chamber of Commerce echoed his opinion that coverage for agricultural, domestic, and casual workers would be impractical. Abraham Epstein of the American Association for Social Security, however, continued to advocate universal, need-based coverage. The major farm groups did not present testimony before either the House or the Senate. Witte told the Senate Finance Committee he could not recall the Grange's Louis Taber expressing a position on the inclusion of agricultural workers.[33]

As a CES staff summary presented to each house showed, many other countries, including France, Germany, Great Britain, and Italy, included agricultural workers in their old-age insurance systems.[34] Nevertheless, Morgenthau's recommendations were accepted in executive session by Congressman Doughton's Ways and Means Committee. The House committee excluded agricultural workers from coverage, along with domestic servants and employees of religious, charitable, and educational organizations. Exclusion would, in particular, deny benefits to blacks, since three-fifths were either domestic or agricultural workers.[35] Witte concluded that, "In taking this position, the [House Ways and Means] committee apparently was influenced far less by the difficulties of administration than by the fact that it was felt that the farmers would object to being taxed for old age insurance protection for their employees." Frances Perkins "made no attempt to get [exclusion of agricultural and domestic workers] out after it was once inserted in the bill. It was her view that the inclusiveness of coverage was relatively unimportant, because she felt that the law could easily be amended in later years to afford wider coverage."[36]

Eventually the Social Security Act *was* amended to achieve broader coverage, but not nearly as quickly as Perkins had hoped. The extension of coverage to agricultural workers and other initially excluded groups can be attributed in significant part to the development of unusual administrative capacity around the social security program after 1935. As with the AAA, a preexisting, quasi-governmental network of policy specialists

---

[32] Perkins, *Roosevelt*, pp. 297–98 (quote, p. 298); House, *Economic Security Act*, pp. 901–11; Alston and Ferrie, "Labor Costs, Paternalism, and Loyalty," pp. 111–13.

[33] U.S. Congress, Senate Committee on Finance, *Economic Security Act*, 74th Cong., 1st sess., 1935, pp. 220, 509, 915.

[34] House, *Economic Security Act*, p. 78; Senate, *Economic Security Act*, p. 51; Alston and Ferrie, "Labor Costs, Paternalism, and Loyalty," pp. 110–11.

[35] Quadagno, "Welfare Capitalism," p. 643; House, *Economic Security Act*, pp. 796–98; *New York Times*, February 20, 1935.

[36] Witte, *Development*, pp. 153–54.

advocated proposals without mass support, then administered a program based upon them. The social insurance network was centered around John R. Commons and the institutional economists of the University of Wisconsin. It included Edwin Witte, Arthur J. Altmeyer, and Witte's student, Wilbur J. Cohen. These experts emphasized contributory social insurance—operated by government and offering benefits keyed to past wage levels—for unemployment, health, and disability, as well as for old age. They rejected competing proposals for noncontributory public assistance, regulated private insurance, or flat-plan pension systems that would have given all recipients the same benefits without regard to earnings.[37]

The Wisconsin experts' efforts in support of contributory social insurance proposals achieved little political popularity at either the state or national levels before 1935.[38] Other proposals received more mass support. Millions joined clubs set up to advocate the Townsend plan, which would have given two hundred dollars a month to anyone over sixty who agreed to quit work and to spend the money immediately.[39] A looser network of clubs formed around Huey Long's "Share Our Wealth Plan," and it seemed possible a Long third party candidacy stressing the plan would gain as many as six million presidential votes in 1936.[40] The Lundeen Bill, which would have financed generous unemployment, sickness, and old-age benefits by redistributive taxation, was backed by some social workers and labor unions and by Communist-affiliated organizations.[41] Though scorned by the Wisconsin school, these alternatives remained popular even after passage of the Social Security Act.

The social insurance advocates, however, worked within the CES to write the act. These experts then moved over to run the new Social Security Board, which enjoyed considerable bureaucratic autonomy and had the resources to plan policies. Outsiders were henceforth unable to reshape social security policy, despite many attempts from the late 1930s to the early 1950s. Organized labor and advisory bodies were enlisted in support of the experts' vision of the program, while business groups and

[37] Skocpol and Ikenberry, "Political Formation," pp. 51–56; Jerry Cates, *Insuring Inequality: Administrative Leadership in Social Security, 1935–54* (Ann Arbor: University of Michigan Press, 1983), pp. 22–24, 26–31; Weaver, *Crisis in Social Security*, pp. 35–39.

[38] Weaver, *Crisis in Social Security*, pp. 39–56.

[39] Skocpol and Ikenberry, "Political Formation," pp. 61–63; Weaver, *Crisis in Social Security*, pp. 70–71.

[40] Altmeyer, *Formative Years*, p. 110; Weaver, *Crisis in Social Security*, p. 70; Brinkley, *Voices of Protest*, pp. 79, 169–71, 173–75, 179–186, 192–193, 203–8; Williams, *Huey Long*, pp. 696–702.

[41] Skocpol and Ikenberry, "Political Formation," pp. 61–63; Quadagno, "Welfare Capitalism," pp. 638–39.

political executives were frustrated in their attempts to make fundamental changes.[42]

The social insurance experts ensconced after 1935 in the Social Security Board/Administration wanted and expected universal coverage for American old-age insurance. Their arguments stressed the lack of protection for those outside the system and the problems created when workers moved between covered and uncovered employment.[43] But extension of social insurance was also a defense against competing schemes for old-age protection. In particular, the exclusion of potential contributors and beneficiaries in agriculture threatened to drive farm states toward expansion of noncontributory public assistance.[44]

The first in a series of attempts by the Social Security Board/Administration and advisory bodies that shared its conception of social insurance to expand coverage took place in 1938, when a social security advisory council set up to "review" the policies established in 1935 recommended that farm workers and all other private employees be included in the old-age insurance system. The Social Security Board, while recognizing that old-age coverage for all farm workers would pose "great administrative difficulties," concluded that "the inclusion of large-scale farming operations, often of a semi-industrial character, probably would reduce rather than increase administrative difficulties." It proposed that the "agricultural labor" exemption be more narrowly defined to apply only to "the services of a farmhand employed by a small farmer to do the ordinary work connected with his farm." In keeping with its principle of similar coverage for unemployment and old-age insurance, the board recommended that the definition of agricultural labor excluded from unemployment compensation also be restricted. Despite these recommendations, the Ways and Means Committee refused to extend contributory old-age insurance coverage to agricultural workers as part of its 1939 amendments. Instead, the Ways and Means Committee actually broadened the agricultural exemption from old-age and unemployment insurance to include workers in processing.[45]

[42] Martha Derthick, *Policymaking for Social Security* (Washington, D.C.: The Brookings Institution, 1979), pp. 3–292; Skocpol and Ikenberry, "Political Formation," pp. 64–92; Cates, *Insuring Inequality*, pp. 24–26; Weaver, *Crisis in Social Security*, pp. 112–13; Edwin E. Witte, "Organized Labor and Social Security," in Milton Derber and Edwin Young, eds., *Labor and the New Deal* (Madison: University of Wisconsin Press, 1957), pp. 267–72.

[43] Derthick, *Policymaking*, p. 263; Cates, *Insuring Inequality*, pp. 42, 72–73, 92; Weaver, *Crisis in Social Security*, pp. 128–29.

[44] The Social Security Board's efforts to limit public assistance are traced in Cates, *Insuring Inequality*, chap. 5.

[45] "Proposed Changes in the Social Security Act," *Social Security Bulletin* 2, no. 1 (January 1939): 8 (quotes), 12; "Social Security in Review," *Social Security Bulletin* 2, no. 1 (January 1939): 2; "Social Security in Review," *Social Security Bulletin* 2, no. 6 (June 1939):

A second advisory council, created in 1947 in association with a payroll tax increase, again recommended that agriculture be included in social insurance. President Truman endorsed the suggestion in 1949.[46] Altmeyer, as commissioner for Social Security, argued that it was now feasible to collect payroll taxes from the farm population. Extension of benefits to agriculture was also endorsed by farm groups. The Grange said fairness required voluntary coverage for operators, since farmers already paid payroll taxes passed on to them by industry but received no benefits. The Grange also supported coverage for farm workers; its representative told the House Ways and Means Committee that farmers, particularly near urban areas, found it difficult to attract labor to uncovered employment, in which many laborers had worked during World War II. The Farmers' Union, pointing out that rural populations tended to be poorer and older, said farmers would prefer contributory insurance to the humiliation of public relief. The AFBF endorsed the inclusion of farm labor but wanted to postpone extension to farm operators until coverage of other self-employed groups had been tested. All three peak associations, as well as the National Cooperative Milk Producers Federation, agreed with Altmeyer's view that the administrative problems of collecting payroll taxes from farmers could be solved.

Welfare directors from Texas, North Carolina, Alabama, Idaho, Tennessee, Louisiana, and Colorado complained about the costs of old-age assistance and pointed out that many farmers had paid some payroll taxes through covered employment without becoming eligible for insurance benefits. Significantly, the state officials also warned that failure to extend coverage created pressures for an expansion of noncontributory pensions. For example, John H. Winters, director of the Texas Department of Public Welfare, said, "I think we are in grave danger throughout the South and Southwest of ditching the social-security program; that is, if the people had their way about it and going to a straight pension out of current revenues unless the social security is changed and changed immediately."[47] From the perspective of the farm states, extension would replace

6; Altmeyer, *Formative Years*, pp. 92, 97, 103; Weaver, *Crisis in Social Security*, p. 112; Derthick, *Policymaking*, pp. 90–91.

[46] Sources for the 1949–50 extension are Wilbur J. Cohen and Robert J. Myers, "Social Security Act Amendments of 1950: A Summary and Legislative History," *Social Security Bulletin* 13, no. 10 (October 1950): 2–3, 5; *New York Times*, March 4, 1949, January 2, 1950, January 10, 1950, January 14, 1950, January 15, 1950, May 18, 1950, July 16, 1950; U.S. Congress, House Committee on Ways and Means, *Social Security Amendments of 1949*, 81st Cong., 1st sess., pp. 288–93, 1085, 1469–84, 1857–78; U.S. Congress, Senate Committee on Finance, *Social Security Revision*, 81st Cong., 2d sess., pp. 176–93, 195–256, 313–43, 771–75; Altmeyer, *Formative Years*, pp. 182–85; Derthick, *Policymaking*, pp. 91–92, 264; Weaver, *Crisis in Social Security*, pp. 132–34.

[47] House, *Social Security Amendments of 1949*, pp. 291–92.

assistance, for which they paid half, with insurance, for which they paid nothing. From the perspective of the Social Security Administration, extension would ease demands for the expansion of relief. President Truman took up this theme in his 1950 address to Congress, saying that "because the protection of social insurance is so limited, far too many people have been forced to seek public relief," and that his proposals would "gradually reduce the need for public assistance."[48] Doughton, still chairman of the House Ways and Means Committee, remained skeptical of farmers' desire to be included, but the Senate Finance Committee introduced a provision for inclusion of "regularly employed" agricultural workers, and the Senate position was accepted by the conference committee. Regular employment was defined as work for a single employer for one quarter and then for sixty full days in the following quarter; only about 21 percent of farm workers met this requirement for coverage. Farm operators, sharecroppers, and tenants also remained outside the social security system. Overall, the 1950 amendments expanded old-age insurance coverage from 55 percent to 70 percent of the American labor force.

A third advisory board, set up in 1953, followed its predecessors in endorsing the preferences of the Social Security administrators, including expansion of old-age insurance coverage. In 1954, the Eisenhower administration rejected proposals by the U.S. Chamber of Commerce for a conservative flat-plan pension to replace old-age insurance; instead, it endorsed the extension of contributory insurance to additional farm workers, along with farm operators and other self-employed groups.[49] Roswell B. Perkins, assistant secretary of Health, Education, and Welfare, reported that difficulties with the payroll tax had been solved. The AFBF expressed weak opposition to inclusion; the Grange, the liberal Farmers' Union, and the National Milk Producing Federation expressed support. Department of Agriculture officials presented survey results showing that farmers did not have adequate provision for old age, and that they approved of the social security program. A Republican Congress approved mandatory participation for farm operators. Writing in the *Social Security Bulletin*, James E. Marquis explained their inclusion by noting the

[48] *New York Times*, January 10, 1950.

[49] Sources for the 1954 extension are James E. Marquis, "Old-Age and Survivors Insurance Coverage under the 1954 Amendments," *Social Security Bulletin* 18, no. 1 (January 1955): 4–6; *New York Times*, January 4, 1954, January 8, 1854, January 15, 1954, July 9, 1954, August 21, 1954; U.S. Congress, House Committee on Ways and Means, *Social Security Act Amendments of 1954*, 83d Cong., 2d sess., pp. 41, 46–52, 195–223; U.S. Congress, Senate Committee on Finance, *Social Security Amendments of 1954*, 83d Cong., 2d sess., pp. 554–59; Cates, *Insuring Inequality*, pp. 79–82; Derthick, *Policymaking*, pp. 92–93, 264; Altmeyer, *Formative Years*, pp. 216–17, 240–48; Weaver, *Crisis in Social Security*, pp. 135–37.

growing cost of noncontributory old-age assistance in rural areas and farmers' increasingly favorable view of the program, as shown in surveys and in their communications with the Social Security Administration. The Senate, following the recommendations of the Social Security Administration and President Eisenhower, had recommended that 2.6 million farm workers be brought in, while the House extended coverage to only 1.3 million. A conference committee compromise covered 2.1 million additional farm workers. Under the new test, farm workers qualified if they received at least one hundred dollars in cash wages from a single employer in the year. This test increased the proportion of farm workers covered to 85 percent. While other employers were required to report quarterly, farm employers were permitted to report annually in order to simplify record keeping and to avoid interference with planting or harvesting. With extension of old-age insurance coverage to farm operators, farm workers, and other new groups, 90 percent of the labor force was now included in the program.

In sum, by 1954, the extension of social security benefits to agriculture, rejected in 1935 as administratively unfeasible and politically impractical, had been accepted without major controversy. Inclusion of agriculture reflected the rapid development of administrative capacities for politically adroit program expansion around the insurance program. Officials trained in the University of Wisconsin–social insurance network had solved the problems of implementing social insurance in agriculture. They had convinced farmers, along with advisory bodies and key congressional committees, to accept their insurance imagery as reality.[50] And they had redefined economic security issues as technical questions within an accepted program structure. Thus, they could persuade Congress to rewrite the Social Security Act to fit their goal of universal old-age insurance coverage and block the threatened expansion of noncontributory public assistance. Republicans and Southern Democrats went along with the new amendments, noting that extension of national social insurance was less costly to their states in the 1950s than total reliance on federal old-age assistance would have been.

Food Stamps: Farm Subsidy or
Welfare Program?

Thus far we have analyzed the impact of agricultural politics on policymaking for America's core national social insurance program—contributory old-age insurance under the social security system. The exam-

---

[50] The manufacturing of the "insurance" myth is discussed in Cates, *Insuring Inequality*, pp. 31–34, and Weaver, *Crisis in Social Security*, pp. 123–24.

ples of commodity distribution and food stamps, to which we can now turn, reveal agricultural impacts on "welfare," those parts of U.S. social provision devoted to noncontributory assistance for the poor.

Commodity distribution and food stamps are programs that first developed during the New Deal in response to agricultural problems, but they have become important components of the package of benefits the federal government gives the poor. Each of these alternative programs has combined the logic of a farm subsidy with that of a welfare program. The exact mix has been determined by the Department of Agriculture and the House Agriculture Committee. Historically, commodity distributions have increased in times of greatest need, but the commodities distributed have been those farmers have overproduced. As for food stamps, the original New Deal program never made the transition to a welfare program, and it died when its agricultural rationale disappeared. The contemporary food stamps program, established in 1961 and expanded greatly in the 1970s, bore the legacy of the first but gradually did become a major welfare program, the closest the United States has to a national program of income supplements. Unlike other American welfare programs, however, it remains within the jurisdiction of an often unsympathetic agricultural policy system.

Federal commodity distribution began in 1933 with the organization of the Federal Surplus Relief Corporation (FSRC) as an independent corporation under the authority of a combination of recent statutes.[51] Creation of the FSRC followed widespread criticism of the AAA's wasteful and inhumane slaughter of over 6 million baby pigs to reduce pork supplies. Use of surpluses for food relief thus helped to legitimize a farm program whose success would be costly to urban consumers. The purposes of the FSRC were specified as unemployment relief and marketing of surplus commodities. With Section 32 of the 1935 amendments to the Agricultural Adjustment Act, the FSRC became the Federal Surplus Commodities Corporation (FSCC), located within the Department of Agriculture; its purpose was stated in more exclusively agricultural terms than before, and competing goals were subordinated to producers' need for surplus removal. By 1938, the FSCC was distributing over 54 million dollars worth of food. Section 32 distributions of varying size and covering var-

---

[51] The politics of commodity distribution under the FSRC and FSCC are discussed extensively in Poppendieck, *Breadlines*, chaps. 6–12. The next two paragraphs draw on her book and on U.S. Congress, House Committee on Agriculture, *Food Stamp Act of 1976*, 94th Cong., 2d sess., pp. 390–94; Jeffrey M. Berry, *Feeding Hungry People* (New Brunswick, N.J.: Rutgers University Press, 1984), pp. 21, 24, 150–51; Willard W. Cochrane and Mary E. Ryan, *American Farm Policy, 1948–1973* (Minneapolis: University of Minnesota Press, 1976), pp. 281–83; and Kenneth Finegold and Richard M. Valelly, "Reagan 'PIKS' a Farm Program," *Nation* (February 5, 1983): 141.

ious commodities continued until 1974, when all communities began instead to receive food stamps as aid. Under the Reagan administration, however, huge dairy surpluses have led to the distribution, in 1982 alone, of 150 million pounds of cheese and 50 million pounds of butter.

Commodity programs have been criticized since their inception, as welfare workers and others have pointed to the stigmatizing lines for aid and the limited nutritional benefits of a group of foods chosen only for economic reasons. In 1960, for example, recipients were given only lard, rice, flour, butter, and cheese. Commodity distribution has also been criticized by producers, who complain about the pricing and timing of government purchases, and by grocers, who dislike government competition.

The inadequacies of commodity distribution led to the first food stamps program, which was launched in 1939, when surpluses were high and export markets were threatened by war.[52] Among the officials credited with originating the program were Secretary Wallace; Fred Waugh, an economist on Wallace's staff; Louis H. Bean of the Bureau of Agricultural Economics; Milo Perkins of the FSCC; E. F. Bartelt of the Treasury Department; and Carlyle Thorp of the California Walnut Grower's Association. The confusion over who thought of food stamps first, and the reluctance of anyone to claim authorship, provides striking evidence of the unusual administrative capacity and shared orientations within the Department of Agriculture and among those who worked closely with it.[53] Like commodity distribution, food stamps were administratively authorized under a variety of preexisting statutes without explicit congressional approval. As the new head of the FSCC, Perkins was responsible for implementing and publicizing the food stamps program.

The 1939 food stamps program represented a partial alternative to commodity distribution, yet it retained its connection to the surplus problem. Relief recipients in cities covered by the experimental projects could buy orange stamps for the amount of their average food expenditures. These stamps could be used for any foods. For each dollar of orange stamps purchased, the buyer received fifty cents worth of blue stamps. Blue stamps, however, could be used only to buy surplus foods designated by the secretary of Agriculture. The initial list was butter, eggs, flour, cornmeal, oranges, grapefruit, prunes, and dried beans. As Jeffrey Berry points out, "Everything purchased with the blue stamps would represent additional buying and, therefore, additional demand for farm goods."[54]

Despite complaints about cheating by grocers and recipients, the early

[52] Poppendieck, *Breadlines*, pp. 240–41.

[53] House, *Food Stamp Act of 1976*, pp. 394–95; Berry, *Feeding Hungry People*, pp. 21–22. Poppendieck reports similar ambiguity about the origins of the FSRC: Poppendieck, *Breadlines*, pp. 125–26.

[54] Berry, *Feeding Hungry People*, p. 22; House, *Food Stamp Act of 1976*, pp. 395–404.

U.S. food stamps program was popular among both groups and with the general public. In a November 1938 Gallup poll, 70 percent of those with opinions approved of the plan. By 1943, food stamps were distributed in counties encompassing two-thirds of the population of the United States, and as many as four million individuals were participating. Both of the program's aims were being achieved: nutrition was improved and surpluses were reduced. In 1940, both the Democratic and Republican platforms indicated support for the program.[55]

Food stamps did not survive World War II, however. The initial effect of the war was to expand the program: as export markets collapsed, more surplus commodities were available for purchase with blue stamps. But after American entry into the war, food shortages replaced surpluses and the program lost its agricultural rationale. Hunger remained evident; indeed, the rise in food prices due to wartime demand made it more difficult for poor people to obtain an adequate diet. Yet in December 1942, Secretary of Agriculture Claude Wickard announced that the program would end the following spring. Though the food stamps program had been a success and might be resumed in the future, Wickard said, the food surpluses and widespread unemployment that had made it necessary no longer existed.[56]

For the next nineteen years, members of Congress sought to revive food stamps. These attempts were opposed by Southern Democrats, who led and were over-represented on the House Agriculture Committee.[57] Food stamps, like contributory social insurrance, threatened Southern planters' paternalistic control of their labor force. A subsidy to food consumption, moreover, would not directly benefit Southern producers of cotton or tobacco. Conservative agriculture's opposition to food stamps, however, could be blunted by its dependence on trade-offs with liberals over farm aid.

After the end of the New Deal food stamps program, Senators Robert La Follette (Wisconsin) and George Aiken (Vermont) introduced the first of several bills that would authorize a replacement program. Their measure was justified in nutritional terms and was not tied to surpluses of specific commodities. The La Follette-Aiken bill was backed by evidence from the Bureau of Agricultural Economics indicating widespread mal-

[55] Berry, *Feeding Hungry People*, p. 22; House, *Food Stamp Act of 1976*, pp. 404–10, 412–18, 421–27.

[56] Ibid., pp. 411–12, 418–20.

[57] Charles O. Jones, "Representation in Congress: The Case of the House Agriculture Committee," in Robert L. Peabody and Nelson W. Polsby, eds., *New Perspectives on the House of Representatives*, 2d ed. (Chicago: Rand McNally, 1969), p. 157; John C. Peters, "The 1981 Farm Bill," in Don F. Hadwiger and Ross B. Talbott, eds., *Food Policy and Farm Programs, Proceedings of the Academy of Political Science* 34, no. 3 (1983): 160.

nutrition. Nevertheless, it was defeated in 1944 by a 29–46 vote. Southern Democrats voted 16–4 against the measure; non–Southern Democrats opposed it by 19–13, while Republicans split 11–11. No action was taken on later bills along the same lines.[58]

During the 1950s, food stamps became more clearly a cause for urban liberals as well as for farm-state members of Congress. In 1954, for example, twelve representatives introduced thirteen food stamp bills in the House. Six of these sponsors were non–Southern Democrats; the other six were Republicans.[59] Leonor Sullivan, a St. Louis Democrat, became the House's main food stamps advocate. In hopes of winning congressional approval, Representative Sullivan limited her proposal to specific, semi-perishable commodities. Though not a member of the Agriculture Committee, Sullivan convinced its chairman, Harold Cooley, a North Carolina Democrat, to allow hearings in 1955 and to amend the 1956 farm bill to require a report on food stamps by the secretary of Agriculture. Sullivan's efforts were backed by organized labor and social welfare agencies; a 1956 Senate food stamps bill won support from the Farmers' Union as well. But food stamps were opposed by the AFBF and, as was clear from its report, by the Department of Agriculture under Secretary Ezra Taft Benson. Nutritional needs, the department argued, were being met by commodity distribution, which was also a more effective way to dispose of surpluses. Food stamps would be "costly" and unnecessary.[60]

In 1958, Representative Sullivan finally got a food stamps bill out of the House by threatening that she would personally vote against any agricultural subsidy legislation that required unanimous consent to get to the floor. Sullivan's bill received a majority of the vote, but not the two-thirds needed for passage on suspension of the rules. The vote followed party lines, but a higher percentage of rural (mostly Southern) Democrats than of urban or suburban party members opposed the bill. In 1959, the Senate passed a bill actually creating a program. In the House, Sullivan was able to attach an amendment—authorizing the secretary of Agriculture to establish a food stamps program at his discretion—to legislation extending the PL 480 program for foreign sale of surplus commodities.

[58] The vote is given in U.S. Congress, Senate, *Congressional Record*, 78th Cong., 2d sess., 1944, 90, pt. 2:1613. The additional vote for the bill was cast by La Follette, a Progressive. One Southern Democrat and four Republicans were absent but announced against. La Follette and Aiken's food stamp efforts are traced in House, *Food Stamp Act of 1976*, 428–45.

[59] The bills are listed in House, *Food Stamp Act of 1976*, p. 445. Samuel Yorty, then a liberal Democrat from Los Angeles, sponsored two food stamp bills.

[60] Ibid., pp. 455–71; Berry, *Feeding Hungry People*, p. 23; Randall B. Ripley, "Legislative Bargaining and the Food Stamp Act, 1964," in Frederic N. Cleaveland, ed., *Congress and Urban Problems* (Washington: The Brookings Institution, 1969), pp. 282–83; Marjorie L. DeVault and James P. Pitts, "Surplus and Scarcity: Hunger and the Origins of the Food Stamp Program," *Social Problems* 31, no. 5 (June 1984): 546–47.

The conference committee accepted the House's non-mandatory language, but Secretary Benson then refused to use his new authority.[61] Thus, in the 1950s, urban-liberal advocates of food stamps could not quite circumvent farm bloc resistance.

A new, experimental food stamps program was finally established immediately after the inauguration of John F. Kennedy, who had introduced a food stamps bill while in the Senate. On January 21, 1961, Kennedy directed Secretary of Agriculture Orville Freeman to "expand and improve" commodity distribution. On February 2, Kennedy told Congress he was directing Freeman to establish pilot food stamps projects.[62] Because the 1959 legislation was about to expire, the administration went back to Section 32 of the 1935 amendments to the Agricultural Adjustment Act for authorization. Neither Secretary Freeman nor Representative Sullivan had much influence on the details of the new program. It was designed instead by three members of the Department of Agriculture staff: Howard Davis, Sam Vanneman, and Isabelle Kelley. Davis, the head of the Food Distribution Division, and Vanneman were both veterans of the first food stamps program. Kelley had joined the department during World War II after graduate study in agricultural economics. These three members of the USDA–land-grant college nexus dominated the new food stamps program in its early years.

From his experience with the old two-color food stamps program, Davis concluded that a program based on a single coupon would be less cumbersome. Instead of specifying commodities for which stamps could be used, the new program stated which commodities could *not* be bought with food stamps. These included tobacco, alcohol, coffee, tea, cocoa, and bananas. As Davis explained, "This aspect of the present program represented a basic shift in emphasis from the attempt, under the old Stamp Plan, [to] move specific 'surpluses,' to one of generally increasing the consumption of perishables."[63]

Although the relevance of food stamps to agriculture was interpreted more loosely in the 1960s than in the 1930s, it was still not a true welfare program. Recipients had to pay an amount equal to the average monthly food expenditure for their income level. They received stamps for the value of their payment, plus bonus stamps whose value decreased as income increased. (Table 5.1 gives the average number of monthly participants, the total federal contribution, and the federal [bonus] share of the

[61] House, *Food Stamp Act of 1976*, pp. 471–80; Ripley, "Legislative Bargaining," pp. 284–88; Berry, *Feeding Hungry People*, pp. 23–24.

[62] The next three paragraphs draw on House, *Food Stamp Act of 1976*, pp. 481–95; Berry, *Feeding Hungry People*, pp. 24–33, 37–42; and Ripley, "Legislative Bargaining," pp. 287–91.

[63] House, *Food Stamp Act of 1976*, p. 482.

TABLE 5.1 Growth of the Federal Food Stamps Program

Year[a]	Average Number of Monthly Participants (thousands)	Federal Contribution (millions of dollars)	Federal Share of Coupon Value (percent)
1961	49.6	0.4	46.1
1962	142.8	13.2	37.4
1963	225.6	18.6	37.4
1964	366.8	28.6	38.8
1965	424.7	32.5	38.0
1966	864.3	64.8	37.2
1967	1,447.1	105.6	35.6
1968	2,211.5	173.1	38.3
1969	2,878.8	228.8	37.9
1970	4,340.5	549.7	50.4
1971	9,368.0	1,523.0	56.1
1972	11,109.0	1,797.0	54.3
1973	12,166.0	2,131.0	54.9
1974	12,862.0	2,718.0	57.5
1975	17,064.0	4,386.0	60.4
1976	18,549.0	5,327.0	61.2
1977	17,077.0	5,067.0	60.7
1978	16,000.0	5,139.0	62.1
1979	17,652.0	6,478.0	89.7
1980	21,087.0	8,690.0	100.0
1981	22,431.0	10,630.0	100.0
1982	21,717.0	10,209.0	100.0
1983	21,630.0	11,155.0	100.0
1984	20,853.6	11,500.8	100.0
1985	19,899.1	11,624.1	100.0
1986[b]	19,431.5	11,524.8	100.0

SOURCES: United States Department of Agriculture, *Agricultural Statistics, 1971* (Washington, D.C.: Government Printing Office, 1971), p. 591; United States Department of Commerce, Bureau of the Census, *Statistical Abstract of the United States: 1986* (Washington, D.C.: Government Printing Office, 1985), p. 123; United States Department of Agriculture, Food and Nutrition Service.

[a] 1961–76 data for fiscal year ending June 30. 1977–80 data for fiscal year ending September 30. 1975–82 data includes Puerto Rico. 1975–86 data includes Guam and the Virgin Islands.

[b] Preliminary data.

total coupon value for each year of the food stamps program begun in 1961.) This purchase requirement fit Davis, Vanneman, and Kelley's conception of the program, as well as their sense of what Congress would accept, for it ensured that food stamps would boost agricultural demand. But as the pilot projects showed, even a low purchase requirement might be a significant barrier to poor people who could not raise the funds necessary for a month's expenses in advance. For this reason, pilot programs in Cleveland and St. Louis had disappointingly low participation rates, particularly when compared with commodity distribution drives. But Davis, Vanneman, and Kelley insisted the purchase requirement was necessary, and they prevented some projects from reducing the requirement to zero for their poorest recipients. After criticism by Representative Sullivan and welfare workers, the Department of Agriculture administrators did allow recipients to deduct high rents, day-care expenses, and emergency costs from the income used to determine purchase requirements and bonus amounts.[64]

To fully establish the food stamps program beyond the pilot areas, the Kennedy administration proposed a new food stamps bill developed in the Department of Agriculture under Davis's supervision. Southern Democratic support was obtained by combining logrolling with a major concession on the program itself. The concession was that food stamps would be optional: states and counties could continue to sponsor commodity distribution drives instead. (Counties could not offer both programs.) Conservative Southern governments could thus choose the program better suited to their needs. Logrolling began after the House Agriculture Committee tabled the bill in February 1964; liberals forced reconsideration by blocking a rule on a tobacco research program of special interest to Congressman Cooley, the committee chairman. The food stamps bill was reported by an 18–16 vote, though the committee approved an amendment by Albert Quie, a Minnesota Republican, requiring state participation and matching funds, as was the case with such welfare programs as Aid to Families with Dependent Children (AFDC). Then, to obtain approval on the House floor, advocates of food stamps had to link their bill to the pending wheat-cotton subsidy measure. Though no formal trading took place, a widespread perception that the bills were connected developed among members and was spread by the press. The food stamps bill was approved by the House, and the Quie amendment was rejected. The final vote followed party lines: a lower percentage of rural Democrats than of urban or suburban Democrats sup-

---

[64] Sullivan thought the existing purchase requirement was too high, but she believed a minimum requirement was necessary for the dignity of the recipients: Berry, *Feeding Hungry People*, p. 55.

ported food stamps, but, significantly, the gap was less than it had been in 1958. The Food Stamp Act of 1964 was signed by President Johnson in August. As Berry observes, it "legitimized and ratified the administrative guidelines already in effect."[65]

During the remainder of the Johnson administration, hunger was rediscovered as a problem. Urban liberals, led by Senators Robert Kennedy of New York and Joseph Clark of Pennsylvania, tried to reduce food stamps purchase prices and to expand the program to more counties, but their efforts were defeated by, among others, W. R. Poage (Texas), chairman of the House Agriculture Committee; Jamie Whitten (Mississippi), chairman of the House Appropriations Subcommittee on Agriculture; and Allen Ellender (Louisiana), chairman of the Senate Agriculture Committee. In 1966, Representative Sullivan did gain Poage's support for a two-year extension of the food stamps program in return for her cooperation on a peanut subsidy measure, but Sullivan's bill did not include reforms in the food stamps program.[66]

In the 1970s, however, participation, federal costs, and the federal share of the coupon value all increased (see Table 5.1), and the agricultural basis of the food stamps program was challenged. The transformation of food stamps into a large, welfare-oriented program reflected changes in Congress and in the Department of Agriculture. In 1968, the Senate established its Select Committee on Nutrition and Human Needs, chaired by George McGovern of South Dakota, and McGovern became the Senate's leading advocate of food aid after the death of Kennedy and the defeat of Clark.[67] In 1975, Poage became one of three long-time chairmen to lose his position as the Democratic Caucus rebelled against the seniority system; he was replaced by Thomas Foley of Washington. The Ninety-fifth Congress also expanded the House Agriculture Committee from thirty-five members to forty-five. Both these changes shifted power on the committee from Southerners to representatives of the West and Midwest. Farm operators in these regions traditionally have relied more on family labor or cash wages, and less on in-kind paternalistic labor systems, than Southern farmers. Hence they were less threatened by food stamps. Furthermore, while food stamps could not directly stimulate sales of Southern cotton and tobacco, they could increase consumption of the

[65] Berry, *Feeding Hungry People*, pp. 33–35 (quote, p. 35); Ripley, "Legislative Bargaining," pp. 291–310; House, *Food Stamp Act of 1976*, p. 495; DeVault and Pitts, "Surplus and Scarcity," p. 548; Maurice MacDonald, "Food Stamps: An Analytical History," *Social Service Review* 51, no. 4 (December 1977): 648.

[66] Nick Kotz, *Let Them Eat Promises: The Politics of Hunger in America* (Englewood Cliffs, N.J.: Prentice-Hall, 1969), pp. 68–69, 84–102; Berry, *Feeding Hungry People*, pp. 48–49.

[67] Berry, *Feeding Hungry People*, pp. 49–50.

Midwest's key crops, wheat and corn. Moreover, the House Agriculture Committee included, from 1975 until his resignation in 1982, Frederick Richmond, a Democrat from a poor Brooklyn district, who became an effective advocate of and bargainer on agricultural issues. In 1977, Richmond was made chairman of the House Domestic Marketing, Consumer Relations, and Nutrition Subcommittee, responsible for food stamps legislation. The House Agriculture Committee remained commodity-oriented and conservative, but it was more sympathetic to food stamps than it had been when chaired by Congressmen Cooley and Poage.[68]

Within the Department of Agriculture, the first important series of changes came as Davis, Vanneman, and Kelley retired. By 1973, all three had been replaced by administrators whose views had not been shaped by the two-color food stamps program, and who were thus less committed to maintaining a high purchase price.[69] In 1977, Jimmy Carter selected Bob Bergland as secretary of Agriculture. As a Minnesota congressman, Bergland had sought to abolish the food stamps purchase requirement. In his new capacity, he appointed public interest group activists to positions in which they could make food stamps policy, bringing the "hunger lobby" inside the Department of Agriculture for the first time.[70]

During the 1970s, then, both representative and administrative arrangements had undergone changes with important implications for the food stamps program. The food stamps program itself was transformed in three major steps. In 1969, the Senate passed a food stamps bill increasing allotments to the level of the Department of Agriculture's economy diet plan, but in the House, Poage bottled up the bill so that he could use it to trade on the next year's farm bill. Nonetheless, Secretary of Agriculture Clifford Hardin increased the allotments by administrative regulation. Hardin also reduced the purchase price for most recipients. The new rules were announced as President Nixon prepared to address a highly publicized White House conference on Food, Nutrition, and Health. From fiscal 1969 to fiscal 1970, participation increased 50.8 percent, fed-

---

[68] Roger H. Davidson and Walter J. Oleszek, *Congress and Its Members*, 2d ed. (Washington, D.C.: CQ Press, 1985), p. 221; Peters, "1981 Farm Bill," p. 160; Alston and Ferrie, "Resisting the Welfare State," pp. 85–90; Michael Barone, Grant Ujifusa, and Douglas Matthews, *Almanac of American Politics 1980* (New York: Dutton, 1979), pp. 606, 977.

During the 1950s, Victor Anfuso played a role on the House Agriculture Committee similar to Richmond's. But Shirley Chisholm, who, like Anfuso and Richmond, was from a poor Brooklyn district, demanded to be (and was) shifted from Agriculture to Veterans' Affairs, later saying, "There are a lot more veterans in my district than trees": Jones, "House Agriculture Committee," pp. 158, 160; Davidson and Oleszek, *Congress and Its Members*, p. 215 (Chisholm quote).

[69] Berry, *Feeding Hungry People*, pp. 69–70, 78.

[70] Ibid., pp. 90–94, 127–36.

eral spending increased 140.3 percent, and the federal share of coupon values jumped from 37.9 to 50.4 percent (Table 5.1). In 1970, Congress amended the Food Stamp Act of 1964 to incorporate Hardin's reforms. The 1970 amendments also authorized the first free stamps—for families with incomes under thirty dollars per month—and set national eligibility standards. The amendments included work registration requirements introduced by Congressman Poage, but the Department of Agriculture did little to implement these. From fiscal 1970 to fiscal 1971, federal spending on food stamps nearly tripled (Table 5.1).[71]

The next step in the expansion of food stamps was passage of the Agriculture and Consumer Protection Act of 1973, which made the program nationally available by withdrawing from local governments the option to offer commodity distribution instead. The 1973 act was an omnibus farm measure; logrolling between advocates of food stamps and commodity subsidies occurred within the framework of the bill. Extension of the food stamps program has also been interpreted as a response to the failure of Nixon's Family Assistance Plan (FAP) proposal. Since an increasing proportion of their costs were being borne by the federal government, food stamps had become the second-best alternative to a politically unfeasible negative income tax.[72]

The increased federal share of the coupon value also reduced the effectiveness of food stamps as a subsidy to agricultural producers. The purchase requirement ensured that recipients would increase their food consumption above what it would have been in the absence of a food stamps program. As the purchase requirement was eroded, recipients could use a greater proportion of the bonus stamps to substitute for their ordinary food expenditures, freeing up more income for non-food purchases. Department of Agriculture economists estimated that, in the mid-1970s, the food stamps program produced a net increase in retail food purchases of 2 billion dollars, less than 1 percent of total personal food consumption. Receipts in the agriculture, forestry, and fisheries sector were estimated to have increased by 408 million dollars; food manufacturing and wholesale and retail trade received greater increases from the program.[73]

[71] Ibid., pp. 62–64, 68–74; DeVault and Pitts, "Surplus and Scarcity," p. 554; MacDonald, "Food Stamps," p. 649.

[72] Mary Weaver, "The Food Stamp Program: A Very Expensive Orphan," in Anthony Champagne and Edward J. Harpham, eds., *The Attack on the Welfare State* (Prospect Heights, Ill.: Waveland, 1984), pp. 118–19; MacDonald, "Food Stamps," pp. 650–51; DeVault and Pitts, "Surplus and Scarcity," p. 555. MacDonald and DeVault and Pitts draw the connections between the 1973 legislation and the earlier failure of FAP.

[73] William T. Boehm and Paul E. Nelson, "Current Economic Research on Food Stamp Use," USDA Economics, Statistics and Cooperative Service, Washington, D.C., September 1978, p. 3; Paul E. Nelson, Jr., and John Perrin, "Effects of the U.S. Food Stamp and Na-

Food stamps was further transformed from an agricultural subsidy to a welfare program with the abolition of the purchase requirement in 1977. In 1976, Senator McGovern and Senator Robert Dole, a Kansas Republican, sponsored a bill to eliminate the requirement, but it was opposed by Senator Herman Talmadge of Georgia, chairman of the Senate Agriculture, Nutrition, and Forestry Committee, and the Dole-McGovern bill was defeated by the committee's tie vote. 1977 proved to be a more favorable year for food stamps reform. First, President Gerald Ford, who had been hostile to the program, was replaced by Jimmy Carter, who supported it. Carter's Secretary of Agriculture, Bob Bergland, worked to eliminate the purchase requirement. Second, in 1977, as in 1973, farm subsidies were up for renewal. Reform of food stamps again became part of an omnibus farm bill, allowing considerable logrolling to take place in the House. Trades between urban and rural Democrats were put together by Congressman Richmond, whose subcommittee wrote the food stamps bill that was then joined with the farm bill. Rural members endorsed abolition of the purchase requirement; Richmond convinced urban members to support subsidy legislation, including sugar subsidies the Carter administration opposed. Richmond's logrolling also helped to defeat hostile amendments to prevent food stamps from being issued to strikers or from being used to buy "junk" foods. Representative Dawson Mathis, a Democrat from a peanut-producing Georgia district, withdrew his sponsorship of a work requirement amendment after Richmond helped to narrowly defeat a threat to cut the peanut subsidy. As chairman of the House Agriculture Committee, Congressman Foley served as floor manager for the omnibus bill and won support from both urban and rural Democrats. In the Senate, a similar food stamps measure, sponsored again by Senators Dole and McGovern, was approved over Senator Talmadge's opposition.[74]

Abolition of the purchase requirement was a less important influence on participation in the food stamps program than the liberalization of benefits in 1970, the nationalization of coverage in 1973, or the recession of 1975–76.[75] As Table 5.1 shows, the 1977 legislation did increase the

---

tional School Lunch Programs, Fiscal Year 1974," *American Journal of Agricultural Economics* 58, no. 5 (December 1976): 1001–2.

[74] Berry, *Feeding Hungry People*, pp. 94–95; John G. Peters, "The 1977 Farm Bill: Coalitions in Congress," in Don F. Hadwiger and William P. Browne, eds., *The New Politics of Food* (Lexington, Mass.: Lexington Books, 1978), pp. 24–25, 31–33; Linda E. Demkovich, "The 'Odd Couple' Is Whipping Up A New Dish on Food Stamps," *National Journal* (March 19, 1977): 428–29; *Congressional Quarterly*, May 28, 1977, "Senate Votes Food Stamp Overhaul," pp. 1037–39; *Congressional Quarterly*, July 30, 1977, "House Votes Free Food Stamps for Poor," pp. 1565–66.

[75] See Table 5.1 and MacDonald, "Food Stamps," pp. 651–55; Boehm and Nelson, "Current Economic Research," p. 1.

total federal cost of the program. The end of the purchase requirement also further weakened the economic stimulus food stamps provided to farm producers. The Congressional Budget Office estimated that net food consumption would decrease by one billion dollars. Republican opponents of the change, led by Congressman Steven Symms (Idaho) and Senator Carl Curtis (Nebraska) emphasized the extent to which it would shift expenditures away from food. "Whichever way it is calculated," House Republicans wrote in a dissenting statement, "it is obvious that farm income is going to suffer badly because of the provisions of this bill."[76] Abolition of the purchase requirement, however, disproportionately benefited the Southern states, with higher poverty levels and lower AFDC payments.[77]

During the 1980s, the political environment has been less friendly to food stamps. The Senate Nutrition Committee was abolished in a 1977 reorganization. Republican control of the Senate in 1980 made Jesse Helms of North Carolina, a bitter enemy of the program, chairman of the Agriculture Committee. The 1980 election also saw the defeat of Senator McGovern. In 1982, Congressman Richmond resigned amid scandal. Reagan's skillful use of the budget reconciliation process made urban-rural logrolling difficult, as every interest sought to prevent its programs from being cut to meet the overall budget goals. Under Secretary of Agriculture John Block, the Department of Agriculture was less permeable to hunger and consumer activists. Food stamps became a special target in the 1981 budget cuts. Authorized spending was reduced for the first time in the program's history, and several program changes reduced either participation or benefits. Estimates suggest that without the 1981 cuts, one million more each year would have participated, and annual spending would have been two billion dollars higher.[78] The period of food stamps growth has ended: despite continued high unemployment, participation and federal contributions have remained steady during the Reagan years (see Table 5.1).

During the last two decades, both supporters and opponents have come

[76] U.S. Congress, House, 95th Cong., 1st sess., Report No. 95–464, "Food Stamp Act of 1977," pp. 433–34, 852 (quote); Congressional Quarterly, "Senate Votes Food Stamp Overhaul," p. 1039; Congressional Quarterly, "House Votes Free Food Stamps for Poor," p. 1566.

[77] Since AFDC payments are counted as income in calculating stamp values, states with low grant levels receive more food stamp money: Robert B. Albritton, "Subsidies: Welfare and Transportation," in Virginia Gray, Herbert Jacob, and Kenneth N. Vines, eds., Politics in the American States: A Comparative Analysis, 4th ed. (Boston: Little, Brown, 1983), pp. 382–83, 391–95; Patricia Faulkinberry, "Federal Food Dollars Go South," Economic Review (Federal Reserve Bank of Atlanta) 62 (November/December 1977), pp. 137–39.

[78] Berry, Feeding Hungry People, pp. 50, 97–99, 149–52; Weaver, "Food Stamp Program," pp. 124–28.

to see food stamps as a "welfare" program; the abolition of the purchase requirement reflected the acceptance of a welfare rationale in place of the original function of commodity surplus reduction. In the late 1960s and 1970s, the "welfare" rubric was one under which a temporary liberal alliance could greatly expand food stamps. Under the Reagan administration, in contrast, it has rendered food stamps, along with other measures aimed at the poor alone, vulnerable to spending cutbacks.

In the final analysis, though, food stamps remains a welfare program whose politics, administration, and very existence continue to betoken its origin as a farm subsidy. Within Congress, food stamps policy is still set by the agriculture committees. The House and Senate Agriculture Committees are dominated by representatives of agricultural constituencies, who are indifferent or hostile toward food stamps. The result is a peculiar system of unequal bargaining. Food stamps programs, which benefit farm producers and urban consumers at the same time, are traded for subsidy programs that raise commodity prices, benefiting farm producers at the expense of urban consumers.[79]

Not only have food stamps remained under the jurisdiction of congressional agricultural committees, but also they continue to be administered by the Department of Agriculture. In the early years of the Kennedy program, this meant that food stamps were shaped by agricultural experts influenced more by their recollections of the earlier two-color program than by the arguments of social welfare advocates or the experiences of the poor. Bob Bergland, secretary of Agriculture under Jimmy Carter, supported food stamps and brought members of the hunger policy network into the department to run the program; his support was essential to the abolition of the purchase requirement. But hostile secretaries of Agriculture like Earl Butz and John Block have tried to use their regulatory powers to restrict access to benefits.[80] Ironically, opponents of the program, fearing that the costs of food stamps would be "charged" against farmers and would lead to cuts in subsidies, had always argued that it was really a welfare program that belonged in Health, Education, and Welfare. As Harold Cooley said, "we do not want to put the Secretary of Agriculture in the relief business."[81]

Most significantly, that the United States has a food stamps program at all reflects the politics of agricultural policy. Both food stamps programs

[79] The cost of farm subsidies to urban consumers is discussed in Orren, "Liberalism," p. 186.

[80] On Butz, see Berry, *Feeding Hungry People*, pp. 80–90.

[81] House, *Food Stamp Act of 1976*, pp. 447 (Cooley quote), 478; Ripley, "Legislative Bargaining," pp. 295, 303; Berry, *Feeding Hungry People*, p. 81; Don Paarlberg, *Farm and Food Policy: Issues of the 1980s* (Lincoln: University of Nebraska Press, 1980), pp. 114–15.

were established at least in part because of large farm surpluses. These surpluses became major national problems for a Democratic party in which rural Southerners were particularly powerful, and for a Congress that allowed agricultural policy to be made by representatives of agricultural constituencies. As a result, an American can receive a subsidy for food just because he or she is poor. To qualify, poor people do not need to be old, disabled, veterans, or parents, as they do in other welfare programs. A brief contrast highlights how unusual the food stamps program is: In recent years, automobile manufacturers have required federal subsidy just as farmers have, and poor people need transportation as well as food. One economist has estimated that subsidies to automobile ownership and operation by the poor would be more effective and less expensive than further development of mass transit. Yet "automobile stamps," unlike food stamps, remain politically unthinkable.[82] The special leverage enjoyed by American agricultural interests since the New Deal—leverage through the Department of Agriculture, Congress, and the Democratic party—has established a federal commitment to meeting at least one basic need for *all* of America's low-income people.

Conclusions

We can appreciate the influence of agricultural interests on American social provision by considering how the absence of a politically important agricultural sector might have altered the development of the old-age insurance and food stamps programs. Old-age insurance might have been enacted on a universal basis, since even during the 1930s exceptions for agriculture were seen as products of political rather than administrative necessity. The national, contributory social insurance program might have been accompanied by a national, need-based program of old-age assistance, since the old-age assistance program that was enacted granted discretion over eligibility and benefits to state and local governments so that provisions would reinforce employer control over the agricultural labor force. In the absence of a politically important agricultural sector, food stamps might never have been issued, since they were originally designed more to shrink farm surpluses than to feed hungry people, and

---

[82] If only *half* of the funds used to subsidize mass transit in Massachusetts were used instead to subsidize the costs of automobiles for poor people, for example, the state could buy every poor family in Massachusetts a new car every six years or give each poor family $830 every year towards the cost of owning and operating an automobile. These calculations, while interesting, probably do not reflect political realities.

Jose A. Gomez-Ibanez, "Transportation and the Poor," in Manuel Carballo and Mary Jo Bane, eds., *The State and the Poor in the 1980s* (Boston: Auburn House, 1984), p. 161.

they were later traded for urban support of federal farm subsidies. The politics of welfare provision might then have focused upon a more general income subsidy. What happened instead was that agricultural influence led to the initial exclusion of farm workers and farm owners from the social security old-age insurance program, and food stamps became a central program of aid to the able-bodied, non-elderly poor.

Why has agricultural influence had *these* particular consequences, and not any of the others that might be imagined, from fostering the creation of a Swedish-model welfare state to preventing movement beyond the limited social provisions of the 1920s? This essay has argued that arrangements for representation and administration through the state organizations and party systems of the American national government have determined the extent to which agricultural interests would influence social provision, and that state and party have also determined just which agricultural interests would have such influence. State organizations and party systems are abstract forces; power is exercised by real human beings. To trace the influence of agriculture on American social provision, it is necessary to follow the actions of politicians like Franklin Roosevelt, Robert Doughton, and Leonor Sullivan, and of administrators like M. L. Wilson, Arthur Altmeyer, and Howard Davis. Some of these individuals were especially skilled or purposeful. But other individuals with similar administrative or political backgrounds shared their particular skills and purposes. To understand their roles, therefore, we should look at them in terms of the representational and administrative arrangements they embodied.

Representational arrangements in Congress and the party system have chosen among many different sources of agricultural demands and made those of commercial farmers, particularly Southern plantation owners, politically salient. The creation of the New Deal party system made Southerners part of the Democratic majority. The absence of party competition in the South gave Southern members of Congress seniority over other Democrats. The seniority system in Congress made Southern Democrats committee chairmen. Lastly, the decentralization of power within Congress meant that committee chairman would have special say in making policy.

Southern Democratic committee chairmen made policy in the interests of plantation owners; indeed, they were often plantation owners themselves. The economic and political effects of the AAA helped to ensure that other Southern interests would not be represented. The plantation owners' interests lay in the preservation of a paternalistic system of labor control. That system required that agricultural workers be excluded from contributory old-age social insurance, and that food stamps not be provided. Changes in these outcomes reflected either changes in the class in-

terests of plantation owners or changes in the position of their representatives within the policy process. Mechanization, encouraged by the
acreage controls of the AAA and successor programs, made the paternalistic labor system less crucial.[83] Southern Democrats continued to oppose
the expansion of social insurance or food stamps in themselves, but they
became willing to accept social insurance for agriculture if it reduced state
and local expenditures for old-age assistance, and a food stamps program
if it could be traded for extension of commodity subsidies. The ability of
Southern Democrats to control social policies, moreover, was diminished
by the partial revolt against the seniority system, and by the aging of the
New Deal party system, which gave seniority to Northern Democrats too.
These changes meant that representatives of urban and labor interests
could achieve better bargains than before in logrolling with Southern
Democrats.

Administrative arrangements determine whether policies formulated in
Congress can be implemented effectively. But they may also influence the
content of those policies. The Social Security Administration, responsible
for old-age social insurance, and the Department of Agriculture, responsible for food stamps, have drawn upon networks of experts that pre-
dated the New Deal to become exceptionally effective administrative organizations within a generally weak national state. In each case, control
over the language of debate and the techniques of implementation has
allowed experts within the administrative organization to reshape policy
in accordance with their own collectively developed and articulated preferences. Social Security Administration policymakers consistently sought
universal coverage for contributory old-age insurance and achieved this
goal with the extension of the program to agriculture in 1950 and 1954.
The goals of food stamps policymakers in the Department of Agriculture
have been more varied, changing with president and party. The New Deal
food stamps program was administered as a way to reduce agricultural
surpluses more efficiently than through direct commodity distributions;
when surpluses ended, so did the program. Under Eisenhower, the Department of Agriculture became a bulwark of resistance to urban liberal
proposals to revive food stamps. Under Kennedy and Johnson, Department of Agriculture administrators responded to the problems of the
New Deal program at the same time that they continued its emphasis on
agricultural impact and created a second food stamps program with the
purchase requirement as its central feature. Under Nixon, food stamps
became part of welfare expansion, as Department of Agriculture administrators worked to increase participation and erode the purchase require-

[83] Alston and Ferrie, "Labor Costs, Paternalism, and Loyalty," p. 117; Alston and Ferrie,
"Resisting the Welfare State," p. 115.

ment. Under Carter, experts drawn from the hunger policy network expanded the program further and abolished the purchase requirement entirely. Under Reagan, food stamps became part of welfare retrenchment.

To understand the politics of U.S. social provision, many scholars have focused on industrialization and its socioeconomic correlates. This paper suggests that to understand the coverage, benefit levels, and even existence of two crucial social programs, contributory old-age insurance and food stamps, it is also necessary to analyze the politics of agriculture. That analysis can be most fruitful when it combines an understanding of class relations and commodity production in agriculture with an exploration of the institutions of state and party that come between farmers and the policies that shape their lives, as well as the lives of other Americans.

6

From Old-Age Assistance to Supplemental Security Income: The Political Economy of Relief in the South, 1935–1972

JILL QUADAGNO

In the post–World War II era, European nations transformed their pension systems from a minimal program of relief into more comprehensive programs that provided universal benefits.[1] In contrast to the European pattern of development, the United States implemented a joint system of social assistance and social insurance in a single piece of legislation, the Social Security Act of 1935. Old-age assistance (OAA) was shaped as a traditional form of relief, including local administration, means tests, and stringent eligibility criteria.[2] The old-age insurance (OAI) program covered less than half the population, and its benefits were smaller than those under OAA for more than twenty years. It was not until a series of acts were passed between 1969 and 1972 increasing tax rates and indexing benefits that the American system of social insurance provided a basic standard of living rather than a minimal income floor.[3] Even then benefits for the poor and the middle class remained bifurcated: old-age insurance became a program for the middle class, whereas those ineligible for adequate old-age insurance benefits were covered under a separate national

This project was supported by grants from the Kansas Committee for the Humanities, an affiliate of the National Endowment for the Humanities and the American Philosophical Society. I am indebted to Marion Howey, Documents Librarian at Spencer Research Library of the University of Kansas, and Aloha P. South, Judicial, Fiscal and Social Records, National Archives, for extensive help in accessing archival materials. John Myles, Neil Fligstein, Malcolm Bush, Edward Lawlor, and the editors of this volume provided insightful comments on an earlier version of this paper.

[1] John Myles, "The Retirement Wage in Postwar Capitalist Democracies," paper presented to the American Sociological Association, San Antonio, 1984, p. 3.

[2] Jill Quadagno, "Welfare Capitalism and the Social Security Act of 1935," *American Sociological Review* 49 (October 1984): 634.

[3] Martha Derthick, *Policymaking for Social Security* (Washington, D.C.: The Brookings Institution, 1979), p. 357.

program for the poor, Supplemental Security Income (SSI), a reconstituted program of old-age assistance. Hailed as a revolution in the philosophy and financing of relief, what was most radical about SSI was that for the first time in history the federal government had exclusive control of a permanent welfare program.

What processes influenced the transformation of a federal-state program of relief into a national welfare program? The most compelling argument postulated thus far has been presented by Cates, who advocates a "tool view," in which an organization—in this case the Social Security Board—becomes "an instrument in the hands of its leaders, an instrument through which leaders can at times marshal resources to dominate the environment rather than simply responding to and adapting to the environment.[4] Cates argues that program administrators within the Social Security Administration sought to contain the expansion of old-age assistance so that it would not supersede and eventually replace the nascent OAI program that was enacted—along with OAA—as part of the Social Security Act of 1935. Pressures for the expansion of OAA came from "flat-plan" advocates who wanted a universal national pension for the aged. According to Cates, Social Security Board members launched a campaign to control growth in the OAA program as they sought to expand the wage-related insurance program. In the process, old-age assistance was relegated to a residual program of relief.

The problem with this argument is not that it is wrong but rather that the interpretation of factors that shape social policy is narrowed almost exclusively to the activities of officials within the state bureaucracy. Thus, other aspects of state activity as well as fundamental political and economic factors that impinge upon the state are ignored.

In this paper I situate the OAA program in a broader context, arguing that the political economy of the southern racial state in the cotton plantation areas dictated the structure of old-age assistance, guaranteeing maximum local autonomy so that relief would not undermine the control of black tenant labor by landlords. Social policy was shaped by the ability of the southern planter class to wield a disproportionate share of political power in the broader nation-state. Southern planters gained political power through the establishment of a one-party South, which effectively stifled opposition to the dominant planter class, and through the structure of the committee system in Congress, which allowed southern representatives to exercise a controlling negative influence on national legislation.[5]

---

[4] Jerry Cates, *Insuring Inequality: Administrative Leadership in Social Security, 1935–54* (Ann Arbor: University of Michigan Press, 1983), p. 18.

[5] J. Morgan Kousser, *The Shaping of Southern Politics: Suffrage Restriction and the Establishment of the One-Party South, 1880–1910* (New Haven: Yale University Press, 1974), p. 246; David M. Potter, *The South and the Concurrent Majority* (Baton Rouge: Louisiana State University Press, 1972), p. 32.

Changes in the plantation economy, specifically the mechanization of farming, the out-migration of blacks from the plantation region, and the associated aging of the cotton counties reduced the need for local control of old-age assistance and turned the program into an anachronistic burden. Demographic and economic changes occurred in conjunction with a decline in the ability of southern congressmen to exercise negative power in Congress, while the civil rights movement provided opponents to planter rule with a political voice. In the process the southern agenda was changed from a demand for local autonomy to a plea for federal relief.

The New Deal Coalition and the Social Security Act of 1935

Before Franklin Roosevelt was elected president, the Democratic party had been dominated by southerners, who, despite their minority position, maintained a controlling influence on national legislation through the organizational and procedural structure of Congress. At the center of southern congressional power was a committee system through which legislation had to pass. Since a bill could not be brought to the floor of the full House or Senate without favorable committee action, committees had the power to obstruct legislation.[6] Coupled with the committee system was a procedure, established in the middle of the nineteenth century, that used the criterion of seniority as the basis for selecting committee chairman.[7] Southern Democratic congressmen, who often ran for office unopposed, gained seniority and thus control of key congressional committees throughout most of the period from the end of Reconstruction in 1877 until 1963.[8]

Roosevelt's landslide victory in 1932 brought many non-southern states into the Democratic party, eroding southern dominance and creating an uneasy coalition between northern and southern Democrats. Northern Democrats, representing organized labor, favored permanent, national programs operated through a centralized bureaucracy beyond the reach of potentially unsympathetic state governments, whereas southern congressmen consistently opposed any expansion of the powers of central government.[9] The solution to the problem of maintaining a working coalition between two sectors with such different policy goals was the strengthening of the committee system. Early in the New Deal committees became dominated by the interests that fell within the regulatory or distributive scopes of their respective jurisdictions, developing strong norms

[6] Potter, *The South and the Concurrent Majority*, p. 10.

[7] Ibid., p. 16.

[8] Ibid., p. 48.

[9] Richard F. Bensel, *Sectionalism and American Political Development, 1880–1980* (Madison: University of Wisconsin Press, 1984), p. 153.

of reciprocity between them. In practice this meant that members of committee majorities supported the position of other committee majorities during floor consideration. In essence, the committee determined the position on any given piece of legislation for the entire party.[10] Exceptions occurred largely on those issues where there was such a clear differentiation between the interests of northern labor and southern representatives, such as the Wage and Hour bill, that sectionalism rather than committee reciprocity dominated.[11]

The Social Security Act was a compromise piece of legislation that balanced the desires of organized labor for a permanent, bureaucratically controlled old-age pension program with the demands of southern congressmen to keep relief for the aged poor decentralized. The legislation included two different programs to provide economic assistance to the aged. The nationally administered OAI program was financed entirely from payroll taxes collected on employers and employees in industry. The exclusion of the self-employed, farm laborers, and domestic servants meant the exclusion of three-fifths of all black workers on just this basis. In contrast, OAA provided federal funds to the states for old-age pensions to needy persons over sixty-five on a fifty-fifty matching basis up to a maximum federal contribution of fifteen dollars per month.[12]

In the initial formulation of the measure, agricultural workers and domestic servants were included in the OAI provisions. Treasury officials objected, however, on the grounds that keeping track of their work records would pose an insurmountable problem. Although evidence presented at congressional hearings demonstrated that these groups were included in most European schemes, the House Ways and Means Committee, chaired by Robert Doughton of North Carolina and packed with southern Democrats, favored the Treasury Department view.[13] Southern congressmen objected to their inclusion in a program that would be entirely under the jurisdiction of the central state bureaucracy. In the end, agricultural laborers and domestics were excluded from coverage, leaving only 10 percent of the black labor force covered by OAI.[14]

Southern congressmen also influenced the structure of the OAA program. Originally, the OAA title included two clauses implying federal in-

[10] Ibid., p. 150.

[11] Ibid., p. 160.

[12] Margaret Grant Schneider, *More Security for Old Age* (New York: Twentieth Century Fund, 1937), pp. 79–82.

[13] According to evidence provided by Edwin Witte, Austria, Belgium, Bulgaria, Czechoslovakia, France, Great Britain, Italy, the Netherlands, and Spain all had coverage for agricultural workers and domestics. U.S. Congress, Senate Committee on Finance, *Economic Security Act: Hearings on S. 1130*, 74th Cong., 1st sess., 1935, p. 51.

[14] Raymond Wolters, "The New Deal and the Negro," in John Braeman, Robert Bremner, and David Brody, eds., *The New Deal: The National Level* (Columbus: Ohio State University Press, 1975), p. 194.

tervention in states' affairs: a clause specifying that states had to furnish assistance sufficient to provide "a reasonable subsistence compatible with decency and health," and another requiring the state to designate "a single state authority to administer or supervise the administration of the plan and insure methods of administration . . . approved by the Administrator."[15] Southern congressmen objected to both clauses on the grounds that the federal government was attempting to dictate to the states a particular set of standards that would undermine local autonomy.[16]

Roosevelt needed cooperation from the southern coalition, which controlled both the House Ways and Means and the Senate Finance Committees, to get his programs through Congress; thus, in response to southern objections, the legislation was altered to give individual states more control. The "decency and health" provision was eliminated, leaving the states free to pay pensions of any amount and still recover 50 percent of the costs from the federal government. States were also granted the right to impose additional provisions that would make criteria for eligibility more stringent than those stipulated in the bill, such as the ability to exclude people on the basis of age, residence, or citizenship. Finally, through the inclusion of a clause qualifying the original stipulation that the methods of administration satisfy the federal government, states were given the right to select anyone they chose to administer old-age assistance.

The response of southern congressmen to the OAA program was typical of their response to all programs of federal relief. Ravaged by the depression, the southern states desperately needed an infusion of funds, and their congressmen supported vast relief programs. They consistently argued, however, for these programs to be established on a temporary basis or through a decentralized system that worked through state and local organizations, so that "a central state would (not) destabilize the social caste system upon which the economic and political hegemony of the plantation elite was founded."[17] The insistence of southern Democrats on local control for setting standards and administering relief is related to the economic structure of the southern cotton region and the political character of the southern racial state.

The Political Economy of the Cotton Belt

The abolition of slavery after the Civil War created a severe labor problem for the southern cotton-growing region. Although thousands of black slaves were available for agricultural labor, many refused to work in

[15] History of Provision Relating to State Personnel, February 18, 1938. National Archives, RG 47, Records of the Executive Director, Subject Files, Box 47, File 631.31.

[16] Senate, *Economic Security Act*, p. 71.

[17] Bensel, *Sectionalism and American Political Development*, p. 153.

gangs under the conditions that had existed during slavery, thereby creating a need for new forms of labor control. After a period of experimentation with a wage system, planters inaugurated the crop-lien or sharecropping system, through which the majority of southern farmers, black and white, were converted to debtors.[18] Wage labor did not disappear entirely, but the number of wage workers on plantations gradually decreased as the sharecropping system grew in importance.

Sharecropping consisted of a contract between a laborer and a landlord in which the former sold his labor and often that of his entire family in return for half the crop at the end of the season. Tenants held similar arrangements except that a tenant contributed a mule and a plow as well as his own labor in return for two-thirds of the crop. Both classes depended on the landlord for advances of food and clothing until the crops were harvested, and the cost of this "furnish" as well as heavy interest charges were deducted from the proceeds of the croppers' share at the end of the year. Sometimes there was a money balance due the cropper; often there was none, and it was not uncommon for a sharecropper or tenant to find himself continually in debt to his landlord. The indebtedness of the cropper to his landlord forced him to stay for the entire season or forfeit his share of the crop. Thus, the problem of labor turnover experienced by the planter under the wage labor system was almost entirely eliminated.[19]

By 1930 three-fourths of all southern cotton farms were operated by tenants, and a high proportion of all tenants were black. In 1930 28.2 percent of all black agricultural workers in the South were croppers, another 15 percent were tenants, and 36.7 percent were wage laborers. In contrast 42.4 percent of all whites were owners or managers.[20]

Unevenly dispersed throughout the South, these cotton plantations were heavily concentrated in the "black belt" counties of six states—South Carolina, Georgia, Alabama, Mississippi, Arkansas, and Louisiana—which held 80 percent of the plantation acreage in the United States.[21] Plantations also developed in portions of Texas and Oklahoma. In all of the cotton counties at least 50 percent of the population was black, and in many the proportion of blacks was 80 percent or more.

[18] Gunnar Myrdal, *An American Dilemma* (New York: McGraw Hill, 1964), p. 224; Oscar Zeichner, "The Legal Status of the Agricultural Laborer in the South," *Political Science Quarterly* 55 (1940): 412.

[19] Zeichner, "The Agricultural Laborer," pp. 414, 422.

[20] Fifteenth Census of the United States: 1930, Agriculture, vol. ii, part 2, County Table 1. Data on wage laborers are from the Fifteenth Census of the United States: 1930, Population, vol. iv, State Table 11.

[21] Jay R. Mandle, "The Plantation States as a Sub-Region of the Post-Bellum South," *Journal of Economic History* 34 (1974): 733.

The economic system of sharecropping was supported by a legal system guaranteeing white planters domination over black tenants. Laws, such as the lien laws and the Black Codes, which restricted the mobility of labor and enforced the tenant system, were accompanied by the disfranchisement of blacks. Disfranchisement was completed between 1875 and 1908 when all of the southern states enacted legislation restricting the voting rights of blacks and, as a secondary consequence, those of poorer whites as well.[22]

The result of disfranchisement was the reduction of the southern electorate to less than 20 percent and in some places to as little as 12 percent of the adult population in all southern states.[23] What disfranchisement also accomplished was the emergence of the planter-dominated Democratic party as the sole vehicle for political expression, a phenomenon that eliminated opportunities for the mobilization of discontent and meant that for the next half century southern politics would be conducted by amorphous factions within the Democratic party.[24]

Since candidates for political office often ran without opposition in the main election, primaries became the main point at which political choices were made. The winner of the primary could become governor or senator in some instances by receiving votes from less than 7 percent of the electorate.[25] Once in office, politicians had visible advantages over opponents who had no party machine around which to organize a campaign. Thus, southern politicians tended to remain in office for decades, gaining power in Congress through the seniority system.[26] At the local level, planter power was consolidated by constitutional revisions that further reduced the influence of the electorate by favoring the executive over the legislative branch, by increasing the appointive power of the executive and the proportion of appointed over elected offices, and by removing the judiciary from popular influence.[27]

The Administration of Old-Age Assistance

In the early years of the depression, when federal funds for relief became available, landlords, who were often appointed to administrative positions in local government, manipulated these relief funds in a variety

[22] Kousser, *The Shaping of Southern Politics*, p. 239.

[23] C. Vann Woodward, *Origins of New South 1877–1913* (Baton Rouge: Louisiana State University Press, 1951), p. 345; V. O. Key, *Southern Politics in State and Nation* (New York: Alfred A. Knopf, 1949), p. 20.

[24] Key, *Southern Politics*, p. 10.

[25] Ibid., p. 20.

[26] Potter, *The South and the Concurrent Majority*, p. 49.

[27] Woodward, *Origins*, p. 346.

of ways. For example, blacks unilaterally received lower rates of relief than whites in the South, with relief generally kept below the subsistence furnished by the landlord.[28] Not only were rates of relief lower for blacks, but the proportion receiving relief was only half that of southern whites, even though rates of black poverty were substantially higher.[29] Furthermore, at planters' requests, relief offices in many rural counties were closed during the two months of cotton picking.[30] Planters were highly defensive against any direct flow of cash into the system of tenancy that might lessen the dependence of the sharecropper on the landlord.

The enactment of the Social Security Act released federal funds for relief to the aged poor. Fewer than twelve months later, thirty-six states and the District of Columbia had developed plans and were receiving grants-in-aid to help finance their programs.[31] Those states with existing pension laws on the books simply converted these programs to meet OAA guidelines, while those without ongoing programs rapidly developed similar plans so they could meet federal criteria and begin receiving federal funds.

The initial southern response was one of resistance. None of the southern states had state pension laws on the books prior to passage of the Social Security Act, and they were slowest to pass pension legislation. In fact, some black belt congressmen, assuming social security was a temporary measure, at first worked to try to repeal it. When a delegate from the South Carolina House of Representatives wrote the Social Security Board requesting information on "the proportion of white to negro people," which "would be particularly valuable to us at this time in the consideration of old age pension legislation," a confidential memo was circulated documenting the board's concern about how to respond to the South Carolina delegation: "[T]here are strong factors in S.C. trying to kill Social Security, already and a high showing of negroes could make things worse."[32]

As old-age assistance laws were passed, all of the southern states incorporated more stringent criteria into their standards for eligibility than was required, making OAA merely an extension of relief. This pattern was recognized by the Bureau of Research and Statistics of the Social Security Board, which estimated that states with high percentages of recipients drawn from relief rolls stringently interpreted the law, whereas states

---

[28] Thomas J. Woofter, *Landlord and Tenant on the Cotton Plantation* (Washington, D.C.: Works Progress Administration, 1936), p. 151.

[29] Ibid., p. 152.

[30] Ibid., p. 150.

[31] Arthur Altmeyer, *The Formative Years of Social Security* (Madison: University of Wisconsin Press, 1968), p. 59.

[32] Letter from A. J. Hatfield to Frances Perkins, January 22, 1936. Office memo, n.d., National Archives, RG 47, State Files, Box 58, File 092.

with low percentages interpreted the law more liberally.[33] With the exception of Texas, all of the southern states drew more than 60 percent of their OAA recipients directly from relief rolls.[34]

As noted above, in shaping the provisions of the Social Security Act southern congressmen insisted that OAA remain under the control of local authorities. When southern plans were approved, they all included measures that kept decisions about benefits in local hands. For example, Mississippi required an applicant for OAA to be a resident of the *county* in which the application was made, even though the federal law required only residency for five out of the past nine years in the *state*.[35] Georgia was even more adamant in adhering to the principle of local autonomy, with officials refusing to establish any administrative units beyond the county level. The result was high administrative costs and less money available for assistance. Jane Hooey, director of the Bureau of Public Assistance, explained her frustration with the South's adherence to principles of local administration:

> Now you can find a state like Georgia, for example, that had so many counties in that state. Some of them have 200 population, and yet you have the whole plethora of public officials. That would be a waste of money. Yet to get them to join those and have larger limits . . . well, we have no authority.[36]

In one county in Alabama grants were not paid out at all, because local authorities feared they might subsidize black families. The labor control functions were explained by Mrs. Frank Pou of Gordo, Alabama, in a letter to Harry Hopkins, director of the Works Progress Administration.

> As I wrote you, unless the Federal government pays the *entire* amount to the old people it will never be paid in this state. Now I shall trust you never to mention what I shall say to anyone except to our President himself. . . . The *main* reason the Old Age Pension fund will *never* be paid from the *state* funds is that they claim it will effect [*sic*] the labor situation. I have heard some say that they opposed, strongly opposed the Old Age Pension because if they paid them, why the negroes getting them, the entire family would live off of the

[33] Social Security Board Interoffice Communication, March 17, 1937. National Archives, RG 47, Records of the Executive Director, Box 278, File 631.301.

[34] Social Security Board, Bureau of Research and Statistics. National Archives, RG 47, Records of the Executive Director, Box 278, File 631.301.

[35] Mississippi Old Age Assistance Act. National Archives, RG 47, State Files, Box 34, File 600. See also Louisiana—Revised Plans for Old Age Assistance, October 8, 1936. National Archives, RG 47, State Files, Box 26, File 622.203.

[36] Jane Hooey, *Memoirs*, Columbia University Oral History Collection, Butler Library, Columbia University, New York, p. 28.

money, and they could not get them to work for us on our farms. They would be worse about working for us than they have been ever since the government started to hand out to them. They would be too independent if they should get a Federal Old age pension.[37]

In Louisiana in 1937, during the months of June and July when black labor was in heavy demand, the governor arbitrarily ordered that payments to colored recipients be "cut in half, while payments to white recipients were made on the usual basis."[38] Similar incidents occurred in other southern states. Southern insistence on local control of relief was motivated by the fear that direct cash benefits to aged tenants might subsidize entire families and undermine planters' control over their labor force.

As a result of local discretion, grants to blacks were low. As Table 6.1 shows, in all of the southern states the average monthly grant to blacks was less than the average grant to whites. Furthermore, the lowest grants were in the black belt counties. For example, in the cotton counties of Alabama in 1939 the average OAA grant was $7.16, whereas in the non-cotton counties it was $11.42. Similarly, in Mississippi the cotton county grants averaged $6.92 as opposed to $8.07 in the non-cotton counties.[39]

Even though the Social Security Act guaranteed a high degree of local discretion, southern welfare officials were still concerned about possible intrusions on local autonomy by the national Social Security Board. In 1939 administrators of public welfare in the southern states were invited by the commissioner of public welfare for Arkansas to attend a meeting to confront common problems. The agenda was "to coordinate the economic efforts of the southern States, or low-income states with reference to public welfare," and "to urge upon the Social Security Board and the Labor Department to minimize supervisory regulations and to leave to the southern States every possible administrative function, since the states more nearly understand the local problems."[40]

As one mechanism for paying higher benefits to whites than to blacks without violating federal regulations, several southern states used a separate standard for Confederate veterans. Prior to the passage of the Social

[37] Letter from Mrs. Frank Pou to Harry Hopkins, October 20, 1941. Franklin Delano Roosevelt papers, Official Files 494a, Pensions, Hyde Park, N.Y.

[38] Memo from A. D. Smith to Jack B. Tate, Acting General Counsel on Louisiana OAA payments for the months of June and July, December 9, 1937. See also memo from Thomas Bane to Jane Hooey, "Substance of Conversation with Governor Leche," June 8, 1937. National Archives, RG 47, State Files, Box 26, File 600.0413.

[39] Social Security Board, Bureau of Research and Statistics, Bureau Report No. 8, *Trends in Public Assistance 1933–1939*, 1940, pp. 57, 75–76.

[40] Agenda of the Meeting of the Commissioners of Public Welfare from Arkansas, Georgia, Tennessee, Alabama, North Carolina, Virginia, and West Virginia, November 25, 1939. National Archives, RG 47, Records of the Executive Director, Box 272, File 600.

TABLE 6.1 Old-Age Assistance: Comparison of Average Monthly Grants to White and to Negro Recipients Accepted during Fiscal Year 1938–39, in States Accepting 100 or More Negro Recipients

| State | Average Grant per Month per Recipient | | | Amount by which Average Monthly Grant to Negroes Is More (+) or Less (−) than Average Monthly Grant to White Recipients |
	Total	White	Negro	
New York	$21.79	$21.69	$24.30	+ $2.61
Michigan	13.94	13.90	16.20	+ 2.30
Pennsylvania	20.33	20.24	22.20	+ 1.96
Indiana	17.17	17.10	18.63	+ 1.53
Iowa	18.25	18.23	19.51	+ 1.28
Illinois	20.38	20.30	21.26	+ .96
Massachusetts	26.52	26.50	27.37	+ .87
Ohio	21.56	21.52	22.09	+ .57
Missouri	18.69	18.66	19.06	+ .40
Oklahoma	17.59	17.62	17.61	− .01
Arkansas	7.49	7.52	7.42	− .10
California	30.54	30.53	30.24	− .29
Kansas	17.33	17.35	17.01	− .34
Kentucky	7.39	7.44	7.10	− .34
West Virginia	13.54	13.60	12.87	− .73
Maryland	15.82	16.05	15.22	− .83
Tennessee	10.22	10.50	9.40	− 1.10
New Jersey	19.27	19.47	17.91	− 1.56
Virginia	9.42	10.01	8.44	− 1.57
Georgia	7.41	8.14	6.40	− 1.74
South Carolina	7.79	9.14	6.94	− 2.20
Delaware	11.33	11.88	9.51	− 2.37
Mississippi	7.06	8.08	5.71	− 2.37
Alabama	15.56	16.77	14.24	− 2.53
Louisiana	10.66	11.84	9.21	− 2.63
North Carolina	10.45	11.27	8.46	− 2.81
Texas	14.27	14.94	11.88	− 3.06
Florida	12.46	14.04	10.04	− 4.00
District of Columbia	24.57	27.08	22.40	− 4.68

SOURCE: Social Security Board, Bureau of Research and Statistics, Division of Public Assistance Research. National Archives, RG 47, Records of the Executive Director, Box 279, File 632.36.

Security Act, most southern states paid pensions to Confederate veterans under state laws. Beginning with benefits to disabled and diseased veterans of the Civil War, southern states gradually expanded pension systems to include widows and, in some states, servants.[41] In writing their OAA plans, these states incorporated special provisions for veterans, requesting that they be allowed to pay the maximum benefit to all veterans.[42] Although the board could not flatly approve a plan that totally disregarded need, it allowed the states to define "need" differently for veterans (all whites) than non-veterans. In debating how to handle this potentially tricky situation Hooey suggested that

> the statement could be made that the State has decided to meet the needs of veterans more adequately than for non-veterans merely because they do not have sufficient funds to equalize these. The States could be asked as quickly as possible to bring up the average grant of non-veterans to something approximating that of veterans.[43]

This policy was adopted even though it was known that the grant to Confederate veterans ranged from thirty to fifty dollars per month, while the average for non-veterans was only five dollars per month in Mississippi and ten to eleven dollars per month in other southern states.

Historically, the South had feared strong central government, and while the New Deal created a proliferation of bureaucratic agencies, its policy of "cooperative federalism" allowed national policies to vary widely in response to differences in regional politics.[44] In the case of old-age assistance, national authority in program administration was carefully circumscribed. Cash grants to blacks were monitored so as not to undermine prevailing wage rates and to intrude as little as possible into the planter-tenant relationship. Although discrimination was illegal, southern states were allowed to pay blacks lower grants than whites by using different criteria for determining need, and by paying Confederate veterans and their dependents the maximum grant.

The lack of official concern for racial disparity in spite of legal prohibitions against discrimination reflected both the political clout of southern congressmen and the prevailing view that racial differences in income were natural. According to John Corson, director of the Bureau of Old-

---

[41] Charles Henderson, *Industrial Insurance in the United States* (Chicago: University of Chicago Press, 1908), pp. 283–86.

[42] In some states Confederate pensions were set at even higher levels, but regardless of benefit size, the federal government only contributed fifteen dollars per month.

[43] Payment of Federal Funds in Relation to Grants to Needy Confederate Veterans, December 6, 1937. National Archives, RG 47, Records of the Executive Director, Box 273, File 600.045.

[44] Bensel, *Sectionalism and American Political Development*, p. 149.

Age Insurance, blacks earned less than half of what whites earned and women earned only slightly more than half of what men earned, because "[t]hese variations [were] a historical, firmly embedded characteristic of the American wage structure."[45] Lower average payments to blacks were not seen as racial discrimination; they simply conformed to the traditional wage structure.

Old-Age Assistance and the Regional Distribution of Wealth

Although the Democratic party was dominated by a planter class aligned with urban finance and industry, this does not mean that there was no opposition in the South. The center of conservativism was the black belt, but in all southern states, factions, varying in degree of strength and influence, reflected the interests of urban workers, farmers from the hill country, and, in Louisiana, the general voice of Populist protest, filtered through the Huey Long machine.[46] The interests of these factions found expression more readily in the House of Representatives— where congressmen from particular districts were responsive to their constituencies, however limited—than in the Senate. It was from these politicians that protests arose around the issue that had long aggravated North-South relationships—inequities in the regional concentration of wealth arising from the ways federal programs distributed benefits. Depending on such factors as overall population size, the size of the average grant, the percentage of older people in the state, and the percentage receiving relief, some states were eligible for thousands of dollars more than others. As Table 6.2 shows, the amount of federal funds received by the states in 1938 ranged from nearly $17,000,000 in California and over

[45] John Corson, "Insurance Against Old Age Dependency," *Annals of the American Academy of Political and Social Science* 202 (March 1939): 63. Numerous instances of similar remarks appear in the records. For example, I. S. Falk, director of the Bureau of Research and Statistics, acknowledged that "in states in which the average payment to Negroes is higher than to whites it may be assumed that the Negro recipients are more needy. In States in which the average payment to Negroes is lower than to whites in all probability there is a differential in the standards of determining the amount of grant for Negro and white families" (Interoffice Communication from I. S. Falk to Oscar Powell, May 18, 1940. National Archives, RG 47, Records of the Executive Director, Box 279, File 640). Similarly, a report from Industrial Relations Counselors justified lower grants to blacks on the grounds that "for certain racial groups in rural areas of the South and Southwest, long accustomed to an extremely low standard of living, even these small sums undoubtedly represent a standard considerably above that to which they have been accustomed and which are locally considered more than adequate" (U.S. Congress, House Ways and Means Committee, *Hearings on H.R. 6635*, 76th Cong., 1st sess., 1939, p. 807).

[46] Key, *Southern Politics*, pp. 299–301.

TABLE 6.2 Grants to States for Old-Age Assistance, 1938

State	Population 65 Years and Older	Percent Receiving OAA	Total Federal Payment
Alabama	128,000	12	$832,331
Alaska	4,000	20	145,275
Arizona	17,000	18	759,962
Arkansas	99,000	20	1,086,060
California	463,000	19	16,938,074
Colorado	74,000	43	5,769,225
Connecticut	120,000	16	2,288,037
Delaware	22,000	18	196,277
District of Columbia	43,000	19	464,442
Florida	96,000	20	2,222,413
Georgia	141,000	20	1,496,446
Hawaii	11,000	18	126,660
Idaho	29,000	34	1,183,120
Illinois	506,000	28	12,982,696
Indiana	295,000	17	4,038,216
Iowa	222,000	19	4,870,841
Kansas	150,000	20	1,166,302
Kentucky	188,000	20	2,731,308
Louisiana	89,000	30	1,561,516
Maine	88,000	8	326,031
Maryland	112,000	18	1,755,318
Massachusetts	334,000	20	10,906,455
Michigan	290,000	17	6,845,645
Minnesota	197,000	36	8,113,821
Mississippi	89,000	25	431,820
Missouri	319,000	19	6,046,542
Montana	30,000	40	1,412,945
Nebraska	99,000	33	2,169,879
Nevada	6,000	17	290,571
New Hampshire	54,000	9	527,353
New Jersey	256,000	12	2,628,075
New Mexico	19,000	21	264,955
New York	802,000	17	14,247,070
North Carolina	151,000	20	1,045,451
North Dakota	37,000	22	707,167
Ohio	487,000	25	13,795,148

TABLE 6.2 (cont.)

State	Population 65 Years and Older	Percent Receiving OAA	Total Federal Payment
Oklahoma	121,000	50	6,812,088
Oregon	85,000	18	1,869,710
Pennsylvania	632,000	21	13,202,092
Rhode Island	46,000	15	635,660
South Carolina	73,000	21	588,719
South Dakota	43,000	30	1,268,448
Tennessee	156,000	20	949,981
Texas	288,000	50	9,763,265
Utah	27,000	30	1,791,780
Vermont	39,000	16	422,414
Virginia	155,000	20	157,700
Washington	126,000	28	5,162,773
West Virginia	91,000	24	1,811,166
Wisconsin	220,000	18	4,482,796
Wyoming	11,000	27	396,838

SOURCE: National Archives, RG 47, Records of the Executive Director, Box 274, File 622; Box 275, File 622.

$14,000,000 in New York to only $431,820 in Mississippi and $157,700 in Virginia.

This disadvantage did not go unnoticed by southern congressmen, many of whom quickly recognized that the northern states were receiving a disproportionate share of federal funds. Representative A. Leonard Allen of Louisiana explained the South's dilemma.

This Nation has been suffering from too much concentration of wealth for a long time. Where ever wealth is concentrated, power likewise is concentrated. Some sections of our Nation have been the agricultural sections, and some sections have been manufacturing and banking centers, and everyone knows that the tendency has been for wealth to gravitate to the manufacturing and banking centers.[47]

As a means of reducing this inequity, Allen, following the "share the wealth" legacy of Huey Long, put forth a bill to redistribute the wealth of the nation through the payment of a totally federal old-age pension of

[47] House, Hearings on H.R. 6635, p. 764.

thirty dollars a month financed out of general revenues (H.R. 1816).[48] Representative William Colmer, a non–black belt Mississippi Democrat who had protested against the financing provisions in OAA during the original hearings on the Social Security Act, proposed a similar measure for a flat federal pension of fifteen dollars a month to each state per recipient regardless of the state's ability to match dollar for dollar (H.R. 1814), or, if that was unacceptable, having the federal government increase its proportion of old-age assistance to eighty percent.[49]

The Social Security Board also recognized that federal funds exacerbated previously existing inequities in the concentration of wealth among the states.

> Prior to 1931 Federal grants-in-aid never amounted to more than 8% of combined state revenue receipts. . . . Since 1933 it has never been less than 80%, and in 1936 it exceeded state revenues by 24%. . . . The facts and prospects indicate that the old fifty-fifty matching requirement will have to be abandoned if a generalized Federal aid program is not to render the situation of the poorer states worse than ever.[50]

Of equal concern to board members was the unruly growth of the OAA program in several non-southern states, which they attributed to "[t]he percentage grant without any limitation on the amount which the federal government will match. . . . The more the state puts up the more it will get."[51]

Instead of the existing fifty-fifty match, the board proposed that a system of "variable grants" be introduced. Variable grants would establish a basic minimum amount to be paid by the federal government ($7.50 per month was the suggested sum) and an additional federal appropriation on a dollar for dollar basis for all grants over $10 per month, apportioned among the states in ratio to the number of persons over age sixty-five.[52]

Although the Social Security Board and a few southern congressmen pushed for some type of program to balance the apportionment of federal

[48] Non–black belt representatives from Georgia had also passed a resolution supporting a national old-age pension financed solely by federal taxation. Resolution, March 18, 1939. National Archives, RG 47, Central Files, Box 6, File 011.4.

[49] House, *Hearings on H.R. 6635*, p. 2123. I determined Colmer's affiliation, as well as the affiliations of other southern congressmen, by examining the *Biographical Directory of the American Congress 1774–1971*, 92d Cong., 1st sess., Sen. Soc. No. 92–8 (Washington, D.C.: U.S. Government Printing Office, 1971), p. 769.

[50] Variable Grants. National Archives, RG 47, Records of the Executive Director, Box 274, File 622.

[51] Possible Revision of the Formula for Assistance Grants to the States, January 15, 1938. National Archives, RG 47, Records of the Executive Director, Box 274, File 622.

[52] Ibid.

funds to the states, the House Ways and Means Committee, chaired by Representative Thomas Cullin of New York, rejected board chairman Arthur Altmeyer's proposal for variable grants.[53] Like many of the wealthier states, New York stood to lose substantial numbers of federal dollars if a truly variable strategy was enacted. The Senate Finance Committee, controlled by black belt Democrats, discussed Altmeyer's proposal but eventually rejected it.[54] In 1939 the cotton South was simply not willing to establish a minimum level for welfare grants or to relinquish control of a major welfare program. Although bringing in federal funds was important to non–cotton county representatives, the planter class still had a firm grip in most regions of the South.

Pressure from minority factions of southern congressmen continued to increase, and by 1946 the inequity of the fifty-fifty matching was perceived by Congress as a significant enough problem that it attempted to introduce variable grants into the program.[55] The problem was that operationalizing a truly variable strategy still would have meant reducing the percent of the federal share already granted to the larger states, a politically impossible task. Instead, the federal government agreed to pay 80 percent of the first 25 dollars and 50 percent of any amount above 25 dollars up to a maximum of 35 dollars. Under the amendments, to the Social Security Act of 1935, federal funds could contribute an additional 5 dollars per recipient of old-age assistance, but no minimum was established.

The avowed intent of Congress in approving the legislation was for federal funds to be used to increase payments by this amount. Instead, most of the southern states used the more generous federal supplements to increase the number of recipients rather than the amount of money granted to each recipient. For example, Arkansas increased the number of recipients by nearly 45 percent but only increased the average payment by $.94. Alabama increased the number of recipients by nearly 40 percent but actually reduced the average payment by $1.16. Similarly, Louisiana increased the number of recipients by approximately 30 percent but reduced average payments by $1.71. Typically this was accomplished by splitting between husbands and wives payments that formerly were given to each.[56] In contrast, states such as Kansas, Rhode Island, California, Wyoming, Texas, New York, New Hampshire, New Jersey, and Minnesota increased their average payments by at least $4.00, while increasing the number of recipients by fewer than 20 percent.

[53] Altmeyer, *Formative Years*, p. 105.
[54] Ibid., p. 111.
[55] Letter from Homer Atkins, Governor of Arkansas, to Arthur Altmeyer, December 4, 1941. National Archives, RG 47, State Files, Box 5, File 092.
[56] "Public Assistance," *Social Security Bulletin* 10 (December 1947): 29–30.

There are two possible ways to interpret these findings. One is that the overall extent of need was greater in the South than elsewhere in the nation, and that the policies pursued by the southern states represented an attempt to extend relief to as many of the needy aged as possible. The other interpretation is that southern states used this strategy as a means of increasing the amount of federal funds received without increasing welfare payments and thereby undermining control over labor. In all likelihood some truth may be found in both interpretations. The most extensive distribution of relief occurred in Louisiana, where popular sentiment for generous benefits received support from Long and his followers. In other states, which had previously found the funds necessary to provide generous benefits for Confederate veterans, it is more likely that benefits were spread widely while being maintained at minimum levels, both to control labor and to contain pressure for a real redistribution of wealth through tax increases for elites.[57]

In 1958, over the objections of President Dwight D. Eisenhower, southerners on the House Ways and Means Committee pushed through a controversial bill increasing the federal share of public assistance to the aged, blind, and disabled to 65 percent for those states whose per capita income was less than the national average, and increasing to 65 dollars per month the maximum average benefit payment. Thus, without reducing averages to the wealthier states and without setting some minimum payment, the southern states were able to increase their share of federal dollars.[58]

Political and Economic Change in the South

Between 1935 and 1970, a combination of political and economic changes rendered the principle of local control of relief increasingly anachronistic. As a result of government agricultural policies, the increased availability of improved equipment for all stages of cotton production, labor shortages associated with World War II, and other such factors, planters found mechanization an attractive alternative to black tenant labor.[59] Mechanization decreased the number of tenants and increased the number of seasonal day laborers, who were used primarily to

[57] Key, *Southern Politics*, p. 307.

[58] "Social Security," *Congressional Quarterly Almanac* 14 (1958): 157.

[59] David James, *The Transformation of Local State and Class Structures and Resistance to the Civil Rights Movement in the South* (unpublished Ph.D. diss., University of Wisconsin, 1981), p. 158; Neil Fligstein, *Going North, Migration of Blacks and Whites from the South, 1900–1950* (New York: Academic Press, 1981), pp. 139–40; John L. Fulmer, *Agriculture Progress in the Cotton Belt Since 1920* (Chapel Hill: University of North Carolina Press, 1950), p. 58; Richard Day, "The Economics of Technological Change and the Demise of the Sharecropper," *American Economic Review* 57 (1967): 435.

harvest the crops. Simultaneously, it displaced tenants from the land and stimulated the migration of blacks, especially those from the cotton counties, from rural areas to southern towns and cities and to the urban North.[60] As a result, the South experienced a gradual process of urbanization, with the non-urban population declining from 52.3 percent in 1950 to 33.5 percent by 1970.[61] Although the number of agricultural workers in the South decreased by 69.5 percent during this same period, blacks were still more highly concentrated in agricultural occupations than whites.[62] Blacks were particularly likely to be found in the non-mechanized jobs in agriculture, and the income gap between black and white farm operators actually widened in spite of the fact that southern wage levels in general had improved relative to those of the rest of the nation.[63] Thus, the out-migration continued, as limited job opportunities and a decline in relative earnings pushed blacks northward and into cities.

In each decade those who left were more likely to be younger, better educated, and male. Those who remained were more often widowed, older, and illiterate.[64] The economic repercussions of the demise of tenancy and the out-migration of blacks were severe. Rural areas of the cotton belt were left with a small labor force, fewer consumers, and, in many areas, a smaller tax base.

The economic changes in the South were accompanied by political changes that gradually reduced the power of the southern planter class, both within the region and in terms of its ability to influence national legislation. Until Roosevelt's election, the Democratic party was the South. After his sweeping victory in 1932, southern congressmen, for the first time, became a minority faction in the majority party.[65] In every election between 1932 and 1944 Roosevelt's election totals were so great that he could have lost every southern state and still won the election. The same was true of every Democratic president until John F. Kennedy, who had to carry some southern states to win.[66]

Although Roosevelt initially had the support of southern Democrats, many of his policies alienated them, and by 1939 Congress was in full revolt against the president.[67] The rift between northern and southern

[60] Daniel M. Johnson and Rex R. Campbell, *Black Migration in America* (Durham, N.C.: Duke University Press, 1981), p. 118.

[61] Jack Bass and Walter DeVries, *The Transformation of Southern Politics, Social Change and Political Consequences Since 1945* (New York: New American Library, 1976), p. 504.

[62] Ibid., p. 508.

[63] Ray Marshall, "The Old South and the New," in Ray Marshall and Virgil Christian, eds., *Employment of Blacks in the South* (Austin: University of Texas Press, 1978), p. 15.

[64] Ibid., pp. 118, 119, 134.

[65] Potter, *The South and the Concurrent Majority*, p. 60.

[66] Ibid., p. 67.

[67] Ibid., p. 74.

factions of the Democratic party widened in subsequent years over the civil rights and welfare programs of the Truman administration, and in 1948 the split was formalized when the four southern states with the greatest investment in plantation farming (and the highest proportion of blacks in the population) bolted to form the Dixiecrat party. The Dixiecrat revolt, though short-lived, was the beginning of the demise of the solid South. Never again did the South return entirely to the Democratic fold.[68] Republican party growth began in the 1950s and accelerated during the 1960s. By 1972 the Republican party held 31 percent of the southern seats in Congress and 17 percent of the seats in state legislatures: only Mississippi, Louisiana, and Alabama remained one-party states.[69]

One factor that hastened Republican party expansion in the South was the growing unwillingness of organized labor, represented by the northern faction of the Democratic party, to respect the procedural prerogatives of the committee system. Increasing tension developed around issues on which the two factions of the party differed, and by 1960 the desire of the northern Democrats to create a national working-class party made them unwilling to maintain a cohesive stance with southern Democrats in opposing civil rights legislation.[70]

Other changes, some internal and some externally imposed, modified the balance of power in the South, providing a political voice for opposition to planter dominance. The 1944 Supreme Court decision invalidating the white primary began the process of the enfranchisement of the electorate. This decision was followed by the repeal of the poll tax in several southern states during the 1940s, as well as a CIO drive to increase the number of blacks eligible to vote by collecting poll taxes where they were still legal, and to register unionists in southern cities.[71] Thus, even before the civil rights movement transformed the political structure of the South, the proportion of southern blacks registered to vote had increased from 5 percent in 1940 to 28 percent in 1960.[72]

The civil rights movement dealt the final blow to plantation agriculture and to the Democratic coalition. Aided by federal intervention, the movement transformed the state structures of the South, making them incompatible with plantation agriculture.[73] The process began with the voter registration drives, which caused the eviction of hundreds of tenant families as planters drove off their plantations blacks who attempted to reg-

---

[68] Ibid., p. 75.

[69] Bass and DeVries, *Transformation of Southern Politics*, pp. 402–3.

[70] Bensel, *Sectionalism and American Political Development*, p. 242.

[71] Key, *Southern Politics*, pp. 644, 657.

[72] David Campbell and Joe R. Feagin, "Black Politics in the South: A Descriptive Analysis," *Journal of Politics* 37 (February, 1975): 133.

[73] James, *Transformation of Local State and Class Structures*, p. 206.

ister.[74] The movement culminated in 1965 with the passage of the Voting Rights Act, which incorporated blacks into the southern electorate and split the Democratic party into two opposing factions.

Black workers benefited in other ways from legislation passed as a result of the civil rights movement. In 1963 Alabama was taken to court by the federal government on the grounds that it had accepted federal funds in violation of merit system requirements prohibiting racial discrimination in hiring. Although it took five and a half years, the Justice Department finally brought suit against the state in 1968 to force compliance.[75] Gradually, blacks began to gain positions in state and local governments, administering the programs that received funding from the federal government. Among the various federal programs in which nondiscrimination regulations applied, welfare programs were the most integrated, implying that citizen pressures on these programs were strongest and most effective.[76]

Although southern congressmen continued to chair key committees until the late 1960s, within Congress changes in the rules and procedures through which decisions were made reduced the power of the southern coalition. Party caucuses, which had previously made decisions about the fate of bills privately before they ever reached the floor, became less important because southern congressmen no longer formed a majority within the House.[77] Attempts by southern congressmen to bottle up legislation in the Rules Committee were increasingly overridden by discharge petitions, and in the Senate cloture was imposed to prevent southern senators from using the filibuster.[78] Thus, the power of the planter class to impede legislation through negative actions gradually declined.

The out-migration stream of younger blacks from rural areas gradually aged the plantation region. By 1970 a significant proportion of the rural population was composed of older citizens living on meager incomes. For example, in the cotton county of Bolivar, in Mississippi, the aged population constituted only 5 percent in 1940, but more than 11 percent of the population was over 65 by 1970.[79] Thus, local governments in declining rural areas were confronted with relatively high overhead in per capita terms and a limited tax base from which to operate, making the in-

[74] Ibid., p. 300.

[75] David F. Ross, "State and Local Governments," in Ray Marshall and Virgil L. Christian, eds., *Employment of Blacks in the South* (Austin: University of Texas Press, 1978), p. 89.

[76] Ibid., p. 91.

[77] Potter, *The South and the Concurrent Majority*, p. 78.

[78] Ibid., pp. 81, 87.

[79] U.S. Bureau of the Census, *Population: Characteristics of the Population, Part I, United States Summary, Reports by the States* (1940).

creased welfare burden of an aging population more difficult to manage.[80]

It was against this background of a declining tenancy, a transformed political structure, and an increased aged population that the changes in old-age assistance occurred. Step by step, southern congressmen released welfare for the aged poor from local governments, passing control to the federal government as the burden of maintaining aged blacks surpassed their economic value, and as the threat of direct cash payments to older family members subsidizing entire families became less critical to a changing plantation economy. Moreover, changes in the South were accompanied by political and economic changes elsewhere in the country that made the expansion of coverage under OAI a more pressing issue.

The Burden of Old-Age Assistance

Shortly after the Social Security Act of 1935 was passed, an advisory council was formed in response to the concerns of insurance company executives that the accumulation of a large reserve in the old-age insurance account would divert funds from consumer purchasing power to capital investment, adversely affect the capital market, and encourage demands for increased rates of benefits or unwise use of funds for other purposes.[81] One of the solutions for reducing the reserve was to expand OAI coverage to uncovered groups, including agricultural workers. The administrative difficulties of including farm operators (which could include tenants, depending on how this category was defined) were considered too onerous, however, and this group was not recommended for coverage.[82]

Organized labor strongly supported including agricultural workers under OAI coverage.[83] The Social Security Board, however, agreed with the advisory council that extending coverage to agricultural workers was administratively impossible. The southern-dominated House Ways and Means Committee not only continued to exclude agricultural workers but also expanded the exclusion to those involved in the processing of

[80] Arthur M. Ford, *Political Economics of Rural Poverty in the South* (Cambridge, Mass.: Ballinger Publishing Co., 1973), pp. 63–64.

[81] J. Douglas Brown, "Next Steps in Old Age Insurance," in *Social Security in the United States* (New York: American Association for Social Security, 1938), p. 46.

[82] Board Meeting Minutes, February 6, 1937. National Archives, RG 47, Chairman's Files, Box 12, File 011.1.

[83] Statement of CIO before House Ways and Means Committee on Proposed Changes in the Social Security Act. National Archives, RG 47, Chairman's Files, Box 119, File 011.1; Letter from C. H. Jordan, Secretary, Los Angeles Industrial Union Council, to Arthur Altmeyer, June 16, 1938. National Archives, RG 47, Central Files, Box 6, File 011.4.

agricultural products.[84] Thus, when the 1939 amendments to the Social Security Act took effect, old-age relief for southern blacks and poor whites remained under OAA program.

Over the next decade no substantial changes were made in the Social Security program, although pressures were building to extend coverage. Organized labor had continued to press for the extension of coverage to agricultural workers. After a Republican Congress reduced social security coverage in 1948, President Harry Truman made social insurance coverage a major issue in his presidential campaign that year.[85] Members of the Social Security Board, concerned that twice as many persons were receiving old-age assistance as opposed to insurance, reversed their earlier opposition to the inclusion of agricultural workers and began to push for expanded coverage.[86]

After the election, Truman followed up his campaign promises by urging the House to act on several pending Social Security bills. The Democratic-controlled Ways and Means Committee, chaired by Robert Doughton of North Carolina, brought H.R. 6000, a bill that would revise the Social Security Act, to the floor under a gag rule, which meant that no amendments could be added. Although Republicans opposed the gag rule, an attempt to override it was defeated by the Democratic House.[87] H.R. 6000 raised benefits and extended coverage to the non-farm self-employed, provisions that satisfied organized labor, but it continued to exclude farmers and farm labor.[88] Although Republican congressmen from farm states protested that polls of farmers indicated that they wanted coverage, that farmers paid social security taxes anyway in the increased costs of manufactured goods, that periods of non-farm employment in towns were too brief to allow them to qualify for Old Age and Survivors' Insurance (OASI), and that the advisory committee had recommended extending coverage to farm workers, southern Democrats countered that no farmers came to their hearings to argue for coverage.[89] Northern Democrats supported the House Ways and Means Committee position, arguing that while not perfect, the bill represented a significant improvement in Social Security.[90]

When the bill was sent to the Senate Finance Committee, numerous groups testified in favor of extending coverage, including the National

[84] Altmeyer, *Formative Years*, p. 103.

[85] "Social Security Act, HR 6000–P.L. 734, Summary," *Congressional Quarterly Almanac* 6 (1950): 166.

[86] Altmeyer, *Formative Years*, p. 169.

[87] *Congressional Record*, 81st Cong., 1st sess., House, H.R. 6000, 1949, p. 13808.

[88] "Social Security Extension, HR 6000, Summary," *Congressional Quarterly Almanac* 5 (1949): 289.

[89] *Congressional Record*, H.R. 6000, pp. 13817, 13838, 13840, 13845, 13915.

[90] Ibid., p. 13918.

Association for the Advancement of Colored People; representatives from the Food, Tobacco, Agricultural and Allied Workers Union of America; the National Farm Labor Union; the AFL; the CIO; and members of the American Public Welfare Association (APWA), an informal partner of the federal government.[91] Southern APWA officials were the driving force behind the move to extend social insurance coverage, modifying their former insistence on local control of relief when faced with the economic reality of an increased welfare burden. As the public welfare commissioner for Alabama explained: "We have larger and larger numbers of needy old people and correspondingly smaller numbers within the population who can earn and pay taxes. Not only do we have an increasing number of old people, but we are a State with an unusually high proportion of children. . . . Our rate of application for aid also continues to be as high, as there is less and less demand for unskilled and older workers."[92]

Pressure to extend coverage to agricultural workers came from another source—various coalitions of small businessmen and the Chamber of Commerce, who wanted coverage extended to all, so that people would not feel they were getting free pensions. It was the consensus of conservative business opinion that paying for pensions out of payroll taxes was one means of holding costs down and maintaining income maintenance payments to the aged at a basic subsistence level but no higher.[93]

The Senate Finance Committee amended the House bill to include agricultural workers, but only those who were regularly employed. Farm operators were still excluded. When the bill, as passed by the Senate, was returned to the House, House members could not agree to the changes, and the bill was sent to a joint House-Senate conference, in which five of the eleven members were from southern states. After more than a month of debate, regularly employed agricultural workers were finally included.[94] The term *regularly employed* was narrowly defined, however, to include only those who had put in at least three months of steady work for one employer and had then worked at least sixty days and earned at

[91] U.S. Congress, House Ways and Means Committee, *Hearings on H.R. 6000 Social Security Revision,* 81st Cong., 1st sess., 1950, pp. 1929–31, 2365, 195; Daniel Sanders, *The Impact of Reform Movements on Social Policy Change: The Case of Social Insurance* (Fairlawn, N.J.: R. E. Burdick, Inc. 1973), p. 149.

[92] Testimony of Broughton Lamberth, House, *Hearings on H.R. 6000,* pp. 196–97. See also the Testimony of Commissioners of Public Welfare from Louisiana, p. 231; Tennessee, p. 223; and Texas, p. 241.

[93] Testimony of Herschel C. Atkinson, Executive Vice President, Ohio Chamber of Commerce, House, *Hearings on H.R. 6000,* pp. 1489–90.

[94] Wilbur J. Cohen and Robert J. Myers, "Social Security Act Amendments of 1950: A Summary and Legislative History," *Social Security Bulletin* 13 (October 1950): 3.

least fifty dollars during the next calendar quarter.[95] Since average agricultural wages in the South were only forty cents an hour in 1949[96] and since many cotton pickers only worked for a few weeks, few southern farm workers were actually covered.

In 1952, when Republican Dwight D. Eisenhower was elected to the presidency, the Chamber of Commerce agenda to extend coverage re-emerged with renewed vigor. A newly appointed advisory committee, dominated by Chamber of Commerce representatives, recommended mandatory old-age insurance coverage for farm operators and presently ineligible farm workers.[97] As the House Ways and Means Committee began hearings on new legislative recommendations, proposals to extend benefits to farm operators had the support of small business organizations, the Chamber of Commerce, and all major farm organizations except the planter-dominated Farm Bureau. The new bill that emerged from the Ways and Means Committee now included coverage for self-employed farm operators and for farm workers paid at least two hundred dollars in a calendar year.[98] The bill passed with only eight nays, to the embarrassment of the Democrats, who attempted to take credit for the more liberal Social Security measure.[99] The now Republican-controlled Senate Finance Committee broadened coverage generally but still attempted to exclude farm operators, largely at the insistence of Senator Walter George of Georgia, former chairman of the committee and its ranking minority member.[100] Also excluded were all those employed in "a service performed in connection with the production or harvesting of any commodity defined as an agricultural commodity."[101] During debate John Stennis, a Democrat from Mississippi, questioned whether tenants were included under the category of farm workers. When reassured that they were not, he proceeded to suggest an amendment, voted down by a voice vote, excluding all farm workers from coverage.[102] The final version of the Senate bill included only "farm workers paid at least fifty dollars in cash wages by one employer in a calendar quarter."[103]

The bill was sent back to the House and a joint conference was appointed to resolve the differences. The final measure extended coverage

[95] "Social Security Act, HR 6000," *Congressional Quarterly Almanac*, p. 171; Wilbur J. Cohen, Robert M. Ball, and Robert J. Myers, "Social Security Act Amendments of 1954: A Summary and Legislative History," *Social Security Bulletin* 17 (September 1954): 4.

[96] Day, "Economics of Technological Change," p. 441.

[97] Altmeyer, *Formative Years*, p. 241.

[98] *Congressional Record*, 83d Cong., 2d sess., House, H.R. 9366, 1954, p. 7446.

[99] Ibid., pp. 7447, 7448, 7454.

[100] Ibid., p. 245.

[101] *Congressional Record*, 83d Cong., 2d sess., House, H.R. 9366, 1954, p. 14413.

[102] Ibid., pp. 14433–35.

[103] Ibid., p. 14382.

to farm operators (including tenants) and broadened coverage for farm workers to those who were paid at least one hundred dollars in cash wages by an employer in a single year.[104] This bill was passed and signed into law on August 20, 1954, even though Senator George refused to sign the conference report.[105] Although the 1954 amendments did not extend coverage under a federal program to all farm workers and tenants, they did remove substantial numbers from sole reliance on the OAA program administered by local officials, placing their economic security in old age under a national program.

The inclusion of farm operators and agricultural laborers under OAI helped to relieve the welfare burden on the southern states, but it did not eliminate it. Since workers in both categories tended to be in the lowest income group, upon retirement they qualified only for minimum Old Age, Survivors' and Disability Insurance (OASDI) benefits. Thus, all of the southern states still had to supplement the income of most OAI recipients with OAA. For example, in 1959, Louisiana, Mississippi, and Alabama ranked first, second, and third, respectively, in the number per thousand of the aged population receiving OAA, and these states were also highest among those supplementing OASDI payments. In contrast, industrial states like New York and Pennsylvania were ranked fifty-fifth and forty-seventh, respectively, in terms of the proportion of aged receiving OAA or a combination of benefits from both programs.[106]

Welfare Reform and Supplemental Security Income

Concurrent with the civil rights struggle was a precipitous rise in relief rates. The increase in the welfare load was most extensive in the Aid to Families with Dependent Children (AFDC) program,[107] but rising relief rates in one program reduced the funds available for other programs in state budgets. Under increasing pressures for reform, President Richard Nixon introduced a welfare reform bill in 1969, which proposed sweeping changes in the AFDC program as well as in the adult category programs, among them OAA. Under Nixon's plan, old-age assistance along with aid for the blind and disabled poor would have been continued, and a national minimum standard for benefits set, with the federal government contributing to the cost of the minimum payment and sharing the

---

[104] Cohen, Ball, and Myers, "Social Security Act Amendments of 1954," p. 4.

[105] Altmeyer, *Formative Years*, p. 247.

[106] "Money Income Sources of Aged Persons, December 1959," *Social Security Bulletin* 23 (1960): 16.

[107] Frances Fox Piven and Richard A. Cloward, *Regulating the Poor* (New York: Vintage Books, 1971), p. 186.

cost of additional state payments above that amount.[108] Nationally uniform standards for eligibility would also have been prescribed.

On October 31, the Family Assistance Act of 1969, embodying the president's proposals, was introduced into the House of Representatives and referred to the Ways and Means Committee. Among its other goals, the intent of the bill was to remove the tremendous disparity that still existed among states in terms of eligibility requirements and levels of benefits. For example, OAA payments in 1969 in Mississippi averaged $39.80 per month as opposed to $139.00 in Wisconsin.[109] The bill was also intended to provide fiscal relief to the states. The program was structured in a way that would disproportionately benefit the southern states and decrease their welfare expenditures by a substantial amount. In the adult category programs, Alabama would save an estimated $15.7 million, Arkansas $12.4 million, Georgia $22.3 million, Louisiana $1.4 million, and Mississippi 12.7 million. In contrast, many other states would actually have their costs increased in this category, even though the overall impact of the entire program was to categorically reduce state welfare expenditures.[110]

Although the family assistance portion of the bill met with considerable opposition in the House, there was strong support among southern congressmen for the adult category programs. An earlier Supreme Court decision had declared residence requirements for public assistance unconstitutional;[111] agricultural workers were now covered by OAI; blacks had gained administrative positions in welfare programs; and the rural areas of the South were faced with an aging, dependent population in need of extensive welfare benefits. All of the conditions that had favored local administration and financing had altered, and there was no longer any economic or political rationale for keeping OAA as a local program. After several hearings in both the House and the Senate, the bill (H.R. 1) was reintroduced in the Ninety-second Congress with the adult category programs 100 percent federally funded and administered.[112] H.R. 1 passed in the House with the family assistance plan deleted, and OAA became supplemental security income, an income program for the aged poor that provided a basic floor of income support with no relative responsibility tests and more generous income exclusions than had been present in

[108] Congressional Research Service, Library of Congress, "Legislative History, Trends, and Adequacy of the Supplemental Security Income (SSI) Program," in *The Supplemental Security Income Program: A 10-Year Overview* (Washington, D.C.: Special Committee on Aging, United States Senate, 1984), p. 116.

[109] Ibid., p. 117.

[110] Ibid., pp. 151–52.

[111] Ibid., p. 121.

[112] Ibid., p. 140.

many state programs. Supplemental security income came into being with little controversy, because it was packaged within a broader welfare reform bill that generated all of the public attention.

Conclusion

Jerry Cates has effectively demonstrated that bureaucrats within the Social Security Administration had their own ideological reasons for attempting to contain the growth of the OAA program and for expanding OAI. There is no doubt that their activities were important in determining the developing structure of the program as amendments were added. They also experienced significant failures, however, as in the administration of OAA in the South, where program administrators were often unable to enforce their own regulations.

The parameters of the OAA program were not shaped within the isolated confines of the state bureaucracy, subject primarily to the goals of program administrators. Rather, the southern planter class, through its representatives in Congress and its control over state and local government, exerted considerable influence on program formation and implementation. While tenant agriculture dominated the cotton region, planters refused to allow relief to be granted to farm operators or agricultural laborers, since direct cash benefits would interfere with the existing arrangements between planters and their tenants and undermine the control of planters over their labor force. After subsidy and allotment programs by the federal government encouraged the mechanization of cotton farming and indirectly contributed to the demise of the tenant system, the benefits to be gained by maintaining local control of relief were offset by the disadvantages to the southern states in terms of the amount of funds received from the federal government. The initial strategy was to attempt to circumvent this dilemma by demanding greater federal contributions for OAA and increasing the number of relief recipients.

The mechanization of cotton gradually replaced tenants with day laborers and eventually lessened the demand for these workers, too; they then migrated in massive numbers to the industrial centers of the North and Midwest. Left behind were increasing numbers of older blacks and poor whites who created a tax burden on local communities.

As the South industrialized, the political power of the planter class was challenged by industrialists, who wanted a free and mobile labor force and relief from the burden of welfare expenditures, and by organized labor, which increasingly challenged the congressional committee system structured around an uneasy coalition of northern and southern Democrats. The civil rights movement destroyed the alliance between organized labor and the southern planter class and increased the political power of blacks, giving them some degree of direct access to local government. By 1970 old-age assistance had become an anachronistic burden on the southern economy, and southern Democrats led the demand to nationalize relief to the aged poor.

Although the data presented in this paper are limited to the transformation of the OAA program, the thesis developed here has broader implications for the formation of the American welfare state. Many scholars have pointed to the United States as an exception in welfare state development, noting that its programs are not consistent with its level of economic development, and that many European nations with fewer resources have developed more extensive programs with broader benefits. I would suggest that a major factor impeding welfare state growth in the United States was that, contained within the borders of an industrialized, democratic nation with a strong labor movement, existed an agricultural sector, almost feudal in character, in which there was no democracy, and in which a dominant planter class exerted a negative, controlling influence on national legislation until well into the second half of the twentieth century. The formation of the American welfare state, I would argue, was constrained by the political economy of the cotton South, in which the political mechanisms associated with an advanced capitalist economy were manipulated to protect an undeveloped agrarian sector from centralized government authority.

7

Postwar Capitalism and
the Extension of Social Security
into a Retirement Wage

JOHN MYLES

In American social politics old age is unique. Unlike family or health care policy, in this area the United States has developed a truly "modern" welfare state. Because of this, Social Security does its job reasonably well, has acquired a solid basis of political support, and is relatively immune to political efforts to dismantle or erode its basic structure. My purpose in the first part of this paper is to document these assertions, and to describe the development of this "modern" side of the American welfare state. The major step in the development of America's modern welfare state for the elderly, I argue, occurred not under Franklin Roosevelt's administration, but under Richard Nixon's. The reforms of the late 1960s, and early 1970s are responsible for the fact that Social Security now does its job effectively and has developed a political constituency that makes it immune to political attack. When the reforms were complete, as Robert Ball, head of the Social Security Administration, remarked, America had a "new social security program."

Not everyone was happy with the new program, however. During the 1970s and early 1980s, it underwent an astounding assault. American society, it was claimed was about to collapse under the weight of an aging society and rising Social Security entitlements.[1] Ronald Reagan came to power announcing that it would be necessary to slash Social Security in order to save it. In the end, the assault was a failure for two reasons. First,

I wish to thank Gosta Esping-Andersen, Jill Quadagno, Daiva Stasiulis, James Schulz, Theda Skocpol, and David Wolfe for their instructive comments on previous versions of this paper.

[1] At times the imagery reached truly mythological proportions. In the May 26, 1980, issue of *Forbes* magazine, for example, Social Security was portrayed as "the monster that's eating our future."

few of the more radical claims advanced by the critics were able to withstand critical scrutiny.[2] Second, whatever the merits of the criticisms, politicians quickly learned that to tinker with Social Security was to court
electoral defeat.

Though it failed, the attack and its aftermath constitute a watershed in
the history of American social policy. The bipartisan agreement of 1982
that officially brought the "crisis" of Social Security to a close was not
the beginning of a new round of reforms to address the serious problems
that continue to face America's elderly. Neither did it begin an effort to
extend the principles of Social Security to other areas of social life. The
agreement was not a victory but a truce, symbolizing the current impasse
of the welfare state. In the second part of the paper, I elaborate on the
reasons for both the attack and the impasse.

America's Modern Welfare State

The phrase *modern welfare state* has become an integral part of the
contemporary sociological lexicon. But just what is it that defines the mo-
dernity of the welfare state? In an important essay written to commemo-
rate the fiftieth anniversary of the International Labor Organization, Guy
Perrin suggested that the development of social security could be divided
into two major periods: first, the social insurance era prior to World War
II, and second, the period of social security proper, following the war.[3]
Though the beginnings of the social insurance era can be dated to the
German sickness insurance scheme of 1883, social insurance developed
largely in the period between the two great wars, when compulsory insurance schemes (and, less frequently, noncontributory benefits financed
from public funds) flourished in Europe and in several non-European
countries. As Perrin points out, however, the function of these schemes
differed little from that of traditional public assistance programs—to ease
the extreme poverty of the least privileged members of society.[4] Benefits
were low and targeted at those of limited means. The average monthly
benefit of an old-age pensioner in Munich in 1905, for example, was 13.5
marks, significantly below the prevailing public assistance rate of 20
marks.[5] A British investigatory committee reported in 1919 that even

[2] For a review and assessment of this literature, see John Myles, "The Trillion Dollar
Misunderstanding," *Working Papers for a New Society* 8, no. 4 (July/August 1981): 22–
31.

[3] Guy Perrin, "Reflections on Fifty Years of Social Security," *International Labour Review* 99, no. 3 (1969): 249–90.

[4] Ibid., p. 251.

[5] Christoph Conrad, "Aging with a Minimum of Property: The Lower Middle Class and
Working Classes of Cologne, 1830–1930," paper presented at the annual meeting of the
American Historical Association, Washington, D.C., December, 1982, p. 16.

doubling the existing five-shilling pension would be insufficient to provide a subsistence-level income.[6] Nowhere were public pensions intended to provide elderly workers with a level of income sufficient to permit withdrawal from economic activity—that is, to retire—in advance of physiological decline. This traditional welfare state was a welfare state *for the poor*.

The transition to the era of social security involved the gradual implementation of two quite novel principles of distribution. The first was the principle of universality. Coverage and benefits were extended to all citizens or, alternatively, to all members of the labor force. The second was the principle of substitutive benefits; in effect, benefits were related to the worker's former earnings but at a level sufficient to allow continuity in living standards in the event of unemployment, illness, or retirement.[7] This last principle is what distinguishes the modern welfare state from the traditional welfare state. No longer were old-age pensions merely to provide subsistence for those who through age or disability fell out of the labor market. Instead, old-age pensions became a "retirement wage" sufficient to permit (or induce) the older worker to withdraw from the labor market in advance of physiological decline.[8]

The main result of the implementation of these two principles was to break the historic link between public provision and the "poor." "Modern" social security programs were designed to provide income security for the expanding middle strata of the postwar period—workers with average incomes and regular employment as well as the professionals and managers of the "new middle class." The poor were not excluded under this new arrangement; rather, the boundaries of public provision were expanded. This gradual process of middle-class incorporation into the welfare state was subsequently to prove of enormous political as well as economic importance. By virtue, and to the extent of, their incorporation, the growing middle strata became allies rather than enemies of the welfare state.

How well does the transition described by Perrin characterize the American experience? In broad terms, the answer is: not very well. For the most part, the American welfare state continues to be a welfare state for the poor. Instead of a universal system of family allowances, Americans got Aid to Families with Dependent Children (AFDC), and instead of a universal system of national health insurance, Americans got Medicaid. By the mid-1970s, the percentage of families headed by a person aged 25

[6] Hugh Heclo, *Modern Social Politics in Britain and Sweden: From Relief to Income Maintenance* (New Haven, Conn.: Yale University Press, 1974).

[7] Perrin, "Reflections," p. 259.

[8] John Myles, *Old Age in the Welfare State: The Political Economy of Public Pensions* (Boston: Little, Brown, 1984), chap. 1.

to 54 receiving some form of transfer income was only 16 percent in the United States compared with 80 percent in Sweden and 59 percent in Britain. In the United States, 61 percent of transfer income went to the lowest income sextile and only 2.4 percent to the highest income sextile; in Sweden, the corresponding figures were 28 percent and 13.7 percent, respectively.[9] In one sense, the American welfare state is quite efficient: it has the highest proportion of transfers going to the poor. But by the same token it is ineffective: among the advanced capitalist democracies it has among the highest levels of relative poverty.[10] The reasons for this apparent contradiction were noted by Titmuss and his colleagues.[11] Benefit structures created in the poor law tradition that fail to incorporate the middle strata do not generate the broadly based political support necessary to ensure the growth and survival of the welfare state. For middle-aged, middle-income Americans, the welfare state is virtually all cost and no benefit. Consequently, it remains "programmatically underdeveloped, symbolically demeaned and politically vulnerable."[12]

But this is not the case with old-age security. From the base established during the New Deal, Social Security has evolved into a system that provides the major source of income for the vast majority of elderly Americans and is not unlike the most advanced old-age security systems of Western Europe.[13] Evidence for this conclusion is presented in Table 7.1. Panel 1 provides earnings replacement rates of old-age security systems in five countries for workers with a history of average earnings in manufacturing. The earnings replacement rates are computed by dividing social security just after retirement by earnings just prior to retirement. These are hypothetical rates and should not be confused with actual replacement rates that are affected by labor force interruptions and variations in career-cycle earnings. Their main purpose is to demonstrate what would happen to similar workers under different pension regimes. For single workers (or two-earner couples), American replacement rates are modest in comparison with Sweden and Germany but generous in comparison

[9] Lee Rainwater, Martin Rein, and J. Schwartz, *Income Packaging and the Welfare State: A Comparative Study of Family Income* (Oxford University Press, forthcoming).

[10] Peter Hedstrom and Stein Ringen, *Age and Income in Contemporary Society: A Comparative Study* (Stockholm: The Swedish Institute for Social Research, 1985).

[11] Heclo, *Modern Social Politics*, p. 261.

[12] John Ikenberry and Theda Skocpol, "From Patronage Democracy to Social Security: The Shaping of Public Social Provision in the United States," in Gosta Esping-Andersen, Lee Rainwater, and Martin Rein, eds., *Stagnation and Renewal* (Armonk, N.Y.: M. E. Sharpe, forthcoming).

[13] See Richard Tomasson, "Government Old Age Pensions under Affluence and Austerity: West Germany, Sweden, the Netherlands, and the United States," paper presented at the meeting of the Tenth World Congress of the International Sociological Association, Mexico City, 1982.

TABLE 7.1 Selected Indicators for Old-Age Security and the Economic Status of the Elderly in Five Countries

	Canada	Germany	Sweden	U.K.	USA
1. Earnings replacement rates of social security old-age pensions for workers with average wages in manufacturing, 1980					
Single worker	.34	.66	.68	.31	.44
One-earner couple	.49	.49	.83	.47	.66
2. Adjusted disposable income of the elderly in relation to national mean[a]					
Age 65–74	.94	.84	.96	.76	.99
Age 75 +	.81	.77	.78	.67	.84
3. Gini index for adjusted disposable income					
Age 65–74	.309	.298	.143	.266	.342
Age 75 +	.291	.340	.126	.240	.355
4. Poverty rates[b]					
Age 65–74	11.2%	12.7%	0.0%	16.2%	17.8%
Age 75 +	12.1%	15.2%	0.0%	22.0%	25.5%

SOURCES: Panel 1 data from Jonathan Aldrich, "Earnings Replacement Rates of Old-Age Benefits in 12 countries, 1969–80," *Social Security Bulletin* 45, no. 11 (November 1982): 3–11. Panels 2, 3, and 4 data from Peter Hedstrom and Stein Ringen, *Age and Income in Contemporary Society: A Comparative Study* (Stockholm: The Swedish Institute for Social Research, 1985).

[a] After tax income adjusted for family size.

[b] Percentage of persons belonging to families with an adjusted disposable income below half of the median for all families.

with Canada and the United Kingdom. In contrast, American replacement rates for a traditional one-earner couple are high by international standards.

Panels 2, 3, and 4 give us some indication of the actual economic status of the elderly in the United States relative to other countries. These data are drawn from the important analysis of Hedstrom and Ringen based on the Luxembourg Income Study and are constructed from micro-data files from the year 1979 except for the data from Canada and Sweden, which are for 1981.[14] Panel 2 indicates that the American elderly have the highest level of income security among the five countries: their average standard of living differs little from that of the population as a whole. But as Panel 3 shows, security does not imply equality. As indicated by the Gini index, income inequality within the elderly population is highest in the United States. The explanation for this apparent contradiction is straightforward. The American system of income distribution does provide the elderly with a high level of income security, but for the poor this means little since it merely secures them in their poverty. The United States has the highest incidence of relative poverty across all age groups, and this pattern is reproduced among the elderly as well.[15] In sum, the United States does the most effective job of providing income security—continuity of living standards after retirement—but, because it has one of the least egalitarian systems of income distribution prior to retirement, it produces a very high level of relative poverty among the elderly after retirement.

But if Social Security fails to substantially alter the distribution of income in old age, it does maintain it relatively intact, precisely what a modern welfare state based on universal substitutive benefits is intended to do. This explains why Social Security, unlike other sectors of the American welfare state, has proven so resistant to the attacks of the New Right. As Skocpol and Ikenberry conclude, its natural political base is not the "poor" but rather the "better off, stably employed industrial workers and the broad 'middle class.' "[16] As elsewhere, public provision for the elderly in the United States has acquired the form of a retirement wage.

The Origins of the Retirement Wage

In conventional accounts the philosophical foundations of the postwar welfare state are typically associated with the publication in the United

[14] Hedstrom and Ringen, *Age and Income*.

[15] Ibid., p. 23.

[16] John Ikenberry and Theda Skocpol, "The Political Formation of the American Welfare State in Historical and Comparative Perspective," in R. Tomasson, ed., *Comparative Social Research*, pp. 87–148 (Greenwich, Conn.: JAI Press, 1983), p. 141.

Kingdom of the Beveridge Report in 1942. Prepared during wartime, when the costs and risks of war were being borne by rich and poor alike, the Beveridge report became an important symbol of postwar social reconstruction, promising a new era of collective self-help and social responsibility. The state, acting on behalf of all citizens, would provide a safety net below which no member of the community would be allowed to fall. In the spirit of equality, benefits would be equal for all. Reproducing the inequalities of the market was not to be the task of the state. The basic flat-benefit formula proposed by Beveridge guided postwar reforms in many countries, including Britain (1946), Sweden (1946), Holland (1947), and Canada (1951). What is frequently ignored in such accounts is the fundamentally liberal character of the Beveridge proposals. Beveridge did not advocate, and indeed was opposed to, a system of substitutive benefits that would replace the market wage. This was made clear in the third of the three principles he prescribed as the basis for social provision: "The State in organizing security should not stifle incentive, opportunity, responsibility; in establishing a national minimum, it should leave room and encouragement for voluntary action by each individual to provide more than the minimum for himself and for his family."[17] In discussing the problem of employment and old age, Beveridge explicitly rejected the necessity for anything resembling a retirement wage, since the elderly were more able than ever, in his view, to support themselves by their own labor.[18]

In those countries where the flat-benefit Beveridge system was implemented, the eventual creation of a retirement wage to replace the market wage lost upon retirement required a more radical transformation than in those countries where existing benefit structures were already linked to contributions. And, remarkably, Britain, the so-called cradle of the modern welfare state, did not implement such a system until 1978, the result of legislation passed in 1975.

In contrast to Britain's status as a "welfare laggard" in the area of pension reform, America, at first glance, appears to have been remarkably precocious. In William Graebner's account, the retirement wage in the United States can be dated to the Social Security Act of 1935. For Graebner, the Social Security Act of 1935 was first and foremost a piece of "retirement legislation" designed to reduce the massive unemployment of the Great Depression by removing older people from the work force and

[17] William Henry Beveridge, *Social Insurance and Allied Services* (New York: Macmillan, 1942), pp. 6–7.
[18] William Henry Beveridge, *Full Employment in a Free Society* (New York: W. W. Norton, 1945), p. 69.

freeing up their jobs for younger workers.[19] Graebner points to the awareness among many policy advisors of the labor force implications of a system of old-age benefits linked to contributions and, most critically, to a retirement test as a condition for eligibility (an exception among modern welfare states).

It is not my intention here to adjudicate among the many debates over the "real origins" of Roosevelt's New Deal in general, or of the Social Security Act in particular. Undoubtedly, this is an exercise that will preoccupy academics well into the next century. In large measure, these debates are over the proximate forces (the agents and their intentions) that brought the Social Security Act into being. Graebner's important, and lasting, contribution, however, is to draw our attention to what are unquestionably the remote causes of Roosevelt's old-age security legislation, the series of changes within the American political economy that made such legislation an objective possibility. From at least the turn of the century, the search for a means to remove older workers from the industrial labor force had become a key item on the agenda of the "efficiency movement." Modern methods for organizing the labor process, it was concluded, required modern methods for the selection of those workers most "fit" for production. And, as Graebner amply documents, this selection did not include the older, slower members of the work force. The growing awareness of the economic implications of the retirement principle as a means for "rationalizing" labor inputs provided the context within which it became objectively possible to consider seriously a program for the superannuation of elderly workers. And with the massive unemployment of the 1930s, possibility was transformed into probability.

But if it was the intent of the reformers of the 1930s to establish a retirement wage, then their victory was only a partial one. The provisions of the Old-Age Insurance (OAI) program were set up so that benefits would not exceed minimum wage levels.[20] And by 1949, the average benefit of the Old-Age Assistance (OAA) program—a program designed in the poor law tradition—was 70 percent higher than the average primary insurance benefit.[21] Though perhaps designed as a piece of "retirement legislation," the Act itself did not provide for a "retirement wage," a benefit that would allow withdrawal from economic activity in advance of physiological decline. But what the act did provide was a policy framework of

[19] William Graebner, *A History of Retirement* (New Haven, Conn.: Yale University Press, 1980), p. 184.

[20] Jill Quadagno, "Welfare Capitalism and the Social Security Act of 1935," paper prepared for the annual meeting of the American Sociological Association, San Antonio, Texas, 1984, p. 9.

[21] Martha Derthick, *Public Policy for Social Security* (Washington, D.C.: The Brookings Institution, 1978), p. 26.

earnings-related benefits that allowed subsequent generations of reformers to construct a system of retirement wages through what would appear to be a series of incremental reforms rather than through a radical transformation of the policy structure itself. In short, in the United States the road to the retirement wage was made smoother by virtue of the fact that reforms could be presented as a series of improvements on an already existing benefit structure. This "ratchet" approach to social reform appears to have been a deliberate strategy of the program's chief executives almost from inception.[22] Elsewhere (Sweden, Canada, Great Britain), comparable results could be achieved only through radically new policy initiatives to construct an earnings-related system on top of the existing flat-benefit structure.

During the first two and one-half decades of the U.S. system's operation, the major changes in it were directed at achieving the first of the two objectives identified by Perrin as characteristic of a modern welfare state, namely, universal coverage. This objective was accomplished through a series of Social Security amendments in 1950, 1954, 1956, and 1965.[23] Coverage was extended to regularly employed farm and domestic workers, state and local government workers, farm operators, most self-employed professionals, and members of the armed forces. In contrast, the benefit increases that were legislated during this period were aimed at merely maintaining the real value of benefits against price increases.[24] The enormous benefit increases of 1950 (77 percent) simply restored the purchasing power that had been lost since the plan's inception. The result was that during the period between the end of the war and the mid-1960s, there was a continual erosion of the economic status of the American elderly.[25] Benefits did not keep pace with the general rise in the standard of living or replace the labor market income being lost through a rising retirement rate. The combination of low benefits and a rising number of retirees was progressively pauperizing the American elderly.

If we adopt Perrin's conception of universal substitutive benefits as marking the transition to a "modern" welfare state, then, as I stated at the beginning of this paper, it is the administration of Richard Nixon, not of Franklin Roosevelt, that marks this development in American social history. Because the transformation that occurred in the period from 1969 to 1972 did not require the addition of a major new program to America's old-age security network, the drastic character of the changes

---

[22] Ibid., p. 26.

[23] James Schulz et al., *Providing Adequate Retirement Income: Pension Reform in the United States and Abroad* (Hanover, N.H.: University Press of New England, 1974), p. 8.

[24] Ibid., pp. 8–9.

[25] Fred Pampel, "Changes in the Labor Force Participation and Income of the Aged in the United States, 1947–1976," *Social Problems* 27, no. 2 (December 1979): 135.

introduced during this period was less noticeable than the legislative in-novations that marked comparable developments in Sweden (1958), Can-ada (1965), and the United Kingdom (1975). But when the transforma-tion was complete, as Robert Ball remarked, America had a "new social security program."[26]

The process of transformation had begun modestly under the Johnson administration with a 13 percent increase in benefits in 1967 and an in-crease in the level of covered earnings from $4,800 to $7,800. But under the Nixon administration major increases in benefits were legislated in 1969 (15 percent), 1971 (10 percent), and 1972 (20 percent). The result was a real increase in benefits (i.e., net of inflation) of 23 percent in just three years. Of equal importance was the fact that the 1972 legislation added indexing against inflation. The results were soon apparent. In 1965, the income replacement rate for a retired worker with a dependent spouse who had average earnings before retirement was .44. By 1975 it was .57, and by 1980 it had risen to .66.[27] And, not surprisingly, after 1965 the relative economic status of the elderly began to rise again until, in the mid-1970s, it was approximately at the level it had been after the war.[28]

Launching the Counterattack:
American Business and the Crisis
of Social Security

Until 1972, the relationship between American business and the Social Security program had always been an ambivalent one. A number of im-portant business leaders had supported the initial Roosevelt reforms and, according to Derthick, took the lead in pushing through the amendments of 1939 that extended benefits to aged dependents and survivors, as well as in urging universal coverage for the aged in 1953.[29] In those sectors of the economy in which strong labor unions were able to demand high cor-porate pension benefits, many corporate leaders became enthusiastic sup-porters of the system, seeing in it a means of offsetting corporate labor costs. But throughout most of the program's history, the dominant strat-egy of business and conservative critics was not to dismantle Social Se-curity but merely to "hold the line, wherever that line might be at the

[26] Quoted in Derthick, *Public Policy*, p. 339.

[27] Leif Haanes-Olsen, "Earnings-Replacement Rate of Old Age Benefits, 1965–75, Se-lected Countries," *Social Security Bulletin* (January 1978): 3–14; Jonathan Aldrich, "Earn-ings Replacement Rates of Old-Age Benefits in 12 Countries, 1969–80," *Social Security Bulletin* 45, no. 11 (1982): 3–11.

[28] Pampel, "Changes in the Labor Force," p. 135.

[29] Derthick, *Public Policy*, chap. 6.

moment."[30] Until 1965, this was a successful strategy; after 1965, it failed and failed massively. By 1972 the modernization of America's welfare state for the elderly was a *fait accompli*. And throughout the rest of the decade, corporate America set out, in concerted fashion, to undo the damage. As a result, the "crisis" of Social Security was discovered.

At first, it might appear that corporate America had fallen asleep during the 1969–72 period, only to reawaken, like Rip Van Winkle, to discover the world had changed in the interlude. In reality, both the transformation of the U.S. Social Security system and the subsequent attack on it correspond to one of the most dramatic turnarounds in class politics in American history. As Derthick points out, the traditional conservative strategy of merely "holding the line" reflects the fact that to "oppose, rather than merely to resist change, would have required internal consensus and considerable organizational effort," a consensus and organizational capacity that was generally absent in postwar corporate America.[31] But after 1965, even the capacity to resist popular demands disintegrated. As Edsall demonstrates, during the period after 1965 corporate America was in retreat. The civil rights and anti-war movements made corporate America a special target of their protests. And the consequence of reports of corporate corruption and, finally, Watergate was that "public confidence in the chief executives of major corporations fell like a stone from the mid-1960s to the mid-1970s. The percentage of the public describing themselves as having a great deal of confidence in corporate leaders dropped from 51 percent in the 1966–67 period to an average of 20 percent in the 1974–76 period."[32]

The real weakness of corporate America during this period can be gauged within its own domain as well as in the public sphere. Until 1965, both American labor and American capital had generally adhered to the postwar "social contract" to link wage gains to productivity increases. Indeed, between 1961 and 1965 productivity gains had actually exceeded wage gains for labor. After 1965, however, this relationship was reversed. Between 1966 and 1972 real wages rose 18 percent, while productivity rose only 13 percent.[33] The result of this changing balance of power was a rise in labor's share of the national income and a profit squeeze.[34] The

[30] Ibid., p. 132.

[31] Ibid., p. 133.

[32] Thomas Edsall, *The New Politics of Inequality* (New York: W. W. Norton, 1984), p. 113.

[33] Paul Scheible, "Changes in Employee Compensation, 1966 to 1972," *Monthly Labor Review* 98 (March 1975): 10–16.

[34] Samuel Bowles, David Gordon, and Thomas Weisskopf, *Beyond the Wasteland: A Democratic Alternative to Economic Decline* (Garden City, N.Y.: Doubleday, 1983), p. 103.

seriousness of this reversal in the balance of class power in America is indicated by the program of wage controls the Nixon administration introduced in August 1971 to halt the erosion of corporate profits. But what the administration offered to business with one hand, it withdrew with the other. In the following year, Americans won the largest real increase in their "retirement wages" in the history of the Social Security program.

The seeming contradiction between imposing limits on market wages while simultaneously expanding social wages can be reconciled when we recognize another special feature of the "retirement wage." Whereas any increase in market wages must be paid for immediately, the retirement wage is a deferred wage, an income entitlement to be claimed at some point in the future. The real "Social Security wealth" of the vast majority of Americans was dramatically increased by the reforms of 1972, but only those already retired began to consume that wealth immediately.[35] In the short term at least, a deferred wage—a promise to deliver a benefit at some point in the future—provided a non–zero-sum solution to the problem of mounting wage pressure. Workers won real wage gains—because deferred retirement benefits eventually have to be paid—while employers avoided the cost of significant increases in current real wage bills. In the case of the 1972 reforms, these savings were enhanced by the fact that the benefit increases were not accompanied by increases in contribution rates.

The American experience shows a marked resemblance to the pattern of policy reform that emerged during this period in Europe, where labor entered into formal agreements with governments to forego increases in market wages in exchange for increases in social wages. A case in point was the British pension reform of 1975, the direct result of an agreement between organized labor and the British government in 1974. Similarly, the Italian reforms of 1969 were the product of a formal truce with labor following three general strikes in 1968–69. While the Nixon reforms of 1972 were passed with an eye to an impending election rather than as part of an effort to bring a powerful labor movement to heel, the logic of reform was similar. In the short term at least, workers/voters could be appeased with expanded social benefits at the same moment that market wages were being subjected to restraint.

After 1972, the balance of class power in America began to shift again. As Edsall writes:

During the 1970s, the political wing of the nation's corporate sector staged one of the most remarkable campaigns in the pursuit of polit-

---

[35] For a discussion of the concept of "Social Security wealth," see Martin Feldstein and Anthony Pellechio, "Social Security Wealth: The Impact of Alternative Inflation Adjustments," in Colin Campbell, ed., *Financing Social Security* (Washington, D.C.: American Enterprise Institute, 1979), pp. 91-118.

ical power in recent history. By the late 1970s and the early 1980s, business, and Washington's corporate lobbying community in particular, had gained a level of influence and leverage approaching that of the boom days of the 1920s.[36]

Edsall dates the origins of this mobilization of corporate America to November 1972, when two business organizations whose main purpose was to restrict the influence and bargaining power of organized labor joined to form the Business Roundtable, a policy forum and lobbying agency for America's largest corporations. In the latter half of the 1970s, this mobilization was manifested by the revitalization of the Chamber of Commerce, in which "many of the principals in the formation of the Roundtable participated."[37] What made this revitalization remarkable was not the amount of corporate activity in the political arena but, rather, the content of this activity. Unlike the situation Derthick describes as being typical of an earlier period, business now "refined its ability to act as a class, submerging competitive instincts in favor of joint, cooperative action in the legislative arena."[38] Rather than using up their political capital by competing with one another for a larger share of the government pie, corporations now joined together in the struggle to advance interests they shared in common—defeating consumer protection and labor law reforms, enacting favorable tax legislation, and rolling back America's recently modernized welfare state for the elderly.

Among the most important elements of the attack on Social Security was the extremely successful effort by corporate America to provide an institutional environment for the development of a conservative, probusiness intelligentsia. With a few notable exceptions (William Buckley, Milton Friedman), a major weakness of American conservatism until the 1970s was the absence of a critical mass of intellectuals, literati, and academics capable of presenting the conservative case in a coherent and persuasive fashion. In fact, the "new class" of America's educated elite was targeted as one of the main enemies of traditional business interests.[39] To turn this situation around, business began to put large sums into the creation of think tanks and policy institutes to nurture scholarship and research that could be drawn upon to support its case at all levels of society. These organizations included not only such well-known agencies as the American Enterprise Institute and the National Bureau of Economic Research but also more specialized agencies such as the Employee Benefit Research Institute, which, after its foundation in 1978, poured out hundreds of carefully done analyses demonstrating the problems associated

---

[36] Edsall, *New Politics*, p. 107.
[37] Ibid., p. 123.
[38] Ibid., p. 128.
[39] B. Bruce-Briggs, *The New Class?* (New Brunswick, N.J.: Transaction Books, 1979).

with a publicly financed old-age security system and the advantages of shifting responsibility for this activity to the private sector.

Great care was taken to ensure that Social Security's critics backed up their claims with research that met rigorous academic standards, and that the results of this research were disseminated in an appropriate form to a wide range of audiences. The work of Martin Feldstein, director of the National Bureau of Economic Research from 1977 until his appointment in 1982, as chairman of President Reagan's Council of Economic Advisors, can usefully serve as an example. In 1974, Feldstein launched a spirited debate in U.S. economic circles with an article based on sophisticated econometric methods demonstrating that Social Security had reduced the capital stock of America by a dramatic 38 percent since its inception, a result of its effects on personal savings.[40] In the context of the discussions that followed in the late 1970s about the "deindustrialization" of America, a process blamed on America's historically low rate of saving, this was powerful stuff indeed.

To ensure that the message was communicated, various versions of this and similar articles prepared by Feldstein and his associates appeared in the *Public Interest*, a major disseminator of conservative economic and political views, and in the op-ed pages of America's major newspapers, and they were widely cited in major articles on Social Security appearing in the business press (*Forbes, Fortune, Business Week*). In the end, Feldstein's main numbers were shown to be the result of a programming error which, when corrected, suggested (somewhat implausibly) that Social Security had actually increased the savings rate.[41] But what is significant here is the pattern of intellectual production: from learned journal (replete with sophisticated econometric analysis), to political essay (without numbers) for the American literati, to the business press, and, finally, to the mass media. It was a pattern repeated many times in the late 1970s and early 1980s. The claims varied—Social Security was going broke, Social Security was a bad buy, Social Security was too generous—but the pattern of intellectual production and dissemination of ideas did not. By 1981, when the Reagan administration came to power, the "crisis" of Social Security had successfully penetrated American culture, both high and low. According to Henry Aaron, 80 percent of all Americans were reported to have less than full confidence in Social Security and disillusionment was particularly pronounced among the young.[42]

[40] Martin Feldstein, "Social Security, Induced Retirement and Aggregate Capital Formation," *Journal of Political Economy* 82 (September-October 1974): 905–26.

[41] Dean Leimer and Selig Lesnoy, "Social Security and Private Saving: New Time-Series Evidence," *Journal of Political Economy* 90 (June 1982): 606–42.

[42] Henry Aaron, "Advisory Report on Social Security," *Challenge* (March/April 1980): 12–16.

When placed against the backdrop of the actual cycle of policy innovation, on the one hand, and the shifting balance of class forces in the American political economy, on the other, the timing of the attack on Social Security is understandable. But by themselves these factors do not account for the special significance of Social Security in the efforts of corporate America to reassert its dominance after 1972. In the end, most of the claims of the critics were discredited.[43] Even Martin Feldstein admitted that so long as the voters were prepared to support it, Social Security could not go broke; and all available evidence suggested that the voters were prepared to do just that.[44] In the following section I shall argue that the claims the critics advanced about the long-term implications of the Social Security "debt," while misleading in their emphasis, do point us in the right direction.

Capital, Labor, and the Retirement Wage

The fact that modern welfare states continue to reproduce market-based inequalities is often construed as evidence of the fundamentally "capitalist" character of such provisions. Ironically, however, it was labor, not capital, that provided the political support for the principle of substitutive benefits in the postwar capitalist democracies. As Perrin observes, the first systematic articulation of the substitutive principle is to be found not in the pronouncements of liberal policy reformers but rather in Recommendation 67 passed by the International Labor Organization at its twenty-sixth meeting in Philadelphia in 1944. "Real security" for the worker, Perrin notes, required benefits related to former earnings at a level that would allow the worker and his family to maintain their normal standard of living.[45] Demands for a government-sponsored pension program based on the principle of earnings replacement was advocated by the Swedish Labor Organization as early as 1944, by the Canadian Congress of Labour in 1953, and by the British Trade Union Congress in 1957—all in countries where the more egalitarian flat-benefit formula was in place. Perhaps even more instructive is the fact that in these nations the major opponents of any departure from the flat-benefit principle came from the business community.[46] The great virtues of a flat-benefit

---

[43] Henry Aaron, *Economic Effects of Social Security* (Washington, D.C.: The Brookings Institution, 1982).

[44] Employee Benefit Research Institute, "Louis Harris Survey of the Aged" (Washington, D.C.: Employee Benefit Research Institute, 1981).

[45] Perrin, "Reflections," p. 259.

[46] This point has been made in a large number of national studies, including Gosta Esping-Andersen, *Politics Against Markets* (Princeton: Princeton University Press, 1985); Heclo, *Modern Social Politics*; Anne Menzies, "The Netherlands," in Thomas Wilson, ed., *Pen-*

system were that it kept benefits low and left untouched the lucrative and growing private pension market among middle- and upper-income earners.

For labor, the institutionalization of the retirement wage was a victory that went far beyond income security in old age. Embedded in the retirement wage was an achievement that has tended to be devalued by liberal and leftist critics alike—the right to cease working before wearing out. The remarkable fact about old age in the late twentieth century is that while the elderly generally are not allowed to work, neither are they required to do so. And as the opinion polls amply demonstrate, the right not to work in old age is just as important to most workers as the corresponding denial of the right to continue working.

Now in principle, a retirement wage could have been established simply by having the employer or some other market actor retain control over the deferred wage for distribution during the retirement years. And in part, this was precisely what occurred, as witnessed by the dramatic growth of the private pension industry during the postwar period. But for a variety of reasons, governments in all countries quickly nationalized the bulk of this "new industry"; everywhere, responsibility for administering the retirement wage bill was assumed by the state.[47] And despite national differences in political ideology and social structure, public pensions are now the major source of income for the retired in all capitalist democracies. This development was an event of enormous significance in the evolution of the distributive practices of these nations. For despite frequent protestations to the contrary, a state-administered pension scheme is not just another big insurance company. Instead, an ever-growing and increasingly important portion of the national wage bill is removed from the market and made subject to a democratic political process, one in which workers, in their capacity as citizens, are able to claim a share of the social product that is independent of any claims they possess in their capacity as wage earners. While a democratic polity may choose to respect the norms of the market—that is to link benefits to contributions—it is by no means constrained to do so and, in general, has not done so. All national pension systems, as they have evolved during the past decades, have incorporated democratic principles of equality, need, and adequacy into their distributive practices; all redistribute income—to a greater or lesser degree—from high wage earners to low wage earners; the majority make allowance for need in the form of supplements for

---

sions, *Inflation and Growth* (London: Heinemann, 1974), pp. 110–54; and Barbara Murphy, *Corporate Capital and the Welfare State: Canadian Business and Public Pension Policy in Canada since World War II* (unpublished master's thesis, Carleton University, Ottawa, 1982).

[47] Myles, *Old Age*, chap. 1.

dependent spouses and survivors; and, historically, the majority of countries have legislated increases for the elderly to provide them with a larger share of a growing economic pie. In effect, the retirement wage was transformed into a citizen's wage, an income entitlement partially independent of the commodity value of the worker's labor power. The extent of this transformation varies from country to country, a result of differential levels of working-class power inside the state, but the tendency has been universal.

The retirement wage has aided labor in other ways. As Bowles and Gintis observe, the social wage increasingly insulates the working class from the reserve army of the unemployed.[48] By absorbing the unemployed, the welfare state also absorbs much of the downward pressure on wages that a rise in unemployment would otherwise produce. And among the first to be absorbed in periods of rising unemployment are the elderly: more workers retire and more choose to take advantage of early retirement provisions. Between 1970 and 1979 the labor force participation rate of males aged 55 to 64 declined from 83 to 73 percent.[49]

But the main problem for capital lies in the deferred character of the retirement wage, for unless it can find political or other means to renege on its promises, the deferred wage bill must eventually be paid. Irrespective of how it is financed or whether it is public or private, the cost of today's benefits must ultimately be paid for out of current production, and tomorrow's benefits must be paid for out of tomorrow's production. The real issue lying behind the trillion dollar Social Security deficit once projected for the next century was not that it could not be paid but, more simply, that it would have to be paid. And irrespective of how it is financed, future benefits promised to today's workers represent real wage costs to employers, a fact that is obvious to any elementary economic and business student exposed to "present value theory."

In short, expanding the retirement wage does not actually reduce the wage bill; it simply pushes an increasing portion of the wage bill into the future. And as it expands, so too does the portion of future real wage costs that are fixed in advance. In the language of Marxian economics, a portion of variable capital is in fact no longer variable, and the capacity of capital as a whole to manipulate the total wage bill (market wages + social wages) in response to changing economic conditions is increasingly constrained. This represents a fundamental change in the social character of the capitalist allocation process.

Under capitalism, as Przeworski observes, the trade-off between cur-

---

[48] Samuel Bowles and Herbert Gintis, "The Crisis of Liberal Democratic Capitalism: The Case of the United States," *Politics and Society* 11, no. 1 (1982): 51–93.

[49] Robert Clark and David Barker, *Reversing the Trend Toward Early Retirement* (Washington, D.C.: American Enterprise Institute, 1982), p. 13.

rent wages and current profits is a societal trade-off that affects every-one.[50] Future wage gains are as dependent as future profits on the reten-tion and reinvestment of today's profits. But, Przeworski argues, the actual allocation of increases in the social product created by reinvesting today's profits is, in principle, indeterminate. It may be returned to labor in the form of wage gains, consumed by capital, or exported elsewhere: there is "nothing structural" in the capitalist system that determines this allocation in advance. The advent of the retirement wage bill, however, changes all this. The institutionalization and expansion of the retirement wage in the capitalist democracies mean that the allocation of wealth to be produced in the future is increasingly fixed in advance. And, indeed, actuaries and economists have been busy generating estimates of this fixed portion of tomorrow's wage bill well into the next century. As a *New York Times* article observed, defined benefit plans are "a blank check against corporate assets."[51] In short, the rules of the allocation process under capitalism are changed. In terms of traditional market prin-ciples, a growing share of the national economy is "out of control."

Now it is important to recognize that securing the future incomes of the elderly in this way poses no inherent problem so long as other sectors of the economy are similarly secured. And, indeed, it was just such long-term stabilization of markets, for both labor and capital, that the Keynes-ian system of macro-regulation had provided the American economy dur-ing the preceding decades. The emergence of this system of market stabi-lization and its demise during the 1970s have been thoroughly documented elsewhere.[52] Suffice it to say that by the early 1970s, a whole series of shocks and transformations in the national and international economies were signaling that these conventional mechanisms for long-term market stabilization were breaking down. With inflation and un-employment rising together, Keynesianism was losing its force.

A key element of this macro-regulatory structure was the welfare state itself. It had been intended not merely to stabilize the "wages" of the elderly and the poor, but also to provide a counter-cyclical stimulus that would stabilize the economy as a whole by sustaining demand during eco-nomic downturns. In sum, stabilizing wages, whether for active or retired workers, was acceptable so long as this served to stabilize corporate prof-its as well. When it appeared that wage stabilization was no longer serv-ing to stabilize long-term corporate profits, the *raison d'être* of these

[50] Adam Przeworski, "Material Bases of Consent: Economics and Politics in a Hegemonic System,'" *Political Power and Social Theory* 1 (1980): 21–66.

[51] Deborah Rankin, "The Fading of the Fixed Pension Plan," *New York Times*, March 20, 1983, p. F–15.

[52] Michael Piore and Charles Sabel, *The Second Industrial Divide* (New York: Basic Books, 1984).

mechanisms disappeared, and indeed they became counterproductive. In the language that began to emerge during this period, welfare and efficiency could no longer be construed as compatible principles of economic organization.[53]

Thus, the modernization of America's welfare state for the elderly occurred at almost the same moment when the system of macro-regulation for the economy that could legitimate such a program was beginning to break down. And Social Security was all the more visible a target due to its uniqueness within the American welfare state structure. Within this context the special significance that Social Security acquired in the conservative offensive becomes understandable. The future incomes of today's workers had been secured—that is what income security means—while future profits had not. The projected increase of America's elderly population simply exacerbated this problem. From the point of view of corporate America, a growing share of the national income was "out of control," and the problem would become even more severe in the future. Accordingly, the wages of the elderly, like the wages of the young, would have to be subjected to the rigors of market disciplines once again and be returned to the private sector.

Conclusion

If the attack on Social Security was successful in generating widespread alarm about the long-term viability of the system, it was less successful in achieving its objectives. American public opinion proved remarkably resistant to demands that the system be dismantled or significantly cut back. In 1981, Louis Harris polls showed the majority of Americans thought government should be doing more for America's elderly and were prepared to pay higher taxes to ensure the viability of the program.[54] As a result, the Reagan administration was forced to back away from the more radical proposals that had been advanced to "save" the system. In the United States, as elsewhere, the modern welfare state that constructs broad political coalitions between lower- and middle-income earners has proven to be highly resistant to such direct assault. But this resistance also points to the fact that the long-term viability of Social Security depends less on demographic developments than on the viability of the political coalitions that sustain it.

The attack on Social Security demonstrated that the "modern welfare state," one that incorporates a broad section of the middle classes as well

[53] Theodore Geiger and Frances Geiger, *Welfare and Efficiency* (London: Macmillan, 1978).
[54] See Employee Benefit Research Institute, "Louis Harris Survey."

as the poor, cannot easily be dismantled. It is less certain, however, that it is immune to a long-term process of slow erosion. Cuts were made during the first term of the Reagan administration, and, though modest, the cumulation of many such small "adjustments" can seriously erode the program over the longer term. This, after all, was how America's modern system of retirement wages was constructed—through a series of incremental changes to the base established in 1935. This, as Derthick has pointed out, was a deliberate strategy of American policy reformers. There is nothing to prevent those who would dismantle the welfare state from adopting a similar strategy.

III

SOCIAL POLICY, RACE, AND
THE "POVERTY PROBLEM"

The distinctive configuration of public social provision launched by the New Deal and extended during the 1960s and 1970s greatly increased the economic security of many Americans. At the same time, however, it left others vulnerable to changes in the national economy and to new patterns of social organization. Nowhere were the limits of American social and economic policy more telling than among black Americans. The essays in this section examine the intersection between race and social policy, exploring the complex and volatile matrix of issues that set the agenda for the Great Society and remains at the heart of social policy debates today.

To make sense of the assumptions that guided policymaking and shaped the policy of the Great Society, we look to the pattern of social and economic intervention launched during the New Deal. The operation of policy feedbacks are thus central to the issues discussed in this section. The critical feature of New Deal social policy that would continue to shape public intervention for the next half century was the bifurcation of policy into two tiers: a top layer of increasingly generous, politically legitimated social insurance programs and a bottom layer of politically vulnerable programs aimed at the poor. Once established, this pattern of policy channeled the development of federal government capacities along particular lines and affected possibilities for alliances of social interests.

The bifurcation of social policy would have its most profound impact on black Americans. As the Skocpol essay points out, the framers of Social Security conceived the system in a regionally divided federal democracy that gave little political leverage to blacks. By denying coverage to those in agricultural and service occupations, the Social Security Act effectively excluded most blacks from its old-age and unemployment provisions. Moreover, the two-tiered framework established by New Deal social policies proved insufficient to meet the changing needs of rural and urban blacks, disproportionately located at the bottom of the social and economic system. Skocpol, Orfield, and Slessarev each discuss aspects of the effort to address the problems of black Americans within this two-tiered system of social policy.

Skocpol argues that the achievements and omissions of the Social Security Act are critical for understanding the lines along which social policy developed after the 1930s. She points to the distinction between welfare and social security as a central legacy of the New Deal. Believing that all Americans would eventually be covered by contributory social insurance programs, the framers of the Social Security Act did little to bolster the public assistance programs also provided for in the new legislation. In fact, in their desire to build up the legitimacy of social insurance, Social Security administrators sought to ensure that public assistance programs would remain relatively ungenerous and stigmatizing. Despite the obvious miscalculations of New Deal policymakers, the central distinctions established during the New Deal would hold in the 1960s when the rolls of the main public assistance program, Aid to Families with Dependent Children (AFDC), exploded. As benefits for the elderly and disabled clients of social insurance programs steadily increased, the low-income women and children primarily served by public assistance repeatedly found themselves the targets of budget cutters.

Another New Deal legacy emphasized by Skocpol is the federal government's failure to embrace a policy of full employment. When Roosevelt's Committee on Economic Security established the framework for the Social Security Act, it predicated its social policy recommendations on accompanying proposals for ensuring full employment. Yet with the defeat of the Full Employment Bill in 1945, social policy was left to shoulder an exceptionally heavy burden. This rejection of the full employment–welfare state reinforced a sharp disjuncture between social and economic policy, and it narrowed the scope of what subsequently would be considered legitimate economic policy.

Spurred by the demands of the civil rights movement and the formal extension of full political rights to blacks, the Great Society sought to add onto the existing framework of social programs new policies aimed at the poor and, in particular, urban blacks. The Great Society thus did little to alter the basic two-tiered structure of social policy in America. Instead, the new "poverty programs" highlighted and further entrenched the bifurcated pattern of public social provision inherited from the New Deal. As the essays in this section detail, the Johnson administration launched a range of new initiatives that included Medicaid, federally subsidized housing, and job training. Unlike the older social insurance programs established in the New Deal, the new anti-poverty policies were not meant to be universal programs; they were directed at the poor. Nor did these new policies seek to question the established bounds of economic policy. As both Orfield and Skocpol point out, the social programs of the 1960s assumed that no fundamental changes in national economic management were necessary to address the "leftover" problem of poverty.

The potential ability of the Great Society to end poverty was never fully tested, as social programs directed at the poor, particularly the black poor, quickly became the targets of cutbacks. Skocpol, Orfield, and Slessarev each offer a perspective on the political vulnerability of the race-specific policies launched during the Great Society. Skocpol argues that without collective justification, social policies have little defense against anti-statist attacks claiming to speak in the name of individual rights and freedom. Particularly in periods of economic distress, social policies that have not been legitimated as expressions of collectively held values will come under mounting pressure. This, she argues, is what happened to the lower tier of social welfare policies during the 1970s and 1980s.

Orfield expands on this theme, chronicling the collapse of the liberal agenda on racial issues. Arguing that the urban ghetto had come into being as a result of longstanding governmental neglect of blacks, he maintains that race-conscious remedies aimed at integrating blacks and breaking down the ghetto were the only way to address the social and economic problems facing blacks. Education and housing, two policy realms central to social and economic mobility, were among the most important areas in which the strategy of integration was attempted. Orfield argues that, despite strong black support for integration, sustained action along these lines never materialized. Faced with substantial white opposition, strong measures to promote integration were abandoned before they had even gotten underway. The liberal coalition that had supported civil rights in the South fractured when confronted by the more complex social and economic issues linked with race in the North.

White backlash created special problems for Democrats, as both Orfield and Skocpol show. Counter to many expectations, the Johnson administration initially provided considerable support for the southern civil rights movement and, in 1965, was on the verge of offering a new set of policy initiatives directed at the social and economic problems affecting blacks in the North as well as in the South. These proposals were stillborn, however. White resistance to integration escalated dramatically in the mid-1960s, as urban riots rocked the major cities of the North. Attentive to the concerns of its white constituents and frustrated by its inability to control the urban turmoil, the Johnson administration quickly retreated from the ambitious agenda of racial policies it had only recently outlined. Orfield argues that the abandonment of blacks reshaped liberal politics and policy in a number of ways. He traces the rise of the black power movement to the desertion of blacks by liberals; with little hope for federal support for social and economic remedies, arguments for black self-reliance became increasingly attractive (although Orfield points out that a majority of blacks continued to support integration). Among white Democrats, the retreat from racial issues laid the groundwork for a new set of understandings that interpreted the problems confronting blacks in terms of the failure of individuals. Seen in this light, the social and economic problems confronting blacks were no longer amenable to government action.

Slessarev offers yet another perspective on the politics of race and social policy by examining the pattern of budgetary cutbacks during the first Reagan administration. Focusing on Medicaid and subsidized housing—both lower tier social programs that target poor, disproportionately minority recipients—she argues that three factors determine how well programs will survive periods of retrenchment. Programs that are hastily passed or enacted with much contention at the end of a cycle of reform are likely to be targets of cuts. When such programs threaten the racial status quo and remain outside established institutional networks, they are likely to be met with vocal opponents and few strong sources of support. Thus, subsidized housing, a program enacted as a quick response to the upheavals of the 1960s, found its budget eviscerated in 1981, while Medicaid, a longstanding item on the Democratic agenda throughout the 1950s, remained relatively intact. Slessarev shows that, unlike Medicaid, which simply distributed reimbursements to recipients, subsidized housing was charged with racial implications because the 1968 Housing Act had explicitly sought to promote racial integration. Finally, Medicaid had accumulated a strong support network among hospital administrators and state officials who had come to rely on Medicaid revenues. Lacking a comparable structure of institutional support, subsidized housing found few allies to defend it against proposed cuts.

Without a supportive political coalition, social policy issues relevant to blacks were largely dropped from the U.S. national agenda by the early 1970s. With inflation eating away at AFDC payments and black unemployment rates soaring, the economic position of poor blacks steadily eroded as national attention was directed elsewhere. In recent years, however, worries about a persistent "culture of poverty" have sparked concerns about the adequacy of existing social policies to address the problems of the black poor. As Orfield and also Neckerman, Aponte, and Wilson indicate, much of the commentary has interpreted rising illegitimacy, unemployment, and school dropout rates as evidence of individual irresponsibility that current programs only exacerbate. The essays by Bane and Neckerman, Aponte, and Wilson take up this issue, suggesting that the problems underlying the persistence of urban ghettos are far more complex and will require new forms of public intervention if they are to be solved.

Bane analyzes the new face that poverty has taken since the Great Society. Increasingly, the poor are composed of women and children, with minority women and children particularly vulnerable to poverty. But, she shows, the "feminization of poverty" actually encompasses two separate problems. For white women, poverty is more often the result of a change in family situation, such as divorce, and is more likely to be short-term. Among black women, however, poverty is less associated with changes in family composition, since black women and their children are more likely to be poor both before and after any change in family situation. Their poverty is, therefore, usually more long-term than that of white women. Bane's analysis suggests that any simple policy approach to the feminization of poverty will not work. In particular, she points out, child support programs may benefit white women whose former spouses can afford to pay, but such programs will have little impact on the poverty of black women. If the new feminization of poverty is to be addressed, the longstanding problem of chronic poverty in the black ghetto must be tackled.

Neckerman, Aponte, and Wilson's analysis complements that of Bane and suggests that the federal government needs to rethink the relationship between race and social policy. Their essay asks why it is that black women are more likely to be part of female-headed households so susceptible to poverty. They suggest that the answer has much to do with the high rates of unemployment among black males. Rejecting the argument that welfare incentives account for the growth of female-headed households among blacks, they construct an index of the "male marriageable pool" and show that high rates of black unemployment have contributed to a marked decline in the number of economically stable—"marriageable"—black men. These findings, they argue, show that the social policy focus of the past has been misplaced. Like Bane, they believe that attention must be directed to increasing employment among the poor with a broad range of programs designed to promote economic growth and create tight labor markets. They also call for the replacement of the current welfare system with a variety of social programs available to working- and middle-class Americans, as well as to the poor. Such universal programs coupled with appropriate economic policies, they argue, are more likely to attract widespread popular support than did the race-specific policies of the past.

The structure of social policy inherited from the New Deal proved an inadequate framework for creating further policies to address the needs of Americans at the bottom of the economic ladder. Each of the chapters in this section underscores the political vulnerability of the "poverty programs" that emerged during the 1960s and 1970s within the bifurcated structure of U.S. social policy. They also show that the narrow definitions of economic policy established after World War II placed an overwhelming burden on social programs in America. Taken together, the essays suggest that the persistence of poverty, particularly among black Americans, can be addressed only by new universal policies—and correspondingly broad political coalitions—that transcend the limits of the New Deal system.

8

The Limits of the New Deal System and the Roots of Contemporary Welfare Dilemmas

THEDA SKOCPOL

During the past two decades, the social policies of the U.S. national government have been the focus of heated political controversies that have gone well beyond mere tinkering with the terms of the 1935 Social Security Act, the charter legislation for America's social insurance and public assistance programs. These controversies are far from over. Debates about the rising costs of old-age insurance and medical coverage, about the adequacy or efficacy of welfare, and about the basic legitimacy of national public efforts to cope with social dependency promise to be with us for some time to come. The United States is unmistakably in the midst of a watershed in its public social policies.

From the 1960s through the early 1970s, the United States looked to many observers as if it might soon complete—in its own peculiar way—a belated progress toward a European-style welfare state.[1] The "War on Poverty" of Lyndon Johnson's Great Society promised to address the special needs of groups left beyond the reach of the New Deal's social legis-

Final revisions of this paper benefited from astute comments and criticisms by Christopher Jencks, Jennifer Hochschild, Robert Kuttner, and Craig Reinarman.

[1] Until recently, the comparative social science literature on welfare states has been remarkably evolutionist, assuming that sooner or later all welfare states would establish a full array of five types of programs—accident, old-age, sickness, unemployment, and family allowance—and expand benefits and population coverage for each type of hazard. In addition, welfare states were expected to integrate such programs with universally available public assistance for low-income people, overcoming the lingering stigma attached to public assistance from the era of pre-industrial poor laws. Sweden, Great Britain, and other Western European nations were implicitly the models for "full welfare state development," and the United States and other industrial or industrializing nations were expected, perhaps with delays due to peculiar national values or class relations, to follow in their footsteps.

lation.[2] An array of special programs was launched to address the difficulties faced by inner-city blacks and inhabitants of non-urban "depressed" areas, and efforts were made to nationalize income supports for the poor. Manpower and public employment programs were fashioned to cope with "structural unemployment." Reformers inside and outside of government hoped that national health insurance would soon follow the enactment of Medicare for the elderly and Medicaid for the poor.

But the liberal-reformist controversies of the 1960s soon gave way to the conflicts over social policy retrenchment that dominated the national political agenda after the 1980 presidential election. During the 1970s, formerly liberal academics led the way in attacking Great Society programs as overambitious and costly failures, and Keynesian tenets of macroeconomic management came under increasing criticism from economists and publicists who argued that excessive government spending and regulation hurt economic growth.[3] An effort at national welfare reform petered out during Jimmy Carter's presidency.[4] Thereafter, the main preoccupation of social policy advocates became the shoring up of existing programs, especially retirement insurance and Medicare for the elderly, in the face of rapidly rising costs.

Political forces gathered to reverse the trends of thirty years of social policymaking. In 1975, David Stockman, the man who became President Reagan's budget director in 1981, attacked what he called the "great social pork barrel" and called for major cuts in federal social spending on the grounds of equity and economic efficiency.[5] Once in power, the Reagan administration found that it was not politically feasible to cut major middle-class entitlement programs such as social security. But the first Reagan administration did manage to achieve other domestic spending cuts, primarily by shrinking programs that were started or expanded dur-

[2] For overviews of Great Society efforts, see Sar A. Levitan and Robert Taggart, *The Promise of Greatness* (Cambridge, Mass.: Harvard University Press, 1976), pts. 1 and 2, and James T. Patterson, *America's Struggle Against Poverty, 1900–1980* (Cambridge, Mass.: Harvard University Press, 1981), pt. 3.

[3] For representative critiques of the Great Society efforts, see Henry Aaron, *Politics and the Professors* (Washington, D.C.: The Brookings Institution, 1977), and Daniel Patrick Moynihan, *Maximum Feasible Misunderstanding* (New York: The Free Press, 1970). The retreat from Keynesianism is discussed in Ira Katznelson, "A Radical Departure: Social Welfare and the Election," in Thomas Ferguson and Joel Rogers, eds., *The Hidden Election: Politics and Economics in the 1980 Presidential Campaign* (New York: Pantheon Books, 1981), pp. 313–40.

[4] Laurence E. Lynn, Jr., and David deF Whitman, *The President as Policymaker: Jimmy Carter and Welfare Reform* (Philadelphia, Pa.: Temple University Press, 1981).

[5] David A. Stockman, "The Social Pork Barrel," *The Public Interest* no. 39 (Spring 1975): 3–30.

ing the Great Society period.[6] During its second term, moreover, the Reagan administration conducted an in-house review of all public assistance programs for the poor, with the rhetorical emphasis upon finding ways to "reduce welfare dependency" while de-emphasizing the role of the national government.[7]

The unsettledness of American social politics from the 1960s to the present must be understood in relation to what the Social Security Act did, and did not, achieve—and, indeed, in relation to the whole array of social and economic reforms that the New Deal did, and did not, accomplish. The New Deal's accomplishments and shortcomings created the matrix for subsequent political struggles over public social policies in America. Only against this historical background—with history understood not just as past events but as processes over time leading into the present—can we properly understand the nature of the contemporary political debates about U.S. social provision.

In the following sections, I analyze social and political patterns that can help us to understand the present controversies over public social provision. Rather than attempt a single chronological narration, I move back and forth between the New Deal era and the period since the 1960s, suggesting under a number of thematic headings how earlier institutional and policy patterns have fed into the ongoing dilemmas of contemporary U.S. social politics.

"Social Security" versus "Welfare": A Legacy of the New Deal

Social scientists may use the term *welfare state* to refer to the entire set of social insurance and public assistance programs operating in virtually every industrial nation, the United States included. Obviously, though, the term has an inappropriate ring about it in the case of the United

---

[6] See David A. Stockman, *The Triumph of Politics: The Inside Story of the Reagan Revolution* (New York: Avon Books, 1987); Jack Meyer, "Budget Cuts in the Reagan Administration: A Question of Fairness," in D. Lee Bawden, ed., *The Social Contract Revisited* (Washington, D.C.: The Urban Institute, 1984), pp. 33–64, and Edward J. Harpham, "Fiscal Crisis and the Politics of Social Security Reform," in Anthony Champagne and Edward J. Harpham, eds., *The Attack on the Welfare State* (Prospect Heights, Ill.: Waveland Press, 1984), esp. pp. 26–32.

[7] *Up From Dependency: A New National Public Assistance Strategy*, Report to the President by the Domestic Policy Council Low Income Opportunity Working Group (Review Draft, December 1986). During the mid-1980s, in fact, state governments became the chief loci of debates over such social policy initiatives as reforming welfare by adding work requirements. See the discussion of several states' programs in Michael Wiseman, "Workfare and Welfare Policy," *Focus* (Newsletter of the University of Wisconsin's Institute for Research on Poverty) 9, no. 3 (Fall and Winter 1986): 1–8.

States. For in practical political rhetoric, Americans make a sharp conceptual and evaluative distinction between "social security" and "welfare." *Social security* refers to old-age insurance and the associated programs of survivors', disability, and medical coverage for the elderly; and these programs are seen as sacred governmental obligations to deserving workers who have paid for them through "contributions" over their working lifetimes. *Welfare*, by contrast, is often discussed as a set of governmental "handouts" to barely deserving poor people who may be trying to avoid honest employment—trying to get something for nothing.

"Welfare state" as a political slogan originated in Britain during World War II.[8] It indicated an aspiration to integrate all forms of income assistance, social services, and social insurance into a complete system of social protection for all British citizens, and it was held up as an ideal worth fighting for in the conflict with Nazi Germany. Tellingly, no such ideal has ever gained currency in American social politics. Americans do not think of the federal government's public benefits as adding up to an integrated system, applicable to *all* citizens. Instead, they sharply distinguish welfare programs from social security. And only social security has positive legitimacy as a state activity and comes close to being identified with full citizenship rights for Americans.

The exact programs connoted by social security versus those connoted by welfare have shifted over time since the 1930s, but the bifurcation itself was implicit in the original Social Security Act and was deliberately emphasized by the administrators of the act after 1935.[9] The framers of the Social Security Act made sure that unemployment insurance and old-age insurance would start to pay out benefits only after workers or employers had paid in taxes for some years. And they tried to minimize the federal government's outlays for public assistance to the poor by putting one-half to two-thirds of the fiscal obligation onto the hard-pressed states and leaving the states responsible for setting benefit levels and eligibility rules. Those who formulated the Social Security Act hoped that, over time, most Americans would earn protections from contributory social insurance programs and cease to need public assistance at all.

After the Social Security Act was passed, its administrators worked hard from 1936 through the 1950s to build up contributory old-age insurance, the only fully national program they controlled, and simultaneously to reduce the popular appeal of federally subsidized old-age public

---

[8] Peter Flora and Arnold J. Heidenheimer, "The Historical Core and Changing Boundaries of the Welfare State," in Flora and Heidenheimer, eds., *The Development of the Welfare State in Europe and America* (New Brunswick, N.J.: Transaction Books, 1981), p. 19.

[9] This draws upon Theda Skocpol and John Ikenberry, "The Political Formation of the American Welfare State in Historical and Comparative Perspective," *Comparative Social Research* 6 (1983): 92–119.

assistance.[10] This was not easy. Until the 1950s, more older Americans received old-age assistance (one-half funded by their states, one-half by the federal government) than were covered by contributory old-age insurance. Moreover, there were recurrent political efforts by Townsend movement advocates of flat-rate pensions, by Keynesians, and by conservatives to substitute need-based old-age pensions for contributory insurance. But in their dealings both with the public and with Congress, the Social Security administrators presented old-age insurance as an "earned right," an honorable "contract" between each working citizen and the government. What is more, they used administrative discretion to make sure that public assistance remained niggardly, as well as difficult and demeaning to obtain. Many states, especially in the South, treated welfare in this way without federal encouragement; but the Social Security administrators also reined in would-be liberal states like California to make sure that public assistance did not become too easily available or too appealing.

During the 1950s, beneficiaries of social security old-age insurance finally overtook those receiving welfare assistance for the elderly, as more and more retiring workers became eligible for social security payments. Social security was becoming politically popular and sacrosanct. Under Republican and Democratic administrations alike, working alliances between the Social Security Administration and key congressional committees led to the expansion of coverage, higher benefits, and the addition to social security of a new disability and medical-insurance programs.[11] By the early 1970s, social security was sufficiently extended and liberalized to function as a true retirement wage for regularly employed workers, including many middle-class Americans.[12]

Meanwhile, a public assistance program that had been quite minor at the time it was brought into the Social Security Act of 1935 expanded greatly in response to unanticipated social and economic changes. This program—Aid to Families with Dependent Children (AFDC), whose rolls grew steadily in the 1950s and early 1960s and exploded after that[13]—primarily dispenses grants to mothers without husbands to support them

[10] Jerry R. Cates, *Insuring Inequality: Administrative Leadership in Social Security, 1935–54* (Ann Arbor: University of Michigan Press, 1983).

[11] Martha Derthick, *Policymaking for Social Security* (Washington, D.C.: The Brookings Institution, 1979).

[12] On social security as a retirement wage, see the paper by John Myles in this volume (Chapter 7).

[13] Winifred Bell, *Aid to Dependent Children* (New York: Columbia University Press, 1965); Patterson, *America's Struggle Against Poverty*, chap. 11. As Patterson points out (p. 171), the "number of Americans on public assistance grew from 7.1 million in 1960 . . . to 14.4 million in 1974," and "all of this growth came in the numbers on AFDC, which increased from 3.1 million in 1960 . . . to 10.8 million by 1974."

and their children. Since the 1950s, AFDC clients have been marginal participants in labor markets and thus not able to build up social insurance rights of various kinds.

By the 1960s, AFDC became the visible embodiment of welfare understood in contrast to social security, and Great Society programs targeting the poor tended to be incorporated into the welfare rubric. Ironically, the efforts the Social Security Administration had made over the years to differentiate two kinds of old-age coverage were in effect transferred into the bifurcations of the current period—between public benefits for the elderly, on the one hand, and public benefits for the unemployed and underemployed poor, on the other. As the first years of the Reagan administration clearly demonstrated, this symbolic and programmatic bifurcation built into the American scheme of public benefits really matters. Even though low-income public assistance programs accounted for less than 18 percent of federal social spending, far less than the proportions for social security and Medicare, these welfare programs took the brunt of the Reagan efforts to trim the "social pork barrel."[14] The expanding ranks of the poor, primarily mothers and children, have suffered while the elderly clients of social security have continued to improve their economic standing.[15]

The Failure of Social Keynesianism and Full Employment

The Social Security Act of 1935 was originally planned in 1934–35 by a body of Roosevelt administration officials and selected expert advisors called, not incidentally, "the Committee on Economic Security." Although the committee's report to the president was careful to maintain throughout a firm distinction between "social insurance" for nondependent, employable people and "relief" or "public assistance" for dependent unemployables, it was also eloquent in insisting that this approach would work only if the federal government permanently committed itself to providing guarantees of suitable public employment for willing workers who exhausted unemployment benefits, or were not covered, or could

[14] John Palmer and Isabel Sawhill, *The Reagan Experiment* (Washington, D.C.: The Urban Institute, 1982), p. 373.

[15] See Samuel H. Preston, "Children and the Elderly: Divergent Paths for America's Dependents," *Demography* 21, no. 4 (November 1984): 437–57, and the overview of current findings on "The Relative Well-Being of the Elderly and Children: Domestic and International Comparisons," *Focus* (Newsletter of the University of Wisconsin's Institute for Research on Poverty) 9, no. 3 (Fall and Winter 1986): 10–14. See also Irwin Garfinkel and Sara McLanahan, *Single Mothers and Their Children: A New American Dilemma* (Washington, D.C.: The Urban Institute, 1986).

not find private employment.[16] Patterns of social-welfare provision, in short, were seen as inextricably tied to complementary public policies to ensure full employment. Such plans and hopes of the Committee on Economic Security were not realized, however.

At the time the Social Security Act was proposed, its formulators thought that the appropriate larger economic framework could be institutionalized simply through extensions of New Deal public works and public employment programs, and through the establishment of the National Resources Board as a permanent executive agency for social and economic planning by the federal government. Later, beginning in the late 1930s, many liberal New Dealers also became "social Keynesians," adopting the view that permanently high levels of federal social spending should be coordinated with macroeconomic stimulation to ensure steady growth with full employment.[17] During World War II, social Keynesians drew up the Full Employment Bill of 1945.[18] This measure would have reorganized federal budgeting and economic planning capacities and unequivocally committed the national government to using public spending and other appropriate governmental means to ensure jobs for all Americans willing to work.

But the New Deal did not culminate in social Keynesianism or in government guarantees to pursue full employment through public action (for reasons that Margaret Weir has explored in Chapter 4 of this volume). Instead, from the late 1940s to the 1970s, mainstream American Keynesians with the greatest academic prestige and most access to national policy planning through the Council of Economic Advisors stressed the fine-tuning of fiscal and monetary adjustments within relatively limited parameters of government action and domestic social spending.[19] Such "commercial Keynesians" understood their finest moment to be the decision by President John Kennedy in 1962 to cut taxes in order to stimulate economic growth.[20]

The New Dealers who originally planned and proposed the Social Security Act believed that unemployment was the most basic hazard that

---

[16] *Report to the President of the Committee on Economic Security* (Washington, D.C.: U.S. Government Printing Office, 1935), p. 1 and passim.

[17] See Dean L. May, *From New Deal to New Economics: The American Liberal Response to the Recession of 1937* (New York: Garland, 1981); Richard V. Gilbert et. al., *An Economic Program for American Democracy* (New York: Vanguard Press, 1938); and Robert M. Collins, *The Business Response to Keynes* (New York: Columbia University Press, 1981), chaps. 1 and 2, esp. pp. 10–12 and 51, on "stagnationist Keynesianism."

[18] On the Full Employment Bill, its background, and its fundamental modification before passage, see Stephen Kemp Bailey, *Congress Makes a Law: The Story Behind the Employment Act of 1946* (New York: Columbia University Press, 1946).

[19] Collins, *Business Response to Keynes*, pt. 3.

[20] Robert Lekachman, *The Age of Keynes* (New York: Vintage Books, 1966), chap. 11.

would be addressed by the nascent American welfare state they were launching; yet the timid commercial Keynesianism with which the federal government addressed this problem after the defeat of the Full Employment Bill of 1945 fell far short of the guaranteed "employment assurance" originally envisaged by the Committee on Economic Security. Nevertheless, following World War II the U.S. national economy was reasonably healthy. Its steady growth with but moderate inflation and unemployment was propelled by limited federal efforts at macroeconomic management, by wage and benefit bargains in the private corporate sector that kept consumer purchasing power high, and of course by the temporarily privileged position of the U.S. economy within the postwar international economy.[21]

The postwar U.S. political economy, including the New Deal's social security system, worked well enough to meet the expectations of the majority of American workers who were steadily employed. As more and more employees became covered by contributory old-age insurance, they could look forward to basic public support in retirement, perhaps supplemented by private-sector benefits gained through union bargaining. Federal unemployment insurance was markedly uneven across the states and not easily coordinated with Keynesian macroeconomic management; nevertheless, it served the steadily employed as a back-up for temporary periods of unemployment.[22]

Even during the 1950s and 1960s, however, the lack of a U.S. national commitment to ensure full employment was telling for those unlucky people who were willing to work but unable to to so regularly or at adequate wage levels. For such Americans, including residents of depressed regions and blacks migrating out of the rural South, the New Deal's social programs were left to bear much more weight than their formulators had ever intended. The persistent ranks of black males marginal to the labor market and the growing ranks of dependents on AFDC were indications, even in the prosperous parts of the postwar era, of the prescience of those New Deal reformers who had doubted that social security's social insur-

[21] See Michael J. Piore and Charles Sabel, *The Industrial Divide* (New York: Basic Books, 1984), chap. 4, and Charles S. Maier, "The Politics of Productivity: Foundations of American International Economic Policy after World War II," in Peter Katzenstein, ed., *Between Power and Plenty* (Madison: University of Wisconsin Press, 1978), pp. 3–49.

[22] On the unevenness of unemployment coverage, see Joseph M. Becker, "Twenty-five Years of Unemployment Insurance," *Political Science Quarterly* 75 (1960): 481–99; on the difficulties of meshing unemployment insurance with Keynesian macroeconomic management, see Edward J. Harpham, "Federalism, Keynesianism, and the Transformation of Unemployment Insurance in the United States," in Douglas Ashford and E. W. Kelley, eds., *Nationalizing Social Security in Europe and America* (Greenwich, Conn.: JAI Press, 1986), pp. 155–79.

ance programs could be adequate without what they called federal "employment assurance."

Briefly during the 1960s, federal labor market and job training programs emerged as part of the Great Society's War on Poverty, yet these programs remained adjuncts of the predominant "anti-poverty" and "welfare reform" themes of the period.[23] Equally damaging, these policies were never accepted as part of overall federal strategies for managing the economy as such. Commercial Keynesian macroeconomists remained in charge—until the puzzlingly persistent "stagflation" of the 1970s raised questions about their ability to predict and manage the national economy.

The discrediting of Keynesian certainties in the 1970s was accompanied by the rising political credibility of "monetarist" and "supply-side" arguments that too much—not too little—"government spending" and "interference with the free market" lie at the root of any U.S. economic difficulties.[24] By the 1980s, it became apparent that even periods of economic recovery and growth were unlikely to bring the United States as close to full employment as it was in the 1950s and 1960s. For the foreseeable future, unemployment rates—which do not even include the large numbers of "discouraged workers" who have dropped out of the labor market altogether—seem unlikely to drop below 5 or 6 percent at best. And structural declines in heavy industries are displacing many formerly privileged industrial workers. Yet even in the face of these developments, calls for the federal government to devise bold, new full employment strategies have been but faintly heard in academic and political discourse.

In historical perspective, this is not surprising. Back during the founding period of its modern interventionist state, from 1930 through 1946, the United States originally opted *not* to closely coordinate "social" and "economic" interventions. Throughout the postwar period, U.S. macroeconomic managers de-emphasized public spending and did not work to coordinate manpower and labor market interventions (or any other sectorally specific interventions) with the fiscal and monetary adjustments used to encourage economic growth. The technical and intellectual capacities of the federal government to devise and implement targeted industrial or labor market interventions were not improved during the era of commercial Keynesian dominance. Little intellectual or political legitimacy was built up for the notion that the federal government could—or should—pursue economic, employment, and social-welfare objectives

---

[23] See the paper by Margaret Weir in this volume (Chapter 4).
[24] See Katznelson, "A Radical Departure."

through the same public policies or through deliberately coordinated public policies.

Thus, when economic growth faltered and stagflation persisted in the 1970s, moderate Democrats and conservative Republicans understandably perceived trade-offs between economic growth and social protection (including protection against unemployment). Predictably, too, they responded—starting during the Democratic presidency of Jimmy Carter—by advocating at least the appearance of a reduced role for government in relation to the economy. Under President Reagan, many de facto Keynesian measures certainly were used to stimulate economic demand, but they were not labeled as such. And the labeling was significant, for it was part of an overall effort by conservatives in the 1980s to de-legitimate public spending and governmental interventions as "economically inefficient."

In one sense, of course, such Reagan administration tactics reacted against the logic of American public policies in the commercial Keynesian era of the 1940s to the 1970s. But, in another sense, they were an understandable culmination of the original failure of the New Deal to institutionalize social Keynesian policies and full employment guarantees as complements to social policies premised on the notion that all able-bodied Americans would be able to work at well-paid jobs in a growing national economy. The commercial Keynesianism with which the postwar United States muddled through was, it is now clear, only a fair-weather support for the social needs of American workers. By downplaying the role of the state in coping with economic problems, the policies and rhetoric of the commercial Keynesian era paved the way for further retreats from public solutions once their own efficacy became questionable.

The Unstable Place of Blacks in the New Deal System

If the framers and—especially—the administrators of the Social Security Act established a bifurcation between "social security" and "welfare," the New Deal as a whole laid the basis for the eventual politicization of this division along racially charged lines. This politicization would become especially bitter in a political economy without the will or the means to ensure full employment, since blacks are disproportionately the victims of insufficient employment opportunities for the least skilled and poorest Americans.

In effect, blacks were only marginally included in the social security programs launched by the New Deal, for in the 1930s they were still mostly at the bottom of a racial caste system and a backward economy in the South. Yet New Deal economic interventions ended up facilitating structural transformations in the southern economy that would urbanize black poverty. What is more, the Democratic party that sponsored and benefited from the New Deal began to mobilize urban blacks into electoral coalitions. By the 1960s, the Democratic party would have to cope with political contradictions engendered by the shifting socioeconomic status and rising political demands of blacks. From the Great Society to the recent efforts to revitalize Democratic coalitions to do battle with Reagan Republicans, the Democratic party has grappled with these racially charged political contradictions.

The core social insurance programs established by the New Deal—old-age insurance and unemployment insurance—did not reach most American blacks. The agricultural and service occupations open to most blacks at that time were simply excluded from social insurance taxes and coverage. Had this not been done to propitiate politically powerful southern Democrats and representatives of commercial farmers, it is doubtful that the Social Security Act could have gotten through Congress.[25] Likewise, the Social Security Act's institutionalization of federally subsidized public assistance programs gave free rein to state-level variations in benefits and eligibility, and allowed state and local officials to exercise administrative discretion. This meant that blacks in the South could be deprived of adequate welfare assistance. Southern economic interests were left free to enforce labor discipline on their own terms and retain competitive advantages in relation to higher-wage industries in the North.

Although Franklin Roosevelt and the New Deal facilitated and benefited from the expansion of urban liberalism in the Democratic party during the 1930s, they never could escape dependence on the southern party oligarchs whose local sway partially rested on the exclusion of blacks from electoral politics. When it came to appealing to black voters, the New Deal Democrats confined their efforts to the northern cities, where they were building multi-ethnic coalitions in tandem with the growing trade unions. Northern blacks were the last and the most marginal group to join the New Deal electoral coalition.[26] Fatefully for the future of the Democratic party, they had gained a toehold through which black demands could be pressed more aggressively in the future, after black urban populations grew.

Ironically, New Deal agricultural programs facilitated major transformation of southern agriculture that ultimately helped to undermine segregation and swell the ranks of urban blacks, leading to new demands on

[25] See Edwin E. Witte, The Development of the Social Security Act (Madison: University of Wisconsin Press, 1963), along with Jill Quadagno's essay in this volume (Chapter 6).

[26] Kristi Andersen, The Creation of a Democratic Majority, 1928–1936 (Chicago, Ill.: University of Chicago Press, 1979), chap. 6; Harvard Sitkoff, A New Deal for Blacks (New York: Oxford University Press, 1978), esp. chap. 4.

the national Democratic party for civil rights and economic assistance. Among New Deal liberals were radical reformers who wanted to aid tenant farmers and agricultural laborers, including southern blacks; but these reformers were defeated by the American Farm Bureau Federation and by allied officials in Congress and the Agriculture Department.[27] From the mid-1930s onward, federal farm subsidies and other interventions in the agricultural sector aided richer commercial farmers and spurred the mechanization of southern farming. During World War II, moreover, military spending promoted urbanization and industrialization in the South.

From the 1940s through the 1960s, blacks migrated in huge waves into southern and northern cities.[28] The shift of blacks from a predominately rural South to heavily populated urban areas located in the South and the North created the preconditions for the civil rights struggles of the 1950s and 1960s.[29] At last, American blacks had won the right to vote in all areas of the nation, and from the 1960s to the Jesse Jackson movement of the current period they have been mobilizing for fuller participation in local and national politics.

Yet the migration of blacks from the rural South transformed their electoral status more thoroughly and quickly than it changed their economic status. For blacks arrived in America's central cities and heavy industries at a point when opportunities for upward mobility after starting in unskilled industrial jobs were much less available than they were for earlier ethnic immigrants into American cities.[30] Thus urban blacks experienced extraordinary rates of unemployment or marginal employment, and to survive economically they called in disproportionate numbers upon welfare programs, especially AFDC.

By the 1960s, blacks were pressing the federal government and the

[27] See Richard S. Kirkendall, "The New Deal and Agriculture," in John Braeman, Robert H. Bremner, and David Brody, eds., *The New Deal: The National Level* (Columbus: Ohio State University Press, 1975), pp. 83–109; Raymond Wolters, "The New Deal and the Negro," in Braeman, Bremner, and Brody, eds., *The New Deal: The National Level*, pp. 170–78; Paul E. Mertz, *New Deal Policy and Southern Rural Poverty* (Baton Rouge: Louisiana State University Press, 1978); and Christiana McFadyen Campbell, *The Farm Bureau and the New Deal* (Urbana: University of Illinois Press, 1962).

[28] See Doug McAdam, *Political Process and the Development of Black Insurgency, 1930–1970* (Chicago, Ill.: University of Chicago Press, 1982), Tables 5.2 through 5.4, pp. 78–80.

[29] Ibid. McAdam's overall argument connects the changing structural circumstances of blacks to the development of the civil rights protests.

[30] Stanley Lieberson, *A Piece of the Pie: Blacks and White Immigrants Since 1880* (Berkeley: University of California Press, 1980), esp. chap. 10 and 11; John D. Kasarda, "The Changing Occupational Structure of the American Metropolis: Apropos the Urban Problem," in B. Schwartz, ed., *The Changing Face of the Suburbs* (Chicago, Ill.: University of Chicago Press, 1976); John D. Kasarda, "Caught in the Web of Change," *Society* 21 (November-December 1983): 41–47.

Democratic party for expansion of the few social programs within the New Deal system for which impoverished blacks were eligible—and for new programs to address their special needs. Reformers of the 1960s realized that the original New Deal framers of the Social Security Act had been wrong to suppose that contributory old-age insurance and contributory unemployment insurance would, over time, include virtually all Americans and leave only shrinking ranks of non-employable and truly destitute people dependent on public assistance. This comfortable illusion of the social security framers had been premised upon the exclusion of most blacks from America's nascent and partial welfare state—and the illusion crumbled as soon as blacks gained political rights and black poverty gained urban visibility. The Democratic party, above all, had to do something to cope with the contradictory socioeconomic and political tendencies that the New Deal had fostered.

The Great Society programs of Lyndon Johnson's War on Poverty can be understood as an effort by the national Democratic party to address the political demands and economic needs of blacks—especially urban blacks—by tacking onto the social security system a whole new layer of programs especially targeted for the poor, both whites and blacks.[31] The idea was that healthy growth in the U.S. economy would allow the continued expansion of social security protections for the elderly and increased funding for social programs appealing to the predominately white middle classes, at the same time that new, ostensibly nonracial programs to overcome poverty were launched. Although AFDC rolls continued to expand, reformers during the Great Society period and for some years afterward hoped to do better than just expand the demeaning welfare programs originally established by the New Deal. Rather, they hoped to use programs such as Food Stamps, Medicaid, federally subsidized housing, and job training to overcome racial divisions by eliminating poverty once and for all.[32] Many reformers also intended to nationalize and reform public assistance into permanent, universal income subsidies for the working and non-working poor.

In *America's Hidden Success*, John Schwarz argues that Great Society anti-poverty efforts did achieve remarkable successes, reducing poverty by about half compared with what it would have been in the absence of

[31] Carl M. Brauer, "Kennedy, Johnson, and the War on Poverty," *Journal of American History* 69 (1982): 98–119; Frances Fox Piven and Richard Cloward, *Poor People's Movements* (New York: Pantheon Books, 1977), chap. 5; Guida West, *The National Welfare Rights Movement: The Social Protest of Poor Women* (New York: Praeger, 1981).

[32] See note 2. Along with Medicare, Medicaid was considered by its proponents to be a "second best" alternative to national health insurance, and many reformers hoped that national health insurance would then soon follow.

such federal interventions in the private economy.[33] Newly upwardly mobile black politicians and middle-class professionals also gained employment opportunities through these efforts.[34] With some justice, Schwarz argues that the failure of the Great Society to eradicate poverty was due as much to the under-funding and early abandonment of many of its programs as it was to fundamental flaws in their conception.

Nevertheless, political time-bombs were built into these special anti-poverty efforts from the start. Federal interventions further provoked rather than propitiated black demands—demands both for "affirmative action" to benefit the employed and for more generous assistance to those on welfare. In turn, black demands continually aroused fearful reactions among established white groups, especially the working-class ethnics who are socially closest to blacks in urban residential and employment settings.[35] In addition, Great Society reformers did not foresee that the Vietnam War and America's shifting international economic position in the 1970s would undermine their original supposition that ever-increasing federal funding could be made simultaneously available for middle-class programs and anti-poverty efforts. As soon as fiscal constraints did become an issue, politicians responding to white working- and middle-class fears could easily castigate the Great Society's anti-poverty programs for being costly and unnecessary welfare handouts (this criticism was usually accompanied by the unstated presumption that these programs benefited only overly demanding and often undeserving blacks). Such programs were all the more vulnerable because they clearly had not achieved the apocalyptically declared objective of "abolishing poverty" in America.

Originally an effort to correct for the New Deal's omissions and short-comings in public social provision, the Great Society ended up reinforcing the programmatic bifurcation of social security and welfare and deepening American political divisions along racial lines. It is hard to avoid the conclusion that the Great Society's attempt to complete by rhetorically overblown patchwork the partial system of social protections inherited from the New Deal inadvertently opened the door to powerful critiques of the aims and practices of public social provision in the United States. It especially opened the door to attacks against those policies implicated

[33] John Schwarz, *America's Hidden Success: A Reassessment of Twenty Years of Public Policy* (New York: Norton, 1983), pp. 32–35.

[34] Michael K. Brown and Steven P. Erie, "Blacks and the Legacy of the Great Society: The Economic and Political Impact of Federal Social Policy," *Public Policy* 29 (Summer 1981): 299–330.

[35] On "white backlash," see Jonathan Rieder, *Canarsie: The Jews and Italians of Brooklyn Against Liberalism* (Cambridge, Mass.: Harvard University Press, 1985).

in the troubled realm of welfare for the unemployed or marginally employed.[36]

The Vulnerability of Social Policies
without Collective Justification

To the degree that any nationally organized political force is actively working in the 1980s to defend the lines of social provision launched in the New Deal, it is the Democratic party. Yet we have seen that the Democratic party of today is laboring to overcome the ulterior political effects of tensions built into the New Deal's original accomplishments and shortcomings: the bifurcation of social insurance and public assistance, the holding out of political promises to blacks not originally included in New Deal social provision, and the failure to join full employment and social spending in a socioeconomically comprehensive welfare state. Finally, the party must cope with yet another problematic legacy of the New Deal: the absence of effective collective symbols to legitimate the social policies with which it is identified.[37]

In an excellent essay entitled "The New Deal and the American Anti-Statist Tradition," James Holt has analyzed the evolving symbols and arguments that were invoked by New Dealers during the 1930s to characterize and justify their new federal interventions. Holt explores "the difficulty of explaining and defending a complex and novel program of federal action in the face of deeply entrenched anti-statist traditions" in the United States.[38]

The New Deal was up against anti-statist traditions in the 1930s not just because Americans were ideologically prejudiced against strong public authority, but also because, historically, they had not experienced for good or ill the impact of a bureaucratic national state. There was no such thing in nineteenth-century America, and even though realms of public administration did expand markedly in the first decades of the twentieth century, Congress and the federal system always circumscribed direct, co-ordinated "national state" activities.[39] Americans thought of political

[36] A vivid example of the kind of sweeping attack against federal social programs that can be launched by those who stress the failures of the Great Society efforts is Charles Murray, *Losing Ground: American Social Policy, 1950–1980* (New York: Basic Books, 1984).

[37] This section draws from my "Legacies of New Deal Liberalism," *Dissent* (Winter 1983): 33–44.

[38] James Holt, "The New Deal and the American Anti-Statist Tradition," in Braeman, Bremner, and Brody, eds., *The New Deal: The National Level*, pp. 27–49.

[39] See Stephen Skowronek, *Building a New American State* (Cambridge, England, and New York: Cambridge University Press, 1982).

sovereignty as divided and considered ultimate sovereignty to reside abstractly in "the law" and "the Constitution," because these ideas in fact made the most sense of the actual political organization within which they lived.[40]

The New Deal made direct federal governmental activities an immediate reality for all Americans, *and the justification and portrayal of the new economic and social programs in New Deal rhetoric was a portentous ideological development in U.S. history.* As Holt shows, in the early New Deal, Franklin Roosevelt and his political allies relied heavily on images of social cooperation combined with constant emphasis on the "experimental" activism of federal governmental efforts. Things had to be done to promote economic recovery and relieve distress; only a distant, heartless federal government would fail to act boldly. Roosevelt's government would "roll up its sleeves" and "keep them rolled up," acting not out of ideological or intellectual certainties, but out of value of neighborliness that would bring the whole nation together in response to the emergency. As Holt astutely points out, this early New Deal rhetoric, although rather thin and expedient in many ways, did have a component of moral regeneration. For early New Dealers called upon Americans to put aside selfish, competitive individualism in the name of solidarity across regional and class lines.

Yet as the early New Deal—launched around the ultimately unsuccessful National Recovery Administration—gave way to the second, reformist New Deal of 1935 and after, the official rhetoric changed. It became more focused on *political conflict*—the people against the "economic royalists"—and on *social security* for "the one-third of a Nation ill-fed, ill-housed, ill-clothed." In these ways, the rhetoric of the later New Deal became undeniably more radical. But as Holt underlines, in another way it simultaneously became more conservative. For the New Deal after 1935 mostly gave up the rhetoric of collective solidarity as an antidote to excessive individualism and instead sought to justify New Deal reforms as better means for achieving or safeguarding traditional American individualistic values of liberty and "getting ahead." Their socioeconomically interventionist state, later New Dealers told Americans, was not the attack on basic American values that conservatives were saying it was. Rather, it was merely an excellent instrument for furthering those values because it struck down the excessive privileges and power of "economic

---

[40] See the discussions of American political culture in J. P. Nettl, "The State as a Conceptual Variable," *World Politics* 20 (1968): 559–92, and in Ira Katznelson and Kenneth Prewitt, "Constitutionalism, Class, and the Limits of Choice in U.S. Foreign Policy," in Richard Fagen, ed., *Capitalism and the State in U.S.–Latin American Relations* (Stanford, Calif.: Stanford University Press, 1979), pp. 27–33.

autocrats" and relieved economic necessity so that Americans could really be free to exercise their individual rights to equality of opportunity.

This approach to legitimating the new state activities established by the New Deal was probably the surest way to stabilize and moderately extend such policies in U.S. domestic politics from the 1930s to the 1970s. Between 1937 and 1940, liberal New Dealers were not able to best conservatives in head-on collisions, so rhetorical retreat was prudent. After World War II, liberal Democratic gains usually depended upon taking advantage of the rosy climate of national economic expansion and international hegemony to push through social spending programs that would benefit not only blue-collar workers and the poor but also the more middle-class and suburban groups who might swing to the Republicans.[41] In these circumstances—even during the breakthroughs of the War on Poverty—it was politically safest to avoid collectivist visions of a welfare state in favor of suggestions that social policies could help every individual and category of individual to get ahead in a non–zero-sum economy.

But when the political going gets rough for public social policies, as it has in the United States since the 1970s, policies that lack clear political and cultural legitimation as expressions of social compassion and collective solidarity are difficult to either defend or extend against individualist, market-oriented, and anti-statist attacks. Hard public choices are called for now that federal interventions are no longer automatically associated with a steadily growing economy. In this situation, the vulnerabilities of instrumentally justified social policies become apparent—especially to the political heirs of the New Deal in the Democratic party. Political coalitions become difficult to sustain across urban and rural populations, Northeast and Southwest, blacks and whites, and middle class and poor. For Americans are not habituated to the notion that, as Michael Walzer eloquently puts it, "the welfare state . . . expresses a certain civil spirit, a sense of mutuality, a commitment to justice."[42]

The rhetoric of the 1984 presidential campaign revealed that the Democrats of the present are, indeed, seeking new moral imageries to overcome the vulnerabilities of instrumentally justified social policies. In his widely praised keynote address to the Democratic National Convention in July 1984, Governor Mario Cuomo invoked the notion of "the family of America" to "explain what a proper government should be."

> We believe we must be the family of America, recognizing that at the heart of the matter we are bound to one another, that the problems

---

[41] The political constraints on liberal Democrats and the policy patterns that resulted are cogently discussed in John Mollenkopf, *The Contested City* (Princeton, N.J.: Princeton University Press, 1983).

[42] Michael Walzer, "The Community," *The New Republic* (March 31, 1982): 11.

of a retired school teacher in Duluth are our problems. That the future of a child in Buffalo is our future. The struggle of a disabled man in Boston to survive, to live decently is our struggle. The hunger of a woman in Little Rock, our hunger. The failure anywhere to provide what reasonably we might, to avoid pain, is our failure.

Obviously, Cuomo was invoking a new political metaphor in order to justify a Democratic defense of activist government under attack: "We believe in only the government we need, but we insist on all the government we need."[43]

Yet the rhetoric of Cuomo and of the Democratic party's 1984 nominees also indicated how cautious they felt they had to be in defending America's threatened social policies in the current conjuncture. Presidential nominee Walter Mondale talked mostly about budget deficits and about the need not only to raise taxes but also to cut public spending for the sake of the economy. Vice-presidential nominee Geraldine Ferraro both discussed and symbolized the hope that the traditional American and Democratic theme of opening the doors for individual achievement might be realized one more time, for women. Even the family imagery invoked by Cuomo was, after all, minimally solidaristic—much less so than the rhetoric of neighborliness, national community, and mutual sacrifice invoked in the early New Deal.

Tellingly, Governor Cuomo tried to join in one ambiguous image the conservative, almost patriarchal notion of each individual family struggling to get ahead as a single unit with the more collectivist idea of a national family "feeling one another's pain. Sharing one another's blessings. Reasonably, honestly, fairly, without respect to race, or sex, or geography, or political affiliation." But the analogy was severely strained, for families do not bridge races (except in very few cases); nor do families operate by public principles of fairness. It also remains to be seen whether many Americans can be persuaded to extend the protective feelings they have (or feel they should have) toward their own children, siblings, parents, and spouses to encompass the "other people's children," disproportionately Hispanic or black, who along with their mothers now crowd the ranks of the American poor.[44]

In sum, Governor Cuomo's imagery (which he continued to use well after 1984) revealed the problematic thinness of the collective vision invoked by mainstream Democrats as they currently try to revitalize broad support for a strong federal social role.[45] In the shifting political circum-

---

[43] Governor Cuomo's address is reprinted in the *New York Times*, July 17, 1984, p. A16.

[44] Preston, "Children and the Elderly" (see note 15).

[45] See the "Transcript of Cuomo's Inaugural Address for His Second Term," *New York Times*, January 2, 1987, p. B4.

stance of the 1980s, advocates of a revitalized American system of social provision have yet to find political metaphors of collective compassion simultaneously appealing to blacks and whites, to traditional and newly structured families, and to the middle classes and the poor.

Conclusion

Ironically, especially for the Democratic party, many of the contradictions that now bedevil efforts to build strong social policy coalitions across races and social strata represent the playing out of the New Deal's partial accomplishments in shaping and justifying nationwide patterns of public social provision for the United States. As this discussion has tried to show, only if we understand historically the limits and the internal contradictions of modern U.S. public purposes and social policies—with the New Deal as the pivot of our analysis—can we properly understand the roots of the critical juncture those purposes and policies face today.

The legacies of New Deal achievements and, even more, the problems left unresolved by its shortfalls, have interacted with postwar changes in American society and politics to produce passionate debates—from the 1960s through the present—about what government should do for poor women and children, for unemployed black youths, and for displaced industrial workers. Neither the Democratic party nor any other national political force—including the Republicans under Ronald Reagan—has as yet come up with politically self-sustaining solutions. Consequently, the unresolved dilemmas posed by the Great Society's efforts to transcend the limits of the New Deal system continue to arouse intellectual and political conflict. Alternative possible futures for social policy in the United States remain very much at issue.

9

Race and the Liberal Agenda: The Loss of the Integrationist Dream, 1965–1974

GARY ORFIELD

Race is the most fundamental cleavage in American history. Black and white experiences have been separate and unequal in important ways, and political conflicts over how to describe and explain the separation and subordination remain central. The conflict over slavery divided American political, intellectual and spiritual leaders for generations before the Civil War. In the southern and border states, where most blacks lived, the Jim Crow system of segregation became mandated by state law and was accepted by American political and intellectual leaders by the late 1880s, and it was not seriously challenged for half a century. In one of the greatest triumphs of American liberalism, this system was exposed, and an ambitious program to overturn the whole structure of southern segregation law was developed and incorporated into national law during the 1960s.

A third system of racial separation and control, the urban ghetto, emerged with the substantial black migration to the cities. The urban ghetto had a very different status in public discussion: it received little serious attention until the mid-1960s and was not clearly defined as a major problem by either intellectuals or legal institutions. By the late 1960s, the civil rights movement, urban riots, and research had helped to bring the ghetto crisis into focus, but white liberals failed to develop a coherent reform program to deal with the problems.

By the early 1970s efforts to make structural changes in the ghetto system had been rejected by all three branches of the federal government. As in the period after Reconstruction, this, the dominant form of racial separation, was accepted as natural, and anyone suggesting more than incremental changes was the object of intense political and intellectual criticism. Liberals turned to other issues.

After a brief and extraordinary period in the 1960s, many white liberals returned to a position of noninvolvement with civil rights. During most of American history liberalism has attempted to ignore the question of race. The New Deal, for example, greatly expanded the activities of national government but left the southern racial system virtually intact. Earlier, during Woodrow Wilson's New Freedom, a progressive administration had imposed segregation on the federal bureaucracy. In fact, opposition to Jim Crow did not become part of mainstream American liberalism until the 1948 Democratic convention. Only after the triumph of the decades-long struggle of the National Association for the Advancement of Colored People (NAACP) in the 1954 *Brown* decision did the process of political, social, and intellectual change really begin.

At its peak the liberal consensus on the central nature of the problem of race was broad and highly effective. The black community was mobilized more than at any point in U.S. history. A virtual consensus developed among northern Democrats, with broad support in the labor movement, among major religious leaders, and on the campuses. With public opinion and congressional attention focused by the great civil rights marches in Birmingham and Selma, a period of only two years, from June 1963 to early August 1965, saw the introduction, debate, and final enactment of laws incorporating the entire reform agenda devised during the previous two decades to end de jure segregation in the South. The measures rapidly changed some basic elements of southern race relations.

Between 1965 and 1966, however, the civil rights movement and its allies went from the astonishing triumph of the Voting Rights Act, which surpassed the fondest hopes of the recent past, to confusion, conflict, and defeat. The issues changed, the central symbols changed, the northern wing of the Democratic party began to divide seriously on racial issues as the Republican party moved into opposition, and the civil rights forces began to lose in Congress. The focus of racial issues had suddenly moved from the rural and small-town South to the ghetto.

After the conservative victory in the 1968 election, these new issues of urban discrimination and desegregation would virtually disappear from American politics, except as targets for attack. Civil rights groups and researchers still report problems and make proposals, but they receive no significant attention. Liberalism, which had embraced the goal of integration for the South, turned away when the extent of change such a goal would imply in the North became apparent. Increasingly, civil rights was discussed as an issue that had been resolved in the 1960s. White liberalism turned its back on the problem of the ghetto, despite abundant signs that social and economic conditions in the ghettos had deteriorated rapidly and severely, even amid the unprecedented prosperity of the 1960s.

The ease with which white liberals turned away from civil rights requires an understanding of the logic of the color line. In a society with intense racial consciousness and a rigid color line, all kinds of resources and opportunities are distributed in ways that benefit the dominant group. If one looks only at the resulting inequalities, one's natural conclusion is that something is wrong with the people who are on the wrong side of the color line. Only if the nature of the line of separation is understood and its impacts analyzed is it possible both to explain the unequal results and to understand the kinds of changes that would attenuate them.

When no effective explanation is presented, the political and social initiative is decisively with those who assert that the subordinate group's inferior position is caused by some kind of inherent personal or group inferiority. The tendency is to conclude (often in euphemisms) that the dominant group deserves to be dominant, that nothing much can be done about the unhappy reality, and that attacks on the structure of separation are disruptive and misguided. This is precisely what has happened since liberals forgot the insights of the civil rights movement into the nature of discrimination in the ghetto.

This paper will explore the causes of the removal of race from the agenda of the Left. The analysis will challenge the view that this change originated within the black community, in the black power movement; rather, it will show that it occurred only after a great many failures of a unified black integrationist movement in the cities. It will explore the dynamic of change within the black groups and the turn in white opinion about civil rights. It will show the growing understanding in the late 1960s and early 1970s of the causes of and possible remedies for the ghetto system, and it will explain the conditions under which the proposed remedies were rejected. The paper will discuss the implications—for both the future of social policy and American race relations—of the liberals' abandonment of a structural explanation for racial differences and of their inability to create or win support for a policy of resource transfer across ghetto lines. Once they abandoned an analysis rooted in an understanding of the history of white prejudice and the need for fundamental change in the ghetto system, the ground shifted in the entire debate on compensatory programs. These programs were seen as beneficence by the white middle class rather than as a right. When blacks asked for more, they were accused of ingratitude.

The Success of
the Civil Rights Movement

In 1960 the dream of integrating the South seemed highly implausible. Six years after the 1954 *Brown* decision, only a fraction of 1 percent of black students in the South went to white schools, and no white students in the South had ever been enrolled in black schools. Entire states remained completely untouched by the decision. Congress and the executive branch had been passive bystanders as the resistance of southern states and local officials rendered the *Brown* decision largely ineffectual. There had been few major mass movements of southern blacks besides the historic Montgomery, Alabama, bus boycott. Efforts to obtain positive action in Congress had been largely futile, and the voting rights provisions of the weak 1957 and 1960 Civil Rights Acts did not work.[1] The best analysis of the experience of the 1950s seemed to be that the courts could produce only symbolic change, and that there were overwhelming barriers to forceful action by the other branches of government. A persistent system of segregation with slowly growing symbolic levels of access for a few blacks was the likely future of the South.

The 1960s began with a change in the mood of the national government and a great surge of black protest movements in the South. The Kennedy administration transformed the posture of the executive branch from one of disinterest to one of national leadership. The driving force behind the change in the political agenda, however, was the civil rights movement and its capacity to arouse and focus public concern, and to generate a coalition for major change in national policy. It galvanized white liberalism.

The Johnson administration brought strong, consistent, and highly effective presidential leadership, which succeeded in writing virtually the entire rights agenda of the southern protest movement into federal law in 1964 and 1965. Discrimination in hotels and restaurants was outlawed and almost immediately ceased. Federal power over local elections was extended in fundamental ways to produce a rapid and broad expansion of the black electorate in the Deep South. The Justice Department was authorized to sue on behalf of minority plaintiffs in civil rights matters, and the federal government moved from its neutral posture to one of powerful support of the civil rights movement in the courts. Discrimination was forbidden in all institutions receiving federal aid, and the regulations implementing these provisions greatly accelerated the integration of schools and other institutions in the South. Job discrimination became illegal.

These and other changes transformed many significant features of life in the southern and border states. In a surprisingly short period of time many of the most obvious differences between the South and the North were eliminated. By 1970, for example, southern schools were, and have since remained, more integrated than those in any other region.[2]

[1] Reed Sarratt, *The Ordeal of Desegregation* (New York: Harper and Row, 1966); Jack W. Peltason, *Fifty-Eight Lonely Men* (New York: Harcourt, Brace and World, 1961); U.S. Congress, House Committee on the Judiciary, Subcommittee on Civil Rights Oversight, *Hearings on the Enforcement of the Voting Rights Act*, 92d Cong., 1st sess., 1971.

[2] Gary Orfield, *Public School Desegregation in the United States, 1968–1980* (Washing-

As is often true in social revolutions, the solution of one set of problems on which a consensus had been laboriously constructed, ending Southern segregation laws, revealed another, underlying set of structural racial barriers to integration and equality, particularly in the urban South. In fact, this set of barriers began to come into focus not only in the South but across the nation.

As the federal courts and the Department of Health, Education, and Welfare (HEW) acted, for example, to strike down the school segregation laws in the seventeen states that had been operating dual school systems, it rapidly became apparent that reassigning students to the closest school would integrate most of the rural and small-town South but leave segregation almost untouched in the region's big cities. Even with the supporting legal structure removed, the complex historical forces that had produced and maintained the ghetto as the basic form of black urbanization meant that the racial segregation of public education would be substantially unaffected. Telling children that they were now segregated de facto instead of de jure would change nothing about their experience. If there was to be any substantial urban integration, additional forceful governmental action against the system of ghettoization and its consequences would be required.

A fundamental political and social problem was that the civil rights movement had been based largely on a common-sense opposition to the explicit racial policies embodied in the southern statute books but confronted in the urban ghettos a system that would yield only to explicit racial policies of mandatory integration across the ghetto line. Many who had been readily persuaded of the need for the first set of policies did not understand or accept the necessity of the second set. It was also, of course, almost immediately apparent that the first set of principles raised few questions of any consequence for northern race relations, while the second set could trigger questioning of the whole system of urban society, since blacks were separate and unequal everywhere.

The Collapse of
Integrationist Objectives

The extremely forceful and successful social movement launched by blacks in the early 1960s inevitably carried the battle to the second set of racial barriers. In fact, almost as soon as there was a serious protest movement in the South, nonviolent direct action spread to the North. Since

ton, D.C.: Joint Center for Political Studies, 1983); U.S. Commission on Civil Rights, *Civil Rights '63* (Washington, D.C., 1963); U.S. Commission on Civil Rights, *Federal Civil Rights Enforcement Effort* (Washington, D.C., 1971).

northern blacks were almost all urban, the movement there was against urban racial policies. There were usually no state laws to protest against, but there were comprehensive systems of separation and inequality. The initial focus of the movement was squarely on the urban color line; and the overwhelming demand was for access and integration, primarily in the key mobility systems of education and choice of residential neighborhood.

These issues were intrinsically difficult. There was strong white resistance to any serious threat to the accepted prerogatives of communities on the white side of the color line. Added to these difficulties, however, was the following set of historical circumstances that made the struggle in the North quite different from that in the South.

1. The lack of a developed program for change.
2. Disagreement among black groups about fundamental goals.
3. Urban riots and the "white backlash."
4. Vietnam War budget constraints and the impossibility of creating major new federal programs after the mid-1960s.
5. The declining political strength of President Johnson and congressional liberals by 1966.
6. The geographical extent of segregation, and the fact that local government institutions often are all white or overwhelmingly nonwhite.
7. The complex interaction between major forms of private discrimination and supporting government policies that appeared neutral on the surface but reinforced private segregation.

Even with strong leadership, changing the established processes of ghettoization would have been difficult. The ghettos in the large cities were vast, and blacks had already missed the opportunity to become homeowners during the early postwar period when conditions were highly favorable and returns for investments in housing were often extremely high. Income and wealth were, on average, much greater on the white side of the line, though there was much overlap in black and white income distributions. A half century of extremely destructive processes of ghetto development in large northern cities had created deeply rooted fears and expectations that would not easily be changed, no matter what the policymakers said. Because housing is more than nine-tenths in private ownership, while schools are almost nine-tenths in the public sector, government had far less leverage over housing than over schools. Conditions were anything but favorable for change by 1966.

It is important to sort out the forces operating during this period, because certain assumptions that the record of the period does not support have often been read into the turn away from integrationist goals. Three of the most important of these assumptions are (1) that strong integration policies were attempted in the big cities and did not work; (2) that whites abandoned the policies only after blacks, with the emergence of the Black Power movement, changed their demands; and (3) that there was or is some kind of substantial alternative policy that worked or could work more effectively.

The actual sequence of events was different in all fundamental respects. Blacks strongly demanded urban integration in many cities, and they demanded it year after year as the black movement reached its peak. Their policies calling for more than merely symbolic levels of change in school and housing patterns met almost monolithic resistance by city and school officials. Higher levels of government, including the courts, not only failed to provide enough backing for integrationist policies to make changes possible in the face of local resistance, but also, in a number of critical turns, actually reinforced local opponents.

Black organizations turned toward different policies because of actions they regarded as betrayals of integrationist goals. The New York City school decentralization movement, which arose when the school district failed to keep its promise to integrate a new school in Harlem, was one extremely important case in point. Apart from isolated local instances, no successful alternative policies that would produce fully integrated or substantially equal schools, housing and neighborhoods, and access to employment have been devised. Despite the failure of the integrationist movement in the cities, its abandonment by a number of black intellectuals and politicians, and an increasingly hostile national white leadership, blacks have remained overwhelmingly committed to integrationist goals during the two decades since the civil rights movement peaked and began its rapid decline. Even during periods when actively hostile national administrations held office and there was no hope for integrationist policies, black goals did not significantly change.

The Civil Rights Movement
and Integration

The extraordinary visibility of the civil rights movement of the 1960s makes it relatively simple to point to the peak of the movement. Between the Birmingham demonstrations in the spring of 1963 and the signing of the Voting Rights Act in August 1965, civil rights dominated the national agenda as no domestic issue has since. Although the great legislative battles were over the future of southern society, the leaders of the movement were already looking to the next step—dismantling the ghetto system. Martin Luther King, Jr., the leader of the Southern Christian Leadership Conference (SCLC), spoke about it in 1964.

Until the Harlems and racial ghettos of our nation are destroyed and
the Negro is brought into the mainstream of American life, our be-
loved nation will be on the verge of being plunged into the abyss of
social disruption. No greater tragedy can befall a nation than to leave
millions of people with a feeling that they have no stake in their society.[3]

King was not asking for access to money or sharing of assets held only
by whites. He was urging the same kind of fundamental structural change
in race relations that he had been fighting for in what was widely seen as
a hopeless battle in the South. King was not alone. In fact, his goals reflected those of virtually all major black organizations at that time. Radical groups within the black community were not distinguished from the
mainstream civil rights organizations by their goals, but by their tactics
and their sense of urgency about forcing a confrontation with the worst
of the northern segregationist leaders and institutions to bring on more
rapid and comprehensive change.

The tremendous surge of black protest in the South from 1961 to 1963
generated a parallel activism in the cities of the North and West. The great
demonstrations against southern segregation prompted a mobilization of
northern black and white civil rights supporters, first in support of the
southern movement but soon turning to fight local discrimination. (There
were also many local organizations not directly related to the national
movement. They mushroomed spontaneously, particularly during 1963.)
National Urban League and NAACP chapters that had been quietly pursuing modest change for decades began to raise fundamental questions.
Support for nonviolent direct action tactics, like those used in the South,
produced a sudden expansion of the Congress of Racial Equality (CORE)
across the United States following the 1962 CORE Freedom Rides through
the Deep South. Activists eager to apply the lessons of the southern struggle to their own communities were soon sitting in at school board offices,
picketing businesses with no black employees, and mobilizing against segregated real estate developments.

Public attention focused on the South not because of the absence of
activity in the big cities, but because the South received the primary emphasis from national civil rights and political leadership, and because the
issues seemed much clearer and the public support much broader in the
South. Retrospectively, however, the popular understanding and the civ-
ics textbook view of the period is one of a southern movement with
southern objectives that solved the problems of race in America. It is as if

[3] Thomas L. Blair, *Retreat to the Ghetto: The End of a Dream?* (New York: Hill and
Wang, 1977), p. xx.

the many facets of the movement that were defeated never existed and there had been no northern movement.

Meier and Rudwick's history of CORE, however, gives a very different view of the period. To many, moving from "supportive demonstrations for the southern campaigns into northern employment and housing projects was a natural progression."

> Mainly . . . the chapters developed techniques to fight northern racism through trial and error. . . . During 1961 and 1962 most of them expended more effort on housing campaigns than on any other activity. Job discrimination also had a high priority, and by 1963 it became the most popular target for CORE demonstrations. De facto segregated schools and police brutality were also objects of concern, but did not achieve salience until 1963 and 1964.[4]

The NAACP had been involved in litigation against northern segregation for many years and had played an important role in the development of campaigns for local ordinances in support of fair housing and in local school desegregation fights. During the 1960s it expanded its activities on the legal front and became much more actively involved in local protests for civil rights. Even with this expansion, it was often criticized for not doing enough.

There were differences in approach among the different black organizations. The NAACP, for example, had been active in the fight against residential segregation since 1915, and in 1917 it had succeeded in winning a critical Supreme Court decision invalidating the mandatory racial zoning ordinances adopted in many U.S. cities early in the twentieth century. When the system of racial covenants enforced by state courts developed as the practical equivalent of racial zoning, the NAACP carried out a protracted legal attack that resulted in the 1948 Supreme Court decision *Shelley* v. *Kraemer*, 334 U.S. 1 (1948), which invalidated racial covenants.[5] The group became actively involved in the early open housing litigation in New York City that helped create the national fair housing movement.[6] The approach of CORE, however, was more direct; it included sitting in at rental offices, picketing realtors, and demanding immediate change.[7]

The most cautious of the major black groups, the National Urban

---

[4] August Meier and Elliott Rudwick, *CORE: A Study in the Civil Rights Movement* (Urbana: University of Illinois Press, 1975), p. 182.

[5] Clement E. Vose, *Caucasians Only: The Supreme Court, the NAACP, and the Restrictive Covenant Cases* (Berkeley: University of California Press, 1967).

[6] Arthur Simon, *Stuyvesant Town, U.S.A.* (New York: New York University Press, 1970), p. 59.

[7] Meier and Rudwick, *CORE*, pp. 184–86.

League, engaged in job placement through its local chapters. Closely tied to local business leadership, these chapters had been quietly documenting and reporting on ghetto conditions and urging changes. By the early 1960s, the new sense of urgency and hope in the black community brought involvement of the League with activist struggles.[8]

School desegregation was a central goal of black organizations in cities across the North and West at the peak of the civil rights movement. The campaign covered the spectrum of activities from resolutions to reports to litigation to large-scale protest and huge school boycotts in a number of the nation's largest school districts. It is probably true that there were more community protests over school segregation in the North than in the South. The difference was not in what was demanded, but in how the institutions of government, particularly the federal courts and the federal executive branch, responded to these black demands.

The U.S. Civil Rights Commission summarized the mounting protest movement in a 1963 report.

> In the North and West, Negro protests until recently took the form of petition. . . . However, segregated schools have now become targets of public demonstrations, picketing, sit-ins, and school boycotts since the summer of 1961. . . . Negroes have picketed in suburban Philadelphia and in Boston, Chicago, and St. Louis.[9]

Detailed studies of individual communities show active black leadership campaigning for school integration in many parts of the country, often with the most militant integrationist demands coming from CORE.[10] The Student Nonviolent Coordinating Committee (SNCC) was making similar demands for immediate change in the South, where civil rights lawyers struggled against enormous odds until the federal government entered powerfully on their side.[11] The most fervent and impatient integrationists (and the most integrated themselves) were the very groups of young black activists who would embrace separatism a few years later.

There was tremendous optimism as the activist phase of the urban civil rights movement began outside the South. If the ultimate bastion of discrimination was crumbling in Dixie, surely it would be much easier to

---

[8] Guichard Parris and Lester Brooks, *Blacks in the City: A History of the National Urban League* (Boston: Little, Brown, 1971), pp. 410–21.

[9] U.S. Commission on Civil Rights, *Civil Rights '63*, p. 53.

[10] T. Bentley Edwards and Frederick M. Wirt, *School Desegregation in the North: The Challenge and the Experience* (San Francisco: Chandler Publishing, 1967); Raymond W. Maci, *Our Children's Burden: Studies of Desegregation in Nine Communities* (New York: Random House, 1968); Anna Holden, *The Bus Stops Here: A Study of Desegregation in Three Cities* (New York: Agathon Press, 1974).

[11] Howard Zinn, *SNCC: The New Abolitionists* (Boston: Beacon Press, 1964); Peltason, *Fifty-Eight Lonely Men.*

achieve change in a region where few publicly endorsed segregation and there were active white supporters taking part in the movement. In most cases, protest involved very little of the physical and financial risk that was often present in the South. The North was convinced that it was fundamentally different from and better than the South. Black leaders and their allies hoped that was true.

The results of the northern protest movement, however, were bitterly disappointing. Thousands marched, promises were made, committees were appointed, there was intense media coverage of the protests—but nothing happened. School and housing segregation remained virtually untouched. No dramatic remedies were imposed from Washington. Often, criticism was redirected from the conditions the movement wished to change to the movement itself. The protesters were blamed for disrupting the social order and for pursuing unworkable remedies.

The 1960s would end with an increase in residential segregation in the metropolitan areas of the United States. A study of 130 metropolitan areas found, for example, that between 1960 and 1970 the percentage of blacks living in intensely segregated tracts (more than 70 percent black) increased in all regions, with the most rapid rise in the North Central states. The percentage of whites living in the neighborhood of the average black dropped in all regions.[12] More and more of the largest school districts were becoming predominantly black without ever having experienced significant desegregation. By 1970 the northern schools would be substantially more segregated than those in the South.[13] There were none of the statistics showing dramatic and sudden declines in segregation levels that followed the enactment of civil rights laws and regulations which affected southern school segregation, voting rights, and other issues. The movement had very little measurable impact.

One reason was the very different role of the courts. The NAACP and its allies filed cases in the North as they had in the South. After a victory in the 1961 *New Rochelle* school integration case, civil rights groups hoped the courts would give the northern movement the same kind of legitimacy that the *Brown* decision had provided the southern struggle.[14] In the big cities, however, the civil rights groups lost with monotonous regularity, including widely publicized and influential cases in Gary, Indiana; Cin-

[12] Ann B. Schnare, "Residential Segregation by Race in U.S. Metropolitan Areas: An Analysis Across Cities and Over Time," Contract Report No. 246–2 (Washington, D.C.: The Urban Institute, 1977).

[13] U.S. Commission on Civil Rights, *Fulfilling the Letter and Spirit of the Law: Desegregation of the Nation's Public Schools* (Washington, D.C.: Government Printing Office, 1976), pp. 2–13; Gary Orfield, *Public School Desegregation in the United States.*

[14] *Taylor v. Bd. of Education*, 191 F. Supp. 181 (S.D.N.Y. 1961).

cinnati, Ohio; and Kansas City.[15] "The court," wrote NAACP lawyer Lewis Steel, "refused to review a series of conservative lower-court decisions which upheld what school officials described as accidental segregation in Gary, Ind., Kansas City, Kan. and Cincinnati. As a result, the schools of the North have become segregated faster than southern schools have been desegregated."[16] The Supreme Court refused to hear any northern urban case until 1973. There was a similar reluctance, even on the Warren Court, to impose desegregation requirements on local urban renewal and housing officials.[17]

At the height of the civil rights movement, there were few clear successes outside the South. The hope for voluntary local action was not realized. Only one large American city, Seattle, would ever implement a city-wide desegregation plan without a court order. Integration did not seem a real possibility to the activists, as frustration and failures accumulated. It was against this background that the period's dominant black leader, Martin Luther King, Jr., went to Chicago to assemble the largest protest campaign outside the South during the civil rights era. Before Dr. King's campaign began, however, circumstances began to change rapidly and in fundamental ways.

The Turning Point:
From the Voting Rights Act to Black Power

Within a few days in the summer of 1965, the civil rights movement went from perhaps its most triumphant moment to the beginning of its rapid decline. During those same days, a portentous shift in white attitudes toward blacks began to take shape, both among the public and among government leaders.

Seldom in the history of political trends can political change be linked so unequivocally with a brief period of time. The civil rights issue is a dramatic exception. The likely turning point, which began to transform a powerful movement into an embattled movement with a far smaller constituency, came between August 6, when President Johnson signed the sweeping Voting Rights Act, and August 11, when the worst race riot in a generation erupted in Los Angeles. There was a sudden shift in mood. The implications of the change would not be broadly apparent for an-

---

[15] Bell v. School City of Gary, 213 F. Supp. 819 (N.D. Ind.), aff'd 324 F. 2d 209 (7th Cir. 1963), cert. denied, 377 U.S. 924 (1964); Deal v. Cincinnati Bd. of Ed.: Downs v. Bd. of Ed., 336 F. 2d 988 (10th Cir. 1964), cert. denied, 380 U.S. 914 (1965).

[16] Lewis M. Steel, "Nine Men in Black Who Think White," in Leonard Levy, ed., The Supreme Court under Earl Warren (New York: Quadrangle, 1972), p. 86.

[17] Ibid., pp. 86–90.

other year or more, but the possibilities for civil rights progress had suddenly become far more limited than they had been.

The first half of 1965 was a triumphant period for the civil rights movement and for the reform administration of Lyndon Johnson. In his remarkable "We Shall Overcome" speech Johnson urged rapid congressional approval of a voting rights measure that would have been inconceivable a year earlier. The president acted only two months after Dr. King's Selma campaign began, and the measure was law fewer than five months later—extremely rapid action for a measure that transformed the politics of the South.

Even in the midst of the voting rights struggle, Johnson gave clear signs that he wished to press on to the next set of racial barriers, those afflicting urban blacks. In an address at Howard University, he called for a White House conference on civil rights to work on the new agenda, and he began to outline a whole new set of issues beyond the traditional southern concerns. Rejecting the widespread white belief that it was unfair to give special aid to blacks, Johnson insisted that the black experience was fundamentally different from that of other immigrants. In fact, he declared, the black community had "been twisted and battered by endless years of hatred and hopelessness" growing out of white racial feelings, "a feeling whose dark intensity is matched by no other prejudice in our society."[18] Urban blacks, he said, were a "separated people," living involuntarily in depressing slums.

> Men are shaped by their world. When it is a world of decay, ringed by an invisible wall, when escape is arduous and uncertain, and the saving pressures of a more hopeful society are unknown, it can cripple the youth and it can desolate the man.
>
> There is also the burden that a dark skin can add to the search for a productive place in society. Unemployment strikes most swiftly and broadly at the Negro, and this burden erodes hope. Blighted hope breeds despair. Despair brings indifference to the learning which offers a way out. And despair, coupled with indifference, is often the source of destructive rebellion against the fabric of society.
>
> There is no single easy answer. . . . Jobs are part of the answer. They bring the income which permits a man to provide for his family. Decent homes in decent surroundings and a chance to learn—an equal chance to learn—are part of the answer. . . . And to all these fronts,—and a dozen more—I will dedicate the expanding efforts of the Johnson Administration.[19]

[18] Congressional Quarterly, *Congress and the Nation, Vol. II, 1965–68* (Washington, D.C.: Congressional Quarterly, Inc., 1969), p. 397.
[19] Ibid.

Roy Wilkins, the leader of the NAACP, by far the largest civil rights group, felt great optimism for the future at this point. He wrote:

During the spring and early summer of 1965, the civil rights movement seemed to be at the very apex of its power. That June President Johnson called me before his Howard commencement speech to tell me that he was ready for an all-fronts assault on the problems of race. I was astonished by his fervor and by his daring. . . . No President before had ever been so enlightened or bold in facing up to these truths.[20]

The ceremony in the Capitol rotunda when President Johnson signed the Voting Rights Act into law was one of the high points of an ebullient civil rights movement. Participants recall the mood of great hope among the assembled civil rights leaders, legislators, and administration officials. The president called the law "a triumph for freedom as huge as any victory that has ever been won on any battlefield." The law, he said, would "strike away the last major shackle of those fierce and ancient bonds." Now that Congress had acted against "the last of the legal barriers," the country would begin to deal with the effects of "centuries of oppression and hatred," such as "families that are imprisoned in slums and poverty."[21]

SIGNS OF TROUBLE

Even at the great moment of the voting rights victory, however, the first signs of trouble to come appeared. Dr. King tried to persuade the president to announce an immediate attack on ghetto poverty and an end to federal control of the predominantly black city of Washington, D.C. Johnson replied that the time was not ripe.[22] Because CORE had openly criticized the administration's growing involvement in Vietnam, President Johnson refused to give its director, James Farmer, a pen from the historic ceremony until he was strongly urged to do so by the heads of the NAACP and the National Urban League.[23] (Dr. King soon would become a great anti-war leader.)

Three days after the signing of the Voting Rights Act, in a summer of

[20] Roy Wilkins with Tom Mathews, *Standing Fast: The Autobiography of Roy Wilkins* (New York: Viking Press, 1982), p. 311.

[21] Lyndon Baines Johnson, *Public Papers of the President* (Washington, D.C.: Government Printing Office, 1965), pp. 840–43.

[22] Jim Bishop, *The Days of Martin Luther King, Jr.* (New York: G. P. Putnam's Sons, 1971), pp. 403–4.

[23] James Farmer, *Lay Bare the Heart: An Autobiography of the Civil Rights Movement* (New York: Arbor House, 1985), p. 300.

legislative accomplishments unequaled since the New Deal, the president signed the law creating the Department of Housing and Urban Development (HUD), giving the United States the capacity to develop an urban policy for the first time in its history. He promised new housing initiatives and set the goal of "a home of dignity and a neighborhood of pride" for every family.[24] The first secretary of HUD, Robert Weaver, was also the first black cabinet member in U.S. history and an expert on housing discrimination and the black ghetto.

In the next few weeks, however, things would begin to come apart. "It took a long time," wrote *New York Times* correspondent John Herbers, "to make the Negro revolution of the 1960s. It took only a few months, weeks really, to do it in."[25] Only days after the voting rights ceremony the president was speaking to the nation in a very different way. The Los Angeles ghetto had erupted in the largest of the postwar race riots, which the president said reflected "violent, willful disregard of law" and could threaten the basis for black progress.

> To resort to error and violence not only shatters the essential right of every citizen to be secure, . . . it strikes from the hand of the Negro the very weapons with which he is achieving his own emancipation.

> Those who strike at the fabric of ordered liberty also erode the foundation on which the house of justice stands.[26]

Riots would occur each year for the remainder of the Johnson administration. Soon Congress would be debating anti-riot proposals rather than civil rights measures. In the nation's largest state, California, the 1965 Watts riot helped elect Ronald Reagan as governor: the riot had encouraged Los Angeles Mayor Sam Yorty, who blamed the riot on civil rights groups, to challenge incumbent Governor Pat Brown in the Democratic primary; he seriously hurt the governor, who lost to Reagan in the general election.[27] Reagan was a harsh civil rights opponent. He had supported the 1964 California referendum outlawing fair housing in the state, and he strongly opposed the 1964 federal civil rights measures.

In the general election campaign, Reagan attacked the Johnson civil rights laws as "grandstand stunts" for black support. Shortly before the election he told the California Real Estate Association that fair housing was wrong, because the "rights of an individual to ownership and disposition of property is inseparable from the right of freedom itself." He said

[24] Johnson, *Public Papers of the President*, 1965, pp. 861–63.

[25] John Herbers, *The Lost Priority: What Happened to the Civil Rights Movement in America?* (New York: Funk and Wagnalls, 1970), p. xiv.

[26] Johnson, *Public Papers of the President*, 1965, p. 882.

[27] John C. Bollens and Grant B. Geyer, *Yorty: Politics of a Constant Candidate* (Pacific Palisades, Calif.: Palisades Publishers, 1973), pp. 152–59.

that many blacks protesting housing segregation really did not want the housing in the white areas and were only "causing trouble."[28] In another speech he attacked "arson, rioting, looting and bloodshed" and the unnamed leaders who, he said, claimed these were a part of black rights.[29] California chose a leader who symbolized white reaction. Riots, Reagan said, were caused by misguided black leaders; government should do less, not more; strong civil rights enforcement threatened white liberty. These were the kinds of position embraced by the GOP's presidential candidate in 1964, Barry Goldwater, and they became the prevailing positions of the party that would control the White House for sixteen of the twenty years after Lyndon Johnson went home to Texas.

The riots created a crisis for American liberalism. Advocates of an integrated society found themselves without a convincing program and trapped between growing racial polarization, both within the left of the civil rights movement and within moderate to conservative white leadership. Even if the anti-war movement had not emerged as the principal liberal concern, the profound ideological disarray would have weakened liberal efforts.

The political problem was severe. No administration since Lincoln's had so invested its political capital in black progress, and none had made *more* progress. Never had Congress acted on such a sweeping social policy agenda in the absence of great crisis. Poverty was falling rapidly for blacks, as well as whites. Yet, though there had been no serious black riots since World War II, a series of huge upheavals was beginning in the cities. Social scientists could offer theories about the way increasing opportunities and belief in the possibility of change triggered protests, but the political advantage went to the conservatives, who could attack black leaders and denounce social programs as unsuccessful and counterproductive. Liberals could not outbid the conservatives in promising stronger police action, and they had found no way to explain the need for basic changes in the ghetto system.

Johnson tried to straddle the line that Democrats would find themselves walking in the 1968 presidential campaign against Nixon. He spoke of the "melancholy life" in "slum houses, in crowded schools, in the desolate streets where unemployment and boredom lead hopeless men to crime and violence." The riots, he said, "bore no relation to the orderly struggle for civil rights that has ennobled the last decade."[30] Expressing his disappointment after a decade of battles for civil rights laws, he lectured black leaders:

[28] George H. Smith, *Who is Ronald Reagan?* (New York: Pyramid Books, 1968), pp. 96, 165.
[29] Ibid., p. 95.
[30] Johnson, *Public Papers of the President*, 1965, pp. 897–98.

We cannot . . . in one breath demand laws to protect the rights of all our citizens, and then turn our backs, or wink, or . . . allow laws to be broken. . . .

A rioter with a Molotov cocktail in his hands is not fighting for civil rights any more than a Klansman with a sheet on his back. . . . They are both lawbreakers, destroyers of constitutional rights and liberties, and ultimately destroyers of free America.[31]

The liberal view seemed weak and defensive in contrast to a clear and aggressive conservative defense of law and order, and of firm action against violence. Liberals were depressed, worried and divided among themselves.

The riots and the increasing evidence of severe social problems in cities that had already received extensive poverty program funding created a political and intellectual crisis for liberalism. The liberal program for urban poverty in the 1960s was built around preschool and compensatory education, job training, access to higher education, increased social services, and community organization and empowerment through community action agencies. The basic assumption was that no fundamental economic or racial change was essential. Opportunities existed; the need was simply to prepare blacks for them and forbid discrimination. Civil rights required only relatively weak fair employment and fair housing laws to deal with individual cases of discrimination. The assumption was that the economic boom and low overall unemployment rate of the 1960s would continue, and that there would be ample work for the minority job seekers who received adequate training.

The many riots, and the intense, fearful scrutiny of ghetto communities that followed, suggested that the analysis was wrong and the problem underestimated. The riots also created a climate in which whites were far less ready to consider additional government action. The evidence accumulating from the ghetto was that the separation of blacks from white society was much more profound, both in racial and economic terms, than the liberal program had presumed. The unambiguous evidence of the riots was that there was a profound racial gulf in the cities, and that mass violence was a real threat even amid the greatest and most liberal social policy changes ever directed toward the problem of black inequality. Black leaders and some white liberal politicians and intellectuals demanded much more radical government intervention both to deal with the ghetto system itself and to directly change the economic situation of black workers and families. Many whites, however, including a substantial portion of the moderate supporters of civil rights in the South, reacted

[31] Ibid.

very differently, emphasizing the reestablishment of social control and the punishment of lawbreakers. Liberals faced the burden of explaining why the riots occurred after so many of the things which they had promised would solve the problems had already been done. They faced accusations that they were unwilling to uphold public order and were proposing to reward rather than punish communities that had spawned mass violence. Politically, liberals suddenly found themselves on the defensive, no longer occupying the high moral ground. Intellectually, they were far from certain about what was required or what would work.

Black Separation
and the Goal of Integration

Black leaders were deeply divided about how to respond to the unrest, and the moderates resented the implication that they were somehow responsible for it. Some radicals perceived a pre-revolutionary situation. With the great protest campaigns in the South, the civil rights movement, particularly its direct action groups, had created the basis for a major change in attitudes and law. The movement had crystallized action by liberal leaders and pushed civil rights to the top of the national agenda. Through their unity and forcefulness, the six major black groups—the NAACP, National Urban League, SCLC, SNCC, CORE, and National Council of Negro Women—had played a crucial role in the development of a program and a strategy that produced a liberal agenda. The U.S. Civil Rights Commission had done much to document inequalities and to translate reform ideas into proposals for legislative and administrative change. During the 1965–66 period, however, two of the leading protest groups, CORE and SNCC, moved toward black separatism, which resulted in severe internal division and rapid institutional collapse, leaving Dr. King's group, the SCLC, as the only major direct action organization committed to an integrated society. The result was a spectacular ideological conflict, a conflict that bore little relation to the actual structure of black opinion. With some of the most eloquent and dynamic young black leaders attacking integration policies, liberalism was unable to develop and effectively defend a coherent policy toward urban race relations.

Serious tensions had developed within CORE and SNCC by 1964, tensions produced by the failure of many campaigns and the growing criticism by some blacks of the leadership roles held by whites in the integrated groups. As separatism became the policy associated with radicals, the left of the civil rights movement was forced into a vicious choice between being denounced as out-of-date or adopting policies that expelled important white support and alienated integrationist blacks in the name of a more authentic black constituency that never materialized.

As early as 1964, CORE leader James Farmer had come under increasing attack for his philosophy of nonviolence and integration, as well as for not expelling the remaining white leadership from CORE. There were parallel attacks on white participation in many local chapters, and white membership fell quickly. A drive to become more closely identified with ghetto problems and to drop what were seen as middle-class concerns intensified the pressure. By 1965, when Farmer resigned, CORE was fading away and about to be taken over by a radical separatist faction. As integrationists left the group, opposition to the black power philosophy melted away. Membership and contributions plummeted, and most chapters ceased functioning. The remaining black separatists took over.

The Congress of Racial Equality's 1966 convention rejected integration as a goal in favor of "racial coexistence through Black Power."[32] As its old constituency disappeared, the organization's rhetoric continued to escalate. At the time, the energy of the rhetoric was often interpreted as a symbol of the strength and vitality of the new focus. Only later did it become apparent that there was little backing.

It is clear in retrospect that the segregationist black leadership was not leftist but rather, moved toward the right or dissolved in incoherent radicalism. For example, CORE leader Roy Innis, who attacked NAACP leaders as "house niggers" and the Congressional Black Caucas as "incestuous" and "outdated," later endorsed Richard Nixon for President. As the NAACP and other groups were leading massive battles against Nixon's Supreme Court nominations and his dismantling of civil rights and social programs, CORE had become a Nixon ally emphasizing segregation and black capitalism.

The Student Nonviolent Coordinating Committee was rapidly declining and moving toward separatism during this same period. Tension between white students and black rural organizers, as well as severe disappointments in a number of struggles, including that of the Mississippi Freedom Democratic Party at the 1964 Democratic National Convention, produced strong attacks on the organization's integrationist strategy. As in the case of CORE, the contact of organizers with the anger and extreme isolation of the ghetto was a major influence in SNCC's move toward separatism.

The organization was rapidly declining in participation and in fundraising ability by the end of 1965, in both the North and the South. When, after a divisive contest, Stokely Carmichael was elected by the group's staff in 1966 and SNCC embraced separatism, SNCC rapidly lost many of its former leaders and its capacity to generate any kind of local mass movement. The Los Angeles and New York campaigns, for example,

[32] Meier and Rudwick, *CORE*, pp. 410–18.

floundered. The leaders of the early, and much larger, movement left the organization.

Leaders of SNCC who urged violence in the midst of riots in various cities faced criminal charges. Carmichael left the country for Africa. The group's strategy for creating a mass base in the ghetto failed.

Although the organization that became committed to separatism rapidly vanished in most communities, the "Black Power" movement had much broader political importance for both blacks and whites. The dramatic slogan captured national attention after it was popularized by SNCC leader Stokely Carmichael in a Mississippi civil rights march in mid-1966. The Mississippi march proved to be a disaster for integrationists, as the image of Carmichael shouting "Black Power" to excited crowds of young blacks and openly challenging fellow marcher Martin Luther King, Jr., dominated national press coverage. The march drew attention away from Dr. King's Chicago campaign and led to a widespread perception of integrationist civil rights leaders as spokesmen for a tired and old-fashioned position in contrast to the exciting and provocative views of the nationalists. The largest black organizations, the NAACP and the National Urban League, were often described as irrelevant. Debate over the meaning and significance of "Black Power" would preoccupy the movement for years.

Leaders of SNCC and CORE rejected nonviolence and, sometimes, openly supported violence. Carmichael told an Atlanta riot mob that he wanted to "tear this place up."[33] His successor, H. Rap Brown, predicted a "race war" and threatened to "blow Atlanta up" over police issues. In Cambridge, Maryland, shortly before a riot began, he spoke to an angry black crowd about burning down white stores.[34] Though SNCC was evaporating, the statements of these young leaders and those of newly emerging groups like the Black Panthers received spectacular publicity at a time when racial violence and fear were important national issues. The significance of intensely publicized statements by black groups rejecting integration in a society in which white support for further government action on desegregation was rapidly shrinking is obvious. Whites could oppose further racial reform on the grounds that they could not submit to threats of violence, and also on the grounds that new black leaders did not want it.

The black power movement, of course, had many dimensions. Whites were offended by what appeared to be an anti-white tinge to the rhetoric of some of the leading spokesmen. The movement could also be viewed as a call for pride in black culture and black heritage or as a platform for

[33] William Brink and Louis Harris, *Black and White* (New York: Simon and Schuster, 1967), p. 61.

[34] Clayborne Carson, *In Struggle: SNCC and the Black Awakening of the 1960s* (Cambridge, Mass.: Harvard University Press, 1981), pp. 254–55.

the expansion of black political power or black business activity. Its influence, in at least some of these dimensions, was pervasive. In retrospect it is clear that it gave birth to extremely varied kinds of politics, ranging from revolutionary black nationalism to conservative black capitalism. In between there was a wide range of consequences, from reinforcement of black activism inside traditional two-party electoral politics to a revival of interest in black history. When the movement first emerged, however, it was perceived by whites and by some critical black leaders as an explosive and negative movement, symbolized by young black radicals screaming "Black Power," renouncing nonviolence, and demanding the expulsion of whites from the civil rights movement.

Although the black separatist movement received a great deal of attention and was often cited as justification for curtailing civil rights activity, most blacks rejected its support of separation throughout this period. According to consistent findings by various public opinion surveys, they remained strongly integrationist, right through the period of white reaction, the urban riots, the murder of the era's greatest black leader, and the election of presidents who received virtually no black votes and were actively hostile to civil rights enforcement. In other words, no matter how hopeless it might seem, commitment to the goal of an integrated society was fundamental. The objective was unchanging despite substantial division over such tactics as busing and affirmative action.

Blacks surveyed in 1966, as the black power movement was emerging, were even more integrationist than those surveyed at the peak of the civil rights movement in 1963. Eighty percent of those expressing an opinion preferred integrated neighborhoods, and there was a seven to one margin in favor of integrated schools. Three in five saw Martin Luther King as an excellent leader, two in five said the same about the NAACP's Roy Wilkins, but only one in fourteen thought the same about the leaders of SNCC and CORE. By an overwhelming thirteen to one margin, blacks disapproved of black nationalism; and only 11 percent thought that blacks "should give up working together with whites and just depend on their own people."[35] The Survey Research Center at the University of Michigan took surveys in fifteen big cities at the peak of the riots and black power agitation. These surveys revealed that only 8 percent of blacks preferred living in an all-black neighborhood, only 5 percent wanted all-black friends for their children, only 6 percent wanted their children to attend "all or mostly black schools," and only 10 percent believed that black schools "should have mostly Negro teachers."[36] Black goals have remained remarkably

[35] Brink and Harris, *Black and White*, pp. 232–34, 244–52, 260–62.
[36] Angus Campbell and Howard Schuman, "Black Views of Racial Issues," in Marcel L. Goldschmid, ed., *Americans and White Racism: Theory and Research* (New York: Holt, Rinehart and Winston, 1970), p. 347.

consistent since that time. A 1984 survey showed that only 7 percent of blacks believed it would be better "if blacks lived separate and apart from whites," and 82 percent said that public schools would be better if they were integrated.[37] Black separatists, in other words, never had a substantial mass following in the black community, but their policies did tend both to dissipate white support and strengthen white opposition to racial change. They failed to mobilize blacks, but they did help to mobilize white opposition and undermine white liberals.

Political Impact of the White Backlash

Whites had turned notably less sympathetic to the black movement by 1966. Though they did not reject the general goal of equal treatment for blacks, even as fears of urban violence increased sharply, many fewer than before saw civil rights as an important national issue, and the view that government had already done enough for blacks became widespread. The political climate in Washington soon reflected the new mood.

Although whites continued to support abstract goals such as integrated education and nondiscrimination in employment, there was a growing gap between white and black views on whether discrimination was still a serious issue. Whites tended to believe that the problems had been solved, and they saw no necessity for further government action. Many whites gave priority to the need for laws to control urban violence. During the twenty years after 1965, except for a brief period following Dr. King's assassination, the polls would show no surge of public concern for civil rights. Particularly distressing was the tendency of white opinion to crystallize in a strongly negative way around the new issues of discrimination in the urban setting—issues involving race-conscious remedies for deeply rooted discriminatory practices. These remedies included busing, affirmative action, scatter-site public housing, and changes in suburban zoning. No significant white support developed for policies that would open to blacks the middle-class schools and the suburban neighborhoods and job opportunities that were the keys to mobility in metropolitan society.

White concern for civil rights simply evaporated between the mid-1960s, when it was the nation's preeminent issue, and the middle of the first Nixon administration, when it virtually disappeared from the list of serious issues. Gallup Poll data from 1963 to 1971 indicate the change (see Table 9.1).

In any case, it is one thing to be concerned about a problem and quite another to believe that government should try to do something about it. There were always many Americans who believed that the national administration was "pushing integration too fast." This was true even in

[37] Survey by Black Data Opinion Polls, Inc., *Ebony* (January 1985): 115.

TABLE 9.1 Importance of Race as a National Issue, 1963–1971

Date	Proportion of Americans Seeing Race as Most Important Issue (percent)	Leading Issue When Race Is Not
April 1963	4	International
July 1963	49	problems
April 1964	41	
June 1964	47	
August 1964	40	
March 1965	52	
May 1965	23	
November 1965	17	Vietnam
May 1966	9	Vietnam
August 1966	24	Vietnam
November 1967	21	Vietnam
May 1968	25	Vietnam
June 1968	13	Vietnam
August 1968	20	Vietnam
January 1969	16	Vietnam
February 1971	7	Vietnam
July 1971	7	Vietnam
September 1971	7	Economy
November 1971	6	Economy

SOURCE: Gallup Polls, 1963–71.

the early 1960s, before the first major civil rights bill had been sent to Congress. Throughout the Kennedy-Johnson years, at least one-third of the public held this view. After Kennedy asked for sweeping legislation, the proportion of the public thinking that things were going too fast went up to 50 percent—even before the law was enacted. Even though Lyndon Johnson actually put far more emphasis on civil rights, many fewer people thought at first that he was going "too fast," perhaps because of the trauma of the Kennedy assassination, because Johnson was a southerner, and because of his political skill in making issues sound less controversial. By the fall of 1966, however, after two summers of rioting and the emergence of the black power movement, more than half the public thought change was happening too fast (see Table 9.2).

Even more revealing than the general trends of white attitudes are the

TABLE 9.2 Percentage of Americans Believing National
Administration Was Pushing Integration Too Fast,
1962–1968

	National Total	Northern Whites
BEFORE KENNEDY CIVIL RIGHTS BILL		
May 1962	32	
June 1962	36	
AFTER CIVIL RIGHTS BILL		
July 1963	38	
August 1963	50	
September 1963	50	
DURING JOHNSON ADMINISTRATION		
February 1964	30	28
March 1965	34	28
April 1965	45	
July 1965	40	36
September 1965		36
June 1966	46	44
September 1966	52	52
AFTER KING ASSASSINATION		
April 1968	39	

SOURCE: Gallup Polls, 1962–68.

changes in attitudes of those northern whites who were strongly in favor
of action against southern discrimination. As the issues moved north and
the political climate changed, there was a sharp and steady rise in opposition among northern whites, beginning before the Watts riot and becoming the opinion of the majority by late 1966. Table 9.2 shows that
the fraction of northern whites who thought Washington was forcing integration "too fast" nearly doubled. Since northern congressmen had
been the key to the civil rights coalition's successes, this shift in constituency opinion was critically important.

Although the Eighty-ninth Congress (1965–66) was probably the most liberal in U.S. history on social policy and civil rights, reaction soon became apparent on Capitol Hill. The 1964 Democratic landslide had created extremely favorable conditions for liberals, producing a net gain of thirty-eight seats in the House; and most of the newcomers were activist liberals with strong civil rights commitments.[38] This Congress enacted an astonishing array of major new federal policies, including the Voting Rights Act in its first year, but it had turned against further civil rights change by 1966, as white support fell and northern discrimination issues began to come into focus.

For the first time since 1954, the House began to pass measures that would actually shrink existing civil rights protections. It eviscerated President Johnson's 1966 fair housing proposal, passed amendments to limit school desegregation, voted to provide sweeping anti-riot powers to local police, and blocked Johnson administration plans that could have begun action on problems of metropolitan segregation.

President Johnson had promised leadership on the next generation of civil rights problems in his widely hailed 1965 Howard University address. When the first new initiatives reached Congress, however, the mood was much less supportive. For example, Johnson had named a Task Force on Urban Problems to design new solutions for cities, stating that he wanted a plan for "rebuilding the slums." The task force's basic proposal was for a national competition that would award grants for designing and carrying out a comprehensive urban strategy in a few cities. Plans were to incorporate "measures to eliminate social and racial segregation including assurance of equal opportunity in housing." This recommendation became part of draft model cities legislation, which included a call for plans to "counteract the segregation of housing by race or income." The president's message to Congress warned of the widening city-suburban gap and the problem of blacks trapped in ghettos.[39] The bill, which became known as "Model Cities," included provisions requiring compliance with federal civil rights laws and the appointment of a federal coordinator for each metropolitan area selected, whose job it was to convince the various federal agencies to provide the resources to carry out the local plan.

New York Republican Congressman Paul Fino, however, successfully assailed the civil rights provisions, reflecting the changing mood in Congress. After he claimed that the coordinator could be a "commissar or czar" forcing unwanted changes, that requirement was eliminated. The fair housing provisos were weakened, and federal agencies were forbid-

[38] Jeff Fishel, *Party and Opposition* (New York: David McKay, 1973), pp. 10, 64–94.
[39] Bernard J. Frieden and Marshall Kaplan, *The Politics of Neglect: Urban Aid from Model Cities to Revenue Sharing* (Cambridge, Mass.: MIT Press, 1975), pp. 35–39.

den to withhold funds to force compliance with civil rights requirements.[40] By the time it came out of Congress, the most important urban
policy initiative of the Great Society had no effective provisions against
urban discrimination and segregation. In the final version of the bill, the
money was spread much more thinly over cities in many congressional
districts.

The backlash was even more apparent in Congress's treatment of Johnson's 1966 fair housing proposal. The climate was so negative that a
number of civil rights groups criticized the president for submitting hopeless legislation rather than doing what he could through an executive order. Though Johnson's strategy would eventually succeed in 1968, after
Martin Luther King's assassination, the 1966 experience shows the terri-
ble decline of the civil rights coalition. The bill came out of the House
with such limited fair housing provisions and so many anti–civil rights
amendments that Dr. King said it was not worth passing. It included anti-
busing language, a prohibition against "outside agitators" crossing state
lines to encourage riots, and other provisions that could be used against
civil rights groups. It recognized not only the right of individual families
to discriminate in home sales, but also their right to require their realtors
to do so.[41]

Things were even worse in the Senate. Republican leader Everett Dirk-
sen led the opposition to any fair housing law, calling it a threat to the
country and insisting that the problem was not white discrimination but
the behavior of blacks moving into white areas. Only ten Republican senators voted for fair housing, and supporters did not come close to cutting
off the conservative filibuster.[42] The coalition that had enacted voting
rights the year before no longer existed, even though the same members
were in Congress.

The 1966 session was a turning point for both northern modern Democrats and Republicans, particularly in the House. House Republicans
shifted decisively into opposition, and they were to become a powerful
anti–civil rights bloc on many votes. Northern Democratic moderates
would be far less reliable civil rights supporters in the future.[43] The issues
were changing from questions about the South to policies that could force
change on white urban constituents. The 1966 congressional elections
made things worse, greatly increasing conservative strength in Congress.

[40] Ibid., pp. 59–63; *Congressional Record*, October 14, 1966: 26922–27.

[41] *Congressional Record*, July 1966; August 3, 1966: 17326–30; August 5, 1966: 17594–
97; *Washington Post*, August 8, 1966.

[42] Congressional Quarterly, *Congress and the Nation, 1969* (Washington, D.C.: Congressional Quarterly, Inc., 1969), pp. 368–73.

[43] *Congressional Quarterly*, March 12, 1971.

Martin Luther King
and the Chicago Campaign

As a wide variety of negative trends threatened the integrationist movement, its dominant leader, Dr. Martin Luther King, attempted to prove the viability in the northern urban setting of both his goals and his methods by launching a great campaign in a citadel of northern segregation, Chicago. He sought to produce a decisive and symbolic conflict like those in Birmingham and Selma, which had helped generate the historic federal legislation attacking the bases of southern segregation.

Chicago seemed a logical testing place for several reasons. Local civil rights groups had sustained an extraordinary long-term mobilization over a school integration fight in which white resistance was as hostile and unyielding as in the South. In fact, the situation contained many of the ingredients that had led to breakthroughs in the South—active resistance, a distinct villain, an aroused and organized black community, extreme segregation, obvious inequality, and strong news media interest. After visits showing a strong local response, Dr. King and his staff decided that Chicago would be the testing ground for the next stage of the civil rights movement. The nonviolent integrationist movement turned squarely against the ghetto system.

Protest over separate and blatantly unequal schools in Chicago was important since quality education could provide a means of escape from the urban ghetto. The school fight was particularly bitter because Chicago School Superintendent Benjamin C. Willis was adamantly opposed to even the most modest concession to black demands. When the school board ordered the transfer of twenty-four black students to white schools in 1963, Willis resigned and provoked an intense political crisis in the city. The board brought Willis back and rescinded the directive.[44] Willis's decision to place large numbers of mobile classrooms in the playgrounds of black schools rather than permit the transfer of students from crowded buildings increased resistance.

The school fight precipitated the formation of the Coordinating Council of Community Organizations (ccco), which organized scores of demonstrations, protests, and giant school boycotts, setting the stage for the Chicago Freedom Movement, King's last major campaign. During his time in Chicago, King spoke much about the nature of the urban color bar and about the overwhelmingly depressing impact of the ghetto even on his own children. On many occasions, he spoke of problems that would stay with him into some of the last speeches of his life. Some of his Chicago comments offer the clearest statements the nation's preeminent

[44] Joseph Pois, *The School Board Crisis: A Chicago Case Study* (Chicago: Educational Methods, Inc., 1964), pp. 109–13.

black leader was to make about the nature and severity of the country's most important remaining racial barrier—the urban ghetto system.

King spoke of the "slow, shifting death of concentration camp life." His own children, he said, began to change "only a few days" after they moved into the West Side of Chicago. He found himself "struggling constantly against the depression and hopelessness which the hearts of our cities pump into the bloodstream of our lives."[45] He described aspects of the cycle of ghettoization such as blacks receiving far less income than whites but having to pay far more for housing, financing, groceries, and other necessities of life. Urban renewal was continuing to take black homes, he said, while there were no efforts to construct new housing for blacks outside the ghetto.[46]

> It is a vicious circle. You can't get a job because you are poorly educated, and you must depend on welfare to feed your children; but if you receive public aid in Chicago, you cannot own property, not even an automobile, so you are condemned to the jobs and shops which are closest to your home.[47]

The only real way of getting out was through education. But the public schools in the ghetto were seriously inadequate compared with white schools in the city, to say nothing of the suburban schools that trained most white children.

> In this way the system conspires to perpetuate inferior status and to prepare the Negro for those tasks that no one else wants, hence creating a mass of unskilled, cheap labor for the society at large. . . . Already in childhood their lives are crushed mentally, emotionally and physically, and then society develops the myth of inferiority to give credence to its lifelong patterns of exploitation, which can only be defined as our system of slavery in the twentieth century.[48]

King defined the ghetto system as a type of "internal colonialism," a "reservation." It was a system with separate education and a separate economy, where a vastly disproportionate part of the society's unemployment was concentrated. The police functioned differently on opposite sides of the racial line, and the courts treated people differently according to race.[49]

[45] Martin Luther King, Jr., *The Trumpet of Conscience* (New York: Harper and Row, 1968), pp. 134–35.

[46] Ibid., pp. 136–37.

[47] Ibid., p. 137.

[48] Ibid., p. 136.

[49] Ibid., p. 131; Stephen B. Oates, *Let the Trumpet Sound: The Life of Martin Luther King, Jr.* (New York: Harper and Row, 1982), p. 390.

The white resistance to the fair housing marches in Chicago was intense and violent. "I've been in many demonstrations all across the South," said King, "but I can say that I have never seen . . . mobs as hostile and hate filled."[50] His biographer, Stephen Oates, writes, "He could not shake the image of all those maniacal faces, taunting and screaming at him."[51]

King's sweeping and often majestic rhetoric frequently took on an apocalyptic cast when he was discussing the black ghetto: the ghetto was a prison, it was this century's form of slavery, it doomed its children. He wanted to bring down the walls and open the paths into full participation in American society. Oates writes: "For him, the future of integration—of the movement, the country, and perhaps humankind itself—was increasingly on the line in this perilous hour."[52]

After his drive to organize the slums failed, Dr. King turned to fair housing marches, as did the parallel ghetto mobilization campaigns of SNCC, CORE, and other groups in large cities. Neither King nor any other black leader could sustain power and organization in communities devastated by economic and social collapse. But King could stir an upswelling of black protest by turning his attack on the wall around the black community.

Once he turned against the color line itself, he soon faced the kind of nationally publicized violent confrontation between peaceful marchers and violent white segregationists that had revolutionized the civil rights movement in the South. There were screaming people with swastikas and "White Power" signs, and largely Catholic mobs stoned columns of marchers, screaming at priests and nuns in the line. In the South, exposing this kind of race hatred and violence had gravely undermined the moral and political position of white segregationists and triggered powerful national action. In Chicago, however, the protest cast into glaring relief a structure of imposed physical separation that was widely considered legitimate. Many white politicians rushed not to file new civil rights bills, but to criticize the protesters for making trouble.

Both before and after King came to Chicago, civil rights groups appealed to Washington for action against the city's segregation, as had their southern counterparts. In 1965, a lengthy complaint was filed alleging numerous specific violations of the nondiscrimination requirements of the 1964 Civil Rights Act. Officials inside HEW decided that the charges were serious enough to withhold federal aid from the Chicago schools until an investigation could be conducted and the necessary desegregation plan prepared.

[50] Oates, *Let the Trumpet Sound*, p. 413.
[51] Ibid., p. 418.
[52] Ibid., p. 406.

Action in the North, however, had legal and political ramifications fundamentally different from action in the South. There were no Supreme Court decisions on northern segregation, and northern mayors were a key part of President Johnson's political coalition. Conditions might be similar, but the law had not recognized the similarity. The high court said nothing about northern urban segregation until nineteen years after the *Brown* decision. The very next year, 1974, it acted to protect the white suburbs of the North from integration.

President Johnson's domestic policy chief, Joseph Califano, recalls the President's reaction on learning of the action withholding education funds from Chicago.

> I remember the day [HEW Secretary] Gardner notified the city of Chicago. President Johnson was in New York to welcome Pope Paul VI to the United States. . . . Earlier that day, Johnson had heard that HEW Secretary Gardner had announced his intention to cut off federal funds to Chicago's school system. Mayor Richard Daley, also in New York to meet the Pope, had already called Johnson to express his angry astonishment. Johnson was extremely agitated and instructed me to have Gardner and Attorney General Katzenbach in his Oval Office on our return to Washington.[53]

The funds were restored to Chicago after five days, and a face-saving agreement was developed but never honored. Soon there was a new commissioner of education in Washington, and the change was attributed in part to the Chicago fiasco. There would be no significant enforcement of the desegregation requirements of the 1964 Civil Rights Act in any big city outside the South for twelve years, until a 1977 attempt to begin desegregation in Kansas City led to congressional action outlawing such enforcement.[54]

The federal government refused to act in the Chicago school desegregation case. In housing, things were even worse. The housing issues were predominantly federal responsibilities. Both public and private housing in Chicago and its suburbs had been developed under federal policies that accepted and subsidized residential segregation. Chicago's public housing was a spectacular example of government-financed segregation. The giant high-rise projects, stretching for miles in the heart of the city's South Side ghetto, were notorious across the United States.

---

[53] Joseph A. Califano, Jr., *Governing America: An Insider's Report from the White House and the Cabinet* (New York: Simon and Schuster, 1981), pp. 221–22.

[54] Gary Orfield, *The Reconstruction of Southern Education: The Schools and the 1964 Civil Rights Act* (New York: Wiley, 1969), pp. 151–207; Gary Orfield, *Must We Bus? Segregated Schools and National Policy* (Washington, D.C.: The Brookings Institution, 1978), pp. 279–318.

If things had worked in the Chicago campaign the way they had in the South, the marches in Chicago should have given a positive impulse to the drive for fair housing. The white violence, however, had no such effect. The House of Representatives weakened the fair housing bill so severely that Dr. King said its passage would only "increase despair."[55] The polls showed a rapid decline in public support for the president's civil rights policies.[56] Five of every six whites thought the marches were hurting racial progress.[57] The demonstrations were consolidating opposition, not mobilizing sympathy.

After his campaign came to an end, Martin Luther King's Chicago Freedom Movement was attacked as a failure. Although there were divided opinions, King himself was deeply affected by the experience and became considerably more pessimistic, though he never gave up his commitment to integration. However, King decided that the direct action protests could not work in the North.[58]

Actually, it could be said that King's Chicago campaign was a success in the same way his southern campaigns had been successes. He had mobilized the community to a massive protest, focused immense publicity on the problems, created a dramatic symbolic confrontation that revealed the underlying prejudices, and forced the city leaders into a negotiation process to end the escalating protests. The summit agreement was itself comparable to what he had won from southern officials. The critical difference was that the southern campaigns had stimulated national action by Congress. The Chicago movement had not. The southern movement required no action that would directly affect northern whites. Once urban whites were threatened, the politics changed.

The Chicago experience convinced King that the movement had seriously "miscalculated" the intensity of northern discrimination. Segregation in the North was untouched and expanding even as life was changing in the South.[59]

As he told David Halberstam later, Chicago convinced him that whites did not really want integration, did not really want the Negro as a brother. . . . Up to now he had thought he was reaching for the best in white America. After Chicago, though, he decided that only

[55] *Washington Post*, August 6, 1966.

[56] *Washington Post*, September 12 and 29, 1966; Johnson, *Public Papers of the President*, 1966, pp. 859–60.

[57] *Washington Post*, October 12, 1966.

[58] Oates, *Let the Trumpet Sound*, p. 415.

[59] Martin Luther King, Jr., *Where Do We Go from Here: Chaos or Community?* (New York: Harper and Row, 1968), pp. 15, 22.

a small minority of whites—mostly college students—were committed to the cause of racial equality.[60]

Partly because of the disappointment of the Chicago campaign, King did not launch new protests against urban segregation in his last years. The problem of the ghetto, however, was central to his thoughts, as he explained in an article in *Look* that was published after his death.

> I'm convinced that if something isn't done to deal with the very harsh and real economic problems of the ghetto, the talk of guerrilla warfare is going to become much more real. . . . White America has allowed itself to be indifferent to race prejudice and economic denial. It has treated them as superficial blemishes, but now awakes to the horrifying reality of a potentially fatal disease. . . . The seams of our entire social order are weakening under strains of neglect.[61]

Growing Understanding, Shrinking Support

After the Chicago campaign, there were no more major national protests against urban segregation; in fact, the entire direct action wing of the civil rights movement was in a severe decline that would become a collapse after the failure of the 1968 Poor People's Campaign in Washington.

There had been, however, a devastating series of urban riots and increasingly clear and stark warnings from many directions about the fundamental instability and inequality of urban race relations. Year after year, a deepening sense of crisis and social danger was building. Before the 1960s ended, there were numerous local, state, and national reports documenting profound social and economic problems in the inner cities. By the late 1960s, a great deal of knowledge had been accumulated about the situation of urban blacks and the kinds of issues that would have to be faced if the underlying trends were to be reversed.

The civil rights laws of the mid-1960s created institutions and expertise in enforcing racial change that the government had never before possessed. The laws and institutions were aimed at southern conditions, but the reform impulse also focused attention on northern urban issues. In public education, for example, President Johnson, in late 1965, requested the U.S. Civil Rights Commission, the institution that had helped create the policy agenda for transforming southern race relations, to make a nationwide study of segregated schools. The commission's 1967 report, *Racial Isolation in the Public Schools*, documented serious increases in segregated education in many central cities and strong tends toward pre-

---

[60] Oates, *Let the Trumpet Sound*, p. 418.

[61] Charles Fager, *Uncertain Resurrection: The Poor People's Washington Campaign* (Grand Rapids, Mich.: Eerdmans Publishing Co., 1969), p. 16.

dominantly minority central city systems. It recommended national legislation outlawing urban segregation and providing substantial aid to help achieve successful desegregation.[62]

The Civil Rights Act prompted national collection and publication of segregation statistics for the first time in U.S. history. Although HEW did not cut off funds from northern cities, it did launch many investigations and accumulate a great deal of evidence about the history of segregation in those cities. By the late 1960s it was clear that much of the "de facto" segregation in northern schools was actually the result of a history of discrimination by local school districts. In the final months of the Johnson administration, the Justice Department filed its first lawsuits aimed at desegregating urban schools in the North.

There was also a developing understanding of the need for a variety of actions to deal with the housing segregation that was a root cause of the ghetto. In 1967–68, the first significant efforts were made within HUD to redirect the policies of housing authorities and the Federal Housing Administration (FHA) that had led to urban segregation. In the final months of the Johnson administration, Congress passed both the largest housing subsidy program in U.S. history and a broad fair housing law with few teeth. Effective coordination of these two laws could have had a major positive impact.

Four different presidential commissions warned of the great urban racial issues still to be faced as the 1960s ended. The National Commission on Urban Problems, the President's Commission on Urban Housing, the National Advisory Commission on Civil Disorders (the Kerner Commission), and the National Commission on the Causes and Prevention of Violence (the Eisenhower Commission) all conducted massive studies, reported severe problems, and proposed broad recommendations for more far-reaching urban policies dealing explicitly with problems of the ghetto.

The reports were delivered, however, to a lame duck administration that had little political strength and was facing serious problems financing the Vietnam War. The most important of the broad descriptions of the urban racial situation was the March 1968 report of the National Advisory Commission on Civil Disorders, which had investigated the causes of scores of urban riots from 1964 to 1967. The commission concluded that the urban ghetto system was threatening American society. "Segregation and poverty," it said, "have created in the racial ghetto a destructive environment totally unknown to most white Americans."[63] Deepening polarization was occurring.

[62] U.S. Commission on Civil Rights, *Racial Isolation in the Public Schools* (Washington, D.C., 1967).

[63] U.S. National Advisory Commission on Civil Disorders, *Report of the National Advisory Commission on Civil Disorders* (New York: Bantam Books, 1968), pp. 1–2.

The nation is rapidly moving toward two increasingly separate Americas. Within two decades, this division could be so deep that it would be almost impossible to unite. . . .

The Negro society will be permanently relegated to its current status, possibly even if we expend great amounts of money and effort in trying to "gild" the ghetto. . . .

We cannot escape responsibility for choosing the future of our metropolitan areas and the human relations which will develop within them. It is a responsibility so critical that even an unconscious choice to continue present policies has the gravest implications.[64]

The commission found that all the Great Society programs had been insufficient. For example, at the peak of the economic boom of the 1960s, there had been depression-level joblessness for young blacks and a dropout rate three times the level for whites. Many inner city blacks had obtained neither the education nor the job experience needed for mobility. They were becoming permanently detached from the opportunities outside the ghetto. In particular, teenage blacks in 1966 were six times as likely as their white counterparts to be unemployed.[65] In the midst of a great economic boom and after the enactment of a law against job discrimination, they still had depression-level unemployment though there were few whites without jobs.

Much as Dr. King had, the commission recommended both broad efforts to improve ghetto institutions and a sustained attack on urban segregation. It called for incentives for and strong enforcement of school integration. It proposed a massive expansion of subsidized housing to build mostly small-scale scattered-site housing outside the ghettos.[66]

The commission's report and the assassination of Martin Luther King the next month initiated the last period of strong national focus on racial conditions for many years. Though both contributed to the enactment of the fair housing law then pending in the House of Representatives, neither stimulated any new proposals from the White House. Three weeks after he received the Kerner Commission report, Johnson told a press conference that he had already asked Congress for as many programs as he thought he could get.[67]

A basic problem, Johnson wrote in his memoirs, was that the commission's recommendations would have cost $30 billion.

That was the problem—money. At the moment I received the report I was having one of the toughest fights of my life trying to persuade

[64] Ibid., pp. 407, 408.
[65] Ibid., p. 414.
[66] Ibid., pp. 425–82.
[67] Johnson, *Public Papers of the President*, 1968, pp. 434–35.

Congress to pass the 10 percent tax surcharge without imposing deep cuts in our most critical Great Society programs. I will never understand how the commission expected me to get this same Congress to turn 180 degrees and appropriate an additional $30 billion for the same programs that it was demanding I cut by $6 billion. This would have required a miracle.[68]

Conflict over the war costs meant that Johnson had little power and no money to begin anything new. Although a sympathetic president received an unvarnished warning about threats to the future of American urban society, he thought nothing could be done. Before the end of the year, the issues would totally disappear from the national agenda.

Nixon and the Assault on Civil Rights

The 1968 presidential campaign was the last in which there was a serious debate about the problems of the urban ghetto. Though the campaign was dominated by the Vietnam War and the division in the Democratic party, the electorate was offered an extraordinary range of positions on race relations by Hubert Humphrey, Richard Nixon, and George Wallace.

Humphrey was the leader of the activist civil rights wing of his party. He had led the 1948 convention fight to commit the Democrats to civil rights, and his greatest Senate triumph was the successful struggle to enact the 1964 Civil Rights Act. Just before the 1968 election, he published a book on civil rights, sharply challenging Richard Nixon's "Southern Strategy" and warning of the threat of serious regression from civil rights accomplishments that he believed it posed.[69]

George Wallace ran as a segregationist candidate, committed to dismantling the entire structure of civil rights reform, including what had already been accomplished in the South. Wallace won more than nine million votes in an election in which the major party candidates were separated by only a half million votes. Earlier in the campaign support for Wallace was far higher, peaking at 29 percent of the electorate.[70]

When Richard Nixon adopted the "Southern Strategy" for his campaign, he harshly criticized busing, promised to end cutoffs of federal aid that had been designed to impose desegregation, criticized aspects of the

[68] Lyndon Baines Johnson, *The Vantage Point: Perspectives on the Presidency, 1963–1969* (New York: Holt, Rinehart and Winston, 1971), p. 173.
[69] Hubert H. Humphrey, *Beyond Civil Rights: A New Day of Equality* (New York: Random House, 1968), pp. 8–9.
[70] Gallup Poll, *Richmond Times-Dispatch*, June 19, 1968; *Washington Post*, July 15, 1968.

Voting Rights Act, and promised to name conservative "strict construc-
tionists" to the Supreme Court. Nixon and Wallace together received almost three-fifths of the vote. Humphrey had an almost unanimous vote
in many black areas.[71] It was a pattern of racial polarization that would
be characteristic of national elections through 1984. No Democrat would
carry the white vote during this period. No Republican would receive a
significant black vote.

The historic significance of the 1968 election did not become fully apparent until the mid-1970s, when the remaining ideological battles within
the GOP had been resolved and the Supreme Court had changed direction.
The GOP, the national party that would win the White House in four of
the five elections after 1964, committed itself strongly against any further
governmentally imposed racial change and promised to use its power to
make it impossible for either the courts or the bureaucracy to require
more. No liberal would be named to the Supreme Court in the next generation, and there would be no significant effort to integrate urban society. Six years after this decision, when whites constituted fewer than half
the students in more than two-thirds of the nation's largest school districts, it was clear that protecting the suburbs from integration orders
often meant that there could be no real integration. Segregation would be
accepted as natural, and the power of government would be directed
against those who attacked it.

The Nixon administration's failure to control either house of Congress,
the continuing influence of senior Republican moderate senators who
supported civil rights, the presence of officials representing a considerable
ideological spectrum in the initial Nixon cabinet, and the time lag in gaining a generally supportive Supreme Court majority tended to obscure the
consequences of the changes for some years. The Supreme Court, for instance, rejected transparently political efforts to delay school desegregation in the South in 1969 and imposed busing on the urban South during
the first Nixon years. Other federal courts found the Nixon administration guilty of refusing to enforce the Civil Rights Act, and they weakened
White House control over school and college desegregation activities in
the South. Congress enacted legislation providing financial aid to desegregating school districts. These actions accounted for the final major
surge of school integration in the South, from 1968 to 1972. After 1972
the momentum of change was largely spent (see Table 9.3).

By the time the cases critical to the future of equal education in the big
northern cities reached the Supreme Court, however, the four Nixon justices and the Justice Department played dominant roles in blocking fur-

[71] William J. Keefe, *Parties, Politics, and Public Policy in America*, 3d ed. (New York:
Rinehart and Winston, 1980), p. 118.

TABLE 9.3 Percentage of Southern Black Students in Desegregated Schools, 1968–1984

Year	In Predominantly Minority Schools	In 90 to 100 Percent Minority Schools
1968	80.9	77.8
1972	55.3	24.7
1976	54.9	22.4
1980	57.1	23.0
1984	56.9	24.2

SOURCE: U.S. Department of Education data.

ther reform. In its 1973 *Keyes* decision, the Court divided on a major school issue for the first time since 1954, but it opened the way for northern school desegregation orders under some circumstances. The next year, however, the Court confronted the dilemma posed when a central city school district has violated the rights of black children, and desegregation of that district would require involving suburban as well as city schools. Since most large northern cities had public schools with a rapidly declining white minority, this was the most important question for school integration. By a five to four vote, the Court raised massive barriers to metropolitan integration orders.[72] The four Nixon justices all voted against city-suburban desegregation. This meant that most central city black children would remain segregated.

The early 1970s had brought an extremely active campaign of school finance litigation; however, in 1973, the Supreme Court cut off a major reform effort intended to win equal funding for school districts within states. It decided by a five to four majority that there was no duty to provide equal resources among school districts (*San Antonio Independent School District* v. *Rodriguez*, 411 U.S. 1 [1973]). This decision had little immediate importance for most big cities, since many still had relatively favorable fiscal situations. It meant, however, that as the cities became poorer relative to their suburbs, more overwhelmingly minority, and considerably weaker in state legislative competition for funding, there would be no protection against steadily increasing inequalities. When school districts in Chicago, New York, Cleveland, and elsewhere experienced extremely severe fiscal crises and major cutbacks later in the decade, there was no possible leverage through the federal courts to guarantee that sep-

[72] *Keyes* v. *School Dist. No. 1, Denver*, 413 U.S. 189 (1973); *Milliken* v. *Bradley*, 418 U.S. 717 (1974).

arate would be somewhat more equal. Fiscal inequality would grow in the 1980s.

As the school integration movement and the drive for equal resources were coming to dead ends in the Supreme Court, critical housing policy decisions were taking shape within the executive branch. The Nixon administration inherited the largest housing subsidy program in U.S. history. The 1968 housing program was in its crucial start-up phase. Since the program relied on the private market for housing, it offered possibilities for integration not present under traditional public housing authorities. In a society in which the average family moves every six years and the residence of a substantial fraction of the poor is determined by government, a serious fair housing policy combined with a large subsidy program could have a strong impact in a few years. At its peak, this new law was producing one-fourth of all new housing under construction in the United States. It included programs for the purchase or subsidized use of existing private housing as well. It was the first housing program subject to the directive of the 1968 fair housing legislation requiring that all federal housing programs be administered in a manner fostering fair housing. The new secretary of HUD, former Michigan Governor George Romney, had a record of strong support for civil rights. He proposed to use HUD programs and HUD housing investments to force communities to permit construction of housing outside ghettos and in white suburbs.[73]

The HUD integration efforts, of course, produced loud local protests. President Nixon then announced that he was opposed to "forced integration of the suburbs." Nixon drastically limited HUD initiatives. One of his first actions after reelection in 1972 was to end all possibility of using housing programs as leverage for integration by imposing a moratorium on the operation of all federal housing construction programs.[74] Since that time federal housing production has not even approached the levels of the early 1970s. No president since the 1960s has advocated suburban housing integration. Even the one Democratic president, Jimmy Carter, spoke in favor of the "ethnic purity" of neighborhoods in his successful 1976 primary campaign, though he later apologized and worked unsuccessfully for a modest strengthening of fair housing law.

The Supreme Court in the 1970s rejected the major campaign of litigation intended to deal with the problem of suburban racial and economic exclusiveness—the battle against exclusionary zoning and subur-

[73] Anthony Downs, *Federal Housing Subsidies: How Are They Working?* (Lexington, Mass.: Lexington Books, 1973).

[74] Congressional Quarterly, *Nixon: The Third Year of His Presidency* (Washington, D.C.: Congressional Quarterly, Inc., 1972), p. 23; Congressional Quarterly, *Nixon: The Fifth Year of His Presidency* (Washington, D.C.: Congressional Quarterly, Inc., 1974), p. 28-A.

ban rejection of all subsidized housing through various land use and building controls. The Supreme Court's decisions during the 1970s made bringing such litigation in the federal courts very difficult and recognized a broad range of permissible local discretion in zoning decisions, even if those decisions had the effect of excluding the great majority of nonwhite households from a community on economic grounds. The courts put no pressure on local, state, and federal agencies to come to terms with the social and racial implications of a system of mandatory economic separation through housing controls; in fact, their decisions legitimized suburban actions.

Accepting the Ghetto and Blaming Its Victims: 1975–1985

The decisions of the Nixon and Ford administrations and the Burger Court were remarkably effective in redefining the policies and politics of urban race relations. The ghetto was accepted as normal, much as the Jim Crow system had been after Reconstruction. Policies that attacked it structurally, rather than permitting a few individuals to cross the color line, were rejected as unworkable and counterproductive. A Booker T. Washington–style philosophy of black development within segregated communities without equal resources was imposed on the black community as its only alternative. As at the end of Reconstruction, state and local officials who had a consistent record of inaction on or opposition to civil rights were given more control and discretion over domestic programs. Federal institutions with a capacity to devise and enforce desegregation policies in cities either lost legislative authority, were dismantled, or were turned over to officials actively opposed to civil rights laws. By the early 1980s, for instance, in federal courts across the United States, the Department of Justice was actively representing the interests of whites opposed to school integration and affirmative action. In 1986 President Reagan chose the Supreme Court justice with the most consistent record of opposition to civil rights, William Rehnquist, as the new chief justice.

After the end of Reconstruction, the issue of racial equality rapidly disappeared from the political agendas of both major parties, and scholars and political leaders alike produced explanations of black inequality that strongly emphasized the deficiencies of blacks and their communities. Political sympathy and philanthropic support usually went to "responsible" black leaders who accepted the basic structure of imposed segregation and developed non-threatening programs for working within it to address what whites defined as the black deficiencies.

With the important, but transitory, exception of the Carter administration, which was more sympathetic than the Republican administrations but very cautious, much the same has happened in U.S. political and intellectual life since the end of the civil rights movement. Neither party has offered any major proposals to implement a plan on the scale of the Kerner Commission proposals, or to develop a policy that would provide blacks confined to the urban ghetto with substantial access to white housing and school and job opportunities. No president since Johnson has even made a major speech on the issues. A great deal of policy attention has been focused on issues such as black teenage pregnancy, welfare dependency, the "black underclass," the collapse of the black family, the lack of black small business development, and the problems of black mayors and school administrators. But questions about structural racial barriers have largely disappeared from public discussion. For example, many discussions about the need for job experience or about the lack of job motivation among young blacks never mention the fact that there has been a continuing and massive transfer of jobs from the black to the white side of the color line in metropolitan areas, and that in many markets virtually all new job creation is taking place in outlying white areas largely inaccessible to ghetto workers.

The ultimate stage of the process of turning the issues inside out comes with the claim that what is wrong with blacks now is the result not of discrimination or segregation, present or past, but of excessive welfare programs that have destroyed their incentive to be productive. This has been a major theme in President Reagan's analyses of the situation of blacks.

The vacuum in liberal thought and Democratic party policy is directly related to the abandonment of the understanding of urban race relations that had developed by the late 1960s. The problem is not that the intellectual framework was incorrect, or that it did not work. In fact, it had very strong predictive power, accurately forecasting the increasing inequalities and joblessness that have developed in the past two decades as ghetto boundaries spread rapidly to cover large parts of many central cities. The framework was abandoned by politicians because it was unpopular, and because it implied a need for restructuring urban institutions in ways that were strongly opposed by the increasingly dominant white suburban middle class.

Once one accepts the ghetto as natural and agrees with the closely related proposition that people in communities with systemic differences in income, employment, educational background, availability of local jobs, level of public education, exposure to crime, number of poor, female-headed households, and other major social problems have substantially the same opportunities for mobility in the society, a variety of policies appear logical that may have dangerous and perverse consequences when put into practice. To cite only one example, many states have recently decided to deal with a perceived decline in the level of education by increasing high school graduation requirements and imposing minimum competency tests on students receiving diplomas. Clearly, there is a real problem. In bankrupt central city school systems serving low-income student bodies with dropout rates already at 50 percent or more, however, the most likely result of imposing such requirements is an increase in the dropout rate and a further reduction in the employability of ghetto youth. To understand and justify the need for providing such schools with major additional resources or for moving students out of them and into better financed, more competitive middle-class schools, we need to have a theory about the impact of the ghetto society and economy and its direct relationship to historical and contemporary inequalities.

Similarly, to assess contemporary theories about business reinvestment as an ultimate solution, we need to know the historical and present significance of the urban color line in urban investment and disinvestment decisions made by private business. To ignore such issues is to adopt policies that will fail and whose failure will be blamed on the victims of the urban racial system.

To develop a more adequate theory of urban social problems and a more effective agenda, we must consider anew insights of the integrationist leaders of the civil rights movement and the conclusions that had been reached by much of the academic and government establishment by the end of the 1960s concerning the nature of the ghetto and the race-related vicious cycles that were eroding the future of central cities and polarizing race relations in the great metropolitan areas.

Several kinds of work would contribute to this reconsideration and to a reformation of the liberal agenda that would reincorporate a structural theory of racial inequalities. The social trends within and outside the ghetto should be studied to determine the extent to which predictions of the 1960s have come true and have validated the theories of ghettoization. Existing data are strongly supportive. Race, particularly racial characteristics of geographic areas, should be used as an important variable in social policy analysis, and the results should be carefully analyzed. There should be careful longitudinal measurement of conditions within ghettos to show the direction of change in social and economic conditions and in educational opportunities.

Since the dominant white middle- and upper-class population is now extremely isolated from ghetto conditions in many metropolitan areas, it is extremely important for researchers to describe the conditions of life in the contemporary ghetto, and to compare the life situation and opportunities of its residents with those in typical white communities. Without such information and without evaluations of those experiments designed to change basic ghetto realities—experiments such as metropolitan school desegregation, scattered-site housing and special housing mobility programs, stably integrated residential communities with positive programs to maintain integration, public employment projects, and a variety of other attacks on basic features of the ghetto system—a new integrationist program cannot be constructed. Determining which of the experiments has worked and under what conditions is critical if there is to be a credible alternative set of policies.

Conclusion

The civil rights movement and the vast changes in southern racial patterns that it engendered in the 1960s disclosed a second set of structures of racial inequality as important and as deeply rooted as the Jim Crow laws that were successfully overturned in the South. Black groups demanded change in urban segregation with remarkable consensus and force, until the mid-1960s, when it became apparent that there was deep resistance and no will to implement serious changes at any level of government. By the time the executive branch of government had developed an understanding of the severity of the problems, as well as the capacity to act, black groups were bitterly divided, urban riots were seriously shaking the liberal constituency, the Vietnam War was draining resources and political energy, and conservatives were beginning a long upsurge of support and power, during which an increasingly anti-black Republican party was to exploit racial polarization.

The period's most important black leader, Martin Luther King, Jr., could not successfully convey to whites, at a time when blacks and whites were moving apart, his understanding of the ghetto and the great virtues of an integrated society. His Chicago campaign was a watershed, marking a turning away from the integrationist dream, not a symbol of new hope for breaking down the color line. White leaders rejected the appeal for fundamental change in the ghetto system.

Conservatives promised that if the integrationist efforts to reconstruct urban society would only be abandoned, the money and energy that were being consumed by the battle would be redirected to upgrading black institutions. Some black nationalists made the same argument. When the conservative civil rights opponents captured the national government, however, things turned out differently. Freed from the threat to white prerogatives, they saw no reason to transfer increasingly scarce resources across the color line. The dominant policy, in fact, became one of defining segregation as normal, blaming problems within the black community on blacks, and rapidly reducing social programs. This has always been the logic of the color line. The minority victims, not the institutions of racial separation, are blamed. Rebuilding a viable liberal explanation of urban society and an agenda that works will require recapturing and bringing into the present what was learned with such great effort during the civil rights movement.

10

Racial Tensions and Institutional Support: Social Programs during a Period of Retrenchment

HELENE SLESSAREV

Ronald Reagan's election to the presidency marked the collapse of the liberal consensus that had guided American social policy since the New Deal. As a presidential candidate, Reagan had vowed to follow through by eradicating much of the Great Society's social legislation, while shrinking social insurance programs to a scope approximating their New Deal origins. No longer would government be used to correct the inequities of the private sector. Instead, individuals would be left to make their way in the market economy.[1]

Although the president announced that his proposed budget cuts would preserve a "safety net" of social programs for the poorest people in the country, in reality his seven sacred programs largely benefited the non-poor. Reagan proposed to save $35.2 billion by reducing funds for seventeen federal programs. Targeted for major cuts were many of the remaining Great Society programs. The proposals included both reductions in expenditures and restrictions in eligibility for many Great Society entitlement programs. Defense spending was to be untouched and the main Social Security programs were off-limits, so that the bulk of the cuts had to come from the means-tested programs benefiting the poor. This meant that the cuts would disproportionately fall on Afro-Americans, especially black women and children.[2]

[1] For a fuller understanding of Reagan's philosophy, see Martin Anderson, *Welfare: The Political Economy of Welfare Reform in the United States* (Stanford, Calif.: Hoover Institute, 1978); Jack Kemp, *An American Renaissance: A Strategy for the 1980's* (Falls Church, Va.: Conservative Press, 1979); and Robert Carlson and Kevin Hopkins, "The Reagan Rationale," *Public Welfare* (Fall 1981): 13. For critical accounts of Reagan's philosophy, see Philip Green, *The Pursuit of Inequality* (New York: Pantheon Books, 1981), and Edward J. Nell., ed., *Free Market Conservatism: A Critique of Theory and Practice* (London: George Allen and Unwin, 1984).

[2] For more on Reagan budget cuts, see John Palmer and Isabel Sawhill, eds., *The Reagan*

This paper focuses on two social programs—Medicaid and subsidized housing—that have repeatedly been targets of the Reagan budget axe. Medicaid has experienced relatively modest cuts since 1981, while subsidized housing has suffered among the most severe cuts of any social program. The goal of this paper is not only to provide an explanation of why these two programs experienced such differing treatment but also to suggest more general features that have enabled certain programs to survive a period of retrenchment. The two cases are similar enough in their general parameters to allow for a close examination of the differences between them that led to their different fates.

The Reagan Cuts in Medicaid
and Subsidized Housing

Both of these programs were established in their recent forms during the 1960s, when much of the country's social legislation was for the first time oriented toward the needs of the poor. They are both a part of the lower tier of American social welfare programs. They both provide in-kind benefits and are targeted, means-tested programs. Furthermore, in contrast to the social insurance programs that compose what is commonly known as Social Security, there is a broad similarity in the characteristics of each program's recipients. This can be seen clearly from Table 10.1. In terms of class, race, and age, the recipients of benefits under Medicare are strikingly different from those receiving benefits under the two means-tested programs. The overwhelming majority of Medicare recipients are elderly, white, and non-poor, in contrast to the large percentages of poor minority recipients covered by subsidized housing and Medicaid. Nearly half of the beneficiaries of subsidized housing and Medicaid are below the poverty line, while only 18 percent of Medicare recipients are poor. Although Medicaid serves 8.6 percent more whites than does subsidized housing, both programs, with well over one-third minority recipients, are far more racially identifiable than Medicare, which is only 12.5 percent minority. It should be noted that the subsidized housing program serves a much smaller number of total recipients than do Medicaid and Medicare, and, furthermore, that the most visible of the federal housing programs, public housing, has a higher proportion of black recipients than all other subsidized housing programs combined.

Both subsidized housing and Medicaid came under fire by conservatives in the Reagan administration for being too costly and inefficient.

Record (Washington, D.C.: The Urban Institute, 1984); Alan Gartner, Colin Greer, and Frank Riessman, eds., *What Reagan is Doing to Us* (New York: Harper and Row Publishers, 1981); and Anthony Champagne and Edward Harpham, eds., *The Attack on the Welfare State* (Prospect Heights, Ill.: Waveland Press, 1984).

TABLE 10.1 Characteristics of Households Receiving Selected In-kind Benefits

Type of Household	Subsidized Housing (thousands)	(percent)	Medicaid (thousands)	(percent)	Medicare (thousands)	(percent)
White	1,473	59.0	5,403	67.6	16,508	89.1
Black	967	38.5	2,417	30.2	1,823	10.0
Hispanic	202	08.0	726	09.0	474	02.5
Female-headed	867	34.5	2,893	36.2	1,738	09.4
Aged 65 or over	863	34.3	2,652	33.2	15,040	81.2
Below poverty level	1,170	46.6	3,799	47.5	3,330	18.0
Total	2,511		7,993		18,526	

SOURCE: "Characteristics of Households Receiving Non-Cash Benefits, 1979," *Current Population Reports, Special Series*, Bureau of the Census, Series P–23, no. 110, March 1981.

The 1981 budget proposals sought a $10 billion dollar cut in the budget authority for subsidized housing, far in excess of cuts in any other program. The budget proposal constituted a 40-percent cut in the Section 8 program of the 1974 Housing and Community Development Act that authorized new construction. The administration requested funding for the construction of only 175,000 subsidized housing units in 1982, a sharp drop from the Carter administration's plan for 260,000. Section 312, which provided 20-year loans at 3 percent interest to be used for housing rehabilitation, was to be completely repealed. The Reagan administration also proposed increasing the percentage of income that public housing tenants were required to pay from 25 percent to 30 percent, with the increase stretched out over five years.[3]

The budget proposals submitted in 1981 also called for significant cuts in Medicaid. The most substantial of these cuts came in a proposal to place a 5-percent cap on the growth of the federal Medicaid share that would be paid to the states. Previously, an average of 55 cents of every dollar spent by the states came from federal contributions; but with the cap, each marginal dollar would come totally from state revenues. State governments facing their own budgetary constraints would invariably respond by making deeper cuts into vital services and raising eligibility requirements. In essence the administration sought to end the entitlement nature of Medicaid, making it more like a close-ended block grant pro-

[3] Tom Joe, "The Poor: Profiles of Families in Poverty" (unpublished report, The Center for the Study of Welfare Policy, March 27, 1981).

gram. In addition to the Medicaid cuts, the administration was proposing a 25-percent cut in other health and prevention programs, such as community and migrant health centers, child immunization, family planning, mental health, and alcohol and drug abuse programs.

On the whole the Democrats mounted little opposition to the Reagan administration's first round of budget cuts in 1981. Many of them accepted Reagan's call for a restructuring of social priorities, some believed Reagan held an electoral mandate to make the proposed changes, and others were concerned that any opposition to a popular president would be labeled as obstructionist. The Democrats' own alternative budget accepted three-fourths of the Reagan cuts. They attempted to save 3,000 subsidized housing units from being cut, and they rejected the proposed Medicaid cap, calling instead for reductions in federal payments to the states of 3 percent in 1982, 2 percent in 1983, and 1 percent in 1984.[4] While the administration continued to press for both the subsidized housing and Medicaid cuts, a group of moderate Republicans from the Northeast and the Midwest emerged; they opposed the Medicaid cuts and became part of a bipartisan coalition, consisting of liberal Democrats, moderate Republicans, and southern Democrats, which forced the administration to retreat on the Medicaid cuts. No comparable support emerged for subsidized housing; Congress ultimately approved housing cuts that actually exceeded those originally proposed by the administration.

In 1982 Reagan proposed even more radical changes in the subsidized housing programs. The administration requested almost complete termination of all funding for new construction of subsidized housing. The only new housing construction would be for the elderly and handicapped. While Congress did not make cuts as deep as those requested by the administration, the latter received most of what it wanted. As a result of consecutive years of cuts, the nominal budget authority for housing assistance plummeted from $26.1 billion in 1981 to $3.9 billion in 1983 to $2.1 billion in 1985. Since 1983 the Department of Housing and Urban Development (HUD) has authorized construction of only 10,000 new units per year, exclusively for the handicapped and elderly—over 90 percent fewer than in 1981.[5]

Reagan also renewed efforts to cut back on Medicaid in 1982 and 1983. Again he was unsuccessful in placing a cap on federal expenditures for Medicaid. However, Congress did enact provisions that allow the states greater flexibility in deciding how to control Medicaid costs. Many

[4] House of Representatives, U.S. Congress, Report of the Committee on the Budget, *The Omnibus Reconciliation Act of 1981*, June 19, 1981, p. 287.

[5] Joseph Pechman, ed., *Setting National Priorities: The 1983 Budget* (Washington, D.C.: The Brookings Institution, 1983), p. 121.

states have used this new discretionary capacity to arrange for fixed-rate payments to health care providers rather than reimbursing them for costs. The changes have resulted in a rate of budget growth for Medicaid that is one-third that of previous years.[6]

Three factors may explain the divergent outcomes experienced by the two programs. The empirical sections of the paper will be built around an examination of the differential effects of these three factors.

1. *The historical circumstances of each program's enactment.* The origins of a social policy can continue to affect its development long after initial debates have subsided. Whether the policy's adoption was contested or consensual, whether it was the product of a prolonged period of discussion or passed quickly during a moment of crisis, can have enduring consequences in terms of the depth and the firmness of the political support a program enjoys. The way the architects of a new policy attempt to situate it in relation to past policies may also determine how well-established it will become. Programs that can be interpreted as an addition to earlier efforts are more readily defended than those that represent an entirely new endeavor. How a program fits into a sequence of reform may determine the kind of support it is likely to receive and how wide a range of beneficiaries it is likely to serve. Policies passed at the beginning of a reform cycle are more likely to have the opportunity to establish themselves than those enacted just as a reform cycle is ending.

2. *Policy goals: income support versus social intervention.* Earlier federal social programs allocated additional federal funding to states while allowing local officials a high degree of administrative autonomy over implementation. Such programs, operating within the confines of the accepted local status quo, often resulted in only limited benefits to those recipients intended to receive aid. More recently, as the federal government often explicitly set out to alter the local status quo, it established programs that imposed uniform national standards and sought to change longstanding economic and political relationships. Federal programs can alter local social structures in a number of ways; for example, setting minimum standards for benefits can challenge the wage structure of local labor markets, and setting personnel standards can disrupt established channels of hiring. But the most controversial types of interventionist programs are those that have explicitly sought to end racial segregation and discrimination. Such programs have endeavored to disrupt well-entrenched economic, political, and social practices that systematically maintain racial inequality. In the face of such controversial goals, local politicians may attempt to ignore the intentions of such programs, or they

---

[6] Palmer and Sawhill, *The Reagan Record*, p. 17.

may simply conclude that the additional funds are not worth the threat created by the new programs.

3. *The development of an institutional support structure.* The relationship of a social policy to existing institutions is critical in determining the type of support it can hope to build. If a new policy becomes incorporated into established institutions, linking their survival with its continuance, the new program will be difficult to cut, even in periods of retrenchment. Conversely, if a program remains isolated from and marginal to larger centers of institutional power, it can be much more easily terminated.

Historical Circumstances
of Each Program's Enactment

The first striking difference between the two programs that accounts for their divergent outcomes is the set of historical circumstances under which each program was enacted. Medicaid, passed together with Medicare as amendments to the Social Security Act, was the first piece of legislation passed following the landslide Democratic victory in the 1964 elections—a victory which gave the Democrats a better than 2 to 1 margin in both houses of Congress (68–32 in the Senate and 295–140 in the House). In the past, even though the Democratic party held the numerical majority, the mild attempts at reform by its liberal Northern wing had met with defeat by a coalition of Southern Democrats and Republicans. Yet, in 1964 these conservatives were overwhelmed by liberal Democrats riding the strength of public support for racial equality and social reform. The result was a brief period of tremendous legislative change. No president since Franklin Roosevelt in his first term had operated with fewer constraints than President Johnson did between 1964 and 1966.[7]

Medicare and Medicaid were part of the unfinished agenda of the New Deal, since health insurance had originally been a component of the Social Security Act. When vehement opposition to health insurance threatened the entirety of the Social Security Act, the Roosevelt administration decided to drop those previsions. After 1939, bills proposing the establishment of a compulsory health insurance program were annually introduced into Congress. In a bid to gain greater acceptance for the proposals

[7] The period from 1965 to 1967 saw the passage of Medicare-Medicaid; the Elementary and Secondary School Act of 1965; the Higher Education Act of 1965; the Housing and Urban Development Act of 1965; the Equal Opportunity Act, which was the heart of the War on Poverty; the Model Cities Act; and the Voting Rights Act of 1965. From Sar Levitan and Robert Taggart, *The Promise of Greatness* (Cambridge, Mass.: Harvard University Press, 1976). For more on the Great Society, see Robert Haveman, *A Decade of Federal Anti-Poverty Policy: Achievements/Failures and Lessons* (New York: Academic Press, 1977); Theodore Lowi, *The End of Liberalism* (New York: Norton & Co., 1979); and Henry Aaron, *Politics and Professors: The Great Society in Perspective* (Washington, D.C.: The Brookings Institution, 1978).

among conservatives, the top administrators of the Social Security Administration had decided to propose legislation that would restrict health insurance to the elderly who were already beneficiaries of the Old Age and Survivors' Insurance (OASI) program. With this strategy, additions to existing insurance programs would reinforce the bias—established by the original Social Security Act—of aiming social programs at the middle class who had "earned" their benefits, rather than at those most in need. This approach sets the United States apart from most other countries, where health insurance programs typically began by protecting low-income workers.

Some form of comprehensive health insurance had long been a part of the Democratic liberals' policy agenda, but it was not until 1965 that they were able to secure the votes needed for passage in Congress. That year, the liberal reformers placed their standard health insurance bill as the first item of business before the new Congress. Given the new balance of power in Congress, it was a certainty that some form of health insurance would be passed. Considering the favorable conditions in Congress, it is significant that the reformers did not introduce a more comprehensive proposal than their standard bill which was restricted to OASI beneficiaries. The American Medical Association (AMA) sponsored a counter bill that would provide benefits only to those too poor to afford private health care. In an effort to compromise between the two proposals, Congress drafted a new bill that simply combined the two separate ones. Title 18 of the Social Security Amendments (now Medicare) contained the old health insurance proposals of the reformers. Title 19 was an expansion of the AMA's public assistance program, now extended to all persons who qualified for public assistance or who were found to be "medically indigent." As with all public assistance programs, Title 19, or Medicaid, was to be administered by the states. Eligibility was set at 133⅓ percent of each state's eligibility levels for Aid to Families with Dependent Children (AFDC).[8] This meant that variations among states would continue, since those states with restrictive AFDC eligibility standards, especially those in the South, would also have restrictive Medicaid standards.

The passage of Medicare/Medicaid took place under atypical circumstances. Although health insurance had been a centerpiece of the Democratic party's legislative agenda for thirty years, it took only the vigorous opposition of the AMA and congressional conservatives to prevent its earlier enactment. The massive Democratic majorities following the 1964 election had altered the incentives and disincentives facing the former opponents. A close link was formed between the more favored Medicare program and the public assistance Medicaid program. By covering the medical needs of the poor, Medicaid contributed to the strengthening of

---

[8] Theodore Marmor, *The Politics of Medicare* (Chicago: Aldine Publishing Co., 1970).

Medicare as an elite program restricted to the elderly and survivors who were also recipients of OASI. For Medicare recipients who were also eligible for Medicaid, states could use Medicaid funds to pay for deductibles or other optional benefits not automatically covered by Medicare.

Public housing also has its origins in the New Deal. From its inception it has had the dual and at times contradictory purposes of providing shelter for homeless families and stimulating the economy by providing federal funds for housing construction. During the 1950s federal funds were made available for urban renewal projects being initiated by local politicians and businessmen, who were designing the major post-industrial urban centers. Federal money was increasingly channeled away from housing into downtown redevelopment projects. Studies done in the mid-1960s showed that as a result, in some cities, demolition of housing for the poor far exceeded new construction.[9]

The complete segregation of the private housing market, combined with the very small scale of public housing construction and its high degree of concentration, forced Afro-Americans and other poor to live in substandard housing concentrated in inner cities. According to the 1960 census, 45 percent of nonwhite-owner (Latinos are counted as white so this means, essentially, black-owner) households were poverty families. But these households occupied 72 percent of substandard, nonwhite-owner housing. Among nonwhite renters, 62 percent lived in substandard housing, compared with 35 percent of whites.[10] The Kaiser Commission, formed by President Johnson in 1967 to evaluate the country's housing needs, estimated that, nationwide the need among blacks for low-income housing was almost three times as acute as the need among whites.[11] After more than a third of a century of federal efforts, only one-tenth of the nation's housing needs had been met.

The poor housing conditions of low-income blacks first achieved high visibility as a result of the ghetto rebellions in the North between 1966 and 1968. The riots that broke out in dozens of cities across the country during this period created a crisis atmosphere. In its report on the causes of the urban riots, the Kerner Commission Report on Civil Disorders warned in 1968 that, unless remedies were found soon, the country would continue to move toward "two societies, one white, one Black—separate and unequal."[12]

[9] National Commission on Urban Problems, *Building the American City* (New York: Praeger Publishing, 1969), p. 86.

[10] Ibid., p. 70.

[11] President's Committee on Urban Housing, *A Decent Home* (Washington, D.C.: Government Printing Office, 1968), p. 42.

[12] National Advisory Commission on Civil Disorders, *Report of the National Advisory Commission on Civil Disorders* (New York: Bantam Books, 1968), p. 1.

In their book on the urban rebellions of the late 1960s, Feagin and Hahn outline two responses by government officials to the urban riots. The conservative approach called for the use of massive police repression, while the liberal approach called for increased spending on social welfare programs aimed at ghetto blacks.[13] The 1968 Housing Act embodies the liberal approach, which was well articulated by moderate Republican Senator Charles Percy during the Senate debate on the bill.

There has been sufficient evidence of late of the graveness of urban problems. These problems will not be basically solved by increasing our police force. . . . Unless the Negro can deploy the means whereby he can obtain decent housing in the suburbs, we shall only have additional and more serious unrest. By providing the means whereby families can own their own homes, we are providing more than a decent shelter. We are permitting individuals to have pride in themselves.[14]

The idea that federal money for housing would contribute to an end to urban disorder was also articulated by Henry G. Parks, a spokesman for the National Urban League, who testified at the House hearings on the 1968 bill. He stated that "the 1968 Housing and Urban Development Bill with the safeguards we are suggesting, could possibly be one of the most important steps taken to curb the civil disorders of recent months."[15] The same opinion was repeated by another black activist who spoke as the chairman of the National Committee for a Confrontation with Congress (CWC).

The CWC is convinced that there is no single solution to the racial crisis. We are equally convinced that important steps can be taken to ease the present situation; to bring hope to the slums; to channel anger into constructive action and to get black Americans headed down the road to progress that seemed so promising just a few years back. HR 16266 [1968 Housing Act] is, we believe, an extremely important first step towards this goal. This bill tackles two major problems at the same time—jobs and housing.[16]

[13] Joe Feagin and Harlan Hahn, *Ghetto Revolts: The Politics of Violence in American Cities* (New York: Macmillan, 1973).

[14] *The Congressional Record*, May 24, 1968, S–14969, Senator Charles Percy's Statement.

[15] U.S. Congress, House Subcommittee on Housing of the Committee on Banking and Currency, Statement by Henry G. Parks, Chairman of the Housing Committee of the National Urban League, 90th Cong., 1968, p. 1035.

[16] U.S. Congress, House Subcommittee on Housing of the Committee on Banking and Currency, Statement by James Haughton, 90th Cong., 1968, p. 1049.

The 1968 bill was a massive reorientation of federal housing programs toward the needs of low-income people. Its passage was a bipartisan effort, cosponsored by Democrats and moderate Republicans like Percy. The principal new programs were Sections 235 and 236. Section 235 was designed to enable low-income families to purchase their own homes by providing a federal subsidy that could bring down the effective interest cost of the purchaser's home mortgage. The program had been conceived of by moderate Republicans the year before but had not passed Congress because of Democratic opposition. But now, suddenly, increased home ownership was seen as the way to uplift blacks living in the ghettos. The bill also expanded the rent supplement program for low-income people and called for the construction of six million new low-income housing units in the next ten years. The law prohibited the future construction of new high-rise public housing for families. This marked the end of a period of high-rise public housing construction, in favor of more dispersed forms of private housing construction and the use of existing private housing stock. Urban renewal was now also reoriented toward low-income people, as at least 50 percent of all housing built was to be low-income. The new law placed primary emphasis on the mobilization of private construction capacity to meet the goals of the program. The government would play a supportive role, making it easier for the poor to meet their housing needs on the private market.

The new legislation resulted in dramatic increases in the number of housing units committed to subsidy during the next few years. Table 10.2 shows that over two times as many subsidized housing starts occurred in 1970 as in the year before. In 1970 subsidized housing starts made up almost 30 percent of the total number of housing starts that occurred in the country. However, already by the following year the number of new starts began to decline, and by 1972 it had been reduced to only 14 percent of the total number of housing starts. In 1973, President Nixon put a complete halt to all further subsidized housing construction for one and one-half years. In his speech declaring the moratorium, Nixon announced that the "crisis" in American cities was over.

While Medicaid emerged as the result of a prolonged debate over what form of public health coverage the country should adopt, the reorientation of housing programs toward the poor came about very rapidly in the midst of a crisis atmosphere. Health insurance, which has long been a component of the liberal Democrats' policy agenda, was enacted as soon as these Democrats had the necessary majority in Congress. Medicaid was enacted during the beginning of the reforms generated by the civil rights movement. In contrast, by the time the 1968 Housing Act was passed, the movement had lost much of its strength. Instead, spontaneous rioting in Northern cities had created a crisis. By then, even those politi-

TABLE 10.2 Annual Housing Production, 1967–1972 (in thousands)

Year	Total	Non-Subsidized	Federally Subsidized	Subsidized as Percentage of Total
1967	1,321.9	1,230.5	91.4	6.9
1968	1,545.4	1,379.9	165.5	10.7
1969	1,499.5	1,299.6	199.9	13.3
1970	1,469.0	1,039.2	429.8	29.3
1971	2,084.5	1,654.5	430.0	20.6
1972	2,378.5	2,039.7	338.8	14.2

SOURCE: U.S. Department of Housing and Urban Development, *Housing in the 1970's* (Washington, D.C.: Government Printing Office), p. 4.4.

cians who favored the use of social programs rather than police saw these programs primarily as a means of regaining control over inner city ghettos. Once the rioting ended, the crisis was declared to be over and housing programs became expendable. In 1965 conservatives favored reform programs such as Medicaid, whereas by 1968 most conservatives were abandoning their support of social programs altogether in favor of "law and order" policies. Even though the 1968 Housing Act was passed by a substantial majority, it received only one-third of the appropriations requested by HUD. The department had wanted authorization to enter into contracts of up to $75 million each for the home ownership and the rental assistance programs, but the same Congress that passed the 1968 act agreed to only $25 million for each—an indication that even at the time of its passage, support for the bill was not nearly as strong as it had appeared, but that many Congressmen were reluctant to openly oppose the measure.

Policy Goals: Income Support
versus Social Intervention

The New Deal's relief programs and the Social Security Act of 1935 established a pattern of service delivery in which federal social programs were administered in ways that were least disruptive to local class and race relations. The New Dealers believed that the purpose of their new social programs was to help all Americans, including Afro-Americans. For these reformers,

> the solution to the "negro problem" ultimately hinged upon the interplay of a number of factors—expanded economic opportunities and security, the power of education to modify traditional beliefs, the steady rise in Black standards, and the eventual decrease in white bigotry. Within this complex interrelationship there were established limits on the government's activities in dealing with racial questions. Those limits involved basically the degree to which the white population would accept the inclusion of blacks in New Deal housing, labor, education and health programs.[17]

In keeping with this perspective, the New Dealers accepted the decentralized implementation of their social programs that allowed local officials to leave existing racial barriers intact. Since blacks were still restricted to marginal employment, they often did not qualify for the upper tier of the social insurance programs. Eligibility for the public assistance programs was narrowly defined so as to restrict large numbers of blacks from access to those programs. Benefits in the South were set well below levels found in the North to ensure that the assistance programs would not interfere with the maintenance of a large low-wage labor pool.

In challenging Southern race policies, the civil rights movement successfully pushed national politicians to impose national standards on a resistant South. In addition to the 1964 Civil Rights Act and the 1965 Voting Rights Act, which abolished the legal forms of racial inequality in the South, Congress established new social programs that sought to remedy the de facto discrimination experienced by urban blacks across the country. Although not prescribed by law outside of the South, longstanding discriminatory barriers existed in education and in the housing and employment market throughout the nation. These new programs differed substantially from the earlier social insurance programs, whose primary purpose was income support. They sought to break down remaining discriminatory barriers as well as to compensate Afro-Americans for past inequalities by providing programs especially designed to uplift the inner city poor. For the first time, the elimination of black inequality became the central policy objective. To be successful, programs that sought to alter local racial practices required extensive federal control over program implementation as the means of forcing reluctant local leaders to carry out the new national policy goals.

This new approach to social policy was never fully accepted. The con-

---

[17] John Kirby, *Black Americans in the Roosevelt Era* (Knoxville: University of Tennessee Press, 1980), p. 94.

servative wing of the Republican party believed that the government's obligation to end racial discrimination was met with the passage of the Civil Rights and Voting Acts of 1964 and 1965, respectively. Any actions beyond these constituted preferential treatment of minorities. Furthermore, as the civil rights movement had expanded beyond the South to take up issues of poverty, discrimination, and segregation in Northern ghettos, the urban Democratic politicians who had supported civil rights legislation as long as it focused on the South now began to side with conservative Southern politicians.

While Medicaid followed in the noninterventionist pattern of the traditional social welfare programs, the 1968 Housing Act sought to alter local segregated housing market patterns by providing easy access to home ownership for Afro-American families who could not afford to buy a home on their own. Earlier federal housing programs had conformed to local patterns of racial housing segregation, which in most urban areas served as a basic component of a system of political and economic inequality for blacks.

In 1961 the U.S. Commission on Civil Rights found that as a result of racial segregation, "housing . . . seems to be the one commodity in the American market that is not freely available on equal terms to everyone who can afford to pay."[18] The Civil Rights Commission went on to state that even though the federal government had been involved in virtually all aspects of mortgage credit, it had made no effort to exert its authority to secure equal access to housing for blacks. While the provision of Federal Housing Administration (FHA) and Veterans Administration loans after World War II had facilitated the large-scale movement of whites into the suburbs, blacks were intentionally prohibited access to these same low-interest loans because of fears that they would lower surrounding suburban property values. Thus, by preventing the movement of Afro-Americans into the suburbs, government policies in the 1940s and 1950s had played a significant role in increasing their segregation in inner city ghettos.

Since its origins in the New Deal, public housing routinely had been built either as all black or as all white. The federal government had agreed to leave decisions concerning housing sites in the hands of local officials, thereby almost guaranteeing that housing would be built on a segregated basis. Local housing authorities had two choices, either to build on vacant land, mostly located on a city's periphery, or to clear sites in the inner city. Decisions to build on vacant land could have served to break down existing patterns of racial segregation. In the early 1950s, debates in

[18] United States Civil Rights Commission Report, *Housing* (Washington, D.C.: Government Printing Office, 1961), p. 145.

Northern cities over where public housing was to be located were closely connected to the question of whether residential segregation of blacks was to be maintained. According to case studies done on Chicago, race appeared again and again in the deliberations of those who supported public housing and those who opposed it.[19] In Chicago, as in other cities, this debate was resolved by deciding to build major projects only in inner city ghetto areas. "The conclusion is inescapable that the locations for new projects were selected by CHA [Chicago Housing Authority], and by the political leadership of Chicago, to contain and segregate the poor, black population."[20] Local political leaders sought to contain the black population within compact areas of the city, since their own power base rested upon the maintenance of a sizable white voting population. When blacks did move into all white neighborhoods, the old residents rapidly fled to the suburbs. As the black urban population expanded, its demands for equal political representation in city government, along with equal shares of city services, increased. Local politicians were soon caught between the growing demands of blacks and the demands of white voters that the status quo be maintained.

Since the cost of inner city land was so high, planners could stay within federal per-unit cost ceilings only by constructing high-rise buildings. Between 1957 and 1968, the CHA completed 15,591 family units, of which all but 696 were in high-rise buildings in the inner city. As early as 1955, two-thirds of all CHA residents were Afro-American; by 1959 the numbers had increased to 85 percent.[21] Similar trends occurred in the rest of the country. By 1967 50.5% of all public housing in the country was occupied by black families. If Mexican and Puerto Rican families are added as minority groups, the proportion of public housing occupied by minorities was roughly three-fifths to two-thirds of the total.[22]

By the early 1960s the high concentration of Afro-Americans and Latinos in public housing served to make it "one of the least popular federal welfare programs . . . devoid of all capacity for major expansion."[23] The opposition to public housing was also recognized by the Douglas Commission that reported to President Johnson on the lack of decent housing for the poor. The commission concluded that "the public housing program has been slowed to a faltering walk by economic class and racial

[19] Martin Meyerson and Edward Banfield, *Politics, Planning and the Public Interest: The Case of Public Housing in Chicago* (New York: Macmillan, 1965), p. 25.

[20] Devereux Bowly, Jr., *The Poorhouse: Subsidized Housing in Chicago, 1895–1975* (Carbondale: Southern Illinois University Press, 1978), p. 112.

[21] Ibid., p. 112.

[22] National Commission on Urban Problems, *Building the American City*, p. 114.

[23] Gilbert Steiner, *The State of Welfare* (Washington, D.C.: The Brookings Institution, 1971), chap. 4.

antagonism."[24] The decisions to build segregated public housing, which then necessitated building high-rise projects, resulted in a concentrated and intensified version of ghetto life. Many housing experts knew from the start that the high-rise buildings with hundreds of apartments would be unsuitable for families with small children.[25]

The national crisis created by the urban riots resulted in the first major reorientation in housing policies since 1949. The 1968 Housing Act not only redirected housing programs toward the poor, but also now tied public housing construction to new federal civil rights enforcement efforts. The Civil Rights Act of 1964 had barred discrimination under any federally aided program. This was followed by additional legislation aimed especially at housing discrimination. Title VIII of the 1968 Civil Rights Act prohibited discrimination in the sale, rental, advertising, or financing of housing.

Also included in the 1968 Housing Act was the decision to end the construction of high-rise public housing, in favor of more dispersed forms of construction. A mandate was written into the law that new family public housing could not be located above the third floor. By 1968, it was the old-line political forces who opposed racial integration who were the principal supporters of high-rise projects. Liberals had become the severest critics of high-rise construction, and the decision to end such construction was a manifestation of the markedly liberal character of the 1968 legislation. The provisions of the civil rights acts and the decision to end high-rise construction meant that much of the new family construction had to be built outside the inner city. Such efforts have been vehemently opposed by white neighborhoods and suburban communities.

Tying civil rights efforts to federal housing programs created the possibilities for breaking down the private market barriers that prevented blacks and other minorities from living anywhere they chose. For the first time housing programs could be used as a tool to alter existing social and economic relations, rather than simply reinforcing private market trends as they had done in the past. They had the potential of being used actively to pursue a national goal of civil rights enforcement, rather than simply serving as a source of funding for local governments to do with what they wished.

The civil rights goals of the 1968 Housing Act have largely gone unrealized. Despite the existence of fair housing legislation, a 1985 nationwide study of forty-seven cities, conducted by the *Dallas Morning News*, found that white families and the elderly received the majority of all hous-

[24] National Commission on Urban Problems, *Building the American City*, p. 130.
[25] Gary Orfield, "Federal Policy, Local Power, and Metropolitan Segregation," *Political Science Quarterly* 89, no. 4 (Winter 1974–75): 787.

ing built under the new housing programs since 1968.[26] Whites occupied almost 3 out of 4 of the more than 2.53 million apartments provided under the new subsidized rental programs, with the elderly occupying 45 percent. Whites occupy 85 percent of all Section 8 housing. Meanwhile blacks remain concentrated in the older, decaying projects in the inner city. The *News* found that whites and blacks live in federally subsidized housing that is both separate and unequal. They concluded that "the pattern in most cities is a throwback to the days of the antebellum South: The deteriorating, barely habitable housing goes to blacks, the newer, well-maintained and sometimes lavish housing goes to the whites."[27]

To avoid implementation of the required civil rights provisions, hundreds of suburban communities have refused to accept any subsidized housing in their communities, thereby perpetuating their overwhelmingly white character. Other communities have made conscious decisions to build public housing only for the elderly rather than for families, knowing that the demand for family housing is much greater among blacks than the demand for housing for the elderly. At times, HUD reports, it has been unable to give away federal money earmarked for the construction of family housing. A survey by HUD found that out of twenty cities that did build Section 8 family housing, twelve of them had located 90 percent of it in low-income areas.[28] In the face of stiff opposition from local communities and politicians, the federal government has done little to enforce housing desegregation in the two decades since the laws were first enacted.

By the mid-1960s, liberals recognizing that the building of high-rise projects in ghetto areas was a failure were able to stop such construction. Conservatives who had supported the program as long as projects were restricted to inner cities now began to condemn subsidized housing as a form of class and race integration that would only result in the social disruption of middle-class communities.[29] Central city politicians who in the past had benefited from urban redevelopment funds that could be directed into downtown projects now found that much of the money was restricted for use in controversial low-income projects. This made the federal housing money much less attractive to them. The net result was to further narrow the basis of support for subsidized housing, making its construction on a large scale politically infeasible. Today the Reagan

[26] Craig Flournoy and George Rodrigue, "Separate and Unequal," *Dallas Morning News*, February 10, 1985, p. 1A.

[27] Ibid., p. 26A.

[28] Craig Flournoy and George Rodrigue, "Stuck in the Ghetto," *Dallas Morning News*, February 13, 1985, p. 14A.

[29] George Gilder, *Wealth and Poverty* (New York: Basic Books, 1981), pp. 92–93.

administration has virtually stopped all subsidized housing construction, with the exception of housing for the elderly.

In contrast to the increasingly interventionist character of urban housing programs, Medicaid retained the characteristics of the New Deal social programs, providing federal funding within the traditional structure of private medicine. As a result of the AMA's strong influence in framing the 1965 amendments, Medicare and Medicaid were established explicitly to function within the existing system of private health care provision. The program was designed to permit clients "freedom of choice" in selecting doctors and hospitals. The government was required to provide physicians and hospitals with "reasonable cost reimbursement," which meant that both groups were free to charge what they wished for services rendered, with the federal government repaying them in full. There were no federal requirements stipulating that Medicaid had to ensure equal medical services to all its patients; neither was there any regulation of the quality of health care to be provided within poor inner city communities.

Development of
an Institutional Support Structure

Social programs targeted to serve the poor, and particularly those programs designed to alter racial inequality, are vulnerable to political attack even in the most auspicious political and economic circumstances. Since these programs are aimed at sectors of society that remain largely excluded from legitimate, regularized avenues of political expression, they must find support among other, more powerful sectors of society that are willing to defend them against attack. The experience of Medicaid and subsidized housing during the Reagan era of budget cuts reveals the extreme vulnerability of targeted programs that have operated in isolation from more powerful institutional networks.

One of the most striking aspects of the implementation of Medicare and Medicaid is that it greatly benefited those who had been most opposed to the enactment of the two programs—physicians and the AMA. The tremendous strength of the AMA had enabled it to give both programs a strong private market orientation by channeling them through the system of private health care delivery. As a result, physicians' fees increased between 5 to 8 percent annually following the implementation of the program.[30]

Medicaid is a vendor payment program; that is, the funds go directly to the provider of services for the care rendered. In Illinois almost one-half of all Medicaid payments go to hospitals, nearly $400 million in fis-

[30] Marmor, *The Politics of Medicare*, p. 123.

cal 1982. This makes the program an important source of revenue for hospitals. In the city of Chicago in that same year, Medicare and Medicaid together accounted for more than 56 percent of the patient days in the city's hospitals. Eighteen Chicago hospitals that are considered to be in financial difficulty (eight are in danger of closing) received in 1982 an average of 36.9 percent of their funds from Medicaid patients. Twelve of the eighteen are located on the city's predominantly black South and West sides. All totaled, these eighteen hospitals in 1982 owned 5,592 beds, served 191,403 patients, contributed almost $709 million to the city's economy, and employed 19,779 workers.[31]

That Medicaid funding plays a crucial role in keeping many hospitals from closing was an argument made again and again by hospital administrators who testified in opposition to Reagan's proposed cap on Medicaid. They argued that the cap would have severe effects on both private and public hospitals. Public hospitals would be forced to accept indigent patients who no longer had Medicaid coverage, with the states absorbing the total costs. Even large private hospitals, such as the University of Chicago Hospitals, would have been faced with as much as $5 million in losses in its outpatient programs alone. According to David Bray, executive director of the University of Chicago Hospitals:

> Because the cutbacks will be concentrated on a few, already financially troubled institutions, the simultaneous nature of the cutbacks of federal services funding under the health block grant and the proposed federal retrenchment from Medicaid cost-sharing may be sufficient to collapse what remains of the health care system for Chicago's inner city.[32]

There was also considerable state-level opposition to Reagan's proposed Medicaid cuts. Following the pattern of other public assistance programs such as AFDC and old-age assistance, Medicaid eligibility and services were determined by each state. Because of a lack of interest in the program at the Department of Health, Education, and Welfare, the states had carved out a substantial degree of autonomy and control over Medicaid while still receiving a large proportion of the needed funding from the federal government. Certain states even opted not to participate in the program at all, while others chose to provide just the mandatory services to the eligible population. Since eligibility for the mandatory component of Medicaid was tied to welfare eligibility, which varied tremendously among states, the proportion of a state's poor population receiving Med-

[31] Center for Health Systems Development, *Health Care in Chicago: The Problems and the Solutions* (Chicago: Center for Health Systems Development, Philip Davis, Executive Director), p. 8.

[32] U.S. Congress, House Subcommittee on Health and the Environment of the Committee on Energy and Commerce, Statement by David Bray, 97th Cong., 1st sess., p. 182.

icaid also varied significantly from state to state. Those that had established generous welfare provisions usually also had large Medicaid programs with numerous optional services. Other states that sought to restrict welfare coverage maintained small Medicaid programs.

As states increasingly experienced fiscal difficulties during the 1970s, many of them began to cut their Medicaid programs. Some states eliminated optional eligibility groups such as unemployed parents, while many allowed their programs to shrink simply by not increasing welfare eligibility standards in the face of high inflation.[33] Other states cut back on optional services such as providing payments for drugs and dental care. State control over the Medicaid program allowed state officials the flexibility to alter the program to fit their priorities, rather than requiring them to meet uniform national standards of eligibility and services. Not surprisingly, Medicaid came to have strong support among states and local politicians. The major adjustment made in Medicaid during the Reagan administration has increased still further state flexibility in administering the program: the states are now required to pay only "reasonable and adequate rates" needed to meet the costs of "efficiently and economically operated facilities." This adjustment has increased the ability of the states to force hospitals and physicians to adopt cost-saving measures, thereby lowering Medicaid expenses without causing the states themselves to suffer cuts in federal Medicaid money.

In many states Medicaid is the largest program in the state's entire budget, while it is the predominant item in *every* state's health care budget. Therefore, cuts in the amount of federal funding for Medicaid would have had serious repercussions for the states' budgets, since there was little remaining fat to be trimmed from the program. The strength of state-level opposition is shown in a letter to Congress written by Republican Governor of Michigan William Milliken, stating his opposition to large Medicaid cuts.

> While I support the President's efforts for reducing the budget, it is essential that these actions be taken in ways that are fair. Medicaid is a major budget expense for the Michigan state government. Unduly large reductions in the federal government's share of these costs would have grave consequences. Given the Administration's position of record to date, I urge you to support the Energy and Commerce Committee proposals as submitted. by Chairman Dingell [the Democratic proposals].[34]

---

[33] Randall Bovbjerg and John Holahan, *Medicaid in the Reagan Era: Federal Policy and State Choices* (Washington, D.C.: The Urban Institute, 1982), p. 27.

[34] *Congressional Record*, June 26, 1981, H–3369, Letter from the governor of Michigan, William Milliken.

It is remarkable that in a year when Reagan received virtually unanimous Republican congressional support for his cuts, a Republican governor would openly call for support of the Democratic alternative.

The close linkage established between Medicaid and Medicare at the time of enactment served as another source of support for the public assistance program during the Reagan budget cuts. Since there were significant numbers of Medicaid recipients who were also eligible for Medicare, cuts in Medicaid would have meant that the cost of Medicare would increase. This was the reason given by Jim Jones, the Democratic chairman of the House Budget Committee, when explaining his committee's rejection of the cap.

> We heard from Governors from across the country and from those familiar with Medicaid and Medicare and we felt it was an unwise cap and we could cut elsewhere. Why did we do it? Well, take just one example. Four million people who are now eligible for Medicaid are also eligible for Medicare. We received a great deal of evidence that indicated that there would be a shift of the burden from that program, from the broader based, tax supported Medicaid program to the payroll tax based Social Security–Medicare program and if you put further pressure on the Social Security system you were putting further pressure on the government to raise Social Security taxes again in the very near future to keep that Social Security system from going bankrupt.[35]

Apparently legislators felt that in order to protect the privileged Medicare program, the public assistance programs had to be maintained. This is a continuation of the pattern, begun with the establishment of Social Security in 1935, of protecting and building upon the insurance programs. It indicates that the ability to maintain the privileged programs in their present form rests upon the minimal maintenance of a lower tier of public assistance programs.

In sharp contrast to Medicaid, subsidized housing programs served relatively few people and were isolated by the time of the 1981 budget cuts. During the 1981 budget hearings powerful business interests such as the National Association of Home Builders, the Mortgage Bankers Association, and individual realtors and bankers displayed little concern about the effects of the proposed cuts in subsidized housing. Instead, they testified in favor of the continuation of FHA and Governmental National Mortgage Association (GNMA) mortgage programs, along with programs such as federal flood insurance. Repeatedly, the high cost of the housing

---

[35] *Congressional Record*, April 30, 1981, H–1601, Statement by Representative Jim Jones.

programs in relation to the small number of people served by them were cited as examples of their inefficiency.

It is true that only a small fraction of those eligible for housing assistance have received it. An unpublished 1984 HUD study discovered that in 1981 in excess of 23 million households lived in substandard or overcrowded conditions or paid a disproportionate amount of their income in rent. Yet, 83 percent of poor households remain unserved by subsidized housing. The study also found that among the poorest families—those with an income that is less than 10 percent of the national median—federally assisted rental programs "accomplish almost nothing—94 percent remain unserved."[36] Housing programs have remained small in part because they are closely connected to the maintenance of racial housing patterns, but also because housing construction is costly. This is especially true when the majority of construction is carried out by private contractors who build for a profit. Building large amounts of low-income housing at a profit has repeatedly been shown to be politically infeasible. As a result, the programs become easy targets of politicians who argue that housing for the poor can just as well be provided by the private market.

Conclusion

The changes made in social programs during the first years of the Reagan administration represent the most sweeping policy reversal in the thirty-five years since the New Deal. The cuts reduced or eliminated dozens of programs. It is in this context that the case histories of Medicaid and subsidized housing take on particular significance, providing important insights into both the boundaries of social reform and the political conditions that allow certain programs to survive a period of retrenchment.

Medicaid was saved from the Reagan axe by an exceptionally strong coalition of support that came to its rescue. The coalition consisted of neither Medicaid recipients nor the AMA. In fact, during the 1981 congressional budget hearings, the AMA, which has always dominated health care policies, came out in support of the Reagan cuts. Medicaid's base of support lay instead among state politicians, local hospital administrators, and the program's close connection to the "safety net" Medicare program. In part the program had secured such a strong base of support because its design allowed it to become incorporated into the existing structure of private health care delivery and into the priorities of state governments.

While the civil rights movement had helped to pave the way for the

[36] Flournoy and Rodrigue, "Separate and Unequal," p. 24A.

passage of Medicaid, the program's emergence was not in direct response to the movement's demands for black equality. For thirty years health insurance had been a centerpiece of the Democratic party's legislative agenda. Throughout the 1940s and 1950s the health proposals were carefully nurtured by the administrators within the Social Security Administration, who sought to expand social welfare coverage by building upon the upper tier of social insurance programs. As a result, once the needed congressional majorities finally materialized, the new health programs were incorporated into the traditional pattern of program delivery.

The new reform initiatives of the 1960s sought to force conservative local politicians to redirect programs toward the needs of the poor, especially Afro-Americans. This was to be accomplished by imposing a uniform set of national program standards on all localities. Without federal intervention, local leaders had been reluctant to serve poor blacks, since they were not a component of their own constituent base. Frequently these local politicians had maintained their own power by restricting black mobility and political power. By the late 1960s the conservative backlash that had emerged against the Great Society made a return to local control one of its major rallying cries. In the name of "states' rights" and returning control to the people, it launched an attack on the new interventionist social policies. Beginning with Nixon's "New Federalism" and revenue sharing proposals, policy began to swing back to the traditional pattern of local discretion over program implementation. In this new political climate programs that enjoyed the support of local and state politicians proved to be much more durable than those that did not. Yet local support could be obtained only by allowing programs to function in a way that served the interests of local-level politicians and businessmen. As was evident from the case of subsidized housing, policies that enforce civil rights often have not been in the interests of local politicians and therefore have had little support at that level.

The history of Medicaid shows that in a period of conservative retrenchment, social programs can survive when they are closely connected to important institutions at the local level if the well-being of those institutions would be threatened by the program's elimination or if they have the political power to organize congressional support. The experience of subsidized housing shows the degree to which not only class but also race forms a boundary on the extent of welfare coverage in the United States. From the enactment of the Social Security Act in 1935 when AFDC and old-age insurance provisions were written so as to preserve Southern racial inequality, it has been a significant factor in setting the contours of American social policies. Only in the mid-1960s when Afro-Americans attained formal political equality throughout the country, were major programs enacted to meet their needs. By the late 1960s conservatives had begun calling for a halt to programs aimed at correcting the injustices suffered by blacks and other minorities. Housing and job programs, along with many civil rights programs, have met with strong opposition from conservative politicians who believe that government responsibility to end discrimination was fulfilled with the passage of the 1964 Civil Rights Act. In general, social programs designed to alter the racial status quo have come under much greater attack than programs that operate within existing racial norms.

The cuts in subsidized housing suggest that the social programs that were a direct response to the highly visible urban crisis in the 1960s are particularly vulnerable in periods of retrenchment. In reality, the crisis of American cities has become only more severe in the last fifteen years, with the steady transference of jobs and middle-class residents to the suburbs, the economic recession of the 1970s, and the continual cuts in federal aid to cities. Yet today, many of the urban problems that Great Society programs sought to remedy are viewed as intractable by liberals and conservatives alike. The challenge ahead remains the establishment of programs targeted to the urban poor that have the political strength needed to endure beyond peaks in the reform cycle.

11

Politics and Policies of
the Feminization of Poverty

MARY JO BANE

In the early 1980s, depending on the year and the state of the economy, between twelve and fifteen percent of the American people were classified as poor, according to the standard definition of the Census Bureau. About half of the poor were women living alone or members of households headed by women: women in these circumstances constituted a much greater proportion of the poor than of the population as a whole. This fact is the basis of concern about the "feminization of poverty," and about the responsiveness of policy to the plight of poor women.

This paper deals with these issues. The first section describes the character of contemporary poverty with particular emphasis on the "feminization of poverty." It argues that the feminization of poverty is a complicated phenomenon, with different policy issues raised by different groups among the poor. The most difficult issues arise around the poverty of single-parent families. While some of their poverty is temporary, caused by changes in family structure and alleviated when the new family is back on its feet, much of the poverty of single-parent families, especially among blacks, appears to be chronic poverty that existed before the break-up of the family and persists afterward.

The second section of the paper describes the major developments in poverty policy since about 1965, particularly as they affected the different groups that contribute to the feminization of poverty. It suggests that while income transfer policy was quite successful in dealing with the poverty of the elderly and disabled, it has been much less successful with single-parent families. This failure resulted partly from ambivalent public attitudes about whether poor mothers should work and partly from the inherent difficulty of the problem of chronic poverty.

The third section of the paper, which asks where the politics and poli-

This paper is a revised version of one presented at a conference on "The Changing Situations of Blacks and Women," held at the University of Chicago, April 1985.

cies of poverty may be going over the next decade, assesses some of the suggestions from current welfare reform efforts.

The Nature of Contemporary Poverty

Although the deep recession of the early 1980s drove many ordinary families into poverty, the demographic composition of the poor remained quite different from the rest of us in ways other than simply having less money.[1] The major difference is that members of female-headed families and women living alone are disproportionately represented among the poor.

The feminization of poverty is seen most dramatically in data from 1979, before the beginning of the recession of the early 1980s. (Later sections of this paper will provide data for 1959 to 1985.)[2]

* *While three-quarters of the American population in 1979 lived in husband-wife or male-headed families, only 40 percent of the poor lived in such families.*

In 1979, 12.3 percent of the population lived in female-headed families and 6.6 percent were women living alone. In contrast, 51.2 percent of the poor were members of female-headed families (36.5 percent) or women living alone (14.7 percent).

* *Blacks were much more likely than whites to be living in female-headed families in 1979, and these families were a much larger proportion of the black poor than of the white poor.*

In 1979, 40.8 percent of all blacks were living in female-headed families or were women living alone; these two groups made up 69.3 percent of the black poor. In contrast, among the white population, 15.8 percent were members of female-headed families or women living alone, both groups making up 43.6 percent of the white poor.

---

[1] The analysis summarized in this section is laid out more fully in Mary Jo Bane, "Household Composition and Poverty," in Sheldon Danzinger and Daniel H. Weinberg, eds., *Fighting Poverty: What Works and What Doesn't* (Cambridge, Mass.: Harvard University Press, 1986).

[2] The data reported here and in the following section come from published reports of the U.S. Bureau of the Census, particularly "Characteristics of the Population Below the Poverty Level: 1979," *Current Population Reports*, P–60, No. 130, 1981 and "Characteristics of the Population Below the Poverty Level: 1983," *Current Population Reports*, P–60, No. 147, 1985 (Washington, D.C.: Government Printing Office). They are reported more fully in Bane, "Household Composition and Poverty."

THE FEMINIZATION OF POVERTY

The family composition of the poor has changed quite dramatically since 1960. If we include in the definition of feminization of poverty women living alone and members of female-headed households, it is clear that poverty has become more and more feminized.

- *Members of female-headed households and women living alone almost doubled as a proportion of the poor between 1959 and 1979. Both the level of feminization and the amount of change were much greater among blacks than among whites.*

Members of female-headed families and women living alone made up 26.3 percent of the poor in 1959, rose to 51.2 percent of the poor in 1979, and decreased slightly to 47.0 percent of the poor in 1983. By far the greatest increase in poverty between 1959 and 1979 occurred among members of female-headed families. In the early 1980s, poverty increased proportionately more among husband-wife families. During recessions, it appears that members of female-headed families and men and women living alone decline as a proportion of the poor, presumably because economic hard times push a disproportionate number of male-headed families into poverty.

Looking at the data from the perspective of race, the proportion of the poor white population who were members of female-headed households or women living alone increased from 25.0 percent in 1959 to 43.6 percent in 1979. Among blacks, the proportion of the poor in these households more than doubled, from 29.3 percent in 1959 to 69.3 percent in 1979.

These increases in the proportion of the poor who were women living alone or members of female-headed households result from the combined effects of changes in the family composition of the population as a whole and changes in the relative poverty rates of various household groups. During the 1970s and 1980s, marital breakup, births to unmarried women, and an increasing tendency for various groups (especially elderly widows) to live alone changed the family composition of the population quite dramatically.[3] At the same time, poverty rates were changing. In general, poverty rates were falling between 1959 and 1979, from 22.4 percent in 1959 to 11.7 percent in 1979; they then rose to 15.3 percent by 1983 and fell to 14.0 percent by 1985. The most dramatic declines in poverty rates during the 1960s and 1970s were among elderly whites living alone and among black two-parent families, for whom poverty rates

---

[3] A detailed analysis of changes in family composition, and of the causes and effects of these changes, is contained in Irwin Garfinkel and Sara S. McLanahan, *Single Mothers and Their Children: A New American Dilemma* (Washington, D.C.: The Urban Institute, 1986).

fell from 50.9 percent in 1959 to 14.8 percent in 1985. The poverty rates for members of female-headed families, in contrast, fell relatively less, from 49.4 percent in 1959 to 37.6 percent in 1985.

An analysis of the reasons for the increased feminization of poverty suggests that about 40 percent of the increase is accounted for by changes in relative poverty rates and about 60 percent by changes in population composition. Changes in relative poverty rates were considerably more important for blacks than for whites.[4]

This is an important finding. Especially among blacks, as more female-headed families were formed, the two-parent families left intact were far less likely to be poor than they had been in earlier times. This suggests that a good deal of black poverty was simply reshuffled, with poor two-parent families breaking apart into poor female-headed and single-person households, while better-off families remained together. Among whites, the data are more suggestive of a pattern in which families that were well-off before a split became poor after it.

Transitions to Female-Headed Households

These observations are supported by data on transitions to female-headed and single-person households. The Panel Study of Income Dynamics, a fifteen-year longitudinal study that began in 1968 with a sample of five thousand households, provides us with such data.[5]

One question that can be asked about the poor single-parent families that form when a marriage breaks up is whether the family would have been poor had it not broken up. We may learn the answer to this question by looking at whether the family was poor before it broke up. The data show very different patterns for blacks and whites.

• *Among whites who were poor in the first year after moving into a female-headed household, about three-quarters became poor simultaneously with the transition. In contrast, of those blacks who were poor after the transition, about two-thirds had also been poor before.*

A similar result appeared in an analysis of poverty rates among young children who were still living with their unmarried mothers in the grandparental households. Since most unmarried mothers do live at home for some period after having their first child, poverty rates while they are still

---

[4] These calculations are explained in detail in Bane, "Household Composition and Poverty."

[5] The analysis of the Panel Study is reported more fully in Bane, "Household Composition and Poverty." The analysis of children born to unmarried women is reported in Mary Jo Bane, "The Feminization of Poverty Among Children," a paper presented to the American Association for the Advancement of Science, May 1986.

at home give an indication of their own family's economic status and a hint of the economic status of the young men they might have married. The analysis found that 20 percent of white children and 51 percent of black children in three-generational households were poor. It seems unlikely that independent households formed by the marriages of young unmarried mothers to young men from families like their own would have been poor less often than the households from which the unmarried mothers came, since young people starting out on their own are, on the whole, less well-off than their parents. On the basis of these data, therefore, one can speculate that perhaps *half* of the black children born to unmarried mothers, but perhaps only one-fifth of the white children of unmarried mothers, might have been poor at birth even if their mothers had married.

These data clearly suggest the association between poverty and the split-ups of two-parent families among whites, but the much lesser importance of "event-caused" poverty among blacks. Perhaps half of the poverty of female-headed households is best characterized as "event caused"; that is, the members were not poor before the family structure changed, but they were poor afterward. Usually, this kind of poverty is relatively short-term.[6] The rest of the poor in female-headed households seem to have been born poor both before and after the family change: their poverty is simply "reshuffled." This kind of poverty is most likely chronic and of longer duration.

The problem of the feminization of poverty, to the extent that it results from the formation of female-headed households, is thus in reality two different problems: one of mostly temporary poverty for women whose poverty follows directly from a family change, and one of mostly chronic poverty for women who came from situations that offer opportunities for neither men nor women. Sensible policies to reduce the number of poor female-headed families would have to reflect this distinction. Unfortunately, policy responses have not always taken it into account.

Policy Responses in the 1960s and 1970s: What Was Done and Why?

The changes that were taking place in the characteristics of the poor and in the economic situations of various demographic groups were not independent of what was happening in the policy arena. This issue is

---

[6] Some of the characteristics of the short- and long-term poor are discussed in Greg J. Duncan, *Years of Poverty, Years of Plenty* (Ann Arbor: Institute for Social Research, University of Michigan, 1983), and in Mary Jo Bane and David T. Ellwood, "Slipping into and out of Poverty: The Dynamics of Spells," *Journal of Human Resources* 21, no. 1 (Winter 1986): 1–23.

sometimes framed as whether policy changes contributed to the dramatic changes that took place in family composition, especially among blacks.[7] Here, however, I am more concerned with the question of how policy responded, consciously or not, to changing demographic and economic circumstances.

Demographic changes produced larger numbers both of elderly women and of female-headed families at risk of poverty. Changes in these groups as a proportion of the population were not, however, the only changes contributing to the feminization of poverty. The other main contributor was the slower decline of poverty rates for female-headed families vis-à-vis two-parent families, a trend only partly countered by an improvement in the relative poverty rates of elderly women. A crucial question, therefore, is whether policy was contributing or failing to respond to these changes in relative poverty rates.

It seems quite clear that the dramatic reduction in poverty among two-parent families during the 1960s resulted almost entirely from economic growth, productivity improvements, and the increasing number of wives entering the labor force.[8] Two-parent families, with the exception of those that contain an elderly or disabled member, receive negligible government transfer payments. In contrast, government transfers—Aid to Families with Dependent Children (AFDC) and other welfare programs—are a much more important component of income among single-parent families and women living alone. Welfare policy therefore has a greater potential impact on the feminization of poverty.

Three themes characterized the development of income transfer policy as it affected poverty among female-headed families and women living alone during the 1960s and 1970s. These themes grew out of the historical circumstances and politics of the period during which the programs developed, and they reflect changing but ambivalent attitudes about who among the poor was indeed "deserving" of public support. The result has been that poverty among certain groups, particularly the elderly and the disabled, has been addressed, but it has not been adequately dealt with among other groups, particularly chronically poor communities and female-headed households.

The first theme characterizing the development of poverty policy dur-

[7] See, for example, Charles Murray, *Losing Ground: American Social Policy 1950–1980* (New York: Basic Books, 1984). For the other side of the issue, see David T. Ellwood and Lawrence Summers, "Poverty in America: Is Welfare the Answer or the Problem?" in Danzinger and Weinberg, eds., *Fighting Poverty*; David T. Ellwood and Mary Jo Bane, "AFDC and Family Structure," in Ronald G. Ehrenberg, ed., *Review of Labor Economics*, vol. 7 (Greenwich, Conn.: JAI Press, 1985); and Neckerman, Aponte, and Wilson in this volume (Chapter 12).

[8] Data are presented in Ellwood and Summers, "Poverty in America."

ing the last few decades reflects a historical tendency to categorize the poor.

- *Income support programs for the poor solidified around categorical distinctions between those able to work and those not able to work, and they dealt quite generously with those categories of people whose inability to work was both widely agreed upon and easy to document. The disabled and the elderly, especially elderly women, benefited from this distinction.*

Official attitudes toward the poor have long distinguished those able to work from those unable to do so, resulting in different policies for dealing with the aged and infirm on the one hand and the able-bodied on the other. The most successful public solutions to the poverty problem were the programs for the aged and disabled.

Social Security is one of the great social welfare success stories of all time. During the last several decades, the program's coverage has expanded to include almost all elderly people.[9] In addition, benefits are indexed to maintain their real value. The average benefit received by a retired worker relative to the poverty line for a single-person household grew from about half the poverty line in 1959 to slightly greater than the poverty line in the 1980s.

The indexing of Social Security benefits occurred in the early 1970s and was firmly in place during the high inflation of the late 1970s. The result has been dramatic. Whereas twenty years ago 35 percent of the elderly were poor, the poverty rate of the elderly today is slightly below that of the population as a whole. Social Security payments are clearly responsible for pulling a large proportion of the elderly, especially elderly women, out of poverty. Supplemental Security Income, (ssi), a means-tested program for the elderly and disabled who are not covered through the contributory Social Security program, also has benefit levels indexed close to the poverty line. Thus it is not just the insurance nature of Social Security that has led to its success. Part of its appeal must lie in the fact that the elderly and disabled are perceived as a deserving group, relatively straightforward to identify, who are unable to work and are deserving of public support.

A second theme in the development of poverty policy reflects the difficulty of applying the able/unable-to-work distinction across-the-board.

- *The history of the* AFDC *program, in contrast to programs for the elderly and disabled, reflects deep public ambivalence about the ability and*

[9] Data on program coverage and benefit levels come from the U.S. Department of Health and Human Services, Social Security Administration, *Social Security Bulletin, Annual Statistical Supplement, 1983* (Washington, D.C.: Government Printing Office). The population data come from the sources listed in note 2.

responsibility to work among single mothers, and about the responsibility of society for mitigating the results of family breakup. The result has been deteriorating levels of transfer payments and few work programs for poor female-headed families.

Given the reliance of income transfer policy on categorical programs that distinguish between those able and those unable to support themselves, it is instructive to examine three categories of women who are often grouped together in discussions of the feminization of poverty. One group consists of non-elderly adult women living alone, who in 1979 made up 7.4 percent of the poor. These women are often in transition, having recently moved out of their parents' homes or separated from their husbands. They receive very low levels of transfer payments, unless they are disabled or eligible for unemployment benefits. They are eligible for food stamps. Like unattached, able-bodied males, they are expected to support themselves. Their poverty tends to be temporary, and their poverty rates fluctuate with the business cycle. There is little enthusiasm, probably rightly, for expanding transfer payments for this group.

A second group consists of elderly women living alone, who in 1979 made up 7.3 percent of the poor. This group has been a primary beneficiary of the expansion and indexing of Social Security and ssi benefits. In the 1980s, about 70 percent of the elderly who have pre-transfer incomes below the poverty line are moved out of poverty by transfer payments.[10] The relatively low current poverty rate of elderly women (relative to their situation two decades ago and to other groups in the population) testifies to the proposition that transfer payments can indeed be an effective weapon against poverty.

The third group, and the largest and fastest growing contributor to the feminization of poverty, consists of members of female-headed families, mostly with children, who in 1979 made up 36.5 percent of the poor. Among this group, only about 14 percent of the pre-transfer poor were moved out of poverty by transfer payments. The major income support program for this group, AFDC, has contracted rather than expanded in terms of the number of children covered.

Rather than being indexed in federal law, AFDC benefit levels are subject to annual appropriations by state legislatures, which tended not to raise benefits during the high inflation years of the 1970s. As a result, real benefit levels have fallen dramatically since the early 1970s. Even when they were at their highest, AFDC benefit levels were not high enough in

[10] The analyses of pre- versus post-transfer poverty reported here come from Sheldon Dansinger, Robert Havemen, and Robert Plotnick, "Antipoverty Policy: Efforts on the Poor and the Nonpoor," in Danzinger and Weinberg, eds., *Fighting Poverty*.

any state to push single-parent families with no other income out of poverty.

Why has the transfer payment mechanism not been used to move single-parent families with children out of poverty, as transfer payments have been used for the elderly? The answer cannot lie simply in the cost. The AFDC program cost $13.5 billion in 1984, constituting about 1 percent of total government spending. The poverty gap for female-headed households, which presumably could be filled by an expansion of AFDC, was $15.1 billion.

The answer almost certainly lies in public ambivalence about parental responsibility for children—ambivalence that has arisen from changing behavior and changing attitudes toward marital permanence and women's participation in the labor force. In times past, everyone assumed that marriages would stay together, that women would stay home, and that men would support their children. If marriages dissolved through death or, in a few cases, desertion, public aid would replace the earnings of the fathers, enabling the mothers to continue to stay home with the children. This conception provided the basis for the original AFDC program.

Those patterns clearly have changed. Female-headed families are now only rarely formed through widowhood, but result instead from marital breakups or from births to unmarried mothers; two living parents are available to support the children. In addition, work has become a normal activity for mothers as well as for fathers. But as I have argued in more detail elsewhere,[11] the current welfare system seems to incorporate the worst of both the old and the new worlds. Men are tacitly assumed to have divorced their children if they leave or do not marry their children's mothers, and, at least until recently, support obligations have been enforced in a quite desultory manner.

At the same time, though the majority of non-welfare mothers of preschool children work in the paid labor force, welfare mothers of young children not only are exempt from work requirements but also are excluded from many training and employment programs. The public cannot seem to decide whether it expects or even wants mothers of young children to work. Instead, the AFDC program takes over the financial support responsibilities of both parents. Perhaps because almost everyone is profoundly uncomfortable about this governmental assumption of parental responsibility, the levels of support for female-headed families are stingy and the harassment great.

No good solution to this dilemma has been found. In the past few years, increasing federal and state attention has focused on child support

[11] See Mary Jo Bane, "Income Transfers and the Poor," in Manuel Carballo and Mary Jo Bane, eds., *The State and the Poor in the 1980s* (Boston: Auburn House, 1984).

collection, with tough new legislation now in the process of being imple-mented. This legislation should have positive effects on the poverty rates of children whose fathers are not chronically poor, and it should alleviate some of the "event-caused" poverty that results from marital breakup. Recent years have also seen some new efforts in the area of work require-ments and in programs for "employable" mothers, that is, those who are not disabled and whose youngest child is over six.[12] These efforts too should have positive results, but it is important to note that "employable" mothers make up only about one-quarter of AFDC applicants. Neither ef-fort speaks to the problem of chronic poverty among either mothers or fathers, a theme to which I now turn.

• *Policy during the past few decades has virtually ignored the problem of chronic poverty. This inattention has had the most serious effects on those female-headed families, especially ones headed by blacks, whose poverty seems to be independent of family change.*

During the 1970s, discussions of chronic poverty became unfashiona-ble, partly due to new empirical evidence, available from longitudinal studies of family income, that documented for the first time the consid-erable turnover within the poverty population. There was also a vehe-ment reaction from minorities, civil rights activists, and liberals to reports that seemed to "blame the victims" for their poverty, for example, Daniel Patrick Moynihan's report on what he called the "tangle of pathology" reflected in black family structure. These intellectual currents helped to focus policy attention on the transitory poor and programs that would aid them.[13]

Not coincidentally, perhaps, the problem of transitory poverty among female-headed families is much easier to solve (or, alternatively, to ig-nore) than that of chronic poverty. If people are only poor for short pe-riods, they may not need help at all, and if they do, temporary income support is the answer: time-limited unemployment benefits, food stamps, or cash benefits. One does not need to worry that generous transfer pay-

[12] Employable AFDC recipients have been required to participate in the Work Incentive Program (WIN) since that legislation was passed in the 1960s. Community Work Experience Programs (CWEP or workfare) for AFDC recipients were made a state option in the Omnibus Budget Reconciliation Act of 1981.

[13] The evidence on turnover came largely from the Panel Study of Income Dynamics and was reported on in a series of articles and papers by researchers at the University of Michi-gan's Institute for Social Research. A recent overview of this Michigan work is contained in Duncan, *Years of Poverty, Years of Plenty*. The famous "Moynihan Report" was Daniel Patrick Moynihan, *The Negro Family: The Case for National Action* (Washington, D.C.: U.S. Department of Labor, 1965). Some of the more thoughtful critiques appeared in Lee Rainwater and William L. Yancey, *The Moynihan Report and the Politics of Controversy* (Cambridge, Mass.: MIT Press, 1967). On this issue, see also Henry J. Aaron, *Politics and the Professors* (Washington, D.C.: The Brookings Institution, 1978).

ments to the temporarily poor will become overly expensive or foster dependency, since these poor are not prone to long-term dependency. Benefits to the short-term poor can afford to be adequate and can be delivered automatically and with minimal intrusion. One does not need massive employment efforts or supportive services of the sort that have proven themselves notoriously difficult to design and manage effectively. Dealing with chronic poverty, in contrast, raises all these difficulties.

Whether consciously or not, the development of policy for the non-elderly, non-disabled poor during the 1970s seemed to be based on the assumption that poverty, even among single-parent families, was indeed temporary. Public employment, training, and job development efforts were always small and were virtually abandoned in the 1980s. In the AFDC program, an older "social work" orientation, in which services and advice accompanied cash grants tied to needs as defined by the case-worker, was replaced by flat grants, eligibility workers who were more like clerks than service providers, and court-generated proscriptions against intrusions in clients' lives.[14] Benefit levels were kept quite low, perhaps on the implicit rationalization that people would not have to live on them for long.

Unfortunately, intellectual or policy preferences for dealing with temporary poverty do not make chronic poverty go away. Bane and Ellwood show that almost half of the poor at a given point in time are in the midst of spells of poverty that will last at least eight years.[15] Neckerman, Aponte, and Wilson (Chapter 12 in this volume) have raised renewed concern about chronic unemployment among young blacks and its relationship to the poverty of the women they might otherwise have married. The analyses reported above suggest that, especially among blacks, much of the poverty of single-parent families is not caused by a family event, but by a chronic, underlying poverty that carries across changes in family structure. Thus, serious efforts to counter the feminization of poverty would have to take on the problem of chronic poverty.

Where Do We Go from Here?

If the analysis presented above is correct, it would appear that poverty policy since 1960, while successful for certain groups among the poor, left the most serious problem underlying the feminization of poverty un-

[14] The history of the administration of welfare programs is extremely interesting. For glimpses into it, see Frances Fox Piven and Richard A. Cloward, *Regulating the Poor* (New York: Pantheon Books, 1971), and Michael Sosin, "Legal Rights and Welfare Change: 1960–1980," in Danzinger and Weinberg, eds., *Fighting Poverty*.

[15] Bane and Ellwood, "Slipping into and out of Poverty." This finding is not inconsistent with earlier findings on turnover among the poverty population. The difference comes from looking at the poor at a point in time rather than looking at anyone who ever becomes poor.

resolved. It would also appear that the reasons for this are not simply lack of will or of understanding; rather, they reflect deep-rooted but ambivalent attitudes about whether poor mothers should work, and the inherent difficulty and complexity of the problem of chronic poverty. If these attitudes do indeed underlie the continuing feminization of poverty, what can we expect from the politics and policies of the next decade?

One possibility is a renewed interest in non–means-tested "family policy" programs—perhaps refundable tax credits, children's allowances, or large expansions of day care or subsidized parental leave. Renewed interest in such programs seems unlikely in a time of large federal deficits, though the persistent small voices that argue for children's allowances (from Senator Moynihan to George Gilder) may, at some point, be successful. Even if a children's allowance were to be put in place, however, it is extremely unlikely that it would be set anywhere near high enough to keep a family with little other income out of poverty.

Another possibility is an increase in AFDC benefits within that program's current basic structure. Several proposals from welfare reform groups and a few pieces of legislation would set a federal minimum for benefits that would increase to a proportion of the poverty line and be indexed to the annual inflation rate. Interestingly, most of the proposals would raise benefits only to something like 70 percent of the poverty line. While it can be argued that supplemental non-cash benefits make this level of benefits almost the equivalent of the poverty line, it would not move people out of poverty in the traditional sense. Nor would it deal with the structural defects of the AFDC program as a way of dealing with either transitory or chronic poverty.

TRANSITORY POVERTY AMONG SINGLE-PARENT FAMILIES

A third possibility is a restructuring of the AFDC program to make it a better instrument for alleviating the transitory poverty that characterizes part of the feminization of poverty. Although it can be argued that the present array of programs is not too bad an approach to transitory poverty, even that of single-parent families, this is mainly because transitory poverty is short-term, and problems can be expected to go away by themselves. There are several aspects of the AFDC program, in addition to the low benefit levels, that make it a less than optimal response to transitory poverty.

For a program to be effective against transitory poverty, it should be easy to get on it, easy to get off it, and easy to make a transition to other sources of income—in this case, earnings and child support. None of these characteristics apply to the AFDC program. There was a time when it was easy to get on AFDC—in the early and mid-1970s, when welfare rights advocacy and a series of court cases resulted in something very close to a self-declaration of eligibility. These "reforms" also resulted in extremely high overpayment rates (25 percent overpayments in New York State, for example) and the inevitable resulting pressures for control of fraud and abuse. Today the application and eligibility determination process for AFDC in most states requires extensive documentation and cross-checking. Ironically, the process is most difficult for applicants who work or have other sources of income, and who must therefore provide substantial detailed documentation that their income is in fact below the eligibility level.

Once on AFDC, a client finds almost no incentive to work or obtain child support and has almost no expectations of doing either. Other income reduces benefit levels almost dollar for dollar. There are no work requirements—not even job search or employment registration—for the vast majority of AFDC recipients who have children under six. In addition, the periodic reports and interviews that are required to maintain AFDC eligibility are more difficult for continuing clients, as for applicants, who work or have other sources of income. As a result, AFDC is the sole source of support for the vast majority of AFDC clients.

These features of the AFDC program make a gradual transition to other income sources extremely difficult. There is also another feature of AFDC that makes it hard to get off the program. In most states, going off AFDC also means losing Medicaid coverage either immediately or shortly thereafter. Medicaid is an enormously valuable benefit, and the loss of it would seem to serve as a serious deterrent to going off the program.

The characteristics of AFDC that make it inappropriate as a temporary income support have often been identified as problems. And at least some of them appear to be solvable. Recent federal legislation not only toughens child support obligations but also provides incentives for meeting them. States are moving toward employment and training programs for women with younger as well as older children. Welfare administration increasingly emphasizes the reciprocal responsibilities of the system and the clients, with obligations defined not simply as honest reporting but also as the development and carrying out of a plan of activities aimed at independence.

A farther-reaching approach to the solution of these problems is a guaranteed child support system. This approach, advocated by analysts at the University of Wisconsin and analogous to the guaranteed maintenance systems of several European countries, would combine automatic wage withholding for child support payments with a state guaranteed minimum payment to the custodial parent. The benefit would not be means-tested and would be sufficient when combined with part-time work to bring the family to or above the poverty line. The structure of the program would provide powerful incentives to both work and pay child support, and thus it would enable governmental programs to serve their proper role as reinforcers of parental responsibility.[16]

All of these proposals for restructuring AFDC, even the seemingly radical Wisconsin proposal, may well generate substantial intellectual and political support. As family breakup becomes more and more common, coping with transitory poverty in female-headed families will become widespread and more and more, a "middle-class" issue. There could well be considerable public support for governmental initiatives to deal with poverty in these situations, as there has been broad middle-class support for child support enforcement legislation. The proposals outlined here are consonant with American attitudes toward self-support and parental responsibility, and they recognize the changing nature of family relationships. They may well represent an emerging consensus about the direction the AFDC program should take.

CHRONIC POVERTY

Unfortunately, the proposals described above speak to the easy problem. The hard part of the problem of the feminization of poverty, that of chronic poverty, remains. It is more difficult to discern an intellectual or political consensus involving proposals for dealing with chronic poverty.

Charles Murray has recently argued that the welfare system was an important part of the problem of chronic poverty during the 1960s, providing incentives for families to break up and for young people to stay out of the labor market. Whether or not one agrees with this analysis, it is easy to agree that the welfare system ought to be more a part of the solution than it now is.[17] Just as the welfare system ought to be designed in a way that makes it easy to get on for temporary relief and easy to get off, it ought also to be hard to stay on welfare for long periods of time. This is most humanely accomplished not through harassment or arbitrary time limits but through specifications of client responsibilities. These can take the form, perhaps, of requirements stipulating that clients participate in activities that are part of a jointly agreed upon plan for movement toward self-support. The notion of a contract in which clients agree to participate in job search, education, training, and work experience programs, and in which welfare departments agree to provide and support

[16] Irwin Garfinkel has written extensively about the rationale and model for a guaranteed child support system. See, for example, Irwin Garfinkel and Elizabeth Uhr, "A New Approach to Child Support," *The Public Interest* no. 75 (Spring 1984).

[17] Murray, *Losing Ground*. There have been many critiques of the Murray argument, including a powerful criticism of the book by Christopher Jencks, in his review of it for *The New York Review of Books*, May 9, 1985.

these opportunities, is gaining increasing acceptance. After a certain period, recipients could switch to a program that provided work in return for benefits, an idea that is also being developed by many states.

The welfare system, of course, cannot be the whole solution to chronic poverty, just as it is not the whole problem. The key to a more lasting approach is jobs not only for the women who end up on welfare but for the other men and women in their communities. Self-sufficiency for men, women, and families requires that they have jobs, which in turn requires that jobs are available, and that men and women have the skills and motivations to hold them. General economic development, stimuli to develop specific job intensive industries, and careful management of public sector employment are all parts of this solution. Education, job training, and employment readiness programs for potential workers are other parts.

Unfortunately, experience with employment programs over the last two decades has not been uniformly positive.[18] Indeed, there is a widespread public perception that public service employment programs were at best ineffective and at worst wasteful and fraudulent. Moreover, many of the educational and training programs mounted during the War on Poverty were not demonstrably cost-beneficial. Therefore, there has been extreme reluctance on the part of both federal and state governments during the past few years to undertake new job development in the public sector. There has also been considerable caution about investing extensively in education and training programs, with the result that recent efforts have been small-scale and have focused on those groups that are relatively easy to deal with.[19]

One reaction to the perceived failure of public employment efforts during the 1960s has been the Reagan administration's reliance on general, untargeted economic development as a solution to the problem of jobs. There seems to be increasing evidence, however, that the benefits of the last period of economic recovery did not, in fact, "trickle down" to the most disadvantaged among the unemployed.[20]

Thus, none of the "solutions" that have been tried since 1960, taken individually, seems to be especially powerful. But there are few new ap-

[18] For a good, recent review of the literature on employment and training programs, see Laurie J. Bassi and Orley Ashenfelder, "The Effects of Direct Job Creation and Training Programs on Low-Skilled Workers," in Danziger and Weinberg, eds., *Fighting Poverty*.

[19] As an indication of federal disinterest in this issue, one can observe that budgeted federal spending on employment and training went from $10.3 billion in fiscal year 1980 to $5.3 billion in fiscal year 1984. The main federal effort is now the Job Training Partnership Act, which provides funds to private industry councils in the states.

[20] For documentation of the Reagan administration's programs and its effects, see John L. Palmer and Isabel V. Sawhill, eds., *The Reagan Record* (Cambridge, Mass.: Ballinger Publishing Company, 1984).

proaches on the horizon that would seem to be any more effective. Both the demand side and the supply side of the labor market would seem to require some sort of public intervention. Continued experimentation with programs of various sorts seems to be the only way to proceed.

The political attractiveness of "more of the same" is extremely limited. Thus states have been trying to develop new angles or to put new labels—the most catchy being "Massachusetts' E.T." (for employment and training)—on their employment services packages. In addition, careful program evaluations are beginning to provide good information about the most effective programs for different groups of clients.[21] These efforts, combined with a strong emphasis on mutual responsibilities in welfare programs, may result in programs that are attractive enough to deserve political support.

Whether they will get it may depend on what alliances can be forged among the groups who traditionally advocate for "liberal" programs, and on whether these groups can agree on notions of mutual responsibility and the need for cost-effective programs. Were the civil rights groups to find common cause with children's advocates, women's groups, and the churches around a set of proposals, a powerful coalition could conceivably develop. For such a coalition to develop, it probably has to include women. In recent years, the women's movement has taken up some causes that bear on the feminization of poverty—particularly child support, day care, and job opportunities for women. Progress against chronic poverty, however, almost certainly requires greater emphasis on job opportunities for minority men. Unless we move into a period of labor shortages, therefore, it may be difficult for the groups to become political allies.

In short, it is possible to imagine programs that, combined with a growing economy, could make some progress in the fight against chronic poverty. It is not easy to see, however, where the political impetus for such programs will come from, since the programs are neither simple nor sexy, and the political coalitions that might support them are tenuous. Nonetheless, the seriousness of the issue compels our attention.

---

[21] The best are being done by the Manpower Development Research Corporation, in its evaluations of supported work and of the work welfare demonstration programs.

12

Family Structure, Black Unemployment, and American Social Policy

KATHRYN M. NECKERMAN, ROBERT APONTE, AND WILLIAM JULIUS WILSON

The problem of family disintegration among poor black Americans has grown so rapidly since 1970 that the Moynihan report, *The Negro Family: The Case for National Action*, which was the subject of stormy controversy in the late 1960s, is now seen in a growing number of circles as a prophetic document.[1] In the years since *The Negro Family* was released to the public, the proportion of out-of-wedlock births among blacks has risen to 57 percent.[2] At the same time, the family instability originally identified as a problem in the black community has become increasingly common among whites. As larger proportions of the poverty population have come to be members of female-headed families, the "feminization of poverty" has become the focus of considerable public concern.

Uncertainty over the cause of these changes in family structure has hindered the development of a coherent policy approach to the related problems of poverty, welfare dependency, and teenage pregnancy. Despite insufficient evidence, the conviction that welfare incentives underlie trends

This is a substantially revised version of a paper by Robert Aponte, Kathryn M. Neckerman, and William Julius Wilson, prepared for presentation at the colloquium on "The Changing Situations of Black Americans and Women," held April 25–27, 1985, at the Center for the Study of Industrial Societies, University of Chicago, and published as "Race, Family Structure, and Social Policy," *Working Paper 7: Race and Policy* (Washington, D.C.: National Conference on Social Welfare, 1985). Research for this paper was supported by grants from the Ford and Spencer Foundations. The authors wish to thank Christopher Jencks and Pastora San Juan Cafferty for their comments on an earlier version of this paper.

[1] Daniel P. Moynihan, *The Negro Family: The Case for National Action* (Washington, D.C.: Department of Labor, Office of Policy Planning and Research, 1965).

[2] Moynihan, *The Negro Family*; U.S. Bureau of the Census, *Current Population Reports*, Series P–20, No. 388, "Household and Family Characteristics: March 1983" (Washington, D.C.: Government Printing Office, 1984); National Center for Health Statistics, "Advance Report of Final Natality Statistics, 1980," *Monthly Vital Statistics Report* (Washington, D.C.: Department of Health and Human Services, 1982).

in family structure has dominated the policy discussion of the past twenty years. The high rates of welfare receipts among black female-headed families, as well as the coincidence of the rise in female-headed families with increased expenditures for social programs, appear to support this view, and economic theories of family behavior lend theoretical backing.[3] Charles Murray's book *Losing Ground* is the most prominent example of the perennial appeal of this argument.[4]

In addition, the considerable racial disparities in family structure have inhibited frank discussion of the issue. Liberal social scientists, social workers, journalists, policymakers, and civil rights leaders have until recently been reluctant to refer to race when discussing female-headed families, teenage pregnancy, and out-of-wedlock births, for fear of appearing racist or seeming to "blame the victim." The current discussion of the "feminization of poverty," based on the family structure changes emerging in the general population, is often cast in terms of the problems of female-headed families in general, with little reference to racial differences.

This neglect of race is not wholly misguided: the rise of female-headed families among blacks and whites does share some common features. Contrary to popular assumptions, the two-parent nuclear family was the predominant family type among both whites and blacks in the late nineteenth and early twentieth centuries.[5] The proportion of families headed by women began to rise only in the 1950s and 1960s. In contrast to the earlier part of the century, when most women heading families were widows, today most are separated, divorced, or never-married. In addition, single mothers are increasingly likely to establish their own households rather than live in subfamilies (households headed by another person).[6]

---

[3] Gary S. Becker, *A Treatise on the Family* (Cambridge, Mass.: Harvard University Press, 1981).

[4] Charles Murray, *Losing Ground: American Social Policy, 1950–1980* (New York: Basic Books, 1984).

[5] Herbert G. Gutman, *The Black Family in Slavery and Freedom, 1750–1925* (New York: Pantheon Books, 1975); Frank F. Furstenberg, Jr., Theodore Hershberg, and John Modell, "The Origins of the Female-headed Black Family: The Impact of the Urban Experience," *Journal of Interdisciplinary History* 6 (Autumn 1957): 211–33; Paul J. Lammermeier, "The Urban Black Family of the Nineteenth Century: A Study of Black Family Structure in the Ohio Valley, 1850–1900," *Journal of Marriage and the Family* 35 (August 1973): 440–56; Elizabeth H. Pleck, "The Two-Parent Household: Black Family Structure in Late Nineteenth-Century Boston," *Journal of Social History* 6 (Fall 1972): 3–31; Crandall A. Shifflett, "The Household Composition of Rural Black Families: Louisa County, Virginia, 1880," *Journal of Interdisciplinary History* 6 (Autumn 1975): 235–60.

[6] Mary Jo Bane and David T. Ellwood, "Single Mothers and Their Living Arrangements," working paper, supported by U.S. Department of Health and Human Services Contract No. HHS-100-82-0038, 1984; Phillips Cutright, "Components of Change in the Number of

These similarities obscure marked racial differences in the prevalence and character of families headed by women. In the past, primarily because of high black male mortality rates, black families were twice or three times as likely as white families to be headed by women. This difference persisted as separation, divorce, and out-of-wedlock birth became more frequent: between 1960 and 1983, for example, the proportion of female-headed families with children rose from 6 to 14 percent for whites and from 21 to 48 percent for blacks.[7] Reasons for family headship also differ by race. Most of the increase in black female-headed families stems from a dramatic decline in marriage rates, in combination with high rates of out-of-wedlock births. Although marriage rates have dropped and out-of-wedlock birth rates have risen among whites as well, marital disruption is the more important contributor to the increase in white female-headed families. And because white women are more likely than black women to marry or remarry, female family headship is more transitory among whites than among blacks.[8]

Because so many first become single mothers through teenage out-of-wedlock childbearing, black single mothers are younger, less educated, more likely to be never-married, and less likely to receive child support than white single mothers. Their poverty rates are higher: in 1983, 60.7 percent of black female-headed families with children lived below the poverty line, compared with 39.8 percent of white female-headed families.[9] And because they have greater difficulty escaping poverty through either marriage or employment, black female-headed families are likely to be persistently poor (or poor over a number of years). In fact, black female-headed families, who are only 5 percent of the total non-elderly population, are 46 percent of the non-elderly persistently poor.[10]

Female Family Heads Aged 15–44: United States, 1940–1970," *Journal of Marriage and the Family* 36 (November 1974): 714–21.

[7] U.S. Bureau of the Census, *U.S. Census of Population: 1960*. Characteristics of the Population, Part 1. U.S. Summary (Washington, D.C.: Government Printing Office, 1961); U.S. Bureau of the Census, *Current Population Reports*, 1984.

[8] Mary Jo Bane and David T. Ellwood, "Single Mothers and Their Living Arrangements." For evidence that spells of family headship tend to be shorter among whites than among blacks, see Heather L. Ross and Isabel Sawhill, *Time of Transition: The Growth of Families Headed by Women* (Washington, D.C.: The Urban Institute, 1975), and Mary Jo Bane and David T. Ellwood, *The Dynamics of Dependence: The Routes to Self-Sufficiency* (Washington, D.C.: Department of Health and Human Services, 1983).

[9] U.S. Bureau of the Census, *Current Population Reports*, Series P–60, No. 147, "Characteristics of the Population Below the Poverty Level: 1983" (Washington, D.C.: Government Printing Office, 1985).

[10] Greg J. Duncan, *Years of Poverty, Years of Plenty* (Ann Arbor: University of Michigan Press, 1984). For evidence that black women have more difficulty escaping welfare dependency through marriage, see Mary Jo Bane and David T. Ellwood, *The Dynamics of Dependence*.

Some analysts have suggested that changes in family structure are a major factor driving up poverty rates.[11] This argument has validity for white women, who tend to enter spells of poverty following an event such as the breakup of a marriage or the birth of a child.[12] Among blacks, however, trends in marital status and family formation that underlie the rise in female-headed families are concentrated among women who are already poor. For example, out-of-wedlock births are most common among low-income black women, particularly those from families whose poverty is compounded by problems such as poor neighborhood quality.[13] Marriage delay and marital disruption have increased most among black women with less than a high school education.[14] Bane shows that most black female heads were poor prior to the event—whether out-of-wedlock birth or marital breakup—that led to their heading a family; for blacks, she emphasizes, changing family structure does not so much cause poverty as "reshuffle" it.[15]

As we consider measures to address these problems, it is crucial that we not gloss over the question of race. Although changes in family structure have taken place in all racial and class groups, black women heading families remain more prevalent and more disadvantaged than their white counterparts. While they certainly do not characterize all blacks, the problems of the black urban underclass—long-term poverty, welfare dependency, teenage pregnancy, and out-of-wedlock births—are qualitatively different from the problems of most white female-headed families. While a race-specific approach to policy may not be desirable, examining the social structural bases of racial differences will lead us to a more sound interpretation of the problems of female-headed families.

We argue here that scholarly and policy discussion of the increase in female-headed families has been misled by an overemphasis on welfare incentives. Despite evidence of a modest effect at best, both academics and policymakers continue to emphasize the role of welfare. The evidence we review suggests an alternative explanation: that racial differences in

[11] Gordon Green and Edward Welniak, *Changing Family Composition and Income Differentials*, Special Demographic Analyses CDS-80-7 (Washington, D.C.: Government Printing Office, 1982).

[12] Mary Jo Bane, "Household Composition and Poverty: Which Comes First?" in Sheldon H. Danziger and Daniel H. Weinberg, eds., *Fighting Poverty: What Works and What Doesn't* (Cambridge, Mass.: Harvard University Press, 1986).

[13] Dennis P. Hogan and Evelyn M. Kitagawa, "The Impact of Social Status, Family Structure, and Neighborhood on the Fertility of Black Adolescents," *American Journal of Sociology* 90 (January 1985): 825–55.

[14] Reynolds Farley, *The Growth of the Black Population* (Chicago: Markham Publishing Co., 1970); Andrew J. Cherlin, *Marriage, Divorce, Remarriage* (Cambridge, Mass.: Harvard University Press, 1981).

[15] Mary Jo. Bane, "Household Composition and Poverty."

family structure stem primarily from the disadvantaged economic status of black men, who have been disproportionately affected by recent shifts in labor market conditions. This evidence calls for a reorientation of both research and policy agendas on the question of poverty and family structure.

Welfare and Family Structure

Charles Murray is the most prominent recent exponent of the view that the liberal social welfare policies of the Great Society era have reduced the incentive to work and to maintain stable two-parent families. In *Losing Ground*, he argues that policies intended to reduce poverty have instead created more poverty, as the disadvantaged reject the traditional avenues of mobility in favor of short-term gains derived from welfare and crime.[16] Murray claims that during the 1960s and 1970s rising welfare payments and non-cash benefits such as food stamps and Medicaid posed ever greater financial disincentives to marry. Work incentives under the Aid to Families with Dependent Children (AFDC) program, which were intended to prod welfare recipients into the labor market, instead lured the working poor onto welfare. These and other changes in the political, social, and legal climate are blamed for growing family instability, joblessness, welfare dependency, crime, and school failure. For these reasons, according to Murray, progress against poverty slowed in the early 1970s and reversed by the end of the decade even as social spending increased.

Although Murray's book provides no rigorous test of the effects of welfare, his interpretation merits attention here because it has been so widely accepted. A few months after the book appeared, for example, an editorial in the *New York Times* noted that "this year's budget-cutter bible seems to be 'Losing Ground,' Charles Murray's book appraising social policy in the last 30 years. The Reagan budget . . . is likely to propose deep reductions in education, child nutrition, and housing assistance, and elimination of programs like the Job Corps, revenue sharing, and urban development grants. In agency after agency, officials cite the Murray book as a philosophical base for these proposals."[17]

To illustrate his argument, Murray cites the case at two points in time—1960 and 1970—of a fictional young unmarried couple, Harold and Phyllis, who live in Philadelphia. Phyllis is pregnant and the couple must decide between remaining unmarried and thus qualifying for AFDC or marrying and subsisting on Harold's minimum wage earnings. In 1960, the welfare package would barely have supported Phyllis and her

[16] Charles Murray, *Losing Ground*.
[17] "Losing More Ground," *New York Times*, February 3, 1985.

child. Moreover, AFDC regulations did not permit payment of welfare benefits if the couple were to share a household, regardless of their marital status. In that situation, Murray suggests, Harold and Phyllis would have been likely to marry and live on his earnings. By 1970, however, the situation has changed: not only is the income from the welfare package comparable to Harold's minimum wage earnings, but the couple can collect it while they share a household, provided they do not marry. The couple's best alternative is to remain unmarried and combine Phyllis's welfare benefits with Harold's pay, but because of more liberal AFDC and Unemployment Insurance benefits, Harold need not work steadily. Thus, Murray argues, by 1970 low-income couples with (or expecting) children would tend to favor welfare, perhaps combined with occasional employment, over marriage and stable employment in low-wage jobs. These incentives changed little during the 1970s, according to Murray; average AFDC payments continued to rise in real terms until around mid-decade, when they stabilized.

Murray's example is appealingly simple and, as he notes, sidesteps the controversial issue of the culture of poverty; the behavior of the poor is claimed to be solely the result of the changing rules and incentives that govern their lives. However, this account misrepresents the economic choices facing Murray's fictional family. His comparison for 1970 of the family's income from AFDC and other transfers with income from Harold's minimum wage earnings takes insufficient account of non-cash benefits such as food stamps that working poor intact families can receive. In addition, Murray concludes that income tax and Social Security deductions reduce Harold's earnings below the family's potential welfare income, but he gives no estimates of these deductions in his presentation of the couple's alternatives. Without this information, the reader cannot assess Murray's claim that welfare paid more than work in 1970.

Murray also neglects the deterioration after 1970 in the relative advantage of welfare over work. The real value of AFDC benefits (a better measure than average payments) has fallen substantially since the early 1970s. Adjusted for inflation, the value of AFDC plus food stamps dropped 16 percent between 1972 and 1980, and by 1984 it was only 4 percent higher than in 1960.[18] The 1975 enactment of the earned income tax credit further increased the advantages of work for low-income families. In 1980, Greenstein estimates, Harold and Phyllis's income would have

---

[18] Real average AFDC payments did rise until the mid 1970s, then rose little if at all in most states. Average payments, however, may be biased by changes in the composition of the AFDC population; benefit levels (the payment guaranteed to a family with no income) are a better indicator of the generosity of the AFDC program. For estimates on declines in the value of AFDC benefits, see Sheldon, Danziger and Peter Gottschalk, "The Poverty of Losing Ground," *Challenge* (May/June 1985): 32–38.

been one-third higher in Pennsylvania (and higher still in other states) if Harold had worked than if the family had relied upon welfare. Accordingly, he concludes, "if perverse welfare incentives in the late 1960s actually led to family dissolution and black unemployment, as Murray contends, then these trends should have reversed themselves in the 1970s, when the relative advantage of work over welfare increased sharply. They didn't. The number of female-headed households continued to surge, and black employment declined."[19]

A good deal of research supports Greenstein's claim that changes in welfare benefit levels alone cannot explain family disintegration. Over the past fifteen years, many empirical studies have examined the relationship of variations in AFDC benefits to out-of-wedlock births, marital dissolution, and female-headed families. Cross-state differences in benefit levels as well as changes over time in welfare payments provide a natural experiment for studying the effects of welfare benefits on family structure. There is no comparative research on the availability of welfare itself, since public assistance programs exist nationwide. Nevertheless, because the inauguration of AFDC in 1935 predates the increase in black female-headed families by about twenty years, it is unlikely that welfare causes family breakup. Rather, as Murray would argue, it is perhaps the liberalization of AFDC regulations and the increase in benefit levels during the 1960s and early 1970s that may have stimulated out-of-wedlock childbearing and marital dissolution. It is this period that researchers have focused on.

There is no evidence, first of all, that high welfare benefits stimulate out-of-wedlock childbearing. Research examining the relationship between AFDC benefit levels and measures of illegitimate births across states and over time has consistently shown no significant association between these variables.[20] Other studies of low-income women suggest that

[19] Robert Greenstein, "Losing Faith in 'Losing Ground,' " *New Republic* 192 (March 25, 1985): 12–17.

[20] For cross-state comparisons, see Phillips Cutright, "Illegitimacy and Income Supplements," Joint Economic Committee of the Congress, Subcommittee on Fiscal Policy, *Studies in Public Welfare*, Paper No. 12, Part 1 (Washington, D.C.: Government Printing Office, 1973); A. Fechter and S. Greenfield, *Welfare and Illegitimacy: An Economic Model and Some Preliminary Results*, Working Paper 963–37 (Washington, D.C.: The Urban Institute, 1973); C. R. Winegarden, "The Fertility of AFDC Women: An Econometric Analysis," *Journal of Economics and Business* 26 (Spring 1974): 159–66; and Kristin A. Moore and Steven B. Caldwell, *Out-of-wedlock Pregnancy and Childbearing*, working paper (Washington, D.C.: The Urban Institute, 1976). For longitudinal studies, see Cutright, "Illegitimacy and Income Supplements," and David T. Ellwood and Mary Jo Bane, *The Impact of AFDC on Family Structure and Living Arrangements* (Washington, D.C.: Department of Health and Human Services, 1984).

women on public assistance want and have fewer children than those not on welfare.[21]

Studies of the relationship between welfare benefits and marital dissolution or female family headship produce more mixed results. Among the studies using aggregate data, Honig and Danziger et al. each found that AFDC payments had positive effects, Minarik and Goldfarb reported insignificant negative effects; Ross and Sawhill found significant positive effects for nonwhites but not for whites; and Cutright and Madras found that AFDC benefits did not affect marital disruption but did increase the likelihood that separated or divorced mothers would head their own households.[22] Hoffman and Holmes, in their analysis of the Panel Study of Income Dynamics (PSID), reported very modest effects of benefit levels on marital dissolution. However, Sawhill et al. found no effect at all in their analysis of the same data.[23]

In recent work that may prove definitive, Ellwood and Bane develop three different types of cross-state comparisons to control for cultural or other unmeasured influences on family structure that might have confounded the effect of welfare in other state-level analyses.[24] Their results were remarkably consistent across method: welfare benefits had a modest

[21] S. Polgar and V. Hiday, "The Effect of an Additional Birth on Low-Income Urban Families," *Population Studies* 28 (November 1974): 463–71; Harriet Presser and Linda S. Salsberg, "Public Assistance and Early Family Formation: Is There a Pro-Natalist Effect?" *Social Problems* 23 (December 1975): 226–41; P. J. Placek and G. E. Hendershot, "Public Welfare and Family Planning: An Empirical Study of the 'Brood Sow' Myth," *Social Problems* 21 (June 1974): 660–73.

[22] Marjorie Honig, "AFDC Income, Recipient Rates, and Family Dissolution," *Journal of Human Resources* 9 (Summer 1974): 303–22; Sheldon Danziger, George Jakubson, Saul Schwartz, and Eugene Smolensky, "Work and Welfare as Determinants of Female Poverty and Household Headship," *The Quarterly Journal of Economics* 97 (August 1982): 519–34; Joseph J. Minarik and Robert S. Goldfarb, "AFDC Income, Recipient Rates, and Family Dissolution: A Comment," *Journal of Human Resources* 11 (Spring 1976): 243–50; Ross and Sawhill, *Time of Transition*; Phillips Cutright and Patrik Madras, "AFDC and the Marital and Family Status of Ever Married Women Aged 15–44: United States, 1950–1970," *Sociology and Social Research* 60 (April 1976): 314–27.

[23] Saul Hoffman and John Holmes, "Husbands, Wives, and Divorce," in James N. Morgan, ed., *Five Thousand American Families*, vol. 4 (Ann Arbor: University of Michigan Press, 1976); Isabel Sawhill, Gerald E. Peabody, Carol A. Jones, and Steven B. Caldwell, *Income Transfers and Family Structure* (Washington, D.C.: The Urban Institute, 1975).

[24] David T. Ellwood and Mary Jo Bane, *The Impact of AFDC.* Ellwood and Bane compare marital dissolution and living arrangements among mothers likely and unlikely (because of their socioeconomic status) to be AFDC recipients and among women who are or are not mothers (and thus are eligible or are not eligible for AFDC), and they compare changes in marital dissolution and living arrangements over time, in high- and low-benefit states. In their analysis of illegitimate births, they compare births to women likely and unlikely to be AFDC recipients, and they examine changes over time, in high- and low-benefit states. Note that because these comparisons are of groups *within* states, unmeasured differences *between* states do not affect the analysis.

effect on the incidence of single motherhood and on divorce and separation, and virtually no influence on illegitimacy. They did report a relatively large effect on living arrangements: high welfare benefits increased the likelihood that young single mothers would live in their own households rather than with a relative. Overall, however, welfare had little impact on the proportion of families headed by women: in 1975, their analysis indicates, a 100-dollar increase in monthly benefits was associated with a 5-percent difference in single motherhood and a total 15-percent difference in the number of female-headed households because of changes in young mothers' living arrangements.

Ellwood and Bane observe that "the more significant the family structure or living arrangement change, the less influence AFDC seems to have."[25] Childbirth involves more serious consequences for women than changes in living arrangements, or even separation or divorce. As the emotional and financial importance of these decisions increases, they reason, welfare figures less prominently. The greater influence of AFDC on younger women is amenable to a similar interpretation, since the marriages of older women are likely to be of longer duration and to involve more significant ties.

Although Murray does not discuss much of this literature (it should be noted that the Ellwood and Bane research appeared after *Losing Ground* was in press), he does cite the income maintenance experiments as evidence of the strong effects of welfare on family structure. These experiments, conducted over a number of years in the 1970s, indicated that guaranteed incomes increased marital dissolution by more than 50 percent. Murray's reference to the income maintenance experiments in this context has several problems. The experimental effects were not consistent across payment levels: at the highest income level, the income maintenance payments had no significant effect on marital stability.[26] In addition, Cain notes, the effects of the income transfers were not distinguished from those of the experimental training program, which increased marital instability; the magnitude and direction of the effects of the income transfers alone are unclear.[27] Finally, these experiments are not directly generalizable to AFDC. Unlike AFDC, the income maintenance experiments provided income support to two-parent as well as one-parent families, and in cases of marital breakup both parents received income support. Lack of stigma, lower transaction costs, and better information for clients were also said to distinguish the income mainte-

[25] Ellwood and Bane, *The Impact of AFDC*, p. 6.

[26] *Final Report of the Seattle/Denver Income Maintenance Experiment*, vol. 5 (Menlo Park, Calif.: SRI International, 1983).

[27] Glen Cain, "Comments on August 18th Version of Marital Stability Findings, Chapter Three," mimeo, September 2, 1981.

nance program from welfare.[28] In fact, because the control group for the experiments was subject to AFDC incentives, what the experiments demonstrated was a significant difference between income maintenance payments and AFDC. Although the findings of these important experiments cannot be ignored, it is not clear what implications they have for the existing welfare system.

The argument that welfare policy is responsible for family dissolution has gained renewed attention at precisely the time that empirical research to address it has become available. The evidence reviewed in this section is clear: although welfare may play a minor role in marital breakup and a more significant role in single mothers' decisions to establish independent households, by itself it cannot account for the marked shift to single-parent families among blacks or whites. We must look elsewhere for an explanation of changing family structure.

Joblessness and Family Structure

The focus on the effects of welfare on family formation in recent years has resulted in both scholars and policymakers ignoring evidence of the importance of male employment for family stability. A variety of empirical studies suggests a positive relationship between male economic status and family stability. Classic studies of black communities, such as DuBois's *The Philadelphia Negro*, Drake and Cayton's *Black Metropolis*, Liebow's *Talley's Corner*, and Rainwater's *Behind Ghetto Walls*, consistently point to the role of male economic status in the delay or dissolution of marriages.[29] Research on family life during the depression documents the deterioration of marriage and family life following male job loss.[30] More recent, the Moynihan Report noted the association between unemployment and out-of-wedlock births.[31] Multivariate analyses also show that indicators of male economic status are related to marital instability or the incidence of female-headed families. For instance, Sawhill et

[28] Lyle P. Groeneveld, Nancy Brandon Tuma, and Michael T. Hannan, "The Effects of Negative Income Tax Programs on Marital Dissolution," *Journal of Human Resources* 15 (Fall 1980): 654–74.

[29] W.E.B. DuBois, *The Philadelphia Negro: A Social Study* (Philadelphia: University of Pennsylvania Press, 1899); St. Clair Drake and Horace Cayton, *Black Metropolis: A Study of Negro Life in a Northern City* (New York: Harper and Row, 1945); Elliot Liebow, *Talley's Corner* (Boston: Little, Brown, 1967); Lee Rainwater, *Beyond Ghetto Walls* (New York: Aldine Publishing Co., 1970).

[30] W. E. Bakke, *Citizens Without Work* (New Haven, Conn.: Yale University Press, 1940); Glen H. Elder, Jr., *Children of the Great Depression* (Chicago: University of Chicago Press, 1974); Mirra Komarovsky, *The Unemployed Man and His Family* (New York: Octagon Books, 1940).

[31] Moynihan, *The Negro Family.*

al. reported that male unemployment, fluctuations in income, and lack of assets are all associated with higher separation rates; for a subsample of low-income black families, level of husband's earnings also has an effect. Controlling husband's age, Cohen found a positive effect of husband's earnings on marital stability for the entire sample.[32]

Researchers have also found that the low ratio of men to women among blacks raises the incidence of female-headed families. The low sex ratio among blacks reflects both high mortality and the census under-count of black males, and thus it is in part a result of the unstable attach-ment to household or labor force that characterizes the under-enumer-ated population. A complex of interrelated factors such as joblessness, crime, incarceration, substance abuse, and high mortality is likely to con-tribute to the low *measured* sex ratios that Darity and Myers find to be key in their analysis of the rise of female-headed families.[33]

Scholars have used male economic status to explain cross-sectional black-white differences in family structure. More recent research extends those insights to an interpretation of trends over time in family structure. When the increasing joblessness of black men is combined with high rates of incarceration, premature mortality, and other problems, it becomes clear that the ability of black men to provide economic support is even lower than official employment statistics convey.[34] The full extent of the worsening marriage market faced by black women is captured by Wilson and Neckerman's "male marriageable pool index" (MMPI), or the ratio of employed men to women of the same age and race.[35] Trends in the MMPI

[32] Honig, "AFDC Income, Recipient Rates, and Family Dissolution"; Ross and Sawhill, *Time of Transition*; Sawhill et al., *Income Transfers and Family Structure*; Hoffman and Holmes, "Husbands, Wives, and Divorce"; John H. Bishop, "Jobs, Cash Transfers, and Marital Instability: A Review and Synthesis of the Evidence," *Journal of Human Resources* 15 (Summer 1980): 301–34; Alan Cohen, "Economics, Marital Stability, and Race" (Ph.D. diss., University of Wisconsin–Madison, 1979).

[33] William Darity, Jr., and Samuel L. Myers, Jr., "Changes in Black Family Structure: Implications for Welfare Dependency," *AEA Papers and Proceedings* (May 1983): 59–64.

[34] William Julius Wilson and Kathryn M. Neckerman, "Poverty and Family Structure: The Widening Gap between Evidence and Public Policy Issues," in Danziger and Weinberg, eds., *Fighting Poverty*. See also Tom Joe, "The Flip-side of Black Families Headed by Women: The Economic Status of Black Men," working paper (Washington, D.C.: Center for the Study of Social Policy, 1984). For evidence on black male incarceration and mortal-ity, see Alfred Blumstein, "On the Racial Disproportionality of United States' Prison Popu-lations," *The Journal of Criminal Law and Criminology* 73 (Fall 1982): 1259–81, and Reynolds Farley, "Homicide Trends in the United States," *Demography* 17 (May 1980): 177–88.

[35] Men and women are matched by age and race because most marry within their own race and near their own age. Because of the census undercount of black men, the MMPI sets a lower bound on the ratio of men to women. If most of the black men not counted in the census are not employed, then their omission from the MMPI does not bias the measure significantly. The MMPI figures include estimates of the number of men in the armed forces,

TABLE 12.1 Male Marriageable Pool Index (Ratio of Employed Men Aged 20–44 to Women of the Same Age Group) and Percent of Women Aged 15–44 Heading Families, by Race and Region, 1960–1980

Region	White			Black		
	1960	1980	Change	1960	1980	Change
NORTHEAST						
MMPI	86.9	84.7	−2.2	67.5	56.3	−11.2
Women Heads	3.5	6.5	+3.0	13.4	25.4	+12.0
MIDWEST						
MMPI	90.6	87.0	−3.6	68.8	56.3	−12.5
Women Heads	2.9	6.2	+3.3	13.4	25.5	+12.1
SOUTH						
MMPI	84.4	86.8	+2.4	71.2	65.1	−6.1
Women Heads	3.7	6.1	+2.4	10.0	19.1	+9.1
WEST						
MMPI	87.7	86.8	−0.9	69.7	67.0	−2.7
Women Heads	4.7	7.9	+3.2	14.1	22.9	+8.7

SOURCE: Adapted from Robert Aponte, Kathryn M. Neckerman, and William Julius Wilson, "Race, Family Structure, and Social Policy," *Working Paper 7: Race and Policy* (Washington, D.C.: National Conference on Social Welfare, 1985).

for the nation as a whole show that unlike white women, black women, and particularly younger black women, face a shrinking pool of economically stable or "marriagable men." These findings provide additional support for the hypothesis that the rise of black female-headed families is directly related to increasing black male joblessness.

Trends in the MMPI were compared with trends in family structure by region in order to test this hypothesis more directly and to highlight the role of broad economic shifts in changing family structure.[36] Data presented in Table 12.1 show changes between 1960 and 1980 in the MMPI and in the proportion of women heading families. Changes in the MMPI among whites have been minimal, with modest declines in the Northeast

---

allocated among the regions according to the proportion of the total population (by race) residing in each region.

[36] Robert Aponte, Kathryn M. Neckerman, and William Julius Wilson, "Race, Family Structure, and Social Policy," *Working Paper 7: Race and Policy* (Washington, D.C.: National Conference on Social Welfare, 1985).

and Midwest and some increase in the South. On the other hand, the black MMPI figures have fallen substantially in the Northwest and Midwest, with smaller declines in the South and West. In the Northeast and Midwest, among both whites and blacks, the increase in the proportion of women heading families corresponded roughly to the drop in the MMPI. In the South and West, however, the proportion of women heading families rose more than would be expected simply on the basis of a drop in the MMPI, with substantial deviations in the case of southern whites and western blacks.

These deviations highlight regional differences in social climate, divorce laws, and demographic factors that may also be influencing trends in family structure. For instance, in the South, rapid urbanization and a relatively slow fertility decline between 1960 and 1980 may have boosted the proportion of women heading families. In the West, black women heading families are more similar in their social and economic characteristics to white female heads than to black female family heads elsewhere. Compared with black female family heads in other regions, the black women who head families in California (where four-fifths of western blacks live) have higher average incomes, and they are more likely to head a family because of divorce than because of out-of-wedlock birth or separation. Given the relative similarity between white and black women heading families in the West, it is likely that the reasons for their high rates of marital dissolution are also similar and involve selective migration or factors specific to the West, where divorce rates have historically been high.[37]

In addition, increasing marital instability may stem from the increasing economic independence of women, as indicated by their rising employment rates and improving occupational status. Studies find that labor force participation and independent income are associated with marital dissolution among white women, although the findings for black women are not as consistent.[38] Given the dramatic increase in labor force participation among white women and the relative stability in employment indicators among white men, it is especially likely that women's economic independence is related to white marital instability. The influence of this factor should not be neglected for blacks, however, and the especially rapid increase in black women's employment in the South and West may help explain family structure trends in those regions.

More research is needed to untangle the influence of these different factors on the rise of female-headed families. But the evidence discussed here,

[37] Ibid. For related evidence, see Ross and Sawhill, *Time of Transition*.

[38] Danziger et al., "Work and Welfare"; Hoffman and Holmes, "Husbands, Wives, and Divorce"; Ross and Sawhill, *Time of Transition*.

as well as the results from a growing body of empirical literature, indicate a relationship between male economic status and family stability. Simple associations between joblessness and family structure do not establish the causal direction of this relationship: marital instability might undermine a man's attachment to his job just as his unemployment might undermine a marriage. Both marital instability and joblessness are complex phenomena undoubtedly influenced by many factors. Ethnographic research on work and family life in low-income families has established, however, the major role of male unemployment in marital delay and dissolution. Further, the profound forces reshaping urban labor markets are likely to play a major role in the joblessness among central city men. At any rate, it is clear that scholars' and policymakers' focus on the impact of welfare is misplaced, and that the falling employment rates among minority males deserve greater attention.

Changing Economic Organization and Black Male Joblessness

The decline in minority male employment that drives the MMPI has taken place as economic activity has shifted from the central cities to the suburbs, and from the Northeast and Midwest to the South and West, or abroad. Over the past two decades, the Northeast and Midwest have experienced substantially less employment growth than the rest of the country (see Table 12.2). Manufacturing, wholesale, and retail jobs have become scarcer particularly in the nation's largest cities, where blacks are heavily concentrated. Between 1947 and 1972, the central cities of the 33 most populous metropolitan areas (according to 1970 figures) lost 880,000 manufacturing jobs and 867,000 jobs in retail and wholesale trade, while blue-collar employment in their suburbs expanded dramatically.[39] The decline in demand for low-skilled labor has been most severe in the older central cities of the north. The four largest (New York, Chicago, Philadelphia, and Detroit) lost over a million jobs in manufacturing, wholesale, and retail enterprises between 1967 and 1977 alone.[40] While the black populations of these central cities were growing substantially, white and middle-class residents were migrating to the suburbs. Populations of many of the older northeastern and midwestern cities became minority-dominant. The source of much of this urban black popu-

[39] John D. Kasarda, "The Implications of Contemporary Redistribution Trends for National Urban Policy," *Social Science Quarterly* 61 (December 1980): 373–400.

[40] John D. Kasarda, "Caught in the Web of Change," *Society* 21 (November/December 1983): 41–47.

TABLE 12.2 Percent Change in Employment by Region

Region	Period 1950–1977	1970–1977
NORTHEAST		
New England	44.6	6.3
Middle Atlantic	28.4	−1.1
MIDWEST		
Eastern region	52.8	8.5
Western region	71.8	15.6
SOUTH[a]		
South Atlantic	128.1	20.1
East South Central	107.5	21.9
West South Central	133.0	29.8
WEST		
Mountain	185.5	36.8
Pacific	155.0	21.0
TOTAL		
UNITED STATES	70.3	8.6

SOURCE: Bernard L. Weinstein and Robert E. Firestine, *Regional Growth and Decline in the United States* (New York: Praeger Publishers, 1978).

[a] Between 1970 and 1977, all southern states experienced job growth of at least 10 percent, while the District of Columbia had a loss of 16.1 percent.

lation growth was the exodus of rural southern blacks.[41] Displaced from a marginal existence in southern agriculture, these migrants were likely to be relatively uneducated, unskilled, and unprepared for the transformations in production awaiting them in the cities.

As Kasarda's figures suggest, job loss is concentrated in sectors with modest educational and skill requirements, and particularly in manufacturing. The manufacturing jobs that were the economic foundation of the older industrial cities have also been the mainstay of the working-class black population. Although historically blacks were over-represented in service occupations, it was mainly opportunities in manufacturing that attracted black migrants to the cities and represented their major avenue

[41] C. Horace Hamilton, "The Negro Leaves the South," *Demography* 1 (Spring 1964): 273–95; Neil Fligstein, *Going North: Migration of Blacks and Whites from the South, 1900–1950* (New York: Academic Press, 1981).

TABLE 12.3 Number of Manufacturing, Retail, Wholesale, and Selected Service Establishments in Chicago City and Metropolitan Area, 1963 and 1982

Type of Industry and Location	1963	1982
CHICAGO CITY		
Manufacturing	9,221	5,203
Retail[a]	19,023	12,503
Wholesale	9,248	4,748
Services[a]	10,371	15,312
CHICAGO METROPOLITAN AREA		
Manufacturing	13,956	13,905
Retail[a]	33,696	33,974
Wholesale	12,206	14,364
Services[a]	35,231	39,390

SOURCES: U.S. Bureau of the Census, *Census of Manufactures, 1963* and *Census of Business, 1963* (Washington, D.C.: Government Printing Office, 1966); U.S. Bureau of the Census, *1982 Census of Manufactures* (Washington, D.C.: Government Printing Office, 1985); U.S. Bureau of the Census, *1982 Census of Retail Trade, 1982 Census of Service Industries,* and *1982 Census of Wholesale Trade* (Washington, D.C.: Government Printing Office, 1984).

[a] Figures refer to establishments with payroll only.

to economic stability and advance. Manufacturing has to some extent been replaced with service industries, which have changed the skill requirements and wage structure of employment opportunities.

All these developments—job loss from central cities, the growing dominance of suburban and exurban areas in the metropolitan economies, and the decline of manufacturing—are evident in the example of Chicago, typical of northern industrial cities adversely affected by recent economic and demographic trends. In 1960, the city of Chicago contained 57 percent of the population in the six-county Chicago metropolitan area; by 1980, because of suburban growth and some central city depopulation, that proportion had fallen to 42 percent. Forty percent of the city's population was black in 1980, compared with 23 percent in 1960. As Table 12.3 shows, the number of manufacturing, retail, and wholesale firms located in the city declined in absolute terms between 1963 and 1982. In addition, Chicago's share of the metropolitan area's manufacturing firms fell from 66 percent to 37 percent, its share of retail firms fell from 56 percent to 37 percent, and its share of wholesale firms fell from 76 percent to 33 percent. Although the city experienced absolute growth in the number of service establishments, its share fell from 64 percent in 1963 to 39 percent in 1982. Chicago now has a higher proportion of the metropolitan population than it has of the metropolitan area's economic activity. Commuting across city limits results in a further loss of jobs to the city: suburban residents take almost 200,000 more jobs in Chicago than city residents take in the remainder of the metropolitan area.[42]

As the case of Chicago suggests, central city declines in blue-collar employment have been partly offset by expansion in other sectors. Employment in fields such as advertising, finance, brokering, consulting, accounting, law, and other "knowledge intensive" enterprises has grown. But job opportunities in positions requiring minimal human capital input, such as hotel work, auto repair, and personal services, have become more limited.[43] More recent research by Kasarda provides evidence of a severe mismatch between the skills of inter-city black men and the opportunities available to them.[44] The number of "entry level" positions (those requiring less than a high school diploma) fell by over 30 percent during the 1970s in New York, Philadelphia, and Baltimore, while "knowledge intensive" employment (requiring over 2 years of college) increased significantly. Although black and white educational attainment is converging, racial differences persist, especially among older men. Inner-city black males are especially poorly prepared for these employment trends. In 1982, among central city males aged 16 to 64, 40 percent of all blacks and 26 percent of all whites had not completed high school, while 42 percent of whites and only 25 percent of blacks had attended at least one year of college. Consistent with the implications of this research, youth employment problems are concentrated among the less educated, among blacks, and among residents of central cities and poverty areas, or ghettos.[45] Accordingly, Kasarda argues, "chronically high unemployment will

[42] U.S. Bureau of the Census, *Census of Manufactures, 1963* and *Census of Business, 1963* (Washington, D.C.: Government Printing Office, 1966); U.S. Bureau of the Census, *1982 Census of Manufactures* (Washington, D.C.: Government Printing Office, 1985); U.S. Bureau of the Census, *1982 Census of Retail Trade, 1982 Census of Service Industries,* and *1982 Census of Wholesale Trade* (Washington, D.C.: Government Printing Office, 1984).

[43] Kasarda, "Implications of Contemporary Redistribution Trends."

[44] John D. Kasarda, "Urban Change and Minority Opportunities," in Paul E. Peterson, ed., *The New Urban Reality* (Washington, D.C.: The Brookings Institution, 1985).

[45] David T. Ellwood and David A. Wise, *Youth Employment in the Seventies: Changing Circumstances of Young Adults,* Working Paper No. 1055 (Cambridge, Mass., National Bureau of Economic Research, 1983); S. L. Friedlander, *Unemployment in the Urban Core: An Analysis of Thirty Cities with Policy Recommendations* (New York: Praeger Publishers, 1972); Richard B. Freeman, "Economic Determinants of Geographic and Individual Varia-

plague large portions of the urban underclass so long as the demographic and job-opportunity structures of the cities continue to conflict."[46]

In addition, a recent assessment of the implications of the sectoral shifts in production calls into question the benefits to workers of service sector expansion. Based on an analysis of trends in the distribution of earnings by industry, Stanback and Noyelle argue that the employment opportunities created by the rise of the service sector are characterized by a polarization of pay scales and restricted opportunities for advancement.[47] Their analysis also shows that in 1975, blacks were concentrated in a few of the lower-tiered occupations. The high rate of job turnover that the authors found among service workers suggests that these workers are dissatisfied with their employment conditions.

Overall, then, changes in the location of economic activity have reduced employment opportunities in the older central cities where blacks are heavily concentrated. Most service enterprises replacing the manufacturing industries in the central cities offer unstable employment and low wages to those with inadequate education and training. Moreover, labor market crowding due to the entry of increasing numbers of white women and illegal immigrants into the labor force, and to the large size of recent cohorts of young adults, may have exacerbated the job shortage in central city areas. More research is needed on the contribution of each of these factors to the declining employment of minority males. It is clear, however, that the eroding industrial base of the older central cities is a formidable obstacle to low-skilled minority males seeking stable employment and decent pay.

Conclusions

Over the past two decades, explanation of the sharp rise in female-headed families among blacks has focused on the incentives that welfare programs provide. Charles Murray is simply the latest and perhaps the most prominent representative of this point of view. But while the welfare hypothesis was plausible in the early 1970s, following the simultaneous sharp increase in proportions of female-headed families and the unprecedented expansion of welfare, it can no longer be sustained. Sophisticated empirical research on the subject shows only modest effects of AFDC on family structure. Welfare benefit levels appear to have their greatest influ-

tion in the Labor Market Position of Young Persons," in Richard B. Freeman and David A. Wise, eds., *The Youth Labor Market Problem: Its Nature, Causes, and Consequences* (Chicago: University of Chicago Press, 1982).

[46] Kasarda, "Caught in the Web of Change," p. 44.

[47] Thomas M. Stanback, Jr., and Thierry J. Noyelle, *Cities in Transition* (Totowa, N.J.: Allenheld, Osmun and Co., 1982).

ence not on the incidence of out-of-wedlock births or on rates of separation and divorce, but on the living arrangements of young single mothers. The experience of the past ten years confirms this research: the proportion of families headed by women has continued to rise even as the real value of welfare benefits has fallen.

As the welfare hypothesis had proven unfruitful, the effect of black male economic status is again receiving attention. In historical and ethnographic studies as well as in multivariate analyses of survey data, male economic status is consistently related to family stability. Recent research indicates that increasing black male joblessness, in combination with the high mortality and incarceration rates of black men, has resulted in dramatic declines over the past twenty-five years in the ratio of employed men to women, or the "male marriagable pool index."[48] Not only are national trends consistent with the hypothesis that male joblessness is related to the rise of female-headed households, but also, when these data are disaggregated by region, they show that in regions where the black MMPI fell the most—the Northeast and Midwest—the proportion of black female-headed families also increased the most. The more modest increase in families headed by women among whites is accompanied by little change in white MMPI values.

Recent economic shifts are likely to be a major factor in the increasing joblessness of black men. Regional differences in the change in MMPI discussed earlier point to the particular importance of industrial transformations occurring in the Northeast and Midwest. The shift from manufacturing to services and the geographic shifts in production activity have altered both the number and the characteristics of jobs available in areas where blacks are concentrated. Most inner-city blacks cannot qualify for high-skilled positions in the finance, real estate, and information-processing sectors; low-skilled service jobs, however, are characterized by low wages, restricted opportunities for advancement, and unstable employment.

Despite the consistent evidence linking male economic status to family stability, until recently most scholars and policymakers have overlooked joblessness in their discussions of changing family structure. Because official unemployment statistics do not take into account discouraged workers, or those who have dropped out of the labor force, they understate the increase in black male joblessness; thus it is possible that the extent of the problem has escaped the notice of social scientists concerned with the black family. A more likely explanation, however, lies in the sensitive and highly politicized nature of the debate over the black family. Although previous historical and ethnographic accounts had often por-

---

[48] Wilson and Neckerman, "Poverty and Family Structure."

trayed the lower-class black family as unstable or disorganized, Moynihan's *The Negro Family* generated a tremendous amount of controversy, and this criticism had a chilling effect on research on the black family. Most scholarly writing that addressed the subject at all emphasized the resilience and adaptability of lower-class black families in the face of overwhelming disadvantage.[49] Ironically, this focus had led to a neglect of traditional liberal concerns, such as problems of racial isolation and restricted economic opportunity and the impact of these problems on the family, even as the economic and demographic shifts of the 1970s have made these concerns increasingly timely. Conservative scholars, who were not inhibited by this ideologically tinged criticism, came to dominate the debate with their arguments of welfare dependency and the culture of poverty.[50]

Research agendas on the family must be broadened to take account of macrostructural forces such as employment trends. Although we have evidence that male economic status is related to family stability, much work remains to be done. Still unresolved is the role of factors such as ethnicity, class, and community in mediating the influence of male unemployment on marriage and family relations. Those concerned with contemporary family problems may be able to draw on the insights of a rich and growing literature in history of the family.[51]

Even as this research proceeds, however, we must develop new policy approaches to female-headed families and the related problems of welfare dependency and teenage childbearing. Although the liberal social welfare programs of the 1960s cannot be blamed for the increase in black female-headed families, they also have been helpless to stop it. Further, these Great Society programs have shown only limited success in alleviating the poverty of female-headed families; even when poverty rates are adjusted for receipt of non-cash benefits, one-fourth of all female-headed families are still poor.

One major component of a policy approach to the problems of female-headed families must be a comprehensive economic reform package designed to promote and enhance employment among the disadvantaged—

[49] Andrew Billingsly, *Black Families in White America* (Englewood Cliffs, N.J.: Prentice-Hall, 1968); Robert B. Hill, *The Strength of Black Families* (New York: Emerson Hall, 1972); Joyce Ladner, *Tomorrow's Tomorrow: The Black Woman* (Garden City, N.Y.: Doubleday, 1971); Joyce Ladner, ed., *The Death of White Sociology* (New York: Random House, 1973); Robert Staples, "The Myth of the Black Matriarchy," *Black Scholar* 2 (January/February 1970): 9–16.

[50] William Julius Wilson, "Cycles of Deprivation and the Underclass Debate," *Social Service Review* 59 (December 1985): 541–59.

[51] For an introduction to this literature, see Andrew Cherlin, "Changing Family and Household: Contemporary Lessons from Historical Research," *Annual Review of Sociology* 9 (1983): 51–66.

both men and women. Fundamental to this approach are policies that will foster economic growth and create a tight labor market. The logic of supply and demand indicates that policies to create a tight labor market may also raise wages; historically, in addition, other employer concessions such as company-sponsored day care have also been provided when labor is scarce. However, without protectionist legislation or measures such as employee ownership/control, unskilled or semiskilled workers, especially those in production, are vulnerable to the same economic shifts now devastating the older industrial cities. Low-skilled workers who are paid well enough to escape poverty are for that very reason likely to lose their jobs, either to mechanization or to international competition. To address the problem of joblessness, we need macroeconomic and labor market policies sophisticated enough to come to terms with this dilemma.

This problem points as well to the importance of measures such as adult education, on-the-job training, and apprenticeship to raise the skill levels of the disadvantaged. Wide disparities in education and training perpetuate inequality in the American labor force and represent a formidable obstacle to anti-poverty efforts. Lack of skills also leaves workers vulnerable to fluctuations in economic conditions and to future technological change. Improved manpower policies would ensure that the disadvantaged are not permanently trapped on the lowest rungs of the job market.

Employment policies are not typically seen as an answer to the problems of female-headed families. Research shows that a rising tide does not raise all boats equally: Economic growth helps male-headed families more than female-headed families.[52] Our work suggests that these employment policies will address the problems of female-headed families indirectly, by improving the job prospects of men and enhancing the stability of low-income two-parent families. But even under our current set of social policies, economic growth improves the economic status of women who head families, and it will do so more effectively with policy efforts to improve child care services and child support enforcement. The majority of women heading families are in the labor force, and more can be drawn in by more attractive job prospects and better child care. In addition, in combination with better child support enforcement, economic growth helps custodial parents, mostly women, by raising the earnings of absent parents.

In the foreseeable future, however, employment by itself may not raise a family, whether single-parent or two-parent, out of poverty. Many fam-

[52] Rebecca Blank, "Disaggregating the Effects of Economic Growth on the Distribution of Income," Discussion Paper #780–85 (Madison, Wis.: Institute for Research on Poverty, 1985).

ilies will still need income support. Therefore, these economic policies must be supplemented with a program of welfare reform and related measures to address the problems of the current income transfer system: inadequate levels of support, cross-state inequities, work disincentives, and lack of provisions for poor two-parent families. At the very minimum, a national AFDC benefit standard, adjusted each year for inflation, is certainly needed. Income support for single-parent families might take the form of the Child Support Assurance Program, developed by Irwin Garfinkel and currently underway on a demonstration basis in Wisconsin.[53] Under this program, a minimum benefit per child is guaranteed to single-parent families regardless of the income of the custodial parent. The absent parent's earnings are taxed at a fixed rate, and if the resulting payment is less than the minimum benefit, the state contributes the rest out of general revenues. This program provides a more adequate level of income support—less stigmatized, with no work disincentives, but with little or no additional cost to the state.

Some Western European countries provide support through family or child allowances. Moynihan has recently noted that tax expenditures through the Earned Income Tax Credit and standard deductions are a form of child allowance already available to American families—one that has been severely eroded by inflation, but one in place nevertheless.[54] It may be easier to make incremental changes in this arrangement than to institute an entirely new program. Even more important than Moynihan's specific policy recommendations, however, may be this reminder that "no government, however firm might be its wish otherwise, can avoid having policies that profoundly influence family relationships. This is not to be avoided. The only option is whether these will be purposeful, intended policies or whether they will be residual, derivative, in a sense concealed ones."[55]

These policies are likely to enjoy more widespread political support than the set of means-tested programs presently targeted at the poor. "Universal programs," those available to working- and middle-class segments of society as well as to the poor, are more likely to attract political support, and therefore more generous and stable funding, because all classes have a stake in them. Means-tested programs, on the other hand, are associated with a low-income and minority constituency, and thus they are not programs that most voters identify with. Economic growth and tight labor market policies, child allowances, and child support en-

[53] Irwin Garfinkel and Elizabeth Uhr, "A New Approach to Child Support," *The Public Interest* no. 75 (Spring 1984): 111–22.

[54] Daniel Patrick Moynihan, *Family and Nation, The Godkin Lectures, Harvard University* (New York: Harcourt Brace Jovanovich, 1986).

[55] Moynihan, *Family and Nation*, pp. 116–17.

forcement are programs that all segments of society might participate in or benefit from, even though the most disadvantaged groups (such as the ghetto underclass) would reap disproportionate benefits.

An emphasis on universal programs to attack problems in the black community that historically have been related to racial subjugation represents a fundamental shift from the traditional approach of addressing problems associated with race. It is true, as we have tried to show in this paper, that the growth in the proportions of families headed by women, and the related problems of poverty, long-term welfare dependency, and teenage out-of-wedlock childbearing, are for historical reasons concentrated in the black community. And, as we have also noted, failure to address racial differences in family structure will distort the debate over changes in family structure and lead to neglect of the plight of the black urban underclass. However, to stress the prevalence of these problems among blacks does not mean that race-specific policies are the only or the most effective way to address them. Indeed, race-specific policies such as affirmative action traditionally have aided the most advantaged members of the minority population, have difficulty attracting widespread popular support, and have failed to address the fundamental source of recent black family disintegration—the economic shifts have fallen most heavily on the truly disadvantaged segment of the black community. America's future challenge in social policy, therefore, is to improve the life chances of groups such as the ghetto underclass by emphasizing programs to which the more advantaged groups of all races can positively relate.

The Future of Social Policy in the United States: Political Constraints and Possibilities

MARGARET WEIR, ANN SHOLA ORLOFF, AND THEDA SKOCPOL

The future of social policy in the United States is becoming a matter of intense national interest and debate. Since the late 1970s, the foundations of postwar social provision have come under newly energized political and intellectual challenges from the right. Maintaining that federal government "interventions" fashioned in the New Deal and (especially) the Great Society have hurt rather than helped both "the underclass" and the nation, neoconservatives call for sharp cutbacks in social spending and for strengthened market rewards or administrative requirements for individual work efforts in a revitalized "opportunity society." Some even advocate that the federal government remove itself altogether from promoting social welfare or managing the national economy through other than monetary means.[1]

Those not persuaded grope for ways to respond to this resurgent and self-confident American right. Certain "neo" liberals have largely accepted the premises of conservative critiques, bowing to arguments that the limits of government effectiveness have been reached, while looking

---

A number of people commented on this essay in ways that helped us to sharpen our arguments. Thanks go to Fred Block, Kenneth Finegold, Hugh Heclo, William Hixson, Jennifer Hochschild, Craig Reinarman, and Jim Shoch, none of whom should be held responsible for the positions we take here.

[1] Among the most prominent of the recent conservative critiques have been George Gilder, *Wealth and Poverty* (New York: Bantam 1982); Charles Murray, *Losing Ground: American Social Policy, 1950–1980* (New York: Basic Books, 1984); and Roger A. Freeman, *The Wayward Welfare State* (Stanford, Calif.: Hoover Institution Press, 1981). See also David Stockman, *The Triumph of Politics: Why the Reagan Revolution Failed* (New York: Harper and Row, 1986).

for ways to retain some trimmed and reformed social programs.[2] Other liberals continue to defend the conglomeration of social and economic policies that make up America's version of the Western welfare state. Arguing that Great Society programs were partially successful in reducing poverty, these older-line liberals refuse to grant credence to conservative critiques and are digging in their heels for a dogged and, if necessary, protracted defense of inherited lines of policy development.[3] Finally, various voices are faintly heard from further to the left, some advocating a wholehearted commitment to an American "full employment welfare state," others advocating greatly expanded income transfers to the disadvantaged.[4]

Sharp and wide-ranging debates over public social provision are, therefore, currently underway in the United States. Yet—as we shall see in greater detail below when we return to a closer examination of some current policy proposals—those engaged in the debates are remarkably unselfconscious about the political forces that have shaped American social policies in the past. Arguments about policy possibilities for the future need to become better anchored in an understanding of the forces that have previously shaped public social provision in the United States, especially from the New Deal to the present. From such a vantage point, we can see the improbability of any wholesale dismantling of all existing social policies. At the same time, we can see why American public social provision cannot be revitalized on the same political bases that have sustained its development since the 1930s—although it *might* be revitalized through alternative broad alliances cutting across social strata in today's United States.

As the essays in this volume have shown, the United States has no comprehensive "welfare state" in the European sense. Instead, it has developed a disjointed patchwork of programs bifurcated into two tiers. In the realm of social transfers, the upper tier is "social security." Since the 1950s, this portion of public social provision has been politically protected by a strong bureaucracy and a broad base of public support made possible by its relatively universal scope. In contrast, the lower tier of

[2] Charles S. Robb, former governor of Virginia, and elected officials in the Democratic Leadership Council have taken a prominent role in arguing that the Democratic party should adopt a more "centrist" agenda. See "Democrats Urged to Reassess Impact of Public Welfare Programs," *New York Times*, June 24, 1986.

[3] See John E. Schwarz, *America's Hidden Success: A Reassessment of Twenty Years of Public Policy* (New York: W. W. Norton, 1983), and Sar Levitan and Clifford M. Johnson, *Beyond the Safety Net: Reviving the Promise of Opportunity in America* (Cambridge, Mass.: Ballinger Publishing Company, 1984).

[4] See Michael Harrington, *The New American Poverty* (New York: Penguin Books, 1984), and the essays in Alan Gartner, Colin Greer, and Frank Reissman, eds., *Beyond Reagan: Alternatives for the '80s* (New York: Harper and Row, 1984).

social transfers includes programs grouped under the rubric of "welfare," programs that have been far less popular and much more vulnerable to political counter-pressures than those considered part of the "social security" system. Meanwhile, in the realm of economic policy, a parallel division has bifurcated macroeconomic management, the legitimate means of promoting aggregate "full employment" and "economic growth," from microeconomic interventions that (in the U.S. context) became targeted on problems of "poverty" and have been relegated politically and administratively to close association with "welfare" measures.

These parallel bifurcations of social and economic policies have been reinforced by the ways U.S. governmental institutions have intersected with social and political interests seeking to shape American public social provision. The representative and administrative arrangements of the federal government have functioned to enhance the influence and unity of some groups and to minimize the impact of others, with important consequences for policy outcomes. In addition, the division of policies into an upper and lower tier has been recurrently reinforced, as the unintended but decisive consequences of earlier policy decisions have shaped future political alliances and policy debates. The timing and packaging, first, of the New Deal's measures, and then of the Great Society's programs created subsequent "policy feedbacks" that further channeled U.S. social politics and policy outcomes in bifurcated ways.

Drawing on the insights offered throughout this volume, we can distinguish analytically—and descriptively flesh out in turn—three interrelated dimensions along which the bifurcation of policy grew from the New Deal to the present. First, the agenda of issues debated in postwar U.S. social policy was reshaped as problems became redefined and solutions were transformed in response to earlier government interventions; yet the antinomies of U.S. social provision were recapitulated in the new debates. Second, the emergence of political coalitions around domestic policy interventions also served to reproduce rifts in social welfare and economic policies. Earlier policy interventions created possibilities for joining some interests and discouraged alliances among others, while the structure of the U.S. state itself—and, in particular, the processes of congressional decision making—had an important impact on the possibilities for coalition formation. Third and finally, the two-tiered configuration of policy was reinforced by the continuing patterns of state building set into motion by particular policy innovations during and after the New Deal.

The Social Policy Agenda since the New Deal

Since the New Deal, processes set in motion by the array of policies already in place have helped to determine the guise in which new social problems appeared as public issues, reinforcing the central bifurcations of American public social provision. Policymakers define problems and construct remedies in the context of earlier interventions. By grouping particular problems and policies together and segregating others, entire networks of experts and politicians establish distinct criteria for addressing the various dilemmas they perceive. In the postwar United States, social policy issues of concern to experts and politicians have often been quite narrowly and rigidly defined, and the possibilities—or impossibilities—for developing lines of communication between and across "issue networks" have strongly affected the range of policy alternatives debated at any given point.[5]

The emergence of "poverty" as a national issue in the 1960s provides a striking example of how an apparently very new policy agenda was actually structured in ways that reflected and reproduced previous bifurcations in U.S. public social provision. During the New Deal and World War II, reform-minded experts and politicians attempted to forge close links between, on the one hand, national economic planning and social security programs and, on the other, federal government commitments to deal with (variously caused) problems of unemployment. Had the National Resources Planning Board and its strategies endured, or had the Full Employment Bill of 1945 been passed and successfully implemented, the postwar United States might have been better prepared to address structural labor market issues and the socioeconomic side effects of black migrations out of the South as aspects of national economic management and social security.

Instead, however, between the late 1940s and the early 1960s, the commercial Keynesians associated with the Council of Economic Advisers— typically recruited on a temporary basis from networks of academics who theorized strictly in terms of aggregate processes and macroeconomic rather than microeconomic interventions—built up prestige as the "high priests" of national economic growth. America's commercial Keynesians reached their peak of policy influence with presidents just as the United States had to start facing the problems of newly urbanized (and newly enfranchised) blacks. From the point of view of the Council of Economic Advisers, these were not problems involving the national economy as such. Instead, they became marginal issues of "poverty" to be addressed by much less academically prestigious groups of labor economists and sociologists—types of experts restricted, moreover, to marginal or tem-

[5] For a discussion of "issue networks," see Hugh Heclo, "Issue Networks and the Executive Establishment," in Anthony King, ed., The New American Political System (Washington, D.C.: American Enterprise Institute, 1978), pp. 87–124.

porary niches within the federal bureaucracy and unable to alter the main lines of policy advice set by the Council of Economic Advisers.

The category "poverty" restricted the way the problems of low-income citizens were understood, and it redefined the range of remedies deemed appropriate for solving the problems of such people. As many of the essays in this volume have documented, the separation of poverty policy from overall economic policy had far-reaching consequences for low-income black Americans in particular. By defining black unemployment as a problem outside the realm of central economic concerns, the discovery of poverty transformed black joblessness into a "welfare" problem to be remedied by the least powerful and most poorly organized sectors of the national government. This interpretation of the problem limited the range of tools that could be used to alleviate black unemployment, despite its persistence at very high rates in the prosperous economy of the late 1960s.

What is more, once the problem had initially been interpreted in this manner, it became very difficult to reorient policy in fundamental ways, even after the War on Poverty petered out, far short of victory. The dominance of macroeconomists at the center of economic policymaking and the apparent success of their efforts to reduce aggregate unemployment undermined possibilities for constructing an employment policy centered on microeconomic interventions; unemployment that remained after the Keynesian tax cut of 1964 could be explained away by reference to the characteristics of those without work. At the same time, the vitalization of a national network of "poverty researchers" ensured the generation of new research that respected the policy divisions separating anti-poverty measures from economic policy. As this community of policy experts became more established, it produced the most technically sophisticated research on poverty in the world but remained guided by a limited research mandate.[6] Poverty researchers devoted little attention to unemployment; and throughout the 1960s and 1970s poverty was rarely linked to the processes generating unemployment. Instead, considerable attention was devoted to questions of work incentives for individuals and to the relationship between income maintenance and work efforts by the poor.[7]

The poverty framework has had an enduring influence on the ways in which policymakers think about the problems of many black Americans. The most important consequence has been an emphasis on policies that

[6] See the discussion by Walter Korpi, "Approaches to the Study of Poverty in the United States: Critical Notes from a European Perspective," in Vincent T. Covello, ed., *Poverty and Public Policy: An Evaluation of Social Science Research* (Boston: G. K. Hall, 1980), pp. 287–314.

[7] Ibid.; see also Henry Aaron, *Politics and the Professors* (Washington, D.C.: The Brookings Institution, 1978), chap. 2.

aim to change the personal characteristics of poor blacks and a neglect of policy tools designed to reorganize socioeconomic arrangements more broadly. By creating the new category of poverty policy, policymakers of the 1960s ensured that black unemployment would be addressed through "special interest" programs directed at a particularly vulnerable constituency. Segregating the economic problems of unemployed or underemployed blacks into the category of "poverty" has, in turn, made it easier to construe such matters as the proliferation of black female-headed households or the persistence of a marginal urban "underclass" in terms of the deficient individual values of the poor, and not as a consequence of more inclusive economic or institutional insufficiencies in American life. Thus, as Neckerman, Aponte, and Wilson argue in this volume, the focus on "welfare incentives" had dominated the research and policy discussions about female-headed households, opening the door for Charles Murray's declaration that Aid to Families with Dependent Children (AFDC) should be abolished because it has discouraged labor force participation and weakened family ties among the poor.

In short, emphasis on the individual characteristics of the poor as the solution to poverty grew naturally from the policy agenda set into motion by the War on Poverty. Despite a greater willingness to expend resources on the poor than at any time since the New Deal, the labor economists and sociologists who became the architects of poverty programs in the 1960s saw efforts to change the behavior of poor people as the most promising route to ending poverty—for poverty was, by definition, not a national economic problem. When the poor did not go away, it was only a short step for less generous policy analysts to advocate some form of coercion to impose behavioral, if not value, changes on the poor. Thus, increasingly, elements of coercion, in the form of work requirements, have been built into welfare programs.[8] Proposals for instituting "workfare" nationwide rest on individualistic assumptions about the causes of poverty, as do extreme right-wing proposals for abolishing income support programs and subjecting former recipients to the discipline of the market. By contrast, arguments for changing social and economic arrangements to promote fuller employment have been relegated to the fringes of policy discussion, their assumptions radically at odds with the policy framework that has shaped thinking about poverty since the 1960s.

---

[8] For reviews of some of the major "workfare" programs, see Mickey Kaus, "The Work Ethic State," *The New Republic* (July 7, 1986): 22–33, and Michael Wiseman, "Workfare and Welfare Policy," *Focus* (Newsletter of the University of Wisconsin's Institute for Research on Poverty) 9, no. 3 (Fall and Winter 1986): 1–8.

Political Coalitions in
American Social Policymaking

Just as the evolving policy agenda has reproduced the bifurcation of U.S. public social provision, so, too, have political coalitions solidified around the divisions built into American social politics since the New Deal. To make sense of the political alliances that have sustained and shaped social policy, it is important to recall in the first place that the U.S. state structure has given some interests special leverage in setting the orientations of political alliances. Beyond that, existing policies, like institutional arrangements, may encourage the formation of groups and alliances that differ from any supposedly based on purely economic interests. Policy-created advantages may call forth a constituency to defend those benefits, or they may inspire coalitions to press for the extension of those benefits to new groups. Conversely, policy-created costs to some constituency, or else perceived inequities in the targeting of benefits across groups, may produce political demands for cuts in old policies or for new programs to help those previously left out. In sum, certain political alliances are more likely than others to be formed within a given configuration of economic and social interests; yet state institutions and preexisting policies also accentuate or attenuate differences between groups, and thus reinforce or undercut their willingness and capacity to ally with one another in ongoing political struggles.

In the postwar United States, the coalitions that came together in support of social security and commercial Keynesianism defined the limits of public social provision by discouraging alternative policies that might have more fully bridged the interests of blacks and whites and those of lower-income and relatively better off working- and middle-class people. Although certainly affected by cultural outlooks and economic interests, the coalitions that developed over time to support social security and commercial-Keynesian economic management were not simply given. Rather they were politically shaped and reshaped in the context of U.S. political institutions and previously established policies.

We have seen that reforms during the New Deal and World War II were ultimately stopped short by the disproportionate political leverage enjoyed by southern landlords. Early New Deal agricultural interventions had the unforeseen effect of strengthening conservative agricultural alliances bridging the South and Midwest. Similarly, business and commercial farmer groups opposed to national economic planning and a more comprehensive welfare state were strengthened at the expense of potential worker-farmer alliances, in significant part because of the extra leverage southerners gained from the congressional committee system, from their region's limited democracy, and from the decentralization of American party politics. Until well into the 1960s, southerners had sufficient leverage to block any efforts to expand and nationalize the parts of U.S. public social provision that affected their local economic or political interests.

In the interim, postwar U.S. social provision became increasingly bifurcated into "social security" versus "welfare," in significant part because of the feedback effects of New Deal policies. After 1935, and especially after the late 1940s, Social Security administrators worked effectively not only within the federal executive but also with congressional committees to build up contributory social insurance. At key junctures when it seemed as if noncontributory assistance might become more popular than contributory insurance, the Social Security administrators and their congressional allies extended coverage or raised benefits prior to raising taxes (which, in any event, were labeled "contributions"). Over time, moreover, the maturing social insurance programs actually paid out benefits to more and more regularly employed Americans who had been enrolled for many years.

From the late 1950s, social security encompassed contributory old-age, survivors, and disability insurance, and it developed a remarkably solid base of congressional and electoral support. Behind the banner of social security were grouped not only all retired employees currently collecting benefits, including many middle-class and even wealthy people, but also their families who might otherwise have had to support them, along with the bulk of the working-aged population, who as they made payroll "contributions" gained a stake in the future benefits to which they now felt themselves "entitled." This was exactly the kind of virtually universal coalition of citizens that the Social Security administrators had deliberately tried to fashion to make contributory insurance politically secure. Their efforts proved so successful that by the 1980s, when retrenchment of social expenditures is supposedly the order of the day, many conservative congressional representatives actually vie with the most liberal of their fellows to be seen as the staunchest defenders of social security.

Perhaps inevitably, the consolidation of such support for social security was also accompanied by the political marginalization of programs assisting those Americans not adequately included in contributory social insurance. For one thing, from the late 1930s into the 1950s, the Social Security administrators sometimes deliberately worked to denigrate and restrict the generosity of public assistance measures (especially old-age assistance) that were potentially more popular than contributory insurance.[9] Equally to the point, the expansion of contributory insurance—to

[9] See Jerry Cates, *Insuring Inequality: Administrative Leadership in Social Security, 1935–54* (Ann Arbor: University of Michigan Press, 1983).

cover more and more of the elderly in place of old-age assistance, and (after 1939) to cover widows and orphans of employed workers in place of Aid to Dependent Children—meant that social security siphoned off the most socially appealing categories of public assistance recipients, leaving "welfare" with politically weak clients, including many from culturally disapproved categories such as unwed mothers. Thus, as the scope and inclusiveness of social security expanded, so did its supporting political coalition, while the possibilities for securely extending generous social assistance to those beyond its fold correspondingly diminished.

Briefly in the early 1960s, reexaminations of national economic policy apparently offered an opportunity to create full employment programs that could have bridged those on the bottom of society with the working class. However, in the context of the federal institutional arrangements and macroeconomic strategies put into place back in the 1940s, tax-cutting commercial-Keynesian policies understandably became the preferred means for boosting aggregate employment. Allowing for only the most blunt forms of government intervention into particular labor markets, the macroeconomic policy choices of the early 1960s could not solve the problems of the unemployed or marginally employed; and the specially targeted programs added on by the War on Poverty failed to build bridges between the interests of the unemployed and those of more regularly employed Americans. In fact, the War on Poverty ended up increasing the potential for political conflict by so visibly aiming (largely ineffectual) federal employment measures at "the poor" alone.

Parallel to what happened in the realm of economic and employment policies, the extensions of social welfare that came in the late 1960s and early 1970s followed the inherited divisions within U.S. public social provision. Contributory social insurance expanded through the passage of Medicare in 1965 and through the cost-of-living indexing of old-age benefits that transformed them into a retirement wage in the years 1969–72. These changes represented the working out of plans long ago prepared by the Social Security Administration and its congressional allies for a propitious political conjuncture. And, of course, politicians understood them to be appealing to the broad coalition of middle- and working-class Americans already appreciative of social security benefits for themselves and their parents.

Remarkably, some improvements in public assistance for the poor also occurred. For the working-aged poor, the major victory of this period was the dramatic expansion of food stamps; yet as Kenneth Finegold reveals in this volume, this victory depended upon a temporary alliance of bureaucratic, urban-liberal, and agricultural forces willing to expand an in-kind program specifically offering food benefits. In addition, Medicaid passed along with Medicare in 1965, and it was followed in 1972 by

Supplemental Security Income, effectively a nationally guaranteed income for elderly and disabled people not sufficiently covered by contributory insurance. Again, the Social Security Administration was behind both of these innovations, taking advantage of the national polity's temporary sense of urgency about overcoming poverty and racism to put long-laid plans through Congress. As Jill Quadagno's contribution to this volume demonstrates, changing socioeconomic conditions in the South had finally dissolved the opposition of politically well-situated southern representatives to nationally standardized old-age assistance. In any event, given the prior inclusion of most Americans in contributory insurance, newly nationalized Supplemental Security Income was not a major welfare commitment. By the 1960s, AFDC had become by far the largest public assistance program, and it was *not* nationalized or displaced by any guaranteed income for the working-aged poor.

In the end, the political energies mustered for social reform in the 1960s and early 1970s were channeled into programs that did not function to draw together the constituencies separated by the social policy decisions of the 1930s, but instead worked to increase the *political* isolation of the poor, especially the black poor, from the working and middle classes. Whatever the social policy gains, therefore, a bitter legacy of the War on Poverty and the reforms of the Great Society and its aftermath was a deepening of the rifts within the ranks of actual or potential supporters of U.S. public social provision. By the mid-1970s, a narrow and beleaguered "welfare" coalition—blacks and the leaders of organized labor, with white workers and much of the traditional Democratic party peeled off—was facing a backlash coalition newly strengthened by the inclusion of working- and middle-class whites increasingly unwilling to "foot the bill" for programs targeting the poor.

The asymmetry in power between the coalition supporting social security and that defending the lower tier of public assistance programs became apparent with the generalized retrenchment of domestic social programs that commenced in the second half of the Carter administration and became the focus for government policy during the Reagan administration. Even when policymakers announced intentions to cut all social spending evenhandedly, programs directly targeting the poor soon proved to be the easiest to eliminate or trim back. As Helene Slessarev suggests in her paper, some of the threatened second-tier social programs have been able to attract more support than others in this period of retrenchment. Direct benefits for poor people, and especially programs like public housing that especially arouse local racial animosities, have been extremely vulnerable to cuts, while programs such as Medicaid in which established third-party institutions or widely dispersed groups of middle-class providers have a stake seem to be better able to hold their own.

In short, within the category of welfare programs as well as between welfare and social security, the basic logic of policy feedbacks and coalition building plays itself out: programs with influential non-poor constituents may cost a lot more than those that directly aid the most needy, but they are much more likely to survive or grow, even in a period of social policy retrenchment supposedly necessitated by budgetary constraints.

U.S. Administrative Capacities and the Development of Social Policies

The bifurcation between social security and welfare in U.S. social policy has been furthered not only by processes of agenda setting and coalition formation, but also by the uneven and limited administrative capacities of the American state. The development of administrative capacities has helped to make certain types of social policy interventions efficacious and politically secure, while undermining other kinds of interventions, most notably those aimed at eradicating poverty among the working-aged poor.

Historically, we have seen that the U.S. federal state was slow to develop administrative capacities, as political reformers and experts advocating modern social and economic policies had to reorganize or bypass the entrenched patterns of nineteenth-century patronage democracy. When new agencies deemed appropriate for administering social legislation were finally established, they were typically isolated islands of expertise within local, state, and federal governments, limited by the ongoing jurisdictional disputes among these levels. Moreover, many areas of American civil administration in the twentieth century have remained partially dominated by patronage-oriented political parties, and all have continued to be plagued by divisions between legislatures and executives, and by divisions among specialized administrative bureaus themselves.

Even so, some islands of administrative expertise in American federal democracy became capable of expanding or improving the social programs under their aegis, when political opportunities for reform and innovation opened up. Examples highlighted by the authors in this volume include the Social Security Administration and the Department of Agriculture. Both of these parts of the U.S. federal bureaucracy have, since their origins, enjoyed unusual jurisdictional autonomy within the national government, and thus they have had the ability to plan new policies and devise their own ideological and technical rationales for favorite policies. Both have also had roots in networks of policy intellectuals long accustomed to mediating between universities and the practical worlds of legislatures and administrative bureaucracies. Thus the Social Security Administration and the Department of Agriculture each established stable ties with key congressional committees and with federated associations of locally influential groups that had a stake in the protection and expansion of certain social policies—especially those favoring old people in the case of the Social Security Administration, and those that could be made beneficial to commercial farmers in the case of the Department of Agriculture.

Beyond the issue of administrative capacities within the national government, capacities to implement social programs in technically and politically viable ways have also mattered. The success of Social Security's primary programs—their eventual ability to greatly diminish old-age poverty and ensure a retirement wage for most Americans—was facilitated by their reliance on simple cash transfers. The federal government has always performed best when administering social programs that involve only a "check in the mail." Although a major federal bureaucracy had to be established to store and update individuals' records and to collect taxes from employers, old-age insurance under Social Security did not involve direct, targeted interventions into the social activities of local communities. Nor did it require dismantling or reshaping governments. When undertakings of such complexity have been required to implement actual—or potential—social policies in the United States, the historical record suggests that the national administrative capacities to carry them out have not been readily available or at all easy to create. Given options between constructing new national bureaucracies and relying on third parties to administer programs in return for subsidies and under loose supervision, the federal government has usually relied on subsidies to third parties—sometimes private organizations and sometimes state and local agencies—to implement its social policies.

Thus after the end of World War II and also during the Great Society of the 1960s, substantial expansions in U.S. social expenditures were effected without proportional growth of the administrative apparatus of the federal government as such. Yet even though reliance on third parties has often provided a way of quickly launching programs without reworking administrative arrangements, this reliance has also undercut the ability of the federal government to control expenditures and to precisely target programmatic interventions—above all, because third-party implementation has typically been accompanied by the dispersion of expenditures across many congressional districts. The federal government's failure to hold down health care costs is one typical consequence of handing administrative control over to third parties. Hospitals, doctors, and state and local governments have all benefited from assorted federal health-related expenditures since the end of World War II. But it has been very difficult for health care planners in Washington to institute rational cost controls or to target facilities or expenditures on the particular communities and populations that need them the most.[10]

In the few instances in which the federal government has attempted to administer programs directly, such efforts have foundered in patronage or in dispute over local versus federal control. The bitter disputes over "corruption" that accompanied the expansion of Civil War pensions, described in Ann Shola Orloff's paper, have been played out anew with different programs and beneficiaries. Most recently, as we have seen, the employment and training programs of the Great Society suffered an extreme version of the chaos that accusations of patronage and bickering between levels of government can produce in the United States. The Labor Department struggled throughout the 1960s to create new federal capacities to alter the functioning of labor markets in ways that would conform to nationally defined objectives concerning employment and underemployment. But the department was handicapped on several counts. The way economic expertise was institutionalized in the immediate postwar period undermined possibilities for assembling executive backing to increase greatly the capacity to administer a national labor market policy. Without such support the department could not hope to extend its authority over the various local and private actors already operating in this arena. Moreover, the creation of alternative routes by the War on Poverty fragmented authority even further. In the end, the employment and training programs that survived became embedded in congressionally mediated local patronage arrangements—yet these only left them vulnerable to subsequent accusations of "corruption" and "inefficiency."

Short of massive income transfers, social and economic programs that might effectively address the multiple problems of America's low-income citizens would surely require the federal government to plan and administer direct and carefully targeted interventions into workplaces and communities. During the Great Society, when new initiatives were launched in the fields of housing, medical care, and employment training, the basic administrative groundwork needed to implement sound programs was neither already available nor (in most instances) successfully created. Several papers in this volume have maintained that "the poverty problem" must be addressed most fundamentally by efforts to combat unemployment, yet embarking on such an effort requires more than amassing political support. It also entails constructing new national administrative

[10] On the difficulties of controlling health care costs, see John L. Palmer and Barbara Boyle Terry, "Health Care Financing and Pension Programs," in Gregory B. Mills and John L. Palmer, *Federal Budget Policy in the 1980s* (Washington, D.C.: The Urban Institute, 1984), pp. 121–53. Reagan's cost controlling measures have experienced little success; see "Medical Costs Continue to Surge; Evasion of Controls Held a Cause," *New York Times* July 26, 1986, p. 1.

capacities in the face of competing actors in the private sector—and within the matrix of a state structure that tends to disperse benefits and undercut central coordination in all realms of American social policy.

The U.S. Polity and
Policy Alternatives for the Future

During the 1970s, the configuration of social and economic policies that grew out of the New Deal and the Great Society proved ill-suited to cope with the human problems of an American economy troubled by recession, inflation, and industrial dislocations. At the same time, changes in racial and family relations further strained the limits of existing social policies, even as new sources of political division undercut national enthusiasm for ever-expanding public social expenditures. The manifest inability of established policies and political alliances to meet new challenges in turn made credible the argument that government itself was the source of America's malaise—rather than the instrumentality through which even better and more just solutions might be sought. In this context, neoconservative politicians have invoked the rhetoric of crisis to attract support for radical surgery on public social provision in the United States.

So far, three alternative policy routes have dominated mainstream discussions about the future of American social policies. One strand of neoconservative thought calls for dismantling most of the structures of social support that have been built up since the New Deal. In place of publicly ensured security, these extreme advocates of laissez faire would have citizens take their chances in a newly unfettered marketplace. A second approach, articulated by voices from the shrinking ranks of mainstream liberals, defends the achievements of past programs and argues for a deepened commitment to the unfinished redistributive agendas of the New Deal and the Great Society. Finally, a line of thought developed by some conservatives and liberals alike argues that governmental authority must be enhanced to regulate the behavior of citizens who shirk their social and economic obligations. Proponents of what we shall label the "new authoritarianism" argue that the state must regulate the behavior of its citizens so that they act in socially responsible ways; rudiments of social welfare provision would remain in place, but individuals would be forced to act in ways culturally deemed to be in their own and society's best interests.

Each of these paths for social policy offers a distinct vision of the proper relationship between the state and the market, and each would have far-reaching implications for the shape of American society and politics. But could any of them be implemented with the results intended?

This volume offers useful insights about the obstacles each approach faces and the unintended effects to which each might lead. For neither conservatives nor liberals can proceed unbedeviled by the effects of past policies or free from the constraints of the particular patterns of state and society characteristic of the United States.

Proponents of laissez faire envision a return to a pre–New Deal America when, they argue, the market provided discipline and encouraged individuals and families to work for their own welfare. One of the most influential recent laissez-faire critiques of American social policy is that offered by Charles Murray in his widely read and fiercely debated *Losing Ground: American Social Policy, 1950–1980*.[11] Quite simply, Murray proposes to do away with all federal social programs for the working-aged poor, save unemployment insurance. Arguing that social welfare programs have actually caused poverty and urban social problems by tampering with the incentives faced by the poor, Murray maintains that nothing short of removing government from the realm of social welfare will re-equilibrate American society, prodding the poor to behave as they should. Although Murray himself is silent on the fate of Social Security's old-age insurance entitlements, other neoconservatives have argued that the current system should be scaled back to reflect the actual contributions of retirees.[12]

Dramatic as it is, the extreme laissez-faire position has attracted a lot of attention and helped to shape a national political climate in which advocates of continued or increased federal social spending are on the defensive. But there is little prospect that wholesale dismantling of social programs could possibly occur, given the common stake of citizens, provider groups, and congressional representatives in sustaining many existing policies. In the real world of American politics, calls for sweeping policy dismantlement translate, at most, into proposals for across-the board budget cuts; these in turn devolve into uneven cuts, differentially targeted on programs for the poor. Universal benefits are left largely intact, and welfare programs that somehow engage middle-class interests or institutional providers also fare better than benefits solely for the poor.

This certainly was what happened during the first Reagan administration. When a brief testing of the waters about possible reductions in social security produced sharp bipartisan outcries, the administration quickly backed off; by default, the second-tier welfare programs became the prime targets for budget cutters. Yet even this selective pattern of re-

---

[11] Murray, *Losing Ground*.

[12] Milton Friedman has been a long-time advocate of dismantling Social Security; see Wilber J. Cohen and Milton Friedman, *Social Security: Universal or Selective?* (Washington, D.C.: American Enterprise Institute, 1972). For a later evaluation, see Peter J. Ferrara, *Social Security: The Inherent Contradiction* (San Francisco: Cato Institute, 1980).

trenchment has its limits. After the initial flurry of budget slashing in 1981, efforts to reduce social spending stalled, as Congress resisted any major inroads into entitlement programs and showed little inclination to do away entirely with subsistence-level welfare benefits. After 1981, agencies and constituencies with stakes in existing programs mobilized intense counter-pressures; and soundings of public opinion that in the early 1980s had shown approval for spending reductions had swung by the mid-1980s to show support for the existing levels of funding, even of welfare.[13]

In the face of recently amplified conservative rhetoric, most liberals have offered only fainthearted defenses of U.S. public social provision. Among the few who have forthrightly defended the achievements of the past and who argue for completing the agenda of the Great Society is policy analyst Sar Levitan.[14] In a survey of social policy at the end of the first Reagan administration, Levitan called for a return to activist government and a renewed commitment to social equity, arguing that liberals should continue to fight for adequate assistance to the working and non-working poor.[15] He faults past social policies for not placing enough emphasis on helping the poor to become economically self-sufficient through comprehensive job training and public employment programs. To make new help for lower-income people affordable, Levitan maintains, it is essential that benefits to the non-needy be reduced. Thus, the various entitlement programs—such as Social Security, Medicare, and veterans programs—that fold middle-class recipients in with the poor should be substantially trimmed back in an overall social policy framework that seeks to improve opportunities for those at the bottom of society.[16] Such a course would be difficult, Levitan acknowledges. Yet, even though he recognizes the obstacles to persuading middle-class citizens that they should foot the bill for helping others, Levitan nevertheless asserts that strong political leadership can re-create broad support for generous and more redistributive measures aimed at lower-income Americans.

Levitan is surely right to argue that previous government interventions have been deficient in helping the poor become economically self-suffi-

---

[13] See the polls summarized in Thomas Ferguson and Joel Rogers, "The Myth of America's Turn to the Right," *The Atlantic* 257 (May 1986): 43–53. The increase in the support for welfare spending from 1980 to 1984 can be seen in The General Social Surveys, National Opinion Research Center. Social Security has retained strong support throughout the Reagan administration; see Robert Y. Shapiro and Tom W. Smith, "The Polls: Social Security," *Public Opinion Quarterly* 49 (Winter 1985): 561–72.

[14] On the failure of liberals to articulate bold alternatives to Republican policy proposals, see Robert Kuttner, "Reinventing the Democrats," *New Republic* 193 (November 18, 1985): 23–26.

[15] Levitan and Johnson, *Beyond the Safety Net*.

[16] Ibid., pp. 22, 177–78.

cient; and he also correctly suggests that programs furthering economic independence are better aligned with public opinion than are simple income transfers for the poor. However, nothing in the history of American social policy suggests that political advocacy by intellectuals and a few politicians alone could bring about the targeted, redistributive social provision envisaged by Levitan. Likely support would come only from congressional representatives of inner-urban and other underprivileged districts.

Throughout American history, from the time of Civl War pensions to the postwar expansion of social security, the most successful public social policies in the United States have been those that combined bureaucratic capacity for innovation and legislative maneuvering with congressional support, in order to deliver benefits directly to a wide array of citizens, regardless of their private incomes and without demeaning "means tests" or other cumbersome application procedures. Only such programs have been able to gain secure support from broad cross-class coalitions in American democracy. Thus, the evidence from the history of U.S. social provision suggests that the kind of close targeting of policies on the poor that Sar Levitan advocates either could not come into being in the first place or, if it did, could not build sufficient political consensus to sustain itself into the future. Even more forcefully, the same practical point could be made in response to those to the left of Levitan, including Fred Block, Richard Cloward, Barbara Ehrenreich, and Frances Fox Piven, who have recently argued (without Levitan's stress on full employment) that existing U.S. public assistance benefits should be made more generous, inclusive, and redistributive for low-income Americans.[17]

The practical problems of the laissez-faire approach toward the poor and the political drawbacks of large-scale redistribution of benefits have shifted public debate away from these alternatives. As solutions based on either extending or radically cutting back the status quo seem increasingly impractical, a new strand of conservative thought has come to the fore, arguing that the state should act with enhanced authority to ensure that citizens behave in socially responsible ways. The reluctance of these new authoritarians to rely simply on the market or on private groups stems from the conviction that failures of individual responsibility entail costs that are borne by the rest of society. Since neither individual transactions nor the discipline of the market can be trusted to ensure that citizens act accountably, the state must step in to enforce particular norms of behavior. Proponents of the new authoritarianism have especially directed their

---

[17] Fred Block, Richard A. Cloward, Barbara Ehrenreich, and Frances Fox Piven, *The Mean Season: The Attack on the Welfare State* (New York: Pantheon Books, 1987).

attention to welfare, arguing that recipients must be required to work in exchange for their benefits.

In *Beyond Entitlement: The Social Obligations of Citizenship*, Lawrence Mead has presented the most thoroughly elaborated case for strict work requirements. Mead faults U.S. social policies of the past twenty years for their "permissiveness," arguing that the failure to enforce standards has compounded the behavioral problems of the poor by fostering a "welfare mentality."[18] He argues that it is up to the government to remedy this situation by forcing the dependent to work. Because society requires of all its adult citizens at least minimal capacities to function, it has an interest in requiring work from everyone—including mothers with children. According to Mead, "low wage-work . . . must be mandated, just as a draft has sometimes been necessary to staff the military."[19] For only when forced out of their passivity will the poor be integrated into American society as true equals.

At first glance, this new authoritarianism seems to overcome much of the political impracticality of laissez faire by maximizing grounds for agreement between conservatives and liberals. For moderate conservatives reluctant to embrace Murray's sweeping proposals to do away with public assistance, work requirements present an attractive means of discouraging some would-be welfare applications and ensuring that the remaining recipients of public largesse "pay" for the aid they receive. At the same time, many liberals find work requirements attractive as a way to preserve welfare benefits for those in need, while allowing supporters of those benefits to avoid the appearance of being "soft" on the undeserving. The political attractiveness of tacking behavioral standards onto social programs has been evident in the various work programs that have been attached to AFDC grants since the late 1960s, and the Reagan administration has greatly accelerated this trend by encouraging the states to set up "experimental" workfare programs.

A broader view of the matter, however, reveals the inherent contradictions of simply "enforcing work" for clients of existing welfare programs. Most of the numerous workfare proposals that have been discussed so far acknowledge that this strategy calls for a much larger government role— even though the declared aim is to "reduce dependency" by welfare clients on the state. Indeed, provision of sufficient numbers of jobs for able-bodied welfare recipients would entail an effort far beyond anything the federal or state governments have previously undertaken with any administrative efficiency or political success. Even if very few of the pro-

[18] Lawrence Mead, *Beyond Entitlement: The Social Obligations of Citizenship* (New York: The Free Press, 1985), p. 65.
[19] Ibid., p. 84.

grams were directly administered by governmental agencies, greatly increased monitoring capacity would still be required to oversee substantial new expenditures and enforce the (frequently unpleasant) work requirements. Increasing the authority of the government to regulate the conduct of citizens inevitably means building up the size and power of the state. That conservative supporters of workfare whose main concern is to deter participants would willingly go all the way with such a massive state buildup is doubtful; that they could do so without inspiring political backlashes is even more dubious. Much more likely is the pattern set by the Work Incentive Program (WIN)—increased registration and certification requirements that serve more to inconvenience and punish some unlucky welfare recipients than actually to promote commitments to work.[20] Yet this sort of outcome would leave U.S. public social provision as unreformed as ever and certainly would fail to realize the professed new authoritarian ideal of better integrating the poor into American society and culture.

Neither the laissez faire nor the new authoritarian approaches could work as promised to overhaul American social policy. All the same, as long as credible alternatives are lacking on the national political agenda, both approaches offer rationales for persistent efforts to reduce U.S. public social provision. The political coalitions that underpin such efforts isolate "the poor" and tend to exclude most black Americans. Implicitly or explicitly, intellectuals and politicians combine the messianic promises of the laissez-faire or new authoritarian approaches with negative racial stereotypes of blacks and allusions to the "immorality" of female recipients of public assistance, seeking to weaken even further ambivalent public support for means-tested public assistance.

Liberal distaste for the coerciveness of the new authoritarianism has combined with an attraction to themes of responsibility and self-discipline to create a new hybrid approach to income support. This neo-liberal variant of authoritarianism has guided a growing array of policy experiments on the level of the states. Sounding themes of economic independence and mutual obligation, a number of governors have inaugurated programs that focus on getting welfare recipients into the labor force, either voluntarily or by added new requirements to AFDC. States that have opted for mandatory work or training requirements have generally sought to provide substantial support services to make the requirements less onerous and more effective. Along with mandatory work requirements, some states provide benefits such as child care and medical insurance to welfare mothers who are enrolled in training and job placement

---

[20] Ibid., chap. 6; see also Mildred Rein, "Work in Welfare: Failures and Future Strategies," *Social Service Review* 56 (June 1982): 211–27.

programs. The most widely heralded of the non-mandatory employment and training programs, the Employment Training Choices Program (popularly known as E.T.) in Massachusetts, likewise seeks to make the work options more feasible and attractive by providing substantial support services, including child care, limited eligibility for Medicaid, and travel allowances.

Because they cover a range of approaches, these policy experiments linking work and welfare have different strengths and weaknesses. To the degree that such programs emphasize the punitive aspect of enforcing work, they are likely to suffer from all the previously discussed drawbacks of the new authoritarianism, creating an alienated population that will not achieve that economic independence workfare proponents claim to support. In contrast to punitive policies, the more generous programs may actually offer some welfare recipients a route to economic self-sufficiency. But they, like the coercive programs, do nothing to address the severe problem of unemployment and underemployment among males not eligible for public assistance.

All of these work-and-welfare programs raise thorny political questions, especially for liberals. Promises to provide such services as child care, Medicaid, clothes, and travel allowances, sometimes continuing even after public assistance recipients find jobs, will surely anger other low-income workers, whose families have to struggle to provide child care and medical insurance on their own. Democratic constituencies, especially, could be set at loggerheads before long, as, once again, relations become embittered between economically pressed lower-middle-class taxpayers—disproportionately white ethnics in two-parent families—and welfare recipients and recent graduates of workfare—disproportionately women of color and their children. Bluntly stated, liberal versions of combining work and welfare threaten to recapitulate the political failings of the Great Society. They target the poor and welfare recipients as a separate group, to be treated differently—more generously or more coercively—than the working and middle classes, deepening the rift between the poor and the rest of the country.

As we have seen, the laissez-faire, redistributive-liberal, and new authoritarian approaches that have thus far dominated debates about the future of U.S. public social provision all face severe obstacles and would become internally contradictory when played out in the American polity. The shortcomings of these approaches leave room for better ideas—including an approach that could draw lessons from the past to respond to new social needs with enhanced rather than diminished commitments to public social provision for all Americans. That is our preference, and so let us conclude this volume with a brief sketch of our own ideas about the future of public social provision in the United States.

A viable route to increasing the public role in securing social well-being must rely on inclusive programs that address the needs of both middle- and lower-income Americans. Although it would not be either desirable or possible simply to convert existing public assistance programs into universal entitlements, changes in social and economic organization may provide new possibilities for addressing through public means problems that affect a wide array of citizens. By searching for emerging areas of common concern, it may be possible—in the spirit of the New Deal's Social Security Act, although being careful not to bifurcate programs into tiers—to build new public interventions that do not segregate the poor into inadequate and politically vulnerable programs. Two important areas that might form the core of an enhanced U.S. system of public social provision are a new national full employment strategy and a new set of policies to support families. For each area, we can point to widely shared needs and to potentially workable measures.

Changes in America's economic structure have created substantial dislocations in the U.S. work force during the past two decades. The collapse of some sectors of industrial production and the rise of a more service-oriented economy have altered the structure of the labor market at the same time that international competition has made economic dislocation an ever-present threat. These changes suggest possibilities for building support for labor market interventions that improve upon the fragmented job training and public employment programs of the past. As formerly well-paid industrial workers are thrust into low-paying service sector jobs, the problems of "the disadvantaged" and "the dislocated" begin to converge, expanding the range of those who would benefit from a national employment policy.[21] Moreover, the political prospects of such a program are enhanced by the support that employment programs enjoy among the American public: public opinion polls have regularly shown that national efforts to make people employable enjoy strong public approval.[22]

What are some possible components of a national full employment strategy? Clearly, it would have to go beyond sheer macroeconomic manipulations along Keynesian lines. In contrast to past efforts, a new strategy would have to focus on both the characteristics of the labor force and the supply of jobs. National labor market policies that offered job training information and relocation assistance to the poor and non-poor alike could provide a basic framework for continually adjusting the labor force

[21] See Forrest Chrisman, "Federal Job Creation: The Moral Issue," *Working Paper 8: Employment* (Washington, D.C.: Project on the Federal Social Role, 1986), p. 1.

[22] See the polls cited in Andrew Levison, *The Full Employment Alternative* (New York: Coward, McCann and Geoghegan, 1980), pp. 193–95, and Connie DeBoer, "The Polls: Attitudes Toward Unemployment," *Public Opinion Quarterly* 47 (Fall 1983): 432–41.

to changing employment opportunities. This approach would differ from past labor market policies in two ways: first, programs would no longer be remedial efforts that served only the poor or unemployed; second, they would be tied more closely to the private sector in order to facilitate the movement of recipients into secure and steady jobs. Labor market measures structured along such lines could establish firm political support by appealing to a broad public, almost any of whose members might need to take advantage of them at one time or another, and by simultaneously establishing support among private employers.

In all likelihood, an important complement to such efforts to improve the supply and adaptability of labor would be a commitment to create transitional public employment opportunities for those unable to find immediate opportunities in the private sector. Considerable popular support for past public employment efforts in the United States suggests that carefully structured public jobs programs could become an accepted feature of national employment policy. Yet it is equally clear that there are dangers of such programs becoming enmeshed in congressionally reinforced local political patronage systems, with the result that they could be credibly attacked as inefficient, costly, and "corrupt." To avoid this, deliberately transitional public employment opportunities must be designed and administered in close conjunction with the nationally oriented labor market policies just discussed.

Administratively, in fact, a truly national set of employment services would need to be established, and fortunately the political obstacles are now much less than they were in the 1930s and 1940s, when southern and other local interests with decisive congressional leverage had overriding socioeconomic and political reasons for blocking a national employment system. What is more, unlike the bureaucracies required for new authoritarian measures, the national employment services we envisage would perform noncoercive functions and would dispense benefits potentially available to *all* Americans, such as training or retraining opportunities, relocation assistance, and generous transitional unemployment benefits.

Adequate employment opportunities can be a starting point for a revitalized public commitment to social welfare, but additional needs remain and must be addressed in other ways. Changes in relationships between men and women and transformations in American families have had social repercussions even more profound than those of the economic shifts of the past decade. As the number of divorces has climbed and the ranks of women entering the labor force have grown, a whole new set of issues relating to child support and the problems involved in mixing work and family have come to concern women—and parents of both sexes—in all income ranges. Thus, substantial room for innovative and universally appealing programs remains in the broad realm of "family policy"—especially because the United States is virtually alone among capitalist democracies (and other industrial or industrializing nations) in not having previously established public measures in this area.[23]

With divorce now so frequent in all ranks of American society, basic problems of adequate child support open some space for establishing a new public role without isolating poor women, as the current welfare program AFDC does. But new policies must be carefully constructed to avoid creating political bifurcations between upper- and lower-income women. The inadequacy of current child support policies has made it an obvious target for reform since the mid-1970s. To date, however, most attempted reforms have sought to enforce payments from non-custodial parents—usually mothers—whose former partners cannot pay, and also without making provision for needy unmarried mothers. The inspiration behind policies that simply aim to make divorced non-custodial parents pay court-mandated child support might be called "new authoritarianism for the middle classes," for it simply seeks to invoke a nostalgic image of the middle-class family to punish divorced fathers who have not lived up to their obligations. Appealing as this is to women, such policies would in political practice tend to divide upper-middle-class divorced mothers from lower-income divorced mothers, as well as from the substantial numbers of never-married "welfare mothers."

One possible exception to a new authoritarian approach to child support is an experiment under way in Wisconsin. This program has been designed with many desirable features, including automatic deductions from the absent parent's paycheck and a minimum benefit for all women.[24] As the program develops, it will be important to note which aspects of it serve to enhance the common interest that all women have in adequate child support and lessen the inequality and stigma usually attached to aid for poor women. An equitable approach to child support would fold all custodial parents into a single system of payments that offers a universal measure of security for children and their caretakers. The costs of such a system need not be excessive, as it could be financed by a combination of funds from absent spouses and general tax revenues.

[23] See Sheila B. Kamerman, Alfred J. Kahn, and Paul Kingston, *Maternity Policies and Working Women* (New York: Columbia University Press, 1983), esp. Table 1.3, pp. 16–22. On the growing problem of single mothers, see Irwin Garfinkel and Sara S. McLanahan, *Single Mothers and Their Children: A New American Dilemma* (Washington, D.C.: The Urban Institute, 1986).

[24] For a description of the program, see Irwin Garfinkel and Elizabeth Uhr, "A New Approach to Child Support," *The Public Interest* 75 (Spring 1984): 111–22, and Thomas Corbett, Irwin Garfinkel, Ada Sykes, and Elizabeth Uhr, "Assuring Child Support in Wisconsin," *Public Welfare* 44 (Winter 1986): 33–39.

In any event, a better national system of child support would help to prevent many problems among American young people, problems that eventually prove very costly indeed to public coffers.

As part of a comprehensive national family policy, new ways must also be found to make domestic obligations more compatible with work. For employed women, paid maternity leaves with rights to return to similar work must be mandated by national legislation, although the financing might well occur through contributory insurance systems as well as through general tax revenues. Beyond guaranteed maternity leave, moreover, flexible work schedules and optional extended parental leaves are policies that would allow employers, fellow employees, and society as a whole to shoulder some of the burden of child care that employed women have borne largely alone.

Also high on the list of new policies must be adequate, publicly encouraged child care provision to help mothers and fathers who work. But public responsibility need not entail an unwieldly federal bureaucracy directly running day care centers in every community. Rather, there could be subsidies to individual parents, supplemented by grants and tax benefits to encourage alternative and decentralized forms of child care facilities. Given everything we have learned about U.S. social policies in the past, we can foresee that this approach would work more efficiently and, at the same time, build public support by allowing input from communities and enterprises into day-to-day decisions.[25]

For employment and family policies alike, the aim of proponents must be to maximize the range of potential recipients and, when possible, to provide assistance in ways that are not at odds with dominant cultural values or with the capacities of the U.S. federal state structure. Universal programs would minimize the over-identification of public social programs with blacks alone, an identification that has bedeviled public intervention since the Great Society. By building broad clienteles, new universal measures could also avoid the political vulnerability of social programs that targeted just the poor. Moreover, making policies that seek to enhance personal responsibility and competence the core of a new American approach to public social provision would help proponents rebut criticisms about the "wastefulness" of social spending and the "undeserving" nature of welfare recipients. Finally, employment and family policies designed along the lines laid out underscore the interdependence of economic and social policy, so that social provision would no longer be seen as a drag on the economy, but instead as an essential contribution to national productivity in an era of intensifying international competi-

---

[25] See the discussion in Ruth Sidel, *Women and Children Last: The Plight of Poor Women in Affluent America* (New York: Viking Penguin, 1986), chap. 10.

tion. This, in turn, would make it far easier to justify the increased federal resources that would need to be committed to new universal programs.

Conservatives have put forward an employment policy that relies on the market or on enforced low-wage work, while their approach to family policy addresses only middle-class needs in culturally nostalgic terms. To date, most American intellectuals and politicians who do not like these approaches have hesitated to articulate bold alternatives that recognize public responsibility for labor market outcomes and acknowledge the changing status of women and of families in our society. Our examination of the ongoing history of U.S. public social provision reveals, however, that new social programs designed to address widely shared needs are politically and administratively feasible, even in the context of the distinctive features of the American state and society. We hope that a new imaginativeness will soon inspire progressive contributions to debates about the future of social policies in the United States. Reforms in U.S. social provision have never come suddenly, without advanced intellectual groundwork. Sustained efforts to design promising programs, taking into account the lessons of the past, are thus essential if proponents of enhanced public social provision are to be able to take advantage of future political opportunities—opportunities that in the American polity come all too infrequently and often unannounced.

NOTES ON CONTRIBUTORS

EDWIN AMENTA is a Ph.D. candidate in Sociology at the University of Chicago. He is the author of "Compromising Possessions: Orwell's Political, Literary, and Analytical Purposes in *Nineteen Eighty Four*," in *Politics & Society* (1986), as well as the co-author of several articles on social policy, including "The Political Origins of Unemployment Insurance in Five American States," in *Studies in American Political Development* (1987). He has been associate editor of the *American Journal of Sociology* and is currently working on a dissertation about U.S. taxing and spending policies in the 1930s and 1940s.

ROBERT APONTE is the project coordinator of the Urban Family Life Project at the University of Chicago. He is an advanced graduate student in the Department of Sociology at the university. He is currently working on a dissertation in which he examines persistent poverty in the nation's largest cities.

MARY JO BANE is professor of Public Policy at Harvard University's Kennedy School of Government. She was formerly executive deputy commissioner of the New York State Department of Social Services. Her publications include *Here to Stay: American Families in the Twentieth Century* (Basic Books, 1976); *The State and the Poor in the 1980s*, edited with Manuel Carbello (Auburn House Press, 1980); and a number of articles on the dynamics of poverty and welfare.

KENNETH FINEGOLD is assistant professor of Political Science at Rutgers University. His publications include "From Agrarianism to Adjustment: The Political Origins of New Deal Agricultural Policy," in *Politics & Society* (1982), and, with Theda Skocpol, "State Capacity and Economic Intervention in the Early New Deal," in *Political Science Quarterly* (1982). The main topics of his current research are progressive reform in New York, Cleveland, and Chicago and New Deal industrial and agricultural policies.

JOHN MYLES is professor of Sociology at Carleton University, Ottawa, Canada. He is the author of *Old Age in the Welfare State: The Political Economy of Public Pensions* (Little, Brown, 1984). He is currently engaged in a comparative study of class structure and class consciousness in Canada, Sweden, and the United States.

KATHRYN M. NECKERMAN is a graduate student in the Department of Sociology at the University of Chicago. She is also associated with the Urban Family Life Project, a large-scale study of poverty headed by Professor William Julius Wilson. She is the co-author of several publications on poverty, family structure, and welfare policy, including *Medicaid and Pediatric Primary Care* (Johns Hopkins University Press, 1987) with Janet D. Perloff and Phillip R. Kletke. Her current research is a comparative historical study of work and family life among blacks and white immigrants.

GARY ORFIELD is professor of Political Science, Public Policy, and Education at the University of Chicago. He is the author of *The Reconstruction of Southern Education: The Schools and the 1964 Civil Rights Act* (Wiley, 1969); *Congressional Power: The Congress and Social Change* (Harcourt Brace Jovanovich, 1975); *Must We Bus? Segregated Schools and National Policy* (The Brookings Institution, 1978); and *Toward a Strategy for Urban Integration* (The Ford Foundation, 1981). He is currently directing the National School Desegregation Project and serving as research director for the Chicago Area Fair Housing Alliance. In addition, he is doing a comparative study of educational and economic mobility in the largest U.S. metropolitan areas from 1975 to 1985.

ANN SHOLA ORLOFF is assistant professor of Sociology at the University of Wisconsin–Madison. A revised version of her dissertation, "The Politics of Pensions: A Comparative Analysis of the Origins of Pensions and Old Age Insurance in Canada, Great Britain, and the United States, 1880s–1930s," will be published in the near future. Her current research projects deal with the relationship between state-formation (especially civil service reform) and welfare reform in the nineteenth century; the political origins of child support laws; and the determinants of successful labor legislation in twentieth-century America.

JILL QUADAGNO is professor of Sociology and holder of the Mildred and Claude Pepper Eminent Scholars Chair in Social Gerontology at Florida State University. She became interested in historical sociology in 1979 when she received a National Science Foundation National Needs Postdoctoral Fellowship to study at Cambridge University with the Cambridge Group for the History of Population and Social Structure. The outcome of that project was *Aging in Early Industrial Society: Work, Family and Social Policy in Nineteenth Century England* (Academic Press, 1982). Quadagno's current research focuses on the historical development of social security in the United States, and she is publishing her results in *The Transformation of Old Age Security: Class and Politics in the American Welfare State* (University of Chicago Press, 1988).

THEDA SKOCPOL is professor of Sociology at Harvard University; she was previously professor of Sociology and Political Science at the University of Chicago. Her books include the prize-winning *States and Social Revolutions* (Cambridge University Press, 1979) and the edited collections *Vision and Method in Historical Sociology* (Cambridge University Press, 1984) and *Bringing the State Back In* (Cambridge University Press, 1985). In recent years, Skocpol has co-authored numerous articles comparing the United States with Britain and Sweden and comparing policy developments among states within the United States. She is currently preparing a book on *The Politics of American Social Provision: From Civil War Pensions to the Crisis of Social Security*.

HELENE SLESSAREV is a Ph.D. candidate in Political Science at the University of Chicago and is finishing her dissertation on the outcomes of employment policies initiated by civil rights organizations during the 1960s. She is co-author of *Job Training Under the New Federalism*, a study of the implementation of current job training programs in Illinois.

BETH STEVENS is assistant professor of sociology at New York University. She is the author of several works on employee benefits, including *Complementing the Welfare State: The Development of Private Pension, Health Insurance and Other Employee Benefits in the United States* (International Labor Office, 1986). She is presently completing research on the interaction between labor market structures, the competing strategies of the AFL and the CIO, and the development of the American welfare state.

MARGARET WEIR is assistant professor of Government at Harvard University. She is the co-author of *Schooling for All: Class, Race and the Decline of the Democratic Ideal* (Basic Books, 1985) and has written several articles on the adoption of Keynesian policies in the United States, Great Britain, and Sweden. She is currently completing a book about employment policies in the United States from the New Deal to the Reagan administration.

WILLIAM JULIUS WILSON is the Lucy Flower Distinguished Service Professor of Sociology and Public Policy at the University of Chicago. He is the author of *Power, Racism, and Privilege: Race Relations in Theoretical and Sociohistorical Perspective* (Free Press, 1973); *The Declining Significance of Race: Blacks and Changing American Institutions* (University of Chicago Press, 1978); and *The Truly Disadvantaged: The Inner City, The Underclass, and Public Policy* (University of Chicago Press, 1987); and he co-authored *Through Different Eyes: Black and White Perspectives on American Race Relations* (Oxford University Press, 1973). He is currently directing the Urban Family Life Project, a comprehensive research project on poverty, joblessness, and family structure in the inner city.

INDEX

Able-unable-to-work distinction, 387–388
Adams, Charles Francis, 60
Administrative expertise, social policy and, 431–434
Adult education, 417
Affirmative action, 306
Aggregate approach to unemployment, 182–183, 186
Agricultural Adjustment Act, 153–154, 204–205, 208; Federal Surplus Relief Corporation and, 218–220
Agricultural Adjustment Administration (AAA): farm subsidies, 203; invalidation of, 158; purge of liberals, 206–207
Agricultural policy: black urbanization and, 303–304; influence on politics and social policy, 200–201; labor and, 156–162, 214–215; landlord-sharecropper system, 24; mechanization of, 252–253; party consensus and, 187–188; politicization of, 23–24, 201–208; production controls and subsidies, 202–204; social policy and, 200; Social Security and, 209–217; southern interests in, 24–25; workers' Social Security provisions, 238–239, 258–261
Agricultural price supports, 8–9
Agriculture and Consumer Protection Act of 1973, 227
Aid to Dependent Children Program, 193. *See also* Aid to Families with Dependent Children
Aid to Families with Dependent Children (AFDC), 260–261, 363–364; abolishment proposed, 426; benefits increase proposed, 392, 402–403; cross-checking of benefits, 393–394; cross-state differences, 404–405; eligibility requirements, 392–394; expansion of, 7; family disintegration, 402–404; feminization of poverty, 386–387; food stamps, 224–225; growth of in 1950s, 297–298; positive benefits and, 404–405; Progressive Era programs, 39–40; state-level administra-

tion, 74–76; substitutive principle and, 267–268; welfare dependency and, 401–402
Aiken, George, 220–221
Alabama, old-age assistance administration, 243–244
Allen, A. Leonard, 249–250
Altmeyer, Arthur, 213, 215, 251
Aluminium Ore Company, 141 n. 60
Amalgamated Clothing Workers, 134–135
American Association for Labor Legislation (AALL), 58, 63–64
American Association for Old Age Security, 64
American Association for Social Security, 64
American Enterprise Institute, 277–278
American Farm Bureau Federation (AFBF), 24, 158–159; agricultural politics, 202–203, 207, 304; Chamber of Commerce and, 160–161
American Federation of Labor (AFL): opposition to social insurance, 55–56; support of private welfare, 137–138; tax reform and, 131–132
American Medical Association (AMA), 24, 363; opposition to national health, 373–374; opposition to Social Security, 75–76
American Public Welfare Association, 258
America's Hidden Success, 305–306
Anfuso, Victor, 226 n. 68
Anti-war movement, 275
Apprenticeship programs, 417
Area Redevelopment Act of 1961, 175–177
Army Corps of Engineers, 165, 167
Arrears Act (1879), 46
Arthur, Chester Alan, 52
Associative state concept, 62–63
Authoritarian policies, 437–438; child support programs, 444–445
Automobile stamp proposal, 195, 231

Library of Congress Cataloging-in-Publication Data

The Politics of Social Policy in the United States.

(Studies from the Project on the Federal Social Role)
Revised papers from the second and third of three conferences held in Chicago throughout
1984–1985, and sponsored by the Project on the Federal Social Role.
Includes index.
1. United States—Social policy—Congresses. 2. United States—Social conditions—
1945– —Congresses. 3. Public welfare—United States—Congresses. 4. United States—
Politics and government—1945– —Congresses. 5. Welfare state—Congresses. I. Weir,
Margaret. II. Orloff, Ann Shola. III. Skocpol, Theda. IV. Project on the Federal Social Role
(U.S.) V. Series.
HN65.P635 1988   361.6′1′0973   87–25702
ISBN 0–691–09436–5 (alk. paper)
ISBN 0–691–02841–9 (pbk.)